Marketing

ELEVENTH EDITION

A Customer-Centric Approach

Montrose Sommers
Special Lecturer and Consultant in Marketing

Jim Barnes
Memorial University of Newfoundland

McGraw-Hill Ryerson

Toronto Montreal Burr Ridge, IL Dubuque, IA Madison, WI New York
San Francisco St. Louis Bangkok Bogotá Caracas Kuala Lumpur
Lisbon London Madrid Mexico City Milan New Delhi
Santiago Seoul Singapore Sydney Taipei

The McGraw·Hill Companies

McGraw-Hill Ryerson

Marketing
Eleventh Edition

ISBN-13: 978-0-07-095186-0
ISBN-10: 0-07-095186-1

1 2 3 4 5 6 7 8 9 10 TCP 0 9 8 7

Printed and bound in Canada.

Editorial Director: Joanna Cotton
Publisher: Lynn Fisher
Senior Sponsoring Editor: Leanna MacLean
Marketing Manager: Joy Armitage Taylor
Senior Developmental Editor: Denise Foote
Developmental Editor: Emma Gain
Editorial Associate: Marina Seguin
Copy Editor: Tracey Haggert
Senior Production Coordinator: Madeleine Harrington
Cover and Interior Design: Dave Murphy/Valid Design and Layout
Cover Image Credit: Dave Murphy/Valid Design and Layout
Page Layout: Valerie Bateman/Valid Design and Layout
Printer: Transcontinental Printing Group (Interglobe)

Library and Archives Canada Cataloguing in Publication

Sommers, Montrose S., 1933–
Marketing / Montrose Sommers, Jim Barnes. — 11th ed.

Ninth Canadian ed. published under title: Fundamentals of marketing / Montrose S. Sommers, James G. Barnes

Includes bibliographical references and index.

ISBN-13: 978-0-07-095186-0
ISBN-10: 0-07-095186-1

1. Marketing. I. Barnes, James G. II. Sommers, Montrose S. Fundamentals of marketing. III. Title.

HF5415.S64 2007 658.8 C2006-906622-1

To Michael, Annie and the memory
of our dear old Jesse
M.S.S.

To Jennifer, Stephanie, and Karen
J.G.B.

About the Authors

Montrose Sommers

Montrose Sommers is an author and special lecturer in marketing. He received his Bachelor of Commerce degree from the University of British Columbia, his MBA from Northwestern University, and his doctorate in marketing and sociology from the University of Colorado. Dr. Sommers has been a consultant to private and public sector organizations involved in petroleum marketing, financial services, telecommunications, various retailing specializations, marketing research, and advertising. His teaching background is extensive; he has worked with Bachelor, Master, and PhD students at the Universities of British Columbia, Texas, Hawaii, Toronto, Guelph, York, Nairobi in Kenya, Witwatersrand in South Africa, Huazhong and Tianjin in China, and the London School of Economics in Great Britain. Dr. Sommers has also served on the editorial boards of the *Journal of Marketing,* the *Journal of International Management and Organizations,* and the *Journal of the Service Industries.*

Jim Barnes

Jim Barnes is Professor of Marketing at Memorial University of Newfoundland. Dr. Barnes holds undergraduate degrees in Commerce and Economics from Memorial, an MBA from the Harvard Business School, and a PhD from the University of Toronto. He has been a member of the faculty at Memorial University since 1968 and served as Dean from 1978 to 1988. He has been a visiting professor at Queen's University, the University of Bath (England), University College Dublin (Ireland), Université de Reims (France), and Macquarie University (Australia). He was co-founder and Chairman of Bristol Group, a full-service Canadian marketing communications and information firm. He has served as consultant to many national and international companies and regularly delivers seminars and lectures on customer strategy and marketing subjects in many countries. In 1997, Dr. Barnes received the national Leaders in Management Education award from the *Financial Post,* and was elected a Fellow of the Marketing Research and Intelligence Association of Canada in 1999. He serves on the editorial boards of the *International Journal of Bank Marketing* and *Managing Service Quality.* His latest book, *Build Your Customer Strategy: a guide to creating profitable customer relationships*, was published in 2006 by John Wiley & Sons.

Brief Contents

Contents

List of Cases

PART 1 Marketing and the Customer

PART 2 Addressing Target Markets

PART 3 Products, Services, and Brands

PART 4 Pricing

PART 5 Distribution

PART 6 Marketing Communications

PART 7 Tying Marketing Together

Preface

Note from the authors

Marketing, as a management discipline, has only been studied in colleges and universities for fifty years or so and has only been a division or department in many large companies since the 1950s. The field is currently undergoing more fundamental and rapid change than at any other time in its brief history. It is truly a dynamic field; one which reveals new subjects for study literally every week.

Marketing is most evident in the advertising that seems to be everywhere and that informs us and persuades us to buy. But marketing is not just the ads we see on TV and hear on the radio, or that pop up on the Internet. It's also not just the new products that we find in attractive retail stores or the "special offers" that catch our eye from time to time. Marketing is all of this and much more.

We see marketing as being very broad in scope. To us, marketing encompasses literally anything that a company does that has the potential to affect customer satisfaction in the long term. So, anything that a company or organization does to make you feel better about dealing with them is marketing. If you work or plan to work in any business or literally any other kind of organization, you need to understand marketing.

This edition of *Marketing* continues with our tradition of making the field of marketing as interesting and relevant to the real world as possible. We are presenting marketing as it is practised in Canadian and international organizations today. With access to more information than ever before, customers have more control now than they ever have. To do marketing well requires a detailed understanding of customers and how they think and behave. It is only with this perspective that marketers can be successful in accomplishing the principal objective of marketing: the creation of long-term customer satisfaction.

To reinforce marketing's commitment to the customer and our commitment to a **customer-centric view of marketing**, we have introduced a new model in this edition — the customer-centric model. This model reflects how marketing is practised today by leading companies, with the customer clearly at the centre. We have also re-organized topics and the flow of materials to continually reinforce this centrality. The new structure and new content of this edition seamlessly integrate new marketing ideas with new technologies and newly emerging concepts and practices — creating a very contemporary and effective learning tool for today's students and tomorrow's practitioners.

The new edition is divided into seven parts to reflect the marketing management process:

- ***Part 1: Marketing and the Customer*** serves as an introduction and includes an introductory chapter, "What's Marketing All About?", our new Customer-Centric Model and a discussion of how it is used, as well as chapters on understanding the customer and the environment for strategic marketing planning.

- ***Part 2: Addressing Target Markets*** is devoted to a discussion of the collection and use of market information, followed by segmentation analysis, targeting and positioning discussions, and a chapter on business-to-business marketing.

- ***Part 3: Products, Services, and Brands*** contains separate chapters on product planning and development, services marketing and customer relationships, and branding and packaging.
- ***Part 4: Pricing*** introduces the real world of pricing mechanisms, pricing policies, and competitive pricing strategies and tactics to gain consumer value.
- ***Part 5: Distribution*** reviews the modern retailing scene and then looks behind retailing to examine the various elements of wholesaling and logistics that, taken together, form channels of distribution and the supply system.
- ***Part 6: Marketing Communications*** covers effective marketing communications and the management of advertising, as well as selling, sales promotion, and public relations, with a chapter devoted to each of these three topics.
- ***Part 7: Tying Marketing Together*** concludes the book with discussions on issues associated with successful marketing implementation and the performance of marketing, and presents our view of future developments.

PEDAGOGICAL SUPPORT

The Customer-Centric Model

The model is presented at the beginning of each of the seven parts of this book with the relevant topics highlighted in the model so that you can see at a glance the coverage of each part and how it relates to the topics covered in the rest of the book. Most importantly, you will be seeing how today's marketing really fits together.

The **customer** is presented in the centre of the model to emphasize that all marketing decisions are made with the customer in mind. Customers are shown to be influenced by a variety of factors: **Internal Drivers** (aspects of the individual's character and situation that affect the decisions they make); **Social Influences** (to which we are very closely linked); **Environmental Influences** (over which we have little control); and **Business Influences** (those factors that the company creating the marketing strategy can control). One of the most important business influences is the **Marketing Mix**, the components of which (Product, Pricing, Distribution and Communication) are listed to the side of the model and are the focus of several chapters. The customer's response to these many and varied influences results in two different sets of outcomes: **Customer Outcomes** (the customer's internal impression of the company) and **Business Outcomes** (the impact the customer's response has on the company).

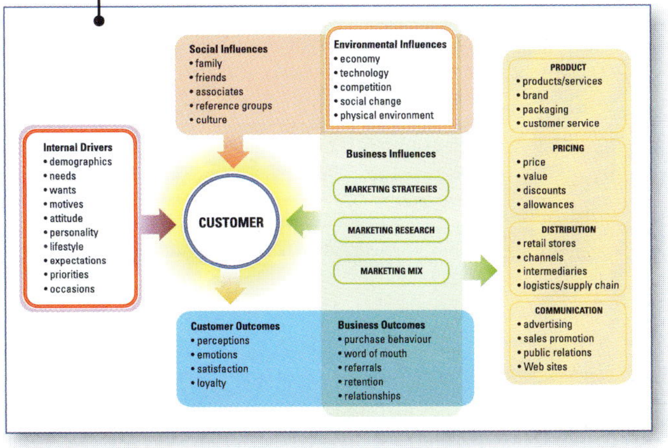

Chapter-Opening Vignettes

Each chapter begins with a contemporary case vignette — 100% of which are new or updated — that introduces some of the concepts, strategies, and techniques covered in the chapter. Some of the companies featured in the vignettes are Apple Canada, Tim Hortons, Canadian Tire, the Royal Bank of Canada, and Disney Studios, with topics ranging from new products and technology to new promotions and marketing strategies and customer responses to marketing influences.

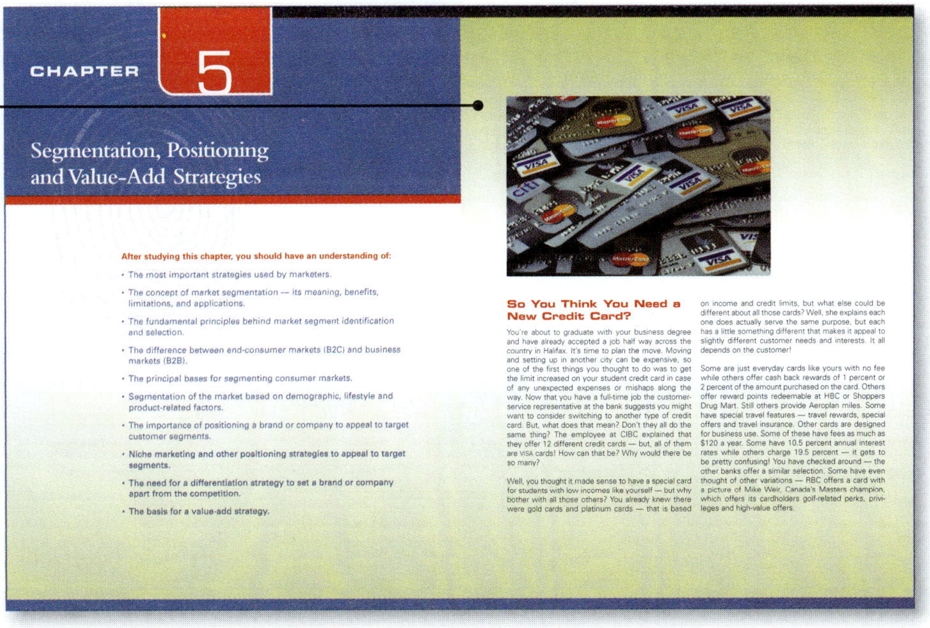
CHAPTER 5

Segmentation, Positioning and Value-Add Strategies

After studying this chapter, you should have an understanding of:

- The most important strategies used by marketers.
- The concept of market segmentation — its meaning, benefits, limitations, and applications.
- The fundamental principles behind market segment identification and selection.
- The difference between end-consumer markets (B2C) and business markets (B2B).
- The principal bases for segmenting consumer markets.
- Segmentation of the market based on demographic, lifestyle and product-related factors.
- The importance of positioning a brand or company to appeal to target customer segments.
- Niche marketing and other positioning strategies to appeal to target segments.
- The need for a differentiation strategy to set a brand or company apart from the competition.
- The basis for a value-add strategy.

So You Think You Need a New Credit Card?

You're about to graduate with your business degree and have already accepted a job half way across the country in Halifax. It's time to plan the move. Moving and setting up in another city can be expensive, so one of the first things you thought to do was to get the limit increased on your student credit card in case of any unexpected expenses or mishaps along the way. Now that you have a full-time job the customer-service representative at the bank suggests you might want to consider switching to another type of credit card. But, what does that mean? Don't they all do the same thing? The employee at CIBC explained that they offer 12 different credit cards — but, all of them are VISA cards! How can that be? Why would there be so many?

Well, you thought it made sense to have a special card for students with low incomes like yourself — but why bother with all those others? You already knew there were gold cards and platinum cards — that is based on income and credit limits, but what else could be different about all those cards? Well, she explains each one does actually serve the same purpose, but each has a little something different that makes it appeal to slightly different customer needs and interests. It all depends on the customer!

Some are just everyday cards like yours with no fee while others offer cash back rewards of 1 percent or 2 percent of the amount purchased on the card. Others offer reward points redeemable at HBC or Shoppers Drug Mart. Still others provide Aeroplan miles. Some have special travel features — travel rewards, special offers and travel insurance. Other cards are designed for business use. Some of these have fees as much as $120 a year. Some have 10.5 percent annual interest rates while others charge 19.5 percent — it gets to be pretty confusing! You have checked around — the other banks offer a similar selection. Some have even thought of other variations — RBC offers a card with a picture of Mike Weir, Canada's Masters champion, which offers its cardholders golf-related perks, privileges and high-value offers.

Back to the Top

The vignettes are referenced throughout the chapter so students can relate what they're reading to the situation they encountered at the beginning of the chapter (look for the Back to the Top icon in the margin). At the end of each chapter, the Back to the Top heading introduces review questions related to the opening vignette.

GUEST MARKETER

Targeting a Very Important Segment

By Heather Tulk

Heather Tulk is Senior Vice President—Marketing at Bell Aliant, responsible for consumer and Small and Medium Business marketing. Heather believes strongly that excellent marketing starts with a deep understanding of the customer, and can only be executed through a focus on the customer experience. Heather is a graduate of Queen's University and Memorial University.

Aliant is an information and communications technology company based in Atlantic Canada. Aliant delivers innovative and traditional communications services, including local and long distance telephony, wireless, Internet, e-commerce, interactive multimedia, data and managed network services, information technology solutions and knowledge-service applications. In addition to serving residential, small-to-medium sized business and larger enterprise customers in its home market, Aliant also serves business customers located in other parts of Canada and the world.

Over the past number of years, the growing importance of the youth segment has become increasingly clear to many companies, including Aliant. This segment, typically defined as anyone under the age of 25, has incredible spending power owing to the fact that most of their income is disposable. These younger consumers are also early adopters of technology and products, heavy users of new services, and key influencers on household spending.

Understanding this customer group is the critical first step to developing a strategy of how a company such as Aliant could successfully deliver solutions. To gain this understanding, Aliant created a youth panel to act as an extension of their marketing te...

Armed with this knowledge, the company concluded that a good youth strategy would not only target younger customers directly but would also target parents. In the first year of the youth program, Aliant's approach was focused in five different areas: creating communications that were much more relevant to this segment; showcasing products, services and promotions in new media and locations; launching new products specifically for them; finding ways to show youth that Aliant cares about their business; and providing gifting options for parents.

Aliant has launched a communications platform for younger customers and created a portal www.aliant.net/youth101 that houses all of the company's youth-relevant information. Aliant has created youth-targeted retail stores and special zones within our stores. These stores provide an opportunity to have an interactive ...

Guest Marketers

New to this edition, five senior marketing executives share their thoughts on the latest marketing practices and how their companies put marketing principles to work to gain desired customer and competitive outcomes. Each Guest Marketer discussion is accompanied by video or audio material. This allows the presentations to be handled as cases using an innovative multimedia approach.

MARKETING AT WORK — 6-3: STRATEGY

Not The Same Jam At All

Everyone knows the Kraft brand. Kraft Foods supplies us with 61 brands of various products. Many of the foods, beverages, and condiments we have grown up with in Canada come from this company, including Kraft Dinner, Tang, Grape-Nuts cereal, Maxwell House coffee, Ritz crackers, and Oreo cookies.

But it is not only in the supermarket that we come across many of the Kraft products we enjoy.

We have all been in a cafeteria, on an airplane, or even at some sort of banquet or function where we have used those small packages of coffee, crackers, jam, or even peanut butter or cream cheese. And most often we recognize the brand on the package — Sanka coffee, Philadelphia cream cheese, Kraft salad dressing. While the contents of these packages are the same as those we can get at our local grocery store, these small packages actually are products that are not available for sale in the consumer marketplace. Kraft offers them only in the B2B marketplace — sold to other businesses for resale — products that enable other companies and organizations to offer their own products and services.

This is an example of a firm that sells to both B2B and B2C markets. And while you may think that strawberry jam is strawberry jam — whether it is in a jar or a single-serving package — you would be wrong! These are actually two different products. Why? Because they each require their own marketing mix. Yes, it is the same strawberry jam, but "'product" also refers to size and packaging, which is a very important detail for creating utility in these two ...

packages will be sold in bulk as a "component" product. Promotion and distribution will differ as well: Sales representatives will attempt to address the very different concerns of different clients — hotel chains and airlines, instead of supermarkets.

QUESTIONS:

1. Would consumers be interested in the product forms that Kraft markets exclusively to the B2B market?
2. Would a particular segment pay more for the added value such portions provide?

Marketing at Work

Ninety percent of the Marketing at Work features are new to this edition and illustrate current developments and successful implementations by recognizable companies and individuals. Some examples: Kraft Canada develops single serving products; Debbie Travis becomes Canada's queen of renovation; Shoppers Drug Mart and its approach to cosmetics marketing; National Car Rental working at building relationships; Toyota Canada's innovative Yaris advertising; Procter and Gamble Canada making cultural diversity work in the office and the market. Each feature highlights a key theme — Strategy, Relationships, Global, Technology, and Ethics. Each is identified with a colourful icon to help students understand the focus and application of each Marketing at Work feature. Each one concludes with a series of questions to aid the student in appreciating and recalling the main points of the discussion.

STRATEGY

TECHNOLOGY

GLOBAL

ETHICS

RELATIONSHIPS

PageUp

PAGE UP!

The PageUp feature allows students to pause as they study a chapter and reflect on what they have read. There are three PageUp sections in each chapter, introduced at appropriate points as major topics are completed. PageUp consists of three review questions that are intended to encourage students to think back over what they have just studied to make sure that they understand the material and concepts.

Cases

Each of the seven parts of the book ends with a set of cases. Almost all of these are new to this edition (a small number of successful cases from the previous edition have been retained and rewritten to reflect current situations). The format of the cases has been changed in response to feedback from instructors across the country. Each of the parts of the text ends with two short cases and one longer one. The short cases capture succinctly a concept or issue from the chapters just studied. They are valuable in that their length allows the instructor to assign them for in-class reading and discussion. The longer case that accompanies each part is more comprehensive in the concepts that it covers. It is appropriate for study and preparation before class, either as a written assignment or for in-depth discussion. The companies and topics presented in the line-up of cases are very student-friendly, dealing with companies with which students will be familiar, including 1-800-GOT-JUNK?, Running Room, and Boston Pizza.

CASE 7-3:

CBC

Dr. Duncan's Other Dilemma

It was Thursday afternoon and Dr. Pauline Duncan had just seen her fifteenth patient of the day. It was the third time Robert McCarthy had been to see her in the past month, complaining about a persistent stiff neck and pain radiating though his right shoulder. Robert was 28 years old and otherwise quite fit and Dr. Duncan had prescribed an anti-inflammatory to deal with Robert's discomfort. Nevertheless, his pain had persisted and Robert had been off work for the past week.

But this third visit was different. Robert had arrived for his appointment with 30 or more pages that he had printed from a number of Internet sites. As soon as he entered the examining room, he said, "Doctor, I've been on the Internet for the past few days, searching through lots of medical sites, and I've found what my problem is; just look! This doctor in England says that he has seen patients with exactly my problem and that this is what is causing it. He prescribes this drug for it. So, I want you to write me a prescription for it."

Dr. Duncan ... al similar experience ... ome to h...

rial that these patients are bringing with them to her clinic. She also knows that she does not have time to go online herself to become aware of all of the information that is currently available on medical conditions, diagnoses and remedies. But, she also has had a few patients get angry when she refused to prescribe the drugs they wanted. A couple even threatened to go to another doctor.

Questions

1. How do you suspect Dr. Duncan feels when presented with such information by patients? How should she handle such situations? How do the patients feel when she refuses to prescribe the drugs they have suggested?
2. To what extent should Dr. Duncan's patients expect to be treated like "customers?" What does this ... in terms of how the doctor deals with them? ... omer alwa...

Multimedia

Fourteen of the 21 regular cases in this edition are tied to a variety of supporting media including CBC video clips, company sponsored clips from Sony, the Running Room, and Mission Hill Family Estate Winery, as well as television and radio commercials featuring Aliant, Envirocoatings, Safeway, Toyota, and others.

CASE 2-4:

GuestLink – Aliant Youth Strategy

In Chapter 5, our Guest Marketer, Heather Tulk, Senior Vice-President – Marketing at Bell Aliant, outlined that company's strategy to reach customers in the youth segment. Let's think about this strategy and why Aliant might want to single out younger customers for marketing attention. What is the market opportunity represented by the "youth market" segment? In fact, is this segment homogenous, or are there several subsegments within the youth market? Is this simple demographic segmentation?

Take a look at the three TV commercials that accompany this case and discuss them in the context of the youth strategy that Heather Tulk has outlined.

Questions:

1. What benefits are "youth" customers seeking from a cellular telephone company? How effectively has Aliant used marketing research to address this question?
2. How has Aliant chosen to position itself to appeal to youth customers? How does it add value for these customers and differentiate its brand from that of Rogers and Telus?
3. How is Aliant's positioning reflected in the three TV commercials? Visit Aliant's youth portal (**www.aliant.net/youth101**) and review how this component of the marketing program also appeals ... customers

In addition to the regular cases, our Guest Marketer feature has been developed in an innovative fashion with what we call a **GuestLink**. Each of the five Guest Marketer presentations included in the text is further developed at the end of the relevant part with a discussion case accompanied by a television or radio commercial. Adding the five new GuestLink cases to our total means there are 26 cases, 18 with multimedia based content available for student use.

Key Terms and Concepts

brand 244
brand awareness 245
brand characteristics 246
brand equity 247
brand extensions 249
brand label 261
brand loyalty 247
brand mark 245
brand name 245
brand personality 246
brand recognition 245
brand relationship 246
brand values 246
branding 244
bundling 260
co-branding 255
eco-labelling 261
express warranty 264
family-brand strategy 257
family packaging 260
grade label 261
implied warranty 264
label 261
multiple-brand strategy 257
multiple packaging 260
national brands 245
packaging 258
private labels 245
service guarantees 264
statutory labelling requirements 261
trademark 245

Key Terms and Concepts

Every chapter contains the definitions of highlighted key terms in margins next to its relevant text. These assist not only in providing precision at a point in discussion but also can be used for quick review as a student works through the text. In addition, the chapter concludes with a complete summary listing of key terms and concepts with chapter page references.

Questions and Problems

1. Explain the terms *retailing*, *retail sale*, and *retailer* in light of the following situations:
   a. Avon cosmetics salesperson selling in offices.
   b. Farmer selling produce door to door.
   c. Farmer selling produce at a roadside stand.
   d. Sporting-goods store selling uniforms to a semi-professional baseball team.
   e. Chapters/Indigo selling books and music through its Web site.
2. What recommendations do you have for reducing retailing costs?
3. Reconcile the following statements, using facts and statistics where appropriate:
   a. "Retailin... ...ll-scale business."

a stronger position than large-scale retailers? Do your findings conflict with the fact that most retail firms are quite small?

5. What course of action might a small retailer take to improve its competitive position?
6. What could a department store do to strengthen its competitive position?
7. "The supermarket, with its operating expense ratio of 20 percent, is the most efficient institution in retailing today." Do you agree with this statement? In what ways might supermarkets further reduce their expenses?
8. "Door-to-door selling is the most efficient form of ..."

Hands-On Marketing

1. Interview a marketing executive and/or consult a corporate Web site to identify how the particular company is applying the principles of CRM as discussed in the boxed item in this chapter. Identify the various components of the company's CRM system. How successful do you believe this company's investment in CRM has been in developing solid relationships with customers? In your report, identify how you believe this company should evaluate the success of its CRM program.
2. Interview three managers in companies near your campus or home and ask them:
   a. How they define marketing in their companies and how marketing may have changed in recent years.
   b. How marketing is organized and who is responsible for it.
   c. What foreseeable developments will have the greatest impact on marketing in their firms over the next five years.
   d. How they think their industry and their company should respond to these developments.

Assignments

Each chapter ends with two types of assignments. The first is a set of approximately 10 Questions and Problems designed to help students discover how to analyze issues and make applications based on the chapter discussion. The second type of assignment is called Hands-On Marketing. These assignments require the students to interact with customers or marketers, as well as make use of the Internet.

TEACHING AND LEARNING SUPPORT

For the Instructor

Instructor's Resource CD-ROM: The new Instructor's Resource CD-ROM for *Marketing* contains the Instructor's Manual, Microsoft® PowerPoint® slides and Computerized Test Bank.

- ***Instructor's Manual*** by Shirley Noseworthy: The *Instructor's Manual* responds to the practical needs of instructors who want to help students learn in the way that works best for them. The goal is to help students learn more effectively by providing instructors with strategy suggestions (such as Internet activities, group work, and case studies) to encourage learning in the context of an introductory marketing course. Case solutions for the text cases are also provided.
- ***Microsoft® PowerPoint® Presentation*** by Janice Shearer: This software includes a set of more than 300 slides. The slides include point-form summaries of key concepts discussed in the text.
- ***Computerized Test Bank*** by Alan McGee: The computerized test bank consists of multiple-choice and true/false questions, as well as caselettes — short, current case descriptions with accompanying multiple-choice questions. The approximately 2000 questions in the test bank are coded to identify the type — concept, definition, or application.

DVDs, including CBC videos: This collection of video and audio clips, featuring CBC programs, corporate videos, and TV and radio ads, corresponds to selected companies or organizations profiled in the book's part-ending cases. They feature a variety of organizations and marketing topics.

Online Learning Centre: Both students and instructors will find the text's companion online learning centre (OLC) to be an invaluable learning support tool. The OLC contains both a student and a secure, password-protected instructor section. The instructor's section contains all the features available to students (quizzes, videos, audio files, *Business Week* podcasts), plus the Instructor's Manual and Microsoft® PowerPoint® presentations. Visit www.mcgrawhill.ca/olc/sommers.

Superior Service

iLearning Sales Specialist: Your Integrated Learning Sales Specialist is a McGraw-Hill Ryerson representative with the experience, product knowledge, training, and support to help you assess and integrate any of the following products, technology and services into your course for optimum teaching and learning performance. Whether it is using our test bank software, helping your students improve their grades, or putting your entire course online, your *i*Learning Sales Specialist is there to help you do it. Contact your local *i*Learning Sales Specialist today to learn how to maximize all of McGraw-Hill Ryerson's resources.

iLearning Services Program: McGraw-Hill Ryerson offers a unique *i*Learning Services package designed for Canadian faculty. Our mission is to equip providers of higher education with superior tools and resources required for excellence in teaching. For additional information, please visit www.mcgrawhill.ca/highereducation/iservices.

Course Management

Visit **www.mhhe.com/pageout** to create a Web page for your course using our resources. PageOut is the McGraw Hill Ryerson Web site development centre. This Web page-generation software is free to adopters and is designed to help faculty create an online course, complete with assignments, quizzes, links to relevant Web sites, and more — all in a matter of minutes.

In addition, content cartridges are available for the course management systems **WebCT** and **Blackboard**. These platforms provide instructors with user-friendly, flexible teaching tools. Please contact your local McGraw-Hill Ryerson *i*Learning Sales Specialist for details.

For the Student

***i*Study** by R. David Nowell: This exciting and innovative online study guide provides students with a completely new way to learn. The motivating interactive exercises are not only enjoyable, but also ensure students' active involvement in the learning process, boosting their ability to retain and apply key concepts. *i*Study includes chapter summaries as downloadable MP3 audio files, interactive quizzes with instant feedback, fun Flash presentations, cases, customer-centric scenarios to exemplify the focus of the text, as well as an interactive case guide. (ISBN: 9780070960169)

Online Learning Centre: Students can access DVD and audio clips to accompany the part-ending cases on the OLC, as well as *Business Week* podcasts specifically chosen to match the topics in the text. They can also benefit from the following features for every chapter of the text:

- True/False Quizzes
- Multiple Choice Quizzes
- Annotated Web links
- Internet-based questions

Visit **www.mcgrawhill.ca/olc/sommers**.

Marketing Magazine: McGraw-Hill Ryerson is pleased to offer special access to *Marketing Magazine's online* archive of marketing articles. It's an unbeatable research tool, invaluable for preparing assignments and exploring the hottest issues in Canadian marketing.

Acknowledgements

Through eleven editions of this book, many people have made important contributions. These include students, colleagues, clients, marketing managers in Canadian firms, and instructors at many universities and colleges. All have provided insights and commentary on the Canadian marketing scene and the teaching and learning of marketing. We sincerely thank them for their advice, thoughtfulness, and support.

We wish to acknowledge several people who provided invaluable research and editorial support that has contributed to the wealth of new material in this edition. In particular, we thank Shirley Noseworthy, Susan Myrden and Peter Dunne, each of whom was instrumental in making this the best edition ever. We are also indebted to the executives who allowed us to write cases on their companies or organizations and to include advertising and other material.

We are delighted to include in this eleventh edition a new feature that further enhances the real-world nature of the book. Our Guest Marketer feature provides a forum for practising marketing executives to share their views on marketing and to give us an inside look at their companies and their responsibilities. The cooperation that we received from Heather Tulk, Bruce Hunter, Greg Pope, John Gardner, and Ralph van Dijk has been exemplary. We thank them most sincerely for their valuable contribution.

Another group that was instrumental in the preparation of this book was the group of reviewers consulted by our publisher. These include the following colleagues:

Harvey Skolnick, Sheridan College
Guillermo Acosta, Humber College
Richard Appleby, Okanagan University College
Brahm Canzer, John Abbott College
Alan Chapelle, Malaspina University-College
William Clymer, Durham College
Brad Davis, Wilfrid Laurier University
Sherry Finney, University College of Cape Breton
Dan Greeno, University of Toronto
Ruth Jaglowitz, Seneca College
Steve Janisse, St. Clair College
Phil Jones, Algonquin College
Kyeongheui Kim, University of Toronto: Scarborough
Henry Klaise, Durham College
Brent McKenzie, University of Western Ontario
Cindy McPherson, BCIT
Lesley Moffitt, Assiniboine Community College
David Nowell, Sheridan College
Janice Shearer, Mohawk College

They provided much useful insight and commentary and we would like to thank each of them.

Finally, we would like to acknowledge with much appreciation the support and cooperation we received from the staff of McGraw-Hill Ryerson. We are grateful to Leanna MacLean, our Sponsoring Editor for this edition, for being there to get things moving. Denise Foote, our Senior Developmental Editor, and Emma Gain, our Developmental Editor, really performed sterling development work. Karen Becker, our Photo Researcher, delivered many of the images that make the text visually appealing. We owe special thanks to Kelly Dickson, Manager, Editorial Services, and Tracey Haggert, Copy Editor, who provided important assistance and information and helped us ensure that this edition will meet the goals and objectives of all those involved.

Montrose S. Sommers
James G. Barnes

PART 1

Marketing and the Customer

An overview of a new view of marketing, one that is truly focused on understanding customers so that we can better meet their needs and earn their loyalty

In **Part 1** of this book, we place the customer squarely at the centre of all marketing activity, and then we examine the various factors that influence customer decision making.

The successful practice of marketing requires an appreciation for the changing society in which we live. It also demands a detailed understanding of customers and what's important to them in their lives and in their dealings with businesses.

Marketing is complex, challenging, rewarding, and always changing! Welcome to the part of the organization where everything comes together, where revenue is generated, and where customers decide what sells and what doesn't.

In **Chapter 1**, we place the customer clearly at the centre of marketing activity, the goal of which is to produce emotional and behavioural responses from customers. In **Chapter 2**, we illustrate that the customer is influenced by his or her own unique internal characteristics and by a series of social factors to which he or she is exposed. Then, in **Chapter 3**, we show that distant and far-reaching environmental factors influence the customer; these also have an impact on how businesses operate.

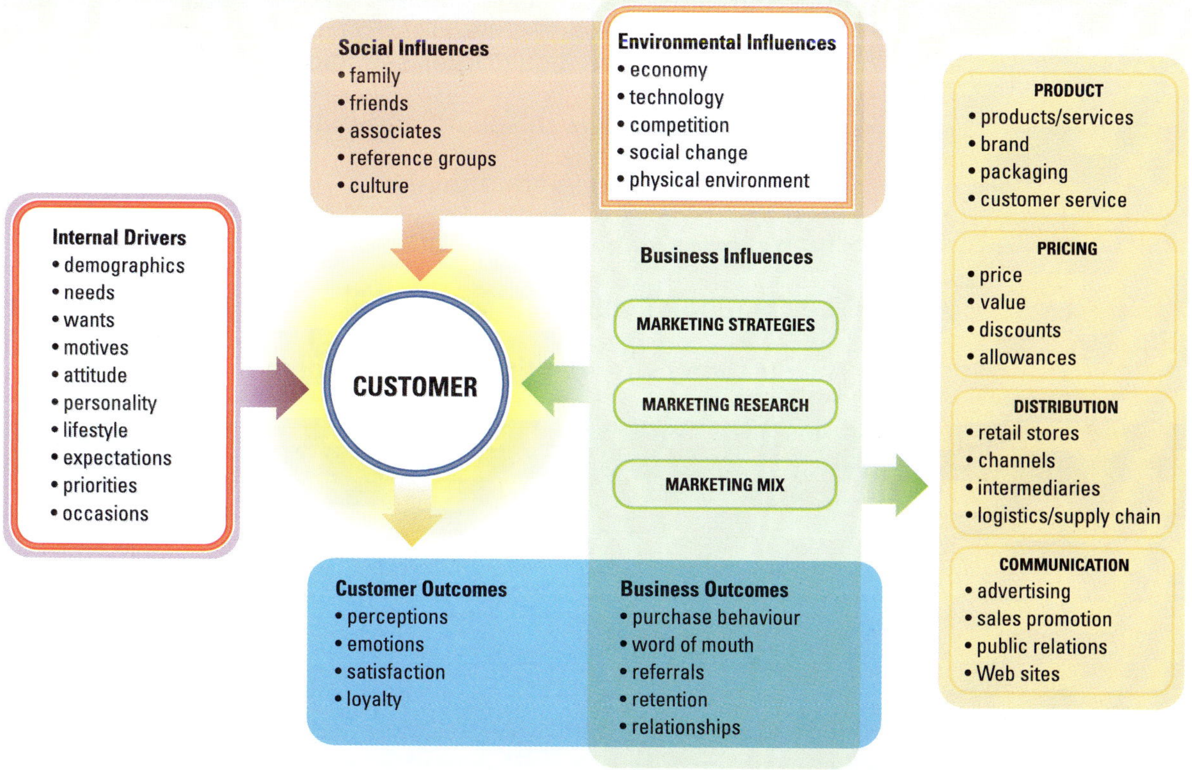

CHAPTER 1

What's Marketing All About?

"What is marketing?" Chapter 1 answers this question — and the answer may surprise you. Marketing today is widely considered to encompass many tasks within a company or organization. It's more than advertising and setting prices. It's more than retail stores and catchy jingles. In fact, it's just about anything that contributes to satisfying customers. After studying this chapter, you should have an understanding of:

- The focus of marketing on customer satisfaction.
- Marketing's emphasis on creating customer loyalty and relationships.
- How marketing applies to business and non-business situations.
- The factors that drive customer satisfaction.
- The difference between selling and marketing.
- The evolution of marketing thinking.
- The modern marketing concept.
- The creation of value, the value proposition, and brand equity.
- The customer's role at the centre of marketing thinking.

It's Not About the Shoes!

It's Saturday afternoon and Sarah has decided to go shopping for a new pair of running shoes. She meets her friend, Colin, at Second Cup for a quick coffee and then they walk down the street to their first stop, Sports Champs, where they notice a display of New Balance running shoes just inside the door, with a sign announcing "20% OFF!"

As Sarah and Colin walk toward the shoe department, they notice that the store is quite untidy, with boxes in the aisles and clothing hanging off racks. Colin comments that the rock music blaring from the speakers in the ceiling is so loud it's almost impossible to carry on a conversation. When they reach the display of shoes, Sarah is pleased to see a good selection and that all New Balance shoes are indeed on sale at 20 percent off. She and Colin select two pairs and then look for someone to serve them.

But, there's no help in sight. Although there aren't many customers in the store and Sarah can see three employees in the distance, dressed in the store's distinctive red-striped uniforms with their names on the back, no one shows any interest in serving her. In fact, the sales staff are gathered at the checkouts, apparently discussing something very important. Another employee walks by carrying an armload of jackets. When Sarah asks if he's busy, he answers, "Yes!" and walks on. Colin decides to approach the group at the checkouts and asks whether anyone is serving in the shoe department. One of the employees says, "That's Ted's department; he should be back soon." Sarah and Colin wait, but Ted doesn't show. After 10 minutes, during which two other employees walk right by them, Colin says, "Let's get out of here."

Three blocks away, Sarah and Colin walk into Blades & Boards. As they enter the store, they are approached by an employee who announces, "Hi! I'm Sandy. What can we help you with today?" Sarah tells her that she is looking for running shoes and Sandy leads her to the shoe department, where Sarah notices that the selection is not as wide as it was at Sports Champs. They do carry New Balance shoes, but the prices are not reduced. Sandy asks what type of shoes Sarah is looking for, and she explains that she has been running a lot lately and is planning to run her first 10K road race next month. Sandy asks what size she wears and what price range she is considering. Sarah tells her she wears size 8 and was hoping to spend no more than $125.

Sandy disappears into the storeroom and emerges with three boxes of shoes: two pairs of Nike and one of Saucony. After trying on the three pairs and walking around the store, Sarah goes back to the display wall to take a closer look at the New Balance shoes. There's one model priced at $119.95 that she and Colin had looked at while waiting at Sports Champs, and she asks Sandy if she has her size in stock. Sandy agrees that these shoes would be very suitable and again goes into the storeroom, emerging with the news that they have an $8\frac{1}{2}$, but no size 8.

Then, Sandy says, "Rather than sell you a shoe that doesn't fit, let me call our other store in the Rosewood Mall to see if they have a size 8. If they have them, I'll get them sent over and you can come in and try them on; we're open tomorrow and I'll be here." She comes back in a couple of minutes to tell Sarah that the size 8 New Balance shoes will be delivered that afternoon and that she can come back later tonight or tomorrow to try them on. Then she says, "By the way, there's a 10 percent discount for students at your school; I couldn't help but notice your knapsack!"

At 2:30 Sunday afternoon, Sarah walks out of Blades & Boards with her New Balance shoes, size 8.

What happened in this typical customer experience that caused Sarah to buy her new running shoes in one store rather than the other? How did Sarah and Colin feel at Sports Champs and at Blades & Boards? How did these feelings influence Sarah's purchase decision? What role did Sandy play? How do you suppose Sarah and Colin now feel toward the two stores? Where are they likely to go when they need to make a similar purchase in the future? What does this have to do with marketing?

The answer is that this example is quite typical of situations that customers face every day. Some customer experiences are positive and others are negative; some are satisfying and others are not; some cause you to vow never to go back and others cause you to tell your friends about how well you were treated. This experience with two retail stores also illustrates how complex something as simple as buying a pair of running shoes can be. There are many factors involved and many things that contributed to Sarah's final decision to buy the shoes and how she felt afterwards. This reflects the complexity of marketing and the importance of the customer's perspective in determining whether a company is successful.

Customer Satisfaction Is the Focus

marketing
An integrated series of activities oriented toward achieving long-term customer satisfaction; involves planning, pricing, promoting, and distributing need-satisfying products and services to target markets in order to achieve success for both customers and businesses/organizations.

customer
An individual or organization involved in making purchase and consumption decisions.

customer satisfaction
The degree to which a customer's experience with a product or organization meets or exceeds his or her expectations.

exchange
The voluntary act of providing a person or organization with something of value in order to acquire something else of value in return.

What is the focus of marketing today? What do we mean when we use the term **marketing**? To what aspects of a company's operations are we referring when we talk about marketing? Different people will have different views when they refer to marketing, and those views have changed over the years. We believe that *marketing* refers to just about anything that a company or other organization does that has an impact on the satisfaction of its **customers**. In other words, marketing is the most customer-focused part of a company and principally involves activities and programs that will contribute to high levels of **customer satisfaction**, through addressing customer needs and wants. In business, the objective of marketing is also to satisfy customer needs and wants at a profit. It is very important, as well, to think about customer satisfaction as a long-term objective, because we want customers to come back over and over again. Therefore, customer satisfaction must be constantly reinforced.

Why are we interested in customer satisfaction (and particularly in *long-term* customer satisfaction) as an objective of marketing? It's really quite simple. Satisfied customers will buy more from us, they will come back again and again to do business with us, and they will often tell their friends and family members about us. A solid group of satisfied customers represents one of a company's most valuable assets — when one considers the potential lifetime value of loyal customers, it is obvious that these customers represent a stream of sales and profits that will last well into the future. Therefore, a marketing focus within a company today involves a long-term view. If we can satisfy a large percentage of customers, they will keep coming back again and again. They represent the future success of the business. Without them, we have to spend a great deal of time, energy, and money continually trying to attract new customers to replace those who are leaving. It's really simple, the more satisfied customers are, the more they will come back to buy again, the more they recommend the company to others, and the more profits the company makes.

How, then, can a company achieve long-term customer satisfaction? The most successful companies accomplish this by giving customers what they want, when they want it, for a price that the customers consider to be acceptable. The best companies make it easy for customers to deal with them and treat them pleasantly and politely. They create the most positive customer experiences. There is a process of **exchange** involved, but what is being exchanged is quite broad. The customer gives the company something and gets something of value in return. We need to consider precisely what this "something" is. It's not as simple as giving money to obtain a pair of jeans or a new tennis racquet. There's much more involved than that. In fact, the tangible components of what is being

THE CUSTOMER GIVES THE COMPANY GETS	THE COMPANY GIVES THE CUSTOMER GETS
Money	Product
Time	Price
Energy	Value
Commitment	Convenience
Referrals	Selection
Past experience	Service
Expectations	Warranty
Knowledge	Brand
Influence	Treatment
Word of mouth	Experience
Support	Comfort
Loyalty	Peace of mind

Figure 1-1: The Give and Get of Marketing

exchanged is often not as critical in creating customer satisfaction as are the intangible aspects, such as the interaction of employees with the customer, how he or she is treated, and how easy the business makes the experience.

Exchanges take place between many different groups and organizations and in different situations. So, marketing as we are discussing it does not apply only to businesses that are offering products and services to customers. There is an exchange involved when you buy a ticket to a concert, when you take a course at your school, when you donate to a charity, and when you visit a museum. In all cases, things are exchanged, some of them tangible, others intangible; sometimes involving the exchange of money, other times not. In all cases, the principles of marketing apply. Customers receive something of value in return for what they are giving. That perception of value is an individual thing and depends on the quality of the product and service, on how conveniently it is made available, on the time it takes to get it, on the price, and on many other factors. When customers perceive that they have received value, a feeling of satisfaction will be experienced, likely leading to a decision to buy, or donate, or visit that company or organization again.

"give and get"
An illustration of the exchange process as both customer and company giving something and getting something in return.

It might be useful to consider the exchange that is involved in marketing as an exercise in "**give and get**" — the customer gives something and gets something in return (see Figure 1-1). What is given and received contributes to the level of satisfaction enjoyed by the customer. It's important to think very broadly about what is being exchanged, because this will help us understand that the scope of marketing itself is indeed very broad.

Think back to the example that opened this chapter. To buy her running shoes, Sarah not only paid a certain price, she also invested time and effort. She had to make a certain commitment in order to obtain the shoes. She may have spent time planning the purchase by looking through magazines, or checking out online stores, or talking with friends. Chances are she has had previous experience buying sports gear and was familiar with many of the brand names available. She may even have owned a pair of New Balance shoes.

BACK TO THE TOP

And what did Sarah get for this commitment of time, energy, and money and for the application of her past experience and knowledge? It's too simplistic to suggest that she got new shoes. She also got the time and attention of Sandy at Blades & Boards. She got the benefit of the selection that was available, the discount for students at her school, and the service involved in sending the running shoes over from the Rosewood Mall store. She received an implicit warranty that tells her that she can return the shoes if she has any problems with them. She also got a certain comfort level that goes with buying a recognized brand name like New Balance. Ultimately, she and Colin had a positive (or even a WOW!) **customer experience** at Blades & Boards.

customer experience
The entire experience a customer has in dealing with a business or organization, including many factors that have the potential to influence whether or not the customer is satisfied, such as how the customer is treated and the setting in which the interaction takes place.

Now, where does customer satisfaction enter the picture? In simple terms, customers are satisfied as long as what they get is at least as much as what they have to give. Where *give* is perceived to be greater than *get*, the customer is generally dissatisfied. Sarah was not satisfied with the service (or lack of service!) at Sports Champs, and she walked out. She was not prepared to give more of her time or make any further effort to get the shoes and the service that went along with them. On the other hand, she was satisfied at Blades & Boards because what Sandy was giving was greater than what Sarah was required to give. In fact, by acting as she did, Sandy reduced the time, commitment, and anxiety that Sarah had to put into the exchange — not to mention the price of the shoes!

By creating satisfaction for customers, or by impressing them with the level of attention and service, companies increase the likelihood that the customer will come back, will tell her friends and others about the experience, and will generally spend more money with that company over time. Therefore, creating customer satisfaction is indeed a long-term proposition. But, customer satisfaction is driven by more than just good products at good prices. There is a very important emotional component of satisfaction. Sarah's satisfaction with Blades & Boards was very much influenced by how she was treated and how Sandy made her feel.

Customer Expectations and Value

customer expectations
What customers expect to encounter when dealing with a company or buying a product or service, based on past experience and desired outcomes.

value
A measure of what customers receive and what companies provide in the exchange. Should be very broadly defined.

BACK TO THE TOP

Two important concepts are evident in this early discussion about marketing. Sandy was successful in making the sale because she was able to exceed the **expectations** that Sarah and Colin brought to the store — they probably didn't expect her to be so friendly and helpful, they didn't expect her to call the Rosewood Mall store and to have the running shoes delivered, and they didn't expect the 10 percent discount. Customer expectations are very important in determining whether customer satisfaction is created.

Then, we must consider the concept of **value**. This is a central concept in marketing, since customers want to receive value when they buy products or services. In fact, it's value that leads to satisfaction. The greater the value that customers perceive they have received, the greater the satisfaction. Sarah bought her shoes at Blades & Boards because she perceived that she was getting value. But, wait a minute! She could have saved 20 percent if she had bought the shoes at Sports Champs — remember, all New Balance running shoes were on sale at a 20 percent discount *and* they had a wider range available.

What this tells us is an important lesson to be learned early: namely, that *value is not only about price*. Customers decide whether they are receiving value by taking into consideration (often subconsciously) all of the factors that are being exchanged: all of the "gives" and all of the "gets." Value for money is only one kind of value. One of the most important roles of marketers is to add value for their customers. Those that succeed in creating greater perceived value are generally more successful. Sandy added very important value by simply being pleasant and helpful, and by surprising Sarah by offering to get the shoes sent over from Rosewood Mall. Companies can increase value for customers by reducing the time and effort the customers have to provide.

What's Involved in Marketing?

marketer
Any business or other organization that desires to create long-term satisfaction among the customer groups it serves.

This book focuses on the activities carried out by individuals, businesses, and other organizations to bring about exchanges that are beneficial to both sides and to develop long-lasting customer relationships. Virtually all organizations are involved in marketing activities, although some have only recently "discovered" marketing and some still practise it more with a sales focus than with an emphasis on creating customer satisfaction and long-term customer relationships. **Marketers** may be business firms in the conventional sense of the word, or they may be non-business, or not-for-profit organizations, such as hospitals, universities, charities, churches, police departments, or museums. Both groups — business and non-business — face the same marketing issues and challenges, and make use of the same marketing principles and concepts.

Our perspective on marketing — applicable in businesses, not-for-profit organizations, and personal situations — is as follows:

> *Marketing is a series of activities and experiences designed to create, plan, price, promote, and distribute need-satisfying products, services, and ideas to selected customer groups in order to achieve the objectives of both the customer and the organization. It involves all aspects of how the organization interacts with the customer that have the potential to influence the customer's long-term satisfaction with the organization and its value proposition.*

This view of marketing has some significant implications when marketing is properly applied:

- The entire series of activities must be customer-oriented and focused on the quality of the customer relationship — customers' needs and wants must be recognized and satisfied effectively. The ultimate objective of marketing is to achieve long-term customer satisfaction.
- It is a dynamic, holistic and integrated definition, which means that it should be understood and applied by everyone in an organization. Effective marketing demands an integrated view of the customer and of how value is created and customer satisfaction achieved.
- The marketing program starts with an idea for a product or service and does not end until the customer's needs and wants are satisfied, which may be some time after the customer actually buys a product or service. This suggests that the process of customer satisfaction is an ongoing one and does not end with a sale.
- An organization's marketing program, often termed the **marketing mix**, has traditionally been viewed in most organizations as consisting of four co-ordinated elements — product, pricing, distribution system, and promotional activities. These have been considered the essential components of what marketing is about.

marketing mix
A combination of the elements — traditionally including product, pricing, distribution system, and promotional activities — that comprise a company's marketing program. Many marketers now consider the service and experience provided to customers to be an additional and extremely important component of the marketing mix.

Marketers have recently begun to express the view that, although getting the components of the traditional marketing mix right is important or even necessary, this may not be sufficient to ensure high levels of customer satisfaction. In other words, as marketers have begun to pay more attention to the application of marketing to service organizations and to the development of long-term customer relationships, they have realized that other factors, such as how customers are treated and how they feel as a result, are important in influencing customer satisfaction. Consequently, in recent years, marketers have begun to consider an expanded marketing mix, one that incorporates customer service, processes, and technology with which the customer comes into contact, and even the employees of the company.

Much of what contributes to customer satisfaction lies outside the traditional responsibilities of the marketing department. The expanded view of the marketing mix has created a situation in some organizations in which there is confusion about the boundaries of what marketing is. Where does marketing begin and end in the modern company and not-for-profit organization?

Traditionally, the role and responsibilities of marketing executives and the marketing department extended principally to the four elements of the marketing mix — product development, pricing, communications, and distribution — so those marketers engaged in activities that dealt largely with these four areas. Such a view was popular until quite recently and many organizations still operate this way. This is a limited view of marketing that is inconsistent with our view that the scope of marketing extends to many other things that have the potential to affect customer satisfaction. Today, marketing in many companies includes the entire experience of customers in dealing with a company and its staff; not just what they want to buy.

BACK TO THE TOP

Progressive organizations have adopted a broad view of marketing. They realize that there is a great deal more to marketing than is suggested by the traditional marketing mix. In fact, it is increasingly accepted that a company could get the four elements of the marketing mix right and still lose a customer. In fact, we saw this in the example with which we opened this chapter. Sports Champs had the shoes Sarah wanted in stock (product and distribution) at a price that she considered attractive. There appears to have been nothing wrong with its advertising or other forms of marketing communications. Yet, Sarah walked out of Sports Champs and bought her shoes elsewhere, mainly because of things that went wrong that lie outside what is generally considered to be part of the marketing mix.

Increasingly, we find companies and other organizations allocating responsibility for customer satisfaction to a number of departments. In what are now often referred to as customer-focused organizations, it is acknowledged that satisfying the customer is a responsibility that must extend outside the traditional boundaries of the marketing department. As a result, we now see evidence that responsibility for achieving long-term customer satisfaction has been extended to include, for example, customer-service departments and cross-functional groups responsible for building long-term relationships with customers.

Long-term focus: Build relationships and loyalty

Next time that Sarah or Colin needs hockey equipment, or tennis balls, or running shoes, where do you think they are going to go? Chances are they will go first to Blades & Boards. The actions of Sandy and the policies and procedures of Blades & Boards suggest that this company has a long-term perspective on marketing. It realizes that it needs more than a good variety of products and attractive prices to satisfy customers and to keep them coming back. It probably realizes that making a customer happy that Saturday afternoon involved more than selling her a pair of running shoes.

Successful marketers look beyond the sale and look for ways to satisfy their customers to such an extent that a sense of loyalty develops. The most successful companies have a solid group of loyal customers who account for the bulk of their business and who act as unpaid spokespersons for the firm. They not only come back again and again, but they also spread positive word of mouth that recommends the company to others. What we are referring to here is often called **brand equity**. It is the value that customers place in the company they are dealing with or brand that they are buying.

brand equity
The value that customers place on a company or brand; its value in their eyes. The higher the sense of loyalty, the greater the level of brand equity.

customer loyalty
A state achieved when a customer not only deals regularly with a company, but also feels an emotional attachment to it and recommends it to others.

customer relationship
A close association between a company or brand and its customers, characterized by strong feelings of loyalty, trust, and commitment; the ultimate connection, based not only on quality of products and service, but also on how the company makes its customers feel.

Customer loyalty is created when companies take a long-term, broad view of marketing. They pay attention to all things that have the potential to influence customer satisfaction. They realize that making a sale is not enough. They know that they must not only offer great products at attractive prices, do good advertising, and have a wide selection to choose from, but that how customers are treated and ultimately made to feel also has a considerable effect on whether they will buy and, more importantly, on whether they will come back again.

What these successful companies are doing is developing relationships with their customers that extend beyond the immediate transaction. **Customer relationships** have become the focus of many companies in recent years, as they have realized the costs and inefficiencies involved in high levels of customer turnover. Those companies that are focused on establishing relationships with their customers have realized that short-term satisfaction is not enough to guarantee their long-term success. If companies can succeed in having large numbers of customers come back willingly (or even enthusiastically!) again and again, they can be far more successful than companies that are constantly having to attract new customers to replace dissatisfied ones who leave to take their business elsewhere. The building of long-term customer relationships and the stronger brand equity that results will be a central focus of this book.

What drives customer satisfaction?

Customer relationships begin with satisfied customers. If customers are satisfied when buying a certain brand of breakfast cereal or jeans or golf balls, chances are that they will buy that brand again. When satisfaction levels are high, there is little incentive to switch. But, the customer must be satisfied with all aspects of what is received from the company.

The example at the beginning of this chapter illustrates the five factors that contribute to customer satisfaction, which could be called the drivers of customer satisfaction (see Figure 1-2).

MARKETING AT WORK 1-1: STRATEGY

Changing Direction

Every now and then, companies have to change the way they approach their business in order to remain competitive and to encourage continued growth. In 2006, two well-known companies had reached important decisions.

WestJet Airlines, faced with continued competition within Canada and constantly increasing energy costs, embarked on a three-year plan to grow its business in the North American airline marketplace. The first component of the new strategy involves WestJet aggressively promoting its service to selected U.S. cities and on U.S.-based travel Web sites. The second part of the strategy will see WestJet cutting expenses, even on small items such as complimentary inflight snacks and drinks that currently account for an annual $7-million expense. Finally, the airline will endeavour to sign more "code-sharing" agreements with other airlines that will allow them to sell tickets on each other's flights.

At the same time that WestJet was making changes, Nike Canada was striking out in some new directions of its own. In an attempt to revitalize its brand in Canada, Nike decided to terminate a 10-year agreement that it had with Athletes World and to launch new Nike stores under the leadership of Marshall Myles, former CEO of Roots. Facing increased competition from Puma and from the recently-merged Adidas and Reebok brands, Nike decided to take matters into its own hands. Having the new Nike stores will allow Nike to take complete control over its brand and image, rather than relying on Athletes World which carries many competing brands.

QUESTIONS:

1. What do these decisions by two quite different companies have in common?
2. What do these insights into strategic decisions tell us about the scope of marketing?
3. How will these decisions result in greater appeal to the customers of the two companies?

SOURCE: Adapted from Brent Jang, "WestJet reveals plans to boost traffic and pare costs," *The Globe and Mail*, April 27, 2006, p. B5 and Marina Strauss, "Nike leaving Athletes World to run with former Roots CEO," *The Globe and Mail*, April 27, 2006, p. B7.

To be genuinely or completely satisfied, a customer must be satisfied at all five levels. At the bottom of the "cone" is the core of the offer to customers — the basic product or service provided by the company. Generally, we tend to think of tangible products as the core because they are easy to visualize, but a service may be the core offering as in the case of Internet service; for a hair salon, the core product is the haircut.

Figure 1-2: Factors that Drive Customer Satisfaction

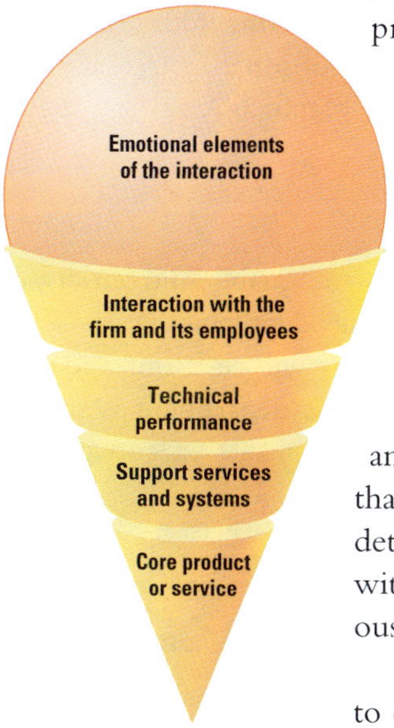

The second level in the "drivers" model is that of support services and systems. It includes such things as the hours when retail stores are open, store location, the variety of models and sizes of products available, inventory control and billing systems, whether the store accepts major credit cards, the availability of staff, and the level of service they provide. Failing to provide satisfactory support services can cause customers to be dissatisfied and not return.

Moving farther up the "cone," the third level involves technical performance, which determines whether the service provider gets the core product and support services right. The emphasis is on meeting the expectations of the customer. Does the company provide the product the customer needs and make it available conveniently and without hassle? Customer dissatisfaction will result from a failure to meet customer expectations that things will go smoothly and as promised. At this level, it is all about delivering as promised — does the firm do what it said it would do?

The fourth level of the model concerns the customer's interaction with the company and its employees. This level can involve both face-to-face interaction and the connection that occurs over the telephone or through e-mail or the Internet. Satisfaction at this level is determined by whether the company makes it easy and pleasant for customers to do business with it. Are customers treated with respect? Is the staff efficient, pleasant, helpful, and courteous? Is the telephone system efficient and the Web site easy to navigate?

Finally, marketers must think beyond the basic elements of the interaction with customers to consider the sometimes-subtle messages that firms send to customers. These messages may create either positive or negative feelings toward the company. Essentially, this final level at the top of the "cone" is concerned with emotional considerations — how the customer feels about dealing with the company. Often, a customer's satisfaction or dissatisfaction has nothing to do with the quality of the core product or service, its price, or how it is provided. Business may be lost because a customer is ignored by employees, an e-mail question is not answered, or some other "little thing" goes wrong and may not even be noticed by staff.

BACK TO THE TOP

It's interesting to remember that, in the chapter-opener example, Sarah bought her running shoes at Blades & Boards, even though the store initially did not have her size in stock, she paid more than she would have at Sports Champs, and she had to make a second trip back to the store to get them. How can that be? Both stores had the shoes that she eventually bought. What caused her to buy them at Blades & Boards?

If we think about the drivers of customer satisfaction, it's obvious that the difference between the two stores lies mainly in the top two levels of the "cone" — Sarah's interaction with employees and how she was made to feel.

PAGE UP!

1. What types of activities are involved in marketing today?
2. When we say that a company has a customer focus, what do we mean?
3. What are the five drivers of customer satisfaction?

Evolution of Marketing Thinking

Although they didn't call it marketing, people have been exchanging things since the beginning of time. However, it was not until the middle of the last century that marketing came to be recognized as an important part of the organization of a company. We make specific reference to companies because the modern view of marketing grew out of businesses. The principles of marketing are now applied to virtually every type of organization, including governments, cultural, charitable, and not-for-profit organizations.

Marketing thinking has evolved through five stages of development or focus: a product focus, a sales focus, an emphasis on the customer, a focus on service, and, most recently, on the development of customer relationships. These five stages reflect not only the development of the field over time, but also the state of mind of those who work in marketing. Although many firms have progressed to the third stage and beyond, the orientation of some firms and some individuals is still in the second or even the first stage, as shown in Figure 1-3.

Product-focus stage

product-focus stage The stage at which a company is focused mainly on producing high-quality products and services.

Fifty or more years ago, most companies were focused simply on the quality and variety of products that they made or sold, and some still are. Firms in the **product-focus stage** place their emphasis on increasing output, while assuming that customers will seek out and buy attractively priced and well-made products. The function of the sales department is simply to sell the company's output at a price usually set by production and finance executives. The

Figure 1-3: Evolution of Marketing Thinking

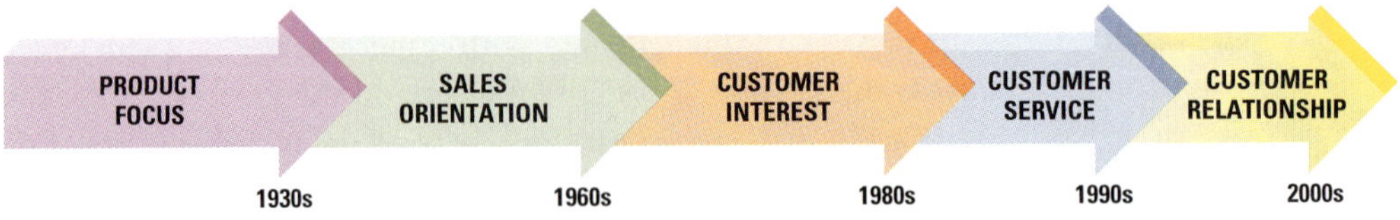

primary focus in business at this stage is to produce large quantities of goods and produce them efficiently. Finding customers is viewed as a relatively minor function. Many companies simply do not understand why customers don't want to buy their perfectly good products. They don't realize that a lot more than great products is involved in producing customer satisfaction and marketing success.

Sales-orientation stage

sales-orientation stage
The stage in the evolution of marketing in which the emphasis is on selling whatever the organization produces.

As the economy grew during the 1960s, it became clear that simply making a better product brought no assurance of success. Firms started to realize that the sale of products required substantial promotional effort. Thus began a **sales-orientation stage** when selling activities and sales executives gained new respect and responsibility. It was also during this period that selling acquired a slightly negative reputation, as "hard-sell" approaches evolved. The emphasis on sales is still a feature of the operations of many retail companies. Employees are rewarded mainly through commissions and bonuses, based on how much they sell.

Customer-interest stage

customer-interest stage
A company realizes that satisfying its customers is critical to its success; generally involves trying to know customers better.

As national and global competition increased during the 1970s, efforts to compete were characterized by aggressive promotional and sales activities. Consumers had become better educated and were less willing to be persuaded, and they had greater variety from which to choose. Consumer organizations were formed and consumer rights legislation was enacted by governments. In the **customer-interest stage** that emerged, many businesses turned their attention to addressing customers' needs. The advent of this stage marked a profound change in marketing, as the orientation turned toward an emphasis on finding out what customers want and then providing them with it. This was a much more sophisticated perspective on marketing, one that was for the first time truly customer-focused. The objective of a company was now to satisfy customers, to meet their needs. In this third stage, firms began to do more of what is now considered marketing, rather than selling.

Customer-service stage

customer-service stage
A company at this stage places emphasis on providing excellent service to its customers, usually through improved systems and employee-customer interaction.

customer-relationship stage
A company actively tries to cultivate long-term relationships with its customers, based not only on great products, price, and service, but also on establishing an emotional connection.

Not until the 1980s did marketing managers really turn their attention to the marketing of services. Until then, marketing had been focused largely on tangible products turned out by well-known manufacturing companies such as General Electric, Kraft Foods, and Bombardier. But, as services began to account for more of the total value of the Canadian economy, firms began to pay greater attention to marketing in industries such as financial services, transportation, and hospitality. Some companies don't sell tangible products; what they offer their customers is entirely intangible. There was increasing acceptance of the fact that services are inherently different from tangible products and that customers approach their purchases differently. There was also a realization in the **customer-service stage** of the fact that all businesses, and indeed all organizations, are in the service business, in that some forms of service accompany the sale of all products. Thus, the era of services in marketing was born, as companies began to ensure that the intangible side of what they offered contributed to customer satisfaction.

Customer-relationship stage

Within the past 10 years, many companies have moved into yet another stage of the evolution of marketing thinking: the **customer-relationship stage**. The main emphasis of a company at this stage is to develop long-lasting relationships with customers, so that they will come back and buy from the company repeatedly and will recommend the company or brand to others. The objective is customer retention, based on the creation of long-term customer satisfaction. This seems to be such an obvious and sensible objective that you might well ask why companies took so long to get to this stage — in fact, it may be argued that many small, local businesses have been operating with this focus for years. They get to know their customers, treat them well, and are rewarded with repeat business. You can probably think of many small businesses that you and your family have been buying from for years, where you are well known to the owners and where you feel welcome or even "part of the family."

Many large national and multinational companies have for many years been motivated by short-term success. It was not until very recently that large companies have been able to use technology to track the business they get and the profits they make from individual customers, and have thereby gained an appreciation for the **lifetime value of customers**. With advances in information systems and customer databases, many companies were able only in the past decade or so to calculate the value of a customer and to realize what they are losing when customers take their business elsewhere. Now these companies can focus on keeping as well as attracting customers. An even more recent extension of this thinking has been directed at creating the most solid relationships possible with customers through the building of an emotional connection with them.

lifetime value of customers
The value to a company of a customer over the lifetime of that customer's association with the firm; more than direct current purchases.

The Modern Marketing Concept

The evolution of marketing thinking from an emphasis on the product to a focus on customer relationships has led to successive steps in the development of a particular philosophy of doing business. Often referred to as the **marketing concept**, this philosophy emphasizes customer orientation and the co-ordination of marketing activities to achieve the mutual long-term objectives of the customer *and* the organization. Although customer satisfaction is important, this focus will work only if it is accomplished at the same time that the organization's objectives are being met; in short, the company has to make a profit. Long-term customer satisfaction leads to the retention of customers, repeat business and referrals, and it generates ongoing profits.[1] Creating and maintaining satisfied customers is therefore an important way to meet the organization's performance objectives. By creating value for its customers, a company is creating long-term payback for its shareholders and securing the future of the company.

marketing concept
A philosophy of doing business that emphasizes a customer orientation and co-ordination of marketing activities in order to achieve customer satisfaction and the organization's performance objectives.

What lies behind the marketing concept?

The marketing concept is based on four beliefs:

- All planning and operations should be focused on creating long-term customer satisfaction. Every department and employee should contribute to the satisfaction of customers' needs. The attitude should be that "everyone is in marketing," because virtually everything that a company or organization does has the potential to affect the satisfaction of customers.
- All marketing activities in an organization should be co-ordinated. Marketing efforts (product and service planning, pricing, distribution, promotion, and customer service) should be designed and combined in a coherent, consistent way, and there should be one overall view of the importance of the customer. Responsibility for the marketing orientation of the company rests squarely on the shoulders of the chief executive officer (CEO) or president. This executive has the responsibility for creating the right culture within the company, one that ensures that customers are treated as

the company's most important asset. Regardless of the department of the company in which employees work, they should be made aware of their roles in supporting a customer focus for the organization.

- Customer-oriented, co-ordinated marketing is essential to achieve the organization's performance objectives, while at the same time meeting the customer's needs. The primary objective for a business is typically to achieve profitability. In not-for-profit organizations, the objective might be to increase the number of people served or the variety of services offered. Since companies began to move into the service- and relationship-focused stages of marketing thinking, there has been a growing awareness that new and different measures of organizational performance are needed.
- Everything is focused on the long term and designed to create an emotional connection with the customer. Thus, an important component of the modern marketing concept relates to creating an environment and an experience for the customer that contributes to the building of a relationship. Concepts such as trust, communication, value, and quality are important parts of what building a relationship means. Thus, truly marketing-oriented organizations have a viewpoint that ensures that they act in a socially responsible manner, that they treat both customers and employees well, and that they behave as responsible members of the communities in which they operate.

The Scope of Marketing Today

Our view of marketing, with its focus on customer satisfaction, means that we will introduce certain concepts and terms that require some explanation and elaboration so we can be sure that our understanding of them is accurate from the beginning.

Marketers take the initiative in trying to stimulate and facilitate exchanges. They develop marketing plans and programs, and implement them in order to create an exchange and an experience that is satisfying to their customers. Marketing, as we have observed, is not simply a business concept, but is used widely in virtually all organizations.

How does an organization such as the Terry Fox Foundation keep alive and share with the rest of the world one young man's dream to run across Canada to raise money for cancer research? How does it inspire and motivate those who organize and participate around the world more than twenty years after the death of the young amputee? As the world becomes more homogenized, so too does the Terry Fox Run. International run locations are organized in more than 50 countries by Canadian Embassies and Consulates, Canadian Forces Bases and many international cancer societies and other dedicated organizations and individuals. To date, more than $360 million has been raised worldwide for cancer research in Terry's name.

Internationally, the Terry Fox Run does not accept sponsorships. Companies that participate, and there are many in the different countries where the run is held, do so on a volunteer basis and the visibility they receive is only through the presence they get from the t-shirts their employees wear when participating. Organization is a large undertaking with scheduling location details and even parking to be arranged for the thousands of participants — it also requires a lot in the way of donations — volunteers, services, refreshments, materials, advertising and promotions, and cold, hard cash!

Even without any official sponsorship title, companies are willing to provide whatever is needed. In far-flung locations such as Abu Dhabi, in the Arabian Gulf, more than 5,000 people participated in the run in March of 2005 — and that was in a rainstorm — something that doesn't happen very often in that part of the world. Next door in Dubai, over 6,000 participants showed up to do their part. On the other side of the world from where it all began, firms line up

MARKETING AT WORK 1-2: ETHICS

"If You've Ever Given a Dollar, You Are a Part of the Marathon of Hope."

How do you market the heroic mission of one young man who lost his personal battle more than twenty years ago? How do you inspire people all over the world to keep his dream alive?

How does the Terry Fox Foundation, based in Chillwack, B.C. continue to raise money for cancer research across Canada and in over 50 countries around the world with the Terry Fox Run 25 years after Terry's death? This is largely undertaken through the use of the Internet. Of course, many people are responsible for the continued success of the Foundation, but the information and resources made available through www.terryfoxrun.org allows the Run to continue growing internationally. The site provides a history of Terry's life, as well as the story of the Terry Fox run and how it has developed since his death. The site is a testament to Terry's unwavering determination to achieve his goal.

The site provides all the information required for people around the globe to organize their own run including downloadable pledge sheets, T-shirt graphics and newsletters. The site also contains links to provincial run pages and a list of times and run site listings. To keep young Canadians and others aware of Terry's battle, video files and photo albums are also available, as well as other resources for educational institutions and the media. The site also makes available Terry's own journal entries expressing his experiences each day as he ran across Canada. As well, the site provides the opportunity for online donations and arranging planned gifts to the Foundation.

QUESTIONS:

1. Why is the Terry Fox Run a good example of marketing in action?
2. Who are the customers?

SOURCES: Adapted from www.terryfox.org, April 10, 2005; Greg Joyce, "Terry Fox's Legacy; runners in many nations raising funds for cancer research," *Canadian Press Online*, April 11, 2005; and http://story.news.yahoo.com.

market
People or organizations with needs or wants to satisfy, money to spend, and the willingness to spend it.

decision maker
The individual in a household or organization who has the responsibility of deciding what to buy.

purchaser
The person in the household or organization who actually makes the purchase of a product or service.

influencers
The people in a buying centre who set the specifications and aspects of buying decisions because of their technical expertise, financial position, or political power in the organization.

to volunteer their services — DHL provided courier services, Mövenpick Hotels provided 4,000 sandwiches, and local newspaper and radio stations provided free promotion of the event.

On the other side of the exchange is the **market**, made up of people or organizations to which marketing programs are directed. Markets are made up of customers — any people with whom a business or organizational marketer wants to do business. While we tend to use the term customers to describe the individuals and entities to which a marketing initiative is directed, this is in fact a general term that is applied to the market for products and services. Markets also include employees, clients, passengers, patrons, donors, students, taxpayers, and patients. Markets may also be other organizations. For example, there are many companies that never sell to end-consumers, but rather market to other businesses and organizations; this is the so-called business-to-business (B2B) market, as distinct from the business-to-consumer (B2C) market.

The people who make up a market, usually referred to as customers, play a number of roles. First, there is the **decision maker**, the individual or organizational unit that has the authority to make the decision to buy something. Then there is the consumer, the one who actually uses or consumes the product or service. The **purchaser** is the person who actually makes the purchase. Finally, there are **influencers**, who affect the decisions of others because of their expertise, position, or power. These definitions are not simply semantic distinctions. These roles are very important in determining how marketers carry out their marketing programs, what information they direct to whom, and what appeals are likely to work for different people in the process.

Suppose your job is to create the marketing for a toy brand, or a toy retailer — who should your marketing speak to? Take a second, it's not as easy as all that! Who buys toys? It

Is this little guy a consumer, or a powerful influencer?

most often isn't children! So…what does that mean for a marketer?

Also, think about all the concern these days about educational toys, gender roles, and childhood socialization. That has to matter, doesn't it? You wouldn't think a toy-buying decision would be a hard one, but in today's environment of political correctness it can be a minefield! How do you decide what to buy your young child? How do you decide what would be acceptable to buy for the child of a friend or family member?

Who, outside of children and family members, impacts the decision of what toys to buy? Sure, advertisers have an influence — that's the whole point of marketing, isn't it? But, in this case the consumers have little to say – in fact, they sometimes can't even talk! Parents, family members and friends buy toys — and they often ask others what the best toys are for their children. Other parents, grandparents, safety advocates, educational experts, even paediatricians get asked for opinions! Who should a toy company try to persuade?

Toy designer Steven Kay faces such issues with his line of mind-maddening and award-winning transformational toys marketed by his company, The Orb Factory. Mr. Kay's product line of brainteasers, orbs, and puzzles appeal to consumers ranging from young children to grandparents... even corporations looking for promotional devices and gifts. While the idea for marketing the products in educational and childhood developmental toy stores may seem to have been a relatively no-brainer decision, reaching a broader target segment than just children, parents, and grandparents was a much greater challenge. With the help of Acadia business graduate Paul Higgins, and thanks to the company's products popping up in television shows such as *Seinfeld* and the *X-Files*, as well as motion pictures such as *I Know What You Did Last Summer*, Mr. Kay's creations also now appeal to individuals seeking unique gift ideas and corporations looking to leave lasting impressions with "corporate keepers" that bear company names, logos, and slogans. In fact, the company that first started out of Mr. Kay's basement in Halifax, now markets internationally to 20 countries with annual sales of over $2-million.[2]

BACK TO THE TOP

In the case of the purchase of running shoes in the example that opened this chapter, Sarah played all three roles of decision maker, consumer, and purchaser, as she was making the purchase of shoes for her own use. Her friend Colin played the role of influencer, and there may have been other influencers — friends with whom she discussed the purchase and others who may have recommended a particular brand of shoes.

needs and wants
The focus of a customer-oriented company who will want to satisfy these in order to achieve customer satisfaction. May be viewed as a combination of functional and emotional needs.

Marketers must also remember that their principal task is to offer customers a product or service that will produce satisfaction. Marketing is a process of satisfying customer **needs and wants** through an exchange process. Technically, customer needs can be viewed in a strict physiological sense (related to food, clothing, and shelter) and everything else can be defined as a want. However, from a customer's perspective, the distinction is not clear. For example, many people consider a television set or a computer to be a necessity. When we speak of customer needs, we are actually extending our use of the term to include wants as well. Technically, it may be argued that most consumers really don't need a large percentage of the products and services that they buy, in the sense that they could continue to exist and get along very well without them. Therefore, we are often talking about wants, but we tend to refer to needs.

We also must remember that customer needs extend well beyond the actual product or service being offered. Customers want to receive satisfaction when they engage in exchanges with businesses. Here, we must return to a comment we made earlier: namely, that we should define what is being exchanged very broadly. So too, we must define customer needs very broadly. Customers shopping for running shoes (or any other product or service) not only need to find shoes that fit and that they like, but also need to find them conveniently located and reasonably priced. These are what may be termed functional needs. But, customers also need to be treated politely and courteously by staff with whom they come into contact, and they need to be made to feel welcome, comfortable and important. It is useful, in fact, to think about how customer needs exist at all five levels of the drivers of customer satisfaction model that we discussed earlier. If the needs that exist at each of these levels are addressed, chances are the customer will be satisfied and will be prepared to buy again and to tell others about the company.

Making the sale is only part of marketing success

As many marketing organizations emerge from an historic focus on sales to a broader view of achieving long-term customer satisfaction, there has been growing acceptance of the fact that making a sale is only part of marketing. In fact, it may be argued that in certain circumstances, it may be better for the company and the customer if no sale is made! How can this be? How can we talk about marketing unless we sell something?

Remember that our objective is to achieve high levels of long-term customer satisfaction. There may be situations where it is better to have customers delay a purchase or even go to a competitor, rather than sell them something that doesn't fit, is inappropriate, or isn't needed, or something with which they will obviously be dissatisfied in the future. But, much marketing attention is focused on the point of purchase, on that interaction between a company and its customers that centres on making the sale. The importance of marketing begins long before this.

Much happens both before and after a sale to create satisfaction or dissatisfaction among customers and prospective customers. In fact, so much happens before a sale that a very large percentage of would-be customers never become customers. Think about situations when you really wanted to buy something. You had seen the advertising, found a certain product on the Internet, or you saw it while walking past a store in a shopping centre. You wanted the product, but you may have encountered a situation such as the one described in the chapter opener — you couldn't find someone to help you. Or you found the Web site so difficult to navigate that you gave up. Or you got so frustrated after being kept on hold with a company's voice-mail system that you hung up.

Some companies make it very difficult for customers and would-be customers to deal with them, even though they have great products and services and through advertising have created an interest in their brands. Customers often do not buy from such companies, because

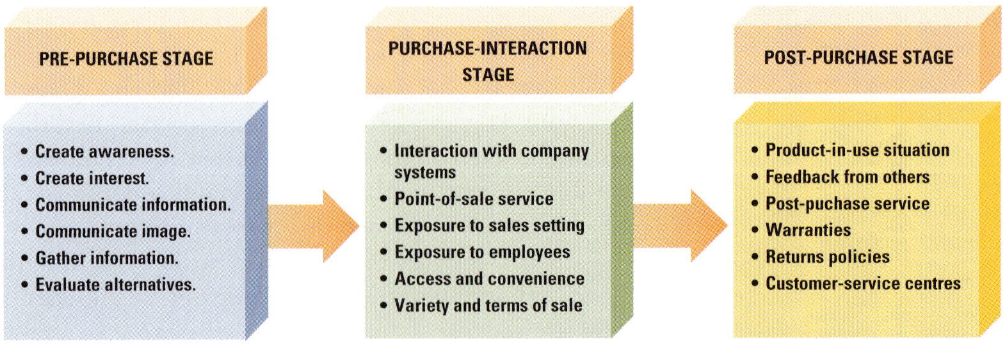

Figure 1-4: Stages of Customer Interaction

the companies have not paid sufficient attention to the second stage of the drivers of customer satisfaction model: support services and systems. They simply make it too difficult for customers to buy. What makes this particularly interesting is the fact that customer dissatisfaction in cases like these has nothing at all to do with the product or with the price being charged. Remember Sarah's purchase of the running shoes? Her final decision had very little to do with the shoes or even with the price. Probably the most important factor that led her to buy them from Blades & Boards was Sandy and the way she handled the situation.

BACK TO THE TOP

Much can go right or wrong at the point of sale, however. Regardless of whether the interaction with the customer takes place over the phone, via the Internet, or face to face, there are many opportunities to create customer satisfaction that will result in the sale being completed, or to dissatisfy customers so that they will abandon the attempt to buy. Success depends on how employees of the company interact with customers. An increasingly important aspect of that interaction is how the company has implemented certain policies. While many customers appreciate the convenience of being able to deal with a bank, for example, through banking machines, the telephone, or the Internet, there are many others who want to deal with real people. Some are likely to leave in search of a company that will treat them like "a real person, rather than a number." Consequently, many companies today are placing a great deal of emphasis on ensuring that the customer's experience when dealing with them is as positive as possible.

product-in-use situation
The stage in the interaction when the customer has bought the product or service and is using or experiencing it; evaluation of the success of the purchase takes place.

What happens after the customer has bought something has as much potential to create satisfaction or dissatisfaction as anything that happens before or during the purchase process. This often relates to the so-called **product-in-use situation**, when a customer may be dissatisfied with a product after it has been bought. The product may actually fail. Friends or family members may not like it. The customer may not know how to assemble it or even how to use it. There is great potential for customer satisfaction or dissatisfaction after the sale. Progressive companies are viewing the customer experience as something that is more broad than simply the interaction between customers and the employees of the firm. It extends to their experience in using the product and enjoying the service, such as a flight on an airline or a stay at a hotel.

As a result, we are seeing more and more companies paying attention to post-purchase service and the treatment of customers after the purchase. This includes increasing the flexibility of return and exchange policies. Increasingly, it is being recognized that it benefits the company to encourage the customer to return a product or complain if not completely satisfied. If you make it easy for your customers, they will return and purchase again, knowing the firm will stand behind its products. The Gap, for example, allows its customers to refund merchandise to any of its stores — Gap, Gap Kids, Gap Maternity — regardless of where it was purchased. A store refund is available for 180 days with or without the receipt. After 180 days customers are entitled to a merchandise exchange or merchandise certificate.

This retailer understands the importance of post-purchase customer satisfaction.

And don't you hate it when something goes on sale right after you have bought it and worn it? Gap stores even offer a one-time price adjustment when an original sales receipt is presented within 14 days of purchase. For online orders the adjustment applies for 14 days from invoice date.[3]

Firms are increasingly utilizing toll-free telephone numbers and Internet sites to provide post-sale support to answer questions, assist with assembly, and other customer requirements. Some are offering guaranteed delivery times and faster service turnaround times, often involving on-site

Sponsorships like this are increasingly important in building brand relationships.

repairs or pick-up and delivery of the item. Such approaches are all about increasing the level of trust and reducing the feeling of risk involved in dealing with a particular company. Some companies are also using post-purchase opportunities to enhance relationships with their customers. Some companies will send gifts to customers after they have made a large purchase such as a new car or living room furniture. Others regularly invite their best customers to special events such as golf tournaments or fashion shows. Thus, sponsorships and events are becoming an important part of marketing for many companies.

PAGE UP!

1. Why is making a sale only part of the job of marketing?
2. Beyond the actual product or service, what are some other customer needs?
3. What are the five stages through which marketing has evolved?

It All Begins with the Value Proposition

We made the observation earlier that marketing involves the exchange of things of value between two parties who we describe simply as a customer and a marketer. We have commented that unless customers perceive that they have received good value from the exchange, satisfaction will not result. Only through the ongoing provision of value to its customers can a company achieve high levels of customer satisfaction, retention, and loyalty.

It is important to note that value, like many other concepts that we will examine in marketing, is intangible and exists largely in the mind of the customer. Value is perceived by the individual customer; where one customer may perceive value, another may see little or no value and may be unwilling to buy or to return to purchase again.

If a company or organization succeeds in creating value for its customers, generally high levels of customer satisfaction will be the result. If the company continues to satisfy its customers, a large percentage of these customers will come back again to buy its products and services — customer

Figure 1-5:
Customer Value Drives Shareholder Value

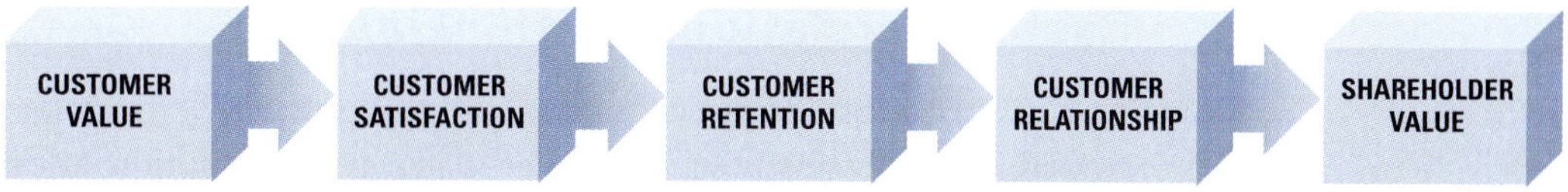

retention will result. If customers are retained over time, they become better known to the company and its employees, a rapport begins to develop, and the customers feel more comfortable dealing with the company — the emotional characteristics of customer relationships begin to show. Once a company has succeeded in creating solid, long-lasting relationships with a large percentage of its customers, it will achieve a state of ongoing profitability and value for its owners. Thus, the creation of shareholder value, a goal of companies the world over, begins with the creation of value for the customer.

Value is, therefore, one of the most fundamental concepts in marketing. The essence of marketing is the creation of value for customers in order to produce high levels of satisfaction and to sustain that satisfaction over time. A central question in marketing deals with how to create value for customers.

value proposition
The sum total of what the company offers the customer, including much more than product and price.

The answer lies in the development of what is termed the company's **value proposition**, encompassing literally everything that the company offers its customers and prospective customers. It is important again to define the value proposition quite broadly. Rather than focus on the core product or service, as we discussed earlier, a company must include in its value proposition everything that it does that has the potential to satisfy or dissatisfy customers. Thus, the value proposition must include not only what is being sold to the customer, but also how the product or service will be made available, what price is to be charged, the processes that will be used to provide the product, the level of post-purchase service to be provided, the way the company communicates with customers, and many other aspects of the total offer.

It is important, finally, not to confine our discussion of value to aspects of the proposition relating to price. The simplest view of value is often expressed as value for money: How much does the customer have to pay for what is received from the company? But much more than monetary considerations influences a customer's decision on whether what is being offered or has been received represents good value. Value involves more than tangibles and more than money.

Think about a situation that would cause you to conclude that you will never go back to a particular restaurant, or a clothing or sporting goods store. We have all had such negative experiences. In fact, one such experience may have been illustrated in the example that opened this chapter. Now, complete the following sentence: "I'll never go back there; it's just not worth the _____." Chances are that you completed the sentence with words like "time," "hassle," "trouble," "aggravation," or "frustration."

Figure 1-6:
Marketing Thinking Drives the Value Proposition

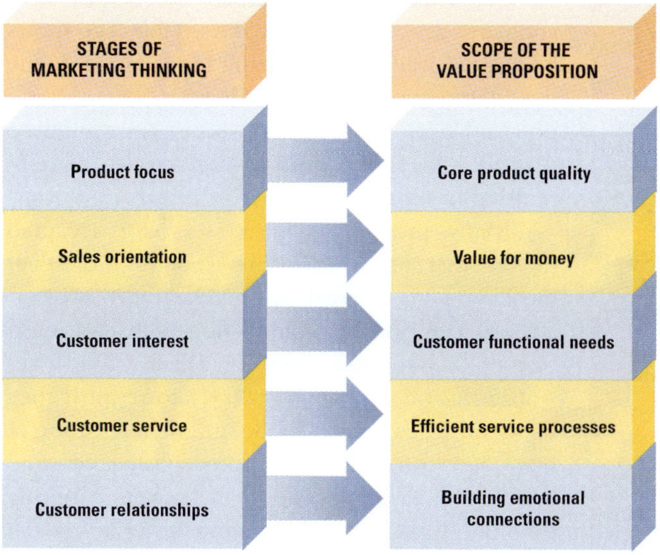

There is a very close connection between the stage of marketing thinking that a company has reached and how it defines its value proposition. Those companies that still have a product focus are most likely to define their value proposition quite narrowly, limiting its scope principally to having great products. As companies move into progressively more advanced stages of marketing thinking, they begin to include a broader range of things in their definition of the value proposition, until ultimately they are focused on the development of solid, long-term relationships with their customers. At this point, they tend to define the value proposition as broadly as possible to include literally everything the organization does that has the potential to influence long-term customer satisfaction.

Customer-relationship thinking

The modern customer-relationship view of marketing is characterized by four concepts that are generally absent at the earlier stages in the evolution of marketing thinking. First, an emphasis on building customer relationships is necessarily a *long-term strategy*. The payback may not be realized for two or three years and will last well into the future, unlike the sales-focused view where the objective is to make the sale today. Second, companies that are focused on developing relationships with customers accept that they must understand the *customer's view* of the relationship, rather than the company's. It is the customer who decides whether quality and value are being offered and whether a solid relationship exists. Third, such companies also accept that they must *define very broadly what they offer the customer*, to include not only the core products or services, but also the service provided and the emotional connection with the customer. Finally, companies operating at this stage of the evolution of marketing *rely on new types of measures* to gauge their success. Rather than measuring success in conventional, short-term, financial terms such as sales, profits, and market share, they assess their performance against measures such as customer satisfaction, loyalty levels, and the strength of their relationships with customers.

Many of the firms that remain in the early stages of marketing thinking are long-established companies that continue to do business as they have done for years. Others have accepted the validity of the modern marketing orientation but have difficulty implementing it, for at least two reasons. First, implementation requires accepting the notion that the needs and wants of customers, not the needs of the company and its management, must direct the organization. Second, moving into the customer-focused advanced stages of marketing thinking requires that managers change their notion of what they offer the customer. Success in marketing today is about more than the products and services that we sell. Modern marketing thinking demands that companies realize that how they treat customers, the level of service provided, and ultimately how the customer feels about the company may in fact be more important in influencing long-term satisfaction and repeat business than the products that the company sells and the prices charged for them.

Helping customers reach their goals.

Placing customers first and taking a long-term view of dealing with customers affects the way a company describes what it does. Table 1-1 shows how some well-known organizations might define their businesses under a product or sales orientation and how differently the businesses would be defined using a more up-to-date service or relationship orientation.

Many progressive businesses have accepted the fact that success in business requires more than great products at great prices. They have adopted a broad view of their interaction with customers that is all about how they can create value. They realize that success is more likely to result if they focus on what they can do for their customers, how they can help them accomplish goals, and look good in the eyes of others. The Running Room, a Canadian retailer with stores across the

TABLE 1-1 What Business Are You In?

Company	Product-Oriented Answer	Marketing-Oriented Answer
ESQ SWISS Watches	We make watches.	We make attractively priced, distinguished timepieces that get noticed.
Bell Canada	We operate a telephone company.	We provide reliable, efficient and inexpensive communications services that allow people to keep in touch.
Esso	We produce oil and gasoline products.	We keep Canadian homes warm.
Samsung	We produce consumer electronics.	We devote our human resources and technology to create superior products and services, thereby contributing to a better global society.
VISA Canada	We provide credit cards.	We help Canadians manage their financial affairs.
Levi Strauss	We make blue jeans.	We make you look great!
Canon	We make digital cameras.	We help you share special occasions.
Ritz-Carlton Hotels	We operate a luxury hotel.	We accommodate the changing needs of a clientele seeking more contemporary design standards and an atmosphere of elegance.
Bombardier Inc.	We make airplanes.	We provide innovative ways of transporting people quickly and safely.
Telus Mobility	We provide cellphones.	We enable people to communicate freely from practically anywhere in the world.
National Hockey League	We deliver hockey games.	We create family entertainment.

country, offers a great example of this approach to business. To its regular customers, The Running Room has become much more than a place to buy shoes and running gear. It has created a partnership with its customers, offering clinics, running groups, and other ways to help customers achieve their personal goals, whether that involves running their first 5K race or training for a marathon.

Free or not-for-profit services also often feel that marketing is unnecessary or inappropriate. Organizations such as The Canadian Federation for Sexual Health (formerly Planned Parenthood) or Canadian Blood Services have missions to fulfil and groups to serve. Such organizations can achieve greater success by understanding the needs of those with whom they deal. Issues of relevance in these cases can include understanding the critical role of empathy and patience when dealing with clients, as well as the importance of staff always conducting themselves with professionalism and providing assurance of confidentiality and privacy. Also, the timeliness, safety, and efficiency of service provision may be of concern to potential users.

Keeping As Well As Getting Customers

The recent focus of marketing on customer service and the creation of customer loyalty have brought about an important change in how marketers view their dealings with customers and prospective customers. In short, there has been a realization on the part of many marketing managers that the provision of the four elements of the conventional marketing mix — product, price, promotion, and distribution channels — is not sufficient to ensure customer satisfaction and repeat business. While we will devote a large portion of this book to coverage of these four components of the marketing mix, it is important to do so in the context of a

"four Rs" of marketing
Guideposts for the new way of thinking in marketing: customer retention, relationships, referrals, and recovery from negative experiences.

new strategic view of marketing, one that focuses on all of the ways that companies create value for their customers, leading to customer satisfaction. We have labelled the components of our new strategic view the **"four Rs" of marketing** — retention, referrals, relationships, and recovery. These components focus our thinking on what the new approach to marketing is designed to accomplish. They also serve to put into context how the elements of the traditional marketing mix should be applied. Marketers today realize that getting the four elements of the marketing mix right is not enough; each of these must be applied in the context of what it does to support the building of long-term relationships with customers.

customer retention
The behavioural connection between regular customers and a company; characterized by repeat buying behaviour, but not yet a relationship because it may be lacking an emotional component.

share of wallet
The share of a customer's total spending in a product or service category that is given to a particular company or brand.

Retention

Most successful marketers today have accepted the principle of **customer retention** — that repeat customers are more profitable and that organizations should pay at least as much attention to keeping existing customers as they do to trying to attract new ones. Recent studies have demonstrated quite clearly that customers become more profitable the longer they continue to do business with a firm. This is the case because satisfied, long-term customers spend a larger portion of their total expenditures (often referred to as **share of wallet**) with a firm to which they are loyal. These customers also cost less to serve, because they are generally more satisfied and don't need to be convinced to buy. They make fewer complaints and are less likely to quibble over price, often being prepared to pay more for good service. And they tell others how satisfied they are.

referral
The process of recommending a company or brand to others; positive word of mouth.

Referrals

This last point leads to the second of our four R's, **referrals**. One of the greatest benefits of satisfying customers is that they will refer their friends and associates to the firm that is providing them with superior value. This is one of the most important benefits to be gained

MARKETING AT WORK 1-3: RELATIONSHIPS

Designer Couture — Who's the Consumer?

Clad in her Burberry coat and diamond choker, Millie strolls the busy streets of downtown Toronto alongside her friend Barb. The girls are off shopping in the trendy Distillery District after a healthy organic breakfast. Barb buys a pink velour hoodie, but they can't find one in Millie's size. So, they try Mona's Pet Boutique where they find the perfect matching hoodie. What? Didn't we mention that Millie was a Yorkshire terrier?

Designer apparel is just one category that has seen great growth in the pet products industry. There is also dentistry, holistic medicine, and pet magazines. New food choices include organic, vegetarian, and low-carb varieties as well as a selection of savoury low-cal gravies for dry dog food. Then there's daycare, spas and salons, and high-end boarding accommodations — even hotels that cater to pet owners. Sheraton, Westin and W Hotel properties in Canada have doggie beds, bowls, room service, and grooming services for its furrier guests.

Every year, Canadian pet owners spend $3 billion on goods and services as varied as travel, gourmet baked treats and pet insurance. What is different about the pet industry today is that it has evolved into a diverse, mature, and high-value category.

The Boutique's clients range from empty nesters, to gay couples, and single women. Pet ownership crosses all boundaries in Canadian society — from families housing hamsters to seniors with posh Persian kittens. Another customer comes in to exchange a sweater received as a gift. It's not quite the dog's style, she says. "I don't want her to feel humiliated in any way. I want her to feel proud and comfortable."

QUESTIONS:

1. How does a company like Mona's Pet Boutique cater to the relationship between Canadians and their pets?
2. Where's the emotional connection between this company and its customers?

SOURCE: Adapted from Michelle Halpern, "Heavy Petting," *Marketing Magazine Online*, marketingmag.ca/magazine/current/feature/article, March 21, 2005.

They'll tell their friends about this customer experience.

word of mouth
The process of customers discussing companies and brands with which they have come in contact; may be either positive or negative.

viral marketing
The planned promotion of a product or service by a company taking advantage of the attention and credibility that often accompanies word of mouth communication.

Sweetspot

from satisfying customers. Through positive **word of mouth**, satisfied customers can produce large volumes of new business. Conversely, a dissatisfied customer will either spread negative word of mouth or will simply never return. Companies that provide a high level of value to their customers always keep in mind the potential for existing customers to bring in new ones.

Some companies use word of mouth to introduce new products and generate interest. Today, a planned approach to generating word of mouth is often referred to as **viral marketing**, a topic we will return to later in the book. Once the public's attention is drawn to the company or the brand through some event or promotion, then it becomes something that people talk about and tell others — it starts a 'buzz' about the product. The media begin to cover it and it gets talked about on talk shows and in chat rooms and blogs. In that sense, information about the brand spreads like a 'virus' through the potential target market.

Is personal conversation online more believable?

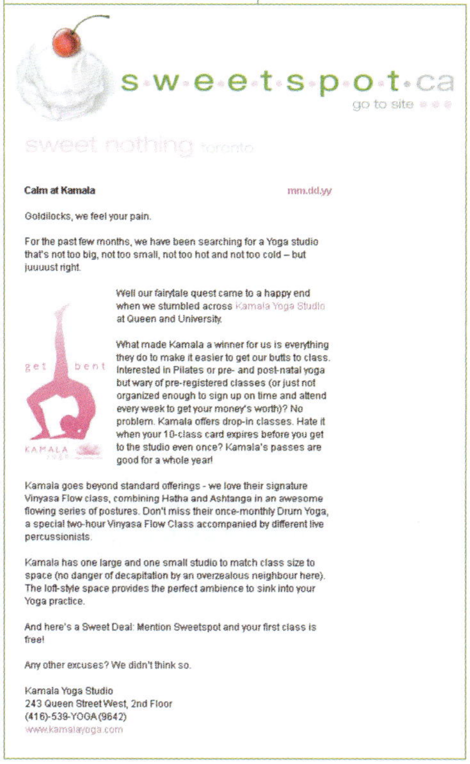

sweetspot.ca
go to site
sweet nothing toronto

Calm at Kamala mm.dd.yy

Goldilocks, we feel your pain.

For the past few months, we have been searching for a Yoga studio that's not too big, not too small, not too hot and not too cold – but juuuust right.

Well our fairytale quest came to a happy end when we stumbled across Kamala Yoga Studio at Queen and University.

What made Kamala a winner for us is everything they do to make it easier to get our butts to class. Interested in Pilates or pre- and post-natal yoga but wary of pre-registered classes (or just not organized enough to sign up on time and attend every week to get your money's worth)? No problem. Kamala offers drop-in classes. Hate it when your 10-class card expires before you get to the studio even once? Kamala's passes are good for a whole year!

get bent
KAMALA

Kamala goes beyond standard offerings - we love their signature Vinyasa Flow class, combining Hatha and Ashtanga in an awesome flowing series of postures. Don't miss their once-monthly Drum Yoga, a special two-hour Vinyasa Flow Class accompanied by different live percussionists.

Kamala has one large and one small studio to match class size to space (no danger of decapitation by an overzealous neighbour here). The loft-style space provides the perfect ambience to sink into your Yoga practice.

And here's a Sweet Deal: Mention Sweetspot and your first class is free!

Any other excuses? We didn't think so.

Kamala Yoga Studio
243 Queen Street West, 2nd Floor
(416)-539-YOGA (9642)
www.kamalayoga.com

The Web is a fertile breeding ground for gossip, and its ability to foster immediate communication is a blabbermouth's dream. So, it's no surprise that as a means of marketing it has become a vehicle for the organized spread of messages you would typically expect to hear from your clued-in friends. Sweetspot.ca (**www.sweetspot.ca**) is urban, affluent, and about avid consumption — the latest sale or that trendy new product. The short, punchy newsletter is mailed out to about 3,500 shopaholics daily and is meant to sound like tidbits of advice from one of your most in-the-know friends. It reports the newest brand of jeans only available at one small retailer in Toronto, or the best restaurants in the area for a first date. Retailers don't pay for the online plugs, but the site is a gold mine for small trend-setting retailers as they rely heavily on word of mouth for their reputations and their success.

Several such 'newsletters' have developed in Canada and the United States in the past couple of years. "I find Sweetspot a little more personal," one subscriber says. "When I get it, I read it and go 'oh yeah, I do need that'…It makes me, the consumer, feel special."[4]

Customer relationships

One of the most important developments in marketing in recent years has been the attention now being paid to the establishment of relationships with customers. This is an aspect of marketing that is linked very closely to the notion that long-term customer satisfaction is a direct result of the provision of superior customer value. The customers' definition of value very often extends to the establishment of a close relationship with a company — they come to value the relationship itself. However, the establishment of a long-term customer relationship is not a simple task and should be approached following much study of how the firm's customers define a relationship.

Home Depot

Many companies are now introducing relationship-marketing programs to try to get closer to their customers, so that customers feel more a part of the company and that the company is genuinely interested in helping them achieve what they want to do. Home Depot (**www.homedepot.ca**), like the Running Room, offers classes and seminars to equip customers with the know-how to get their desired projects completed. Would you like to install a faucet or build your own headboard? Well, Home Depot wants to help you do it. How-to seminars are offered throughout the week and on weekends for anything from wallpapering to plumbing to laying ceramic tile. There are do-it-herself workshops as well as ones for kids. As well, the Web site offers a number of step-by-step instructions with diagrams to assist with everything from gardening basics to gutters and siding. You can do it, and they can help!

Recovery

service recovery
The process of correcting the situation when a customer is dissatisfied with service provided. A company may attempt to recover from a poor service experience by apologizing or by offering the customer a price reduction or other form of compensation.

The final element in our four Rs of marketing relates to **service recovery** — what a company can do to recover customer satisfaction when something has gone wrong. It is inevitable that customers will encounter problems and poor service when dealing with some companies. Even the most meticulous companies cannot completely avoid delivering poor service on occasion. The issue is: What can and should a company do when something goes wrong? Certainly, the answer is not "Do nothing." In recent years, managers have been paying increasing attention to the development of procedures to deal with service problems as they arise, with a view to solving customers' problems before they decide to take their business elsewhere. Therefore, service recovery becomes an important component in a company's program to establish and maintain customer relationships. Taking the necessary steps to deal with customers' problems efficiently and effectively will lead to those customers being satisfied, even to the point that they will be more loyal than they would have been if the service problem had never occurred!

A Comprehensive View of Marketing

This first chapter has presented a view of how marketing is addressed in today's businesses and organizations. A number of key points should be obvious from this early discussion of marketing. The first and foremost is that the modern approach to marketing starts with the customer and all decisions made in a marketing context must be made with the customer in mind. Therefore, it is extremely important that managers and executives in marketing have a detailed understanding of customers.

The marketing model introduced at the beginning of this chapter illustrates how the customer is at the centre of modern marketing thinking. It also illustrates how various factors influence the customer and the kinds of outcomes that are likely to result. Each of these topics will be discussed in detail in the remaining chapters of the book.

We will see in these chapters how customers are influenced by certain unique characteristics that are internal to themselves and that drive their view of the world and their behaviour. These include their personalities, needs, wants and expectations — all unique to the individual customer.

Other people with whom they associate, either directly or indirectly, also heavily influence customers in the purchase of certain products and services. These may be as close as family members, friends and next-door neighbours or as distant as the culture to which they belong.

Then, of course, customers are influenced in a marketing context by the activities of those businesses and other organizations that wish to attract them as customers and to retain their business. These influences include all of the various components of the marketing mix, as well as the broader view that includes how a company treats its customers and how they are made to feel as a result.

In between are a number of what we term environmental influences that affect both customers and the companies that wish to attract and retain them. These are largely outside the control of both customers and businesses but are important influences on customers' lives and on how companies conduct their business. These include the state of the economy, advancing technology, and the competitive nature of the marketplace.

Finally, as a result of this complex array of influences, we observe certain customer outcomes. In the first place, customers experience outcomes that may be internal to themselves and generally not observable. These include their perceptions of the options available to them, their opinions of brands and companies, their level of satisfaction and sense of loyalty or relationship.

There is another set of customer outcomes that are closer to the company and may be more easily observed because they generally involve behaviour on the part of customers. These outcomes represent the behavioural result of the internal outcomes and include purchasing, repeat buying, and the referring of other customers.

The model presented suggests a comprehensive view of what is involved in marketing and of the knowledge that managers need if they are to practise marketing effectively. It starts with an understanding of the many influences that act upon people in the context of their decision making as customers. Those influences come from many sources, only some of which are under the control of the marketing company or organization. To obtain positive outcomes from the perspective of the company, managers must understand customers, the many influences on their behaviour, and how to create value for them.

Marketing has changed a lot in recent years. This is because marketing is an extremely dynamic field — it is always changing, because customers and the competitive environment are always changing. Marketing is all about satisfying customers, and these customers are influenced by many trends and changes in their lives. This is what makes marketing one of the most exciting fields of study.

An important point that should be reiterated to end the chapter is that marketing must be integrated throughout an organization. Many concepts have to be reflected in the marketing thinking of the modern organization. Management in a marketing-oriented company understands that virtually everything that the company and its employees do must be oriented toward the creation of value for customers and the development of a solid base of loyal customers.

PAGE UP!

1. The essence of marketing is the creation of ____________ for customers.
2. What four concepts characterize the customer-relationship view of marketing?
3. What are the four Rs of marketing?

Key Terms and Concepts

brand equity 8
customer 4
customer expectations 6
customer experience 5
customer-interest stage 11
customer loyalty 8
customer relationship 8
customer-relationship stage 11
customer retention 22
customer satisfaction 4
customer-service stage 11
decision maker 14
exchange 4
"four Rs" of marketing 22
"give and get" 5
influencers 14
lifetime value of customers 12
market 14
marketer 6
marketing 4
marketing concept 12
marketing mix 7
needs and wants 15
product-focus stage 10
product-in-use situation 17
purchaser 14
referral 22
sales-orientation stage 11
service recovery 24
share of wallet 22
value 6
value proposition 19
viral marketing 23
word of mouth 23

Questions and Problems

1. What does it mean to say that marketing is intended to facilitate, or encourage, exchange? What is it that is being exchanged in such transactions?
2. a) What is the "give and get" in each of the following exchanges:
   1) A municipal election.
   2) The sale of shares in a company.
   3) A donation to the Canadian Cancer Society.

   b) Why are the objects of each of these considered exchanges of value, and how do they create customer satisfaction for the 'customer' in each situation?
3. a) What are marketers talking about when they consider, or discuss, customer expectations? Why is it important to consider customer expectations?
   b) What is the impact of customer expectations on designing the marketing mix?
4. a) What is the relationship between the concept of value and the concept of price?
   b) What are the different components of any product or retailer, other than price, that can be considered by a consumer to determine the value he/she has received?
5. a) Who are some of most popular retailers in Canada? Why do you think these retailers are popular? Who represents their target customers?
   b) What stores do you most often patronize? For clothing? Shoes? Grocery items? DVD rentals? Why?
   c) Are there stores that you would rather avoid when looking for these products? Why?
6. a) Explain the five levels in the model of the drivers of customer satisfaction.
   b) Consider a product you have recently purchased or a retailer with which you have recently dealt. Discuss that experience or how that experience could have been better through considering each of these five levels.
7. a) In recent years there has been a great increase in the level of activity in not-for-profit (NFP) marketing. What is NFP marketing?
   b) What are the causes for this increased activity?
   c) What are the challenges faced by marketers who work for such organizations?
8. a) When designing a marketing program for your product it is important to consider that the people that make up the market play a number of roles. What are the roles discussed in the chapter?
   b) Using premium dog food as an example, discuss the different individuals who would fill these roles.
9. a) What is meant by the term viral marketing?
   b) How does such a marketing approach work? Provide examples.
   c) What are the benefits to using such an approach in today's marketplace? Why may it be easier today than ten years ago?

10. The modern marketing concept implies that marketing is in some way a responsibility shared throughout the organization. Provide examples of how people in the following positions could be marketing-oriented in their professional roles:
    a) A production manager.
    b) A human resources manager.
    c) A vice-president of finance.

11. For each of the following organizations what is being marketed?
    a) Toronto Maple Leafs.
    b) Second Cup.
    c) Cineplex Odeon.
    d) Terryfoxrun.org
    e) google.ca
    f) Canadian Blood Services
    g) amazon.ca
    h) The Liberal Party

12. a) What is meant by the term brand equity?
    b) Provide examples of brands that you believe have good brand equity. Why?
    c) Provide examples of retailers that you believe have good brand equity. Why?
    d) Are there any noticeable differences in the reasons provided in (b) and (c)?

13. Is it always in a retailer's best interest to make a sale to a prospective customer? Explain.

14. In today's competitive marketplace is the traditional marketing mix always enough to remain competitive? How can modern organizations use the marketing mix to respond to the changing market environment?

15. What are the potential benefits to the organization that develops ongoing relationships with its customers?

Hands-On Marketing

1. Comparing Web sites for different service providers can illustrate how technology can be used to improve customer satisfaction and build relationships with customers. Visit sites such as amazon.ca, sony.ca, yahoo.ca, and lavalife.com, and compare how these organizations use technology to create portals where customers keep returning.

2. Select a restaurant, hotel, dry cleaner, or other service company near your school and think about how it operates. If possible, observe the operation and interview a manager and some customers to identify: (a) what is being exchanged; and (b) whether the company is product-, sales-, service- or relationship-oriented.

Back to the Top

Think about the customer experience described in the chapter opener and what went on: why Sarah bought her running shoes at one store rather than the other. Think also about the many factors that contributed to her decision — what it was that made her satisfied with her experience at Blades & Boards and with her purchase. Why was Blades & Boards successful in selling her the shoes and Sports Champs was not? Now think about what this tells us about the scope of marketing. Fit the experience Sarah and Colin had into the Customer-centric Model that appears in the part opener for part one of the text. What can marketers learn from this everyday example?

Online LearningCentre

Want to get better grades, tips on how to study more effectively, and up-to-date information on happenings in the world of marketing? Then, visit the Online Learning Centre for practice tests, Study Smart software, *Marketing Magazine,* and much more! **www.mcgrawhill.ca/olc/sommers**

CHAPTER 2

Understanding the Customer

Having looked at the basic principles of marketing in Chapter 1, we now examine the foundation on which these principles rest — the customer. You will see how customers or consumers behave in the marketplace over time, and review the factors that influence this behaviour. After studying this chapter, you should have an understanding of:

- The process customers go through in making buying decisions.
- The roles of motivation, perception, learning, personality, and attitudes in shaping consumer behaviour.
- The importance of commercial and social information sources in consumer decisions.
- The influence of cultures and subcultures on consumer and customer behaviour.
- The direct impact of reference groups on consumer behaviour.
- Family and household buying behaviour.
- The importance of situational factors in buying.

When Did it Get So Hard to Choose a Phone?

You and your friends are registered for another semester of challenging classes, including your favourite — marketing! It's going to be a busy semester and your schedules are all over the place — even night classes! You'll all be spending a lot of time on campus this semester.

You've got your books but what you're thinking about now is that you would all like to have new cellphones to keep connected with everybody on and off campus. You and your friends have been talking about what to do. You've had a Nokia for a while now and it's always worked great, but it's time to upgrade to something with a little more functionality — and entertainment value!

One of your friends, a big music fan, has done a lot of surfing on the Net and thinks an iPod mini is a better idea for passing the time between classes and for nights studying at the library. He thinks that's the best bang for his money and love of music. Your other friend has approached things a little differently. She is finally going to break down and buy her first cellular phone now that she will be at school so much and have to commute such a long distance early in the morning and late in the evening each day. She sees this as more of a practical decision — she sees the phone as a tool, more than anything else.

After talking some more, you've changed your thinking a little — you want something multi-purpose. If you're going to spend your hard earned summer job money, you want all you can get from a mobile phone. But which one should you buy? You know you want to stay with a Nokia because of your past experience with the brand, but there are so many models to choose from — so many features and so many different looks. It has to look good because it has become a fashion accessory on campus, but there's much more to have. They all have video games, but why not go all the way? It'll cost more, but, with Bluetooth, Internet access, mobile TV, a digital camera and an MP3 player, you will have the best of all worlds — fashion, connectivity and entertainment! You decide on the Nokia 9290 with the Symbian operating system — it's much more than you need, but 'WOW' it looks impressive!

Two of your friends are taking somewhat different approaches to the same task. Your music-loving friend has decided to forego a new phone for the iPod mini — he can easily download a ton of music to it from his Apple computer. And your other friend? She doesn't see much difference between brands — she doesn't see much point in doing a lot of research, so she just takes your advice and chooses a Nokia. She opts for the basic 1220 — she just wants a phone!

How did what started as a common need to get ready for a new semester end up with three such different purchases? At the end of the day, will all three be happy with their decisions? Why?

The new semester has created a want (or need) for each of these students. Why do these friends each approach their decision making in different ways? Why do they all shop differently? Why do they ultimately decide on such different products? What kind of decision process leads one to want the most basic, least-expensive option, another to buy a multi-purpose mobile phone (but only as long as it is a Nokia), and yet another to spend a great deal of time researching products and specifications to ensure the best quality and selection of music options? This friend has even decided not to buy a new phone at all! If you look around, watch yourself, your friends, your schoolmates, parents, and others, you will see similar kinds of consumer decision-making.

The foundation for marketing success always depends on knowing what consumers are thinking, doing, and experiencing. In this chapter, we begin by examining the consumer decision-making process. Then, we deal with each of the four specialized environments that influence the process in various ways. Figure 2-1 brings all of the dimensions of consumer behaviour together in a model that provides the structure for our discussion.

The Buying-Decision Process

buying-decision process
The six stages through which a prospective customer goes when faced with a buying problem. The stages differ for consumers and organizations

Consumers are constantly dealing with the surrounding marketing environment. To do this, they engage in a **buying-decision process**. This process can be thought of as a six-stage problem-solving approach. When faced with a buying problem ("I need a new computer before the start of term," "I need a new pair of shoes to wear to my cousin's wedding"), consumers go through a series of logical stages to arrive at a solution or a decision. Table 2-1 presents the stages in this process and some of the variations that commonly occur.

Let's now look at these stages in more detail. Keep in mind that once a buying decision has been made and a product purchased, consumers want their expectations met, value received, and satisfaction to be derived from product possession and use.

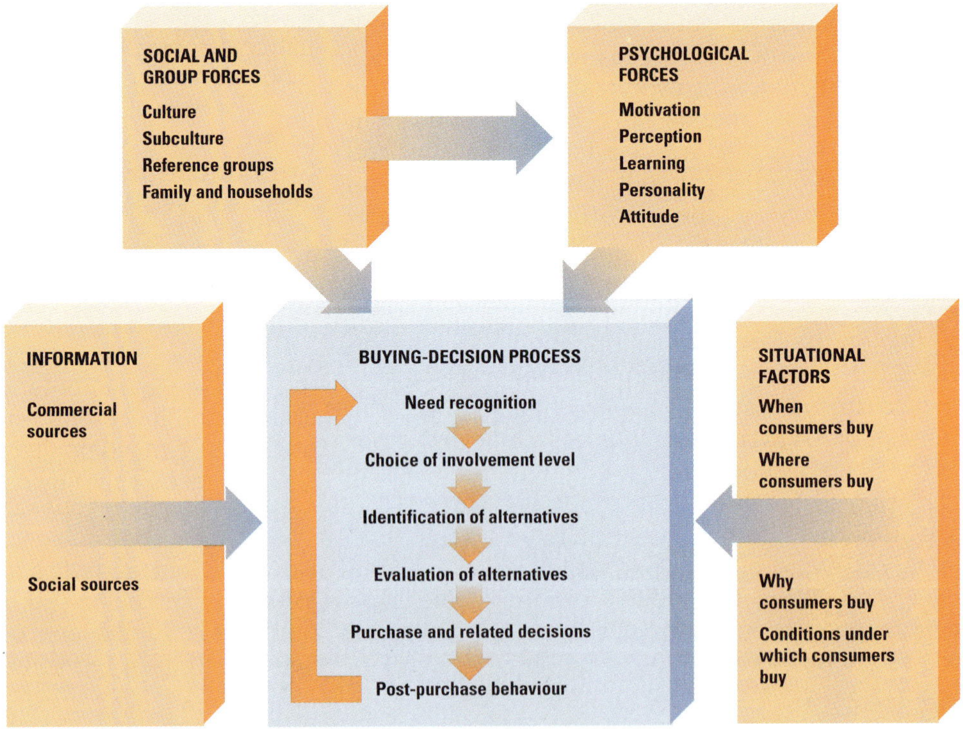

Figure 2-1: The Consumer Decision-Making Process and Its Environment

TABLE 2-1 The Six-Staged Buying-Decision Process and Common Variations

Six Stages of The Buying-Decision Process	Common Variations
1. **Need recognition:** Considering action as a result of an internally or externally generated need. 2. **Choice of an involvement level:** Deciding how much time and effort to invest in satisfying the need and the energy to be devoted to the remaining stages of the problem-solving process. 3. **Identification of alternatives:** Collecting information about products, services, and brands that might satisfy the need. 4. **Evaluation of alternatives:** Weighing the pros and cons of the alternatives identified. 5. **Purchase and related decisions:** Deciding to buy or not to buy. 6. **Consumption experience and behaviour:** Seeking reassurance that the choice made was the correct one, experiencing the product or service in use, assessing whether expectations have been met and satisfaction derived, becoming prepared to develop a relationship with the marketer, determining to engage in the decision process again as the need arises.	• **Withdrawing from the decision process prior to actual purchase:** Need or desire may diminish, no satisfactory alternatives are available; the search is not worth the effort, as when you walk out of a clothing store because you can't find your size in the jeans you wanted. • **Skipping stages:** All six stages are likely to be followed when buying higher-priced, infrequently purchased items; for frequently purchased, familiar products, purchasing is usually routine and is often satisfied by repurchasing a familiar brand, with the third and fourth stages of the process being bypassed. • **Different stages require different amounts of time and energy:** It may take only a moment to recognize the need for a new car, but picking out and evaluating the alternative models may go on for weeks. Sometimes stages can occur simultaneously — when, for example, a consumer identifies and evaluates alternatives at the same time, eliminating unsuitable options as the decision-making process proceeds. • **Not all stages may be performed consciously:** You don't consciously calculate the amount of time and effort you will put into reaching a decision about every purchase. But the fact that you spend more time on some purchases and less on others indicates that level of involvement is part of the process.

It's important for marketers to realize that such variations occur and that customer decision making is highly variable. Literally every customer decision is different.

1. Need recognition

An unsatisfied need creates tension or discomfort for a consumer. This may arise *internally* and have a physiological basis; for example, a person feels hungry or thirsty. Or, the need may be dormant until it is aroused *externally* by a stimulus such as a TV advertisement or the sight or smell of a favourite fast food being eaten by a passerby. Another possible reason to act is dissatisfaction with a product currently being used. Perhaps you realize that as you get into more advanced courses you need a faster computer or some new software.

While hunger represents an actual physiological need that we all experience, the term *need*, as we have pointed out before, also refers to consumers' *wants* — like that new pair of Prada sunglasses with the great shape that you really *need* to buy! — or that top-of-the-line Nokia 9290 cellphone.

Once a need has been recognized, consumers often become aware of conflicting or competing uses for their scarce resources of time and money. Our desire to fulfill all of our needs must be balanced with a sense of practicality and the fact that we never have enough money (and probably never will!) to satisfy all of our wants as consumers. It is the existence of this conflict that forces consumers into some form of decision-making process.

Let's say that one of our friends from the beginning of the chapter is torn between buying a new laptop for school and a completely different purchase with the money remaining from that summer job — let's say a new audio/video system for his car. Perhaps a Sony mobile DVD Dream System and monitor, and an in-dash CD/MP3 receiver/controller with dual cone speakers and a 12-inch subwoofer box. Now that would make the commute to school a lot more entertaining — and it would look really good! But, think of the great laptop that kind of money could also buy — and with the laptop he could work from campus between classes, easily download course notes, and check e-mail. And with a less expensive laptop he could do all that and have money left over to have a social life. After all, that old PC at home is a dinosaur — and downloading music and course notes is painfully slow!

BACK TO THE TOP

Our friend would have to resolve these conflicts before proceeding — he would have to decide what was most important to him — if he doesn't, the buying process stops. If he asks you what to do, what would you recommend? Which of his "needs" is the most important?

2. Level of involvement

high-involvement level
A purchase decision that involves all six stages of the buying-decision process.

low-involvement level
A purchase decision in which the consumer moves directly from need recognition to purchase, skipping the stages in between.

Very early in the process, a consumer can consciously (but most likely, subconsciously) decide how much effort to exert in satisfying a need; in other words, what level of involvement is required. Sometimes, when a need arises, a consumer is sensitive about a product, perceives some level of risk in the purchase, or is concerned with the quantity or quality of information available. Such situations are usually considered to be at the **high-involvement level** and result in extended problem solving, using all stages of the decision-making process. This is like our friend who wants to make sure he makes the best choice for his music listening. If the consumer is comfortable with the information on hand and satisfied that no more is needed (replace your Nokia with another Nokia), or even if the consumer is indifferent about the situation, an unconscious or barely conscious **low-involvement level** results and the decision approach progresses in a routine problem-solving fashion. In this latter situation, the consumer will likely skip directly from need recognition and alternative selection to the purchase, ignoring the intervening evaluation stage. A moderate level of involvement, between the two extremes, leads to limited problem solving — like our friend who wants basic utility and relies on a trusted friend's recommendation of the Nokia brand. Some of the major differences in involvement and problem-solving approaches are presented in Table 2-2.

TABLE 2-2 Behaviour Differences in Involvement and Problem Solving

Level of Involvement	High	Moderate	Low
Problem-Solving Approach	**Extended**	**Limited**	**Routine**
Resulting Behaviour:			
Time Invested	Large amount	Moderate to little	Small amount
Information sources used	Many	Few	None
Response to information	Critically evaluate	Review	Ignore or accept without evaluation
Brands evaluated	Many	Small number	One
Brand attributes evaluated	Many	Moderate number	Few
Sources considered	Many	Moderate number	Few
Interaction with sales, service, and retail personnel	Committed, demanding	Focused, could be sensitive	Nominal

Generally, perceived risk is higher and involvement tends to be greater under any of the following conditions:

- The consumer lacks information about the purchase. It may be a new product on the market or the consumer has no experience with this product or service.
- The product or its attributes and benefits are viewed as being important. Such a product may be heavily relied on to perform each day, or involve safety issues.
- The practical, psychological, or social consequence of making a bad decision is perceived as high. What if it is poor quality, has outdated technology, doesn't look right, or just isn't considered to be cool?
- The need for personal interaction about the purchase is important. Taking part in the interaction can yield important new information, clarify what is known, and generally be informative.
- The interaction process itself is satisfying or even enjoyable and builds confidence when the decision is complicated or difficult.

Most buying decisions for relatively low-priced products that have close substitutes would be low involvement and handled in a routine or limited problem-solving way. Typical examples are the majority of items sold in supermarkets, variety stores, and hardware stores. However, for a wealthy person, the purchase of a car could be low involvement and handled in a routine way, while for a person with a high need for social acceptance, purchasing toothpaste might be highly involving and handled with a moderate or even extended problem-solving approach. Such a consumer may look for new product features such as assurance of whiter teeth and fresher breath. Involvement must be viewed from the perspective of the consumer; it is not a characteristic of the product.

impulse buying
Low-involvement purchase made with little or no advance planning.

What is called **impulse buying**, or purchasing with little or no advance planning, is an important form of low-involvement decision-making. A shopper who goes to the supermarket with the intention of buying only vegetables, soya drinks and twelve grain bread, but on noticing a display of blueberries at an attractive price decides to buy some, engages in impulse buying. Some Internet purchases can also be done with low-involvement; but easy access can also cause high involvement, since consumers find it so easy to spend more and more time searching and comparing products and services, previous low-involvement purchases can become high involvement.

3. Identification of alternatives

Once a need has been recognized and the level of involvement determined, the consumer must next identify the alternatives capable of satisfying that need. First, alternative products and then alternative brands are identified. Product and brand identification usually starts with an internal search or memory scan, since previous personal consumer experiences are obviously important. When a customer was more than satisfied with a brand and really likes it — has an attachment to it or a degree of relationship with it — only one alternative is usually identified. For example, you are with your study group, it's coffee break time, and someone says, "Hey, there are three different places down the block where we could go." You say, "Yeah, but it's Tim Hortons for me — let's go!" In this simple case, a nanosecond of internal or memory scanning yielded a brand alternative that had met a consumer's expectations and provided desired satisfaction and a developed brand-relationship experience.

But when sufficient or appropriate information is not available from memory, a consumer can engage in an extensive external search of the physical or cyber-environment. Suppose a couple decides not to cook but to have a prepared item for their evening meal. Since neither can remember offhand what's in the refrigerator, identifying alternatives might mean first checking the freezer to see if any frozen dinners are on hand, then paging through the newspaper for supermarket specials or discount coupons, or looking in a local magazine or on the Internet to see if there are any reviews of nearby restaurants.

The search for alternatives is influenced by:

- The amount and type of internal information the consumer already has from past consumption and related experiences as well as information from other sources.
- The consumer's confidence in information from external sources.
- The expected benefit or value of additional information or, put another way, what the additional information is worth in terms of the effort, time, or money required to obtain it.

4. Evaluation of alternatives

When a set of reasonable alternatives has been identified, a consumer will evaluate each before making a decision. Approaches to evaluation can range from simple to complex, depending on the consumer's experience as well as product complexity technically and in use. A simple comparison can be determining which of five brands, all well known to the consumer, has the lowest purchase price. A more complex comparison, where the consumer has much less brand experience, could involve the evaluation of each of the seven important product and benefit characteristics of each of the five competing brands. Every evaluation involves establishing some criteria against which each alternative is compared. In the preceding meal example, the decision maker may have a single criterion ("How quickly can we sit down to eat?") or several criteria (speed, taste, nutrition, price, decor, atmosphere). When multiple criteria are involved, they typically do not carry equal weight. For example, preparation time might be more important than nutrition.

The criteria that consumers use in the evaluation result, first and foremost, from their past experience and feelings toward various brands, as well as the opinions of family members, friends, or even experts' comments in newspapers, magazines, or on the Internet. Because experience is often limited or dated, and information from sources such as the Internet, advertising or friends can be biased, evaluations may not be founded on facts. While a consumer may believe that the price of brand A is higher than that of brand B, the opposite may in fact be true.

5. Purchasing and related decisions

After searching and evaluating, the consumer has decided what to buy; the next problem is whether to buy. If the decision is to go ahead and buy, a series of purchasing-related decisions must be made and perhaps the specific types of special features desired must be determined. The consumer must decide where and when to make the actual purchase, how to take delivery or possession, the method of payment, and other issues related to being able to begin using your purchase. So, the decision to make a purchase is really the beginning of an entirely new series of transaction-related decisions that may be as easy or as time-consuming and difficult as the initial one. The outcome of these transaction-related decisions affects satisfaction in an important way. Consumers want their expectations met in terms of product value, the tenor and tone of the actual purchase transaction, and the ease and convenience with which they are able to gain satisfaction from their purchases.

Sources from which to make a purchase can range from Internet sites to manufacturers' outlets. The most common source is a retail store, and the reasons a consumer chooses to buy

MARKETING AT WORK — 2-1: STRATEGY

"Never Achieved Before. At Any Price"

"The end result is an object so carefully crafted, you'll find the obsession worth it and the price tag irrelevant." We should hope so, because at almost US$25,000 for a mobile phone a good price shouldn't be one of the most important issues when evaluating this alternative.

This is how Vertu (www.vertu.com), the luxury division of Nokia, chooses to describe what they make. And perhaps they have a point. After all, for perfect illumination, each and every pivoting key has 546 laser cut microscopic holes filled with transparent resin, the display screen is made from the largest sapphire crystals ever produced, exclusive ceramic technology has created a warm-to-the-touch ear pillow and the bezel holding all of this together is made from enough platinum to make 20 wedding rings! All of this, of course, along with the latest mobile technology...but is technology very important to Vertu's customers?

Cellular, or mobile, phones are marketed much the same as any other product — marketers divide potential customers into groups based on what product attributes are most important to them — it is these attributes that customers consider most important when evaluating their choices and making their purchase decisions. In the mobile phone market there are basically four main groups based on what is most important about the product to those consumers or for what reason they mostly use the product — commonly these segments are referred to as fashion, techie, business, and utilitarian.

QUESTIONS:

1. To which segment do Vertu's customers belong?
2. What criteria do you think potential customers use to evaluate Vertu?

SOURCE: Adapted from "A Broader View," *Gulf Marketing Review*, January 2005, pp. 36-39 and www.vertu.com.

patronage motives
The reasons why a consumer chooses to shop at a certain place or buy from a particular company.

there as opposed to a cyberspace or electronic store are called **patronage motives**. Consumers have a variety of reasons for selecting a retail source for the brand they have decided to buy. Many want to feel comfortable when they shop. This may mean that they want the assurance of being around people like themselves and in an environment that reflects their values or that they can trust. Others may want the convenience, lack of pressure, and anonymity of an electronic store.

Patronage motives can range from something as simple as convenience when you want a bottle of water to something more complex, such as the atmosphere of a restaurant. Patronage motives for e-shopping are as important as those for traditional shopping — but in a slightly modified form. The similarities and differences in patronage motives are illustrated in Table 2-3. The appearance or "look" of a building or Web site matters — each gives an impression of the style and image of the brand. A good impression gives consumers confidence, as do clear

TABLE 2-3 Common Patronage Motives for Selecting Shopping Locations

Buying Patronage Motive	For "Bricks" (offline)	For "Clicks" (online)
Convenient to find/access	Location, name	Memorable URL, easy navigation
Appearance	Physical appeal of premises	Attractiveness of Web site
Product assortment	Reach, touch, feel, try	Clear, useful graphics and text
Service availability	Personal, flexible, range	Impersonal, limited range, fixed
Reliability of product	Inspection, demonstration available	Product brand reputation
Confidence in supplier	Retailer brand, staff reputation	E-tailer brand reputation
Prices, credit, other terms	Fixed but sometimes negotiable	Fixed
Mix of other customers	Visible, known by reputation	Invisible, generally unknown
Reputation for after-sales delivery, service	Easy to find out and evaluate	Difficult to ascertain and evaluate

evidence of security and privacy, and clearly displayed prices and delivery policies. Easy, convenient site navigation and helpful links ensure that customers will stay the course and hit the button to submit an order. If shoppers are frustrated by the quality of the experience as they fill their cybercarts, they can simply "walk away," leaving their carts in the aisle. This is not as easy to do in a physical retail store environment.

6. The consumption experience

What a consumer learns from going through the decision-making process, making the purchase and enjoying the benefits of their purchase has a major influence on how that consumer will behave the next time the same need arises (see Table 2-3). Having decided what to purchase and where, if the customer's expectations throughout the actual purchase have been met, transaction satisfaction results. Transaction satisfaction can arise because of the sales or service person, the retail environment, the Web site or combinations of these. You now have the brand of product you want on terms that are acceptable, and you believe you have received good value. On the other hand, if you end up being unhappy with aspects of the transaction — you feel you paid too much, you felt pressured or insulted — the result is transaction dissatisfaction. You may not want to return to the source in such a case.

Your experience with the product over its useful life — useful as far as you're concerned — will dictate what other satisfactions you may derive. For example, if your experience over the life of a cellphone is negative for whatever reason (functional problems, lack of service when needed, rapid feature obsolescence), your dissatisfaction will feed back to the next need-recognition stage via the feedback loop shown in Figure 2-1. Consumption dissatisfaction will likely cause you to avoid the same brand the next time you buy a cellphone. If your experience had been positive, consumption satisfaction will likely predispose you to the same brand or supplier.

Looking forward to a positive consumption experience.

If the product or service met your expectations, you would favour it in the next decision-making process by feeding back satisfaction information. Satisfaction itself can be derived from the performance or functional aspects of the product. In such a case, a functional relationship is being established. Favouring or preferring a brand does not always lead to it being the only one considered. You may be presented with new functional feature information, causing you to use a limited problem-solving approach and compare features rather than a routine approach that considers only one brand.

When the brand you purchased more than met your expectations and you really enjoyed having it and using it, your feedback of information is based on more than your functional satisfaction. The satisfaction expressed here includes a degree of emotional attachment or liking — an emotional relationship is being established. The greater the degree of emotional information fed back to a need-recognition stage, the more likely the brand in question will be the only alternative considered. The buying-decision process itself will require limited involvement and be routine in nature. The brand name will say it all — a simple and highly satisfactory buying situation for the consumer and a more than happy event for the marketers involved. As long as the consumer's relationship with the brand is maintained or enhanced by marketers, both continue to enjoy the long-term benefits that flow from it. In the chapter opener, it may be concluded that one of these consumers developed an emotional relationship with the Nokia

TABLE 2-4 The Effects on Consumer Experience of Making a Purchase

Consumer Expectations of Brand	Transaction Experience	Consumption Experience	Future Source and Repurchase Predisposition
Meets Expectations	Functional	Functional	Favour same source/brand. Use limited or routine approach.
Fails Expectations	Dissatisfaction	Dissatisfaction	Find alternative source/brand. Use limited or extended approach.
Exceeds Expectations	Relational	Relational	Develop loyalty to source/brand. Use routine approach.

brand and feels that it is a reliable brand that can be trusted. Consequently, this consumer does not bother to consider other brands.

Something else often occurs following a purchase. You went through a careful decision process for a major purchase (perhaps an MP3 player, video game system, or expensive watch), selected what you thought was the best alternative, but then had doubts about your choice after the purchase. You asked yourself if maybe you should have bought the other one you were considering. What you were experiencing is post-purchase **cognitive dissonance** — a state of anxiety brought on by the difficulty of choosing from among several alternatives. Unfortunately for marketers, dissonance is quite common and can easily lead to dissatisfaction with the chosen brand and a weakening of any relationships that existed. You may be unhappy with the chosen product even if it performs adequately.

cognitive dissonance Anxiety created by the fact that in most purchases the alternative selected has some negative features and the alternatives not selected have some positive features.

Dissonance typically increases (1) the higher the dollar value or perceived risk of the purchase, (2) the greater the similarity between the item selected and items rejected, and (3) the greater the importance of the purchase decision to the consumer. Buying a new colour laser printer creates more dissonance than buying the paper for it.

To avoid or reduce post-purchase anxiety, consumers ignore information (such as ads for the rejected products) that is likely to increase the dissonance and seek out information that supports their decision.

Marketers can protect and nurture the relationship they have with consumers by providing dissonance-reducing information. For example, reassuring customers by stressing the number of satisfied owners. The quality of a seller's follow-up and post-purchase service programs can be significant factors in reducing dissonance and strengthening relationships, particularly emotional relationships. Online marketers have a good opportunity to reassure buyers and strengthen any emotional relationship, since they have easy access to all of the customer information they need and can communicate supportive information or direct customers to helpful Web sites and chat rooms, as well as to favourable product reviews.

With this background on the buying decision process, we can now examine specific influences on the buying decision and consumer experience. We'll begin with the sources and types of information used by consumers.

PAGE UP!

1. When a consumer is making a purchase decision, under what conditions is risk perceived to be higher and involvement greater?
2. To what does functional satisfaction refer?
3. ______________________ is a state of anxiety brought on by the difficulty of choosing from among several alternatives.

Psychological Factors

In discussing the psychological component of consumer behaviour, while we continue to use the model in Figure 2-1, we focus on the psychological forces that affect the buying-decision process we have just discussed.

One or more motives within a person stimulate goal-oriented behaviour. One such behaviour is perception — the collection and processing of information. Other important psychological activities are learning and attitude formation. We then consider the roles that personality and self-concept play in buying decisions. These psychological variables help to shape a person's lifestyle and values. The term **psychographics** is used in marketing as a synonym for those variables that include lifestyle and values.

psychographics
A concept in consumer behaviour that describes consumers in terms of a combination of psychological and sociological influences.

Motivation — the starting point

To understand how and why consumers behave as they do, we must first ask why a person acts at all. The answer is "Because the individual experiences a need." All behaviour starts with a recognized need. Security, comfort, social acceptance, and prestige are examples of needs. Thus, a **motive** is a need sufficiently stimulated to move an individual to seek satisfaction.

motive
A need sufficiently stimulated that an individual is moved to seek satisfaction.

A buying decision is often the result of the activating and balancing or ordering multiple motives. Moreover, various motives may conflict with one another. In buying a jacket, a college student may want to (1) please oneself, (2) please a mate, (3) appear fashion-savvy among friends, and (4) fill a gap in a wardrobe. To accomplish all of these objectives in one purchase is not easy. Also, a person's buying behaviour changes because of changes in income, lifestyle, and other factors. Finally, identical behaviour by several people may result from quite different motives, and different behaviour by the same person at various times may result from the same motive. In our example in the chapter opener, all three friends began with a discussion of how it might be useful to buy new cellular phones, but consider how things turned out.

Classification of Motives Psychologists generally agree that motives can be grouped in two broad categories:

- Needs aroused from physiological states of tension (such as the need for sleep).
- Needs aroused from psychological states of tension (such as the need for affection and self-respect).

A refinement of these two categories is Maslow's hierarchy of five levels of needs, arrayed in the order in which people appear to seek to gratify them.[1] **Maslow's hierarchy of needs**, shown in Figure 2-2, recognizes that a normal person is most likely to be working toward need satisfaction on several levels at the same time and that rarely are all needs on a given level fully satisfied. However, the hierarchy indicates that the majority of needs on a particular level must be reasonably well satisfied before a person is motivated at the next higher level. As an illustration, see how the needs of our college student's purchase of a jacket fit into the hierarchy in Figure 2-2. Also note in the figure how the need's hierarchy can be related to types of decision-making that may be used to take care of the needs (horizontal axis) and satisfaction potential at different levels of needs (the vertical axis).

Maslow's hierarchy of needs
A needs structure consisting of five levels and organized according to the order in which people seek need gratification.

You should keep in mind that this is a psychological model and was not originally intended to explain purchase behaviour. While the ideas in Figure 2-2 provide guidance for marketers, they must often go beyond these generalizations to understand the motives specific to the situation. For example, we might observe that a consumer on a shopping trip may be

Figure 2-2:
Maslow's Five Needs Hierarchy: illustrated with **needs** at work in buying a jacket, likely **decision-making approach** used and **satisfaction potential** of purchase

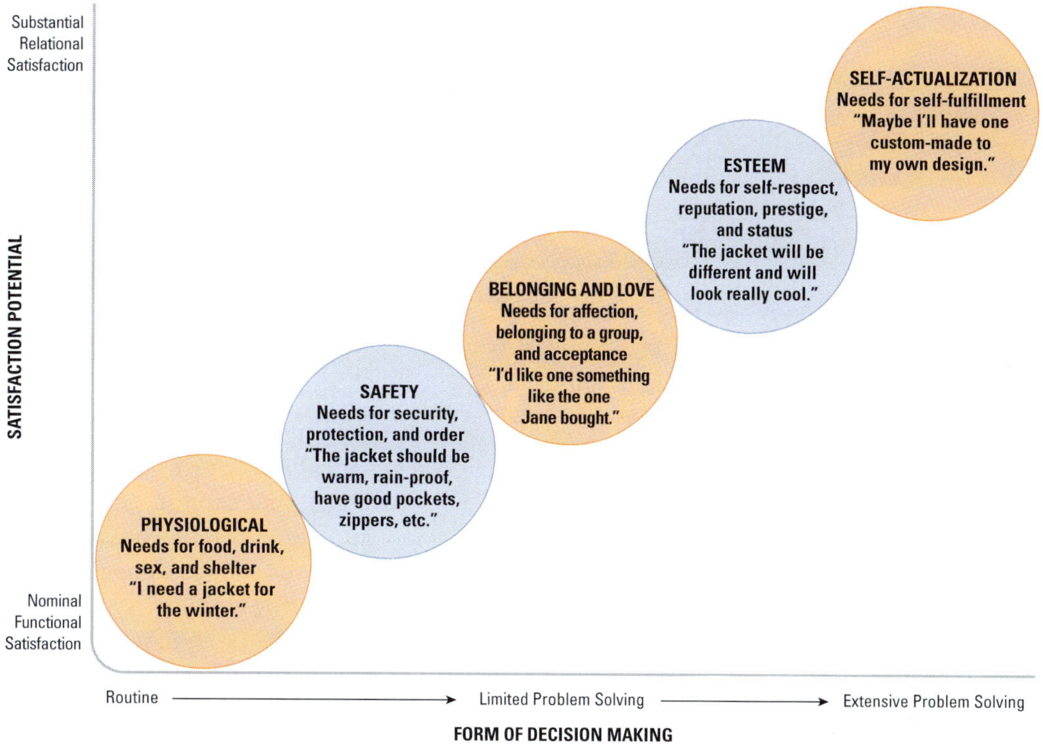

satisfying both physiological and social needs because she buys a jacket *and* talks to friends in the store. More detail is required to capture the specific symbols, terms, language, feelings and relationships involved in the purchase decision to construct messages and approaches that are grounded in the customer's reality.

Perception

perception
Collecting and processing information from the environment in order to give meaning to the world around us.

A motive, as an aroused need, activates behaviour intended to satisfy the aroused need. One form that behaviour takes is collecting and processing information from the environment, a process known as **perception**. We constantly receive, organize, and assign meaning to stimuli detected by our five senses. In this way, we interpret or give meaning to the world of sights, sounds, smells, and tactile feelings around us. Perception plays a major role in the alternative-identification stage of the buying-decision process. Our perception of a company or brand generally will guide our behaviour toward it, whether or not we will consider buying it. Perceptions are slow to change and may or may not have a lot to do with reality. In fact, many marketers agree that the customer's perception of a company or brand is *more* important than reality in terms of guiding a consumer's decision-making and purchase behaviour.

What we perceive — the meaning that we give something we sense — depends on the objects and our experiences. In an instant, the mind is capable of receiving information, comparing it with a huge store of images in memory, and providing an interpretation.

Although important, visual stimuli are just one factor in perception. Consumers make use of all five senses. Scents, for example, are powerful behaviour triggers. Who can resist the aroma of popcorn in a theatre? A recent study of common odours that evoke pleasant childhood memories found that older consumers identified the natural smells of horses, flowers, and hay. However, younger consumers associated pleasant recollections with the scent of Play-Doh and even jet fuel! Marketers are using this type of information to associate odours with products and shopping environments to create positive perceptions.

selective attention
The process that limits our perceptions so that, of all of the marketing stimuli to which our senses are exposed, only those able to capture and hold our attention have the potential of being perceived.

selective distortion
The process of mentally altering information that is inconsistent with one's beliefs or attitudes.

selective retention
The process of retaining in memory some portion of what is perceived.

Every day, we come into contact with an enormous number of marketing stimuli. However, a process of selectivity limits our perceptions. As an illustration, consider that:

- We pay attention by exception. That is, of all of the marketing stimuli to which our senses are exposed, only those with the power to capture and hold our attention have the potential of being perceived. This phenomenon is called **selective attention**.
- We may alter information that is inconsistent with our beliefs and attitudes. Thus, someone may say, "Despite the evidence, I don't believe smoking will be hazardous to my health." This is **selective distortion**.
- We retain only part of what we have selectively perceived. We may read an ad but later forget it. This is known as **selective retention**.

There are many communications implications in this selectivity process. For example, if an ad is too familiar, it will be ignored. On the other hand, if it is too complex, the ad will be judged not worth the time and effort to understand it. A useful communications approach is to create a mildly ambiguous first impression that heightens the consumer's interest.

Selective distortion operates so that we cannot assume that a message, even if it is factually correct, will necessarily be accepted as fact by consumers. In designing a message, the distance between the audience's current belief and the position proposed by the message must be considered. If the distance is large, a moderate claim may be more believable than a dramatic claim and therefore more effective in moving consumers in the desired direction.

For example, to bolster struggling season ticket sales and to capitalize on consumer research showing "that in 80 percent of homes, women decide how leisure time and money are spent," the Toronto Blue Jays are attempting to alter traditionally-held sport beliefs by targeting female fans in an attempt to change female perception of Blue Jays baseball as entertainment rather than just sport. To facilitate this, the organization has revamped its message and placement strategies. The message carries a tagline of "now playing" to deliver a more entertainment-based appeal, while the message placement is refocused on entertainment-based media such as entertainment sections of newspapers and during the hit television show *Desperate Housewives*.[2]

Even messages received undistorted are still subject to selective retention. Consequently, ads are repeated many times. The hope is that numerous exposures will etch the message into the recipient's memory. This partially explains why a firm with very familiar products and advertising, such as McDonald's, spends tens of millions each year reminding consumers that they are still there. In 2005, German Supermodel Heidi Klum signed a two-year contract to be its latest celebrity endorsement playing a role in advertising and public relations events for the all-American company. A company spokesperson said, "Heidi is the best partner (for McDonald's). She's a young mother and represents the modern lifestyle."[3]

Learning

learning
Changes in attitudes and behaviour resulting from previous experiences.

Learning can be defined as changes in behaviour resulting from previous experiences. It excludes behaviour that is attributable to instinct, such as breathing, and temporary states, such as hunger or fatigue. The ability to interpret and predict the consumer's learning process enhances our understanding of buying behaviour, since learning plays a role at every stage of the buying-decision process. The recognition of brand satisfaction and the subsequent development of functional and emotional relationships with the brand are the results of learning from consumer experience. Customers learn about companies and brands in part from prior experience; their own and that of others. While no simple learning theory has emerged as universally workable and acceptable, the one with the most direct application to marketing is stimulus-response theory.[4]

stimulus-response theory
The theory that learning occurs as a person responds to some stimulus and is rewarded with need satisfaction for a correct response or penalized for an incorrect one.

According to **stimulus-response theory**, learning occurs as a person (1) responds to some stimulus and (2) is rewarded with need satisfaction for a correct response or penalized for an incorrect one. When the same correct response is repeated in reaction to the same stimulus, a behaviour pattern or learning is established. Learning is at the root of building positive customer relationships. As the customer learns to expect positive results and treatment from the company or brand, that person will go back and buy again and again.

Once an habitual behaviour pattern has been established, it replaces conscious, wilful behaviour to search for alternatives. This is the same as saying that a consumer, having been satisfied or more than satisfied, develops and continues a relationship with the brand or the seller or both over repeated purchases. The task for a competitor is to find a way to arouse need in a different way or, once need has been aroused, to break into the process and cause the consumer to pay attention to competing information. This would be most easily done when a relationship is weak or is functionally based. It would be more difficult when a strong emotional relationship exists.

Marketers have taught consumers to respond to certain cues:

- End-of-aisle displays and Day-Glo price stickers in supermarkets suggest that an item is on sale.
- Sale signs in store windows suggest that bargains can be found inside.
- Large type in newspaper grocery ads suggests that featured items are particularly good bargains.

But the sad fact for marketers is that what is learned can be unlearned, and effective competitors search the decision-making process and the detail of each stage to find ways of disrupting habitual learned behaviour. Of course, the consumer adds to a marketer's frustration by seeking variety, by being short of time or money and thus prepared to behave differently, or by facing an empty store shelf where a favourite brand should be.

Personality

personality
An individual's pattern of traits that influences behavioural responses.

The study of human **personality** has given rise to many, sometimes widely divergent, schools of psychological thought. As a result, attempts to inventory and classify personality traits have produced a variety of different structures. In this discussion, personality is defined broadly as an individual's pattern of traits that influence behavioural responses. We speak of people as being self-confident, aggressive, shy, domineering, dynamic, secure, introverted, flexible, or friendly, and as being influenced (but not controlled) by these personality traits in their responses to situations.

It is generally agreed that personality traits do influence consumers' perceptions and buying behaviour. However, there is considerable disagreement about the nature of this relationship, that is, about how personality influences behaviour. Although we know that people's personalities often are reflected in the clothes they wear, the cars they drive (or whether they use a bike or motorcycle instead of a car), and the restaurants they patronize, we have not been successful in predicting behaviour from particular personality traits. The reason is simple: Many factors besides personality enter into the consumer buying-decision process.

Self-Concept Your self-concept, or self-image, is the way you see yourself and is a product of your personality and experience. Social psychologists distinguish between (1) the actual self-concept (the way you really see yourself) and (2) the ideal self-concept (the way you want to be seen or would like to see yourself).

self-concept
A person's self-image.

We know that people generally prefer brands and products that are compatible with their **self-concept**. Our friend in the chapter opener decided on the iPod because it was a better

actual self-concept
The way you really see yourself, as distinguished from ideal self-concept.

ideal self-concept
The way you want to be seen or would like to see yourself, as distinguished from actual self-concept.

fit with his love of music than a combination phone and music product. The compatibility is what allows brand relationships to develop, and the greater it is, the more emotional the relationship. There are mixed reports concerning the degree of influence of the actual as opposed to the ideal self-concept on brand and product preferences. Some researchers contend that consumption preferences correspond to a person's **actual self-concept**. Others hold that the **ideal self-concept** is dominant in consumers' choices.

Perhaps there is no consensus here, because in real life we often switch back and forth between our actual and our ideal self-concepts. A middle-aged man may buy some comfortable but not fashionable clothing to wear at home on a weekend, reflecting his actual self-concept. Then, later, he buys some expensive, high-fashion exercise clothing, envisioning himself (ideal self-concept) as a young, active, upwardly mobile guy. This same fellow may drive his old, beat-up minivan for his weekend errands (actual self-concept), but he'll drive his new, European sports sedan to work, where he wants to project a different (ideal) self-concept. Self-concept theory argues that individuals express themselves in the artifacts that they acquire, or would like to acquire, thus representing personality by the kinds of things they own and use. While this show-me-what-you-have-and-I'll tell-you-what-you-are notion is appealing and we can easily think of examples of people we know who would seem to fit this abstraction, this is but one force acting on consumers in their purchase decisions.[5]

One company that definitely appeals to the ideal self-concept of its customers is Nike. This brand continuously plays to the ideal self-concept in the commercials that feature professional athletes, including Tiger Woods. It makes many people want to be like Tiger.

Attitudes

attitude
A learned predisposition to respond to an object or class of objects in a consistently favourable or unfavourable way.

Attitude is traditionally defined as a learned predisposition to respond to an object or class of objects in a consistently favourable or unfavourable way. In our model of the buying-decision process, attitudes play a major role in the evaluation of alternatives. Numerous studies have reported a relationship between consumers' attitudes and their buying behaviour regarding both types of products and services selected and brands chosen. Surely, then, it is in a marketer's best interest to understand how attitudes are formed, the functions they perform, and how they can be changed.

Attitudes are also critically important in the formation of customer relationships. Since relationships are based to a very great extent on how customers feel toward a company or brand, their attitudes represent an important component of those feelings. They represent the deeply held views and opinions that customers have toward the companies and brands that they encounter in the marketplace.

All attitudes have the following characteristics in common:

Salon

- ***Attitudes are learned***. The information individuals acquire through their direct experiences with a product or an idea, indirect experiences (such as reading about a product in *Wallpaper** magazine or at **www.salon.com** on the Internet), and interactions with individuals in their social groups all contribute to the formation of attitudes. For example, the opinions expressed by a good friend about diet foods, plus the consumer's favourable or unfavourable experience as a result of using diet foods, will contribute to an attitude toward diet foods in general.
- ***Attitudes have an object***. By definition, we can hold attitudes only toward something. The object can be general (professional sports) or specific (Toronto Raptors); it can be abstract (college life) or concrete (the computer lab). In attempting to determine consumers' attitudes, it is very important to carefully define the object of the attitude, because a person might have a favourable attitude toward the general concept (exercise) but a negative attitude toward a specific dimension (running).

- ***Attitudes have direction and intensity***. Our attitudes are either favourable or unfavourable toward an object. They cannot be neutral. In addition, they have strength. For example, you may mildly like this textbook or you may like it very much (we hope!). This factor is important for marketers, because strongly held positive attitudes are the foundation of strong emotional relationships and are difficult to change.
- ***Attitudes are arranged in structures that tend to be stable and generalizable***. Once formed, attitudes usually endure, and the longer they are held, the more resistant to change they become. People also have a tendency to generalize attitudes. For instance, if a person is treated well by a salesperson in a particular store, there is a tendency to form a favourable attitude toward the entire store and develop a relationship with it.

A consumer's attitude does not always predict purchase behaviour. A person may hold very favourable attitudes toward a brand but not buy it because of some inhibiting factor. Typical inhibitors are not having enough money or discovering that your preferred brand has been replaced by a new model or is out of stock when the purchase must be made. Under such circumstances, purchase behaviour may even contradict attitudes.

As the preceding discussion suggests, it is extremely difficult to change strongly held attitudes. Moderately held or weakly held attitudes are much more amenable to change. Marketers need to know what consumer attitudes are to many aspects of their products, services, personnel, and advertisements, as well as the strength of such attitudes. Only then can they determine the bases for either satisfaction or dissatisfaction and where their relationships with consumers are vulnerable. When a company is faced with strongly held negative or unfavourable attitudes, it has two options. The first is to try to change the attitude to be compatible with the product. The second is to change the product, or more likely its image, to match attitudes. Ordinarily, it is much easier to change the product image than to change consumers' strongly held attitudes.

Nevertheless, in many situations, attitudes have been changed. Consider how negative attitudes have changed in favour of trucks and sports utility vehicles, how positive attitudes have changed about tobacco products, and how yellow tennis balls and off-season vacations have been accepted.

Values and lifestyles

lifestyle
The way in which a person conducts his or her life — activities, interests, and opinions.

One of the most valuable ways of looking at customers involves consideration of their values and **lifestyles**. Marketers develop programs based not only on how old their customers are or where they live, but also on how they spend their leisure time, what type of movies they like to watch, and what things they consider to be important in their lives — what they hold near and dear. This is an integral part of the concept of market segmentation, which will be discussed latter in the text. Essentially, the Canadian market is made up of many types of people. Once we can identify how these various groups think and live, we can do a better job of developing products, services, advertising, and other marketing techniques to appeal to them.

The field of psychographic research was developed through the study of thousands of consumers by measuring their opinions, interests, attitudes, values, beliefs, and activities in a variety of different areas. Today, psychographic research is considered by many in marketing to have transcended the demographic categories of age, gender, religion, social class, and ethnicity.

In the book *Sex in the Snow*, author and pollster Michael Adams provided one approach to lifestyle segmentation. He divided the Canadian population into three sections: Elders, Boomers, and GenXers. Each of these three categories can be further divided by distinguishing the fundamental motivators, key values, words of advice, and icons of each of the defined groups. Take a look at the categories on the next page to determine where you fall in Michael Adams' social tribes.

The Social Value "Tribes" of Canada

The Elders (now about 60+)

Rational Traditionalists (54 percent of Elders)

Motivators: financial independence, stability.

Key values: primacy of reason, deferred gratification, duty, and guilt.

Sayings: "Better safe than sorry," "A woman's place is in the home," or "A bird in the hand is worth two in the bush."

Extroverted Traditionalists (26 percent of Elders)

Includes a higher-than-average proportion of women and individuals from the Maritimes and Québec.

Motivators: social status, institutions, traditional communities.

Key values: religion, family, fear, respect for tradition and institutions.

Sayings: "Duty above all else," "A woman's work is never done," and "A penny saved is a penny earned."

Cosmopolitan Modernists (20 percent of Elders)

Includes a higher-than-average proportion of British Columbians, are over 50, have post-secondary education.

Motivators: traditional institutions, experience-seeking.

Key values: education, innovation, and a global perspective.

Sayings: "Take time to smell the roses," and "The world is my oyster."

The Boomers (now about 40-59)

Autonomous Rebels (25 percent of Boomers)

Motivators: personal autonomy, self-fulfilment.

Key values: freedom, individuality, sceptical of traditional institutions.

Sayings: "To each his own," "Knowledge is power," and "I did it my way."

Anxious Communicators (20 percent of Boomers)

Motivators: traditional communities, institutions, social status.

Key values: family, community, respect, fear.

Sayings: "Wisdom comes with age," and "Children are our future."

Disengaged Darwinists (41 percent of Boomers)

Includes a higher proportion of men and blue-collar workers.

Motivators: financial independence, stability, security.

Key values: fear, nostalgia for the past.

Sayings: "Look out for number one," and "Every man for himself."

GenXers (now about 25-39)

Aimless Dependants (27 percent of GenXers)

Motivators: financial independence, security, stability that their parents, members of the Boomers, possessed.

Key values: independence, fear.

Sayings: "What's the point?" "I couldn't care less," and "What's the system going to do for me?"

Thrill-Seeking Materialists (25 percent of GenXers)

Motivators: traditional communities, social status, experience-seeking.

Key values: desire for money, material possessions, respect, and admiration.

Sayings: "Live dangerously," and "Money is power."

New Aquarians (13 percent of GenXers)

Motivators: new experiences, new communities.

Key Values: hedonism, ecologism, egalitarianism.

Sayings: "There is no being, only becoming," and "Unity is diversity."

Autonomous Post-Materialists (20 percent of GenXers)

Motivators: personal autonomy, self-fulfilment.

Key values: freedom, respect for human rights.

Sayings: "It's my life," "Image is nothing," and "There is more to life than money."

Hedonists (15 percent of GenXers)

Motivators: seek new experiences, new communications.

Key values: immediate gratification, sexual permissiveness, hedonism.

Sayings: "Party hard," "If you look good you feel good," and "Don't worry, be happy."

GenYers (now about 12-24) the latest and not included in Adams' discussion.

Born between 1977-1995, the sons and daughters of the Boomers. Still formulating, much more diverse and amorphous than Gen X, some similar, some the opposite. At home with the digital revolution, Internet is medium of choice, more group oriented than GenXers, use rapid fire communications, subject to greater parental oversight in many cases, less hung up on race, gender ethnicity, extremely diverse, materialistic, less interested in traditional brands, hard to reach by marketers.

SOURCES: Adapted from Michael Adams, "The Demise of Demography," *The Globe and Mail,* January 18, 1997, p. D5, and based on *Sex in the Snow: Canadian Social Values at the End of the Millennium* (Toronto: Penguin Canada, 1997). GenY material adapted from online reports of a Northwestern University Marketing Department Conference on "Ygen," 2002.

The social-value tribes classification gives marketers a quick, comprehensive, and integrated multivariate view of the basic segmentation of the country. Many large firms develop similar approaches that are more specific to their purposes. This kind of information signals who is interested in what kinds of products and services, their location, their preferred information themes, their orientations to product claims, and the kinds of events they would likely attend.

Information and Purchase Decisions

Consumers constantly need to know more than they already know about what products and services are available, which brands offer what features and benefits, what services are available to support the purchase, who sells them at what prices, where they can be purchased, and what kind of follow-up service is likely. They need to add to what they have already learned and kept in memory. Without new information to learn for the first time or to update what they already know, there wouldn't be any decision to make.

commercial information environment
All marketing organizations and individuals that directly or indirectly communicate with consumers.

social information environment
Family, friends, and acquaintances who directly or indirectly provide information about products.

Recall from Figure 2-1, two information sources — commercial and social — enabled the buying decision process. The **commercial information environment** includes all of the marketing organizations and individuals that attempt to communicate with consumers — manufacturers, retailers, advertisers, e-commerce Web site sponsors, and sales and service people.

The social information environment is made up of family, friends, and acquaintances who directly or indirectly provide information about products. Think how often your conversations with friends at the coffee shop or in a chat room deal with purchases you are considering or those you have made. You probably have more discussions about products, brands, and services in a day than the number of commercial messages to which you pay attention. Also, it is interesting to note that people report negative experiences with products and services to other people more often than they report positive experiences.

Advertising is the most common type of commercial information. Other commercial sources are direct sales efforts by store clerks, telemarketing, and direct mail and e-mail to consumers' homes and computers, as well as consumers' physical involvement with products (examining packages, trial product use, and sampling).

The most important kind of social information is word-of-mouth communication — two or more people simply have a conversation about a product or service. The proliferation of product review sites and special-topic discussion groups and chat rooms on the Internet has enhanced word-of-mouth activity. Other social sources include your observations of others using products and your exposure to products in the homes and offices of others.

It's estimated that the typical adult is exposed to about 300 ad messages a day — almost 10,000 per month.[6] To understand how this information affects the buying decision process, we begin by examining the social and group forces that influence the individual's psychological make-up.

Social and Group Forces

The way we think, believe, and act is determined to a great extent by social forces that surround us and the groups with which we are involved. Note that the arrows in Figure 2-1 extend from the social and group forces in two directions: to the psychological make-up of the individual and to the buying-decision process. Our discussion begins with cultural and sub-cultural forces since all other group effects take place within cultural boundaries.

culture
A complex of symbols and artifacts created by a given society and handed down from generation to generation as determinants and regulators of human behaviour.

Definition of culture and cultural influence

Culture is the complex of symbols and artifacts (which includes goods and services) created by a society and handed down from generation to generation as determinants and regulators of behaviour. The symbols may be intangible (attitudes, beliefs, values, languages, religions) or

Cultural complexity represents a tremendous marketing opportunity.

tangible (tools, housing, products, works of art). Culture implies a totally learned and "handed-down" way of life. It does not include instinctive acts. However, standards for performing instinctive biological acts (eating, eliminating body wastes, and sexual relationships) can be culturally established. So, while everybody gets hungry, what people eat and how they act to satisfy the hunger will vary among cultures.

Our sociocultural institutions (family, school, language, religion) provide behavioural guidelines for us. "Culture . . . regulates our lives at every turn. From the moment we are born until we die there is constant conscious and unconscious pressure upon us to follow certain types of behaviour that [others] have created for us."[7] People living in a culture share a whole set of similarities and beliefs — and these often differ from those living in or originating from other cultures.

Canada: A culturally complex society

Compared with many other countries, Canada is a culturally complex society — it has many **subcultures**, as opposed to being relatively homogeneous such as Japan. Our subcultures are based on factors such as race, nationality, religion, geographic location, age, and urban-rural distribution. Ethnicity, for example, is a cultural factor that has significant marketing implications. According to Dr. Elizabeth Hirschman of New York University, "Ethnicity contributes to consumers' imaginal tendencies and sensory arousal-seeking, and that affects consumption motives and preferred leisure activities."[8] Concentrations of Middle or Eastern Europeans in the Prairies provide a market for some products that would go unnoticed in Italian or Chinese communities in Toronto, Montréal, or Vancouver. In this sense, people with distinctive cultures can form cultural markets from a business perspective.

subculture
Groups that exhibit characteristic behaviour patterns sufficient to distinguish them from other groups within the same culture.

The cultural diversity of Canada continues to be of increasing importance for business. In the past, marketers frequently ignored ethnic and linguistically based groups. However, as they grew in size as well as diversity, differences became emphasized, marketplace competition escalated and segmentation or treating groups differently became accepted as a viable marketing strategy. Besides the large French Canadian population, there are also large communities of Italian, Chinese, German, Portuguese, and South Asians in this country. Although many of these people have been here for many years, language loyalty continues to remain high, indicating the pervasive influence of original cultures within our cultural mosaic. In fact, only about 12 million Canadians identify their ethnic origins as being Canadian.[9]

Of the 5.4 million immigrants in Canada (a number expected to continue to grow), 42 percent currently live in Toronto, 37 percent in Vancouver, and 17 percent in Montréal. The four largest foreign-born groups in the greater Toronto area alone — South Asian, Chinese, Italian, and Portuguese — account for more than $36 billion in annual expenditures.[10] The most obvious marketing efforts to reach ethnic market segments are, therefore, found in these markets. In Toronto, for example, Fairchild Radio reaches 24 percent of the Chinese population, while CHIN reaches 11 percent. The OMNI.2 television system in

Omni Television

Ontario (**www.omnitv.ca/omni2**) boasts the number-one Cantonese language newscast in Ontario, with a 71 percent weekly reach. OMNI.1 and OMNI.2 also broadcast Armenian, Filipino, Greek, Iranian, Japanese, Korean, Macedonian, Maltese, Polish, Russian, South Asian, and Ukrainian productions. In the 10 largest Canadian cities, the proportion of visible minorities is more than 20 percent of the population.[11] The ethnic market is highly concentrated, with four-fifths of visible minorities living in Ontario (50 percent), British Columbia (17 percent), and Québec (15 percent).

According to a recent OMNI TV study, 66 percent of the Chinese market learn about brands and services from Chinese television; 35 percent are more likely to buy products or services if they saw them advertised in Chinese, and 54 percent watch less than seven hours of English TV per week. Fifty percent of Asians say their opinion of a company would improve if they saw the ads on Asian TV.[12]

Interestingly, younger Chinese consumers, who are fluent in English, say they would respect companies more if they made the effort to communicate with them in their own language. As a result, Rogers Wireless is making a special commitment to make its products and services "more culturally relevant so (customers) think we really understand them," says Madonna Lee, Ethnic Marketing Manager at Rogers in Toronto. Simply an initiative to tap into the $20 billion that Chinese-Canadian consumers spend every year.[13]

Television and newspapers are available to the Chinese communities in Vancouver, Toronto, Montréal, and elsewhere. Toronto's Spanish-language *El Popular* is targeted at the area's 250,000 Spanish speakers and is distributed from Québec to British Columbia. Edmonton's Aboriginal Media Services sells airtime for its Native radio station as well as advertising space in its 70 Native newspapers. These and similar media represent attractive advertising outlets for companies who want to reach growing subcultural and linguistic market segments.

The most consequential subcultural market of concern to marketers is portrayed in the attitudinal and behavioural differences between English- and French-speaking communities on a countrywide basis, including Acadian markets.

MARKETING AT WORK — 2-2: GLOBAL

Leveraging Cultural Diversity

More than 800 employees who work for Procter & Gamble Canada in Toronto, representing 40 different countries and speaking over 30 different languages, celebrated the company's first diversity day. And this was not just a wave the flag feel-good day. For P&G, the continued success it has in marketing Crest, Mr. Clean, Pampers, Swiffer, Tide and a host of other household products is tied directly to the increased innovativeness, productivity and relationship building capacity that a diversified workforce brings to its marketing as well as other company efforts.

It is too easy for companies, P&G included, to fall into simple stereotyping when creating information for different ethnic or cultural groups. Tim Penner, President of P&G Canada, says that diversifying the workforce is now a core strategic mission. Diversity gives employees a better understanding of their customers. The concept goes beyond the idea that "...someone who is black can market better to black people, or that French people can market better to French people, that women can market better to women." It helps create understanding across the company, an acceptance of differences and results in more productive and innovative teamwork when it comes to putting together marketing programs. Work colleagues now can much more easily reach out for perspectives and advice from colleagues with different ethnic, racial, religious and sexual backgrounds than has been the case in the past.

QUESTIONS:

1. How does the P&G relationship building approach result in better customer relationships?
2. Are there disadvantages to using this approach within the firm?

SOURCE: Adapted from Virginia Galt, "P&G leverages its cultural diversity," *The Globe and Mail*, April 7, 2005, pp. B1, B18.

The Québécois market

While French Canada is technically and politically for some, a subculture, its sheer size, homogeneity, main geographic location, purchasing power, and social and political orientation makes it a cultural rather than a subcultural market. No other ethnic or non-English-speaking linguistic group comes close to comprising 14 percent of the Canadian population (in total, approximately 31 percent of the population of Canada speaks French).[14]

Quebec is the major French-speaking market with a long-established and fully developed set of cultural, social, artistic, and legal institutions. Québec consumers consistently exhibit consumption patterns unlike those in the rest of Canada. Some examples of such generalized consumption differences are:[15]

- Better acceptance in Québec of premium-priced products, such as premium-grade gasoline and liquors.
- Willingness to pay higher prices for convenience items.
- Greater popularity in Québec of coupons and premiums.
- Greater per-capita expenditure in Québec on clothing, personal-care items, tobacco, wine, and beer. There is a lower consumption of "hard" liquor, although stronger brands of beer are preferred.
- Greater per-capita consumption of soft drinks (regular, not diet), maple sugar, molasses, candy, and pre-sweetened cereals in Québec than in the rest of Canada — and lottery tickets, as well.
- More time spent watching television and listening to radio in Québec compared to the rest of the country.
- Women in Québec show different patterns of cosmetics use, including more use of perfumes, colognes, and hair-colouring products.

It's easy to reach different cultural groups through the Web.

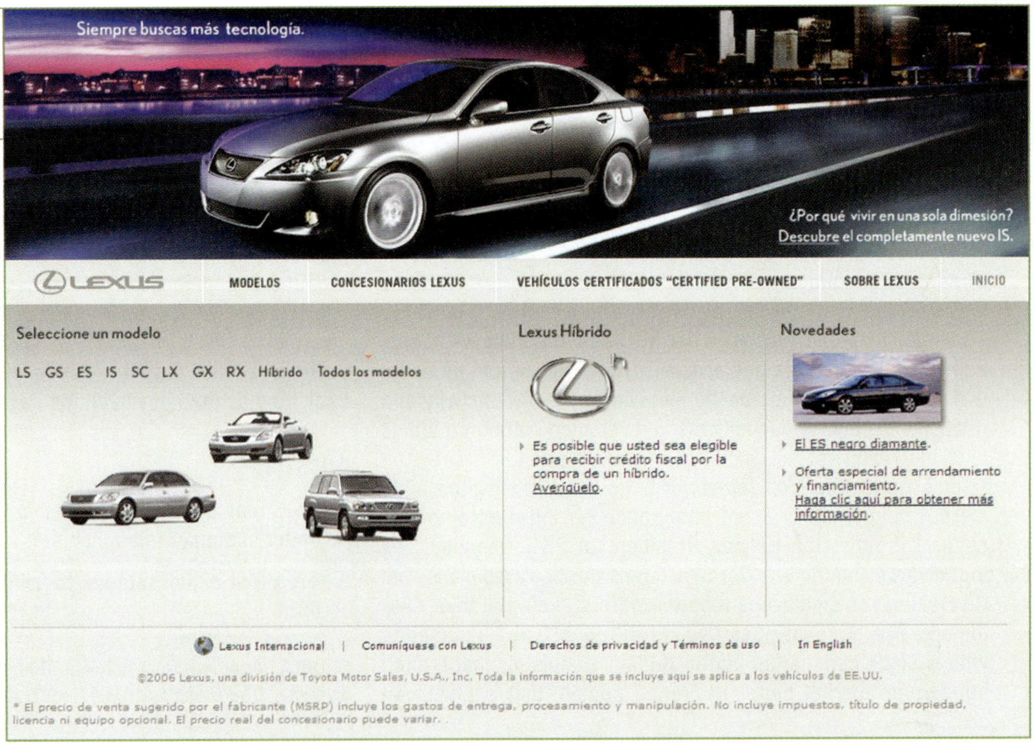

The impact of cultural differences on marketing

The fact that French Canada as well as the various other cultural communities in Canada represent distinctively different markets ideally requires that marketers develop specialized programs in order to be effective. Because most of these communities are so much smaller in both scale and purchasing power than Francophone Québec, the scope for and amount of marketing program adaptation that is feasible for firms to engage in is frequently limited to advertising in the appropriate language and using, where possible, culturally acceptable symbols, themes and illustrations. For example, the large Asian population represents a most attractive market but there are intricacies that must be considered. Within this group, there are differences in origin that are significant: people from Hong Kong primarily speak Cantonese; those from Taiwan primarily speak Mandarin and Taiwanese; those from China primarily speak Mandarin or standard Chinese.[16] Burger King faced language concerns head-on with its "Now we're speaking the same language" campaign, in which they chose Cantonese as it is the most common dialect in the Canadian Chinese community. Colours are important in advertising since their symbolic significance varies from cultural group to group. White flowers, for example, are a sign of death in Chinese culture and may have been incorrectly used in the background of advertisements — the result can be that unintended meanings can too easily be communicated. Marketers must know the target culture or risk making needless errors.

Reference Group Influences

reference group
A group of people who influence a person's attitudes, values, and behaviour.

Consumers' perceptions and buying behaviour are also influenced by the **reference groups** with which they associate. Influences can result from either direct group membership or from identification with a group. After all, it is from the association with such groups that one learns the meaning of most things. In general, reference group influences are stronger in their effects than are cultural influences. Most reference groups — but not all — with which you associate are likely within the same cultural group.

Small group effects

Influential reference groups may include family, sports clubs or teams, or a circle of close friends from school, work, or the neighbourhood. Each of these groups has its own standards of behaviour that serve as guides or frames of reference for actual or aspiring members. A person may agree with all of the ideas of the group or only with some of them. Also, a person does not have to belong to a group to be influenced by it. Actual and potential reference groups operate to influence a person's attitudes, values, and behaviour.

Studies have shown that personal advice in face-to-face reference groups is much more effective in influencing buying behaviour than is advertising in newspapers, television, and other mass media. That is, in selecting products or changing brands, you are more likely to be influenced by advice, comments, or word of mouth from satisfied (or dissatisfied) customers in your reference group. This is true especially when you consider the speaker to be knowledgeable about the particular product or service or about the problem a product or service is designed to address. There is now growing awareness of the importance and influence that Internet-based reference groups or special-interest communities have on those who spend a significant amount of time in online conversations with individuals as well as in chat rooms — either in giving opinions or monitoring them. Notoriously popular among today's 'tween generation (between child and teenager, ages 9 to 13), online groups and chat rooms make 'tweens feel empowered. The experience allows their creativity to roam wild, and unleashes their imagination as they role-play while communicating with faceless individuals at the other end.[17]

Advertisers rely on reference group influence when they use celebrity spokespersons. Professional athletes, musicians, models, and actors can influence people who admire them or want to be like them in some small way. Recent examples include McDonald's new global focus on healthy living featuring Canadians Wayne Gretzky and speed skater Bonnie Blair as well as tennis stars Venus and Serena Williams. English-born and Canadian-raised actress Kim Cattrall, of *Sex and the City* fame, has even gotten in on the action for, of all things, Tetley Tea TV advertisements in the UK where she plays her infamous man-hungry character 'Samantha' from the hit HBO series.

In 2005, Reebok beat out rivals Nike, Bauer, and Mission to sign 17 year-old Rimouski Oceanic hockey sensation Sidney Crosby from Cole Harbour, N.S. to a five-year endorsement deal reported to be worth US$2.5 million.

A variation on this is marketers who actually supply professional organizations with their products. Bauer Inc., for example, as part of its parent company Nike's sponsorship deal with the International Ice Hockey Federation, dressed Team Canada in Bauer uniforms and equipment.[18]

The importance of reference group influence is evident when charities and not-for-profit organizations use endorsements by well-known figures to champion their causes in print and broadcast media advertising. A recent example of a star who has spoken out to educate the public and promote research support for a cause close to him is Michael J. Fox's campaign for Parkinson's Disease, from which he suffers.

Reference group influence in marketing is not limited to well-known personalities. Any group whose qualities a person admires can act as a reference. The physically fit, the environmentally conscious, and the professionally successful have all served as reference groups in advertisements. Another useful reference group factor pertains to the flow of information between and within groups — it tends to flow horizontally from group to group on a similar social level, rather than trickle down from high-status to lower-status groups.[19]

innovator
The first member of a reference group who is most likely to adopt something new (good, service).

The proven role of small groups as behaviour determinants, plus the concept of horizontal information flow, suggests that a marketer is faced with two key problems. The first is to identify the relevant reference group likely to influence a consumer in a given buying situation. The second is to identify and communicate with two key people in the group — **the innovator**

A celebrity with credibility adds support to a good cause.

opinion leader
The member of a reference group who is the information source and who influences the decision-making of others in the group.

(the early buyer — which one of your friends got "it" first) and the influential person — the person you would ask for advice (the **opinion leader**) about a specific topic. Every group has a leader — a taste-maker or opinion leader — who influences the decision-making of others in the group. The key is for marketers to identify, communicate with, and convince that person of the value of their products or services. The opinion leader in one group may be an opinion follower in another. A person who is influential in matters concerning music, because of a special interest or skill in that area, may follow the opinions of another when it comes to buying software, or clothing.

Family and household influence

family
A group of two or more people related by blood, marriage, adoption, or common practice, living together in a household.

A **family**, usually the most important reference group, is still commonly viewed as a group of two or more people related by blood, marriage, adoption, or common practice, living together in a household. During their lives, most people will belong to at least two families — the one into which they are born and the one they form at marriage, partnering, or living together. The birth family primarily determines core values and attitudes. In contrast, the marriage family or other family forms, have a more direct influence on specific purchases. For example, household size is important in the purchase of a car; perceived household permanence is important in making costly expenditures on furnishings.

household
A single person, a family, or any group of unrelated persons who occupy a housing unit.

A **household** is a broader concept than a family. It consists of a single person, a family, or any group of unrelated persons who occupy a housing unit. Thus, an unmarried homeowner, college students sharing an off-campus apartment, and people who are cohabiting are examples of households.

Since households are not necessarily composed of a couple with children, sensitivity to household structure is important in designing marketing strategy. It affects such dimensions as product type and form (semi-processed or prepared gourmet meals for singles or busy working couples), product size (how large a serving for older couples, how large a refrigerator or microwave oven), and the design of advertising (who should be depicted in a TV ad: A traditional family or a couple? What kind of couple?).

In addition to the direct, immediate impact households have on the purchasing behaviour of members, it is also interesting to consider the buying behaviour of the household as a unit. Who does the buying for a household? Marketers should treat this question as five separate ones, because each may call for different strategies:

1. Who influences the buying decision?
2. Who makes the buying decision?
3. Who makes the actual purchase?
4. Who uses the product or service?
5. Who follows up on service and performance concerns?

The answers to these questions allow marketers to design programs that take into consideration the nature of the interaction patterns within the household and thereby create effective marketing programs. Different household members may assume these various roles, or one individual may play several roles in a particular purchase.

More than ever before, teenagers and young children are important decision makers and influencers in family buying, as well as being active shoppers in their own right. In Canada, 2.5 million 9- to 14-year olds spend $1.7 billion of their own money each year, and that's nothing compared the $20 billion they influence their families to spend. The diversity of their interests and their access to information means that they could be exposed to just about any

Hilary Duff is a big Sony fan.

Milk producers want to get her to drink more.

message and their money could just about go anywhere![20] This certainly is enough to warrant the attention of many manufacturers. Even very young children influence buying decisions today, because they watch TV advertising and ask for products when they shop with their parents. Children are also making their way onto the Internet and "window shopping" — there have yet to be reports of them making massive use of parents' credit cards on an unauthorized basis.

The power this market holds is evidenced by changes in retail offerings aimed at this group. Some retailers have focused on young girls who are in control of Mom's credit cards. Le Château and La Senza have developed product lines and marketing for this segment. Zellers has even jumped on the bandwagon carrying the new line of clothing from teen movie and pop star Hilary Duff. Most recently, attention has turned toward the males in this age group. Winnipeg-based *What!* Magazine has split its publication into *What's His* and *What's Hers* following the lead of many other North American youth magazines. Unilever has also recognized a previously untapped need for its Axe deodorant with teen males. The approach of the "Camp Touch" ad campaign laced with innuendo is on the importance of fragrance on "getting the girl." "Thirteen to 14-year old boys think Axe is great," a company spokesperson says. "They're going out, playing sports, having fun with their friends, and when they are out with the gang they know they should smell good in front of the girls. On the other hand, they don't have a great ability to manage how to do that. So they spray on the scent."[21]

When children aren't influencing the process, purchasing decisions are often made jointly by the household heads, male and/or female. New couples are much more likely to make buying decisions on a joint basis than are older couples. Apparently, the longer a couple lives together, the more each partner feels able to trust the other's judgement.

Knowing which family member is likely to make the purchase decision will influence a firm's entire marketing approach. For example, children are often key decision makers, concerning breakfast cereals. Obviously, a manufacturer will produce something that tastes good to children, design the package with them in mind, and advertise on Saturday morning cartoon shows. Even sedate and wholesome products such as milk and yogurt can have added appeal with a packaging makeover. Canada's major dairies have in recent years launched loudly packaged, single-serving milkshakes and flavoured milks, whose cool design, advertising, and convenience aim for strong teen appeal. Yogurt products have had similar makeovers, making them more convenient to carry and even possible to drink from the package, eliminating the need to arm oneself with a spoon. Other strategies to broaden the appeal of yogurt include adding cream or cereal products to reduce the sharp taste and hopefully making it more appealing to younger consumers. Such strategies are employed regardless of who actually makes the purchase and who else (besides the children) in the household might eat cereal or yogurt.

MARKETING AT WORK 2-3: RELATIONSHIPS

Where the Boys Are

"My clothes, they have to represent me. I listen to hip hop, so I wear stuff like Sean John, because P. Diddy makes it, and Shady, ltd., because that's Eminem's line." — Ricky, 13.

The 'tween and teenage markets are not new targets for marketers, but there is a growing interest in understanding the males in these groups as it has remained a largely untapped market for many brands.

Here's some of what we do know about how boys buy....

Who They Look to for Ideas About Trends:

34% Friends

27% Television

13% Stores

12% Magazines

45% of boys report that the brand name of the clothes they wear is either important or very important to them.

63% of them have the same brand of shoes they had a year ago.

What Makes a Brand Cool:

21% Quality

16% Colour

12% Advertising

30% Have entered a contest in the past three months.

40% Have been offered a free sample in the past three months.

QUESTIONS:

1. Which is the most important reference group for male 'tweens and teens?
2. Why do you think contests and samples influence them?

SOURCE: Adapted from Kathleen Martin, "Where the Boys Are," *Marketing Magazine Online*, www.marketingmag.ca, January 17, 2005.

PAGE UP!

1. Which social force has the most direct impact on our individual buying decisions?
2. Consumers from which province consistently exhibit consumption patterns unlike those in the rest of Canada?
3. For the marketer, what is the difference between a family and a household?

Situational Influences

situational influences
Temporary forces, associated with the immediate purchase environment, which affect behaviour.

You know that you and your friends act differently in a classroom from the way you act in your favourite coffee shop. The same holds true of buying behaviour. You might get a haircut because of an upcoming job interview when you would not get one otherwise. On vacation, you might buy a souvenir that seems very strange when you get home. For a close friend's wedding gift, you might buy a more prestigious brand of small appliance than you would buy for yourself. These are all examples of how temporary forces associated with the immediate purchase environment affect behaviour. Situational influence tends to be less significant when the consumer has a strong relationship with a brand and when the consumer is highly involved in the purchase. However, it often plays a major role in buying decisions. The five categories of **situational influences** and their effects are explained next.

Time effects — when consumers buy

Consumer buying is greatly influenced by the time dimension: by the season, week, day, or hour of purchase; by the impact that past and present events have on the purchase decision.

The time dimension of buying has implications for promotion scheduling since it makes sense that promotional messages reach consumers when they are in a decision-making frame

Lots of growth in the family restaurant sector.

of mind. Marketers also adjust prices in an attempt to even out demand. For instance, supermarkets may offer double coupons on Wednesdays, usually a slow business day. If seasonal buying patterns exist, marketers can sometimes extend the buying season. There is obviously (or so you'd think) little opportunity to extend the buying season for Easter bunnies or Christmas ornaments, although some "Christmas" stores operate year round. Even the traditional season for vacations has been shifted to such an extent that winter and other "off-season" or "shoulder-season" vacations are now quite popular.

As for the impact of past or future events, the length of time since you last went out to dinner at a nice restaurant may influence a decision on where to go tonight. Or the significance of an upcoming event, such as a vacation trip to a resort area, could result in a greater than normal level of clothing purchases. Marketers need to know enough about the targeted consumers to anticipate the effects of these past and future events.

Dual-income households find it difficult to make time in their busy schedules to prepare meals at home, yet they can afford to take the family out to eat at a restaurant that offers something more in terms of quality than do the mainstream fast-food outlets such as McDonald's, Burger King, and Harvey's. Rather than standing in long lines for burgers and fries, these families head for restaurants that offer a wider menu selection, table service, and a family atmosphere. There has been considerable growth in the sector of the restaurant business labelled "family restaurants," which include Swiss Chalet, White Spot, and Golden Griddle, and in the slightly more pricey casual-dining sector, where we find East Side Mario's, Jack Astor's, and such regional chains as Milestone's or Joey Tomato's.[22]

The growth and popularity of fast-food restaurants, quick-oil-change outlets, highly specialized Web sites, and catalogue retailers are marketers' responses to consumers' time pressures. Two working household heads, more commuting and mandatory leisure-time activities (such as carpooling children to social and sports events) leave little time for relaxed shopping. The results are measurable. In 1988, the average consumer spent 90 minutes on a mall shopping trip. Today, this figure has fallen below 65 minutes. Some photo-processing operations return developed prints by mail or e-mail, or send them to their customer's Web site to save time and effort. Internet-based marketers are open for business 24 hours a day. Whether purchases are of the pure "click" or "click and brick" variety, time of buying can and is being changed.

Where consumers buy — the physical and social surroundings

Physical surroundings are the features of a situation that are apparent to the senses, such as lighting, smells, weather, and sounds. Music can be an important element in a store's strategy. Colours, smells, and sounds can all be engineered to control consumers' retail experience and attempt to influence their behaviour.

The social surroundings are the number, mix, and actions of other people at the purchase site. You probably would not go into a strange restaurant that has an empty parking lot. And in a crowded store with other customers waiting, you probably ask the clerk fewer questions and spend less time comparing products.

Surroundings also impact experiences on the Internet. The ease with which product information can be obtained and orders can be placed in the virtual surroundings will decide if a site will be considered for future purchases. The Internet also places greater control in consumers' hands. Wherever the purchase is made, consumers can now arm themselves with huge quantities of technical and pricing information that allows greater leverage when making unfamiliar and/or large purchases. This knowledge combined with information regarding actual and virtual locations to buy a product helps to prevent a consumer from being taken advantage of, or simply making uninformed purchasing decisions.

How consumers buy — the terms and conditions of the purchase

How consumers buy refers to the terms and conditions of sale as well as the transaction-related activities that buyers are willing to perform. More retailers sell on credit today than just a few years ago. Not only do consumers use credit for instalment purchases (to buy things today with future income), but many now use credit for convenience. The ability to use VISA or MasterCard or debit cards to make a wide variety of purchases while not carrying cash is an attractive option to many consumers, particularly college students. The growth of catalogue distribution and e-commerce has enabled consumers to buy everything from food to a new house without setting foot outside the door.

Finally, with increasing pressures on our time, the trend toward one-stop shopping has encouraged traditional retailers to add unrelated items to their basic mix of products. Consider, for example, the wide variety of goods found in what we call a drugstore. Many Shoppers Drug Mart locations carry household cleaning supplies and grocery items and have postal outlets. Gas bars have added convenience foods and sundries. E-tailers attempt to design and develop Web sites that carry more and more items.

Conditions under which consumers buy — states and moods

Sometimes consumers are in a temporary state that influences their buying decisions. When you are ill or rushed, you may be unwilling to wait in line or to take the time or care that a particular purchase deserves. Your expectations and decision-making are different when you want to grab a quick lunch with a fellow student than they are when you go out for dinner with family or friends to celebrate a special occasion. Moods can also influence purchases. Feelings such as anger or excitement can result in purchases that otherwise would not have been made. In the exciting atmosphere of a rock concert, for example, you might pay more for a commemorative T-shirt than you would under normal circumstances. Salespeople must be trained to recognize consumers' moods and adjust their presentations accordingly.

What about the impact of catastrophic events such as 9/11, SARS, or even the tsunami that hit Southeast Asia in early 2005? Airlines, hotels, and other travel- and tourist-related services immediately felt a tremendous impact. And not just in the areas directly affected. People were afraid to travel for different reasons in each case, but the result was the same: Would they ever feel safe again? Would people refrain from using public transportation unless absolutely required? People became afraid to invest in large purchases because of the uncertainty of what would happen next.

PAGE UP!

1. What is selective distortion?
2. What are the four common characteristics of attitudes?
3. What three major generational divisions exist in Canada?

Key Terms and Concepts

actual self-concept 42
attitude 42
buying-decision process 30
cognitive dissonance 37
commercial information environment 45
culture 45
family 51
high-involvement level 32
household 51
ideal self-concept 42
impulse buying 33
innovator 50
learning 40
lifestyle 43
low-involvement level 32
Maslow's hierarchy of needs 38
motive 38
opinion leader 51
patronage motives 35
perception 39
personality 41
psychographics 38
reference group 49
selective attention 40
selective distortion 40
selective retention 40
self-concept 41
situational influences 53
social information environment 45
stimulus-response theory 41
subculture 46

Questions and Problems

1. For each of the following type of products, provide an example of when each could be a high-involvement purchase and when a low-involvement purchase. Consider the different possible uses for the products, the different occasions when they are purchased, and the different types of consumers that exist in the market.
   a. A laptop or personal computer.
   b. An automobile (e.g.: car, van, pickup truck).
   c. A watch.
   d. An expensive item of jewellery.
   e. A hotel room.
2. In Figure 2-1 illustrating the consumer-decision-making process and its environment, two arrows flow from the "social and group forces" box in the diagram. Explain why there are two arrows from this box and what this means.
3. What happens when a product or service provider fails to meet the expectations of a customer? In what different ways might customers respond to such experiences?
4. Sometimes a product or service provider exceeds the average customer's expectations for quality or value. Is there any disadvantage for a marketer whose product causes the consumer's experience to greatly exceed expectations? What future challenges might this create for that company or brand?
5. From a consumer-behaviour perspective, is it more practical, or appropriate, to consider the population of a relatively small country like Canada as a uniform marketplace? Why or why not?
6. From a consumer-behaviour perspective, is it correct to view the European Union or the countries of Asia as single markets? Why or why not?
7. Explain how your family or household might influence your choice of a product or brand for the following items:
   a. Toothpaste.
   b. Auto tune-up.
   c. Haircut.
   d. Breakfast cereal.
8. How would a soft drink company market its product to the Québécois market? How would the company's marketing activities differ in Québec, compared with the rest of Canada?
9. Explain how self-concept might come into play in the purchase of the following products:
   a. Eyeglasses.
   b. New suit.
   c. Perfume or cologne.
   d. College or university education.
10. List three products or services for which usage would not be greatly affected by cultural or ethnic differences. List three that would be affected by such differences. Explain how.
11. How could you assess your product for its appeal to different cultures or subcultures in or outside of your own country? In other words, how do you find a market for your product?

Hands-On Marketing

1. Interview the manager of a store that sells big-ticket items (furniture, appliances, electronic equipment) about what methods, if any, the store uses to reinforce purchase decisions and reduce the cognitive dissonance of its customers. What additional methods can you suggest?
2. Have a friend describe a high-involvement purchase that he or she recently made. Show how each of the six stages described in this chapter are reflected in the description. Identify the primary social influences that played a part in the decision.

Back to the Top

Think about the decisions that our friends made in the beginning of the chapter regarding their purchases. Apply some of the concepts covered in this chapter, so that you can better explain what went on in the minds of our three friends. What were their 'motives'? How were they different? What evidence is there that 'motives' were at work? Is there any evidence of reference group influence? What information sources were used? Where is there evidence of learning having occurred? What are the implications of all of this for marketers in the cellphone business? How does information like this about customers help marketers do a better job?

Online Learning Centre

Want to get better grades, tips on how to study more effectively, and up-to-date information on happenings in the world of marketing? Then, visit the Online Learning Centre for practice tests, Study Smart software, *Marketing Magazine*, and much more! **www.mcgrawhill.ca/olc/sommers**

CHAPTER 3

The Dynamic Marketing Environment

In this chapter, we'll examine how a company plans its total marketing program. After studying this chapter, you should have an understanding of:

- The concept of monitoring a firm's environment (environmental scanning) and how forces outside a company play a role in strategic marketing planning.
- The role of internal company factors (the internal environment) in guiding and supporting marketing strategies and their implementation.
- The nature and scope of planning and how it fits within the management process.
- Similarities and differences among mission, objectives, strategies, and tactics.
- The essential difference between strategic company planning and strategic marketing planning.
- The steps involved in strategic marketing planning.
- The purpose and contents of an annual marketing plan.
- How a planning model can be a useful aid in developing a marketing program.

Environmental Change? Yes! ... But Digital Technology? ... At Warp Speed!

Just look at the environment! Customer interests and wishes changing. New businesses to plan for. New competitors to look out for. New marketing programs to develop. And, all at warp speed.

A lot of this change is being driven by technology and particularly, the digital component and those other environmental elements it affects — social and cultural forces as well as legal and political ones. We continue to see startling advances in digitizing almost everything in sight and the most in-your-face evidence is the entertainment industry. And that means, among other things, music. And that means what Apple with its iPod products has wrought. Well over 50 million iPods have been sold since its launch in 2001, 32 million of those were sold in 2005 alone and more to come. One of the more obvious effects, aside from all of us walking around with white cords hanging out of our ears, has been the growth of the iPod accessory market and a host of new accessory businesses based on companion products.

Initially, Apple and a number of small firms built iPod accessories ranging from headphones to cases. But, with explosive market growth, large firms like Belkin, Griffin, Kensington, and Targus quickly focused their attention on the expanding accessories market, developed strategies, plans, products, and executions to take care of the market and marketing changes they observed. Belkin alone planned to sell more than $200 million worth of iPod accessories in 2006 out of a total market estimated at more than $1 billion. Estimates are that for every $3 spent on an iPod, $1 is spent on add-ons. Willi Powell, strategic development manager at Apple Canada, says, "There are people spending more money on their headphones than on their iPods."

As the market grows, more new businesses appear, offering microphones, docking stations, high-end earphones, dancing robots, light-up toy dogs, car stereo adapters, cameras, backpacks, clothing, and cars. Levi Straus is designing jeans that will have a docking cradle, retractable headphones, and a joy stick in the coin pocket to act as a wired remote. Roughly 40 percent of new cars sold in the U.S. in 2006 offered iPod docking kit options — this includes Chrysler, BMW, and Jaguar.

Of course, there will be more technological change and more sophisticated environmental scanning, business planning, marketing strategy development, and marketing programming as social and cultural forces change in the face of continued digitization.[1]

In Chapter 1, you were introduced to the ideas that make marketing contemporary and dynamic. You looked at such concepts as customer satisfaction, long-run customer loyalty, the stages of getting and keeping customers, customer value, and shareholder value. In Chapter 2, you reviewed customer behaviour, the buying-decision process, and the forces that influence it. In this chapter, we turn to the marketing organization whose task it is to serve the customer and provide customer satisfaction by putting contemporary marketing ideas to work.

In the first part of this chapter, we describe the environment in which all businesses exist and with which they must deal, regardless of what they do or how big they are. If you know your customers — what's going on in the marketing environment — you can do a better job. Marketing people need to determine what makes up their firm's environment and then monitor it in a systematic fashion. Good monitoring provides the data for developing successful strategies and plans for managing the business.

In the second part of the chapter, we examine three levels of management planning: strategic planning for the business or total organization, strategic planning for the marketing department or functions, and action planning for specific marketing activities. You will see where and how marketing environmental scanning plays a key role in the management process.

The Environment for Strategy and Planning

external macro-environmental forces
Market forces that are mostly beyond the control of companies: demographics, social and cultural trends, economic conditions, competition, technological developments, and political and legal forces.

BACK TO THE TOP

external micro-environmental forces
Forces affecting a particular firm that can be readily influenced by the company: the sets of marketing relationships a firm has with its customers, its suppliers, and the wholesalers and retailers through which the company sells its products and services to customers.

internal non-marketing forces
The environment within a firm composed of working relationships between employees and departments.

The environment in which all organizations operate, regardless of who they are and what they do, is composed of three sets of factors or forces:

- Those that affect all competing firms and that are mostly beyond the control of management: demographics, economic conditions, type and severity of competition the firm faces, social and cultural trends, technological developments, and political and legal forces. These are often referred to as **external macro-environmental forces**. Technology represents an obvious external macro-environmental change that affects many companies today as their customers accept new technologies and abandon old ones. In our chapter opener, the accessories market to support iPods and other MP3 players did not exist a few years ago and is entirely the result of advances in digital technology.
- Those that affect a particular firm and can more readily be influenced by management: the sets of marketing relationships a firm has with its customers, its suppliers, and the wholesalers and retailers through which the company sells its products and services. These forces are often referred to as **external micro-environmental forces**.
- Within the firm itself, an environment exists that is composed of working relationships between employees and departments. These, traditionally, have been referred to as **internal non-marketing forces**, but do influence the ultimate success of the organization.

Sometimes a firm may be able to manage a part of its external environment that is generally not controllable. For example, through corporate and industry lobbying in Ottawa or provincial capitals, or at the municipal level, a company may have some influence on how political and legal forces affect it. In addition, new-product research and development that is on the leading edge of technological innovation can influence a firm's competitive position. In fact, one company's technology may be the external environmental force of technology that is affecting other organizations.

The six interrelated macro-environmental forces that are generally beyond the control of management are presented in Figure 3-1: demography, social and cultural forces, economic conditions, competition, technology, and political and legal forces. Each force is then discussed, described, and illustrated. Keep in mind that the forces and their magnitude keep changing. When they change, it can be at different rates — not all markets or consumers are affected by a given change in the same way, and sometimes, through industry and company pressure, some

Figure 3-1:
Relationship-Insensitive External Environmental Forces
Six largely uncontrollable external forces influence an organization's marketing activities.

of these forces can be influenced. Such forces could be said to be **relationship-insensitive**, meaning that they do not afford a firm a particular advantage or the opportunity to develop particularly strong bonds or connections with its customers.

relationship-insensitive forces
Forces that do not afford a firm a particular advantage or the opportunity to develop particularly strong bonds or connections with its customers.

Demography

Demography is the statistical study of human population and its distribution. People who have similar demographic characteristics (such as age, geographic location, or income level) often share other relevant characteristics, creating a potential group of customers or market for a particular product or service.

demography
The statistical study of human population and its distribution.

The Ever-Present Boomers Born between 1946 and 1966, Baby Boomers account for a larger percentage of the population of Canada than is the case in any other country (32 percent of the entire population — more than nine million people in 2005).[2] They are now passing through their middle years (early 40s to early 60s) bringing changes in "middle-aged" values, tastes, and concerns — indulging in well-earned vacations and luxury cars instead of family minivans. Boomers have lots of spending capacity and lots of customer experience.

Seniors For the first time in history, there are more people aged 65 and older than there are teenagers in Canada (more than 4.1 million in 2005). By 2031, the number of people aged 65 and over will range between 8.9 million and 9.4 million, while the number of children will range between 4.8 million and 6.6 million.[3] The cruise ship industry benefits greatly from this growing market, as do upscale retirement homes and communities, which are of interest to the mid-seniors. The oldest seniors have the lowest level of affluence and focus on affordable retirement services and products. Dorel, a Montreal-based company that employs 5,000 people in 14 countries, has for many years concentrated on manufacturing products for children and their parents — strollers, car seats, highchairs, and bicycles. Now, the company is turning its attention to a new range of mobility products for seniors, including folding stools, walkers, bathtub security bars, and electric scooters.[4]

Singles Almost 10 percent of Canadian households are made up of people who live alone. Increasingly, products such as single-serving prepared foods are being introduced for young and older singles alike, and homebuilders are designing homes, condominium units, and housing developments with older singles in mind.[5]

'Tweens Youth between 9 and 13 years of age account for approximately 10 percent of the population, and this number will remain fairly consistent in the coming years. Changes in demographics and culture mean that this group of savvy consumers have $1.7 billion to spend and influence another $20 billion in Canada.[6]

Economic conditions

People must have money to spend and be willing to spend it. Consumers and, therefore, the marketing system are especially affected by such considerations as the current stage of the business cycle, inflation, and interest rates.

Stages of the business cycle We think of a three-stage business cycle: prosperity, recession, and recovery. During prosperity, consumers feel confident and intent on spending and firms tend to expand their marketing programs, add new products, and enter new markets.

During a recession, on the other hand, with higher rates of unemployment and reduced consumer confidence and spending, firms typically retrench. Recovery finds the economy moving from recession to prosperity, consumer confidence grows as unemployment declines and disposable incomes increase, and companies expand their marketing efforts to improve sales and profits.

Inflation Inflation occurs when price levels rise at a faster rate than personal income, so that there is a decline in consumer buying power. Although inflation rates have declined to the 2 percent range in recent years from much higher levels previously, a fear of higher rates continued to influence government policies, consumer expectations and business marketing programs in the area of pricing and cost control. With inflation, consumer buying power declines but, at the same time, consumers may overspend today for fear that prices will be higher tomorrow.

Interest rates When interest rates are high, consumers tend to hold back on long-term and large purchases such as housing and vehicles, since it is expensive to borrow money. Retailers sometimes offer below-market interest rates or no payments for a year as a promotional device to increase business.

Unemployment rates These rates reflect the percentage of people who are employed and the percentage who are looking for work. These rates vary from market area to market area and greatly affect the amount of disposable income that consumers have to spend on products and services, as well as their expectations and willingness to spend. Regional variations in pricing and terms of sale may be necessary.

Social and cultural forces

Social and cultural forces, as discussed in the previous chapter, continue to change much more rapidly than in the past. The following are highlights that have significant marketing implications.

Emphasis on quality of life Includes themes such as "Not more — but better value," more satisfaction, more concern about education and health, less about keeping up with neighbours in terms of bigger and better purchases, a growing concern for the physical environment, and discontent with pollution and resource waste. Williams Coffee Pub, which originated in Stratford, Ontario, is capitalizing on an emerging shift back from the traditional

Mom always said we should eat more slowly.

fast-food restaurant culture to a more fast-casual dining experience. While the chain still maintains a focus on consumers' demands for quick service, it also meets their growing desire to once again slow down while they eat.[7]

Immigration and changing values Adds, in both obvious and subtle ways, the unique values and preferences shaped by the cultures of many different home countries. The characteristics of some immigrant groups include a higher degree of control by family elders over purchasing power and buying decisions, a suspicion of government and government-sponsored programs, an aversion to the use of credit cards and the accumulation of debt, and a focus on household and family goals, including securing a job, home ownership, and the education of children.[8]

Roles of men and women The erosion of stereotypes of male and female roles in families, jobs, recreation, and product use continues, affecting all areas of marketing. These effects are particularly noticeable in product design, advertising, and promotion. In 2005, women accounted for 35 percent of the home renovation decision making. Even more astounding, women are

MARKETING AT WORK — 3-1: STRATEGY

Taking the Stink Out of the Boy

What was always thought of as an obsession for some females in our society, body image, has now significantly become a male issue. If you don't believe that, look again! Today's newsstands are bulging with men's "lifestyle" magazines. And what exactly are those? They're the mirror image of what we refer to for women as "beauty magazines." They are about honing the ideal physique, diet, fashion, trends and gadgets, and sure-fire sex tips.

The number of young men having cosmetic surgery is rising and about 83,000 Canadians, mostly young men between the ages of 11 and 18, report using steroids at least once. It's not clear how many have done this knowing the link between use and testicular shrinking and kidney and liver failure. But with the possibility of shedding 11 kg in one month, some may be willing to gamble.

Male "grooming rituals" are becoming more socially acceptable, and it's no longer about which razor blade gives the closet shave — it's face scrubs, moisturizers, fragrances, and hair colour. Look at the popularity among teenage boys of products such as Axe and Tag body sprays!

Times are a-changing and more and more men are going to the cosmetic counter. Research shows that younger professional men, 19 to 34, are much more likely to buy skincare products for themselves and are far more comfortable talking to salespeople about them. While still relatively small, the male personal-care business — hair and skin care — has reported 14 percent year-over-year growth. L'Oréal, for instance, has launched a line of 10 skin-care products for men, including eye cream, cleansers, and moisturizers, which are tailored to men of different ages.

While more and more guys are detoxifying and exfoliating, perhaps the most obvious marketing efforts can be seen in the hair colour aisle. Men's hair colour products are currently one of the largest growth areas in health and beauty products. It's an inexpensive image alteration that can have a big impact — and guys are going for it in a big way. L'Oréal is keenly aware of today's image-conscious male and is doing its bit by providing manly shades such as Camel, Brick, and Black Leather.

QUESTIONS:

1. Do you think changing social roles has something to do with taking the stink out of the boy?
2. Does an increased focus on grooming and body image allow males to be more successful in developing personal and professional relationships?

SOURCE: Adapted from Michelle Halpern, "Taking the Stink out of the Boy," *Marketing Magazine Online*, www.marketingmag.ca, March 14, 2005; "Gillette Gives P&G A Manly Edge," *Marketing Magazine Online*, www.marketingmag.ca, February 28, 2005; Lucy Saddleton, "Marketers Refine Male Beauty Strategy," *Strategy*, May 20, 2002, pp. 36, 38; Rebecca Harris, "Moisturizing Men," *Marketing Magazine*, November 28, 2005.

involved in 80 percent of the decisions on where to shop for these products. Hardware stores have responded. Canadian Tire has recently opened a store with friendly signs, airport style escalators that take shopping carts from one level to the next, opened a gourmet kitchen centre, and even hired TV handywoman, Debbie Travis, as a spokesperson. In addition, Home Depot's new West Vancouver store looks more like an IKEA with its friendly décor and product displays and Lowe's, a giant U.S. chain that targets women with its large appliance department and brightly lit stores, announced its intention to enter Canada in 2007.[9]

Attitudes toward physical fitness and food Increasing consumer expectations concerning health and physical fitness cuts across most demographic and economic segments of society. Stores supplying activity products and service organizations catering to this trend have multiplied. Significant changes in the eating patterns of Canadians continue, as we become more sensitive to the relationship between what we eat and major diseases. McDonald's in the U.S. recently found itself committing to eliminate its "Super Size" options from its regular menu as a result of heightened public pressure related to concern over increases in obesity levels in the U.S. This pressure was greatly spawned by the release of a documentary entitled *Super Size Me* which set out to demonstrate the detrimental health effects of McDonald's offerings.[10]

Emphasis on service and relationship quality Consumers continue demanding to be treated better by businesses. Companies are now beginning to realize that the quality of appropriate customer interaction is important in service delivery, providing desired value, satisfaction, and maintaining and improving customer relationships.

Concern for the environment There has already been a collective outpouring of support for programs and products that allow us to take action to protect the environment: Food manufacturers package products in less wasteful and more biodegradable materials; municipalities across the country have established recycling programs; and supermarkets stock many products labelled "environmentally friendly." Some organizations take it one step further. Not only does beauty products producer Aveda utilize recycled and biodegradable packaging for its hair and beauty products, but it has also incorporated its environmental focus as the main theme in Aveda's corporate mission: "Our mission at Aveda is to care for the world we live in, from the products we make to the ways in which we give back to society. At Aveda, we strive to set an example for environmental leadership and responsibility, not just in the world of beauty, but around the world," says Horst M. Rechelbacher, founder of Aveda.[11]

Desire for convenience Since consumers seem to have less and less time, the desire for convenience continues to increase. Tim Hortons now has double drive-thrus. Products must be ready to use or easy to prepare or assemble; purchasing systems must be convenient; products must be packaged in a variety of sizes, quantities, and forms; stores must be located nearby, easily accessible, and open at virtually all hours; and Web sites must be easily found, user-friendly, interesting, informative, and secure.

Competition

In addition to a company's actual and potential customers, the activities of its competitors are a major environmental influence in shaping its marketing system. Thus, key aspects of relevant competitors' marketing activities need to be monitored. Expanded trade with other countries means that Canadian firms must pay close attention to foreign competition as well as find opportunities for Canadian products and services in foreign markets. A firm generally faces competition from three sources.

Direct brand and store competition from marketers of similar and directly competing products and services The xbox, PlayStation2, and GameCube compete with each other for many of the same gamers, while retailers such as H&M, Gap, and American Eagle compete with each other for many of the same clothing dollars at the local mall.

Indirect competition This form is coming from substitute products that satisfy the same basic need. On any given evening, many people choose either to go to a movie or rent one at a video store, or travel between Montréal and Ottawa by Via Rail or Air Canada. Traditional department stores and clothing retailers realize that their competition is coming not only from other stores down the street or elsewhere in the same town, but also from Internet retailers such as L.L. Bean, Lands' End, and J. Crew, headquartered in other countries.

Competition for the consumer's limited buying power This is the final type of competition, where almost all companies are competing for the same consumer dollars. A marketer of tennis racquets faces competition from other companies that are marketing jeans or shoes or weekend ski holidays. Competition for discretionary spending is one of the greatest challenges for marketers.

Technology

Failing to remain innovative and keep pace with technological advancements in its product category threatens a firm's ability to remain competitive. New materials, television, computers, lasers, miniaturization of components, robotics, compact discs, and closely targeted antibiotics have had a tremendous impact on our consumer lifestyles as well as expectations. Major technological breakthroughs have three primary impacts on marketing:

Start entirely new industries Many new businesses have been started for such products as computers, robots, lasers, fax machines, and microwave ovens. The Internet, PDAs DVD-ROM, futuristic cellphones, and other digital technologies will account for more in the future.

Alter radically or virtually destroy existing industries Television had a significant impact on movies and radio when it was first introduced; compact discs have eliminated vinyl records and most cassette tapes; fax machines and then e-mail cut into the conventional mail business of Canada Post, which now offers its own courier and electronic mail services; sensors imbedded in toll highways, such as on Highway 407 north of Toronto, record cars for toll payment and eliminate toll collectors and toll booths, and have changed road design and building methods;[12] and downloading and ripping hardware and software are changing the music industry's marketing and distribution systems. The iPod is in the process of killing off the home stereo system as we once knew it.[13]

Stimulate other markets and industries not related to the new technology Cellphones, new home appliances and entertainment products have altered the pattern of time use within the home and outside. Portable CD players, iPods, personal video recorders, video games, computer games, and microwave ovens have revolutionized the ways in which consumers use their time. These developments have also led to new industries, providing entertainment and food products used with these new devices that were not available a few years ago.

Political and legal forces

Consumer expectation and behaviour, as well as every company's expectations and conduct, are influenced by political and legal forces. Legislation at all levels exercises more influence on the marketing activity of a business than on any other part of its operations. These influences stem both from legislation and the policies established by a host of government agencies.

MARKETING AT WORK 3-2: TECHNOLOGY

Secure Enough For You?

Pantech has unveiled the world's first fingerprint recognition cellular handset, the Pantech GI100. Fingerprint recognition is fail-safe technology, as no two people have the same fingerprint and the GI100 was designed for customers for whom security is of paramount importance.

Using advanced biometric technology, allowing for more personalized key entries, the GI100 is also intended to be user-friendly. A Secret Finger Dial (SFD) enables the phone to memorize prints from each of the users' fingers and associate each to a specific number, with ten quick-dial numbers in all. Calls made with the SFD remain confidential as no record remains in the phone's call log.

"With mobile phones being increasingly used as more than just a communication device, there is a strong demand for a phone that blocks unauthorized access to stored information or pictures," according to Hyunsoo Jun, vice president of Pantech Global.

Naturally, the GI100 comes with all the 'regular' stuff — a 1.3 megapixel CCD camera with flash, video caller ID and video wallpaper (motion JPEG), dual 260K TFT LCD with 64 polyphonic ring tones, MMS, GPRS, WAP, and finger embedded games ranging from slot machines to car racing.

The product has already been received well in Russia, China, and Taiwan. The third-largest Korean mobile phone manufacturer, Pantech launched its products into Europe in 2005 and anticipated 67 percent growth by the end of 2006.

QUESTIONS:

1. Do you think this technology will destroy some industries?
2. Which industries do you think will adapt or imitate this technology or its effects?

SOURCE: Adapted from Peter Barton, "First Fingerprint Recognition Handset," *Gulf Marketing News,* January 2005, p. 12.

General monetary and fiscal policies The level of government spending, the money supply, and tax legislation affect both consumers and companies.

Legislative framework and government agency codes and policies Human rights codes, environmental legislation, and programs to reduce unemployment or increase national health all work to affect both firms and consumers in various ways. Consumers have the ombudsmen's office to complain to; telephone solicitors and direct marketers, for example, are continually under pressure to reduce 'spam' and unsolicited mail.

Social legislation Social legislation that is intended to protect consumers results in, for example, prohibiting people from smoking in various venues and tobacco firms from certain types of advertising and promotion.

Government relationships with individual industries Governments provide subsidy programs for industries such as agriculture, passenger rail transportation, and many others. In some cases, consumers benefit through employment protection or lower or controlled prices, in other cases, consumer interests are paid lip service only. Governments have also affected the structure and operation of industries by selling publicly-owned firms to the private sector, as well as by deregulating industries such as banking, telecommunications, airlines, and broadcasting. Consumers sometimes gain in increased competition or choice or lower fees and costs.

Legislation specifically related to marketing Marketing legislation is primarily designed to aid and protect consumers — and sometimes actually does. Most is administered by Industry Canada. Table 3-1 contains some examples. Other pieces of legislation dealing with food products and advertising are administered by other government departments and

TABLE 3-1 Marketing-Related Legislation Administered by Industry Canada

• Bankruptcy and Insolvency Act	• Patent Act
• Boards of Trade Act	• Precious Metals Marking Act
• Canada Business Corporations Act	• Radiocommunication Act
• Canada Corporations Act	• Standards Council of Canada Act
• Competition Act	• Statistics Act
• Competition Tribunal Act	• Textile Labelling Act
• Consumer Packaging and Labelling Act	• Trade-marks Act
• Copyright Act	• Telecommunications Act
• National Research Council Act	• Weights and Measures Act

will be discussed in later chapters. While marketing executives do not have to be lawyers, they do need to have an awareness of the major pieces of legislation and regulations and how these impinge on their strategies and tactics.

Provision of information and the purchase of products Illustrating the help provided by governments, Statistics Canada is a prime example of information provision by the government, and government procurement activities provide marketing opportunities for a host of businesses.

Controllable Environmental Forces

Three environmental forces that are external to, but are still a part of a company's marketing system, are the company's customers and potential customers — its market — its suppliers, and other businesses involved in getting the company's products to its market. These forces are considered to comprise the firm's external micro-environment and can be influenced by the firm to varying degrees to help the firm in its efforts to establish ongoing customer and working relationships. The forces can be viewed as being **relationship-sensitive**. They are unlike the uncontrollable environmental forces; they are a part of a firm's marketing system since they can be managed to varying degrees, as opposed to the firm simply reacting to them. A marketing organization, for example, is able to influence its suppliers and other businesses involved in the distribution of its products concerning the services each will provide and the nature and type of information each will make available to the other to aid in strategy development. The better the relationship that exists between the parties, the better the strategy development and implementation. Through its advertising, promotion, and service provision activities, a company is able to influence its different customer groups or markets in a variety of ways to increase perceived value, various forms of satisfaction and relationships. Relationship-sensitive external forces are illustrated in Figure 3-2.

relationship-sensitive forces
Forces that can be managed to varying degrees and therefore are part of a firm's marketing system.

Figure 3-2: Relationship-Sensitive External Environmental Forces

The Market Environment

The customer or market is what marketing is all about — how to reach customers, how to serve markets profitably and how to build trust and relationships by acting in a socially-responsible manner. The market should be the focus of all marketing decisions in an organization. But just what is a market? A market may be defined as a place where customers and sellers meet and where goods and services are offered for sale. As transfers of ownership occur, the foundations for future relationships are established, if they do not already exist. A market may also be defined as the demand made by a certain group of potential buyers or customers for a good or service. For instance, there is an agricultural market for petroleum products and a college market for textbooks.

These definitions are not sufficiently precise to be useful to us here. For business purposes, we define a market as people or organizations with needs or wants to satisfy, money to spend, and the willingness to spend it. In short, the market is made up of customers and prospective customers, so in the market demand for any given product or service, there are three factors to consider:

1. People or organizations with needs or wants.
2. Their purchasing power.
3. Their expectations and buying behaviour.

When we say "needs," we mean what the dictionary says it means: something that is required, desired, or useful. As we pointed out in Chapter 1, we do not limit needs to the physiological requirements of food, clothing, and shelter essential for survival; the words "needs" and "wants" can be used synonymously and interchangeably. Also, we define the market very broadly to include the purchase of many different types of products and services, but also to include other forms of exchange, including the purchase of entertainment and the arts, and contributions to charitable and other public organizations.

Suppliers

To sell a product, you must first make it or buy it. That's why the people or firms who supply the goods or services that a company needs to produce goods are critical to marketing success. And that's why we consider a firm's suppliers as part of its marketing system and sensitive in relationship-building terms. Marketing executives often are not concerned enough with the supply side of the marketing system, but they do become very concerned when shortages or supply service problems occur. A company or organization often has many suppliers on whom it relies for raw materials, operating supplies, electricity, cleaning services, and many other items. If one or more of these fail to deliver what's needed when it's needed and in the quantity and of the quality desired, the company may not be able to meet the needs of its own customers or may even have to cease operations.

Marketing intermediaries

marketing intermediaries
Firms that render services directly related to the purchase and/or sale of a product as it flows from producer to consumer.

Marketing intermediaries are independent business organizations that directly aid in the flow of goods and services between a marketing organization and its customers. There are two types of intermediaries: (1) the wholesalers and retailers and (2) the various facilitating organizations that provide such services as the transportation, warehousing, and financing needed to complete exchanges and facilitate relationships between buyers and sellers. These

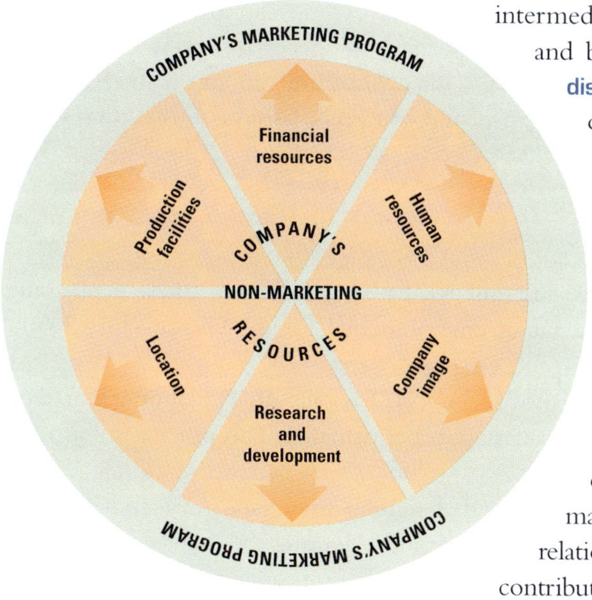

Figure 3-3: Relationship-Sensitive Internal Environmental Forces

A company's internal non-marketing resources influence and support its marketing program.

intermediaries, since they operate between a company and its customers and between a company and its suppliers, are part of what are called **distribution channels**. In some cases, it may be more efficient for a company to take a "do-it-yourself" approach and not use marketing intermediaries. But marketing intermediaries are specialists in their respective fields and often do a better job at a lower cost. Because many companies rely on others to get products and services to market, they pay considerable attention to the cultivation of solid relationships with distribution channel members.

distribution channel
The set of people and firms involved in the flow of ownership of a product as it moves from producer to ultimate consumer or business user.

Internal non-marketing system forces

The internal resources of the firm also have a great influence on an organization's marketing system. These are controllable by management, relationship-sensitive, and require careful organizational relationship building on the part of marketing personnel in order to contribute to the marketing system and its programs.[14] The forces are illustrated in Figure 3-3.

Internal resources and influences can affect marketing programs in a variety of ways:

- Production facilities and capabilities influence the availability of products and their quantities, quality, and costs; these factors also affect whether the marketing department has products available to sell.
- Financial resources play a part in determining marketing and promotion budgets, pricing strategies, terms of sale, and whether money is available to spend on marketing programs.
- Human resource policies and capabilities affect the quality of personnel and their training, job satisfaction, and loyalty, as well as the quality of service and customer contact provided.
- The company image projected to the public affects the acceptance of marketing programs to some extent, as inconsistencies threaten marketing's relationship-building activities and the overall satisfaction, trust and loyalty of customers, suppliers, and intermediaries.
- Research and development activities produce advances in product features, materials, production systems, product costs, packaging, quality enhancements, and overall competitive ability to be an industry leader.
- Location can determine access to markets, transportation costs, service frequency and quality, and even the number and quality of contacts with customers, suppliers, and intermediaries.

All of these factors — not normally considered as marketing variables — have the potential to influence the satisfaction of customers — the overall objective of marketing, as we discussed in Chapter 1. As a result, there is an obvious need for all parts of a business or organization to work together toward the goal of customer satisfaction and to realize that virtually everything that happens in all departments ultimately has the potential to increase or decrease customer satisfaction. Thus, in a firm's internal environment is the constant need to co-ordinate marketing and non-marketing activities. Customer, supplier, and intermediary contacts and communications must be carried out in a planned and consistent fashion in order to achieve the desired quality of relationships. Sometimes this can be difficult because of conflicts in goals and executive personalities. Production people, for example, like to see long production runs of standardized items. However, marketing executives may want a variety of models, sizes, and colours to satisfy different groups of consumers. Financial executives typically want tighter credit and expense limits than the marketing people feel are necessary to be competitive. When customers or suppliers are communicating with various units in an organization, it is important that they be dealt with in an appropriate and consistent fashion, so that their goodwill and loyalty can be maintained and enhanced.

Marketing Planning

All of the environmental forces we have just discussed play a role in marketing planning. Figure 3-4 shows a company's complete set of environmental forces. We now turn to the planning process itself.

Marketing planning, as a management process, consists basically of (1) planning a marketing program, (2) implementing it, and (3) evaluating its performance. This process is illustrated in Figure 3-5.

The planning stage includes setting goals and designing strategies and tactics to reach these goals. The implementation stage involves staffing and orienting the marketing organization and directing its operations according to plan. The evaluation stage consists of analyzing the resulting performance in terms of the marketing goals originally established. This third stage demonstrates the continuous nature of the management process — the results of this stage of the management process are used in planning goals and strategies for future stages.

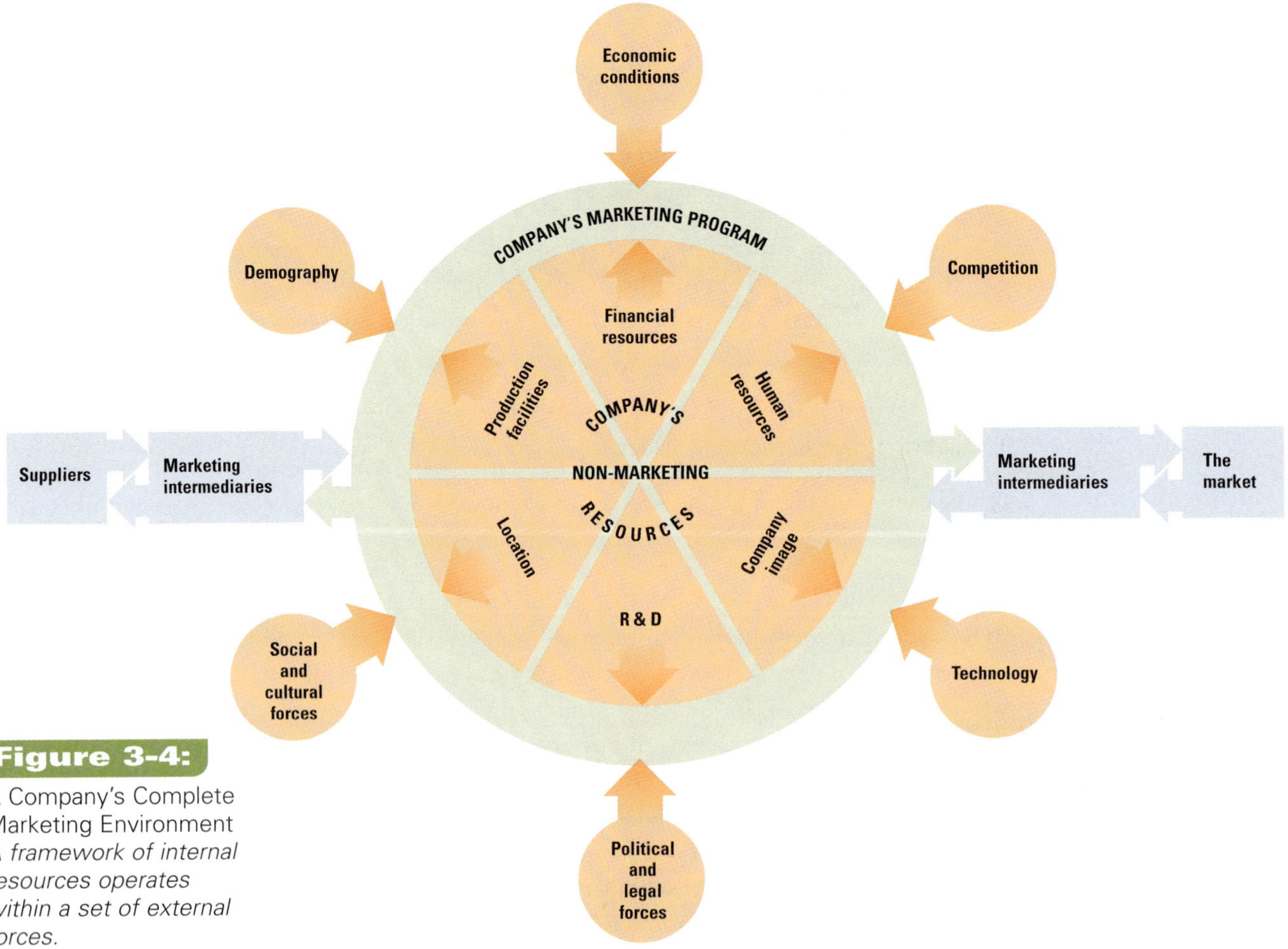

Figure 3-4:
A Company's Complete Marketing Environment
A framework of internal resources operates within a set of external forces.

Figure 3-5:
The Management Process in Marketing

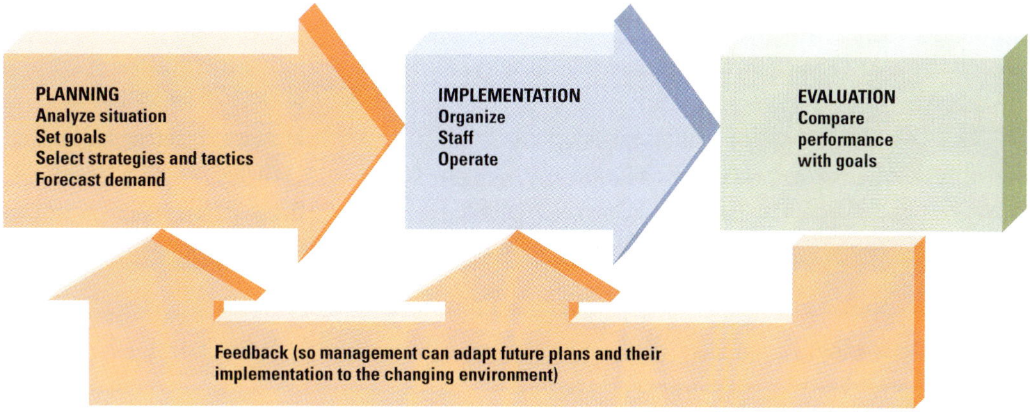

The nature of planning

"If you don't know where you're going, any road will get you there." The point of this axiom is that all organizations need both general and specific plans to be successful. Management first should decide what it intends to accomplish as a total organization and then develop a strategic plan to achieve these results. Given this overall plan, each department or business unit then determines its own plans. Of course, the role of marketing in each of these plans must be considered.

We begin our discussion of marketing planning by reviewing the basic terms used in the planning phase.

mission statement
Indicates the boundaries of an organization's activities.

Mission An organization's **mission statement** details what customers it serves, what needs it satisfies, and what types of products and services it offers, indicating the boundaries of an organization's activities. It should be neither too broad and vague nor too narrow and specific. To say that a firm's mission is "to benefit Canadian consumers" is too vague; to state that its purpose is "to make tennis balls" is too narrow. Neither statement outlines meaningful benefits for customers or provides much guidance to management. Unless the firm's purpose is clear to the various levels of management, strategic planning will probably result in disagreement and confusion.

Some companies still state their mission in production-oriented terms, such as "We make furnaces." Most express their mission in customer-oriented terms — satisfying needs and providing value. Instead of "We produce snowmobiles, ATVs, and small watercraft," Bombardier Inc.'s mission statement could be "We provide safe, comfortable travel for wherever our customer wants, or needs, to go." Recall that in Chapter 1, Table 1-1 illustrated different ways of stating a company's mission to provide more direction for management actions.

objective
A desired outcome; same as goal.

Objectives and goals We treat the terms objectives and goals as synonyms. An **objective** is simply a desired outcome. Effective planning must begin with a set of objectives that are to be achieved by carrying out plans. To be worthwhile and workable, objectives should be:

- Clear and specific.
- Stated in writing.
- Ambitious, but realistic.
- Consistent with one another.
- Quantitatively measurable whenever possible.
- Tied to a particular time period.

Consider the following examples.

Weak (too general)	Workable
Increase our market share.	Increase our market share to 25 percent next year from its present 20 percent level.
Strengthen relationships with our customers.	Increase customer satisfaction, customer retention, and customer loyalty scores by 20 percent.
Improve our company's public image.	Receive recognition awards next year from at least three consumer and/or environmental groups.

strategy
Broad, basic plan of action by which an organization intends to achieve its objectives.

Strategies and tactics A **strategy** is a broad, basic plan of action by which an organization intends to reach its objectives. In marketing, the relationship between objectives and strategies may be illustrated as follows.

Objectives	Possible Strategies
Increase sales next year by 8 percent over this year's sales.	1. Intensify marketing efforts in domestic markets. 2. Expand into foreign markets. 3. Increase customer retention by reducing account closures by 10 percent.

Two companies might have the same objective but use different strategies to reach it. For example, both might aim to increase their market share by 20 percent over the next three years. To do that, one firm might intensify its efforts in household markets, while the other might concentrate on expanding into institutional markets (e.g., food-service organizations). Conversely, two firms might have different objectives but select the same strategies to reach them.

BACK TO THE TOP

It's interesting to examine Apple's strategy for dominating the MP3 universe. Consider the launch of not only the iPod but also of iTunes, enabling consumers to download music from an Apple-branded site. It all fit together and delivered Apple the dominant position in that sector.

tactic
An operational means by which a strategy is implemented or activated.

A **tactic** is a means by which a strategy is implemented. A tactic is a more specific, detailed course of action than is a strategy. If the strategy is to increase customer retention, the tactics spell out how this is to be accomplished. Tactics can change rapidly and cover shorter time periods than strategies. Here is an illustration of tactics related to a strategy:

Strategy	Tactics
Direct our promotion to males aged 25 to 40.	1. Advertise in magazines read by this group. 2. Advertise on television programs watched by this group.
Increase revenue from existing customers.	1. Redesign the customer information system. 2. Create a loyalty program for light and medium users. 3. Retrain account analysts and service personnel.

PAGE UP!

1. The environment of all organizations is composed of what three factors or forces?
2. Six interrelated macro-environmental forces are usually beyond the control of management. What are they?
3. What are the three relationship-sensitive external forces?

Scope of planning

Marketing planning results in marketing strategies, which have taken into consideration the market of customers and potential customers, the social and economic environments and a firm's competitive environment. Planning itself takes place at two different levels:

1. At the company level, senior management defines an organization's mission, sets long-range objectives, and formulates broad strategies to achieve these goals. These company-wide objectives and strategies then become the framework for planning the firm's strategies and tactics in such functional areas as production, finance, human resources, research and development, and marketing.

2. At the marketing unit or department level, the top marketing executives set objectives and strategies for the business's marketing efforts. Strategic marketing planning takes place within the framework of, and co-ordinated with, the company-wide planning level.

Within the marketing unit, a short-term plan of the firm's marketing activities is then developed, based on the marketing strategy. Such a plan covers a specific period, usually a year, and contains the tactics that will be used to implement the strategy for the specified time period.

Strategic Company Planning

strategic company planning
The level of planning that consists of defining the organization's mission, analyzing the situation the company is facing, setting organizational objectives, and selecting strategies to achieve the organization's objectives.

At the company level, strategic planning consists of four essential steps: (1) defining the organization's mission; (2) analyzing the situation the company is facing; (3) setting organizational objectives; and (4) selecting strategies to achieve these objectives. The **strategic company planning** process is shown in the top part of Figure 3-6.

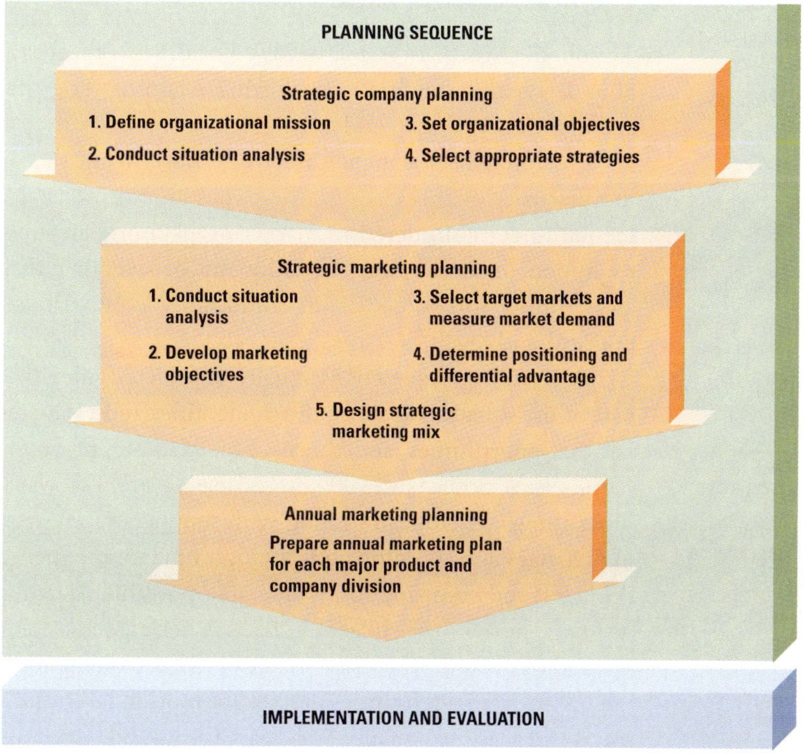

Figure 3-6:
Three Levels of Organizational Planning

Step 1 Define the organization's mission, which influences all subsequent planning. For some firms, this step only requires a review of the existing mission statement to confirm that it is still suitable.

Step 2 Conduct a situation analysis. This is vital, because strategic planning is influenced by many forces both within and external to an organization. **Situation analysis** simply means gathering and studying information that is important to the strategies and tactics of an organization. We'll talk more about conducting a situation analysis in the following section.

situation analysis
The stage in strategic company planning that involves gathering and studying information that is important to the strategies and tactics of an organization.

Step 3 Management must decide on a set of objectives to guide the organization in fulfilling its mission. Objectives also provide standards for evaluating an organization's performance, such as gaining a 10 percent market share within five years.

Step 4 Select appropriate strategies that indicate how the firm is going to get to where it wants to go. Strategies are selected either for the entire company, if it is small and only has a single product, or for each division or business unit if the company is large or has multiple products.

Strategic Marketing Planning

After conducting strategic planning for the organization as a whole, management needs to lay plans for each major functional area, such as marketing and production. Of course, planning for each function should be guided by the organization-wide mission and objectives. **Strategic marketing planning**, as shown in the middle of Figure 3-6, is a five-step process: (1) conducting a situation analysis, (2) determining marketing objectives, (3) identifying target markets and measuring market demand, (4) deciding on positioning and differential advantage, and (5) designing a marketing mix.

strategic marketing planning
The level of planning that consists of conducting a situation analysis, determining marketing objectives, identifying target markets and measuring the market, deciding on positioning and differential advantage, and designing a marketing mix.

Situation analysis

Conducting a situation analysis is critical since the results of this analysis establish the basic boundaries and conditions for further planning. The situation analysis usually has two parts: an environmental scan and a SWOT assessment.

Environmental scanning normally starts with a review of those factors we discussed in the first part of this chapter: the external and internal environmental forces. The environmental forces considered in marketing planning are frequently the same or similar to those examined in developing the company or overall business plan: demographic shifts, social and cultural forces, economic conditions, competitive trends, technological changes, and political and legal forces.

environmental scanning
Gathering information regarding a company's internal and external environment, analyzing it, and forecasting the impact of the conditions and trends that the analysis suggests.

A **SWOT assessment** is usually conducted after the environmental scan. In this second part of the situation analysis, a firm identifies and evaluates its most significant strengths, weaknesses, opportunities, and threats. For example, prior to the financial difficulties leading to Eaton's final closure in 1999, the company's strength was its large size, which gave it — among other things — clout in dealing with suppliers. Weaknesses included its frequent merchandising changes and its comparatively high operating expenses. High inventories and outstanding debts left the company in a vulnerable position. Another fatal weakness for a retailer can be its image in the marketplace — Eaton's heritage as a longstanding pillar of Canadian retailing seemed to make it impossible to shake off the old, staid image that it had — it was unhip and uncool to young consumers despite attempts in later years to change that image in the marketplace. International retailer Wal-Mart (**www.wal-mart.com**), on the other hand, controls its suppliers so that a very efficient inventory supply system has been developed; almost no excess

SWOT assessment
Identifying and evaluating an organization's most significant strengths, weaknesses, opportunities, and threats.

Wal-Mart

Subaru seized an opportunity to launch a luxury SUV.

inventory is carried. Although it is a discount department store, it has developed a relatively attractive image in the marketplace across certain demographic groups.

Opportunities and threats often originate from outside the organization. Subaru is an automobile brand that is set apart from others just a little. Make no mistake, it is a successful brand but one whose image in the marketplace is not so easy to define. Are they cars or are they SUVs? Mostly, they look like station wagons, which aren't really considered to be cool these days. In a competitive market, this can be a weakness. But, one of the brand's strengths is a strong reputation for off-road and rally-driving performance. Given this strength, the company weighed the pros and cons in the marketplace (before the price of gas skyrocketed) of the opportunity of expanding their product line into the growing and highly profitable luxury sector. The decision was to take the opportunity by introducing the 2006 B9 Tribeca, as a new entry into the luxury SUV category complete with 250 horsepower Subaru Boxer engine, leather seating for seven, touch-screen navigation, and a DVD entertainment system. Sounds posh, but this is new ground for Subaru and with so many choices available from brands with more experience in this category, can Subaru make this new entry risk pay off? What are the threats? Will consumers take this product seriously? How will competitors respond? And what about the price of gas and how that will affect customer choice?

Opportunities outweigh threats — a SMART decision.

Table 3-2 illustrates how selected environmental forces might be viewed in a SWOT analysis, using the entry of Mercedes-Benz' Smart brand into the Canadian market in late 2004.

Marketing objectives

When environmental scanning and a SWOT analysis have been completed, the next step in strategic marketing planning is to determine marketing objectives. These should be closely related to company-wide goals and strategies. In fact, a company strategy often translates into

TABLE 3-2 The Smart Car: SWOT Implications for Selected Environmental Forces

The Smart car has come to Canada. After much market research into the North American marketplace, Mercedes-Benz decided to introduce the brand to Canada in late 2004. The first Smart dealership in North America, attached to the flagship Mercedes-Benz midtown store in Toronto, opened in October. The car would also be sold through more than 40 Mercedes-Benz dealerships across the country. The boldly-coloured, three-cylinder, diesel-engined "Smart Coupe" at just 2.5 metres long, was available in three models — pulse, pure, and passion. The "Smart Fourmore" became available in 2006.[15]

Environmental Trend	Market Dynamics	Company Issue
Traditional gender role	Females increasingly continue to independently purchase more vehicles than in the past and to participate in the family decision-making process.	**Opportunity:** Position the fun brand toward the female market with regard to products for individual use or second car for small families using caution not to alienate single male consumers.
State of the economy	Canada moving out of mild recession, with most economic indicators pointing to fair growth trends. Record high fuel prices.	**Opportunity:** Publicize the vehicle not just for its funky looks, but for its low price, high mileage, and economical operating costs. Capitalize on the link with strong parent company — well timed for this market. **Threat:** Although the brand would be familiar to some consumers through its strong reputation and publicity in Europe since 1999 — it may still be seen by some as new and unproven.
Age demographics	The increasing average age of Boomers and seniors — referred to as the "greying" of Canada.	**Threat:** Current brand image is very youthful and may not appeal to Boomers and seniors. **Opportunity:** Sizable portion of young Canadians reaching driving age in the next decade. Could appeal to small segment of seniors looking for small, easy-to-drive vehicle.
Fertility rate/household size	Fertility rates have been decreasing, meaning that the average household has fewer people.	**Opportunity:** With disposable income on the rise, it might be a popular vehicle purchase for well-heeled teenagers. **Threat:** Market size has limited the total potential in this competitive market category. Much smaller market than the U.S.
Concern for the environment	Concern with pollution from burning fuels and the popularity of high consumption vehicles, such as SUVs.	**Opportunity:** Consumer segments exist seeking low pollutant vehicles.
Increasing population centres	Many North American cities are becoming increasingly congested.	**Opportunity:** Many consumers choosing lower-priced, small, easy to manoeuvre and park vehicles.

SWOT conclusion: Many trends are similar across North America. Enter the Canadian marketplace in Fall 2004 (a high-volume sales period for vehicles) with a focus on the two-door coupe emphasizing its distinctive looks, affordability and environmental friendliness. If they are as successful as they have been in Europe, Mercedes-Benz can consider rolling Smart products out to the larger American marketplace in the future.

a marketing goal. For example, to reach an organizational objective of a 20 percent return on investment next year, one organizational strategy might be to reduce marketing costs by 15 percent. This strategy would become a marketing goal. In turn, converting all salespeople from salaried compensation to a commission basis might be one of the marketing strategies adopted to achieve this marketing goal.

Target markets and market demand

Selecting target markets and measuring market demand is the third step in marketing planning. A market consists of people, customers or prospective customers, or organizations with needs to satisfy, money to spend, and the willingness to spend it. For example, many people need transportation and are willing to pay for it. However, this large group is made up of a number of customer **segments** (that is, parts of markets) with various transportation needs. One segment may want low-cost, efficient transportation, while another may prefer luxury and privacy. Air Canada segments the air travel market by offering economy, business, and first-class travel, with each class offering a number of different service bundles that involve different check-in privileges, flexibility on changing travel plans, and different meal options.

segments
Parts of markets or customer groups.

This is not very different from automakers offering products ranging from heavy-duty trucks to luxury cars to economical compact cars. Recently, in an attempt to reach more customer segments (otherwise referred to as market penetration and discussed elsewhere in this chapter) and stimulate demand in different markets across the country, Ford Motor Company added yet another SUV to its already wide selection. Within the SUV category alone, the company produces the Escape, Escape Hybrid, Explorer, Explorer Sport Trac, Expedition, and the Excursion. For 2005, the company introduced yet another SUV product called the Freestyle. But the SUV market became turbulent with the rising price of gasoline and the future looks cloudy unless gasoline drops in price.

target market
A group of customers (people or organizations) to whom a seller aims its marketing efforts.

Ordinarily, it is impractical for a firm to try to satisfy every customer or market segment, since they all have different needs. Instead, a company targets its efforts at one or more of these segments. Thus, **target market** refers to a group of people or organizations to which a firm directs a marketing program. Few companies target a single segment — when they do, they are often said to be following a niche strategy. Designing the actual product is part of that marketing effort.

BACK TO THE TOP

Target markets must be selected on the basis of opportunities. In a new company, management should analyze markets in detail to identify potential target markets. In an existing firm, management should routinely examine any changes in the characteristics of its target markets and alternative markets. A firm must forecast demand — that is, sales, in each market. The results of sales or demand forecasting will determine whether the firm's targets are worth pursuing or whether alternatives need to be identified.

Who do you suppose were Apple's main target segments when it launched the iPod? Do you think that segmentation strategy has changed? Which segments have been buying iPods and how has Apple responded?

To whom is Ford targeting the Freestyle?

MARKETING AT WORK — 3-3: STRATEGY

The Target is Not Just Kids Anymore!

Video gaming has become the second-most popular form of entertainment in the world after the music industry, now attracting more than just traditional gamers.

The latest word in the gaming industry is mobile gaming — portable systems that are significantly larger than a smart cellphone or BlackBerry, but still small enough to stash in a large pocket or purse. Sony has developed the technology to offer a 4.3-inch wide screen providing incredibly sharp images with the capacity to display 16.8 million colours — all for about $300. By March 2006, Sony hopes to have sold five million of the PlayStation Portable (PSP) and is putting much effort into the development of new games and movies for the device.

Wayne Gretzky, who participated in the Canadian product launch, joked that while he didn't write any code for the PSP's Gretzky NHL game, he had chosen the teams' uniform colours.

While technology has allowed the industry to continue attracting new consumers, other trends must explain the demographic changes seen in the industry. The core demographic for video games has changed — it has gotten older and broader — typically 18- to 35-year olds, with a full third of game players being women. The average age of video game players has risen to 29 — very different from a decade ago.

As a result, marketers are aiming campaigns at mainstream consumers and taking cues from Hollywood with many games based on blockbuster movies and heroes. Many of the most popular titles in 2005 were sequels — new versions of successful games but with more impressive images and effects. Consumers are no longer just waiting for new titles, but next-generation technology. They are demanding, and require constant evolution and innovation in their gaming products.

QUESTIONS:

1. Do you think the strategy of basing games on Hollywood blockbusters is a good approach to further expand markets?
2. In what way might the technology involved here develop in order to further attract new gamers?

SOURCE: Adapted from Simon Avery, "Sony Launches PlayStation Portable in North America," *The Globe and Mail Online*, www.globeandmail.com, March 24, 2005, and Greg Hughes, "Video Games Shoot to Record on Popular Titles," *The Globe and Mail*, March 3, 2005, p. B10.

Positioning and differential advantage

positioning
The strategy of creating an appropriate image for a company or brand in the minds of its target customers — what the brand stands for, what it means to customers.

differential advantage
Any feature of an organization or brand perceived by customers to be desirable and different from that of the competition.

Buckleys
Robitussin

The fourth step in strategic marketing planning actually involves two complementary decisions: how to position a product in the marketplace, and how to distinguish it from competitors' products. **Positioning** refers to the image of a company or brand in relation to direct competitors' products, as well as to other products marketed by the same company. **Differential advantage** refers to any feature of a brand or organization that is perceived by customers to be desirable and different from the competition. For example, Buckley's cough syrup (**www.buckleys.com**), developed in a Toronto drugstore in 1919 and long famous for its horrible taste (what can you expect from pine needles!) has used taste to both position the product and to differentiate it: "It tastes awful. And it works." Buckley's competitors do not extol the awful taste of their products — in fact, some of their products even taste good! The Buckley approach has been memorable and successful not only in Canada but also in the United States and other international markets. This is a rare example of how a common strategy can work across international markets. Robitussin (**www.robitussin.com**) on the other hand, has positioned itself as "Mom's trusted partner in cough treatment — enabling her to have complete confidence that she's providing trusted care for her family." This is reinforced through repeated use of the tag line "Recommended by doctors, pharmacists, and 'Dr. Mom.'" Part of this strategy is to reassure the decision maker that the product is alcohol-free and "goes down with a great cherry taste."

Marketing mix

Finally, management must design a marketing mix — the combination of a product or service, its price, and how it is distributed and promoted. Traditionally, the marketing mix has been considered in terms of four elements that must satisfy the needs of the organization's target customers and, at the same time, achieve its marketing objectives, such as creating value for customers and achieving high levels of customer satisfaction. In recent years, as marketers have turned their thinking more toward the customer service and interaction elements that must accompany the sale and marketing of any product or service, some have expanded their view of the marketing mix to include the essential element of customer service. This refers to the way in which the customer is treated, not only by marketing personnel, but also by all

Mix Elements, Strategic Considerations and Illustrations

Mix Element	Strategic Consideration	Example
Product	Managing existing products and services over time, adding new ones, and dropping unsuccessful ones. Determining types and levels of service required to accompany the core product or service. Decisions on branding, packaging, and other product features, such as warranties.	Coca-Cola introduces another diet product to its product line — Coca-Cola Zero in 2005; must decide the future of its mid-calorie lime flavoured diet product, C2, which has had poor market performance since its introduction in 2004.
Price	Determining the prices to set for a company's products and services. Taking into account such things as the location of customers, price flexibility, related items within a product line, discounts to be offered, and terms of sale. Also, pricing strategies for entering a market, especially with a new product, must be designed.	Future Shop remains competitive with its "Lowest Price Guarantee," promising to beat lower prices advertised by Canadian dealers, including on the Internet. 110 percent of the purchase price will be refunded if a competitor advertises the same system at a lower price within 30 days of purchase.
Distribution	Managing the channel or channels by which products and services are transferred from producer to customers. Involves organizing the institutions by which products are moved from the place where they are produced to the place where they are purchased by the final customer. Also involves creating access and convenience for customers.	Mercedes-Benz introduced the Smart brand of vehicles to Canada and decided to take advantage of its existing distribution channel by selling the cars alongside Mercedes-Benz products in more than 40 dealerships across Canada.
Market Communications	Combining individual methods such as advertising, personal-selling, and sales promotion into a co-ordinated campaign that communicates desired value. Adjustments must be made as a product moves from the early stages to the later stages of its life. Decisions must also be made for each individual method of marketing communications.	In launching the new Mini Cooper line of cars, BMW decided traditional promotion wouldn't be enough to get the attention of the desired target market. To get early attention, BMW used fashionably attired actors to drive Minis around trendy nightclub districts in the evenings before the car was actually available for sale.
Customer Service	Determining how customers are to be handled or interacted with as they deal with the company. Considerations are the types and levels of service needed for different target market segments in order to differentiate the company, compete effectively, and to create customer value and strong relationships.	Ritz-Carlton recognized the leading edge technology needs of its guests and provided a 24-hour technology concierge to assist with technical problems and to provide assistance with general computer software and hardware questions.

employees and by the company itself. Let's consider the elements of the expanded marketing mix and some of the concepts and strategies you'll learn about in later chapters. These are presented in the Mix Elements box on the previous page.

The elements of the marketing mix are interrelated; decisions in one area often affect actions in another. When a company relies on pricing as its primary competitive tool, the other elements must be designed to support aggressive pricing. For example, the promotional campaign probably will be built around a theme of "low, low prices." In non-price competition, however, product, distribution, customer and service strategies, and/or promotion strategies come to the forefront. Marketing communications must help create a superior value image for the product if a premium price is to be sustained.

Annual Marketing Plan

annual marketing plan
A written document that details the planned marketing activities for a business unit or product for a given year.

Besides strategic planning for several years into the future, more specific, shorter-term planning is also vital. For this reason, strategic marketing planning in an organization leads to the preparation of an annual marketing plan, as shown in the bottom part of Figure 3-6. An **annual marketing plan**, which is a written document, is the master blueprint for a year's marketing activity for a specified organizational division or major product.

A separate plan normally should be prepared for each major product and company division. Sometimes, depending on a company's circumstances, separate plans are developed for key brands and important target markets. As the name implies, an annual marketing plan usually covers one year, but there are exceptions. For instance, because of the seasonal nature of some products or markets, it is advisable to prepare plans for shorter time periods. In the clothing industry, for example, plans are made for each season, which lasts only several months.

Purposes and responsibilities

An annual marketing plan serves several purposes:

- It summarizes the marketing strategies and tactics that will be used to achieve specified objectives in the upcoming year — it is a "what-to-do" guide.
- The plan also focuses on "how to do it," pointing to what needs to be done. The implementation details provide important basic information that gives direction to evaluation of the marketing program.
- It outlines who is responsible for which activities, when the activities are to be carried out, and how much time and money can be spent.

The executive responsible for the division or product covered by the plan typically prepares it. All or part of the task may be delegated to subordinates.

Preparation of an annual marketing plan may begin nine months or more before the start of the period covered by the plan. Early work includes necessary research and arranging for other information sources. The bulk of the work occurs one to three months prior to the plan's starting date. The last steps are to have the plan reviewed and approved by senior management. Some revision may be necessary before final approval is granted.

The final version of the plan, or relevant parts of it, should be shared with all employees who will be involved in implementing the agreed-on strategies and tactics. Failure to have a plan understood and accepted by those implementing it both within and outside the organization threatens both service quality and the quality of the market relationships ultimately established.

Recommended contents

The exact contents of an annual marketing plan should be determined by an organization's circumstances. For example, a firm in an intensely competitive industry might assess its competitors in a separate section, while a firm in another industry might present this assessment as part of the situation analysis. Similarly, some organizations include alternative (or contingency) plans; others don't. A contingency plan contains the set of steps the firm will take if a competitor introduces a new product, if this is being rumoured.

Annual marketing planning follows a sequence similar to strategic marketing planning. However, annual planning has a shorter time frame and is more specific, both in relation to the issues addressed and the plans laid out. Still, as shown in Table 3-3, the major sections of an annual marketing plan are similar to the steps in strategic marketing planning.

In an annual marketing plan, more attention is devoted to tactical details than is feasible at other levels of planning. While a strategic marketing plan might stress an increased focus on personal selling within the marketing mix, an annual plan might recommend an increased focus on customer retention and provide for training in the tactics necessary for improving customer relations.

It's important to note that an annual marketing plan relates to all of the steps of the management process, not just to planning. That is, sections 5 through 7 in Table 3-3 deal with implementation, and section 8 is concerned with evaluation. We will return to implementation when we discuss the various components of the marketing mix in the chapters that follow.

PAGE UP!

1. What are the four essential steps in strategic planning at the company level?
2. Describe the five steps involved in strategic marketing planning.
3. Explain the difference between positioning and differential advantage.

TABLE 3-3 Contents of an Annual Marketing Plan

1. *Executive Summary.* In this one- or two-page section, the thrust of the plan is described and explained. It is intended for executives who desire an overview of the plan but need not be knowledgeable about the details.
2. *Situation Analysis.* The marketing program for the strategic business unit (SBU) or product covered by the plan is examined within the context of pertinent past, present, and future conditions. It is vital that a reliable assessment of human resource needs and capabilities be part of the analysis. Much of this section might be derived from the results of strategic marketing planning. Additional information of particular relevance to a one-year planning period may be included in this section.
3. *Objectives.* The objectives in an annual plan are more specific than those produced by strategic marketing planning. However, annual objectives must help achieve organizational goals and strategic marketing goals.
4. *Strategies.* As in strategic marketing planning, the strategies in an annual plan should indicate which target markets are going to be satisfied through a combination of product, price, distribution, and promotion.
5. *Tactics.* Specific activities, sometimes called action plans, are devised for carrying out each major strategy included in the preceding section. Tactics answer the question of what is to be done, who will do it, and how the tasks will be accomplished. The who and the how show that a plan is actually implementable, given the finances in section 6.
6. *Financial Schedules.* Normally includes three kinds of financial information — projected sales, expenses, and profits in what's called a pro-forma financial statement, along with the amounts of resources dedicated to different activities in one or more budgets.
7. *Timetable.* Answers the question of when various marketing activities will be carried out during the upcoming year.
8. *Evaluation Procedures.* Addresses the questions of what, who, how, and when connected with measuring performance against goals, both during and at the end of the year. The results of evaluations during the year may lead to adjustments in the plan's strategies and/or tactics or even in the objectives to be achieved.

Using a Planning Model

In this section, we briefly discuss one of the more popular planning models, the Boston Consulting Group matrix. First, however, you need to be more familiar with a form of organization called the strategic business unit.

Strategic business units

Most large and medium-sized companies, and even some smaller firms, consist of multiple units and produce numerous products. In such diversified firms, company-wide planning cannot serve as an effective guide for executives who oversee the organization's various divisions. Consequently, for more effective planning and operation, a multi-business or multi-product organization should be divided according to its major markets, products, or services into **strategic business units (SBUs).** Each SBU may be a major market, product, or service division in an organization; a geographic organization, such as an international or country division; a group of related products; or even a single major product or brand that is marketed globally.

strategic business unit (SBU)
A separate division for a major product or market in a multi-product or multi-business organization.

Bombardier

Bombardier Inc. (**www.bombardier.com**) is a company that was known to Canadians for its recreational vehicles, the Ski-Doo and Sea-Doo. Today, with the recreational vehicle division sold, Bombardier operates two world famous divisions, Bombardier Aerospace (makers of regional, business, amphibious and defence aircraft) and Bombardier Transportation (making rail vehicles, total transport systems, propulsion and control systems). The missions, objectives and strategies of the Aerospace Division (where the strategic business units manufacture a variety of Bombardier aircraft) must be quite different from those that guide the marketing and other activities of the Transportation Division (where the strategic business units manufacture rail and subway cars).

To be identified as an SBU, an entity should: (1) be a separately identifiable business; (2) have a distinct mission; (3) have its own competitors; and (4) have its own executive group with profit responsibilities — as is the case within each of the Bombardier divisions.

Boston Consulting Group (BCG) matrix
A strategic planning model that classifies strategic business units or major products according to market shares and growth rates.

The Boston Consulting Group matrix

Developed by the **Boston Consulting Group (BCG)**, with this model, a company classifies each of its SBUs (and sometimes its major products) according to two factors: its market share relative to competitors, and the growth rate of the industry in which the SBU operates.

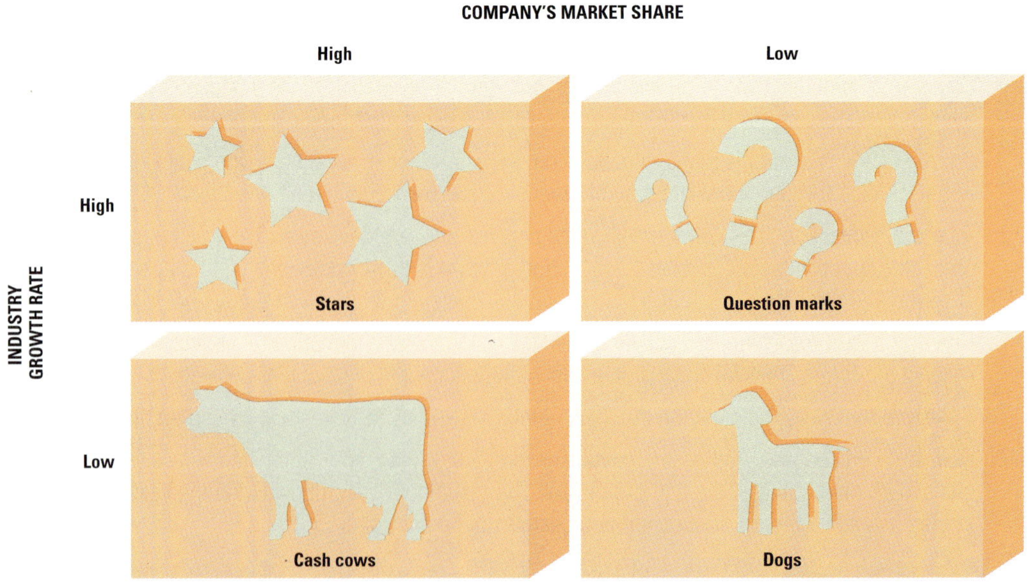

Figure 3-7: The Boston Consulting Group (BCG) matrix

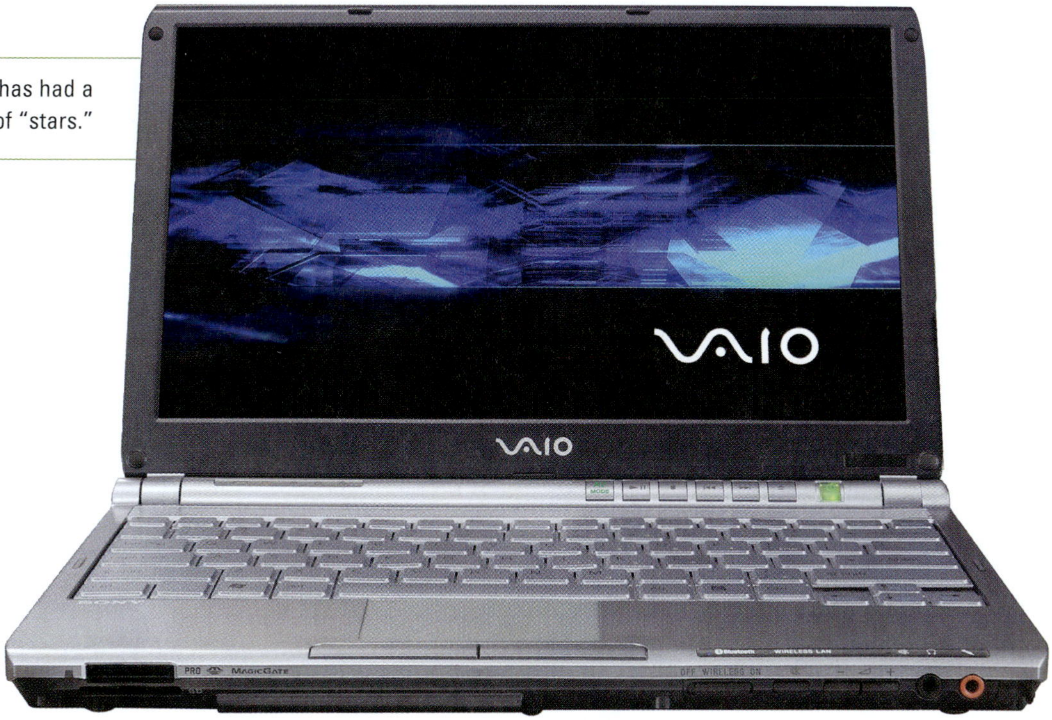

Sony has had a galaxy of "stars."

When the factors are divided simply into high and low categories, a 2-by-2 grid is created, as displayed in Figure 3-7. In turn, the four quadrants in the grid represent distinct categories of SBUs or major products: stars, cash cows, question marks, and dogs. The categories differ in relation not only to market share and industry growth rate, but also to cash needs and appropriate strategies.

stars
Strategic business units characterized by high market shares and high industry growth rates.

- **Stars** have high market shares and high industry growth rates. They also require lots of cash to remain competitive in growing markets. Aggressive marketing strategies are imperative for stars to maintain or even build market share. Adding new customers and retaining existing ones are both crucial at this stage. Examples of this category are Microsoft's Xbox (**www.xbox.com**) and Windows XP (**www.microsoft.com**) software packages, Ford Motor Company's Explorer SUV (**www.ford.ca**), and Sony's Vaio laptop computer (**www.sony.ca**).

cash cows
Strategic business units that are characterized by high market shares and do business in mature industries (those with low growth rates).

- **Cash cows** are SBUs that have high market shares and do business in mature industries that have low growth rates. When an industry's growth diminishes, stars for which the strategies and tactics have resulted in the building of strong customer relationships move into this category. Because most of its customers have been with it for some time and remain satisfied and loyal, a cash cow's marketing costs are not high and it generates more cash than it needs. As a result, cash cows can be "milked" to support the firm's other SBUs that need more resources. Marketing strategies for cash cows seek to defend market share by maintaining or increasing perceived value, as well as by continuously improving customer relationships and reinforcing customer loyalty. For example, The Jeep line of vehicles, now owned by DaimlerChysler continues to be very popular today. The long heritage of the Jeep TJ has attained almost cult status, spawning the development of a four-door version called Liberty. Even low-priced food items can be cash cows; products such as Wrigley's Juicy Fruit gum and Kraft Dinner continue to reap big profits.

Xbox
Microsoft
Ford
Sony

question marks
Strategic business units characterized by low market shares but high industry growth rates.

- **Question marks** (sometimes called "problem children") are SBUs that have low market shares but high industry growth rates. A question mark has not achieved a strong foothold in an expanding but highly competitive market. The question surrounding this type of SBU is whether it can gain adequate market share and be profitable. If management answers "No," then the SBU should be divested or liquidated. If management instead answers "Yes," the firm must come up with the cash to build market share — more cash than the typical question mark generates from its own profits. Appropriate marketing strategies for question marks focus on creating an impact in the market by displaying a strong differential advantage that enhances perceived value, thereby, building customer support. Coca-Cola is certainly a successful company but it too can stumble. Its mid-calorie diet soda flavoured with lime, C2, flopped. However, the company continued through 2005 to develop new ways to promote the product in the hope it would find a home with some market segment.[16]

dogs
Strategic business units that are characterized by low market shares and operate in industries with low growth rates.

- **Dogs** are SBUs that have low market shares and operate in industries with low growth rates. It would be unwise to invest substantial funds in SBUs in this category. Marketing strategies for dogs are intended to maximize any potential profits by minimizing expenditures or to promote a differential advantage to build market share. The company can instead say, "Enough's enough!" and divest or liquidate an SBU that's a dog. Air Canada has had many challenges in recent years, not the least of which was having to disband its Tango division aimed at price-conscious flyers. With ticket prices as much as 80 percent below full economy fares and tickets available only through the Internet, the airline lasted less than two years. Perhaps, as in many other product categories, Internet shoppers are often not bargain hunters. General Motors' Oldsmobile was once a crown jewel (that is, shiny like a star!). However, as the oldest brand in the U.S. automobile industry, its dull image lost favour with consumers and the product line-up was discontinued.

Ordinarily, one firm cannot affect the growth rate for an entire industry. An exception might be the leading firm in a fairly new industry. If growth rate cannot be influenced, companies must turn their attention to the other factor in the BCG matrix: market share. Marketing strategies based on the BCG matrix therefore tend to concentrate on building or maintaining market share, depending on which of the four SBU categories is involved. Various strategies require differing amounts of cash, which means that management must continually allocate the firm's limited resources (notably cash) to separate marketing endeavours.

In the financial arena, an investor needs a balanced portfolio in relation to risks and potential returns. Similarly, a company should seek a balanced portfolio of SBUs. Certainly, cash cows are indispensable. Stars and question marks are integral to a balanced portfolio, because products in growing markets determine a firm's long-term performance. While dogs are undesirable, it is rare that a company doesn't have at least one. As a result, the portfolios of most organizations with numerous SBUs or major products include a mix of stars, cash cows, question marks, and dogs.

PAGE UP!

1. An annual marketing plan serves what purpose?
2. According to the BCG matrix, an organization classifies each of its strategic business units according to which factors?
3. What are the main features of a "dog" as defined in the Boston Consulting Group matrix?

Key Terms and Concepts

annual marketing plan 80
Boston Consulting Group (BCG) matrix 82
cash cows 83
demography 61
differential advantage (or disadvantage) 78
distribution channel 69
dogs 84
environmental scanning 74
external macro-environmental forces 60
external micro-environmental forces 60
internal non-marketing forces 60
marketing intermediaries 68
mission statement 71
objective (same as goal) 71
positioning 78
question marks 84
relationship-insensitive forces 61
relationship-sensitive forces 67
segments 77
situation analysis 74
stars 83
strategic business unit (SBU) 82
strategic company planning 73
strategic marketing planning 74
strategy 72
SWOT assessment 74
tactic 72
target market 77

Questions and Problems

1. The size of the average Canadian family has decreased in the past few decades. Some organizations and marketers are only recently beginning to feel the result of this trend.
   a. What are the implications of this for organizations such as private schools, universities, and colleges?
   b. How should these organizations respond to such changes in order to remain viable operations?
   c. Now that you have studied company and marketing planning as discussed in this chapter, what types of objectives, tactics, and strategies would you recommend for the institution you are attending?
2. For each of the following products and services, give some examples of how its marketing program is likely to differ during periods of prosperity as contrasted with periods of recession.
   a. Fairmont hotels.
   b. Smart coupe.
   c. Rollerblade brand in-line skates.
   d. White water rafting holidays.
   e. Nike sportswear/clothing.
3. What have been some of the marketing strategies used in recent years by fast-food restaurants in response to increasing public interest in health and physical fitness?
4. Changes are happening all around us and these events almost always have some sort of implication in the field of marketing.
   a. Provide an example (other than those discussed in the chapter) of a trend that corresponds to each component of the macro-environmental scan that has either recently occurred or is still occurring in North America.
   b. What possible influences might each of these have on marketing practices or impact on the consumption (demand) for certain products?
5. Using examples other than those given in this chapter, explain how a firm's marketing system can be influenced by the environmental force of technology, and particularly by the Internet.
6. Explain how each of the following resources within a company might influence that company's marketing program. How could each be a source or sources of differential advantage and/or disadvantage?
   a. Plant location.
   b. Company image.
   c. Financial resources.
   d. Personnel capability.
7. Should a small firm (either a manufacturer, a retailer, or an online enterprise) engage in formal strategic planning? Why or why not?
8. Considering the impact of changing technology on technology-based industries, should firms involved in these follow the same guidelines and time frames for strategic planning as traditional organizations? Explain.
9. Using a customer-oriented approach (benefits provided or needs satisfied), answer the question "What business are we in?" for each of the following companies:
   a. Air Canada.
   b. Mountain Equipment Co-op.
   c. Subway Sandwiches and Salads.
   d. Roots.
   e. Club Monaco.

10. For each of the organizations listed in the previous question provide an example of a new product idea that represents an extension of what the company currently offers, but is still in line with this strategy.
11. In the situation-analysis step of strategic marketing planning, what specific external environmental forces should be analyzed by a manufacturer of equipment used for backpacking in the wilderness?
12. Using the BCG matrix, identify a major product or strategic business unit that would fit into each quadrant (stars, cash cows, questions marks, dogs).

Hands-On Marketing

1. Talk with a marketing executive at a local firm. Based on the information you obtain, determine the differential advantage or disadvantage of the firm's primary product or service. Indicate how the advantage could be strengthened or the disadvantage alleviated.
2. Go to Gap's Web site (**www.gapinc.com**) and, by reviewing the content of the "About Gap Inc." section, determine Gap's objectives.

Back to the Top

Do you have an Apple iPod or another brand of MP3 player? How did you listen to music before the iPod? What other changes have taken place in your life as a result of recent advances in technology? Think about companies in technology-based industries and how they are serving customers like you today. What changes do you feel must have taken place in their marketing planning in recent years as a result of the marketplace changes outlined in this chapter?

Online Learning Centre

Want to get better grades, tips on how to study more effectively, and up-to-date information on happenings in the world of marketing? Then, visit the Online Learning Centre for practice tests, Study Smart software, *Marketing Magazine,* and much more! **www.mcgrawhill.ca/olc/sommers**

CASE 1-1:

Farm Boy — A SUPERmarket Experience

Today's grocery stores often look like anything but a food store. Gone are the days of the simple supermarket — produce, meat, dairy, canned and packaged goods all under one roof. Today's supermarkets are more like hypermarkets where you'll find electronics, furniture, motor oil, sporting goods, children's clothing, banking services, a pharmacy, a travel agency, home décor items and, yes, food. Time-crunched busy consumers are demanding one-stop shopping and the large grocery chains are delivering. But, there still seems to be a place, and time, for retailers who specialize in groceries.

Take Farm Boy (**www.farmboy.ca**) for instance; a regional Canadian food retailer, headquartered in Ottawa and with eight stores in Eastern Ontario, recognized for its produce, meat, bakery, deli, and dairy product offerings. It finds its uniqueness in providing a "different shopping experience."

Grocery shopping is a $2 billion-a-year business in the Ottawa area and the competition is intense. Since incorporating in 1981, Farm Boy has always provided a different shopping experience than the big box retailers or traditional grocery chains. While the shelves at Loblaws and Sobeys are left without a centimetre of breathing room as they are bursting at the seams with thousands and thousands of products, Farm Boy chooses another approach.

The chain carries a handful of "complementary grocery items," however, that does not necessarily include brand names such as Coke and Tide, nor products like bathroom tissue and paper towels. Farm Boy's concept has stayed true since its inception: providing "perishable, fresh, healthy foods." You will find a butcher on site, a cheese shop, a deli department and a bakery. You can find things like triple-A Alberta beef or private label products like lemon-garlic salad dressing and fresh salsa, with strict adherence to high quality guidelines. You can even request products to order. The company utilizes sophisticated transportation methods to ensure the freshness and quality of its products.

And let's not forget about the fun. Farm Boy provides its customers with well-trained staff and unique animated characters that entertain both children and adults alike. Shoppers may be greeted by a singing Farm Boy and his dog, Barndoor Buddy, a mischievous monkey who does endless flips over the banana display, or Lulu the cow who keeps watch over the dairy section!

Farm Boy understands the importance of both exceptional products and customer service in the food and retail grocery industry. The efforts of Farm Boy's focused and responsive team in understanding food and the service industry are truly impressive.

Can you meet all of your shopping needs at Farm Boy? Generally, no. Many consumers do the bulk of their shopping down the road at the big supermarkets and finish up at specialty stores like Farm Boy. Consumers in the Ottawa area are making three to four food stops in the run of a two-week period — so much for the time-crunched, busy shopper who only wants to make one stop. Seems people will still make time for quality products and service. Whether it's the best deals or the best freshness or some combination of the two, Farm Boy seems quite able to deliver.

Farm Boy isn't trying to compete on promotion either — really how could they? They rely, for the most part, on word-of-mouth, which is why they work so hard to do such an impeccable job. Only one percent of gross sales are devoted to marketing activities. Instead of using an advertising agency, the company produces its ads primarily in-house. The primary advertising medium used to date is radio, simply because of its proven success. Compare this to the large chains' glossy weekly flyers delivered in newspapers and available on the Web. How can Farm Boy and similar retailers compete — not only in Ottawa but across the country?

Questions:

1. What is Farm Boy's competitive advantage? Check out the Web site at **www.farmboy.ca**.
2. What appeal does this company have for grocery shoppers? For what groups of shoppers, in particular?
3. Will Farm Boy be able to stay ahead of the competition in the long-term?

SOURCE: Adapted from Laura Pratt, "Home Grown," *Marketing Magazine — National Capital Region Special Edition*, December, 2005.

CASE 1-2:

Daniel and Jane Stein Dine in Old Montréal

Daniel Stein smiled as he slipped on his sports jacket. The 37-year-old marketing executive was having a great weekend in Montréal, a city he often visits on business. On this particular business trip, however, Jane had been able to take time off work to join him. As this did not happen often, Daniel had made a reservation for dinner at Chez Antoine, an upscale French restaurant in the heart of Old Montréal. He knew the restaurant was very pricey but this was a special weekend for the couple. Both Jane and Daniel had hectic careers and lately, they had not been able to spend much time together.

Although he had several favourite restaurants in Montréal, Daniel had chosen this one for its charming atmosphere and wonderful French cuisine. He was certain Jane would love it too. He had raved to her about Chez Antoine many times and had promised they would go there when she was able to join him in Montréal. They left the hotel on this windy, cold Friday evening in January, jumped into a taxi and headed for Old Montréal, expecting this to be a wonderful evening.

Arriving at the restaurant at 8 p.m., they noticed that it was very busy. Daniel gave his name to the hostess, expecting their reservation to be honoured right away. Instead, the hostess smiled apologetically and explained that a table would be available shortly. Daniel and Jane grew more and more impatient as time went by. They considered leaving for another restaurant nearby but they really had their hearts set on this one. A few minutes later, a couple walked in and gave their names to the hostess. She seated them right away. At this point, Daniel was about to object but as the hostess returned from seating the other couple, she smiled at the Steins and said, "your table is ready now, please come this way." Twenty-five minutes after they had arrived, Daniel and Jane were finally seated and they couldn't wait to order. They ordered their favourite drinks and the server brought them out right away.

Having examined the menu and decided what to order, the couple waited 20 minutes before the server returned. At this rate, they wouldn't be eating until 10 p.m. Jane and Daniel were finished their drinks and looking around impatiently for the server. The server was frantically going from table to table and zipped by the Steins' table a few times without even looking at them. Daniel tried to make eye contact to suggest that they were ready to order but it was to no avail. Finally, he muttered in frustration, "This is unbelievable; I'm going to complain." Jane felt sorry for the server who clearly had too many tables to serve. She felt that the manager was the one responsible for having only two servers working on a Friday evening. She told Daniel that it wasn't the server's fault, and he decided not to complain. Finally, the server came over and described the chef's special to the couple. Daniel ordered lamb, medium rare, and Jane ordered a seafood crepe in a crème sauce. The couple was eager to eat. They had had a light lunch earlier that day, but that was eight hours ago!

While they waited, they couldn't help but notice the quaint décor. Chez Antoine reminded them of a restaurant they had been to in Paris. It brought back memories of their first trip to Europe together. The couple reminisced about the wonderful time they had had and before they knew it, their meals had arrived. The server sprinkled fresh ground pepper on their dishes, asked politely if she could get them anything else and left. Everything looked wonderful. The presentation was very nice and the food smelled terrific. Jane tasted her crepe and commented that it was delicious.

Daniel, however, was not pleased. His lamb was overcooked and the meat was tough. Jane asked him what he thought of his dinner and he answered that it wasn't at all like the lamb he had eaten here before. It was dry and parts of it were even burnt. Jane was disappointed for him. She told him he should complain to the server. Daniel agreed. When the server came back to ask whether they were enjoying their meals, Jane nodded and smiled. The server then looked at Daniel and said, "And how's your lamb, sir?" Daniel thought for a moment, hesitated and finally he said that it was fine. The server was satisfied with this reply and turned to leave. Daniel stopped her and ordered a second bottle of wine.

Jane looked confused. Why hadn't Daniel said anything? Daniel, on the other hand, had decided against complaining when he realized that he would have to wait another 30 minutes if he ordered more lamb. He knew Jane was enjoying her meal and did not want to make her wait longer than she already had. He realized that if the server took the lamb back to the kitchen, they would have to either eat their meals separately or Jane would eat hers cold. He didn't want to go through the trouble and besides, he felt uncomfortable complaining. So he said nothing. The couple finished their meal and realized that the server had forgotten about their second bottle of wine. When the server came to take their plates, they reminded her of the wine she had forgotten to bring them. The server turned red and apologized profusely. The couple told her that they no longer wanted the wine. Instead they ordered dessert. Finally, at the end of the evening, they got ready to leave.

The bill arrived and Daniel glanced at it briefly. It seemed very expensive for what they had ordered. Then he noticed that they had been charged for the second bottle of wine. Daniel was becoming frustrated again. Things were just not going well that evening. He mentioned the extra wine on the bill to the server who again apologized and quickly left to make up another bill. Jane could not believe how poor the service was. She was equally frustrated. When it came time to leave a tip, Jane told Daniel that he should leave a small tip. Daniel felt uncomfortable doing that and even made excuses for the server! Jane felt annoyed at her husband but she didn't want to argue with him, especially not in the middle of this busy, upscale restaurant. The couple left, feeling disappointed by their dining experience at Chez Antoine.

Talin Vartanian has heard of scenarios like this one many times. "Citizen Talin," as she is called, keeps a close watch over the rights of consumers, and she is baffled by customers who won't complain about poor service in restaurants. Restaurateurs insist that when they ask customers "How is everything this evening?" they want to hear the truth. But often, customers simply won't tell the truth. Either they are too timid, too embarrassed or, as in the case of the Steins, they don't want to spoil the mood of the evening. Vartanian insists that customers complain when something goes wrong instead of just putting up with the poor service, leaving a tip and never returning to the restaurant again. A customer who calmly and politely explains the problem to the waiter is much better off. And so is the owner of the restaurant who may not be aware of the problem and may repeat it over and over again. This leads to silent defections. Customers leave quietly, never to return. Their evening is spoiled and what's worse for the restaurateur is that future revenue is lost. The unhappy customers will not give the restaurant repeat business nor will they refer their friends to the restaurant. Worse, they may tell all their friends and family about the poor experience and the restaurant loses more potential customers. The moral of Citizen Talin's story? Complain politely when service is poor and both the customer and the restaurant benefit.

Questions:

1. Which parts of the Steins' service experience were unacceptable? How could the hostess or server have handled these situations differently?
2. If you were Jane or Daniel Stein, how would you have handled the situation? Why did they not complain?
3. Which parts of the Steins' dining experience were good? Which were unacceptable? Why did the couple leave the restaurant feeling disappointed?
4. How do you think the Steins felt towards the hostess, the server, the restaurant, the food, the décor, the whole experience?

SOURCE: Adapted from Talin Vartanian, "Citizen Talin: The case for complaining in a restaurant," CBC Radio, August 18, 2002, www.cbc.ca/consumers.

CASE 1-3:

CBC

Peter Taylor Buys Running Shoes

Peter Taylor was nearing the end of his two-year MBA program at the University of Ottawa and looking forward to moving to Toronto after graduation. There, he was sure he would find a job related to sports marketing, something he found very interesting. Peter had always been athletic and through the years had played many sports. During the gruelling two-year MBA program, however, Peter had often found the workload too demanding to spend much time at sports. He did find some time to swim in the university pool and he also played squash a couple of times a week. Peter fully intended to continue his active lifestyle when he moved to Toronto and had been thinking for some time about which sport would suit his lifestyle once he began working. Having done quite well in middle-distance track-and-field competitions during high school, Peter decided to take running more seriously. While doing his MBA, he had done a little jogging from time-to-time along the Rideau Canal and had enjoyed it. He also realized that running was one physical activity he could do on his own schedule.

Although Peter considered himself quite knowledgeable about most sports, he also felt there was probably more to running than just putting on a pair of sneakers and going out for a jog. Walking through the Rideau Centre one day after an exam, he stopped into a bookstore to buy a running magazine. If he was going to take running seriously, Peter would have to do some research before buying the right pair of running shoes. As he flipped through *Running Times,* Peter realized that he knew very little about the engineering and technology of running shoes. Although he had bought other athletic footwear during the past few years, he had not appreciated the diversity of styles and models available. The wide variety of running shoes and the range in prices and colours made the decision even more complex.

Peter wanted to make sure he bought the right brand of running shoe. As he mulled over his decision, he identified what criteria were most important to him. He was willing to spend more than $100 for a pair of quality running shoes, but his tight budget did not allow him to go much higher. Comfort and protection against injury were critical but colour was not at all important. Peter preferred light-weight shoes as they seemed better for running longer distances.

Having decided more or less what he was looking for, Peter headed to Sports Experts in the Rideau Centre the next day, after his last exam. After he had scanned the huge wall display of running, court, squash, tennis, aerobic, basketball, cross-training and volleyball shoes for a few minutes, a sales clerk approached him and offered her assistance. Peter was looking closely at several Nike and Brooks styles, as he had worn both brands in the past and had been very satisfied with them. He asked Donna, the sales clerk, which of the brands was considered to be the best. Donna proceeded to explain that neither was necessarily the best brand. The decision should be based on comfort and ensuring that the width was neither too narrow nor so wide that his feet shifted from side to side. She felt that price was generally a good measure of the quality of the shoe, but not necessarily of the brand. She recommended that Peter try one style of each of the major brands so he could determine which one fit him best. Donna also suggested that sturdiness could be tested by bending the shoes from right to left, and by ensuring that the heel components of the shoe felt firm.

Peter proceeded to try one Nike, one New Balance, one Saucony, and one Asics running shoe, all within the same price range. He decided that he felt most comfortable with the Air Max Nike shoes because the air cushioning and light weight seemed to offer more spring. The only problem was that they felt a little too narrow on his wide feet. Donna suggested another shoe, the Air Structure Triax and it fit perfectly on Peter. He had finally found what he was looking for. Peter asked Donna to hold the shoes for him until closing. He wanted to make sure that other stores were not offering the shoes at a lower price than $119.99.

Peter decided to head for Elgin Sports on Albert Street, an established Ottawa sporting goods store. There, he found the same shoes for exactly the same price so he quickly left in search of a lower price. He quickly stopped into a nearby Internet café where he logged onto the Running Room Web site (**www.runningroom.com**). He had heard they had a great variety of running shoes. They did in fact have the shoe listed, but again, he found that the price was the same.

Peter then went to Sports-4 (**www.sports4.ca**), a store on Bank Street that specialized more in running shoes. Peter was pleasantly surprised to find that the Nike Air Structure Triax were on a special promotion for $99.99. He asked Geoff Wallace, the sales clerk, whether he had a size 9. Geoff disappeared to the back and returned with a size 9-½ instead. He explained that 9-½ was the smallest size they had in stock. Peter decided to try them on just in case. Maybe the extra ½ size wouldn't matter much. He really wanted to save $30. The extra space in the toe, however, was quite noticeable even with the thick socks that Geoff gave him. Peter shook his head and declined when the clerk offered a different style of shoe to try on. Peter already had his heart set on these sneakers.

It was closer to go to Elgin Sports, but Peter realized that Donna at Sports Experts had been a great help so he walked back to the Rideau Centre. As he walked through the Sparks Street Mall, Peter wondered if he might be able to strike a deal at Sports Experts, considering he should probably also buy a rainsuit anyway. When he returned to Sports Experts, Donna recognized Peter right away and smiled. Peter requested the running shoes that he had asked her to hold for him but expressed dismay over the better deal offered by Sports-4. Peter asked if he might speak to the manager about the possibility of matching the Sports-4 price.

While Donna disappeared to get the manager, Peter spotted a Nike rainsuit that appealed to him and had been marked down in price. As he took the rainsuit off the display rack, he was greeted by the manager. Peter explained his dilemma and asked if Sports Experts would match Sports-4's sale price on the Nike Air Structure Triax, provided that he purchase the rainsuit he had selected. The manager was eager for business and goodwill, especially since he considered Sports-4 to be Sports Experts' main competitor for running and triathalon equipment in the city. He nodded and offered to ring in the sale for him, all the while making conversation about running in Ottawa. Peter appreciated the concession that Sports Experts had made and thanked the manager and Donna, telling them he would be sure to shop at Sports Experts stores in Toronto on a regular basis.

Questions:

1. What objectives do you feel Peter was trying to accomplish in the selection of running shoes? What motivated his final selection?
2. Could Sports Experts have done anything differently in order to make the sale on Peter's first visit?
3. Why did he buy his shoes at Sports Experts? What could Geoff Wallace have done to persuade Peter to buy a different shoe at Sports-4?

PART 2

Addressing Target Markets

The information needed to guide marketing decisions, an exploration of the strategies behind effective marketing, and the nature of business-to-business marketing

In **Part 2**, we introduce those business activities that are involved in marketing; the various research and insight gathering activities that provide the information on which businesses base marketing decisions; the marketing strategies that businesses put in place to plan their marketing program; and the marketing mix, representing the four key tools used to implement marketing.

Chapter 4 discusses marketing research and the ways in which marketers obtain the information they need about customers and markets. Chapter 5 examines the very important strategic principles of market segmentation, differentiation and positioning, and we introduce the increasingly attractive strategy of adding value. In Chapter 6, we examine the business-to-business market, a massive market that many end-consumers rarely see — the one that involves marketing to businesses and organizations.

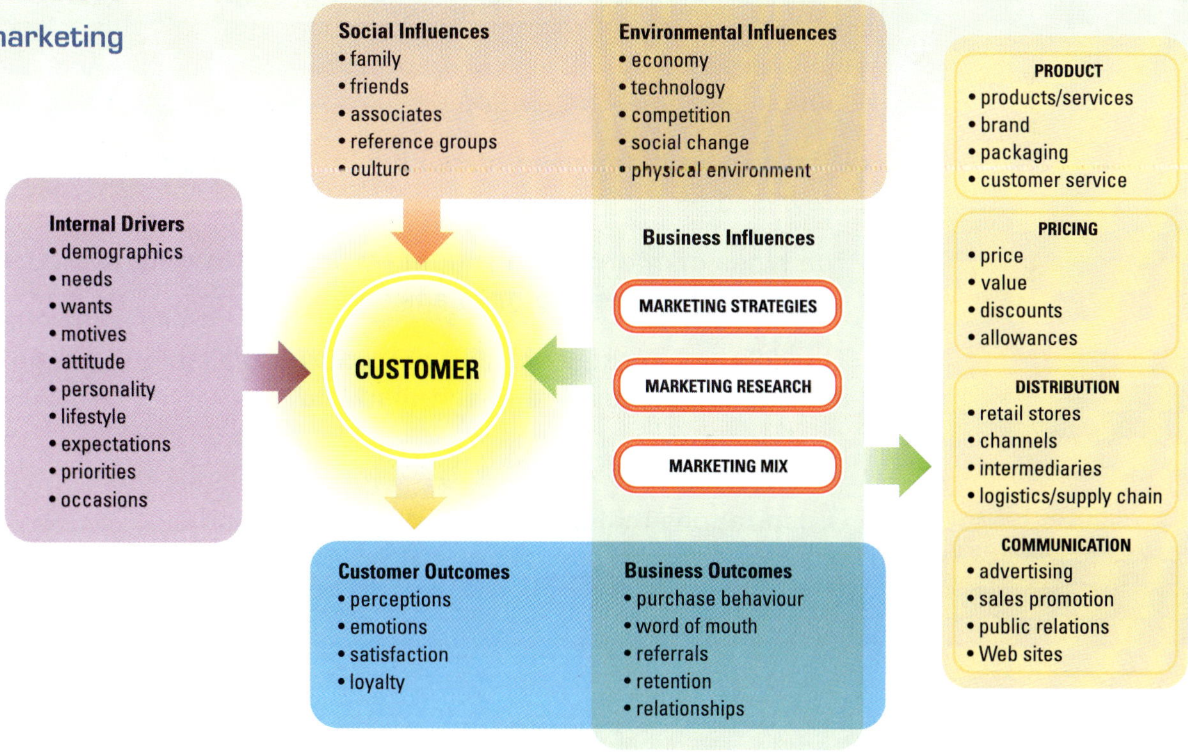

CHAPTER 4

Getting the Marketing Information We Need

The management of any business or organization, whether a major pharmaceuticals manufacturer, a radio station, a retail clothing store, or an art gallery, requires a fundamental input in order to achieve success in a competitive marketplace — accurate and timely information. To be effective, marketing managers need up-to-date information about the customers they are trying to reach, the environment in which their company operates, and the internal and external factors that affect their specific markets. We're about to see where and how this information can be obtained and how it is then used. After studying this chapter, you should have an understanding of:

- Why organizations need marketing information, and the decisions that are based on it.
- The types of information sought by firms — in other words, the questions they need to have answered.
- The different approaches and procedures available to obtain information on customers and markets.
- How to plan and execute a research project.
- Organizations that conduct marketing research.
- The status of marketing research in Canada.

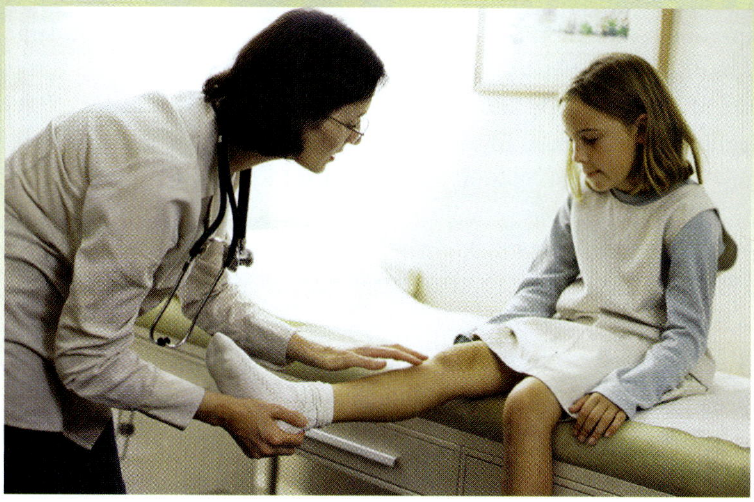

Just What the Doctor Ordered

Deepak Gupta is Director of Marketing Intelligence with PharmaNational, one of Canada's largest pharmaceutical companies. He has just been invited to a meeting in the office of Stella MacIntosh, President and CEO of the company. Also in attendance are Beverley Hotchkiss, PharmaNational's Vice-President of Marketing, and Roberto Dumas, the recently appointed Director of a new project devoted to Patient-Driven Change. The purpose of the meeting is to discuss how to collect information from users of PharmaNational's products that will assist in the development of a patient-focused strategy for the company.

In Canada, where federal laws permit only a very restricted form of advertising to patients, doctors have been the principal decision maker in prescribing medications that are distributed mainly through retail pharmacies. However, in the United States, legislation permits advertising directly to the end user, resulting in consumers being more aware of pharmaceutical products.

As a result, PharmaNational and its competitors have employed many sales representatives who call on doctors on a regular basis. Also, pharmaceutical companies have engaged in a wide range of sponsorship activity, often consisting of inviting doctors (and frequently their families) to conferences where research findings were presented and topics relating to the physicians' speciality discussed. Such conferences were often held in resort locations, thereby affording those attending the opportunity to engage in golf or skiing or other activities.

But, in early 2005, Rx&D (**www.canadapharma.org**), the industry body that represents more than 50 research-based pharmaceutical companies in Canada implemented a strict new code of standards that severely limits the promotional activities of its members. Specifically, the new code prohibits the companies from inviting doctors to conferences or similar activities. This change has sent pharmaceutical companies in search of other innovative marketing techniques.

Stella MacIntosh, President and CEO of PharmaNational, has decided to explore the possibility that the company might base more of its marketing activity on a solid understanding of patients, rather than continuing to direct activities exclusively at doctors. But, she and her colleagues realize that the company has virtually no information on the end users of its products, the patients.[1]

Need for Marketing Information

All organizations, from small neighbourhood vegetarian restaurants to multinational pharmaceutical companies, need information — lots of it — about potential markets, consumer needs and preferences, and marketplace changes in order to develop successful marketing plans and to respond to changes in the marketplace. More than ever before, a large volume of data is available both from external sources and from within a firm. The challenge is how to transform raw data into information and knowledge and how to use it effectively to provide a detailed understanding of customers. To see how to do this, we will begin by briefly discussing why organizations need information and why they need to do research. Then, we will focus our attention on how organizations actually conduct research.

Quite simply, marketing managers have to make many different decisions that will affect the marketing programs of their companies and their attractiveness to customers. To make the best decisions, they need to have access to the most current and reliable information. Consider some of these factors and their relationship to the management of information:

- ***Focus on the customer:*** New ways of viewing customers and of marketing to them demands that companies have as complete an understanding of their customers as possible. Those companies that know and understand their customers best have a distinct advantage when it comes to marketing to them.

- ***Emphasis on retention and relationships:*** As companies have become focused more on building customer relationships and less on making immediate sales, their need for information has changed as well. Companies now have more interest in information on complex concepts such as service quality, perceptions of value, loyalty, and the strength of relationships.

- ***Increased customer expectations:*** Greater competition and better-educated customers have contributed to increased expectations. As customers have experienced better service and quality, they have come to expect more from all companies. To succeed, a firm must know what the customer expects and meet those expectations.

- ***Increased market complexity:*** The marketplace that most companies are facing today is far more complex than it was in the past. As a result, managers must be as informed as possible, armed with information in which they can have complete confidence.

- ***Competitive pressure:*** To be competitive, companies must develop and market new products and services more quickly and effectively than ever before. Pressures continue to build as the Internet eliminates geographic borders, drawing new competitors from around the globe.

- ***Cost of a mistake:*** Launching and marketing a new product or service is enormously expensive. A failure can cause severe — even fatal — damage to a firm. Even making modifications to existing products and service is a risky business. Knowing what to change and when are decisions that should not be made without input from customers.

Managers in a wide variety of organizations make important marketing decisions on many different subjects. It is obvious that the best decisions are based on the best available information. Before embarking on marketing decisions related to the introduction of a new product, changes in the customer service program, the launch of an advertising campaign, or a program to target new customer segments, the marketing manager needs information. In most organizations, the necessary information is not generally available and must be obtained from some external sources. This is where marketing research comes in.

The information obtained through marketing research guides strategic decision-making. However, in order for the marketing manager to have complete confidence in the information, the research must be conducted professionally and in accordance with certain standards that will ensure as little bias as possible and that the results accurately reflect the situation the manager is facing. Many managers view marketing research as an important tool that will help them make the right decisions, thereby contributing to the success of their brands and companies.

What is marketing research?

marketing research
The process of specifying, assembling, and analyzing information used to identify and define marketing opportunities and problems; generate, refine, and evaluate marketing actions; monitor marketing performance; and improve the understanding of customers and of marketing as a process.

Marketing research includes all of the activities that enable an organization to obtain the information it needs to make decisions about its marketing mix and its present or prospective customers. More specifically, marketing research involves the development, interpretation, and communication of decision-oriented information to be used in the strategic marketing process. Businesses and other organizations spend millions of dollars each year obtaining information to improve the quality of decision-making. Obviously, research is an important part of marketing.

Marketing research is an important function within a business because it is responsible for providing accurate, timely information that can be relied on by management in making decisions related to marketing. Most firms don't conduct marketing research all of the time, however, and the vast majority are not large enough to employ research staff on a full-time basis. Only very large firms have a marketing research department; most rely on outside specialty firms to conduct research projects for them.

Therefore, most managers need to know when they require research information, and they need to know how to get research projects done. They rely on marketing research to help them reach accurate conclusions and make the best possible decisions in understanding their customers, in planning their marketing programs, in implementing those programs, and in determining how successful the programs have been. Marketing research is more than designing a questionnaire and collecting data. It must be very well planned to obtain the information that's really needed by marketers.

Scope of Marketing Research Activities

Marketing managers need a great deal of accurate information to better understand the marketplace in which they are operating, the customers who represent the target segments for their products and services, and what is or is not working. The challenge is to put in place a marketing research program that will deliver the required information in a timely and accurate way. Let's start by outlining the types of information that are needed by marketing managers in most organizations. This is not meant to be a complete or detailed list, but it will provide an overview of the kinds of information that are usually obtained.

The information that is generally collected extends from information about the marketplace and what marketers need to know about planning an entry into that market, to customers and how they buy, to how to plan the marketing mix, to evaluating how well the firm has performed and how satisfied its customers are.

What's happening out there? Companies must have a solid understanding about what is happening in the marketplace and the characteristics of the markets they plan to enter. Such information generally deals with the size of the market, the level of competition, changes that are occurring that will affect customer buying power, and other factors discussed in Chapter 3. Keeping up to date on trends and changes is critical if a company is to respond appropriately.

What's going on in our market? The marketer must have detailed information about the specific markets in which the firm operates — information about direct competitors, new brands entering the market, price and distribution changes, and new consumer interests. They also need to know how well they are doing against competitors, what their market share is, sales trends, and much more. The marketplace is constantly changing. If marketers are not up to date on what's going on, they can be left behind very quickly.

What are our competitors doing? All companies need to keep an eye on the competition. Some larger firms have created formalized competitive intelligence programs that are intended to collect information on competitive activity. Today, a great deal of information on the competition and on what other firms in the industry are doing is available on the Internet and through the business media. Some companies employ industry experts to prepare regular reports on competitive activity.

Does anyone want to buy this? Before launching a new product or service, or even before changing an existing product, marketers need to know how consumers will react. A very large percentage of new products that are introduced into the market each year fail, mainly because the companies that introduce them have not done sufficient research to know whether the customer is even interested.

What are the customers like? The more a firm knows about its customers and prospective customers, the better the job it can do in marketing to them. There is a great deal to know. Profiling customers is a major role of marketing research, telling the marketing staff about customers, including their characteristics, needs, attitudes, lifestyles, and likes and dislikes. Understanding the various segments that exist is also of critical importance.

What's important to them? To satisfy customers — the ultimate objective of marketing — a company must understand what customers consider to be important when buying its products and services. Some customers think obtaining a low price is very important, while others may be prepared to pay higher prices if they can access the product quickly and conveniently.

What do they buy and where? A firm needs to know a great deal about customer buying patterns: what they currently buy, what brands, how often, what quantities and sizes. Do they buy from the same stores all of the time, or is location not particularly important? Customer buying patterns, if they are well established, may be difficult to break if a company is trying to unseat an existing brand.

Do they like our products? A company needs to know how customers respond to the various elements of its marketing program, in particular, to its products or services. Unless customers find these attractive, the company has little chance of success. Therefore, much marketing research is devoted to assessing customer reaction to existing and planned products, identifying strengths and weaknesses so that modifications can be made to make the product as attractive as possible.

Do they like our advertising? Advertising and other forms of promotion are also tested through research. A firm needs to know whether its planned advertising and promotions will be attractive to customers before the company spends possibly millions of dollars producing them. After advertising has run in the market for a time, it is tested again to determine customer reaction and the advertising's effectiveness.

Do they think our prices are fair? Much pricing research is devoted to finding out what prices customers are prepared to pay for the products and services being offered. As we will discuss in Chapter 10, the real objective of such research should be to find out what customers value, what they will or will not pay for, and what will represent good value for them.

Do we make it easy for them? A fundamental issue for most customers is how easy it is to deal with a company. Most want their interaction with a company to be hassle-free, convenient, and quick. This means that a company needs to know how customers want its products distributed or made available for them to buy. Research on various aspects of the firm's distribution and customer service system is critical to make sure that customers find it convenient.

Do they like dealing with us? Much marketing research is devoted to determining customers' perception of the quality of products and services offered by a company, and the customers' overall satisfaction with those products and with the service provided by the firm. Customer satisfaction research is important in that it provides the company with feedback on how well it is doing in serving its customers.

What do they think of us? A company needs to know about its image and reputation among customers and the general public at large. Many companies conduct public opinion research that is not directed at specific products and services or at aspects of the marketing program, but rather at how the company is regarded as a member of the community or as a place to work.

How solid are our relationships? Finally, a firm needs to know how well it is doing in developing a base of loyal customers and in building solid relationships with them. As the attention of marketing shifts more toward customer retention and loyalty-building, companies are increasingly interested in measuring the health of their relationships with customers.

Examples of typical marketing research projects are described briefly in Table 4-1.

TABLE 4-1 Typical Marketing Research Projects

Project	Objective
Concept test	To determine if a new product idea is attractive to potential customers, or to determine how targeted customers will respond to advertising concepts.
Copy test	To determine if the intended message in an advertisement is being communicated effectively.
Price responsiveness	To gauge the effect a price change would have on sales of a brand.
Market-share analysis	To determine a firm's proportion of the total sales of a product or service and whether that share is increasing or declining.
Segmentation studies	To identify distinct groups within the total market for a particular product or service, so that these groups may be targeted with specific marketing programs.
Customer satisfaction studies	To monitor how customers feel about an organization and its products or services, and how they are treated by the company.
Usage and attitude studies	To study a firm's own and their competitors' customer attitudes and rates of usage of relevant products and brands.

The Path to Customer Understanding

Ultimately, the role of marketing research is to provide the marketing executive with a better and more in-depth understanding of customers and the markets that they comprise. It is useful to think about a path that will lead to that better understanding. That path leads from the collection or availability of data to the obtaining of insight into customers and their lives. To have a complete understanding of customers and markets, research should ensure stops at several points along this path.

In most companies today, there is a great deal of data collected — every time a credit or debit card is swiped or a long-distance call made. Data are also collected by research companies through surveys. We tend to associate the term "data" with large volumes of numbers. In many companies, the data that exist in large databases remain unanalyzed and uninterpreted. So, the mere availability of data does little to provide an understanding of customers. A women's clothing store in a shopping centre, for example, will likely have lots of data in its customer database that reveals exactly what each customer has purchased. But, the data are of little value until someone analyses them.

Value is added to data when they are analyzed and interpreted. The question is asked, "What are the data telling us?" At this point, we begin to extract information from data. Once data are ordered in certain ways and the results for one group compared with another, we start to get information. For example, we may find that customers in certain neighbourhoods make more purchases of leisurewear, or (assuming we have household data in our database) that women with children under the age of five make more trips to the store than other demographic groups. At this point, we have extracted information from the data.

Now, we ask "so what?" What is this information telling us that we can apply to the explanation or solution of a marketing-related question or problem? We now have to extract knowledge from the information. How can we use the information that we have to address the research question? We may decide that the reason that young mothers are shopping in our store so frequently is simply to get out of the house or to take their kids for a walk in the mall when the weather is bad. As a result, we may determine that young mothers are an important

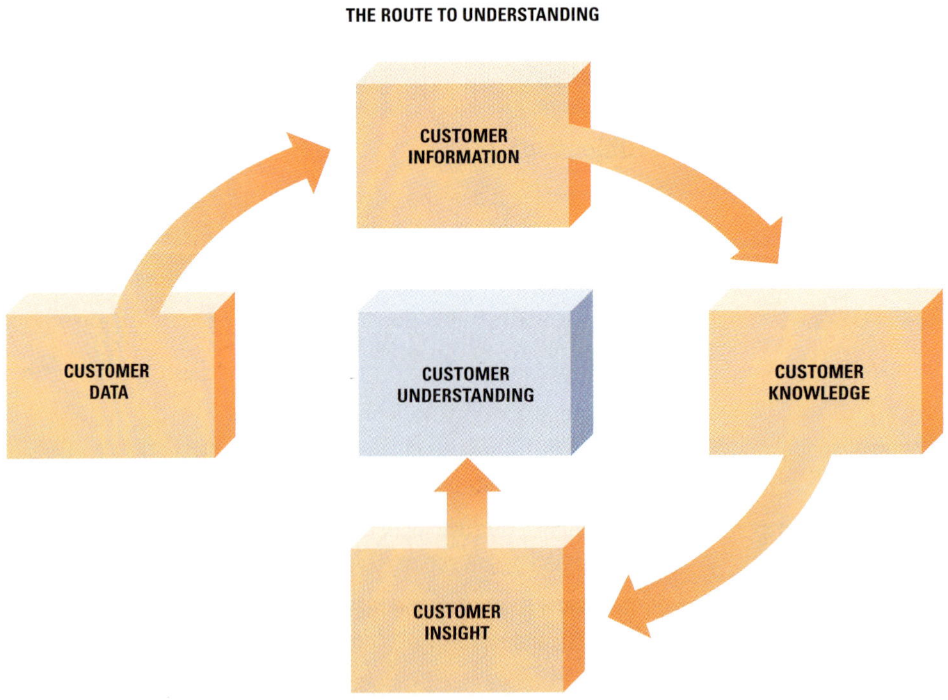

Figure 4-1:
The Path to Customer Understanding

target segment for our store and then decide to organize a "moms and tots" program in the store one morning each week or to provide a children's play area near the change rooms.

Finally, we may decide that we need to probe even more deeply into the minds and lives of customers so that we can truly gain insight into how we can create value for them. This search for deeper insight usually involves qualitative research and the kind of probing that is only possible through in depth interviews and focus groups. For example, the search for a better understanding of young mothers may lead us to do focus groups. In those groups, we are likely to learn that women will avoid dealing with retail clothing stores where the mirrors are outside the change rooms. This is insight that shows that we now understand our customers a little better and can make changes that will likely lead to increased customer satisfaction.

PAGE UP!

1. What is marketing research?
2. What are the different types of questions that market research tries to answer?
3. Discuss the progression from data collection to customer understanding, discussing the importance of each step along the way.

Customer Databases

database
A set of related data that is organized, stored, and regularly updated in computer files. Much of the data are automatically "captured" through the ongoing monitoring of card swipes, billing data, etc.

A great deal of data is available in most companies today; much of it is automatically collected by various systems. These data are organized, stored, and updated in computer **databases**. Often, a database will contain separate data modules on such topics as customers, competitors, industry trends, and environmental changes.

Internally, data are provided by the sales force and by the marketing, manufacturing, and accounting departments. One of the most valuable sources of customer data, for example, already exists in customer accounts and billing files, which provide information on what

MARKETING AT WORK 4-1: STRATEGY

Do-It-Yourself Shopping

Well, the results are in and the research clearly shows that Canadians are becoming increasingly more comfortable with all aspects of self-service retailing, including checking out and bagging their own groceries. In an Ipsos Reid study conducted for NCR, 56 percent of Canadians are more likely to shop at stores with self-service than those without. In 2004, only 27 percent said they preferred stores with self-service checkouts.

Kent Porter, NCR's director of self-service solutions, suggests that the increase is a result of the fact that Canadians are now much more familiar with the technology. They are now much more accustomed to self-serve and it seems we accept new technology very quickly in this country.

In fact, it would appear that Canadians want even more of their shopping experience to go high-tech, mainly because they are seeking greater convenience. For example, 62 percent like it when they can check prices themselves.

They also like it when they can get into and out of a retail store quickly. We Canadians are making more retail trips per week than ever before — 89 percent make between one and seven shopping trips per week — and most often we are buying fewer items per trip. More than 50 percent said they get frustrated standing in line at checkouts.

All of this is leading to a much more automated and high-tech shopping environment in Canadian retail stores; all in the interest of speeding the shopper on her way with a minimum of delay.

QUESTIONS:

1. What are your thoughts about the results of this research study?
2. Could you have predicted many of the results?
3. What questions would you ask Ipsos Reid about how the research was conducted?

SOURCE: Adapted from Rebecca Harris, "Confident Customers," *Marketing Magazine*, April 10, 2006, p. 6.

predictive modelling
Procedures for analyzing data so as to predict, based on past purchase behaviour, the types of products and services customers may be interested in buying, so that targeted marketing programs may be developed.

customers have purchased, when and what they paid for it. Such detailed data is available in large organizations, such as banks and telephone companies, for example. Some users of databases use this kind of data for **predictive modelling**, which seeks to determine which customers would be interested in a particular type of product or service. For example, by scanning its database of credit card customers for individuals who have used their cards to purchase a computer in the past year, a bank could develop an excellent list of customers who would probably be interested in online banking and investment services.

data warehouse
A large collection of data from a variety of internal and external sources, compiled by a firm for use in conducting transactions.

Some organizations move beyond databases to create large and complex **data warehouses** that comprise enormous collections of data from a variety of internal and external sources. These are typically compiled by firms that are conducting transactions with millions of customers. For example, large companies such as banks, major retailers, telephone companies, and credit card companies maintain massive data warehouses that contain data files on each customer, including detailed records of each and every transaction, right down to each use of the credit card, each ATM transaction, and each telephone call.

data mining
Method used to identify patterns and meaningful relationships in masses of data that might be unrecognizable to researchers.

The data in data warehouses can be analyzed in the same way as databases, searching for predetermined patterns in the data. But, because of their size, this would be a slow and cumbersome process. Therefore, more advanced statistical and artificial intelligence techniques are utilized for such processes. Referred to as **data mining,** these techniques have the capability to identify patterns and meaningful relationships in masses of data that otherwise might be overlooked or unrecognizable to researchers.

The way in which a company analyzes and combines the data from databases determines their usefulness in planning and implementing marketing strategy. An impressive example of data mining lies in the use of customer data by the Hudson's Bay Company and Zellers. The HBC Rewards loyalty programs is likely the most comprehensive and potentially far-reaching customer database in Canada. And size is everything — about 85 percent of Canadians go through the doors of The Bay or Zellers every year and the product selection covers approximately 80 percent of the things Canadians buy. When someone buys children's clothes at either store, the retailer has the ability to identify details that effectively identify the gender and age of the customer's children. With data-mining techniques, the company can link and understand cross-shopping behaviour in a way that it may not have been able to understand before. "The loyalty programs give us a snapshot of what customers are buying, where they shop, when they shop, and whether they are full price or discount shoppers," according to Gord Soddenberg, Senior Vice-President of Marketing. Such information has led the company into successfully using what is referred to as 'custom publishing' to specifically target different groups of loyal customers. In this case these publications are 'lifestyle' magazines with editorial content but that focus mostly on showcasing the retailer's products and services. *Living Spree* is distributed to over 500,000 shoppers of The Bay, Zellers, and Home Outfitters targeting the moderate family-oriented segment, while The Bay distributes over 325,000 copies of *Belle*, targeted toward their higher-income, style-conscious customers aged 45 to 55. According to Soddenberg, the information collected through the loyalty programs combined with retail scanner information has provided "a very fine customer loyalty database that allows us to speak to the customer directly."[2]

retail scanner
The electronic device at retail checkouts that reads the bar code on each item, thereby capturing detailed data on every transaction.

Research has allowed marketers to move from undifferentiated, mass marketing to focusing on well-defined market segments. It is now suggested that, through the management of databases, marketers will be able to reach the ultimate level of segmentation — the individual. For example, many online retailers, such as Chapters and Indigo, the major book retailers, (**www.chapters.indigo.ca**) greet returning visitors by name, make recommendations and special offers based on previous purchases, and can hold items in your "shopping cart" between visits, while you are deciding whether or not to buy. The Chapters/Indigo loyalty

Chapters and Indigo

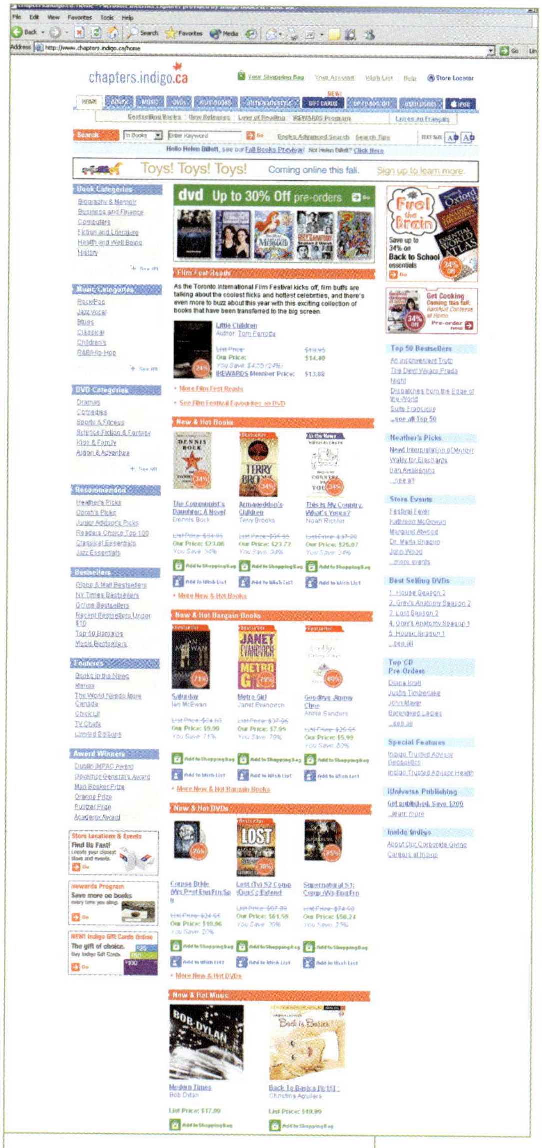

Chapters-Indigo captures data every time you visit their Web site.

program, iRewards, is accepted for online purchases and visitors can even create a wish list of movies, music, and books they would like to eventually own. Online retailers have the ability to monitor and log which site pages were visited and for how long, as well as what site you came from when you came to their sites. These data can be used to prepare special offers to a market of one — especially if you join their mailing list.

Perhaps the most important data source for databases is the **retail scanner**, the electronic device at retail checkouts that reads bar codes located on each product that is purchased. Originally, these were meant simply to speed up the checkout process and reduce errors in supermarkets. With unique bar codes on each item indicating price information, prices did not need to be memorized or checked, and no keying errors could be made entering the price. However, it was soon discovered that the scanner could also be used to improve decisions regarding inventory control and the allotment of shelf space for products.

Many retailers quickly discovered how to extend the use of this technology as a marketing tool and developed what are known as frequent-shopper or loyalty programs. Some benefit or convenience is offered to a consumer for carrying a store's program card and allowing this card to be "swiped" at the time of purchase. To receive the card, the customer provides some personal information that the store retains in a data file. This system enables the store to combine data stored on the card about household demographics and lifestyle with the shopper's scanned purchases. The store is then able to relate product choices to household characteristics and plan product assortment and store layouts to maximize sales potential.

There is an important distinction between data or information that are automatically collected and reside in corporate databases and marketing research projects that are conducted by businesses to obtain answers to specific questions. We now turn our attention to the complex task of obtaining accurate marketing research information.

Approaches to Marketing Research

There are many ways to carry out marketing research — however, there is no single right or wrong way to obtain the information that a company needs. The answer to what research approach should be used depends on the objectives of the research, the information needed, and many practical considerations, such as how much time and money the company has available to devote to the project. **We will discuss the four main approaches to marketing research here, and then present a detailed example of how a marketing research project is actually conducted later in the chapter.**

Essentially, there are four approaches to carrying out marketing research: quantitative, qualitative, observational, and experimental. The approach chosen by a marketer to collect the required information depends on the nature of the problem or question being examined. A major point is that they are not competing approaches. In other words, a marketer or researcher rarely would have to decide whether to use qualitative research or an experimental approach. The approach selected will be dictated by the nature of the problem.

Quantitative or survey research

quantitative research
A form of marketing research that is intended to obtain statistical information about a sample of customers or members of the public; usually relies on surveys to collect the data.

benchmark
The process of comparing a company with its competitors and others in related industries, or comparing the results of one time period with those of another.

survey
A method of gathering data by interviewing a limited number of people (a sample) in person, by telephone or mail, or over the Intenet.

Quantitative research is so named because it involves the measurement of concepts using standard numeric measures such as time, frequency, or monetary units, or specific measures that have been developed to assess customer- or marketing-related concepts, as when we are asked to express our satisfaction with shopping at Loblaws on a 10-point scale. Unlike qualitative research, which is intended to capture the deeply held views of customers, quantitative research has the advantage of using numbers that allow for statistical calculations and comparisons. For example, if a company measures customer satisfaction every six months, it can calculate average satisfaction scores for various groups of customers, compare its performance on customer satisfaction over time, and can then **benchmark** itself against other companies that also measure customer satisfaction.

Most forms of quantitative research involve carrying out a **survey** of customers or prospective customers. A survey consists of gathering data by interviewing people or by having them complete a questionnaire of some type. What distinguishes a survey from qualitative research, such as focus groups or depth interviews, is that, in a survey, the information is usually collected from a fairly large sample of customers, generally several hundred or more, and the results are entered into computer files for analysis. The results of survey research are quantitative in nature because they involve statistical analysis. The advantage of a survey is that information is first-hand. In fact, it may be the only way to determine the opinions or buying intentions of a group of customers or prospective customers.

Certain limitations are inherent in conducting surveys. There are opportunities for error in the construction of the survey questionnaire and in the data collection process. Moreover, surveys can be costly, and they take some time to complete. Other possible weaknesses are that potential respondents sometimes refuse to participate, and the ones who do respond often cannot or will not give accurate answers. **We will discuss surveys in greater detail later in this chapter as an example of how to conduct a marketing research project.**

Quantitative research provides data, but they are data that have been collected to address specific questions. Therefore, the kind of data that are provided through surveys also delivers a great deal of information, thereby moving us farther along the path of customer understanding than is generally possible through automatically collected data that reside in customer databases.

Qualitative research

qualitative research
A form of marketing research intended to provide greater insight into customers' deeply held views, opinions, and feelings; includes focus group interviews and one-on-one depth interviews.

individual depth interview
An approach to qualitative research that involves a one-on-one interview with a customer, usually lasting 90 minutes or more, intended to explore attitudes and opinions in considerable depth.

focus group
An approach to qualitative research that involves interviewing customers in groups of 8 to 10, usually lasting 90 minutes or more, intended to reveal deeply held views.

When research is intended to probe more deeply into opinions and attitudes, qualitative techniques are usually required. **Qualitative research** involves interviewing relatively small numbers of people in considerable depth and for as long as 90 minutes or two hours. The two most widely used qualitative research techniques are the **individual depth interview** and the **focus group** interview.

Qualitative research allows the marketer to gain more insight than is possible using quantitative techniques. Depth interviews and focus groups are valuable when a company wishes to explore in detail and depth an area that they have not looked into before. For example, Deepak Gupta, in our chapter opener, might suggest qualitative research to gain a better understanding of end customers in the pharmaceutical industry and to explore such complex topics as doctor-patient relationships. Qualitative techniques are also often used when marketers want to gain additional information about customer needs and perceptions prior to designing a survey project.

An individual depth interview is used when the researcher wants to probe the customer's thoughts concerning purchase and use of a certain product or service. It is conducted with an

BACK TO THE TOP

individual rather than with a group, because sometimes the topics to be discussed are sensitive ones or because the people are difficult to reach and would be unlikely to attend a focus group session. For example, an individual depth interview is often used to interview business executives and professionals. If Deepak wanted to gain a deeper understanding of the views of doctors toward their patients' use of prescription drugs, he would almost certainly have to use individual depth interviews. Such interviews will generally take more than an hour to complete and range over a number of topics. The interviewer usually conducts the interview using a prepared interview guide.

In the case of a focus group interview, approximately 8 to 10 people are "recruited" to participate. They are usually selected to meet certain criteria relating to demographic characteristics, the use of a particular brand, frequent visits to certain vacation destinations, or similar criteria of interest to the researcher and client. The focus group interviewer or moderator orchestrates the discussion using a loosely structured interview guide, rather than the more structured questionnaire of the typical telephone or Internet survey. Many interesting and enlightening findings are revealed through focus group interviews; this has become one of the most widely used techniques in marketing research.

These are qualitative marketing research techniques, so their results are completely non-quantifiable; typically, no statistics are generated and research reports do not contain any numbers. They do however produce valuable insights into how consumers feel about certain concepts and why they make decisions as they do. The principal use of the focus group interview, for example, is to allow the marketer to really understand why customers are buying one brand over another, why this brand of soap and not that one, why this locally owned fitness centre and not a national chain. The research explores what customers like and dislike about each, and what would have to happen for them to switch to the alternative. The loosely structured focus group is intended to provide marketers with insights that they simply cannot obtain through the more structured answers provided by survey research. Focus groups represent one of the most widely-used marketing research techniques because they are invaluable for gaining the kind of customer insight that is simply not available through surveys.[3]

Online focus groups are becoming more commonplace. Depending on the product and the target group of consumers, in many parts of the country as many as 90 percent of target segment customers are online. The stumbling block has been that until recently marketers have been uncomfortable with the fact that they can't see the research participants. Recent growth and advancements in broadband technology has made possible the interactivity and flexibility to make such an approach more effective — real-time interactivity and the ability to show concepts, videos and virtual 3-D images.

With the use of Webcams and instant messaging, today there are clear benefits to online research: focus groups can be drawn from all corners of the country without the participants having to travel; a geographically-dispersed client-specific sample can be recruited within 24 hours; clients can observe the interaction from their own desks, queries can be answered almost immediately, and online panels are also more affordable. For periodic access to 10 people over a month's time, the price tag can be as low as $5,000.

In the online environment, a focus group would be like a focused chat room with a moderator. Unfortunately, not much research has been conducted to gauge the effectiveness of this focus group format.

Online research requires that participants be technologically savvy — which today means from about 12 years to somewhere around 40 years of age. Of course, this age range will broaden with time, as today's 40-year-olds become 50 and then 60-year-olds. So, while there are legitimate concerns that these groups currently are not representative of the overall

Focus groups provide marketers with valuable insights.

population, it is an effective means of targeting certain consumers and certain age groups. And the validity of this type of research continues to increase as the population becomes increasingly familiar and comfortable with the technology.

Also, there is the question of how participants in focus groups will represent themselves online. While there are those who argue that people are more honest and expressive in this forum because of the anonymity afforded, studies have found that people often misrepresent themselves — perhaps as part of the entertainment value of the Internet. As for being expressive, these focus groups lack the richness of the traditional format, because moderators are unable to observe the group dynamics, facial expressions and body language of participants.

So, while 70 percent or more of Canadian households are online, many marketing researchers are still uncomfortable about seeming to leave out that other 30 percent or so. Many marketers are quickly realizing, however, that amongst their target customers, Internet usage is often at 90 percent or higher. Think, for example, about your group of friends and even about your parents and their friends. Is there anyone who is not actively online? As a result, the use of online research is increasing at a rapid rate in response to the availability of new remote technologies and greater high-speed access.[4]

Observational method

observational method
Gathering data by observing personally or by using technology the actions of a person.

In the **observational method**, data are collected by observing some action of the respondent. No interviews are involved, although an interview may be used as a follow-up to obtain additional information. For example, if customers are observed buying beer in cans instead of bottles, they may be asked why they prefer that form of packaging. We should not adopt a too-restricted view of what constitutes observational research. We can include any form of research that involves the automatic capture of information, where the customer or consumer is being observed by a machine or by technology rather than by another person. In each case, the information is often being collected without the customer's knowledge, which may raise ethical issues.

MARKETING AT WORK 4-2: ETHICS

The Recruiter

Although online focus groups show a great deal of promise, this doesn't mean that the days of watching participants from behind a one-way mirror are over. According to Michele Erskine, of Toronto-based Solutions Research Group Consultants, "You still need to do focus groups in person every now and then, because group dynamics play a factor in real life."

Enter 'The Recruiter,' Dawn Smith. Mild mannered and pleasant in demeanour, this woman knows how to do focus groups. A job she takes very seriously! A few years ago, the Toronto marketing research community started noticing a familiar face in focus groups. Sometimes uninvited, this shady figure would show up in different disguises that even crossed genders. It soon became clear they were dealing with a focus group junkie, whose presence could easily taint research results. It took a while, but Smith and her colleagues were able to identify the person and his "habit" was nipped in the bud!

Smith doesn't mince words when she says she considers it her personal mission to protect the reputation of all marketing research recruiters, because "Recruiters are at the bottom of the food chain," as Smith puts it. They often get caught in the crossfire when things don't work out as they should. Every now and then, a loose screw falls between the cracks — like that often-bearded focus group junkie, who was eventually flagged with 30 names and 15 different telephone numbers — but that doesn't happen too often.

Being a recruiter takes patience and good telephone skills. Recruiters rely on and build their databases most successfully by referral. Good respondents are later asked for potential contacts among friends and family. Of every 10 telephone calls made to referrals, about six people are interested, whereas cold calls average a 1-in-10 success rate.

Focus groups are an easy target for criticism because of the monetary incentive involved. However, while some do it for the money, others do it for the social aspect and yet others like the sense of having participated in the decision process. When recruiting over the telephone, Smith tries to determine how articulate, expressive, and creative the recruit is, but that's not easy. While a screening questionnaire is utilized, that doesn't prevent something from going awry. As Smith says, "It's impossible to tell what people look like, their level of personal hygiene — not to mention whether they'll show up drunk, which can and does happen."

QUESTIONS:

1. Why is it so important to recruiters that individual participants not attend focus groups too often?
2. How can recruiters ensure that they get the "right" people in a focus group?
3. Who are the right people?

SOURCE: Adapted from Lisa D'Innocenzo, "Focus Groups For a New Age," *Strategy,* April 2005, p. 10, and Lesley Young, "The Recruiter," *Marketing Magazine*, July 16, 2001, pp. 8, 9.

In using this approach, researchers may collect information by personal or mechanical observation. In one form of personal observation, the researcher may pose as a customer in a store. This technique is often referred to as "mystery shopping" and is useful in getting information about the calibre of the salespeople or in determining what brands they promote. One example of mechanical observation is the use of an electric cord laid across a highway to count the number of cars that pass during a certain time period. Technology has advanced so rapidly that data are now captured by technology in many different settings. Whenever we use banking machines, we enable the bank to capture a lot of information. The scanners that speed up the process of checking through our groceries at supermarkets also are automatically collecting information about what was purchased. If your supermarket has a frequent-shopper club, the system uses the list of items purchased to update your personal data file. The resulting databases that most large retail firms and others now maintain on their customers are a direct result of data captured through such technology-based observation.

Retailers also find that watching the customer is a valuable way to gauge reactions and attitudes toward store displays and merchandise. In fact, there has been a resurgence of observational research over the past five years, often involving watching customers doing tasks in their own homes. In doing research to develop its Dryel home dry-cleaning product, for example, Procter & Gamble watched people sort laundry in their own homes and Sico watched people paint rooms. Sometimes it's a little sneaky, such as video-recording customers'

Urban Outfitters

reactions without their knowledge; this has also provided valuable input. Urban Outfitters (**www.urbanoutfitters.com**), the specialty clothing and home accessory store, likes to use observation as a marketing research tool. By videotaping and photographing customers in its stores, Urban Outfitters doesn't plan to find out what customers are saying, but rather what they are doing. Managers are then able to determine what customers are wearing and their reactions to displays, etc. This helps them make future merchandise decisions.[5]

Marketers have even found a way to keep an eye on us when we are surfing the Internet. Through the use of "cookies," inactive data files are placed on a visitor's hard drive when the person visits a particular Web site. The cookie records the visitor's activity while connected to the site — which pages were visited, how long was spent in which areas and the links used. The cookie allows the visitor to be identified and welcomed back, making the log-in process quicker; it can keep track of shopping-cart items, or provide customized news, weather, or sports information. Sometimes, based on past purchases, suggestions may be made about other products or services of possible interest. It is only when companies link this information with individual e-mail addresses and make this available to third parties that your personally identifiable information is accessible to other marketers. A common complaint that arises out of this practice concerns consumers' privacy, but there is another issue that should make marketers question its effectiveness. The cookie tracks the activity of the machine, not the actual person using it, so pop-ups and e-mails may be blindly sent to those not in the target group. Another scenario: You search the Web to find a gift for a niece or nephew and suddenly you're receiving banner ads for everything from toys to diapers. The problem: You don't actually have any children.[6]

The observational method has several advantages. It can be highly accurate. Often, it removes all doubt about what the consumer does in a given situation. Consumers are usually unaware that they are being observed, so presumably they act in their usual fashion. The observation technique also reduces interviewer bias. However, the technique is limited in its application: Observation tells what happened, but it cannot tell why. It cannot delve into motives, attitudes, or opinions.

Experimental method

experimental method
A method of gathering primary data in which the researcher is able to observe the results of changing one variable in a situation while holding all others constant.

The **experimental method** involves the gathering of primary data in which the researcher is able to observe the result of changing one variable in a situation while keeping all others constant. Experiments are conducted in simulated or laboratory settings and in the field. In marketing research, the word laboratory is used to describe an environment over which the researcher has complete control during an experiment.

Consider the following example. A Vancouver film producer wanted to determine whether Canadian films would be rented more frequently from video stores if they were identified as being Canadian. To assess this, he set up an experiment with ten Vancouver-area video stores, supplying them with a stock of Canadian videos to put on their shelves. In three stores, the DVDs were mixed in with other films. In another three stores, the Canadian films were displayed separately on their own rack and identified as being Canadian. The remaining four stores, known as the promotional group, put the Canadian films in their own section, stuck little bar signs on each DVD, and promoted them with stickers and posters. Rentals were tracked over six months, and the results indicated that people rented more Canadian films when they were identified as such, and 45 percent more when they were promoted. These results, incidentally, conflict with the conventional view that Canadians are not interested in films made in this country — information that is of great interest to the Canadian film industry.[7]

Laboratory experiments can be used to test virtually any component of marketing strategy. However, it is important to recognize that the setting is unnatural and that consumers' responses may be biased by the situation.

test marketing
A marketing research technique in which, before committing to a major marketing effort, a firm markets its product in a limited geographic area, measures the sales, and then, from this sample, projects (a) the company's sales over a larger area and/or (b) consumer response to a strategy.

An experiment carried out in the field (that is, under actual market conditions), is called **test marketing**. It is similar to a laboratory experiment but is conducted under more realistic conditions. The researcher therefore has less control. In test marketing, the researcher duplicates real market conditions in a small geographic area to measure consumer response to a strategy before the company commits itself to a major marketing effort. Test marketing may be undertaken to forecast sales or to evaluate different marketing mixes. Test marketing methodology is used to test new products before a national launch, to evaluate pricing strategies, to obtain feedback on aspects of an advertisement, or to establish the effectiveness of an advertising campaign in influencing buying behaviour. Advertising testing is sometimes done by running two versions of the same advertisement and assessing changes in purchasing behaviour in each area.

The advantage of field experiments over laboratory experiments is their realism; however, there are several disadvantages. Test marketing is expensive (spending $500,000 or more to complete a test is not uncommon), time-consuming (9 to 12 months is normal), and impossible to keep secret from competitors (who may intentionally disrupt the test by temporarily changing their marketing programs). Another problem is the researcher's inability to control the situation. For example, a company that is test marketing a new product may encounter a certain amount of publicity while the product is in the test market, simply because of the innovativeness of the product. Although such publicity would normally be considered a good thing, when faced with it in a test market situation, the marketer is not sure about the extent to which the publicity has distorted the sales results. In other words, what volume of sales resulted from the product and the regular marketing efforts of the company (what was actually being tested), and what resulted from the publicity that was generated?

PAGE UP!

1. What is predictive modelling?
2. What is data mining and in what ways is this information collected?
3. Name the four approaches that a firm can use when it conducts marketing research.

Conducting Marketing Research Projects

The carrying out of occasional marketing research projects is a major part of marketing research. Some of these projects are non-recurring, in the sense that they are conducted only once to address a particular issue, such as a decision on a new package design. Others are repeated periodically, as they are intended to update management's knowledge about a particular subject; for example, a company may have a policy of measuring aspects of customer satisfaction and loyalty every 12 months. Examples of marketing research projects were described briefly in Table 4-1. Most marketing research projects follow the procedure outlined in Figure 4-2. Let's examine what goes into conducting a marketing research project. **We will use a customer survey as our example, simply because survey research will allow us to illustrate all of the various stages and components that go into the making of a reliable research project. Also, survey research still remains the most widely-used approach to research.**

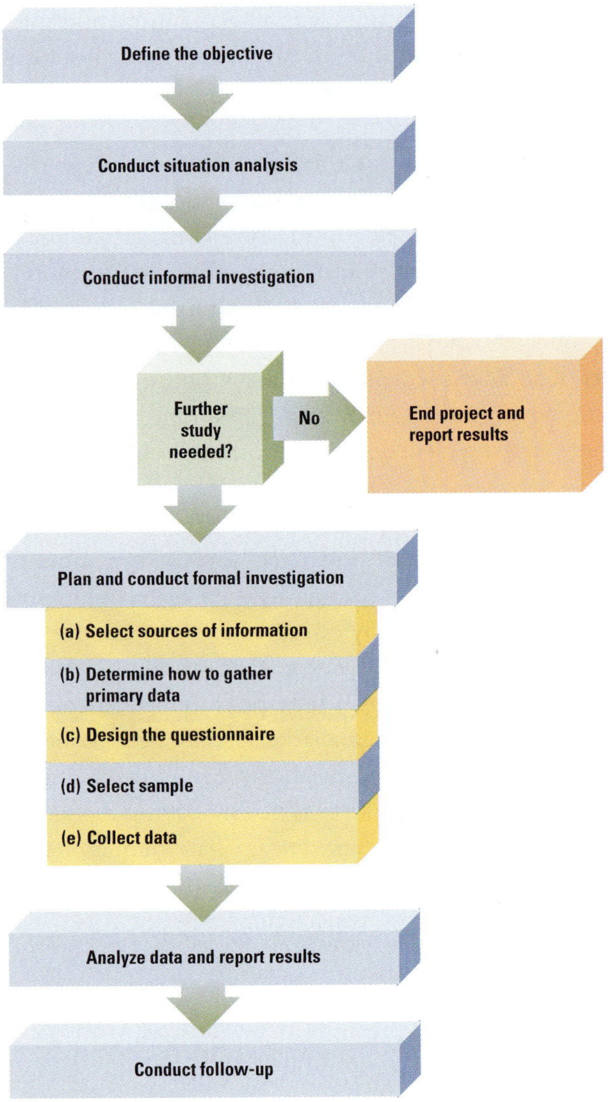

Figure 4-2: Marketing Research Procedure

1. Define research objectives

Marketers need a clear idea of what they are trying to learn — the **research objectives** of the project, why research is needed. Usually the objective is to solve a problem, but this is not always the case. Often the objective is to obtain information that will allow the firm to define the problem. Sometimes it's simply to determine if there is a problem. For example, in our chapter opener, it is important that the executives of PharmaNational determine precisely what it is they need to know about patients in the context of pharmaceutical products. This is an unexplored area for them and they need to make quite clear what it is they want and need to know to allow them to embark on a new approach to marketing. It is critically important that the marketer clearly identifies the research objectives. Failure to do so often means that the most important information is not obtained. After specifying the research objectives, the marketer is ready for the next step — situation analysis.

2. Conduct a situation analysis

Next, the marketer and the researcher who is actually conducting the project will try to get a "feel" for the situation surrounding the problem. They analyze the company, its market, its competition, and the industry in general. Situation analysis is a background investigation that helps in refining the research problem and objectives. It involves obtaining information about the company and its business environment by library research and interviewing company officials. This process generally relies on the use of **secondary data**, meaning that the data already exist in some other form, often available from outside organizations such as Statistics Canada or trade associations.

Secondary data can be especially valuable at this stage of a research project in giving the marketer some additional information about the situation he or she is facing. Secondary data can be obtained from sources such as those presented in Table 4-2 and have the obvious advantage of being readily available at low cost or even free. Much secondary data are "in the public domain," meaning that they are available for anyone's use. This is the case with data from most governments and their agencies.

But secondary data should be used with caution, mainly because they are not likely to pertain directly to the situation the marketer is facing. They represent a good place to start to obtain an overview of the market or of the characteristics of a particular customer segment. For example, a marketer can obtain an understanding of how many people there are aged 25-44 in the Halifax Region, or of how many wholesalers operate in the province of Manitoba. Such information may reveal trends at an industry or regional level and may, as a result, confirm that the company is looking in the right direction. It should always be kept in mind, however, that secondary data were not collected for precisely the reason that the marketer needs information. As valuable as they are, they should always be used with caution.

Marketers may, on occasion, come across studies that have been done by other companies or not-for-profit organizations such as the Conference Board of Canada. Such studies may address subjects that may be closely related to the area of interest of a specific company, but

research objectives
The purpose of conducting the research; questions the marketer and researcher want to have addressed and areas that they want to have explored.

secondary data
Information already gathered by somebody else for some other purpose. They represent a valuable starting point to a research project to provide the marketer with top-line information about a marketing problem or opportunity.

TABLE 4-2 Key Sources of Secondary Data

Information is power, but only if it is the right information. Take the time to learn how to find and evaluate secondary sources.

General Marketing Intelligence

- Canadian Marketing Association, www.the-cma.org — Canada's largest marketing organization with lots of current articles on marketing topics.
- American Marketing Association, www.marketingpower.com — access to AMA publications and more.
- BuildingBrands, www.buildingbrands.com — information on brands and how to build them.
- AllAboutBranding, www.allaboutbranding.com — a very comprehensive site dedicated to examining all aspects of branding.
- Canadian Institute of Marketing, www.cinstmarketing.ca — "Where marketers become professionals through knowledge and experience."
- Marketing Research and Intelligence Association, http://mria-arim.com — a Canadian not-for-profit association representing all aspects of the market intelligence and survey research industry.
- Marketing Profs, www.marketingprofs.com/index.asp — marketing know-how from professionals and professors.
- Marketing Research Association, www.mra-net.org — an association of the opinion and market research profession.

Internal Sources — annual reports, profit and loss statements, sales figures, balance sheets, and prior research conducted by the organization.

- On company Web sites
- At SEDAR, www.sedar.com, for public companies and investment funds which file with the Canadian Securities Administrators (CSA).

OTHER SOURCES OF SECONDARY DATA

The best place to start a search for other secondary sources used to be the library — and it still is. With the growth of the World Wide Web, most libraries have expanded their collections to include digital resources that are accessible from your computer. In addition to books and journals, many statistical resources, especially those from Statistics Canada, are available only to persons with up-to-date library cards/logins.

Current Awareness

- Community/local newspapers.
- Business newspapers:
  The Globe and Mail, www.theglobeandmail.com
  National Post, www.canada.com/nationalpost/index.html
- Canadian Corporate Newsnet, www.cdn-news.com
- Canadian Newswire, www.newswire.ca

Magazines and Journals

- If you just want to read them, use your library's catalogue to find:
  Harvard Business Review
  Journal of Marketing
  Journal of Retailing
  Marketing Magazine
  Strategy Magazine
  American Demographics
- If you are looking for articles on a topic, use an index:
  Business source elite
  CBCA business
  Factiva
  Wilson omnifile

Canadian Government Publications

- Industry Canada, www.strategis.ic.gc.ca
- Statistics Canada, www.statcan.ca/start.html — some available only through a library catalogue.
  Wholesaling and Retailing in Canada (63-236)
  Canadian Economic Observer (11-010)
  Family Food Expenditures in Canada (62-554)
  Market Research Handbook (63-224)
  CANSIM which prepares up-to-date statistics at http://cansim2.statcan.ca/
- Additional information can also be available from specific Canadian (http://canada.gc.ca/main_e.html) or provincial government departments.
- Foreign Affairs Canada at www.dfait-maeci.gc.ca and the Business Development Bank of Canada at www.bdc.ca for Canadian companies researching international business opportunities.

will not be directly pertinent. They are valuable, however, in giving a marketer a "top-line" view of what is going on in his or her market and among target customer groups.

In the situation analysis stage, researchers also try to refine the problem definition and develop hypotheses for testing. A **research hypothesis** is a tentative supposition that, if proven, would suggest a possible solution to a problem. Some examples of testable hypotheses are:

research hypothesis
A tentative supposition that, if proven, would suggest a possible solution to a problem.

- Sales of grocery items are significantly greater when the items are placed in end-of-aisle displays than when they are located only in their normal aisle positions.
- Prescriptions that doctors write for children are more likely to be filled than are those written for elderly patients.
- Bank customers who use ATMs and telephone banking services will accept and adopt Internet banking.
- Demand for MP3 players will increase proportionally to the increasing availability of downloadable music through the Internet.
- Consumers in rural areas of Canada are more inclined to buy locally produced products and services than are those living in larger centres.

The project then turns to generating data that can be used to test the correctness of the hypotheses.

informal investigation
The stage in a marketing research study at which information is gathered from people outside the company, such as distribution channel members, competitors, advertising agencies, and customers.

3. Conduct an informal investigation

Now having a feel for the problem, the researchers are ready to collect some preliminary data from the marketplace. This **informal investigation** consists of gathering readily available information from people inside and outside the company — distribution channel members, competitors, advertising agencies, and customers, for example.

The informal investigation is a critical step in a research project, because it will determine whether further study is necessary. Decisions can frequently be made with information gathered in the informal investigation. For example, a company considering opening sales offices for its computer software support service in western Canada might first talk with representatives of trade associations representing the personal computer industry and with officials of companies that supply computers and software. Before contacting any prospective clients for its new service, the company would be interested in getting a feel for the market and for the extent to which demand for software support is being satisfied. The conclusion at this stage may be that the market is large enough to warrant further investigation. The company's representatives might then meet with office managers or information systems managers of prospective clients in cities such as Edmonton, Calgary, and Vancouver to discuss informally their needs for software support, where they are currently buying such a service, and what they would look for in a new entrant into the market.

Much valuable information is obtained through an informal market investigation. The company not only will learn a great deal about the market it proposes to enter, it will also determine whether further study is needed. A decision on the main problem can often be made with information gathered at the informal investigation stage

Marketers need research to understand why consumers buy products like the Game Boy.

4. Plan and conduct a formal investigation

If the project warrants continued investigation, the marketer and researcher must determine what additional information is needed and how to gather it. This usually involves the part of a marketing research project that we normally think of when we think of research — the actual design and carrying out of the project. At this stage, a series of decisions are made concerning the nature of the project to be conducted: Should it be qualitative or quantitative? From whom will information be obtained? How many people should we talk to? What questions should we ask? And so on. The first step is to decide where the necessary information can be obtained.

primary data
Original data gathered specifically for the project at hand.

syndicated data
Research information that is purchased from a research supplier on a shared-cost basis by a number of clients.

4(a) Select sources of information Primary data, secondary data, or both can be used in an investigation. **Primary data** are original data gathered specifically for the project at hand. Secondary data have already been gathered for some other purpose. For example, when researchers conduct personal interviews, perhaps to have individuals complete questionnaires over the telephone, they are collecting primary data. When they obtain information from Statistics Canada or from the local chamber of commerce, they are using a secondary source.

One mistake often made in marketing research is to collect primary data before exhausting the information available in secondary sources. Ordinarily, secondary information can be gathered much faster and at far less expense than can primary data.

Syndicated data represent a third source of information and are a hybrid between primary and secondary data. Syndicated data are collected by a research supplier and may be purchased from that supplier by a number of clients, some of whom may be in direct competition with one another. The most common form of syndicated data involves the collection of data on a regular basis from an established sample or panel of consumers or retail stores. Clients subscribe to the reports that are produced by the research company and essentially share the cost of collecting the data from the large sample. Although syndicated research does not provide privileged information to a single company, it does allow companies to obtain information on a shared-cost basis.

4(b) Gathering primary data After exhausting the available secondary sources considered pertinent, researchers may still lack sufficient data. If so, they must turn to primary sources and gather or purchase the information. In a company's research project, for instance, a researcher may interview the firm's salespeople, wholesalers or retailers, or customers to obtain the market information needed. Important decisions have to be made regarding from whom the information is to be obtained.

There are four widely used methods of gathering primary data, as we discussed earlier in this chapter: quantitative research, qualitative research, the observational method, and the experimental method. Normally, all four are not used on the same project, although more than one may be. Because each method has strengths and weaknesses, the choice of which to use depends on the nature of the problem, but it will also be influenced by how much time and money are available for the project. **Because it is the most frequently used approach to obtain marketing research information and is usually more complex than other approaches, we will use survey research to illustrate how a research project may be conducted.**

personal interview
A face-to-face method of gathering data in a survey.

Survey data collection is usually conducted either in person, by telephone, by mail, or through the Internet. Personal interviews are more flexible than the other types because interviewers can probe more deeply if an answer is incomplete. Ordinarily, it is possible to obtain more information by **personal interview** than by telephone or mail. Also the interviewer, by observation, (particularly if the interview is being conducted in the respondent's home) can obtain data regarding the respondents' socio-economic status — their homes, neighbourhoods, and apparent standard of living.

mall intercept
A method of gathering data by conducting personal interviews in central locations, typically regional shopping centres.

Rising costs and other problems associated with door-to-door interviewing have prompted many marketing researchers to survey people in central locations, typically regional shopping centres. This technique is called the **mall intercept** method of interviewing. By interviewing people as they pass through a shopping mall, the interviewer is better able to encounter large numbers of people, as the urban mall has essentially become the "main street" of North America. Although data collection is made somewhat easier by this method, the researcher is less confident that a representative sample of the population of interest is being obtained. In such a situation, the ability to access large numbers of people at relatively low cost outweighs concerns about the representativeness of the sample.

telephone survey
A method of gathering data in a survey by interviewing people over the telephone.

In a **telephone survey**, the respondent is contacted by telephone, and the interview is completed at that time. Participants in telephone surveys are usually selected at random from telephone directories or by randomly dialling telephone numbers. If a company wants to obtain information from its own customers, it could provide the researchers with a list from which those to be called may be selected at random. Telephone surveys usually can be conducted more rapidly and at less cost than either personal interviews or mail surveys. Since a number of interviewers can make many calls from a call centre, this method is quite easy to administer. Computer-assisted techniques have broadened the scope of telephone interviewing. These techniques involve automated random-number dialling and a facility for the interviewer to record the respondent's answers directly into computer files as they are received. This technology speeds up the entry and processing of data and the production of reports.

"On a scale from 1 to 10, how interested are you in eating at a vegetarian restaurant?"

A telephone survey can be timely. It can be launched quickly in response to an event that the marketer may wish to explore. For example, a telephone survey may be the most efficient way to get feedback from customers who have been invited to a golf tournament or a fashion show. One limitation of the telephone survey is that interviews cannot be too long, although telephone interviews that take up to 30 minutes to complete are not uncommon. In fact, one of the myths of telephone interviewing is that the questionnaire must be very short, because participants will not be willing to stay on the line for more than a minute or so. This is simply not true, as many Canadians are quite co-operative in participating in telephone surveys that take 5 to 10 minutes to complete.

One difficulty with telephone research is that fewer people are at home today, and those who are at home are becoming more difficult to reach. Although there appears to be no dramatic increase in the frequency of unlisted numbers, more and more people are installing telephone answering machines or subscribing to services such as voice mail and call display. Many people who have such devices or services are using them to screen incoming calls, forcing callers to leave messages, or are choosing not to answer the call if they do not recognize the number or name displayed. As well, more and more Canadians do not have a phone at home and rely exclusively on their cellphones. The result is that telephone interviewers are unable to reach an increasing percentage of the population, thereby making telephone interviewing more costly and resulting in more biased samples. The situation is further complicated by the "do-not-call" legislation that came into effect in Canada in late 2005, mainly to restrict nuisance calls from telemarketing organizations. While marketing research companies are exempt from this legislation, it nevertheless reflects a growing reluctance on the part of Canadians to having their privacy interrupted by unsolicited telephone calls. The low response rates that result generally translate into an under-representation of younger people, males, and professionals or senior executives.[8]

Telephone surveys have been used successfully to reach professionals and executives at work. When preceded by a letter or fax introducing the study and a short call to make an appointment for the actual interview, these surveys can elicit a very high co-operation rate.

mail survey
Gathering data by means of a questionnaire mailed to respondents and, when completed, returned by mail.

Collecting marketing research information through **mail surveys** involves mailing a questionnaire to prospective respondents and having them return the completed form by mail. Since no interviewers are used, this type of survey is not hampered by interviewer bias or problems connected with the management of interviewers. Mailed questionnaires are more economical than personal interviews and are useful in national surveys. If the respondents remain anonymous, they are more likely to give true answers because they are not biased by the presence of an interviewer.

A major problem with mail surveys is the compilation of a good mailing list, especially for a broad-scale survey. If the sample can be drawn from a limited list, however, such as customers of a particular company, or subscribers to a certain magazine, the list presents no problem. Another significant limitation concerns the reliability of the questionnaires returned. The researchers have no control over who actually completes the questionnaire or how thoroughly it is done. In addition, because there is no personal contact with the respondents, it is impossible to judge how much care and thought went into providing the answers.

Another limitation is that there is usually a low response rate to a mail survey. It is not uncommon to receive completed replies from 10 percent or less of those contacted. Techniques for improving mail response rates have been the subject of many experiments. Some of these include making the subject matter of the survey as interesting as possible, offering incentives to the participant to encourage involvement, and guaranteeing anonymity. In the case of mailed questionnaires, a higher response rate can be obtained by paying for return postage and by sending a reminder note or card, or even a second questionnaire, within a week or so of mailing the original.

Because of the lack of control over the process, increased postal rates, low response rates, and the time needed to mail out questionnaires and to receive the completed ones, most marketing researchers are using far fewer mail surveys than was the case several years ago. They are being replaced by surveys that employ technology that makes participating much easier, including "fax-out, fax-back" and the sending of questionnaires by e-mail.

As already discussed, the use of Internet surveys to collect data is rapidly on the rise. Questionnaires can be posted on a firm's Web site or e-mailed to a sample of individuals. Speed and cost are the two most obvious advantages of this approach — transmission is electronic, providing speed and significant personnel and material savings. The technology also allows for the very efficient administration of the survey in that it will automatically skip sections of the questionnaire that do not apply to the respondent.

Internet research
Customer research conducted through the use of surveys administered through the Internet, either by sending questionnaires by e-mail or by having customers enter a secure Web site.

The disadvantages of **Internet research** are decreasing with time as more and more segments of the population can be reached through the Internet. Clearly, the risk of bias still exists with certain age groups and for certain types of products. Not all consumers can be reached through the Internet. But, use of the Internet continues to expand at a rapid pace, with literally 100 percent of customers in some segments now online. For example, this may be the best way for companies such as PharmaNational in our chapter opener to conduct research with business or professional customers. As most doctors' offices are now online, Deepak Gupta may propose doing an online survey of doctors to better understand the image of his company among family physicians and specialists.

Internet-based surveys represent a very cost-efficient way of conducting research amongst specific groups. For example, in business-to-business research, many companies will have a list of their contacts at customer organizations, complete with their e-mail addresses. Similarly, many retail stores are collecting the e-mail addresses of their customers when they register for credit cards. Obviously, Internet retailers like amazon.ca and chapters.indigo.ca automatically have the e-mail addresses of their customers and can easily send surveys to selected groups. Companies that operate frequent shopper or frequent guest programs such as Aeroplan or Delta Hotels can send surveys online to their members. Zoomerang.com is an online research company that operates an online panel of 2.5 million people who have agreed to be available to complete marketing research surveys online.

Despite the rapidly increasing access to the Internet, it is still often not possible to verify the identity of the respondent, quality e-mail address lists of potential participants are hard to find, and it is difficult to provide effective incentives. This new medium also brings with it a new manifestation of bias. Reliability of data is a concern, because people have the tendency to "reinvent" themselves online. Some respondents lie about their identity online. While validity scales are built into almost all surveys to ensure consistency of responses, this is still a major concern with the use of the Internet for research. To promote honest responses, online marketers sweeten the pot with offers of electronic coupons, instant online shopping coupons, contests, and sweepstakes. To participate in these, respondents are required to submit personal information such as e-mail and mailing addresses. As the Internet becomes a more universally used medium, there is no doubt that the use of online surveys will increase.

PAGE UP!

1. What is a research hypothesis?
2. What is the difference between primary data and secondary data?
3. What are some of the challenges and limitations of conducting Internet research?

MARKETING AT WORK 4-3: TECHNOLOGY

TrueLoot! It's True, Loot for Surfing the Net!

When did checking your e-mail become a marketing research activity designed to build customer profiles? There are many Web sites today that are intended to capture marketing research information on behalf of their clients. They send questionnaires through the Web, or they simply track the usage patterns of customers like you as you go about texting or checking out Web sites.

TrueLoot.com wants to reward you for surfing the Web, checking your e-mail, and simply using text messaging on your cellphone! Users earn TrueLoot points for choosing to receive small text ads on your cellphone and surfing your favourite sites. Points can be redeemed for cash and prizes.

In a nutshell, companies pay TrueLoot to advertise to appropriate members, enabling the company to reward subscribers for receiving their special offers. There are three ways to earn points: the TrueLoot AdBar, e-mail advertisements, and/or mobile text ads received on your cellphone. Subscribers choose how they wish to earn points and the types of advertising they wish to receive. But wait, it gets better. Not only will they pay you to use their service, but also pay you when you refer friends — you earn 5 percent of their monthly points earnings! And, you'll be rewarded when your friends sign up their friends!

Receiving and clicking the link in an e-mail ad earns you five points for confirming receipt of the e-mail, and even more points if you act on the offer. Text messaging ads yield you 15 points for replying to the ad and letting TrueLoot know you received the message. As the service grows allowing advertisements to become more and more targeted, the pay rate to users is expected to increase.

QUESTIONS:

1. What types of information do companies such as TrueLoot capture on customers who participate in their programs?
2. To whom is such information likely to be of interest?
3. What are the limitations of this information?

SOURCE: Adapted from Paula Baker, "Online Research — Faster, Easier,...Better?" *Strategy,* February 2005, p. 25, and the TrueLoot Company Website, www.trueloot.com.

questionnaire
A data-gathering form used to collect information in a personal, telephone, Internet, or mail survey.

interview guide
The equivalent of a questionnaire used in qualitative research; a list of semi-structured questions or areas of enquiry designed to guide the depth interview or focus group.

4(c) Designing the questionnaire Whether interviewing or observing subjects, or having respondents complete questionnaires on their own, as in the case of a mail or Internet survey, researchers use a questionnaire or form on which there are instructions and spaces to record responses. It is not easy to design a data gathering form that elicits precisely the information needed. When conducting surveys, researchers use **questionnaires** that are fairly structured and generally provide a number of responses, asking respondents or interviewers to check the most appropriate response or to write in an answer. When conducting focus group interviews or depth interviews, researchers use **interview guides** that are much less structured and ensure that the interviewer raises all of the topics that must be covered during the interview.

Depending on whether questionnaires or interview guides are being used, different considerations apply. If the researcher is to obtain qualitative information through focus groups or depth interviews, no statistical analysis can be performed. The interpretation of these results is quite subjective and will consist of conclusions drawn from the comments made by participants during the interviews. On the other hand, if the researcher chooses to obtain quantitative data, usually through survey research, such information will lend itself quite readily to statistical analysis. Therefore, the appropriate instrument, whether a questionnaire or a less formal interview guide, must be designed in such a way as to ensure that the relevant information is obtained and that it is collected in a form that will allow for analysis.

The following represent some factors that must be considered when designing forms for the collection of research data:

- ***Question wording:*** If a question is misunderstood, the data it produces are worthless. Questions should be written with the potential respondent in mind. Vocabulary, reading level, and familiarity with jargon all must be considered. A common wording error is to inadvertently include two questions in one. For example, the question "How would you evaluate the speed and efficiency of our service?" followed by a rating scale that ranges from "poor" to "excellent" is likely to cause problems. Some respondents may see the service as fast, which is good, but with too many mistakes, which is bad.
- ***Response format:*** Questions asked in survey research are generally designed either for check-mark responses (such as yes or no, multiple choice, agree or disagree scales) or open-ended replies. Open-ended questions allow the respondent to use his or her own words in answering. They are more often associated with depth interviews, are easier to prepare, and frequently produce richer answers, but require more effort from the respondent and therefore lower the level of co-operation. In addition, in a mail survey, it is often difficult to read and interpret open-ended responses. Open-ended questions are used most often in personal or telephone interviews, when the interviewer can probe for explanations and additional details.
- ***Questionnaire layout:*** The normal procedure when constructing a questionnaire for use in a survey is to begin with easy, general questions and move to more difficult, complicated, and specific questions. To understand behaviour, researchers must sometimes ask questions about possibly sensitive topics (for example, personal hygiene) or private matters (age, income). These questions are normally placed close to the end of a questionnaire.
- ***Pre-testing:*** All questionnaires should be pre-tested on a small group of respondents who are similar to the intended sample. **Pre-testing** is designed to identify problems in the design of the questionnaire and to allow for corrections and refinements to be made prior to the actual study.

pre-testing
The process of testing a questionnaire before it is used in a survey, to identify problems and areas of confusion.

Many books have been written on questionnaire design. Extreme care and skill are needed to produce a questionnaire that maximizes the likelihood of obtaining a response while minimizing bias, misunderstanding, and respondent irritation.

sample
A smaller group which is selected to be interviewed or from whom data are to be collected; chosen so as to be representative of the larger population.

population
The group of particular interest to the researcher about which conclusions are to be drawn; usually a specific group or segment of customers.

random sample
A sample that is selected in such a way that every unit in the defined universe has a known probability of being selected. It is usually not possible to obtain a completely random sample. As a result, most research projects will use a sample that is as representative as possible of the population of interest.

convenience sample
A sample that is selected in a non-random way, so that every member of the universe does not have an equal chance of being included.

4(d) Sampling It is, of course, not necessary to interview or observe every person who could shed light on a research problem. It is sufficient to collect data from a sample if its reactions are expected to be representative of an entire group. The key in marketing research is whether the sample provides accurate information.

The fundamental idea underlying sampling is that a small number of items — a **sample** — if properly selected from a larger number of items — a **population** — will have the same characteristics in about the same proportion as the larger group. Obtaining reliable data with this method requires the right technique in selecting the sample. The two main issues to be addressed in selecting a sample are, first, to ensure that the sample is representative of the population of interest and, second, to have a large enough sample to have confidence that the results can be generalized for a larger population.

Improper sampling is a source of error in many studies. One firm, for example, selected a sample of calls from all of the calls made to its call centre and used the information to make generalizations about its customers. Would you be comfortable saying that these callers are a representative sample of all of the firm's customers or even all of the dissatisfied ones? When selecting a sample of Canadians, for example, it is important to reflect Canada's multicultural makeup and to ensure that various cultural groups are represented. It may be necessary to administer such surveys in a number of different languages. Many airlines, hotels, and restaurants also use comment cards to obtain feedback from customers. The danger in generalizing from this information relates to the issue of who completes comment cards. The sample is self-selected and as such has built-in biases.

Although numerous sampling techniques are used, only representative samples of the population of interest are appropriate for making generalizations from a sample to the population. A **random sample** is selected in such a way that every member of the population has a known probability of being included. In fact, unless the researcher has a list of all members of the population, it is virtually impossible to select a random sample. As a result, marketing researchers generally attempt to select a sample that is as representative of the population as possible.

Most of the samples used in marketing research surveys would be considered **convenience samples**. For example, interviews are often conducted in shopping centres, where large numbers of people are conveniently available. These are quite common in marketing research for two reasons. First, random samples are very difficult to obtain. Even though the researcher may select the subjects in a random fashion, there is no guarantee that all of those who are selected will participate. Some will be unavailable and others will refuse to co-operate. As a result, researchers often resort to carefully designed convenience samples that reflect the characteristics of the population as closely as possible. Second, not all research is done with the objective of generalizing to a population. Sometimes the company is interested in interviewing customers who visit a certain store or who telephone for service. In these cases, a convenience sample may be considered representative of the overall population. For example, if we want to assess whether regular users of a shopping centre are favourably disposed to changes in the customer service desk, a convenience sample may be appropriate for this situation.

How large should a sample be? With random sampling methods, a sample must be large enough to be truly representative of the population; thus, the size will depend on the diversity of characteristics of the population. All basic statistics books contain general formulas for calculating sample size. It is not, however, a simple matter to determine the appropriate size of a sample. The choice of sample size is normally made after consideration of a wide variety of factors.

Many researchers have rules of thumb that they use in deciding on sample size. Some, for example, would not consider using a sample of fewer than 400, as this sample size provides an acceptable level of confidence in the results — it is a sample of 400 that provides the confidence often associated with public opinion polls, namely that the results are accurate within plus or minus 5 percent, 19 times out of 20. Generally, a sample of 1,000 or more would be considered acceptable by any standards, as it will provide a high degree of confidence. A problem arises, however, if the marketer wants to examine a subgroup of, for example, Audi or BMW drivers out of a sample of 1,000 owners of luxury cars. If there are only 24 Audi owners in the sample, the research is then very restricted in drawing conclusions about Audi owners because it is based on such a small sub-sample.

4(e) Data collection Earlier in this chapter, we outlined the various approaches that can be used to collect research information. Collection of primary data by interviewing, observation, or distributing a survey over the Internet is often the weakest link in the research process. Ordinarily, in all other steps, it's possible to ensure accuracy. However, these efforts may be lost if interviewers are inadequately trained or supervised. Interviewers must understand the importance of maintaining the integrity of the data collection methods. In other words, if it has been decided that they need to interview every third person entering a store and this is how the sample is being selected, they cannot decide to interview the first 20 people because it is more convenient. Such interference with methodology can significantly bias the results. In their training, interviewers should be given a basic understanding of research methodologies so that they can relate to the importance of the procedures used and understand why these must not be changed in any way.

Motivating interviewers is often difficult, because they frequently are part-time workers doing what is often a monotonous task. As a result, many problems may crop up at the point of data collection. For instance, poorly trained interviewers may fail to establish rapport with respondents or may change the wording of questions. In extreme cases, there have even been instances where interviewers have attempted to fake the responses!

5. Data analysis and reporting

data analysis
The process of extracting relevant information from data collected through research; usually associated with the application of statistical tools.

The value of research is determined by its results. Since data cannot speak for themselves, analysis and interpretation are key components of any project. **Data analysis** software packages have made it possible for researchers to tabulate and process masses of quantitative data quickly and inexpensively. This tool can be abused, however. Managers have little use for large volumes of computer output. Researchers must be able to identify pivotal relationships, spot trends, and find patterns — that's what transforms data into useful information. Proper coding of information assists in this process. Coding enables the researcher to determine how the data are to be presented to ensure efficiency of interpretation. Qualitative data, such as the results of focus groups and depth interviews, are more time-consuming and more difficult to analyze than quantitative data. It is very important to have clearly articulated the research objectives at the beginning of the project. Understanding what questions the research is designed to address makes it much easier to determine what the results are saying. Sometimes trends or patterns will develop that are not anticipated in the planning stages. Good researchers must be able to interpret these findings relative to the research objectives.

The end product of the investigation is the researcher's conclusions and recommendations. Most projects require a written report, often accompanied by a presentation to management. Here, communication skill becomes a factor. Not only must researchers be able to write and speak effectively, they also must adopt the perspective of the manager in presenting research results.

6. Following up

Researchers should follow up their studies to determine whether their results and recommendations are being used. Management may choose not to use a study's findings for several reasons. The problem that generated the research may have been wrongly defined, become less urgent, or even have disappeared. Or, the research may have been completed too late to be useful. Without a follow-up, the researcher has no way of knowing if the project was on target and met management's needs or if it fell short, and an important source of information for improving research in the future would be ignored.

By this time, you have probably realized that doing good marketing research is not easy. It takes a well-designed set of objectives with a research methodology suitable to address these objectives. Unfortunately, research is not always done well. When interpreting research information, you should assess the methods used and be careful not to make generalizations that are not substantiated.

Who Does Marketing Research?

Marketing research can be done by a firm's own personnel or by outside researchers. Sometimes a job is divided, with company personnel doing parts of a project and using an outside research specialist for such tasks as collecting data or developing approaches for the analysis of data.

Within the company

Separate marketing research departments exist primarily in larger companies and are usually quite small. The department might consist of only a single manager or could have as many as four or five professionals in large consumer-products companies. In most of these situations, the marketing research department rarely conducts research utilizing its own staff, but rather contracts the work out to suppliers. The primary role of the marketing research department, therefore, is to organize, monitor, and co-ordinate marketing research, which may be done by a number of different suppliers across the country. The manager of the marketing research department reports either to the marketing director or VP or directly to top management. The researchers who staff this department must be well versed in company procedures and know what information is already available within the company. They must also be familiar with the relative strengths and weaknesses of potential marketing research suppliers.

Outside the company

A sign of the growth in the use of marketing research is the fact that there are a great many companies across the country from which a marketing manager may seek help for marketing research problems. In Canada today, several hundred companies operate in the field of marketing research. When a marketing manager requires information on Canadian marketing research suppliers, a number of sources exist that can be consulted to obtain a list of potential suppliers. One listing of such suppliers is the Research Buyer's Guide available through the newly formed Marketing Research & Intelligence Association (**www.mria-arim.ca**). This directory provides detailed information on companies that operate in Canada in marketing research and related fields.

Mria-arim

Full-service marketing research firms provide a full range of marketing research activities, from the design of a research study to the submission of a final report. In addition to full-service marketing research companies, dozens of smaller Canadian firms operate in various specialized areas of marketing research, such as conducting research by geographic region, by industry, or by service performed. Some concentrate on either consumer or industrial research or carry out studies that involve the application of specialized techniques. Other companies provide specialized marketing research services, such as the analysis of survey data. Some marketing research is also conducted in Canada by advertising agencies and management consulting firms.

Privacy and Other Issues

The field of marketing research has always had to address issues of privacy and research ethics. These are receiving even more attention, as consumers are expressing increasing concern about what happens to their personal information, particularly today when data are automatically captured every time we use a credit card or a banking machine or make a long-distance call. Many consumers want assurance that this information remains confidential and is not used to target them for marketing campaigns. Confidentiality and privacy are particularly important when conducting research related to sensitive areas such as a consumer's medical history and the use of prescription drugs, as we discussed in our chapter opener.

As of January 1, 2004, all Canadian businesses are required to comply with all of the privacy principles set out in the Personal Information Protection and Electronic Documents Act (PIPEDA.) The Act is intended to make consumers feel more comfortable about how their personal information is being used. The legislation applies to all federally-regulated industries, including transportation, financial services, and telecommunications, and to any inter-provincial transfer of personal information for even the simplest information exchange, such as the use of an address for a mailing label.

PIPEDA defines personal information as "information about an identifiable individual" that includes any factual or subjective information, recorded or not, in any form. The following are only some examples of such information: name, address, gender, income, blood type, race or ethnic origin, sexual preference, political opinions, credit records, or the intention to acquire goods or services. However, under PIPEDA, personal information does not include the name, business title, business address, etc., of any employee, i.e., information such as that on a business card.

Under PIPEDA, personal information must be:

- Collected with consent and for a reasonable purpose.
- Used and disclosed for the limited purpose for which it was collected.
- Accurate.
- Accessible for inspection and change.
- Stored securely.

Three levels of consent are recognized by the new law: implied (for example, where personal information may be used to contact consumers regarding renewal of service), negative option (people are given a box to check, indicating whether or not their information may be passed on to other organizations), and express (individuals must give specific consent for use of personal data in cases where the data may be considered sensitive).

PIPEDA compliance is good business. Good privacy practices:

- build customer confidence,
- protect the integrity of the organization's brand,
- increase customer loyalty, and
- contribute to the bottom line.

Good privacy practices can also mean avoiding fines of up to $100,000! Marketers are no longer able to go on "fishing expeditions" for personal information without specifying exactly why the data are being collected. Those who violate the Act will find themselves under investigation by the Office of the Privacy Commissioner of Canada, as Air Canada did when it distributed a brochure to Aeroplan members explaining the ways in which it planned to use members' personal information. The onus was placed on members to "opt out," which violates the legislation requiring individual permission (positive consent) to be sought in order to allow such disclosure. These rules apply to marketers requesting information for contests or promotions, membership drives for loyalty programs, and direct-to-consumer e-mail campaigns.[9]

Status of Marketing Research

Marketing research is a major growth area, partially as the result of advances in technology. These advances include computer accessibility, point-of-sale data collection equipment (such as supermarket scanners), the Internet and its proliferation, and improved data analysis software, all of which have enabled more efficient collection, analysis, and processing of data. The cost of computer technology has plummeted in the last decade to the point where even small businesses can collect and store data in their customer databases. Most large companies now collect considerable amounts of data at each purchase. Frequent-shopper cards, such as those used by The Bay and Shoppers Drug Mart, allow businesses to determine purchasing behaviour and patterns.

The challenge for marketers in the future will be to decide what information is needed and how it is to be integrated into decision-making. Database development and design are critical in ensuring that information is collected efficiently and meets management's needs. The role of managing databases is, therefore, a crucial one, and more emphasis is being placed on proper management. One example of this is the integration of customer files throughout business departments; previously, separate data were often maintained in each. Hotels, for instance, now compile data on their guests that can be accessed at check-in. The individual's file tells the front-desk clerk that the guest may require a smoke-free room, a 6 a.m. wake-up call, and business services, such as access to fax or e-mail. In addition to providing immediate information to management, the integration of this information in research design on lifestyles or travel patterns can identify for marketers the areas to be explored and the types of information to be collected.

As we observed earlier, the marketing environment is changing. For example, increased competition through globalization means new competitors to understand, thereby making it more difficult for some businesses to operate. Lifestyles and value systems are changing. Since marketing research is all about obtaining information to support marketing decision-making, the changing environment is increasing its importance. The more competently marketers can zero in on what is wanted and needed, the more effective they will be in marketing their products and services and in developing high levels of customer satisfaction and loyalty.

It is still true, however, that many companies are spending very large amounts on product-development research and on opening new channels of distribution, without spending enough on determining whether customers find their new offerings attractive or on determining what it will take to ensure high levels of customer satisfaction in the long run. We still find companies that launch new marketing initiatives without having talked with customers in advance. Several factors may explain this less-than-universal acceptance of marketing research:

- ***Predicting behaviour is inexact:*** Because of the many interrelated variables involved, marketing research often cannot predict future market behaviour precisely. When dealing with consumer behaviour, it is difficult to determine present attitudes or motives, let alone predict what they may be next year. As a result, it is difficult to make predictions regarding sales increases for the following period. Unless it is able to convince management of the concrete value of such research, the marketing research department will often not receive enough resources to do a good job.

- ***Conflicting objectives between researchers and managers:*** Poor communication between researchers and managers continues to be a problem. Researchers tend to be product-focused, while managers are usually market-focused. Managers are often forced to make quick decisions in the face of uncertainty, while researchers have been trained to approach problems in a more cautious, scientific manner. It can be appreciated how this leads to disagreements regarding what research to conduct, how long it should take, the way it should be presented, and even what the goals of the research should be.
- ***A project orientation to research:*** Management is often reluctant to treat marketing research as a continuing process and, further, to relate it and decision-making in a more systematic fashion. Too often, marketing research is viewed in a fragmented, one-project-at-a time manner and utilized only when management feels it has a "marketing problem." The expansion of marketing information systems into firms of various sizes will likely improve this situation.

Marketing Research, a magazine dedicated to management and applications issues within marketing, performed its own survey of research professionals, asking what they believed would be the key influences in shaping marketing research in the years ahead. The top responses were as follows: the Internet, globalization of business and research, one-to-one marketing, Internet/online research, privacy issues, computer technology, and e-commerce. As can be seen, the very technology issues that have come up repeatedly throughout this chapter dominate these responses. It is safe to conclude, however, that the future for marketing research is bright, as more and more companies realize the risk associated with making major decisions in the marketing area without good information to back them up.

PAGE UP

1. What is pre-testing?
2. Why do market researchers use convenience samples?
3. What is the primary role of the marketing research department?

Key Terms and Concepts

benchmark 102
convenience sample 116
data analysis 117
data mining 100
data warehouse 100
database 99
experimental method 106
focus group 102
individual depth interview 102
informal investigation 110
Internet research 113
interview guide 115
mail survey 113
mall intercept 112
marketing research 95
observational method 104
personal interview 111
population 116
predictive modelling 100
pre-testing 115
primary data 111
qualitative research 102
quantitative research 102
questionnaire 115
random sample 116
research hypothesis 110
research objectives 108
retail scanner 101
sample 116
secondary data 108
survey 102
syndicated data 111
telephone survey 112
test marketing 107

Questions and Problems

1. Explain how each of the following factors has increased the need for marketing research activities. Provide an example of the type of research that might address each factor.
   a. Increasing customer expectations.
   b. Competitive pressure.
   c. Increasing focus on customer retention and customer relationships.
   d. Increasing market complexity.
2. The consumer electronics company you work for wishes to develop a product that combines the features of many of its existing products — PDAs, mobile phones, and video game systems. What different research projects would be required before this new product would be ready to be placed on store shelves? Remember that market research begins early in the product development stage.
3. An international manufacturer of tinned soup for over 100 years has hired you to provide your professional advice to help the company bring the brand up-to-date in the Canadian marketplace. What different aspects of the brand, and the company, do you think should be addressed and what research methods would you recommend? Explain your choices.
4. Much market research in recent years has been directed toward better understanding customer retention and customer relationships. Suggest what type of information the following companies would seek in this type of research. In other words, what could these companies measure to help them understand the relationships that exist with their customers?
   a. A retail bank.
   b. A dry-cleaning company.
   c. A supermarket chain.
   d. A sportswear manufacturer
5. List as many examples of loyalty programs as you can think of offered by different retailers and service providers in your area. In each example explain the possible value of the information gathered by the firm. Are all of these examples of ongoing market research or are any of them simply a means of offering customer discounts?
6. A questionnaire sounds like an easy thing to design, but it is much more complicated than most people realize.
   a. What types of challenges/problems exist when trying to design an effective list of questions that accurately measure the desired information?
   b. What can researchers do to minimize these potential problems?
   c. How do researchers check to ensure their questionnaires are accurate measurement tools?
7. What are the different types of samples used in research? What types of samples are generally used in market research? Why?
8. How involved should marketing researchers be in setting strategy for their organizations?
9. A group of young wealthy business executives are intrigued with the possibility of developing a large ski resort in the BC Rockies, near the Alberta border. This would be a totally new venture and would be on federal parkland. It would be a complete resort, with facilities appealing to middle- and upper-income markets. A special emphasis would be on younger consumers in these markets. What types of information might the group want to have before deciding whether to go ahead with the venture? What sources of information would be used?
10. Evaluate surveys, observation, and experimentation as possible choices for gathering primary data in the following projects:
    a. A sporting goods retailer wants to determine college students' brand preferences for skis, in-line skates, and golf clubs.
    b. A supermarket chain wants to determine shoppers' preferences for the physical layout of store fixtures and traffic patterns, particularly around checkout stands.
    c. A manufacturer of equipment used in making ice cream wants to know who makes buying decisions for its product among present and prospective users.
11. Using the steps in the research process as presented in this chapter, describe how you would go about investigating the feasibility of opening a used bookstore on your campus.
12. What kind of sample would you use in research projects designed to answer the following questions?
    a. What brand of running shoes is most popular among the students on your campus?
    b. Should retail stores in or near your home town be open all day on Sundays?
    c. What percentage of the business firms in the city closest to your campus have automatic sprinkler systems?
13. Would it be appropriate to interview 200 students as they left your college hockey arena about their feelings regarding funding for athletics, and then generalize the results to the student body? Why or why not?
14. If you were asked to conduct a research project for a venture capital company, what suggestions would you have if your client proposed that you conduct a consumer study to determine the feasibility of introducing a National Basketball Association franchise in Calgary or Montréal?

Hands-On Marketing

1. Assume that you work for a manufacturer of high-end sunglasses that competes with brands such as RayBan and Oakley. Your manager wants to determine the amount of the product that can be sold throughout the country. To help her in this project, prepare a report that shows the following information for your home province and, if possible, your home municipality or region. Carefully identify the sources that you use for this information.
   a. Number of households or families.
   b. Income or buying power per family or per household.
   c. Total retail sales in the most recent year for which you can find reliable data.
   d. Total annual sales of optical stores, sportswear stores, and department stores.
   e. Total number of optical and sportswear stores that sell this type of product.
2. You have just joined the Student Council of your school. You have an idea for a revenue-generating project that you want to present to the Council. You think it might be a good idea to open a DVD and video-game rental kiosk in the school's food court. You need to first gather information to determine if this is a viable idea.
   a. What research questions do you need to answer?
   b. How should the information be gathered?
   c. Design a questionnaire to collect all the pertinent information.

Back to the Top

Go back to the chapter opener and place yourself in the shoes of Deepak Gupta. Now that you have studied how to conduct a marketing research project, what advice would you bring to the next meeting concerning the kind of research that PharmaNational needs to do to better understand the role and attitudes of the patient in the overall market for pharmaceutical products in Canada?

Online Learning Centre

Want to get better grades, tips on how to study more effectively, and up-to-date information on happenings in the world of marketing? Then, visit the Online Learning Centre for practice tests, Study Smart software, *Marketing Magazine,* and much more! **www.mcgrawhill.ca/olc/sommers**

CHAPTER 5

Segmentation, Positioning, and Value-Add Strategies

After studying this chapter, you should have an understanding of:

- The most important strategies used by marketers.
- The concept of market segmentation — its meaning, benefits, limitations, and applications.
- The fundamental principles behind market segment identification and selection.
- The difference between end-consumer markets (B2C) and business markets (B2B).
- The principal bases for segmenting consumer markets.
- Segmentation of the market based on demographic, lifestyle and product-related factors.
- The importance of positioning a brand or company to appeal to target customer segments.
- Niche marketing and other positioning strategies to appeal to target segments.
- The need for a differentiation strategy to set a brand or company apart from the competition.
- The basis for a value-add strategy.

So You Think You Need a New Credit Card?

You're about to graduate with your business degree and have already accepted a job half way across the country in Halifax. It's time to plan the move. Moving and setting up in another city can be expensive, so one of the first things you thought to do was to get the limit increased on your student credit card in case of any unexpected expenses or mishaps along the way. Now that you have a full-time job the customer-service representative at the bank suggests you might want to consider switching to another type of credit card. But, what does that mean? Don't they all do the same thing? The employee at CIBC explained that they offer 12 different credit cards — but, all of them are VISA cards! How can that be? Why would there be so many?

Well, you thought it made sense to have a special card for students with low incomes like yourself — but why bother with all those others? You already knew there were gold cards and platinum cards — that is based on income and credit limits, but what else could be different about all those cards? Well, she explains each one does actually serve the same purpose, but each has a little something different that makes it appeal to slightly different customer needs and interests. It all depends on the customer!

Some are just everyday cards like yours with no fee while others offer cash back rewards of 1 percent or 2 percent of the amount purchased on the card. Others offer reward points redeemable at HBC or Shoppers Drug Mart. Still others provide Aeroplan miles. Some have special travel features — travel rewards, special offers and travel insurance. Other cards are designed for business use. Some of these have fees as much as $120 a year. Some have 10.5 percent annual interest rates while others charge 19.5 percent — it gets to be pretty confusing! You have checked around — the other banks offer a similar selection. Some have even thought of other variations — RBC offers a card with a picture of Mike Weir, Canada's Masters champion, which offers its cardholders golf-related perks, privileges and high-value offers.

Today, when picking out something as simple as a credit card, consumers are faced with many more options than were available just a few years ago. Depending on the consumer, the decision-making process will differ, as will each consumer's perception of the value offered by each card. As consumers, our shopping habits have been altered in recent years, largely as a result of technology and the increasing competition occurring in many industries. We are more sophisticated, knowledgeable, and demanding. Technology has mainly created these changes through advances in service quality and widespread access to the Internet — no longer do most of us let banks tell us what products we want — we tell them. Competition among financial service providers has also made us more aware that there is almost always another way to get a lower rate. The scenario in the chapter opener represents how marketers have responded to consumers with differing needs. These different products appeal to various market segments, all of whom need a credit card but see each of these credit cards as different products with more or less value to them.

To some consumers, a credit card is a credit card and they don't want anything other than the ability to use the convenient credit it makes available when shopping, but others will spend a great deal of time deciding which bundle of options or benefits they want from their credit card.

How different customers think and behave in planning and buying financial products such as a credit card depends on many factors. How financial institutions and credit card companies design and market such products depends on knowing this sort of information. It also helps such companies decide which segments they will target.

What different types of market segments do you believe are being targeted with the various types of VISA cards? How would you describe the different types of customers for these different credit card products? How does knowing such information give us greater insight and knowledge of potential customers?

Thinking and Acting Strategically

In this chapter, we will address some of the most important strategies used in marketing. First, it is important to understand what we mean by strategy and thinking strategically. Essentially, to have a strategy is to have a plan that is based on information. In Chapter 4, we discussed the importance of obtaining solid information on customers and markets. Now we will talk about how we use that information to make strategic decisions.

To have a strategy is to have a good reason to do something. The opposite of a company behaving strategically is to have it going off in all directions, trying things out to see if they work. A strategic company will have collected good information and made decisions to approach its market in a certain way, based on what it has learned. Once a firm has analyzed the market and the needs, attitudes and interests of customers, it is in a much better position to decide more precisely what kinds of customers it wishes to approach and satisfy, what it wants to be known for in the marketplace, how it will set itself apart from its competitors in the eyes of customers, and how it will create added value for those customers. These are the essential marketing strategies and we will examine each of them in this chapter.

The strategies that we will cover in this chapter represent components of a process that marketing managers must follow in making their companies and brands competitive in a very crowded marketplace. First, they must decide what groups of customers they want to deal with; who they will target. Then, they decide how they will have to position the company or brand so as to appeal to those selected customers; what they want their brand to be known for. Finally, they must determine what the company will offer those customers that they will find of value and that will distinguish it from the competition.

Nature of Market Segmentation

The total market for most types of products is too varied — too heterogeneous — to be considered a single, uniform entity. To speak of the market for vitamin pills or disposable razors or education is to ignore the fact that the total market for each product or service consists of sub-groups of customers that differ significantly from one another. This lack of uniformity may be traced to differences in customer buying habits, in ways in which the product or service is used, in motives for buying, or in other factors.

One of the fundamental principles underlying the practice of market segmentation is that most companies and brands cannot aspire to be "all things to all people." If they try to do so, a company or brand will actually mean very little to those looking for specific, and different, characteristics in the products and services that they buy.

Not all consumers want to wear the same type of clothing, use the same brand of shampoo, or take the same holiday. Nor do all business firms want to buy the same computers or delivery vans. Similarly, not all want to have the same kind of relationship with a retail store or bank, or to be treated in the same way. At the same time, a marketer usually cannot afford to provide a different product or service for every single customer. Consequently, market segmentation is the strategy that most marketers adopt as a compromise between the extremes of one product or service for all and a different one for each customer.

market segmentation
The process of dividing the total market for a product into several customer groups, each of which tends to be homogeneous.

Market segmentation divides the total market for a product or service into several segments, each of which tends to be homogeneous in many significant aspects. Management selects one or more of these market segments as the organization's target market. A separate marketing program and approach is developed for each segment or group of segments in this target market.

Benefits of market segmentation

Market segmentation is a customer-oriented approach. We first identify the needs of customers within a sub-market (segment) and then develop an approach to marketing that will satisfy those needs. Segmentation, therefore, benefits customers because they are much more likely to encounter companies and brands that are looking out for their particular needs. There are so many options available in today's market that customers are increasingly likely to find brands and retail stores that seem to have been created "especially for them."

By tailoring marketing programs to individual market segments, management can do a better marketing job and make more efficient use of marketing resources. A small firm with limited resources might compete very effectively in one or two market segments, but the same firm would be ineffective if it aimed for the total market. By employing the strategy of market segmentation, a company can design products, services and approaches to customer interaction that really match customer needs. Advertising media can be used more effectively because promotional messages can be aimed specifically toward each segment of the market. Some of the most successful marketers are small or medium-sized firms that have decided to concentrate on a small number of market segments and to gain a strong market position and greater market share in these segments — an application of the principle of niche marketing, in which goods and services are tailored to meet the needs of small market segments.

Procter & Gamble

Even very large companies with the resources to engage in national advertising campaigns have in recent years abandoned mass-marketing strategies. Instead, these companies have accepted market segmentation as a more effective strategy to reach the many fragments that once were thought to constitute a mass, homogeneous market. Procter & Gamble's (**www.pg.com**) marketing program nicely illustrates these changing conditions. Once the epitome of a mass marketer with innovative but utilitarian products, P&G advertised heavily on network television. But, today, it's a different ball game. Far fewer people are watching network television.

Faced with fragmentation of the television audience, Procter & Gamble developed a variety of marketing campaigns, each designed to appeal to a different target market segment. The company's line of hand and bath soaps alone offers many choices such as Ivory, Zest, Coast, Safeguard, Camay, and Olay. Many of these brands come in different sizes, various colours to match bathroom decor, and different forms — bar soaps, body wash, and liquid soap in pump dispensers. The company is competing in a soap market that is segmented by skin type (oily versus dry, normal versus sensitive), fragrance, aesthetics, the desire for convenience, economy, and the primary benefit sought — clean skin. It is clear that all consumers buy soap for cleansing, but they also expect other benefits from the soap they use. Hence, many segments exist.

Although a market segmentation strategy will involve a firm developing and delivering different products and services for different market segments, it is not necessarily a more costly strategy. Any costs actually represent an investment in a much more efficient approach to marketing. Not to engage in segmentation, but rather, using a broad-brush, mass-market approach, results in much lost effort. Many customers are reached through mass marketing efforts who are not at all interested in the product or service or who do not want any kind of association with the firm. A segmentation strategy increases the likelihood that the marketing effort reaches those who are most likely to be interested in buying.

Conditions for effective segmentation

Ideally, the goal of marketing should be to segment markets in such a way that each segment finds the company's offer attractive and responds positively to its marketing program. Three conditions for effective segmentation will help management move toward this goal.

1. The basis for segmenting — that is, the characteristics used to allocate customers to segments — must be measurable, and the information on those customers must be accessible. The "desire for low levels of cholesterol" may be a characteristic that is useful in segmenting the market for a given food product, but data on this characteristic among customers may not be readily accessible or easily quantified.

2. The market segment itself should be accessible through existing marketing channels — retailers and wholesalers, advertising media, company sales force — with a minimum of cost and waste.

3. Each segment should be large enough to be profitable. In theory, management could treat every customer as a separate segment. But in segmenting a consumer market, a firm must not develop too broad an array of styles, colours, sizes, and prices. Usually the diseconomies of scale in production and inventory will put reasonable limits on this type of over-segmentation. Banks would not introduce a specific credit card targeted at the student segment unless they had determined there was sufficient demand amongst the student segment.

From a customer-oriented perspective, the ideal method for segmenting a market is on the basis of customers' needs, interests and desired benefits. Certainly, using benefits to segment a market is consistent with the idea that a company should be marketing benefits and not simply the physical characteristics of a product. After all, a carpenter wants a smooth surface (benefit), not sandpaper (the product); a young family needs a home, not a mortgage. However, in many cases the benefits desired by customers do not meet the first condition described above — they are not easily measured, because customers are unwilling or unable to reveal the necessary characteristics. For example, what benefits do people derive from clothing that has the designer's label on the outside? Conversely, why do others refuse to wear such clothing?

Selecting Target Segments

target segment
A group of customers (people or firms) to whom a company specifically directs its marketing efforts.

In Chapter 1, we defined a *market* as people or organizations with (1) needs to satisfy, (2) money to spend, and (3) the willingness to spend it. The market is not homogeneous; it is divided into segments that exhibit different needs, characteristics and behaviours. A **target segment** is a group of customers (people or firms) at whom a company specifically directs its marketing efforts. The careful selection, definition and identification of customer segments are essential for the development of an effective marketing program.

This is particularly true because of the changes taking place in the competitive environment. Companies in most industries today are faced with competition from many sources. Not only is the global nature of business creating new competitors from other countries, but customers are now able to buy products from companies with which they would never have dealt a few years ago. With access to the Internet, Canadians can access products from companies all over the world. The e-commerce environment fragments a market by exposing customers to companies with which they were once totally unfamiliar. With this fragmentation of the marketplace and the increased level of competition from local, domestic, and international competitors, most marketers practise a strategy of carving out of the mass market a manageable number of target segments on which they will concentrate. They can't serve them all, so they focus on those for whom they can do the best job and that represent the best fit with their value proposition.

Fresh Oxygen
Holt Renfrew

Firms select target segments that they believe are most likely to be interested in and purchase their products or services. Often, products are specifically designed for a particular group. MuchMusic focuses on a core target of viewers 18 to 24 years of age, while actually attracting an audience ranging in age from 12 to 34. In the last few years, Much has increased the number of channels it offers by developing new stations based on musical taste to better search out specific groups within this larger demographic. Home Depot focuses on men 25 to 49 years of age with its lawn and garden equipment. Degree antiperspirant's new Fresh Oxygen is directed toward women 18 to 34 and was launched with support online at **www.freshoxygen.ca**, which offered free samples and a chance to win a $10,000 Girlfriend's Adventure Getaway. Molson Canadian targets male beer drinkers aged 19 to 24, while Molson Black Label goes for the slightly older beer drinker: 25- to 35-year-olds. Lavalife.com aims its Cupid's arrow primarily at 18- to 40-year-old urban singles.[1]

Guidelines in segment selection

Four guidelines govern how to determine which segments a company should target. The first is that *target segments should be compatible with the organization's goals and image*. One business that is keenly aware of this is Toronto-based Holt Renfrew (**www.holtrenfrew.com**), which changed its emphasis to focus more on national and international brands. This focus is in line with Holt Renfrew's positioning as an upscale store catering to the needs of an elite clientele and those that aspire to such a status with the addition of brands such as Chanel. Holt's has also enhanced its private-label merchandise offering to the point where it comprises about 40 percent of its product mix.

To quote Andrew Jennings, the company's president, "It's all about advancing our goal of being one of the world's leading fashion and lifestyle experiences." This is a clear statement of Holt Renfrew's goals and image, indicating a renewed emphasis on its wealthy clientele supported by multi-million dollar store renovations to keep the store's image trendy. Its glossy magazine named simply *Holt's* features such items as Russian sable jackets and Gucci shirts. While Holt Renfrew targets a wealthier segment, Jennings' view is that, "It's not about expense, it's about perceived value." Holt Renfrew's clientele clearly appreciates the difference.[2]

A second guideline — consistent with our definition of strategic planning — is to *match the market opportunity represented in the target markets with the company's resources*. For example, in examining new product opportunities, 3M considered many options but chose the do-it-yourself

GUEST MARKETER

Targeting a Very Important Segment

By Heather Tulk

Heather Tulk is Senior Vice President—Marketing at Bell Aliant, responsible for consumer and Small and Medium Business marketing. Heather believes strongly that excellent marketing starts with a deep understanding of the customer, and can only be executed through a focus on the customer experience. Heather is a graduate of Queen's University and Memorial University.

Aliant is an information and communications technology company based in Atlantic Canada. Aliant delivers innovative and traditional communications services, including local and long distance telephony, wireless, Internet, e-commerce, interactive multimedia, data and managed network services, information technology solutions and knowledge-service applications. In addition to serving residential, small-to-medium sized business and larger enterprise customers in its home market, Aliant also serves business customers located in other parts of Canada and the world.

Over the past number of years, the growing importance of the youth segment has become increasingly clear to many companies, including Aliant. This segment, typically defined as anyone under the age of 25, has incredible spending power owing to the fact that most of their income is disposable. These younger consumers are also early adopters of technology and products, heavy users of new services, and key influencers on household spending.

Understanding this customer group is the critical first step to developing a strategy of how a company such as Aliant could successfully deliver solutions. To gain this understanding, Aliant created a youth panel to act as an extension of their marketing team. The panel was made up of twelve young Atlantic Canadians, representing both urban and rural areas in all provinces. With the exception of the annual kick-off, all of the panel's work was done online through a secure Web site. This panel's insights and ideas are a major influence in the creation of Aliant's youth strategy. Members of Aliant's Youth Panel are asked to inform Aliant about what they value, where they spend their money, their ideal retail experience, how they spend their time, their media consumption habits and most importantly, how they view Aliant and its competitors.

In addition to the qualitative work with this panel, Aliant conducts quantitative research with Atlantic Canadian youth through online surveys. Through this research, Aliant learned that it is perceived to be the brand in Atlantic Canada that has relevant products for younger customers and that it is leading in top-of-mind awareness. Aliant's marketing team also learned of some interesting youth purchasing habits such as the fact that almost half of this important segment receives their technology products as gifts.

Aliant also monitors secondary research on communicating to and branding for youth, companies targeting younger customers, and best in class promotions to the youth segment. This gives Aliant insight into what other companies in the world are doing and about which initiatives have an impact with this segment. Aliant also works closely within the guidelines of the Canadian Marketing Association to ensure that its activities in this segment reflect the unique responsibility that an organization undertakes when marketing to children and teenagers.

Armed with this knowledge, the company concluded that a good youth strategy would not only target younger customers directly but would also target parents. In the first year of the youth program, Aliant's approach was focused in five different areas: creating communications that were much more relevant to this segment; showcasing products, services and promotions in new media and locations; launching new products specifically for them; finding ways to show youth that Aliant cares about their business; and providing gifting options for parents.

Aliant has launched a communications platform for younger customers and created a portal **www.aliant.net/youth101** that houses all of the company's youth-relevant information. Aliant has created youth-targeted retail stores and special zones within our stores. These stores provide an opportunity to have an interactive experience with our products. The strategy also led to the introduction of youth-designed products such as the Aliant Personal DJ and the Aliant online music store on **www.aliant.net**. Annual promotions such as the Safe Grad promotion and Garage Band promotion don't directly sell to younger customers but provide positive opportunities for them to interact with the Aliant brand.

Key to success in this market was involving the target customers in the creation of the strategy and ensuring that there were ongoing conversations with them through creation and implementation. In addition, the amount of research that was done up-front gave an incredible amount of insight into the segment and helped develop successful program tactics.

As with every good strategy, Aliant's youth strategy is ever changing and updated every year to reflect current market conditions, current competitive realities and recent research results. In 2006 Aliant was working with its fifth annual youth panel and continues to involve the segment in discussion of every opportunity.

Since its launch, the Aliant Youth Strategy has had extremely positive results. A very large number of target customers have gotten involved in the contests and promotions and there have been very positive changes in sales and market results. Members of this younger segment now cite Aliant as having not only great products for them, but also view Aliant as a company that talks to them in the right language and has meaningful things to say. This is a clear example of how being diligent in involving the insight of your customers in the creation of your marketing strategy leads to greater success.

home improvement market because of the marketing economies that could be achieved. The firm's name was already well known to consumers, and the products could be sold through many of the retail outlets already selling 3M products, so entering this market was much less expensive than entering a market in which 3M was inexperienced.

Over the long run, a business must generate a profit. This rather obvious statement translates into our third segment-selection guideline. *Some companies make the mistake of going after sales volume, not profitable sales volume.* Companies that target the higher-yield customer must offer products or services that are perceived by the customer to have value. In some instances, a combination of approaches may be beneficial.

Fourth, a company ordinarily should *seek a market where there are the fewest and smallest competitors.* A company should not enter a market that is already saturated with competition unless it has some overriding differential advantage that will enable it to take customers from existing firms. When the Häagen-Dazs brand of premium ice cream entered Europe and Asia in the late 1980s, it had little competition at the high end of the market. Because per-capita ice cream consumption on these continents is well below that of North America, many viewed the prospects of a high-priced brand in a low-usage market as not very attractive. However, Häagen-Dazs, now with sales well over $500 million, proved the doubters wrong. It wasn't that consumers disliked ice cream; rather, many simply had not been exposed to a high-quality version. By getting to the market first, Häagen-Dazs now has a significant advantage over later entrants.[3]

Market opportunity analysis

Theoretically, a market opportunity exists at any time and at any place where there is a person or an organization with an unfilled need or want. Such opportunities present themselves, for example, when demographics change. As the population ages, more age-relevant products and services will be needed, providing increased opportunities for entrepreneurial firms to create and develop new products and services for an older customer group.

Realistically, of course, a company's opportunity to address certain segments does have restrictions. Thus, selecting target segments requires a realistic appraisal of the opportunities available to the firm. A market opportunity analysis begins with a study of the market forces that affect a firm's marketing program. First, the company must analyze the customers that make up a potential target segment, the number of people or companies in the segment and their buying power. The firm will need to know how well served the segment is at the present time, whose products or services they are currently buying, how much they are spending, and how satisfied they are. Finally, an opportunity analysis should include a thorough assessment of the competition, how they do business and how we can gain a competitive advantage.

When selecting target segments, a company should make quantitative estimates of the sales potential for its product or service. This process requires estimating (1) the total industry potential for the company's product in the target segment and (2) the share of this total market that can be achieved. It is essential for management to also prepare a realistic sales forecast, usually for a one-year period. The existence of a group large enough to target is not a guarantee of equivalent sales. Consumers must become aware of the product or service, be able to obtain it, and then must choose it over the competitors' offer. Knowing that customers buy a certain volume of such products and services is not enough. The firm must give them a reason to buy its product or service.

First Step to Market Segmentation — End-Consumers or Business Users

A company can segment its market in many different ways, and the bases for segmentation vary from one product category to another. At the top of the list, however, is the division of the entire potential market into two broad categories: end-consumers and business users.

end-consumers
People who buy products for their personal, non-business use.

business user
An organization that buys goods or services to resell, use in its own business, or make other products.

The sole criterion for placement of customers in one of these categories is the customer's reason for buying. **End-consumers** buy goods or services for their own personal or household use. They are satisfying strictly non-business needs, and they constitute the "consumer market." This large segment is today often described as the business-to-consumer or B2C market.

Business users are business, industrial, or institutional organizations that buy products or services to use in their own businesses or to make other products. A manufacturer that buys chemicals with which to make fertilizer is a business user of these chemicals. Farmers who buy fertilizer for use in commercial farming are business users of the fertilizer. (If homeowners buy fertilizer to use on their yards, they are end-consumers, because they buy it for personal, non-business use — the fertilizer is very likely to be identical in both situations.) Businesses selling to other businesses and organizations are targeting the business-to-business or B2B market.

The segmentation of all markets into two groups — B2C and B2B — is extremely significant from a marketing point of view because the two markets buy differently. Consequently, the composition of a firm's value proposition will depend on whether it is directed toward the B2C market or the B2B market.

PAGE UP!

1. What is a target segment?
2. What are four general guidelines for selecting target segments?
3. An organization chooses a strategy of ______________________________ when the total market is viewed as a single unit.

Bases for Segmenting Consumer Markets

Dividing the total market into consumer and business segments is a worthwhile start toward useful segmentation, but it still leaves too broad and heterogeneous a grouping for most companies. We need to identify some of the bases commonly used to segment these two markets further. As shown in Table 5-1, the following characteristics may provide bases for segmenting the B2C market:

- Geographic.
- Demographic.
- Psychographic.
- Behaviour toward product or service.

Marketing managers should be particularly aware of trends taking place in the demographic, psychographic, and behavioural characteristics of the markets in which they are operating. For example, if the population of Victoria is increasing because of a large number of people moving there to retire, this has obvious implications for businesses that operate in and around Victoria. Kitchener-Waterloo has been growing as a major centre for the technology industry with resulting changes in the make-up of the population.

Similarly, a company should be interested in knowing if the customers it has been serving are gradually reducing their usage of its product and using more of a competing product. This is precisely what has been happening in the beer market in Canada in recent years, as per-capita consumption of the product has been declining gradually as consumers have switched to more wine and non-alcoholic drinks. Most industry representatives agree that this change in consumption patterns is largely a result of the fact that the percentage of the Canadian population in the heavier beer-drinking age group has been declining over the years as the Baby Boomers grew older and began drinking a lot more wine and less beer.

TABLE 5-1 Bases for Segmenting Consumer Markets

Segmentation Basis	Examples of Typical Market Segments
Geographic	
Region	Atlantic provinces; Québec; Ontario; Prairie provinces; British Columbia: census regions.
City or CMA size	Under 25,000; 25,000 to 100,000; 100,000 to 250,000; 250,000 to 500,000; 500,000 to 1,000,000; over 1,000,000.
Urban–rural	Urban; rural; suburban; farm.
Climate and topography	Mountainous; seacoast; rainy; cold and snowy; etc.
Demographic	
Age	Under 6, 6–12, 13–19, 20–34, 35–49, 50–64, 65–79, 80 and over.
Gender	Male, female.
Family life cycle	Young single; young married; no children; etc.
Education	Elementary school only, high school graduate, college graduate.
Occupation	Professional, manager, clerical worker, skilled worker, salesperson, student, homemaker, unemployed.
Religion	Protestant, Catholic, Jewish, Hindu, Muslim, other.
Ethnic background	White; Black; Asian; British; French; Chinese; German; Ukrainian; Italian; Indian; etc.
Household income	Under $20,000; $20,000–$40,000; $40,000–$60,000; $60,000–$100,000; over $100,000.
Psychographic	
Social class	Upper class, upper middle, lower middle, upper lower, etc.
Personality	Ambitious, self-confident, aggressive, introverted, extroverted, sociable, etc.
Lifestyle	Conservative, liberal, health- and fitness-oriented, adventuresome.
Value perception	Kinds of value the customer finds most attractive.
Relationships	Close, more close, less close, trusting, personal, distant.
Behaviour Toward Product or Service (or Product/Service-Related Bases)	
Benefits desired	Examples vary widely, depending on product or service:
	appliance: cost, quality, life, repairs.
	aerobics class: fitness, appearance, health, fellowship.
	toothpaste: no cavities, plaque control, bright teeth.
	hairdressing: image, style, price, self-confidence.
Usage rate	Non-user, light user, heavy user.
Loyalty/brand recognition	More or less loyal to particular companies and brands.

The key word that marketers should keep in mind when examining such trends or changes in consumption and other segmentation variables is *implications*. Marketers should always look into the implications of such change and seek information to guide an appropriate response to the changing market.

In using the bases outlined in Table 5-1 to segment markets, we should bear in mind two points. First, buying behaviour is rarely a result of only one of these segmentation factors. Including variables from several bases develops useful segmentation. To illustrate, the market for a product almost certainly does not consist of all people living in Québec or all people over 65. Instead, the segment is more likely to be described through a combination of variables, so a market segment for notebook computers might be travelling businesspeople who earn above-average incomes, are well educated, and are older than 30. As another example, one clothing manufacturer's target market might be affluent young women living in larger cities (income, age, gender, geographic).

Another important point to observe is the interrelationships among these factors, especially among the demographic factors. For instance, the age and life-cycle stages typically are related. Income depends to some degree on age, life-cycle stage, education, and occupation.

Geographic segmentation

The geographic distribution and demographic composition of the population are widely used bases for segmenting consumer markets. The reason for this is simply that consumer needs and product usage often are related to where people live, their age and gender, and how much money they have to spend. Geographic and demographic groupings also meet the conditions for effective segmentation — they are measurable, accessible, and large enough. Simply put, it is relatively easy for companies to obtain data on where people live and on their demographic characteristics. Let's consider first how the geographic distribution of population can be used for **geographic segmentation**.

geographic segmentation
The process of segmenting a market into geographic regions and developing a different marketing strategy for each region.

Regional distribution of population

The regional distribution of population (see Figure 5-1) is important to marketers because people within a particular geographic region often tend to share the same values, attitudes, and style preferences. However, significant differences do exist across regions, because of differences in climate, social customs, and other factors. Ontario is a more urbanized province and represents the greatest concentration of people in Canada, especially in the corridor between Oshawa and Niagara Falls. This market is attractive to many marketers because of its sheer size and the diversity of consumers living there. On the other hand, the Atlantic region

Figure 5-1:
Population Projections — Canada, Provinces and Territories

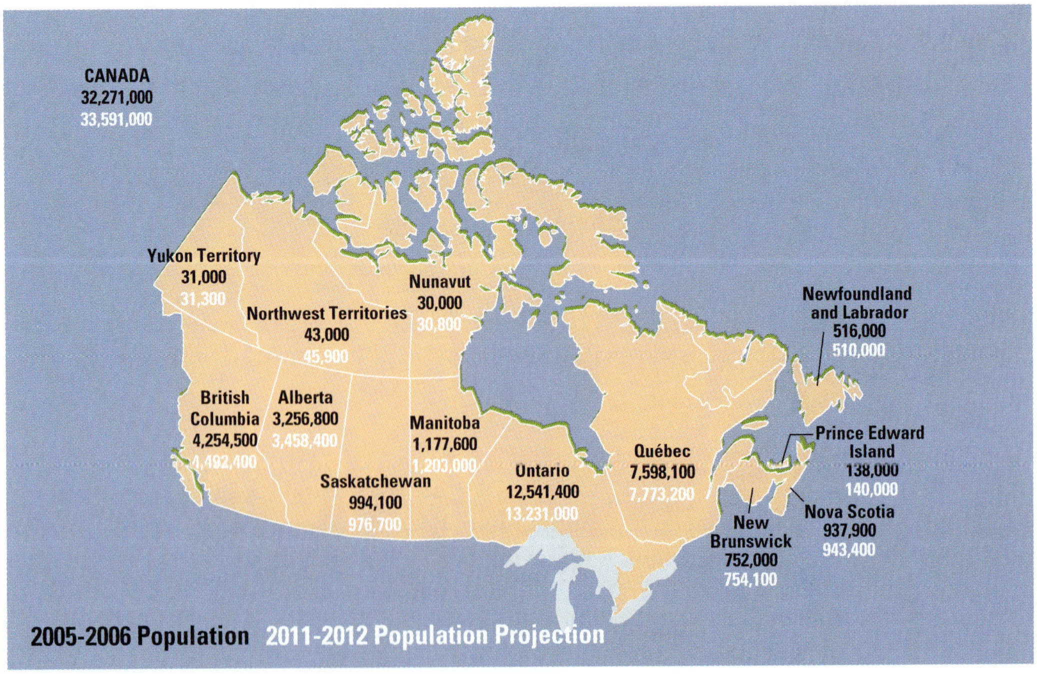

SOURCE: Statistics Canada, *Population Projections for Canada, Provinces and Territories 2005-2031,* catalogue no. 91-520-XIE.

and the Prairie provinces are characterized by a much more relaxed and rural lifestyle, which suggests a demand for different types of products and services. People in the West appear to be more relaxed and less formal than eastern Canadians, and they spend more time outdoors. As the population of Alberta and British Columbia continues to grow, there will be a growth in demand for products associated with an outdoor lifestyle.

Rural and urban population

Census Metropolitan Area (CMA)
One of the major population centres of Canada, as defined by Statistics Canada; generally contains population centres of 100,000 or more.

For many years in Canada, there has been a decline in the rural population and this decline is expected to continue, although smaller communities continue to represent an important market for certain products and services, and many rural Canadians today have easy access to larger population centres. As the rural population has declined, the urban and suburban population has expanded. Statistics Canada established the concept of a **Census Metropolitan Area (CMA)** as a geographic market-data measurement unit. A CMA is defined as the main labour market of a continuous built-up area having a population of 100,000 or more. Table 5-2 indicates the population of each of Canada's CMAs in 2005. These 27 areas account for about 65 percent of the total population of Canada.[4] There has been a notable trend in recent years toward an urbanization of the Canadian population, as reflected in the continued growth of larger CMAs. Immigration is partially responsible for this, as most new Canadians settle in urban areas. Obviously, these Census Metropolitan Areas represent attractive, geographically-concentrated market targets with considerable sales potential.

demographic segmentation
Segmentation of a company's customers based on their demographic characteristics; including most often age, gender, income level, marital status, family composition, etc.

Demographic segmentation

Demographic segmentation involves dividing the population into groups based on some characteristic such as age, gender, family life-cycle stage, income distribution, education, occupation, or ethnic origin. This is, in fact, the easiest way for many companies to think

TABLE 5-2 Census Metropolitan Area Population as of July 1, 2005 (thousands)

Total census metropolitan areas	21030.1	Victoria (B.C.)	334.7
Toronto (Ont.)	5304.1	Oshawa (Ont.)	340.3
Montréal (Que.)	3635.7	Windsor (Ont.)	332.3
Vancouver (B.C.)	2208.3	Saskatoon (Sask.)	235.8
Ottawa–Gatineau (Ont.–Que.)	1148.8	Regina (Sask.)	199.0
Calgary (Alta.)	1060.3	St. John's (N.L.)	182.5
Edmonton (Alta.)	1016.0	Sherbrooke (Que.)	163.7
Québec (Que.)	717.6	Abbotsford (B.C.)[1]	162.8
Hamilton (Ont.)	714.9	Greater Sudbury (Ont.)	161.1
Winnipeg (Man.)	706.9	Kingston (Ont.)[1]	156.2
London (Ont.)	464.3	Saguenay (Que.)	153.0
Kitchener (Ont.)	458.6	Trois-Rivières (Que.)	142.2
St. Catharines–Niagara (Ont.)	396.9	Saint John (N.B.)	126.7
Halifax (N.S.)	380.8	Thunder Bay (Ont.)	126.5

NOTE: Based on 2001 census boundaries.
1. Abbotsford and Kingston became census metropolitan areas in 2001.

SOURCE: Statistics Canada, CANSIM, table (for fee) 051-0034 and catalogue nos. 91-213-XIB and 91-213-XPB. Last modified: 2005-12-21.

about segmenting their markets as data are often readily available on the demographic characteristics of markets. But, it is also a very simplistic way to look at segmentation, one that misses many opportunities to "drill down" to other, more attractive and interesting bases for segmentation.

Age groups

Analyzing the consumer market by age groups is a useful exercise in the marketing of many products and services. Age is one of the most fundamental bases for demographically segmenting markets, as we can see from the large number of products and services directed at seniors, children, teens, young adults, and so on. But marketers must be aware of the changing nature of the age mix of the Canadian population. Looking ahead, we see a rapidly aging population. In 2004, for example, there were almost 4.2 million people in Canada aged between 10 and 19, but by 2016, this will drop to 3.8 million and is forecasted to drop further to 3.5 million by 2026. On the other hand, in 1986, there were only 2.7 million Canadians aged 65 and older. By 2004, this age bracket contained almost 4.2 million, and by 2021, this group will increase in number to 6.71 million and to 8.86 million by 2026.[5]

The youth market (aged roughly 5 to 13) carries a three-way market impact. First, these children can influence parental purchases. Second, millions of dollars are spent on this group by their parents. Third, these children make purchases of goods and services for their own use and satisfaction, and the volume of these purchases increases as the children get older. Promotional programs are often geared to this market segment. Manufacturers of breakfast cereals, snack foods, and toys often advertise on television programs that are directed at children.

The teenage market is also recognized as an important one, yet many companies find it difficult to reach. But, this is actually several markets — the 13 to 16 age group is very different from the 17 to 20 age group. Marketers must understand the teenage market because of the size of the segment and because its members have a great deal of money to spend.

The second-largest teen population in Canadian history will peak this decade at 4.2 million. Teens have more influence than ever over household purchases and have about $19.1 billion dollars in disposable income. Nike, Ecko, Quiksilver, Phat Farm, Tommy, and Brody are among the top brands of clothing for Canadian teens who are "early style adopters." For marketers who set their sights on the much-sought-after 18- to 24-year-old crowd, the university or college campus is the ideal frontier (although many are working, as reflected in Marketing at Work file 5-1): Where else can they find a captive audience so closely matching the desired traits? Marketing activities vary from campus to campus and can range from bathroom advertising to sampling and event sponsorship.

Tons of money to spend.

The aging Baby Boom generation makes an attractive market segment as they move into middle age. They are in their high-earning years and are contemplating retirement; some have already retired, taking advantage of early-retirement packages offered as companies and other organizations have downsized in recent years. Typically, the values and lifestyles of this group are different from those of people in the same age category in previous generations. This generation, with more dual-income families and fewer children, have more money to spend on themselves. As a result, they are a prime market for products that promise convenience and for home and garden and travel services.

MARKETING AT WORK 5-1: STRATEGY

Meet the Gold-Collar Kids! They Live with Their Parents, but Spend Like They're Loaded!

Advertisers seem in constant pursuit of the always-elusive youth market. Yet are companies ignoring the hottest segment among youth, a group happy to purchase $300 sunglasses or spend more than $200 for a tube of skin cream? According to a new Canadian study, the answer is a resounding "yes," and advertisers will be surprised to hear who this group is: 18- to 25-year-olds with just a high school diploma. We are talking about upscale blue-collar youth! How can that be?

These are the folks who are not attending university or college; they are working, often in unionized blue-collar jobs. They have the guys over for a beer to watch the game, and they tend to identify with family and with brands that Mom and Dad also favour — Tim Hortons, Ford, and Bud.

But, nearly a third of this country's working youth seem to have evolved into a new breed of shoppers in recent years according to Synovate Research. They've been termed "gold-collar aspirationalists" by the firm because they buy items you would think they wouldn't be able to afford. This group does not have a strong social identity so they look to consumption — of fashion, premium alcohol, cellphones, even Starbucks — to define who they are. They consider themselves to be early adopters and high-end purchasers in categories such as clothes, handbags, sportswear, beauty and coffee.

Synovate research shows that the average income of working-class youth is below $30,000, so where do gold-collar kids find this excess cash? For starters, most live at home, giving them a much higher level of discretionary income, they don't usually have student loans, and aren't saving money to buy a house. In total, Synovate Research estimates this group to be currently worth about $4 billion a year.

How to reach this group? According to Ian Pierpoint of Synovate's Vancouver office, try launching super-premium limited editions and use endorsements from celebrity personalities. If you give something to Paris Hilton, millionaire moms in Hollywood start buying it, but so do retail store employees in Toronto, according to Pierpoint.

QUESTIONS:

1. To what kinds of businesses is this market segment likely to be of particular interest?
2. What other segments do you think exist within the 18-25 age group?
3. Profile these other segments and point out how they are different from the segment described in this Marketing at Work file.

SOURCE: Adapted from Chris Daniels, "The Other Working Class," *Marketing Magazine*, May 9, 2005, p. 5.

A very important older age group is made up of people over 65 — a segment that is growing both absolutely and as a percentage of the total population. Companies are beginning to recognize that people in this age group are logical prospects for small, low-maintenance housing units, cruises and foreign tours, health-related products and services, and cosmetics developed especially for older people. The Internet is becoming an increasingly attractive way to reach seniors. Of the approximately nine million Canadians aged 50-plus, well over 30 percent are regular Internet users.[6]

They've earned it.

Gender

Gender is an obvious basis for market segmentation. Many products are made for use by men or women, not both. In many product categories (automobiles, for example), women and men typically look for different product benefits. Market segmentation by gender is also useful because either men only or women only have traditionally purchased many products. Today, we are witness to a much more balanced approach to purchasing with a much-increased percentage of purchases being made jointly by men and women. It is still very important for marketers, however, to determine what roles are being played by men and women within these joint decisions and what men and women are looking for when buying. They do approach purchase decisions quite differently!

Family life cycle

family life cycle
The series of life stages that a family goes through, starting with young, single people and progressing through married stages with young and then older children, then ending with older married and single people.

Frequently, an important factor accounting for differences in consumption patterns relates to consumers being in different life-cycle stages. The concept of the **family life cycle** implies that there are several distinct stages in the life of an ordinary family. In addition to the traditional six-stage family cycle there are three alternative stages that reflect significant changes from traditional patterns. In addition to the family configurations represented in Table 5-3, numerous other examples exist, from same-sex marriages to families with shared child custody to cohabitation arrangements between mixed-sex groups. Lifestyles that do not reflect the traditional norm are often more the rule than the exception. We can think of life-cycle position, in any of its various patterns, as a major determinant of buyer behaviour, so it can be a useful basis for segmenting consumer markets.

A young couple with two children (the full-nest stage) has quite different needs from those of a couple in their mid-50s whose children no longer live at home (the empty-nest stage). A single-parent family (divorced, widowed, or never married) with dependent children probably faces social and economic problems quite different from those of a two-parent family. Young married couples with no children typically devote a large share of their income to clothing, vehicles, travel and recreation. When children start arriving, expenditure patterns shift, as many young families buy and furnish a home. Families with teenagers find larger portions of the budget going for food, clothing, and educational needs.

Consumer Income and Its Distribution

personal disposable income
Personal income remaining after all personal taxes are paid.

discretionary purchasing power
The amount of disposable income remaining after fixed expenses and essential household needs are covered.

People alone do not make a market; they must have money to spend. Consequently, consumer income, its distribution, and how it is spent are essential factors in any quantitative market analysis.

What is income? When we talk of consumers and their income, we tend to be most interested in **personal disposable income**, that is, after-tax income available for personal consumption expenditure and savings. We also are interested in a household's **discretionary purchasing power**, the amount of disposable income that is available after fixed commitments (mortgage and loan payments, rent, insurance) and essential household expenditures for food, clothing, household utilities, and transportation have been covered. Compared with personal disposable income, discretionary purchasing power is a better (more sensitive) indicator of consumers' ability to spend for non-essentials.

To obtain full value from an analysis of income, we should study the variations and trends in the distribution of income across regions and customer segments. Different groups clearly have different sources and levels of income and this greatly affects their ability to purchase and their spending patterns.

A genuine income distribution revolution has occurred in Canada over the past 30 years or so — there has been a tremendous growth in the middle- and upper-income segments, and a corresponding decrease in the percentage of low-income groups. The purchasing power of the average Canadian household is expected to continue to increase in the future. It is very likely that more than half of all Canadian families will have a total annual income in excess of $60,000 by the year 2016. The declining percentage of families in very low income brackets, coupled with sharp increases in the upper-income groups, points to growth in discretionary purchasing power. As discretionary income increases, so too does the demand for items that once were considered to be luxuries.

TABLE 5-3 Behaviour Influences and Buying Patterns, by Family Life-Cycle Stage

Bachelor stage: young single people not living at home

Few financial burdens.

Fashion opinion leader.

Recreation-oriented.

Buy: basic kitchen equipment, basic furniture, cars, equipment for the mating game, vacations.

Newly married couples; young, no children

Better off financially than they will be in near future.

Highest purchase rate and highest average purchase of durables.

Buy: cars, refrigerators, stoves, sensible and durable furniture, vacations.

Full nest I; youngest child under 6

Home purchasing at peak.

Liquid assets low.

In some cases, both spouses work outside the home.

Dissatisfied with financial position and amount of money saved.

Interested in new products.

Like advertised products.

Buy: washers, dryers, TV sets, baby food, chest rubs and cough medicine, vitamins, dolls, wagons, sleds, skates.

Full nest II; youngest child 6 or over

Financial position better.

In many cases, both spouses work outside the home.

Less influenced by advertising.

Buy larger-sized packages, multiple-unit deals.

Buy: many foods, cleaning materials, bicycles, music lessons, pianos.

Full nest III; older married couples with dependent children

Financial position still better.

In many cases, both spouses work outside the home.

Some children get jobs.

Hard to influence with advertising.

High average purchase of durables.

Buy: new, more tasteful furniture, auto, travel, non-necessary appliances, boats, dental services, magazines.

Empty nest I; older married couples, no children living with them, head in labour force

Home ownership at peak.

Most satisfied with financial position and money saved.

Interested in travel, recreation, self-education.

Make gifts and contributions.

Not interested in new products.

Buy: vacations, luxuries, home improvements.

Empty nest II; older married couples, no children living at home, head retired

Drastic cut in income.

Keep home.

Buy: medical appliances, medical care, products that aid health, sleep, and digestion.

Solitary survivor, in labour force

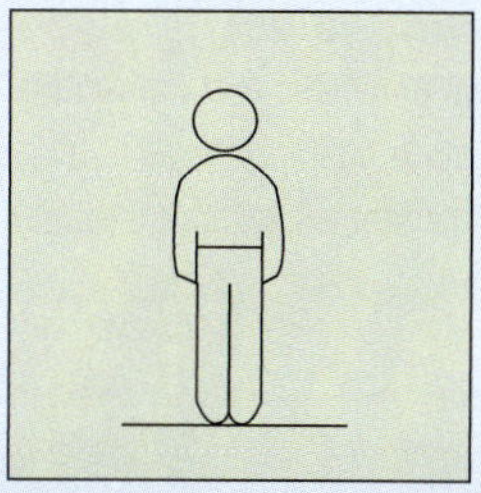

Income still good, but likely to sell home.

Solitary survivor, retired

Same medical and product needs as other retired group; drastic cut in income.

Special need for attention, affection, and security.

SOURCE: William D. Wells and George Gubar, "Life Cycle Concept in Marketing Research," *Journal of Marketing Research,* November 1966, p. 362. Reprinted with permission from the American Marketing Association.

In spite of the considerable increase in disposable income in the past 30 years, many households are still in the low-income bracket or find their higher incomes inadequate to meet all of their needs. Furthermore, many customers are willing to forgo services in order to get lower prices. One consequence of this market shift has been the development of discount houses, dollar stores, and superstores, where the emphasis is on convenience and low prices.

Marketers need to study consumer spending patterns across segments, as well as the distribution of consumer income. Marketers also should be aware of the shifts in spending patterns that have been occurring in recent years. Families have increased the percentage of their total expenditures on housing, health, and utilities. Spending (as a percentage of total income) has decreased for food, beverages, clothing, and home expenses (except utilities). But, expenditure patterns are not the same for all families. These patterns vary considerably, depending on family income levels and life-cycle stage. (See Table 5-3.)

Psychographic and Relationship Segmentation

Demographic data are used to segment markets because these data are related to easily measured and observed characteristics and behaviour. However, demographics are not themselves the causes of behaviour. People don't buy in-line skates because they are young — they buy them because they enjoy an active, outdoor lifestyle, and it so happens that such people are also typically younger. Thus, demographics often correlate with behaviour, but they do not explain it.

Marketers have gone beyond demographic attributes in an effort to understand why consumers behave as they do. Most now engage in a deeper kind of segmentation, which involves examining customer attributes such as attitudes, interests and lifestyles. When demographics and attributes such as these are combined, richer descriptions of segments are produced.

Psychographics The term psychographics was coined to describe a wide variety of psychological and behavioural descriptions of customers. The development of psychographics evolved from attempts by marketers to find factors more directly related to purchase and consumption than demographics are. Lifestyles are often considered to be part of the broad topic of psychographics, although we are treating this subject separately here.

activities, interests, and opinions
The bases of an individual's lifestyle; these characterize how people lead their lives.

Consumer psychographics tends to focus on variables such as customers' **activities, interests, and opinions**. A much deeper view of customers is possible once a marketer better understands their interests and opinions on certain topics and how they spend their time. Research on psychographics includes activities such as media usage, where people go for their vacations, what books they read, and what television programs they watch.

values (as distinct from *value*)
The principles that individuals hold to be important and by which they lead their lives.

Values are another important psychographic descriptor. According to psychologists, **values** are what we hold to be important, so they are a reflection of our needs, adjusted for the realities of the world in which we live. Researchers at the Survey Research Center at the University of Michigan have identified nine basic values that relate to purchase behaviour, which they call the List of Values:

1. Self-respect.
2. Self-fulfilment.
3. Security.
4. Sense of belonging.
5. Excitement.
6. Sense of accomplishment.
7. Fun and enjoyment in life.
8. Being well respected.
9. Having warm relationships.

While most people would view all of these values as desirable, their relative importance differs among customers, and their importance changes over a person's life. For example, people who value fun and enjoyment especially like skiing, dancing, bicycling, and backpacking, and people who value warm relationships give gifts for no particular reason. Thus, the relative strength of these values could be the basis for segmenting a market.

Lifestyles The term lifestyle is a very broad concept, relating to how people lead their lives. Lifestyles relate mainly to activities and interests. They reflect how you spend your time, what books you read, which television programs, specialty channels, or DVDs you watch, video games you play, the sites you surf on the Internet, and where you spend your leisure time and your money. People's lifestyles undoubtedly affect their choice of products and brands. Marketers are well aware of this and often attempt to segment their markets on a lifestyle basis.

Many successful companies have based their entire marketing strategy on appealing to customers who enjoy a certain lifestyle. They have paid close attention to their customers' changing wants and needs, and have earned a reputation as "experts" within a certain category. Mountain Equipment Co-op (MEC) is a favourite of many Canadians, and others, when it comes to climbing, cycling, hiking, camping, paddling, and snow-sports gear and clothing. Alberta-based retailer Lammle's Western Wear is very successful in western Canada with 22 stores in Alberta alone supplying customers with everything imaginable to lead a western lifestyle. The company is the official western wear retailer of the Calgary Exhibition and Stampede carrying a wide selection of product lines such as Wrangler, Skinny Minnie, Jack Daniels, John Deere, and Double D Ranchware allowing them to become the number one western retailer in North America. (**www.mec.ca**, **www.lammles.com**)

Mountain Equipment Co-op
Lammles Western Wear

Relationships With the increased attention being paid to customer relationships, many companies are focusing on segmenting their customer base in terms of the kind of relationship their customers currently have or would like to have with a company or brand. In recent years,

MARKETING AT WORK 5-2: STRATEGY

Magazine Targets Folks with Dough

If your newborn is into French designer sleepers, Italian nursery furniture, and gourmet baby food, there's a new magazine you night be interested in buying.

Advance Publications Inc., publisher of *Vogue* and *GQ* magazine has launched *Cookie* magazine, a parenting publication billed as an "upscale lifestyle magazine for sophisticated parents." The magazine is intended to appeal to parents with a "significantly higher" income than other parenting magazines try to attract. It appeals to sophisticated moms who don't shop for kids' clothes at Wal-Mart. But the magazine isn't just about clothes and imported furniture. According to Mary Berner, CEO of Advance Publications, "It's about quality. Sophisticated doesn't mean you buy things because of the name brands or shop in stores because they are perceived to be upscale."

Few career women read traditional parenting magazines —these appeal to women with a little more time on their hands. Berner says, "I love my children and I'm involved in their lives. But I really don't have time to make the craft projects that take two hours." *Cookie* also talks about family vacations and provides recipes from gourmet chefs for kid-friendly food. At the magazine's Web site, **www.cookiemag.com**, parents can get a little "taste" of *Cookie* with information on topics such fashion, entertainment, and travel.

Karl Moore, business professor at McGill University, thinks the magazine will do well as women are having children later in life and have greater resources and sophisticated tastes. "In a lot of families, out of guilt for not spending enough time with your kids, you buy them things to make up for it..." says Moore. "It's quite shallow but I think we all do that a bit." Ken Wong, marketing professor at Queen's University School of Business, said that there will be no shortage of advertisers wanting to reach the affluent 25-to-45-year-old women the magazine is targeting. The question is whether there will be enough readers!

QUESTION:

1. Discuss the segment that is being targeted by this new magazine and prepare a detailed profile of them. What else do they read? Where do they take vacations? What kind of cars do they drive? What other brands are targeting them?

SOURCE: Adapted from Keith McArthur, "Magazine Targets Folks with Dough," *The Globe and Mail*, March 2, 2005, p. B10, and www.cookiemag.com, January 29, 2006.

many progressive companies have come to realize that the long-term future of their operations is very much linked to their ability to develop relationships with customers. Where a positive relationship exists, customers are more likely to come back again and again, to spend more money with the company, and to refer other customers.

relationship segmentation
The process of segmenting a market on the basis of the types of relationships that customers want to have with a company or brand.

But not all customers want the same kind of relationship. It is extremely important, if a company intends to practise **relationship segmentation**, that the company develops appropriate relationships with customers so that their satisfaction is increased and they remain loyal customers. To do so requires a detailed understanding of the type of relationship that customers will find satisfying and a strategy to develop different types of relationships with different segments of customers.

Behavioural Segmentation

behavioural segmentation
Market segmentation based on consumers' product-related behaviour; typically, the benefits consumers desire from a product, the rate at which they use the product, and situations where it is used.

Some marketers regularly attempt to segment their markets on the basis of the customer's product-related behaviour, utilizing **behavioural segmentation**. This section briefly considers three of these bases for segmentation: the benefits desired from a product, the rate at which the consumer uses the product, and occasions or situations when it is used.

Benefits Desired Different customers look for different things when they buy a product or service. Let's consider a hypothetical division of the toothpaste market based on the benefits desired. The segment names and the benefits sought by each segment might look like this:

- ***Sensories:*** Flavour and appearance
- ***Worriers:*** Decay prevention and plaque control
- ***Sociables:*** Whiteness of teeth
- ***Independents:*** Low price

benefit segments
Segments of customers defined by the benefits they seek or experience from the purchase and use of products and services.

There was a time when a particular brand of toothpaste such as Crest or Colgate was "positioned" to appeal to one of these **benefit segments**. Today, with the concept of brand extension very much in evidence, each of the major brands will have at least one version to appeal to each segment and others.

usage rate
The rate at which people use or consume a product, or participate in the use of a service.

Two things determine the effectiveness of benefit segmentation. First, the specific benefits consumers are seeking must be identified, and then the importance of each benefit must be determined. This typically involves several research steps, beginning with the identification of benefits related to a particular product or behaviour through brainstorming, observing consumers, focus groups, and later, surveys to determine how important the benefits are and how many consumers seek each one.

Usage Rate Another product-related basis for market segmentation is **usage rate** — the rate at which people use or consume a product. Thus, we can have categories for non-users, light users, medium users, and heavy users. Normally, a company is most interested in the heavy users of its product. In most categories, 50 percent or less of users typically account for 80 to 90 percent of the total purchases of a given product or service — which is why most beer brands seem to be targeted at guys aged 19-25. That is not to say that this percentage applies precisely in all product or service categories; rather, it is the principle that is important.

Procter & Gamble targets several different segments with the Crest brand.

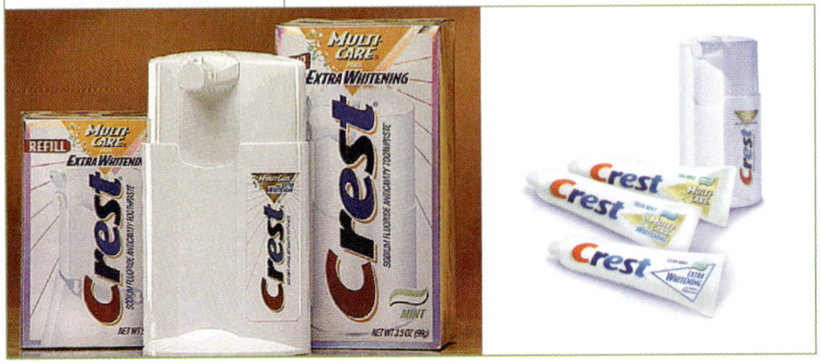

With all these brands available, why does Heinz have such a large share?

Among a company's target segments, there are usually one or two that contain heavier users of the product. These segments represent important target segments. In such circumstances, most companies would prefer to be the market leader among the heavy users, rather than targeting their marketing efforts at customers who use relatively little of the product.

For example, in recent years, lower-priced and private-label ketchup brands have somewhat eroded Heinz's market share. To win back customers, Heinz is going after the heavy half of ketchup users — children and teenagers — with new product variations. The goal is to build an extreme brand personality through extreme products! Introducing Heinz Ketchup in green and purple revived interest in the brand. There was also a special nozzle designed for accurate squirting and an ergonomically smart shape that allowed smaller hands to hold on tight, allowing for some mealtime masterpiece creations from little artists. Limited-time "talking labels" were also introduced, with messages such as "Makes hot dogs chase their tails," "Comes out quicker for curly fries," or "Are your French fries lonely?"[7]

Sometimes the target market is the non-user or light user, and the objective is to woo this customer into a higher-use category. Or light users may constitute an attractive niche for a marketer, simply because they are being ignored by other firms that are targeting heavy users. Once the characteristics of these light users have been identified, a marketer might try to increase usage rates by promoting (1) new uses for a product (baking soda as a deodorant), (2) new times for usage (off-season vacations), or (3) multiple packaging (a 12-pack of soft drinks).

Occasions Another popular approach to benefit segmentation is segmenting the market based on the occasions or situations that customers would associate with the use of a product or service. Certain brands tend to be associated with certain occasions. For example, you may buy one brand of beer if you are taking a six-pack to a party and another if you are at a special restaurant with a friend. Many restaurants and hotels cater to special occasions such as weddings by offering entertainment and all-inclusive rates. This supports the notion that marketers must know a great deal about the context in which various segments of customers use certain products and services, and the situations that they would associate with the use of certain brands.

PAGE UP!

1. Name three bases for demographic segmentation.
2. What is psychographic segmentation?
3. How do people's lifestyles affect their choice of products?

How Many Segments?

Let's assume that a company has segmented the total customer base for its product or service. Now management is in a position to select one or more segments to which it will target its marketing efforts. Despite the concept of a mass market, no company or brand is directed at the entire market, simply because no product has universal appeal or is bought by everyone.

Even commodity products like salt or sugar are marketed to different segments through different package sizes and distribution channels — it's obvious that there are household and commercial markets for products such as these.

A company can follow a strategy of directing its efforts at a single segment, or it can simultaneously target a number of segments. But, before a single- or multiple-segment strategy is decided upon, the potential of the identified segments must be determined, as well as the company's ability to manage more than one segment. This calls for establishing some guidelines for determining which segments to target and how many. Generally, even the largest companies will not spread their marketing efforts too thin by trying to satisfy a very large number of customer segments.

Single-segment strategy

single-segment strategy
The selection of one homogeneous segment from within a total market to be the target market.

A **single-segment strategy** involves selecting as the target market one homogeneous segment from within the total market. One marketing mix is then developed to reach this single segment. A small company may want to concentrate on a single market segment rather than to take on many competitors in a broad market. The decision to direct the firm's efforts at only one segment is often associated with the concept of niche marketing which we will discuss in the section of this chapter that deals with Positioning. Many fashion retailers such as Aritzia and lululemon seem to be targeting one segment in particular.

Companies that have limited resources or that have a particular expertise in a certain speciality will often adopt a single segment strategy. Similarly, some firms will start with a focus on a particular segment, but will then expand into other segments as they grow and develop

lululemon understands its target segment very well.

expertise in other areas. We often see a single-segment strategy employed where a company has several brands, each of which is directed at a single segment.

lululemon, founded in Kitsilano, Vancouver — one of the healthiest places in the world — "focuses on a healthy, balanced fun-filled way of life." Founded in response to the exponential increase of women participating in athletics and yoga, the company's first retail space included a design room that was also shared with a fledgling yoga studio. lululemon has expanded its yoga-inspired athletic apparel line to include products for personal training, running, and dance. In 2005, the company opened yet another location in the trendy upscale Yorkville district. With the number of yoga participants in the U.S. jumping more than five-fold from 3 million in 2000 to 16.5 million in 2005, there seems to be excellent growth potential for this company which plans to open 15 U.S. locations annually over the next five years.[8]

Aritzia began in 1984 as a boutique on the west side of Vancouver. The retail-clothing boutique grew quickly by catering to progressive and aware young women aged 14 to 30 years of age. The product focus is on the latest in urban style for young women who have an eye for the unique. Each boutique is custom-designed with special attention to function, colour, texture, and atmosphere and the Web site is a mix of fashion, music, culture, and arts and crafts with links to such sites as appledolls.org and pixyland.org. Aritzia is the exclusive Canadian retailer for brands such as Talula Babaton, Zoo York, Juicy Couture, and TNA, and carries fashion favourites from California such as Ella Moss and Habitual.[9]

This focused strategy enables a company to concentrate in depth on one segment and to acquire a reputation as a specialist or an expert in a limited market — young consumers who appreciate such brands and feel that the company "gets them." A company can enter such a market with limited resources and, as long as the single segment remains a small market, large competitors are likely to leave the single-segment specialist alone. However, if the small market shows signs of becoming a large market, bigger companies may well jump in.

multiple-segment strategy
A strategy that involves the selection of two or more groups of potential customers as target markets.

The big risk and limitation to a single-segment strategy is that the firm has all of its eggs in one basket. If that single segment declines in market potential, the seller can suffer considerably. Also, a seller with a strong name and reputation in one segment may find it difficult to expand into another segment.

Multiple-segment strategy

Under a **multiple-segment strategy**, two or more different groups of prospective customers are identified as target segments. A separate marketing mix is developed to reach each segment. Most large companies will cater to a number of segments. Even a brand such as Coke or Kraft Dinner which would seem to have almost universal appeal, is in fact marketed differently to several segments.

Fitting new and different segments.

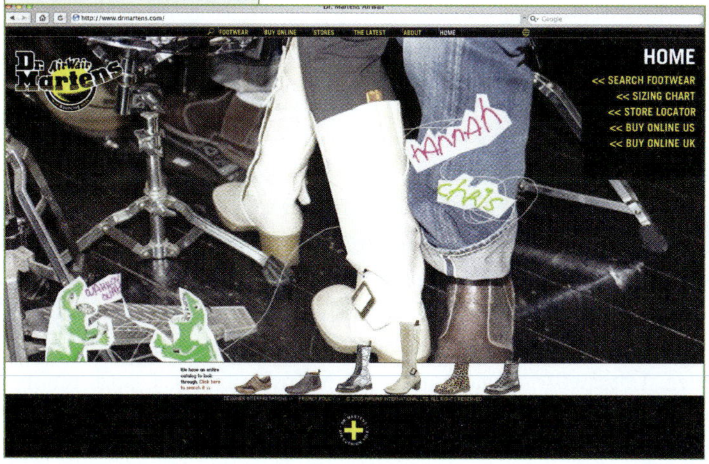

In a multiple-segment strategy, a marketer frequently develops a different version of the basic product for each segment. However, market segmentation can also be accomplished with no change in the product, but rather with separate distribution channels or promotional appeals, each tailored to a given market segment. AirWair, the company that markets and distributes Doc Martens footwear, now develops products for a wider range of target segments. The company's original products (such as the 1460 boot) have always been associated with subcultures such as psychobilly, skins, goth, or grunge. Now older, many from these ranks have joined the adult world and have responsibilities, such as their own children. The company still features its classic lines, but also has developed products for casual business dressing for men, women, and a line for youth. Adult product lines include classic, street, urban, and leisure. The youth line includes boots, shoes and sandals available in a wide range of colours and patterns for these second generation "docmarten" wearers. Still true to their original image, the company participates in the music industry and features an online magazine as well as several documentaries — all intended to represent the voice of youth culture.[10]

Profiling Target Segments

Once a marketer has determined which segments will represent the main focus of the company, it is a very useful exercise to develop detailed profiles of each of the segments. The purpose of the profiling exercise is to prepare as detailed an overview as possible of the customers who make up each of the segments of interest, in terms of their demographic, psychographic, and lifestyle characteristics. The main premise behind this profiling is, "The better we know the customers in each of the segments we plan to target, the more likely it is that we can put together an integrated marketing program that they will find attractive."

Most sophisticated marketing companies will have quite detailed profiles of their target customers, much of it based on knowledge about their personal and family details, and their buying and consumption patterns gleaned from customer databases, and from both qualitative and quantitative research. Comprehensive profiles will contain not only demographic and consumption data, but also details relating to the neighbourhoods where they live, type of car they drive, books they read, vacations taken, children's activities, and a great deal more. Some companies will personalize their segment profiles even more by actually giving them names — for a shopping centre, for example, "Susan" may be a young mother with a three-year old daughter who visits the mall twice a week; while "Fred" may be a recently-retired bank manager who accompanies his wife to the mall once or twice a month to buy things for the grandkids. When these profiles are detailed and done well, they allow marketing and other staff to "get to know their customers" in a way that becomes very personal.

Positioning

positioning
The strategy of creating an appropriate image for a company or brand in the minds of its target customers — what the brand stands for, what it means to customers.

The concept of market **positioning** is closely related to segmentation and to differentiation. A marketer must determine how the company's brands or stores or image is perceived by the public in general and, more particularly, by the customer segments that have been selected as the principal focus for the firm. As part of a company's marketing strategy, decisions must be made concerning how the company and its brands are to be portrayed to convey the correct image to the target segment. Positioning, therefore, relates to the use of various marketing techniques and marketing-mix variables to create the desired image and consumer perception of the company and its value proposition so that they are seen to be different from that offered by the competition.

A company may develop a positioning strategy for a particular brand or group of brands, for a retail store or chain, or for the company itself. The process involves answering questions such as: Who are the target customer segments for this brand or store or company? On what basis do we want to appeal to these segments? What do we want people to think of when they hear our name? What do we want to be known for? What should our brand stand for and what should we mean to people? How do we want to be seen to be different from our competitors or from other brands or companies in the market? In dealing with questions such as these, the company is really asking: What position do we wish to occupy in this market or, more correctly, in the minds of target customers?

One new Canadian retailer, Lotuswear, a Vancouver-based manufacturer and retailer of yoga and activewear clothing, offers its customers a range of clothing under their LOTUSWEAR and LOTUSFRESH brands. After months of study into what women are

Positioned as a "worthwhile" company.

Lotuswear

looking for in yoga and activewear, they learned that customers were looking for fabric that was long-lasting and non-balling and non-pilling; but they also wanted stylish gear that could keep up with their active lifestyles with superior quality and affordable pricing. Most importantly, their research also revealed two distinct groups of female shoppers — the "body-conscious" consumer and the "body-comfortable" consumer. From their launch in 2004, the company set out to produce a product line for each of these segments. The company also has positioned itself as a "worthwhile" company with a higher purpose for its existence, a commitment to the community, and a responsibility to support ethical standards and fair practice. (**www.lotuswear.com**).

Quicksilver's positioning is clear.

Even those firms that sell a more limited range of products — such as clothing — often try to develop a 'personality' for the brand that represents a certain lifestyle — a lifestyle that appeals to their intended target market(s). Quiksilver offers a selection of items for males and females ranging from tops and bottoms to watches and sunglasses. To represent the 'personality' of the brand and these products, the company has associated itself with the boardriding lifestyle — surf, snow or skate. The three often attract many of the same young consumers. The company uses well-known personalities from these sports to endorse its products as well as offering a wealth of information about events and personalities on the company's Web site.[11]

Positioning, therefore, is a strategy for locating a brand or store in the customer's mind in relation to its rating on certain dimensions or attributes that the customer considers important. It involves staking out a place in the collective perception of consumers in which the brand or store or company can establish an image that will be appropriate for certain segments of the market. This image is created through the effective use of marketing-mix variables, including advertising, product design, pricing, packaging, store decor, and level of service.

The creation of the appropriate positioning may be approached in a combination of ways. In the first place, a firm may wish to occupy a position as compared to that occupied by competitors. It may choose a position that is distinct from the one occupied by a competitor or may choose to challenge a competitor directly, thereby trying to occupy roughly the same position. On the other hand, the positioning strategy may be developed to position the brand or firm through the creation of an image tailored to the characteristics, needs, preferences, attitudes, and feelings of a particular segment of the market. This approach is dependent on the company having selected certain target segments. The image of the product, brand, or store is then tailored to appeal to those segments.

Finally, a brand or company may be positioned on the basis of its inherent characteristics. In other words, the marketing staff of the company would have to decide what the brand or retailer is to be known for and set about creating the appropriate image. Such an approach deals implicitly with positioning against competition and meeting the needs of particular segments, but is often undertaken in response to the identification of a market gap, where no company has established a dominant position.

Positioning strategies

Once a company has determined its segmentation objectives and has identified the segments toward which its brands are to be targeted, it may adopt a number of positioning strategies to accomplish its objectives.

1. ***Take on the competition head-on***: By deciding to challenge the market leader or to target large segments of the market with a broad appeal, a marketer is saying, "Our brand is as good as or better than the leader." Such a strategy is exemplified in the so-called "cola wars," in which Pepsi-Cola and Coca-Cola have been fighting for market leadership by attempting to create the widest appeal to attract as many consumers as possible.

MARKETING AT WORK 5-3: RELATIONSHIPS

National Ready for New Relationships

National Car and Truck Rental is ready for a new relationship with customers. The company's latest advertising campaign, "When you're ready, we're ready," focuses on what the company calls "customer-centricity." Frank DeCesare, Vice-President, Marketing for National says, "We really need to build on what we have done to develop and foster that personal relationship with our customers." He adds that because car rentals are based on a specific requirement, a weekend getaway or a sporting event, the ads are about "being able to act on the need and delivering on the need."

The ads are intended to show how National has the solution for whatever your need. In one of the new commercials, called "Low Rider," we see how having the wrong car can set the wrong example in business with a group of business people bouncing down the street arriving at their appointment in a low-rider car. The voiceover tells viewers how National's wide selection of vehicles can help ensure you make the right impression.

As well, the company offers many perks to its Emerald Club members including upgrades, XM radio, and models exclusive to Club members only, along with the usual reward points and express line service.

QUESTIONS:

1. What does this new approach by National Car and Truck Rental tell you about how the company wishes to position itself and how it plans to differentiate itself from competitors like Budget and Avis?
2. How effective do you think the new strategy will be?

SOURCE: Adapted from Rebecca Harris, "National Ready for New Customers," *Marketing Magazine Online*, www.marketingmag.ca, February 14, 2005, and National Car Rental Web site, www.nationalcar.com.

2. ***Occupy a gap in the market***: A number of companies have moved to fill a gap in a market by positioning a brand to appeal to a certain segment of consumers or to take advantage of the disappearance of a competitor. For example, Volvo differentiates its cars from competitors by emphasizing safety.

3. ***Set a brand apart from the competition***: Often a company will decide to employ a strategy that says, "Our brand is not like all of the others; this is why you should buy ours." This involves positioning a brand or store to avoid head-to-head competition with market leaders or with brands that have an established image or reputation and a secure market share. Jumbo Video distinguishes itself with its "guaranteed in-stock" policy for featured new releases while its competition, Blockbuster Video, appeals to another segment with its *End of Late Fees* policy giving members seven days grace to return movie rentals — on the eight day, however, the rental is converted to a purchase and the customer is charged the purchase price of the DVD.

4. ***Occupy a position of leadership***: Some companies that are clearly market leaders are not particularly interested in positioning themselves against the competition, but rather are likely to stake out a position as clear market leader, known to be ahead of the pack and the leader in such areas as product quality, service to customers, profitability, innovations, or technology. Companies such as Loblaws and the Royal Bank of Canada tend to be regarded by many consumers as market leaders whose market franchises are so large and well established that competitors often try to emulate them and to position themselves against them. This approach can also work in cyberspace, as with Google.ca — the Google search engine positions itself to be almost overwhelmingly comprehensive, stating that it searches more than two billion Web pages at each request.

positioning map
A graphic representation of the relative positions that various brands or companies occupy in the minds of their target customers. Positioning maps are based on data collected in customer surveys.

5. ***Position to appeal to lifestyle segments***: Often a company will position itself to appeal to certain segments of the market that are defined not only by demographic characteristics but also by lifestyles. For example, there are two equally large segments of Porsche buyers with quite different lifestyles and reasons for buying the car. One group is driven by power and control. Called "top guns" at Porsche, they buy the car to be noticed. Another group, the "proud patrons," views a Porsche as a reward for hard work. To them, owning the car is an end in itself. They don't need the acknowledgment of others to derive satisfaction from a Porsche. Clearly, an ad that would appeal to the top guns could easily alienate the proud patrons.

Figure 5-2:
Perceptual Map of Jeans Brands

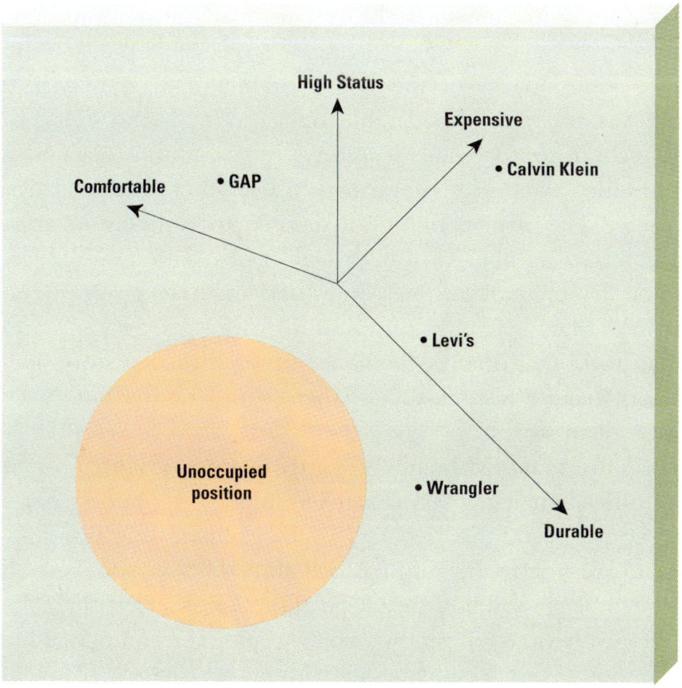

Positioning maps

One of the easiest ways to get a feel for the concept of positioning is to examine products, brands, or stores as they are displayed on a **positioning map**. Such maps are developed through marketing research, which explores the image that consumers have of various brands or stores and rates each competing brand or store on a series of attributes. Once the relevant attributes have been identified, research is undertaken to determine which are most important in influencing the consumer to select one brand over another. Finally, consumers are asked to rate the competing brands or stores in the market on each of the important dimensions or attributes. Such research data allow the researcher to present the brands or stores in a map similar to that shown in Figure 5-2.

The lengths of the lines (or vectors) in the positioning map indicate the relative importance of the attributes, and the position of a brand relative to a vector indicates how closely the brand is associated with the attribute. For example, Calvin Klein jeans are perceived as more expensive than Gap jeans but not as comfortable, while Wranglers are seen as durable but low in status. This map suggests that brands offering comfort and durability at a reasonable price would have little competition from these other brands. Thus, it might be an attractive option.

Positioning maps allow the marketer to see where its brand is perceived to lie in the market in comparison with competing brands, how the brand is rated on various attributes, and where the brand lies in relation to the various identified segments. Typically, a number of brands that are perceived to have similar characteristics are clustered together in close proximity to those large segments of the market that have considerable buying power. Other brands occupy positions in the market where they are seen to appeal to different segments and to display different characteristics.

One benefit of examining perceptual market maps is that the marketer can identify how its brand or store is perceived by consumers in comparison with competitors. Such examination often leads to a decision to reposition a brand, a topic covered later in this chapter. Also, the examination of market maps may lead to the identification of market gaps — positions in the market that are not now filled by existing brands or stores and where untapped market demand may be said to exist.

Repositioning

repositioning
The process of moving a company, store, or brand to a new position in the minds of target customers, usually by changing its image.

Repositioning is a variation of a positioning strategy that involves changing the positioning of a brand or store in response to changes taking place in the broader market environment. The need to reposition a brand or retail store may result from one of three market conditions. First, management may identify a gap in the market that may be filled by altering the image of the store or brand — that is, changing the position it occupies in the minds of consumers. For example, a retailer in a local market may realize that the average age of its customer base is increasing and decide to reposition the store to have greater appeal to an older market segment.

Second, repositioning may be required by an increase in competitive activity. For example, Canada's retail industry has suffered considerable upheaval with the entry of new U.S. competitors. PharmaPlus, a Toronto-based drugstore, is positioning itself as a store that focuses on the core product categories of pharmacy, over-the-counter drugs, health and beauty aids, and baby care. This firm is finding it difficult to compete in non-pharmacy areas because of the increased number of low-priced chains such as Wal-Mart (**www.walmart.com**), who can undercut conventional drugstores in these product categories. Zellers has responded to Wal-Mart by renewing focus on its loyalty program and by introducing "best-value" format stores that offer convenience through smaller store sizes located in densely populated areas, offering less stock variety than regular outlets but "awesome deals" not possible from large chain stores.

www.walmart.com

Canadian Tire is one of Canada's most familiar brands — partly because of what is often jokingly referred to as our second official currency (Canadian Tire money) — but it's not a new one. In fact, it's more than 80 years old and that has been an integral part of its positioning: invoking memories of your first bike, hockey stick, or baseball glove. This sense of being a part of growing up in Canada has often been spun into the fabric of the store's advertising. The store's new positioning is intended to evolve and refresh this, while keeping the equity that has developed with many consumers. It shows people enjoying life with products purchased from

Canadian Tire. It's less about reflecting on past memories and more about creating energy and inspiration — creating new memories.

Third, it may be necessary to reposition a brand or store in response to a change in the demographic characteristics, attitudes, or values of the target consumer market. Packaged-food producers have addressed these trends in recent years as a result of significant changes in eating habits. High-fat foods are no longer appealing to mass markets. This is becoming particularly evident now that labels must carry information about package contents. Heinz, Nabisco, Kraft, and other major packaged-food suppliers are creating new products such as flavoured cream cheeses and ultra-low-fat salad dressings, Linda McCartney vegetarian cuisine (introduced by Paul McCartney's late wife), and Ore Ida Funky Fries in flavours such as cocoa, cinnamon, and sour cream, and colours such as electric blue. Many food manufacturers are now offering products that contain no trans-fats as consumers have begun to take a much more focused interest in additives and other ingredients in foods.

Another change has been in the demand for "convenience" foods or "meal solutions." This has led manufacturers and supermarkets to alter their product offerings. Manufacturers have increased the number of meal "kits" they offer, including prepared frozen main courses that require only cooking or the addition of a certain amount of the consumer's meat of choice. The delicatessen sections of supermarkets have expanded to offer consumers greater selections of home meal replacements: any frozen or fresh meal prepared in-store for immediate consumption at home. This includes items as varied as salad-in-a-bag, to prepared entrées bought by the kilogram, to individual meal packages that have main and side dishes pre-selected.

Niche marketing

niche marketing
A strategy in which goods and services are tailored to meet the needs of small market segments.

BACK TO THE TOP

Some marketers may stake out "niche" positions for their brands; they create an image that is quite distinct and intended to appeal to a fairly narrow segment of the market. This is called **niche marketing**. Within the Canadian beer market, for example, brands such as Schooner and Steam Whistle, imported beers such as Stella Artois, Sol, Guinness, and Corona, and the "handmade" brands are considered to be niche brands, while mainstream brands such as Coors Light, Molson Canadian and Labatt's Blue are positioned to appeal to much larger segments. Many of the credit card products referred to in the chapter opener are in fact targeted at fairly narrow market niches.

Niche brands generally are not positioned to meet major competitors head-on, but rather to be leaders in a very narrow area of the market. Smaller companies often successfully carve out a niche for themselves. To continue with our beer examples, successful microbrewers such as Upper Canada Brewing, Les Brasseurs du Nord, Celtique, Unibroue, and Granville Island Brewery are really niche marketers; they are satisfied with occupying a relatively small position in a very large market by catering to the tastes and preferences of consumers who want something different. Currently, microbrews and imports hold only 5 percent and 8 percent, respectively, of the market. With evolving consumer tastes and preferences for upscale alcoholic products, continued growth is expected for these products.[12]

Niche marketing is generally a successful strategy for smaller companies that do not have the financial and other resources generally available to large companies. To be successful in positioning itself as a niche player in the market, a company or the managers of a niche brand must have identified a segment of the market that is not now being served adequately by the brands and companies that are in the market. That segment must have sufficient potential buying power to warrant the development of a marketing program, it must be sufficiently small that larger companies are unlikely to retaliate if the niche brand is successful, and the niche marketer must have detailed knowledge of the characteristics of the members of the segment and their needs and preferences. One author has suggested that a company should follow four steps in implementing a successful niche marketing strategy.[13]

1. ***Identify an appropriate niche*** through marketing research that will indicate segments of the market that are not being well served by existing brands or where competition is not intense.
2. ***Exploit the niche*** by determining the likelihood of competitive retaliation and the length of time the company will enjoy a competitive advantage.
3. ***Expand the niche*** by meeting changing needs of the market segment, expanding the customer base, and making more effective use of marketing variables.
4. ***Defend the niche*** by continuing to meet the needs of segment members through improving the product and offering better service or lower prices.

Differentiation

Regardless of how many segments a company decides to focus on, or the characteristics and composition of those segments, one unavoidable fact is that the firm will encounter competition. Only in the kinds of monopoly situations found in regulated industries is there likely to be a relative absence of competition. Just about every company, therefore, faces the challenge of gaining an advantage over its competition. To do so, it must be able to differentiate its value proposition from that of the competitors, to set itself apart from the others, to give customers a reason to deal with them.

differentiation
The strategy of setting a company or brand apart from its competition in the minds of its customers or prospective customers.

Differentiation is the strategy by which one firm attempts to distinguish its value proposition from that of competitive companies and brands that are targeted at the same customer segments. By differentiating its products, its quality and level of service, and the way in which it interacts with its customers, a company is attempting to create the impression that what it offers is more attractive to the members of its target segment than the competitors' offer.

At its simplest level, differentiation is focused on creating product differences and on communicating messages to customers that the firm or brand is different. This will usually involve (1) changing some feature of the product (for example, packaging colour or label design), (2) using a promotional appeal that features a differentiating benefit, or (3) using advertising and other promotional strategies to create a differentiating image for the brand, product, or service. Gatorade has used a combination of these to maintain its earnest image and market share in an increasingly competitive marketplace for energy beverages. It has introduced its own line of water, Propel, which is lightly flavoured and "vitamin-packed." It has also introduced alongside its regular thirst quencher products a line of endurance formula beverages, nutrition shakes and energy bars. To promote its image as a serious product for athletes the brand's Web site features information for endurance athletes as well as links and resource libraries for athletic trainers and coaches. As well, the site has a pro athletes page featuring talents such as Abby Wambach, Jennie Finch, Derek Jeter and Yao Ming with career highlights and their favourite Gatorade flavour.[14]

Differentiation is an important strategy in any situation where a company wants to point out or create a difference between what it offers to customers and what is offered by its competitors. It is particularly important in situations where the consumer is unable to understand or appreciate the differences that do exist. Increasingly, companies are turning to service and how they treat customers to differentiate their companies. With so many products now being perceived by consumers to be quite similar, companies that can offer the best service to their customers are getting the business.

With an increased focus on the customer, many companies are looking for new ways to differentiate themselves in the minds of target customers. We are seeing companies make major investments in call centres, help desks, and other resources to provide customer support. Retailers differentiate themselves by employing capable, informed and helpful sales staff to interact with customers. At Running Room, customers are most likely to be served by runners. At Mountain Equipment Co-op, they are likely to deal with people who are themselves avid hikers, climbers and kayakers. The people companies employ to interact with customers represent an important component in a differentiation strategy.

Other companies differentiate in terms of how they help their customers achieve things. Supermarkets like Loblaws and Sobeys offer cooking classes at the supermarket. The Home Depot will teach their customers how to lay ceramic tiles, hang wallpaper, or build a treehouse. By offering such classes, these retailers are setting themselves apart from other retailers, are getting more involved in the lives of their customers, and are contributing to their lives in ways that retailers traditionally have not done. They are striving to be more than just a retail store.

Finally, some firms are differentiating themselves in terms of the customer experience they provide. They consider the experience in two contexts — first, the experience that customers have in dealing with the firm; and second, the kinds of experiences that they can make possible for the customer. In the first place, companies are trying to ensure that the process of interacting with the company is as smooth and pleasant as possible, including interaction in person, through telephone systems and the company Web site. These companies emphasize the accessibility and convenience of their people, systems, and channels of contact, the quality of people they employ, and how they meet and greet customers.

A second approach to differentiation through customer experience relates to the experiences that companies can make possible for their customers. By teaching a homeowner how to build a deck, the Home Depot makes possible fun family weekends. Some companies actually specialize in the provision of experiences and work to ensure that these are as pleasant and memorable as possible. Some holiday providers such as Club Med, Sandals, and Celebrity Cruises ensure that every detail of your 'adventure' is tailored to your individual wants, such as having the same cabin attendant throughout your Celebrity cruise who will remember your meal and drink preferences as well as to get your shoes shined for the next evening's meal in the formal dining room. Other holiday-makers, such as Club 18-30, offer a slightly different experience but with the same strategy in mind. The company has 'reps' who take guests on day and evening outings outside of the resort to local clubs, restaurants and other venues ensuring that they experience the best and wildest of local entertainment and adventure — this can mean anything from a pub crawl through local taverns to finding the best after-hours bars for foam parties and dancing until dawn.

Value-Add Strategies

As we have observed in earlier chapters of this book, marketing may be viewed as the creation of value for customers. The concept of value is much talked about in marketing, but few companies appear to have a coordinated strategy for adding value for their customers. Value creation lies at the heart of marketing — it may be said that this is what marketing is all about, creating increasing levels of value for customers. Customers deal with companies so as to acquire something of value, and they will prefer to deal with companies and brands that offer them more than they can get from other companies. Customers are also prepared to pay more for things to which they attach higher value.

To create value effectively, a company must know a great deal about its customers so as to have a clear picture of what they would value if it was offered. Many companies have failed because they did not have a solid understanding of what their customers were looking for or what would make a difference in their perception of value received. Therefore, value cannot be created from the firm's perspective alone; it must be based on solid understanding of how the customer defines value. A change in the company's value proposition is not really valuable unless it is perceived to be valuable by target customers.

Adding value is actually a differentiation strategy for companies. By adding value more effectively than its competitors, a firm is actually gaining a competitive advantage. But value is also a very complex subject. If we are not careful, we may view value creation very simplistically — it's not just about value for money. Value creation may not involve additions to a product or the reduction of prices. In fact, adding value may have little or nothing to do with price.

Companies need a strategy for creating and adding value for customers at a number of different levels. We have discussed throughout the text that value is the result of a process of give and get. Customers subconsciously weigh what they get against what they have to give to acquire it. Value, therefore, may be represented as an equation — it may be created by increasing what a customer gets or by decreasing what a customer has to give. A firm can create or add value for its customers by adding certain things or by decreasing others. We can add product features or more options for paying bills, or we can decrease time to delivery or the number of steps in an order process.

If we think back to the Drivers of Customer Satisfaction model in Chapter 1, we recall that the factors that influence customer satisfaction may be thought of as existing at five levels. By focusing on value creation at each level of this model, a firm can build a strategy of adding value.

A Broad View of Adding Value

Many companies are guilty of assuming that customers are constantly looking for the lowest price or always trying to save money. This is simply not the case. What customers are typically trying to do is to obtain the best value possible. Where they do not perceive much difference across brands, customers will indeed try to find the lowest price. But, they won't drive across town to save a few pennies, and they aren't prepared to put up with slow or rude service. Time and quality of service are two important factors in a firm's value creation strategy.

It is useful, therefore, to take a very broad view of how companies can add value for their customers. The simplest way is to add product features, or to "bundle" several products or services together for one low, low price. This is the strategy that telephone and cable TV companies have been following for many years.

Bundling is one opportunity for value creation.

But companies create value in many, more creative ways. A supermarket creates value by staying open 24 hours a day. A pharmacy creates value by offering a home delivery service for seniors. Canadian banks have added tremendous value for customers by allowing them to bank and even invest online.

Companies also add value by employing helpful, knowledgeable, friendly employees to deal with customers. They add tremendously to the customer's experience in dealing with a company. Other elements of the service experience represent opportunities to add value, through the reduction in waiting times, improved response times, and more efficient telephone and Web interactions.

Some firms create value simply by providing their customers with valuable information that allows them to get better value out of their products and services. Thus, a laptop manufacturer may include on its Web site tips that tell customers how to use certain features of the computer.

Value may be added when companies create pleasant or surprising experiences for their customers. When a family restaurant offers colouring books and crayons to occupy children while the family is waiting for their meal, it is adding value. When a shopping centre holds a fashion show or a wine tasting in Centre Court, it is adding value.

Companies can also create value by associating with things that are important to customers. The CIBC adds value through its sponsorship of the Run for the Cure. The Home Depot holds classes in its stores that show customers how to build a treehouse or install a new kitchen; Loblaws does the same with its cooking classes. These companies are essentially creating communities that enable customers to join with others in accomplishing goals.

In short, companies need to develop a strategy that will set themselves apart from their competitors by adding value for customers that the customers will find valuable, and that competitors have not thought of adding.

Tying the Strategies Together

In this chapter, we have reviewed the essential strategies that a company must address if it is to practise marketing effectively. While we presented them separately, in fact it is impossible for a company to consider one without the others. A company can not be all things to all customers and must, as a result, decide on the target segments to which it wishes to appeal. But, it cannot do so without at the same time deciding what kind of company it wishes to be and how it plans to be perceived in the marketplace. The segmentation and positioning decisions have to be made together because they have to be consistent with the characteristics and strengths of the company. A company positions itself so as to appeal to its target segments, but it also refines its segmentation to line up with the kind of company it wants to be.

The objective of the company is to gain a competitive advantage over its competitors who are also trying to appeal to its target segments. To do so means that the company must be able to convince customers that they are creating more value for them than competitors are. But the value that a company attempts to add must fit with what the target customers consider to be valuable to them. In other words, it must contribute to meeting their needs or to allowing them to achieve their goals. It must also be consistent with the positioning that the company has chosen for itself, with its image or brand personality. If the value-add strategy is not consistent with the company's positioning, it will not be perceived by target customers to be appropriate or believable.

PAGE UP!

1. What are the three target market strategies that a firm can follow?
2. A firm that develops a different version of the basic product for each segment would use a ________________ target market strategy.
3. How is positioning related to segmentation?

Key Terms and Concepts

activities, interests, and opinions 140
behavioural segmentation 142
benefit segments 142
business users 132
Census Metropolitan Area (CMA) 135
demographic segmentation 135
differentiation 152
discretionary purchasing power 138
end-consumers 132
family life cycle 138
geographic segmentation 134
market segmentation 127
multiple-segment strategy 145
niche marketing 151
personal disposable income 138
positioning 146
positioning map 149
relationship segmentation 142
repositioning 150
single-segment strategy 144
target segment 129
usage rate 142
values 140

Questions and Problems

1. Segmenting the market into different groups can be a very challenging task for a company. What are the benefits a company can expect to gain from segmenting its market?
2. MuchMusic (www.muchmusic.com) has, in recent years, spawned many variations so that there are now a total of five 'Much' music channels offered by CHUM Television. What are the advantages and disadvantages of pursuing such a strategy? Describe what you believe would be the target segment for each channel.
3. In which stage of the family life cycle are families likely to be the best prospects for each of the following products or services?
   a. Cellular phones.
   b. Dental braces.
   b. Hybrid automobiles.
   c. Solar energy panels.
   d. Adventure holidays.
   e. Refrigerators.
   f. Life insurance.
   g. Yoga classes.
4. Using the demographic and income segmentation bases discussed in this chapter, describe the segment likely to be the best market for:
   a. In-line skates.
   b. Good French wines.
   c. Power hand tools.
   d. Birthday cards.
   e. Gas barbecues.
5. Think of examples of brands in each of the following product categories that are targeted at heavy-user segments. Also give examples of brands that are clearly <u>not</u> targeting the heavy user.
   a. Dog food.
   b. Breakfast cereal.
   c. Beer.
   d. Motor oil.
   e. Shampoo.
   f. Soft drinks.
6. Suppose you are Toyota and the network of Toyota dealers across Canada. How is your marketing mix likely to differ when marketing to each of the following market segments? In answering this question, consider the changes that are taking place in how markets are being segmented. Think beyond demographic segmentation.
   a. High school students.
   b. Retired teachers.
   c. Blue-collar workers.
   d. Mothers.
   e. Young single adults.
7. Explain the similarities and differences between a single-segment and a multiple-segment target market strategy. What are the advantages and disadvantages of each strategy?
8. With Apple dominating the MP3 market with its iPod, how can other MP3 manufacturers such as Samsung position their products so as to differentiate themselves from iPod and gain some form of competitive advantage? To what customer segments should these other manufacturers direct their marketing strategy? Why?
9. Identify a number of brands, retailers, or restaurants with which you are familiar that have chosen to occupy a niche in the market. How would you describe the niche that each occupies? Why do you feel each has chosen this niche?
10. Why would a company decide that one of its brands needs to be repositioned? What market conditions are likely to lead to a decision to reposition a brand or company? Can you think of any brands or stores with which you are familiar that have recently been repositioned? What were their original positions? How would you describe the new position that each occupies in the market? How was the repositioning accomplished in each case?

Hands-On Marketing

1. Interview three friends who all own running shoes, but who are from different demographic groups (for example, different education, age, or gender). Using demographic characteristics only, describe in as much detail as possible the market segment each of your friends represents for a running shoe manufacturer. Is yours a very complete segment picture? Why or why not?
2. Consider a number of restaurants in your home town or in the city in which your university or college is located, and describe in as much detail as possible the target market segment that each of the restaurants is serving and the positioning strategy of each of the companies. One of the most interesting industries for which to prepare a positioning map is the restaurant business in any medium-sized to large city. Prepare a positioning map for the restaurants in your town, identifying those restaurants that you perceive to be located "close" to one another and that, therefore, are competing directly with one another. Are certain parts of your map "empty"? Do these suggest that there is a gap in the local restaurant market? If so, what kinds of restaurants might occupy those gaps?

Back to the Top

Knowing what you now know about market segmentation and positioning, think back to the chapter opener on the variety of options available when one applies for a credit card. Think about how financial institutions are addressing the needs of the different market segments. Select three different credit cards that seem to be designed to appeal to three different target segments and outline how they are positioned to appeal to these segments. How do the different banks attempt to differentiate these credit cards? What kind of value is offered by each card?

Online Learning Centre

Want to get better grades, tips on how to study more effectively, and up-to-date information on happenings in the world of marketing? Then, visit the Online Learning Centre for practice tests, Study Smart software, *Marketing Magazine*, and much more! **www.mcgrawhill.ca/olc/sommers**

CHAPTER 6

B2B Marketing

In this chapter, we turn our attention specifically to the situation in which a company is marketing to other businesses and organizations, which today is commonly referred to as B2B (business-to-business) marketing. In many ways, business markets are similar to the consumer markets we examined in the early chapters of this book, but there are also important differences. After studying this chapter, in addition to being able to describe how business markets differ from consumer markets, you should have an understanding of:

- The nature and scope of the B2B market.
- The components that make up the B2B market.
- The characteristics of business market demand.
- The determinants of business market demand.
- The buying motives, buying processes, and buying patterns in business markets.

More Than a Supplier

Natalie Mills and Soren Andersen were excited about their plans to open a restaurant in Natalie's hometown of North Bay, Ontario. They knew the next few months would be extremely busy. They had found an ideal location and now they knew they had to deal with a number of business matters, including financing, before their dream project could become a reality.

Natalie and Soren had met six years ago when both were studying at Le Cordon Bleu Culinary Arts Institute in Ottawa. After graduating from Canadore College with her diploma in Food and Nutrition Management, Natalie had decided to pursue her life-long dream of being a chef. She had enrolled in the Superior Patisserie program at Le Cordon Bleu Institute and graduated with her diplôme de patisserie. There she had met Soren, who had come from Copenhagen to enrol in the Superior Cuisine program at Le Cordon Bleu. They had been together ever since, working in a series of hotel and restaurant kitchens in Eastern Ontario. They decided a year or so ago to move to North Bay to open their own restaurant.

With the help of Natalie's parents, they had identified a building on Main Street in North Bay, which had until recently been the site of a family restaurant whose owners had retired. The building had a fully-equipped kitchen and, with some renovations, would be just right for the new venture. But, Natalie and Soren needed advice on how to put the deal together to buy or lease the building and to get their new business up and running. As they knew that financing would be needed, and that they should at least put their banking arrangements in place, they decided to stop in at the Royal Bank of Canada (RBC) branch, a few doors away from the restaurant on Main Street.

When they asked to see someone about business banking, they were introduced to Dave Matthews. Dave seemed genuinely interested in their plans and thanked them several times for coming in. But he quickly realized that Natalie and Soren had little more than a dream at this point and that they were going to need a lot of help before their restaurant would open down the street.

Dave asked whether Natalie and Soren had prepared a plan for their business, as one would certainly be needed if they were going to arrange financing with the bank or with other investors. When they responded that they had only some general ideas on how they wanted to proceed, Dave offered to work with them to build their business plan. He indicated that RBC would be able to offer whatever accounts and other banking arrangements they would need, but that he also wanted to do whatever he and the bank could to make their business successful. He suggested that they take a look at the RBC Royal Bank Web site where there was a series of pages devoted to "Starting a Business." He made an appointment to meet with them again in a week or so, after they had begun the preparation of their business plan.

This chapter examines the role of companies that market to other businesses and organizations — the business-to-business (B2B) market. It's important to understand the differences involved in marketing in the B2B, as compared with the B2C, market. What is the role of the Royal Bank of Canada in meeting the needs of small businesses such as the new North Bay restaurant? It seems like Dave Matthews wants to be more than a "banker" to Natalie and Soren.

The Nature and Scope of the B2B Market

business and organizational (B2B) market
The market consisting of business and other organizational users; involves business-to-business (B2B) interaction and relationships.

Having discussed consumer behaviour and introduced the role of the relationships between consumers and products and how consumer markets can be segmented and targeted, we now go behind the scenes to examine the business market and how business and organizational buying behaviour works. The **business and organizational market** (we will call it the B2B market), which is full of relationships between businesses and other organizations (many of them with supply chain involvements which are discussed in Chapter 12), consists of all business users — organizations that buy goods and services for one of the following purposes:

Campbell Soup Company
Bombardier

- ***To make other goods and services***: The Campbell Soup Company (**www.campbellsoup.com**) buys fresh vegetables for its Leamington, Ontario, plant; Bombardier (**www.bombardier.com**) in Montréal and its other Canadian and worldwide locations buys a great variety of different materials to make products as varied as its Ski-Doo snowmobiles, Sea-Doo personal watercraft, and regional jets.
- ***To resell to other business users or to consumers***: Loblaws buys canned tuna fish from South America and Asia to sell across Canada; Western Pipe buys lawn sprinkler equipment and supplies from Canadian, U.S., and offshore manufacturers and resells them to sprinkler contractors.
- ***To conduct the organization's operations***: The school that you attend buys office supplies and electronic office equipment (many fitted with Intel chips) for use in the registrar's office; Canadian Tire buys software to co-ordinate and manage its inventory system across the country.

B2B marketing
The marketing of goods and services to business and organizational users, rather than to end-consumers.

The business market deals with both consumer products and business products. **B2B marketing**, then, is the marketing of goods and services to businesses and other organizations, rather than to end-consumers.

Because the business market is largely invisible to the average consumer, its significance is underrated — it is actually huge in total sales volume and the number of firms involved. Approximately 50 percent of all manufactured products are sold to the business and organizational market. In addition, about 80 percent of all farm products and virtually all forest, sea, and mineral products are business goods.

The magnitude and complexity of the B2B market are also evident from the web of relationships and the many transactions required to produce and market a product. Look at your feet. Got your boots on? Think about what goes into getting those thick-soled, leather boots to you and other end-users. First, cattle are sold through one or two intermediaries before reaching a meat packer. Then the hides are sold to a tanner, who in turn sells the leather to a specialized footwear manufacturer. To this point, we are looking at the manufacturer's supply chain. The footwear manufacturer then builds a channel of distribution to sell the finished boots to a wholesaler, who markets them to select retail stores. Finally, they are then available to you, the end-consumer. At least five transactions are involved here, and each sale but the last one is a business-to-business market transaction. Each of the B2B transactions take place in a market that operates for that type of transaction.

Your footwear manufacturer also buys metal eyelets, laces, thread, glue, heels and soles, and zippers, as well as polishes and dyes. Consider something as simple as the bootlaces. Other industrial firms must first buy the raw cotton and then spin, weave, dye, and cut it so that it becomes shoestring material. All of the manufacturers involved have factories and offices with furniture, machinery, furnaces, lights, computer hardware and software, and maintenance equipment and supplies, which also are business goods that have to be produced and marketed. Imagine, then, the number of relationships that have developed and the transactions that have occurred from the cattle and cotton fields to the footwear you are now wearing. In short,

How many B2B markets are involved in getting these boots onto your feet?

hundreds of business products and business marketing activities may come into play before almost any consumer or business product reaches its final destination.

The magnitude and complexity of the B2B market looms even larger when we consider all of the business services involved throughout our "simple" footwear example. Each firm engaged in any stage of the production process probably uses outside accountants, computer systems designers, and law firms. Several of the producers may use advertising agencies. All of these companies will use the services of various financial institutions.

Every retail store and wholesaling establishment is a business user. Every bus company, airline, and shipping company is part of this market, as is every hotel, restaurant, bank, insurance company, software provider, hospital, theatre, and school. In all, there are close to a half million business users in Canada. While this falls far short of the more than 30 million Canadian consumers, the total sales volume in the business market far surpasses total sales to consumers. And it is mostly behind the scenes.

Components of the B2B Market

While Canada's more than 100,000 manufacturers comprise the major component of the business market, there are also five other components of note: resellers, government agencies, service companies, agriculture, and not-for-profit organizations. Although they are often underrated or overlooked because of the heavy attention devoted to manufacturing, each is also a significant part of the business market. And it must be kept in mind that some of Canada's most important and fastest-growing business markets are outside Canada, in the United States and many other countries.

The reseller market

reseller market
Wholesaling and retailing intermediaries that buy products for resale to other business users or to consumers; a segment of the business market.

Intermediaries in the Canadian marketing system — the few hundred thousand wholesalers, retailers, and other organizations — constitute the **reseller market**. Resellers buy products from supplier organizations, for example Nextel buying BlackBerries, and reselling them in essentially the same form to the resellers' customers. In economic terms, resellers create time, place, and possession value, rather than changing the form of the product.

Resellers also buy many goods and services for use in operating their businesses, for example, office supplies, information and communication equipment and materials-handling equipment. In these buying activities, resellers are essentially no different from manufacturers, financial institutions, or any other segment of the business market.

It is their role as *buyers for resale* that distinguishes resellers from their suppliers. To resell an item, you must satisfy your end customers. Resellers must decide what products will be popular or useful to those comprising their end-customer markets. It is more difficult to determine what will please an outside customer than to find out what will satisfy someone in your own organization. When an airline decides to design new foul-weather jackets for its flight crews, it can carefully study the conditions under which the jackets will be worn and ask for the opinions of the people who will be wearing the jackets. As a result, it should be able to select an all-weather jacket that will be lightweight and safe to wear when working, easy to clean, and acceptable to the employees. Contrast that with retailers trying each year to anticipate what outerwear to purchase and place on their shelves. What will be the next trend — short or long, function or fashion — and what about colours and fabrics? In both cases, clothing is being purchased, but the opportunity for interaction with the users and the variety of uses and purposes differ greatly between the groups. This makes buying for resale for the "anonymous" consumer market more difficult and much more risky.

services market
The market for service activities, including all transportation carriers and public utilities; communications firms, financial, insurance, legal, and real estate firms; and organizations that produce and sell services such as rental housing, recreation and entertainment, repairs, health care, personal care, and business services.

The services market

Firms that produce services greatly outnumber firms that produce goods. There are more service firms than the total of all manufacturers, mining companies, construction firms, and enterprises engaged in farming, forestry, and fishing. **The services market** includes all transportation carriers and public utilities, communications firms, and the many financial, insurance, legal, and real estate firms that make purchases to enable them to offer their services. This market also includes organizations that produce and sell such diverse services as rental housing, recreation and entertainment, repairs, health care, personal care, and business services. New businesses, such as the restaurant planned by Natalie and Soren, will need services like those offered by RBC and other suppliers.

BACK TO THE TOP

Service firms constitute a huge market that buys goods and other services. Delta Hotels, for example, buys blankets and sheets from textile manufacturers. Hospitals in Canada and abroad buy supplies from Baxter Healthcare. They also buy legal, advertising, accounting, information technology equipment and systems, and consulting advice from other service marketers. The importance to Canadian marketers of the services market is dealt with in greater detail in Chapter 8.

government market
The segment of the business market that includes federal, provincial, and local government units, buying for government institutions such as schools, offices, hospitals, and research facilities.

competitive bidding
The characteristic form of government procurement, in which a government agency advertises both offline and online for bids, using a format that states the specifications of the intended purchase. The agency must accept the lowest bid that meets these specifications.

The government market

The large **government market** includes federal, provincial, territorial, Native, and municipal governments, as well as various Crown agencies and corporations that spend millions of dollars each year buying for institutions such as schools, offices, hospitals, and military bases. At the federal level, Public Works and Government Services Canada purchases in excess of $199 billion worth of goods and services annually for its own use and for other government units.[1] The largest "consumers" among these are Public Works and Government Services Canada itself and the Department of National Defence. Collectively, however, the other levels of governments are even more important markets than is the federal government.

Government procurement processes are different from those in the private sector of the business market. A unique feature of government buying is the **competitive bidding** system. Much government procurement is done on a bid basis and a large amount takes place online. The government agency advertises both offline and online for bids, using a format that states the specifications of the intended purchase. Any size of firm can usually bid, as individual contracts vary greatly in size across departments. The agency must accept the lowest bid that

Contracts Canada

meets these specifications. Contracts Canada (**www.contractscanada.gc.ca**) is the interdepartmental program assigned to simplify access and improve awareness of federal government purchasing. The potential of the government business market is sufficiently attractive that some firms concentrate almost exclusively on government markets.

The agriculture market

agribusiness
The business side of farming; usually involves large, highly mechanized farming operations.

Both the proportion of farmers in the total population of Canada and the number of farms have been decreasing and probably will continue to decline. Counterbalancing this has been an increase in large corporate or "business" types of farms. Even the remaining "family" farms are expanding in order to survive. Farming continues to be more automated and mechanized, which means, of course, that capital investment in farming is increasing. **Agribusiness** — farming, food processing, and other large-scale, farming-related businesses — is big business in every sense of the word.

Like other business executives, farmers are looking for better ways to increase their productivity, cut their expenses, and manage their cash flows. As farms become fewer and larger, marketing to them effectively requires carefully designed strategies. Some large fertilizer producers have salespeople who visit individual farms and, working with the farmer, analyze the soil and crops to determine exactly what fertilizer mix is best. Based on the analysis, the manufacturer prepares the appropriate blend of ingredients as a special order.

The "non-business" business market

non-business market
Includes such diverse institutions as churches, colleges and universities, museums, hospitals and other health institutions, political parties, labour unions, and charitable organizations.

The **non-business market** includes such diverse institutions or organizations as churches, colleges and universities, museums, hospitals and other health institutions, political parties, labour unions, and charitable organizations. Each of these non-business organizations is actually a business organization. However, our society (and the institutions themselves) in the past did not perceive a museum or a hospital as being a business, and many of those involved still feel uncomfortable thinking of their church, school, or political party as a business organization. Nevertheless, these organizations do virtually all of the things that any business does — offer and consume products and services, collect money, make investments, hire employees — and therefore require professional management.

Not-for-profit organizations also conduct marketing campaigns — although under a different name — in an effort to attract millions of dollars in contributions. In turn, they spend millions of dollars buying goods and services to run their operations.

The international dimension

Since Canada exports more than $180 billion (nearly 30 percent) of its gross domestic product, and since a major portion of this export trade is conducted on a business-to-business basis, the international market, comprising the same components as those that exist within Canada, is a vibrant collection of foreign-based business markets.[2] The value of international B2B commerce being conducted through the use of the Internet continues to increase. It is difficult to predict how quickly both sellers and buyers will adapt to the Internet and how much of their interaction will be conducted through this medium, since traditionally the development of personal relationships has always played an important part in B2B international marketing.

The Internet, however, is invaluable for making international contacts, even if a site does no more than list products or services and contact information. Even sites providing only traditional contact by snail mail or telephone will still turn up in Web search results. However, many B2B buying decisions continue to require face-to-face contact. Marketing to businesses based abroad, whether in the United States, China, India, Europe, or the Gulf states, requires more work on developing relationships than you would expect. This is the case because, whether the marketer is dealing with a foreign subsidiary of a Canadian firm or with foreign firms, the cross-cultural dynamics of negotiation and relationship building cannot be taken for granted. Canadian marketers doing business abroad must become familiar with the values, customs, symbols, and standard practices and expectations of their foreign-based buyers, including the individuals with whom the marketer must negotiate and the firms that they represent. Marketing at Work 6-1, "B2B Relationships in the Global Marketplace," provides a sample of what marketers doing business abroad can expect.

PAGE UP!

1. The business market consists of ______________________________ .
2. What are the six components of the business market?
3. There are more ________________________ firms than firms that produce goods.

MARKETING AT WORK 6-1: GLOBAL

B2B Relationships in the Global Marketplace

As more and more organizations do business across international boundaries, executives are increasingly aware of the non-business factors that influence the ultimate success or failure of their ventures. Consider what marketers going abroad can expect:

- In Germany, executives are thorough, well prepared, and quite systematic. They tend to be assertive — even intimidating — and not very willing to compromise. They are especially punctual and prize efficiency and directness.
- In Egypt, the pace is slow and a "hard-sell" approach will neither be appreciated nor successful. Your counterparts must get to know you and decide they like you for negotiations to go anywhere. Egyptians love language, so they expect a lot of rhetoric, exaggeration, poetics, emotion, and flowery language.
- In France, managers may insist on doing business in French, and because they feel that speaking is an art form, the French don't like being interrupted. Lengthy lunches with lots of wine usually accompany negotiations. Appropriate clothing is suggested, and never use first names without an invitation to do so.
- In the United Arab Emirates some work and most social occasions are segregated. Within same-sex encounters, however, the normally reserved Arabians are much more tactile than westerners in their behaviour. Firm embraces, kissing on both cheeks, and walking hand-in-hand is customary among male business colleagues.
- In Thailand, despite the extreme heat it is expected that suits with full-sleeve shirts and ties will be worn for all business functions. In some organizations, women must wear skirts below the knee, and pants are not acceptable. In some instances, be expected to have to remove your shoes. Having holes in your socks does not go down very well!
- In Mexico, personal relationships are very important, as is face-to-face contact. The idea is to socialize first and work later. To rush business matters when being offered hospitality may be seen as insulting. Businesspeople can be flexible when it comes to trade-offs, but it is often best to negotiate privately in one-on-one conversations.
- In China, small courtesies and follow-up gifts are important in establishing friendships. Meticulous preparation and consistency are important, because the Chinese are very thorough. Again, social engagements will often precede business discussions. Most negotiations will involve government, as there are many joint ventures and state enterprises.
- In Japan, first impressions are critical. Introductions and the exchange of business cards are very ceremonial events, as the order of presentation and business cards is tightly linked to rank. Meetings tend to be large, with many levels involved in decision-making. Non-verbal communication, smiling, laughing, and eye contact are all important communication cues.

QUESTIONS:

1. Do you think that Canadians can be 'trained' for global marketing activities or should locals be recruited in country markets?
2. Does the marketing of highly technical products require the same relationship building as does the marketing of low tech goods, say, commodities?

SOURCE: Adapted from Brian Banks, "English Too," *Canadian Business,* January 1995, pp. 20–35; *Business Culture* (www.businessculture.com), May 2005; *Executive Planet* (www.executiveplanet.com), May 2005.

Characteristics of B2B Market Demand

Four demand characteristics differentiate the business market from the consumer market: Demand is derived, tends to be inelastic, and is widely fluctuating, and the market is better informed.

Demand is derived

The demand for a business product or service is based on (derived from) the demand for the consumer products in which that business product is used. The demand for steel or plastics depends partially on consumer demand for automobiles and refrigerators, but it also depends on the demand for computer graphics boards, butter, and hockey pads and equipment. This is because the tools, machines, and other equipment needed to manufacture these items are made of steel and plastic. When the demand for hockey equipment increases, The Hockey Company — makers of CCM and KOHO — may need more sewing machines and computers — each requiring plastic and steel.

derived demand
A situation in which the demand for one product is dependent on the demand for another product.

There are two significant marketing implications of **derived demand** in the business market. First, to estimate the demand for a product, a business marketer must be very familiar with how it is used. This is fairly easy for a company such as Pratt & Whitney, a manufacturer of jet engines. But what about the manufacturer of rubber o-rings (doughnut-shaped rings of all sizes that are used to seal connections, often referred to as "washers")? Considerable research may be necessary to identify uses, users, and potential new opportunities.

Second, the producer of a business product sometimes engages in consumer marketing efforts to encourage the sale of its buyers' products. Intel consistently advertises to consumers, urging them when buying computers to ask specifically for products with an Intel processor. Further, name-brand computers will often also be labelled, "Intel Inside," which will in turn trigger increases in derived demand for these business products.

Demand is inelastic

inelastic demand
A price-volume relationship in which a change of one unit on the price scale results in a change of less than one unit on the volume scale.

Mountain Equipment Co-op

Another characteristic of the business market is that the demand for business products does not change easily because of price fluctuations. In economic terms, this **inelastic demand** refers to an item's price elasticity — how responsive demand is to a change in the price of a product.

The demand for many business products responds very little to changes in price, as long as the cost of a business product is a small proportion of the product's total cost. In these situations, the demand for the product is relatively inelastic. If the price of a business product such as Velcro fastening materials suddenly rises or falls considerably, how much effect would it have on retail prices at a store such as Mountain Equipment Co-op (MEC)? MEC (**www.mec.ca**) uses these materials in its jackets, pants, vests, and knapsacks. In fact, Velcro is used to some degree in most MEC apparel, so a price increase could mean a significant increase in the company's purchasing cost for this item. Because the fasteners are such a small part of a jacket, pant, or knapsack, however, the price increase would not likely change the retail price noticeably. As a result, Canadians would still flock to MEC and demand for these products would not change. This would also be the case for all other Velcro buyers — a price change in either direction would not alter demand for the business product. But not all business products form a small part of the total consumer product. In such situations, the greater the cost of a business product as a percentage of the total price of the finished good, the greater the elasticity of demand for this business product.

Demand is widely fluctuating

Although the demand for business products and services does not change much in response to price changes, it does respond to other factors. In fact, market demand for most classes of business goods fluctuates considerably more than the demand for consumer products. The demand for installations — major plant equipment, factories, and so on — is particularly subject to change. Substantial fluctuations also exist in the market for accessory equipment — office furniture and machinery, delivery trucks, and similar products. These tend to accentuate the swings in the demand for business raw materials and fabricating parts. We can see this very clearly when declines in demand in the construction and auto industries affect suppliers of lumber, steel, plastics, and other materials and parts.

Fluctuations in the demand for business products can influence all aspects of a marketing program. In product planning, fluctuations in demand may stimulate a firm to diversify into other products to ease production and marketing problems. Changes within the industry, competition, and technology may also cause concerns. For example, in the last few years, IBM has retreated in a major way from mainframe computer manufacturing, has sold it laptop computer business and, using mass-market television and magazine advertising, placed much emphasis on its digitally based consulting services. Companies like Microsoft and Nokia have decided to diversify into more consumer markets by moving into the still relatively untapped, and very lucrative, PDA marketplace to compete with RIM's BlackBerry devices. And Apple decided to used its strong, innovative brand image (also called brand equity) to get into the music business. These strategic decisions in response to changing market circumstances represent not only entries into established markets, but have provided the opportunity to further establish these brands in the burgeoning interactive multimedia market.[3]

Buyers are well informed

In general, business buyers are better informed about what they are buying than are end customers. They know more about the relative merits of alternative sources of supply and competitive products for three reasons. First, there are relatively few alternatives for a business buyer to consider, while consumers typically have many more brands and sellers from which to choose. Consider, for example, how many options you would have in purchasing a TV set. In most business situations, however, a buyer will find only a few firms that offer the particular combination of product features and service desired. Nextel looked hard at competing offerings before choosing RIM. Second, the responsibility of a buyer in an organization is ordinarily limited to a few products. Unlike a consumer who buys many different things, a purchasing agent's job is to be very knowledgeable about a narrowly defined set of products. Third, for most consumer purchases, an error is only a minor inconvenience. However, in business buying, the cost of a mistake can easily be tens of thousands of dollars or even the decision maker's job!

Manufacturers and marketers of business products place a much greater emphasis on product information and personal contact to communicate than do firms that market consumer products. This makes business buyers more reliant on both Internet contact and personal relationships with their suppliers. Business salespeople and service representatives must be carefully selected, properly trained, and adequately compensated. They must give informative and effective presentations, furnish satisfactory service, form relationships with their client firms, and work to build and maintain relationship strength. This is increasingly important, because the Internet makes searching for other suppliers, up-to-date information, and new products easier than ever before.

Determinants of B2B Market Demand

To analyze a consumer market, a marketer would study the distribution of population and various demographics, such as income, and then try to determine the consumers' buying motives, expectations and habits. A firm selling to the business market can use essentially the same type of analysis. The factors affecting the market for business products are the number of potential business users and their purchasing power, buying motives and expectations, and buying habits. In the following discussion, we'll identify several basic differences between consumer markets and business markets.

Number and types of business users

The business market contains relatively few buying units compared with the consumer market. There are approximately 500,000 business users, with about 40,000 of these being manufacturing establishments. In contrast, there are more than 30 million consumers divided among more than nine million households. The business market will seem even more limited to most companies because they sell to only a segment of the total market. A firm selling to meat-processing plants, for example, would have about 45 potential customer plants. If you were interested in providing services to battery manufacturers, you would find about 25 companies as basic prospects. Consequently, marketing executives must try to pinpoint their markets carefully by type of industry and geographic location. A firm marketing hard-rock mining equipment is not interested in the total business market nor even in all firms engaged in mining and quarrying.

North American Industry Classification System (NAICS)
System that allows business marketers to locate codes for present customers and obtain coded lists of similar firms, and provides a rapid, low-cost approach to identifying changes in the growth of various industry sectors.

One very useful source of business market and segmentation information is the **North American Industry Classification System (NAICS)**. This system provides common industry definitions for Canada, the United States, and Mexico, and is consistent with United Nations industry classifications used for measuring global economic activity. NAICS, which replaced the Standard Industrial Classification System that was in use for more than 50 years, comprises 20 industry sectors, with 96 subsectors and many industry groups. Table 6-1 shows the breakdown for one industry — pagers, a segment of the wireless telecommunications industry in the information sector.

The NAICS allows business marketers to locate codes for present customers and obtain coded lists of similar firms, and provides a rapid, low-cost approach to identifying changes in the growth of various industry sectors.

Size of Business Users

Although the business market may be limited in the total number of buyers, it is large in purchasing power. Business users range in size from very small companies with fewer than five employees to firms with staff numbering more than a thousand. A relatively small percentage of firms account for the greatest share of the value-added production by a given industry; slightly more than 1 percent of manufacturing firms — those with 500 or more employees — account for approximately 40 percent of the total value added by manufacturing and for more than 30 percent of the total employment in manufacturing.

The marketing significance of this concentration is that the major buying power in the B2B market is represented by relatively few firms. This market concentration has considerable influence on a seller's approach to target marketing, as well as on policies regarding its channels of distribution and customer contact. Intermediaries in concentrated business markets are not as essential as in the consumer market and the opportunity (in fact, the competitive need) to build strong relationships is very apparent.

Regional concentration of business users

There is substantial regional concentration in many of the major industries and among business users as a whole. A firm selling products usable in oil fields will find the bulk of its market in Alberta, the Northwest Territories, offshore Newfoundland, the United States, and abroad. Rubber-products manufacturers are located mostly in Ontario, shoes are produced chiefly in Québec, and most of the nation's garment manufacturers are located in southern Ontario and Québec. There is a similar regional concentration in the farm market.

TABLE 6-1 NAICS Industry Sectors and the Classification of the Pager Industry

NAICS Industry Sectors		An Industry Sub-Classification	
11	Agriculture, forestry, fishing, & hunting		
21	Mining		
22	Utilities		
23	Construction		
31–33	Manufacturing	513	Broadcast & telecommunications
44–45	Retail trade		↓
48–49	Transportation & warehousing	5133	Telecommunications
51	Information → (513)		↓
52	Finance and insurance	51332	Wireless telecommunications carrier
53	Real estate, rental, & leasing		↓
54	Professional, scientific, & technical	513321	Pagers
55	Management of companies		
56	Waste management		
61	Education		
62	Health care		
71	Arts, entertainment, & recreation		
72	Accommodations & food services		
81	Other services		
92	Public administration		

SOURCE: *North American Industry Classification System — United States, 1997*, U.S. Government Printing Office, Washington, DC, 1997.

vertical business market
A situation in which a given product is usable by virtually all of the firms in only one or two industries.

horizontal business market
A situation in which a given product is usable in a wide variety of industries.

Although a large part of a firm's market may be concentrated in limited geographic areas, a good portion may lie outside these areas. Consequently, a distribution policy must be developed that will enable a firm to deal directly with the concentrated market and also to employ intermediaries (or a company sales force, at great expense) to reach the outlying markets.

Vertical and horizontal business markets For effective marketing planning, a company should know whether the market for its products is vertical or horizontal. If a firm's product is usable by virtually all firms in only one or two industries, it has a **vertical business market**. For example, some precision instruments are intended only for the marine market, but every builder of boats or ships is a potential customer. If the product is usable by many industries, then it is said to have a broad or **horizontal business market**. Business supplies, such as Esso lubricating oils and greases and Canadian General Electric small motors, may be sold to a wide variety of industries, as are the services of financial institutions, including the Royal Bank of Canada.

A company's marketing program ordinarily is influenced by whether its markets are vertical or horizontal. In a vertical market, a product can be tailor-made to meet the specific needs of one industry and personal relationship building can easily be pursued. However, the industry must buy enough to support this specialization and form of customer contact. In addition, advertising and servicing can be directed more effectively in vertical markets. In a horizontal market, a

BACK TO THE TOP

TABLE 6-2 Illustrative Activity Indicators

Indicator	Measure
Manufacturing activity	the number of employees, the number of plants, dollar value added by manufacturing.
Mining activity	number of mines operating, volume of their output, dollar value of the product.
Agricultural activity	cash farm income, acreage planted, crop yields.
Construction activity	number and value of building permits issued, number of construction starts by type of housing, (single-family residence, apartment, or commercial).

product is developed as an all-purpose item, to reach a larger market. In such markets, a strategy of building strong personal relationships may not be as easily accomplished but is still necessary because, given the larger potential market, the product is likely to face more competition.

Buying power of business customers

activity indicator of buying power
A market factor that is related to income generation and expenditures; sometimes, a combined indicator of purchasing power and the number of business users.

Another determinant of business market demand is the purchasing power of business users; measured either by their expenditures or sales volume. Many times, however, such information is not available or is very difficult to estimate. In such cases, it is more feasible to use an **activity indicator of buying power** — that is, some market factor that is related to income generation and expenditures. Sometimes, an activity indicator is a combined indicator of purchasing power and the number of business users.

PAGE UP!

1. What are the four demand characteristics of the business market that differentiate it from the consumer market?
2. What are the factors affecting demand in the business market?
3. What is the difference between vertical and horizontal business markets?

Business Buying Behaviour

Business customer behaviour, like end customer behaviour, is initiated when an aroused need (a motive) is recognized. This leads to goal-oriented activity designed to satisfy the need. Once again, business marketers must try to determine what motivates the buyer, and then understand the buying process and buying patterns of business organizations in their markets.

The importance of business buying

Business buying or purchasing is an important part of overall strategy for at least three reasons:

1. **Companies are making less and buying more.** For example, 93 percent of the cost of an Apple computer is purchased content and, for all manufacturers, purchased content is more than 50 percent of their final products. Managing all of these supply relationships is time-consuming and therefore also consumes additional financial resources. While low price is important, savings can also be found through reducing the number of suppliers and maintaining those who provide dependable, quality service and products. Honda at

one time had different suppliers producing mirrors for the inside and outside of its cars. Very happy with the relationship and working style of the Donnelly Corporation in its agreement to supply interior mirrors, the car company asked that this supplier develop exterior mirrors for its cars, thereby reducing Honda's supplier list by one. This trend can be found across this industry, as there may be up to 2,000 supply relationships to manage in automobile manufacturing.

2. **Firms are under intense quality and time pressures.** To reduce costs and improve efficiency, firms no longer buy and hold inventories of parts and supplies. Instead, they demand that raw materials and components that meet specifications be delivered "just in time" (JIT) to go into the production process. To take advantage of this, Canadian automaker Magna establishes its facilities near its main clients — the Big Three auto producers. This ensures that the automakers' inventories can be kept at a minimum, yet fluctuations in demand will be met with guaranteed on-time delivery. This is achieved through computerized data interchange systems that link suppliers to their JIT clients.[4]

3. **To get what they need, firms are concentrating their purchases with fewer suppliers and developing long-term "partnering" relationships.** This level of involvement extends beyond a purchase to include such things as working together to develop new products and providing financial support.[5]

For example, in September 2005, Ford Motor Company announced it would enter into new long-term agreements with select strategic suppliers globally. The new partnership would apply to safety, technology and design and would differentiate Ford from other automakers and should redefine its relationship with its suppliers in the future. Working with existing suppliers to reduce waste, increase economies of scale and improve customer satisfaction, Ford will move forward by reducing by 50 percent the number of suppliers from which it sources new business for some of its high-impact parts. It is hoped that this new "Aligned Business Framework" will raise Ford's relationships with its suppliers to new levels.[6]

Buying-decision process in business

The buying-decision process in B2B markets is a sequence of six stages similar to the ones followed by consumers, as discussed in Chapter 2. Not every purchase involves all stages. First, we'll illustrate the process by providing an example and then we'll examine some of the details

A low-involvement consumer purchase can require a related high-involvement B2B purchase.

of each stage, as we did in the review of consumer decision-making. Assume that Montréal-based Culinar, Inc., makers of Vachon, Jos. Louis, and May West snack cakes, is considering the use of a fat substitute in a special line of baked goods.

Simple replacement purchases (termed "straight rebuy" and discussed later) are usually low-involvement situations for a buyer, so purchasers typically skip some stages. But the first-time purchase of an expensive product or service is likely to be a high-involvement, total-stage buying decision.

1. Need recognition Culinar's marketing executives are sensitive to the concern of consumers about fat in their diets. They see the strategic opportunity of producing a line of high-quality, good-tasting baked goods without fat as very attractive for segments of the consumer market. Finding the right substitute for fat ingredients is a challenge for those concerned with purchasing.

2. Choice of involvement level The marketing executive who will be responsible for the product development project discusses with production and purchasing personnel the feasibility of finding the right substitute, and the decision is made to carefully research what is available and on what terms, since the firm has no experience with these types of ingredients.

3. Identification of alternatives The marketing staff draws up a list of product-performance specifications for fat-free baked goods — attractive appearance, special features, good taste, and reasonable cost. The product specifications are similar to the expectations that consumers develop. The purchasing department also develops a set of supplier specifications or, in consumer marketing terms, patronage motive criteria. An external search then identifies the potential suppliers and the alternative brands of fat substitutes that generally meet functional specifications.

4. Evaluation of alternatives The production, research, and purchasing people jointly evaluate both the alternative products and sources of supply against the product and supplier specifications. They discover that some brands cannot withstand high temperatures, there are differences in how well they simulate the taste and texture of fat, and some have not received final approval from federal health authorities. The complete evaluation considers such factors as product performance, appearance, and price, as well as the suppliers' abilities to meet delivery schedules and provide consistent quality.

5. Purchase decision Based on the evaluation, the buyer decides on a specific brand and supplier. Next, the purchasing department negotiates the contract, having achieved negotiation satisfaction with the selected supplier. Since large sums are involved, the contract will likely include many details. For example, if Culinar feels confident about the supplier, the contract relationship might go beyond price and delivery schedules. This could include the low-fat substitute producer gaining access, through electronic data interchange to production, quality-control, shelf-life, and product-movement data in order to be able to provide a higher degree of accuracy in product delivery and better-targeted service. A more effective schedule can help ensure a consistently fresher product, perhaps leading to higher product sales. In such a situation, a long-term relationship appears to be in the baking — um, we mean making.

6. Consumption experience Culinar, Inc. continues to evaluate the performances of the fat substitute and the selected supplier to ensure that both meet expectations. Continued dealings will depend on this performance evaluation and on how well the supplier handles the total interaction process. Formal evaluations of the purchase will be made and satisfaction recorded for future reference. A functional relationship is developing. Consumer market success with this product line would increase the likelihood of future projects involving the two firms. Buyer-supplier success in their information interchange, mutual problem solving, and personal communications aid in developing a close working relationship.

In the following sections, we explore several differences between consumer buying behaviour and the business buying behaviour reflected in the Culinar scenario.

Buying motives of business users

buying motive
The reason why a person buys a specific product.

One view of **buying motives** is that business purchases are methodical and structured. Business buying motives, for the most part, are presumed to be practical and unemotional. Business buyers are assumed to be motivated to achieve the optimal combination of price, quality, and service in the products they buy and any relationships that are developed are considered to be functional. An alternative view is that business buyers are human and thus their business decisions are influenced by their attitudes, perceptions, and values and therefore any relationships developed will be emotional in nature. In fact, many salespeople would maintain that business buyers seem to be motivated more toward personal goals than organizational goals, and the two are often in conflict.

As is usual in such cases, the truth is actually somewhere in between. Most B2B relationships are a combination of the functional and emotional. Business buyers have two goals — to further their company's position (in profits, in acceptance by customers) and to protect or improve their position in their firms (self-interest). Sometimes these goals are mutually consistent. For example, the firm's highest priority may be to reduce costs, and the buyer knows that there will be a reward for negotiating a low price. Obviously, the more consistent the goals are, the better for both the organization and the individual, and the easier it is to make buying decisions and develop good relationships.

However, there are often significant areas where the buyer's goals do not coincide with those of the firm, as when the firm insists on dealing with the lowest-price supplier, but the buyer has developed a good personal relationship with another supplier and doesn't want to change. In these cases, a seller must appeal to the buyer both on a rational "what's good for the firm" basis and on a self-interest "what's in it for me" basis. Promotional appeals directed to the buyer's self-interest are particularly useful when two or more competing sellers are offering essentially the same products, prices, and post-purchase services.[7]

Types of buying situations

buy classes
Three typical buying situations in the business market: new-task buy, straight rebuy, and modified rebuy.

new-task buy
In the business market, a purchasing situation in which a company considers buying a given item for the first time.

In Chapter 2, we observed that consumer purchase decisions can range from routine to complex. Similarly, the buying situations in business organizations vary widely in their complexity and, most importantly, in the number of people involved in the decision and the time required to make it. Three **buy classes** or types of business buying situations characterize the field: new-task buy, straight rebuy, and modified rebuy.

- **New-task buy** This is the most difficult and complex buying situation because it is a first-time purchase of a major product. **New-task buys** are not, however, that common. Typically, more people are involved in new-task buying than in the other two situations, because the risk is great. Information needs are high and the evaluation of alternatives is difficult because the decision makers have little consumption experience with the product. Sellers have the challenge of finding out the buyer's needs and communicating their product's ability to provide satisfaction. A hospital's first-time purchase of laser surgical equipment or a company buying robots for a factory (or buying the factory itself) are new-task buying conditions. In these situations, firms with established relationships could work with buyers to help them define the buying task and suggest solutions because these firms are known and trusted. Unknown potential suppliers must provide information and aid in the buying task in a form that engenders trust and allows them to begin the task of establishing a relationship.

straight rebuy
In the business market, a routine purchase with minimal information needs.

- **Straight rebuy** This is a routine, low-involvement purchase with minimal information needs and little or no consideration of alternatives. **Straight rebuys** are very common. The buyer's extensive experience with the seller has been satisfactory or more than satisfactory, so at least a functional and possibly an emotional relationship has been developed. In such a case, there is no incentive to search. An example is the repeat purchase of steering wheels by Freightliner, a truck manufacturer. These buying decisions are made in the purchasing department, usually from a predetermined list of acceptable suppliers. Suppliers who are not on this list may have difficulty getting in to make a sales presentation to the buyer. However, when buyers make use of the Internet to both gather product and service information and actually post their needs and buy online, the predetermined list is easily expanded by asking for bids from a broader base of suppliers.

modified rebuy
In the business market, a purchasing situation between a new-task rebuy and a straight rebuy in terms of time required, information needed, and alternatives considered.

- **Modified rebuy** This buying situation is somewhere between the other two in time and people involved, information needed, and alternatives considered. **Modified rebuys** are also quite common. Where straight rebuys have existed and a degree of dissatisfaction has developed, signalling a possible breakdown of functional performance or personal relationships, a modified rebuy would result. The availability of important new products or product performance information could also cause a modified rebuy. In either case, a new list of acceptable suppliers would be developed. Commonly, two or more suppliers are in constant competition. In selecting diesel engines for the trucks it manufactures, Freightliner considers Cummins and Caterpillar products, among others. However, because these engine makers frequently introduce new design and performance features, Freightliner evaluates each on a regular basis. Close relationships are common in situations where modified rebuys are frequent and, of course, should work to benefit both buyer and seller.

multiple buying influences
A situation in which a purchasing decision is influenced by more than one person in the buyer's organization.

buying centre
All of the people in an organization who participate in the buying-decision process.

users
The people in a buying centre who actually use a particular product.

influencers
The people in a buying centre who set the specifications and aspects of buying decisions because of their technical expertise, financial position, or political power in the organization.

deciders
The people in a buying centre who make the actual buying decision regarding a product and/or supplier.

Multiple buying influences — the buying centre

One of the biggest challenges in B2B marketing is to determine which individuals in the organization play the various buying roles. That is, who influences the buying decision, who determines product specifications, and who makes the buying decision? In the business market, these activities typically involve several people. In other words, there are **multiple buying influences**, particularly in medium-sized and large firms. Even in small companies where the owners or managers make all major decisions, knowledgeable employees are usually consulted before certain purchases are made.

Understanding the concept of a **buying centre** is helpful in identifying the multiple buying influences and understanding the buying process in business organizations. A buying centre may be defined as all of the individuals or groups involved in making a decision to purchase. Thus, a buying centre includes the people who play any of the following roles:

- **Users:** The people who actually use the business product — perhaps a secretary, an executive, a production-line employee, or a truck driver.
- **Influencers:** The people who set the specifications and aspects of buying decisions because of their technical expertise, their organizational position, or even their political power in the firm.
- **Deciders:** The people who make the actual buying decision regarding the business product and the supplier. A purchasing agent may be the decider in a straight-rebuy situation. But someone in top management may make the decision regarding whether to buy an expensive computer.

gatekeepers
The people in a buying centre who control the flow of purchasing information within the organization and between the buying firm and potential vendors.

buyers
The people in a buying centre who select the suppliers, arrange the terms of sale, and process the actual purchase orders.

BACK TO THE TOP

Well-trained purchasing professionals will always be, at the very least, gatekeepers.

- **Gatekeepers:** The people who control the flow of purchasing information within the organization as well as between the firm and potential suppliers. These people may be purchasing agents, secretaries, receptionists, or technical personnel.
- **Buyers:** The people who interact with the suppliers, arrange the terms of sale, and process the actual purchase orders. Typically, this is the purchasing department's role but, again, if the purchase is an expensive, complex new buy, the buyer's role may be occupied by someone in top management.

Several people in an organization may play the same role — there may be several users of the product. Or the same person may occupy more than one role — a secretary may be a user, an influencer, and a gatekeeper in the purchase of office equipment. For example, in the new restaurant that Natalie and Soren plan to open in North Bay, chances are they will not only be the chefs, but will have to play many different roles, at least until their business grows to the point where they can employ other people. Many small businesses in Canada stay small, with the result that their owners have to wear many hats.

The size and composition of a buying centre will vary among business organizations. In one study, the average size of buying centres ranged from 2.7 to 5.1 persons.[8] Within a given organization, the size and make-up of the buying centre will vary, depending on the product's cost, the complexity of the decision, and the stage of the buying process. The buying centre for a straight rebuy of office supplies will be quite different from the centre handling the purchase of a building or a fleet of trucks.

The variety of people involved in any business buying situation, plus the differences among companies, present real challenges to salespeople. As they try to determine "who's on first" — that is, determine who does what in a buying situation and influences which aspect of the decision-making process — sales reps often call on the wrong executives. Even knowing who the decision makers are at a certain time is not enough, because these people may be very difficult to reach and people move into and out of the buying centre as the purchase proceeds through the decision process. This, in part, explains why a salesperson typically has only a few major accounts.

Certainly the challenges presented in the business buying-decision process should suggest the importance of co-ordinating the selling activities of the business marketer with the buying needs of the purchasing organization.

Buying patterns of business users

Buying behaviour in the B2B market differs significantly from consumer buying behaviour in several ways. These differences stem from the products, markets, and buyer-seller relationships in business markets.

Direct purchase In the consumer market, consumers rarely buy directly from the producer, except in the case of services. In the business market, however, direct purchase by the business user from the producer is quite common, even for goods. This is true especially when the order is large and the buyer needs much technical assistance. Computer-chip makers deal directly with personal computer manufacturers because the chip technology is changing so rapidly. From a seller's point of view, direct sale in the business market is reasonable, especially when there are relatively few potential buyers, when they are big, or when they are geographically concentrated. With the Internet readily available, smaller sellers can both concentrate their efforts and work to expand their reach into markets that in the past were too expensive to serve at an appropriate level.

Internet purchase Online buying between businesses is much greater, both in absolute terms and proportionately, than in the consumer market. Business buying is expected to account for 88 percent of all online sales by the end of 2006. While this seems like a lot of sales, this online portion of sales still only represents a relatively small percentage of the total amount of B2B sales that occur. With the promise of saving time and money for all parties involved it is certain that the use of the Internet for order-taking will continue to grow. But in being successful online, one study found that price was one of the least important factors. What's more important is brand reputation, site functionality, information privacy and good service. To that end, the key to a successful B2B business model is nothing new: it's old-fashioned marketing.[9]

value chain
The relationships by which the roles of suppliers, producers, distributors, and end-users contribute to the final product.

Nature of the relationship Many business marketers take a broad view of exchanges. Rather than focus only on the immediate customer, they approach marketing as a **value chain**. That is, they consider the roles of suppliers, producers, distributors, and end-users to see how each contributes value to the final product. This perspective leads to recognition of the importance of all of the parties involved in successfully bringing a product to market and an emphasis on building and maintaining relationships along the chain. For example, Apple Computer, which once relied exclusively on dealers, recognized that many of its larger

MARKETING AT WORK 6-2: RELATIONSHIPS

Do the Tchotchke Tango!

When do a unicycle and juggling balls mean hundreds of thousands of dollars in incremental B2B sales? It sounds like a riddle, but it's actually a lesson. It's when they are relevant, memorable premiums sent out to potential clients. A premium, in this case, is a gift from a company to help remind a prospective customer of the product, service, or brand. All sorts of companies use them, but in the competitive B2B marketplace, marketers are showing that a little incentive creativity can pay off big time. Often it's a pen or a calendar with the company logo.

A business-to-consumer (B2C) campaign typically tries to get top-of-mind awareness, but a B2B campaign is usually just the first touch-point in a series where you're growing relationships. There is another difference: instead of targeting thousands of people, B2B targets key people in a limited number of organizations — usually dozens or maybe thousands of candidates, which means a better per-item budget. In other words... swankier swag, better loot, bigger tchotchkes.

The W Television Network, for example, wanted to reach potential clients with a core message: W is the "marketing to women experts." After developing a list of 250 potential media buyers, it sent out a premium consisting of a W-branded metal first-aid kit billed as containing everything a woman could want at her desk in an emergency. It contained hand cream, clear nail polish for repairing nylons, a hair elastic for bad hair days and a chocolate bar — and a reminder that the network reaches three million women each week.

And what about the unicycle and juggling balls? They were sent to 100 chief information officers by MCI to promote its Web-hosting and IT services. It was meant as a show of understanding of what that job usually entails in most organizations today — a humorous, and memorable, analogy that illustrated empathy and solidarity.

QUESTIONS:

1. Do you think that the use of such promotional materials can actually aid in relationship building or are the items used too trivial or irrelevant?
2. If a 'tchotchke' is personally useful to the recipient, can it cause an ethical problem?

SOURCE: Adapted from Samson Okalow, "Do the Tchotchke Tango," *Strategy*, May 17, 2004, p. 13.

customers needed specialized service. To satisfy this segment of the market and maintain strong ties to these key customers, the firm now has its own sales force calling directly on large accounts. However, many of the orders taken by the sales force are contracted out to dealers to ensure that they are protected.[10]

supply partnerships
A partnership that occurs when a buyer and seller with mutual trust and interests adopt certain policies, procedures, and co-ordinated relationships to lower production and supply costs and increase consumer product value.

Among those businesses where good relationships exist, a **supply partnership** can be created. This occurs when a buyer and seller have developed sufficient trust and mutuality of interest so that, through the mutual adoption of certain policies and procedures, the use of electronic data interchange, and co-ordinated personal and professional relationships, production and supply costs are lowered for both parties and consumer product value is increased.

Wal-Mart, for example, is connected electronically with almost all of its major suppliers, such as Proctor-Silex and Rubbermaid, through an inventory control system that increases efficiency and reduces inventory held at each store. As items are scanned at the checkout, the information about each item is transferred back to manufacturers, so they always have current information about inventories at all locations and are able to better schedule shipments of products to each store. Wal-Mart seldom runs short of a product, ensuring that customers are not disappointed. And by maintaining lower inventories, operating costs are reduced. For suppliers, making the investment in this technology and co-operating with this retailer provides access to an international retail distribution network.

Frequency of purchase In the business market, firms buy certain products very infrequently. Large installations are purchased only once in many years. Small parts and materials to be used in the manufacture of a product may be ordered on long-term contracts, so that a selling opportunity exists as seldom as once a year. Even standard operating supplies, such as office supplies or cleaning products, may be bought only once a month.

Because of this buying pattern, a great burden is placed on the personal-selling programs of business sellers. The sales force must call on potential customers often enough to provide the first-hand information that other media, such as a Web site, e-mail, or fax cannot effectively provide, and to know when a customer is considering a purchase.

Size of order The average business order is considerably larger than its counterpart in the consumer market. This fact, coupled with the infrequency of purchase, highlights the importance of each sale in the business market. A salesperson losing the sale of a pair of shoes to a consumer is not nearly as devastating as Bombardier losing the sale of 10 airplanes.

Period of negotiation The period of negotiation in a business sale is usually much longer than in a consumer transaction. General Electric, for example, negotiated over a five-year period before completing the purchase of a $9.5 million Cray supercomputer to aid in managing operations and research activities in Canada and the United States. Some reasons for extended negotiations are:

- Several executives participate in the buying decision.
- The sale involves a large amount of money.
- The business product is made to order and considerable discussion is required to establish the specifications.

Demand for service The user's desire for excellent service is a strong business buying motive that may determine buying patterns. Frequently, a firm's only differentiating feature is its service, because the product itself is so standardized that it can be purchased from any number of companies. Consider the choice of suppliers to provide elevators for a major office building or hotel. The installation of the elevators is no more important than keeping them operating safely and efficiently. Consequently, in its marketing efforts, a firm such as Otis emphasizes its maintenance service as much as its products.

Sellers must be ready to furnish a continuous service program, not just before or just after a sale. For example, suppliers such as Kraft Foods conduct a careful analysis of a supermarket's customers and sales performance and then suggest a product assortment and layout for the store's dairy department. In the case of office copiers, manufacturers train the buyer's office staff in the use of the equipment and, after the machines have been installed, offer other services such as repairs by specially trained technicians.

Dependability of supply Another business buying pattern is the user's insistence on an adequate quantity of uniform-quality products. Variations in the quality of materials going into finished products can cause considerable trouble for manufacturers. They may be faced with costly disruptions in their production processes if the imperfections exceed quality-control limits. Also, the right quantities at the right time are as important as the right quality. A work stoppage caused by an insufficient supply of materials is just as costly as one caused by the inferior quality of materials. In one study of problems faced by purchasing agents for smaller manufacturers, the problem most often reported was the failure of sellers to deliver on schedule.

The emphasis on total quality management has increased the significance of dependability. Now that it has been established that firms can operate with virtually zero defects, buyers expect a very high standard of performance.

MARKETING AT WORK 6-3: STRATEGY

Not the Same Jam At All

Everyone knows the Kraft brand. Kraft Foods supplies us with 61 brands of various products. Many of the foods, beverages, and condiments we have grown up with in Canada come from this company, including Kraft Dinner, Tang, Grape-Nuts cereal, Maxwell House coffee, Ritz crackers, and Oreo cookies.

But it is not only in the supermarket that we come across many of the Kraft products we enjoy.

We have all been in a cafeteria, on an airplane, or even at some sort of banquet or function where we have used those small packages of coffee, crackers, jam, or even peanut butter or cream cheese. And most often we recognize the brand on the package — Sanka coffee, Philadelphia cream cheese, Kraft salad dressing. While the contents of these packages are the same as those we can get at our local grocery store, these small packages actually are products that are not available for sale in the consumer marketplace. Kraft offers them only in the B2B marketplace — sold to other businesses for resale — products that enable other companies and organizations to offer their own products and services.

This is an example of a firm that sells to both B2B and B2C markets. And while you may think that strawberry jam is strawberry jam — whether it is in a jar or a single-serving package — you would be wrong! These are actually two different products. Why? Because they each require their own marketing mix. Yes, it is the same strawberry jam, but "'product" also refers to size and packaging, which is a very important detail for creating utility in these two different marketplaces. Also, unit pricing will be different because of the packaging and because the small packages will be sold in bulk as a "component" product. Promotion and distribution will differ as well: Sales representatives will attempt to address the very different concerns of different clients — hotel chains and airlines, instead of supermarkets.

QUESTIONS:

1. Would consumers be interested in the product forms that Kraft markets exclusively to the B2B market?
2. Would a particular segment pay more for the added value such portions provide?

SOURCE: Kraft Foods Inc. Web page, www.kraft.com, May 5, 2005.

Leasing instead of buying A growing tendency among firms in the B2B market is leasing business goods instead of buying them. In the past, this practice was limited to large equipment, such as large computers, packaging equipment, and heavy construction equipment. Currently, leasing arrangements include delivery trucks, vehicles used by salespeople, machine tools, and items such as software site licences that are generally less expensive than major installations.

Leasing has several merits for the lessor, the firm providing the equipment:

- Total net income — the income after charging off repairs and maintenance expenses — is often higher than it would be if the equipment was sold.
- The lessor's market may be expanded to include users who could not afford to buy the product, especially for large equipment.
- Leasing is an effective method of getting users to try a new product. They may be more willing to rent a product than to buy it. If they are not satisfied, their expenditure is limited to a few monthly payments.

From the lessee's, or customer's, point of view, the benefits of leasing are:

- Leasing allows users to retain their investment capital for other purposes.
- Firms can enter a new business with less capital outlay than would be necessary if they had to buy equipment.
- Leased products are usually repaired and maintained by lessors, eliminating one headache associated with ownership.
- Leasing is particularly attractive to firms that need equipment seasonally or sporadically, such as food canning or construction.

Bases for Business Market Segmentation

Several of the bases used to segment the consumer market can also be used to segment the broad business market. For example, we can segment business and organizational markets on a geographical basis. Several industries are geographically concentrated, so any firm selling to these industries could easily use this segmentation basis. Sellers also can segment on product-related bases, such as usage rate or benefits desired.[11]

Let's look at three of the bases that are used solely for segmenting business markets — type of customer, size of customer, and type of buying situation.

Type of customer

Any firm that sells to customers in a variety of business markets may want to segment this market on the basis of customer types. We discussed the NAICS codes as a very useful tool for identifying business and institutional target markets. A firm selling display cases or store fixtures to the retail market could use the codes, as could a firm selling janitorial supplies or small electric motors that has a broad potential market among many different industries. Management in this firm could segment its market by type of customer and then perhaps decide to sell to firms in only a limited number of these segments.

Size of customer

In this situation, size can be measured by such factors as sales volume, number of production facilities, or number of sales offices. Many business-to-business marketers divide their potential market into large and small accounts, using separate distribution channels to reach each segment. The large-volume accounts, for example, may be sold to directly by the company's sales force. To reach the smaller accounts, however, the seller may use a telemarketing or Internet approach, a manufacturers' agent, or some other form of intermediary.

Type of buying situation

Earlier in this chapter, we discussed the three types of buy classes — new-task buy, straight rebuy, and modified rebuy. We also recognized in that discussion that a new-task buy is significantly different from a straight rebuy in several important respects. Consequently, a business seller might well segment its market into these three buy-class categories. Or the seller could at least set up two segments by combining new-task buy and modified rebuy into one segment. Then different marketing programs would be developed to reach each of these two or three segments.[12]

PAGE UP!

1. Business buyers have two goals. What are they?
2. What are the three types of buying situations?
3. Who is likely to make up the buying centre in a B2B situation?

Key Terms and Concepts

activity indicator of buying power 169
agribusiness 163
B2B marketing 160
business and organizational (B2B) market 160
buy classes 172
buyers 174
buying centre 173
buying motive 172
competitive bidding 162
deciders 173
derived demand 165
gatekeepers 174
government market 162
horizontal business market 168
inelastic demand 165
influencers 173
modified rebuy 173
multiple buying influences 173
new-task buy 172
non-business market 163
North American Industry Classification System (NAICS) 167
reseller market 161
services market 162
straight rebuy 173
supply partnership 176
users 173
value chain 175
vertical business market 168

Questions and Problems

1. List as many examples of retailers and service providers in your area that:
   a. Serve only business users.
   b. Serve both personal use consumers and business users.
   c. For the companies listed in part (b) explain what differences might exist in the marketing mixes directed at these two different types of customers.
2. More and more B2B marketing and transactions are taking place online. What new, or different, challenges does this create for marketers?
3. All consumers would like to think that they make informed decisions when they purchase products and services. Business buyers, however, are described as being better informed than the average consumer. Why would this be true? How does this impact the marketing process when dealing with such buyers?

4. The final decision to place an order for a product can be impacted by many different individuals — influencers, deciders, gatekeepers, buyers. Consider the purchase of an automobile. What people would fill these roles in the purchase process when it was a business purchase compared to when this was a personal purchase?

5. What are some marketing implications for business goods whose demand:
   a. Fluctuates widely?
   b. Is inelastic?
   c. Is derived?

6. What are the marketing implications for a seller of the fact that business customers are geographically concentrated and limited in number?

7. What differences would you expect to find between the marketing strategies of a company that sells to horizontal business markets and those of a company that sells to vertical business markets?

8. A manufacturer has been selling specialized software to a large oil company in Norway. In which of the three buy classes would you place this buyer-seller relationship? Is there any aspect of the relationship that is likely to fall into the straight-rebuy category?

9. Explain how the six stages of the buying-decision process might be applied in the following buying situations:
   a. New-task buying of a conveyor belt for a soft-drink bottling plant.
   b. Straight rebuy of maintenance services for that conveyor belt.
   c. Modified rebuy of advertising agency services for a hotel chain.

10. How would you go about determining who influences the buying decisions of business users?

11. Steelcase, IBM, Xerox, and other manufacturers of office equipment make a substantial proportion of their sales directly to business users. At the same time, wholesalers of office equipment are thriving. Are these two market situations inconsistent? Explain.

Hands-On Marketing

1. Find an ad for a business product or service that is directed toward the B2B market and another ad for the same product that is directed toward the B2C market (such as an ad for leasing fleets of Chevrolets and an ad for Chevrolet aimed at consumers. Similarly, advertisements for cellular phones, PDAs, or laptop computers). Discuss the buying motives appealed to in the ads.

2. Interview a purchasing agent about buying a product that would qualify as a modified rebuy. Draw a diagram that shows the purchasing agent's perceptions of: (a) the stages of the decision process; (b) who was in the buying centre at each stage of the decision process; and (c) what role or roles each person played at each stage of the process. Comment on how this diagram might be useful to a salesperson representing the product in question.

Back to the Top

Think about the help that Natalie and Soren will need to get their new restaurant open. What role can a very large organization like the Royal Bank of Canada play in helping them realize their dream? Can such a large organization be an effective supplier to a very small, start-up business, as well as being the banker to some of the largest corporations in the country? Visit the RBC Royal Bank Web site (**www.royalbank.ca**) and click on the "go to business banking" link. Check out the various services that the bank offers small business owners, including the "starting a business" section under the Solution Centre. Is this more than you thought the bank would be offering? What role is RBC trying to play in the business lives of its B2B customers?

Online LearningCentre

Want to get better grades, tips on how to study more effectively, and up-to-date information on happenings in the world of marketing? Then, visit the Online Learning Centre for practice tests, Study Smart software, *Marketing Magazine*, and much more! **www.mcgrawhill.ca/olc/sommers**

CASE 2-1:

Multimedia

Envirocoatings (Canada), Inc.

Envirocoatings (Canada), Inc. is the marketing and distribution arm of Envirocoat Technologies, Inc. (ETI), a British Columbia-based manufacturer of high-tech paints and coating products. The company had its start in 1960, when a chemist who had recently immigrated to Canada from Germany developed a new line of coatings designed to protect homes, buildings and other structures from the harsh Canadian climate.

From the beginning, the company's research and product development activities were aimed at finding solutions to the fact that most paints failed to stand up under extreme weather conditions. The persistent, ongoing research paid off, as today Envircoatings offers a range of products based on complex chemical compounds that are acknowledged to be superior to others on the market.

Over the years, Envirocoatings (**www.envirocoatings.com**) has been successful, particularly in the architectural market, where its products became the preferred coatings product for use on commercial buildings in Western Canada and were regularly "written into" the specifications for painting new and renovated buildings. Some office buildings, hotels and apartment buildings that were coated well over 20 years ago still do not need to be repainted, not only retaining their appearance, but also saving their owners a great deal of money through reduced care and upkeep.

The Product Line

Envirocoatings' principal product is the high performance, environmentally safe, water-based Ceramic InsulCoat Exterior Coating Systems intended for use on exterior walls. These products are formulated with "CERYLIUM," a proprietary formula of precision-blended, high-performance ingredients in a complex, 100 percent acrylic suspension that provides superior adhesion, breatheability, elasticity and weatherproofing with a tough, strong coating. These coating products are designed to provide the ultimate protection against ultra-violet degradation and weathering, resulting in significant energy savings, lower maintenance costs and a durable, aesthetically pleasing finish.

The company also manufactures a Ceramic InsulCoat product that is intended for use on the roofs of buildings, providing the advantages of the exterior wall coating, with the added benefit of thermal insulation. Two sealing products round out the product line. SealBond is a polymer-modified acrylic penetrating finishing sealant. It provides significant resistance to dirt and moisture. It can be brushed-on, rolled-on, or sprayed-on. Used undiluted directly from the container, it penetrates deep into porous substrates leaving a virtually invisible, clear protective film. Ceramic InsulSeal is a polymer-modified acrylic penetrating soaker-sealer and bonding agent that can also be brushed-on, rolled-on, or sprayed-on. As it fills and hardens, it provides a myriad of micro-anchoring points in the substrate. It is not a finishing product and must be coated. InsulSeal promotes exceptional adhesion when used in conjunction with the Ceramic InsulCoat Coating System.

The Envirocoatings product is a specialized one, intended for use in situations where exterior surfaces are exposed to extreme weather conditions. While the principal application of the product line is in the industrial and commercial market, there is potential for sales to residential customers. The big question facing management is how to increase sales in both the B2B and B2C markets.

Questions:

1. What are the product advantages offered by Envirocoatings and to whom are these advantages likely to appeal? Who are the target marketing segments for this product in both the B2B and B2C markets?

2. How is the buying decision made for coating products in the commercial and industrial market? Who are the likely influencers for such a decision? What are the implications for how Envirocoatings distributes its products?

3. Why would a homeowner choose to use the Envirocoatings Ceramic InsulCoat Exterior Coating product to paint the exterior of his or her home? How do the factors that drive paint and coatings decisions differ between homeowners and the owners of commercial buildings?

CASE 2-2:

Maison Chaude

It was late Friday afternoon and Geneviève Robert had just returned to her office from a meeting with a prospective new client. Geneviève is a senior research consultant with RCQ Recherche, a regional marketing research firm with four offices in the Province of Quebec. The opportunity facing Geneviève is with Maison Chaude, a distributor of home heating oil in the Montréal area. She had received a call on Wednesday from Serge Leger, Sales Manager of Maison Chaude, who asked if they could meet as he was interested in conducting some marketing research. He had heard of RCQ Recherche from his brother-in-law who is a marketing vice president at a local insurance company.

The problem that Serge is facing and which he wished to discuss with Geneviève is that Maison Chaude's sales had stabilized in recent years, as new homes were being constructed with electric rather than oil heating systems. The problem had become worse as oil prices continued to rise and some homeowners had actually converted their oil heat systems to electricity. There were also the environmental risks, including concerns about oil spills and leaks, that some customers now associate with oil, not to mention the maintenance requirements. Serge was looking for some ideas that might suggest new initiatives that would lead to sales growth. It was mid-September and the company should be preparing for its busiest sales season.

In their meeting in Serge's office on Rue Sainte-Cathérine, Geneviève learned about the history of Maison Chaude; that it had been serving the Montréal region for more than 40 years. Serge had joined the firm only two years ago. Since then, Maison Chaude had been faced with increasing competition from alternate forms of energy and from increasingly aggressive oil distributors, many of whom were prepared to drop prices to retain business. It seemed to Geneviève that Serge was at a loss to know where to turn.

Serge kept referring to the fact that he would like to do a survey of homeowners in the Montréal region. Geneviève was not at all certain that a survey was the right way to go to get the information that she believed Maison Chaude needed to understand its market and to identify how they should compete. It seemed to her that the issues facing Maison Chaude were very complex. The home heating business was changing and the future of oil as a source of home heat was in doubt. The size of the home heating oil market was shrinking and it seemed to Geneviève that Serge had not asked himself a very important question: "Should Maison Chaude be a Home Heating Specialist or remain a Home Heating Oil Distributor?" Maybe this was a question that should be directed to the senior executives of the company.

Depending on the answer, the company would have to develop very different strategies to support future growth. If Maison Chaude is to remain a heating oil distributor, a very aggressive strategy would have to be developed to move or keep customers away from the competition so as to meet the company's growth objective. If the company was open to diversifying and offering other alternatives for home heating, then a strategy to position the company as home heating specialists would be needed. This latter strategy would allow Maison Chaude to be a player in the new home construction market and in home retrofits.

As the discussion progressed, Geneviève observed that Serge did not seem to have a good understanding of the projected trends in home heating and seemed not to have developed a clear picture of what questions he would want to ask in a survey. In fact, he appeared to be unsure as to exactly what he wanted to get from the research. Maison Chaude had never conducted marketing research before. When she asked him what level of budget he had allocated for the project, he hesitated and said he did not have a firm budget, but that he thought he might be prepared to spend as much as $10,000.

Geneviève ended the meeting with the suggestion that she send a formal proposal to Serge by the following Wednesday. As she sat at her desk, she contemplated what she should include in the proposal.

Questions:

1. What information do you think Serge actually needs and what decisions is he likely to have to make?
2. How do you believe Geneviève should propose that RCQ Recherche obtain that information?
3. What role should Geneviève play in helping Maison Chaude, and Serge in particular, achieve success in the future?
4. How does Geneviève deal with the fact that Serge has probably allocated far too small a budget to obtain the information he really needs?

CASE 2-3:

Boston Pizza – The Big Switcheroo

It was Sunday evening and John Yanchus was relaxing after his shift at the Boston Pizza on Warden Avenue in Scarborough. John is in the fifth semester of a three-year Marketing Management program at Centennial College and he has been working part-time at Boston Pizza for the past 18 months. On Sundays, he works through lunch and dinner, and the store had been particularly busy today. He decided to watch a little TV before tackling that Managerial Accounting assignment that was due Monday afternoon.

As he surfed through the channels, he caught a glimpse of a Boston Pizza store and stopped to watch. It was a program on the CBC that followed an employee from a Boston Pizza store as she swapped roles for a week with the CEO of Boston Pizza. John decided to watch — that accounting assignment would just have to wait.

History of Boston Pizza

Boston Pizza is one of Canada's largest and fastest-growing restaurant chains. The Boston Pizza concept was launched in Edmonton, Alberta, in 1964 when Greek immigrant Gus Agioritis opened "Boston Pizza and Spaghetti House." Agioritis achieved success by combining hard work with a business strategy that included a focus on growth through franchising. This strategy established the early success of the Boston Pizza chain, and by 1970 Boston Pizza had 17 locations throughout Western Canada.

One of the first franchisees attracted to the Boston Pizza concept was an RCMP officer named Jim Treliving, who noticed the growing popularity of Boston Pizza and in 1968 opened his first franchise restaurant in Penticton, British Columbia. George Melville, a chartered accountant, became Treliving's business partner in 1973.

Over the next 10 years, Jim and George built a chain of 16 restaurants throughout B.C., giving them the hands-on experience that would prove invaluable in their future position as the franchisor of the Boston Pizza concept. In 1983, Treliving and Melville acquired the chain of 44 Boston Pizza restaurants from then-owner Ron Coyle, who had bought the company from Agioritis in 1978. Boston Pizza was named the official pizza supplier for Expo 86 in Vancouver, and the exposure gained during the World's Fair created significant interest in the franchise opportunity, leading to 17 new franchises in 1987 and 1988. Expansion has continued over the years, and today there are more than 250 Boston Pizza restaurants coast-to-coast in Canada.

The Boston Pizza Concept

The Boston Pizza restaurant provides for "two experiences under one roof," with a full-service, family-friendly casual dining restaurant and a separate sports bar. Most Boston Pizza restaurants also have an outdoor patio to accommodate guests during the warmer months. A typical restaurant is 5,500 to 6,500 square feet and has seating for 180 to 225 guests inside, with another 50 to 75 seats on the patio.

Boston Pizza restaurants offer a casual dining atmosphere with more than 100 menu items, including a unique selection of gourmet pizzas, mouth-watering pastas and a wide variety of appetizers, meal-sized salads, entrees and desserts. The restaurant is perfect for families, teams and groups of all ages and the sports bars feature sports memorabilia, big screen TVs and games in a contemporary setting. The Boston Pizza concept has more locations and serves more than 25 million guests annually — more than any other casual dining restaurant chain in the country.

The Big Switcheroo

"The Big Switcheroo" is a feature of the popular CBC program *Venture*. During a one-hour program, the *Venture* team tracks the lives of the CEO of a major company and an employee of that firm who has been chosen to be CEO for a few days. The CEO and the employee switch roles and the CEO takes the employee's job. In 2006, Venture followed Mike Cordoba, CEO of Boston Pizza, as he switched jobs for three days with Melissa Marchese, an employee of Boston Pizza in Kitchener, Ontario, and an honours French student at the University of Waterloo. It was this program that John had stumbled on as he surfed channels on Sunday evening.

In 2005, *Venture* had profiled Rajesh Subramanian, CEO of FedEx Canada, as he switched jobs with a front-line employee and went to work on FedEx trucks. When asked why he participated in the program, Subramanian indicated that FedEx employee research had indicated a disconnect between management and employees within the firm. Participating in "The Big Switcheroo" was one way that management had chosen to address this problem.

As John watched the *Venture* program, he could identify with the challenges that the food preparers and wait staff faced every day at the Boston Pizza store in Kitchener where Mike Cordoba went to work at Melissa's job. What Mike was dealing with was exactly what faced every new employee. John could recall the confusion and frustration of his first few days on the job.

But he was most interested in how Melissa Marchese was handling Mike's job in Richmond at the Boston Pizza head office. He was surprised at the things that Melissa became involved in: the approval of budgets and new store locations, sampling new menu items, meeting with suppliers at early morning meetings, making unscheduled trips to other cities. He thought, "So, this is what a CEO does!"

Questions:

1. What kind of company does Boston Pizza seem to be? Why would this company, and Mike Cordoba in particular, agree to participate in CBC's "The Big Switcheroo"?
2. How does what you have seen in the video reflect the Boston Pizza philosophy? Based on what you have seen, what do you suspect are the values that guide Boston Pizza?
3. Based on the video and the company's Web site (**www.bostonpizza.com**) and what you know about Boston Pizza, describe in detail the principal market segments that the company is targeting, and outline what you feel is its positioning strategy.
4. What is the role of the CEO and of kitchen and wait staff in influencing customer satisfaction with Boston Pizza?

SOURCE: This case is based in part on information from several sources, including: IABC International Conference — Rajesh Subramanian, June 5, 2006 (www.propr.ca/index.php/category/trust); Sabrina Bowman, "Serving up pizza and corporate power," *Imprint Online*, http://imprint.uwaterloo.ca/print.php?f=2&t=8317&i=&v=f&story=8317, March 17, 2006.

CASE 2-4:

GuestLink – Aliant Youth Strategy

Multimedia

In Chapter 5, our Guest Marketer, Heather Tulk, Senior Vice-President – Marketing at Bell Aliant, outlined that company's strategy to reach customers in the youth segment. Let's think about this strategy and why Aliant might want to single out younger customers for marketing attention. What is the market opportunity represented by the "youth market" segment? In fact, is this segment homogenous, or are there several subsegments within the youth market? Is this simple demographic segmentation?

Take a look at the three TV commercials that accompany this case and discuss them in the context of the youth strategy that Heather Tulk has outlined.

Questions:

1. What benefits are "youth" customers seeking from a cellular telephone company? How effectively has Aliant used marketing research to address this question?
2. How has Aliant chosen to position itself to appeal to youth customers? How does it add value for these customers and differentiate its brand from that of Rogers and Telus?
3. How is Aliant's positioning reflected in the three TV commercials? Visit Aliant's youth portal (**www.aliant.net/youth101**) and review how this component of the marketing program also appeals to youth customers.

PART 3

Products, Services, and Brands

The planning, development, and management of the products and services that represent the essence of an organization's core offer to its customers

The next step in the marketing process is to develop a marketing mix that will achieve the company's goals in its target markets. The marketing mix is a strategic combination of components, all broadly defined — the organization's products or services, its distribution system, the prices it charges, its communications and promotional programs and the value it creates for its customers. Each of these is closely interrelated with the other variables in the mix.

In **Part 3**, we explore that component of the marketing mix that involves the products and services offered by the company, expanding the scope to include brands and the firm's value proposition. In Chapter 7, we define the term product very broadly to incorporate services as well, and discuss the importance of product planning and the new-product development process. Chapter 8 deals mainly with organizations whose core product is actually an intangible service and the importance of service in cultivating customer relationships. Chapter 9 addresses the very important concept of branding and other product features, including packaging and labelling.

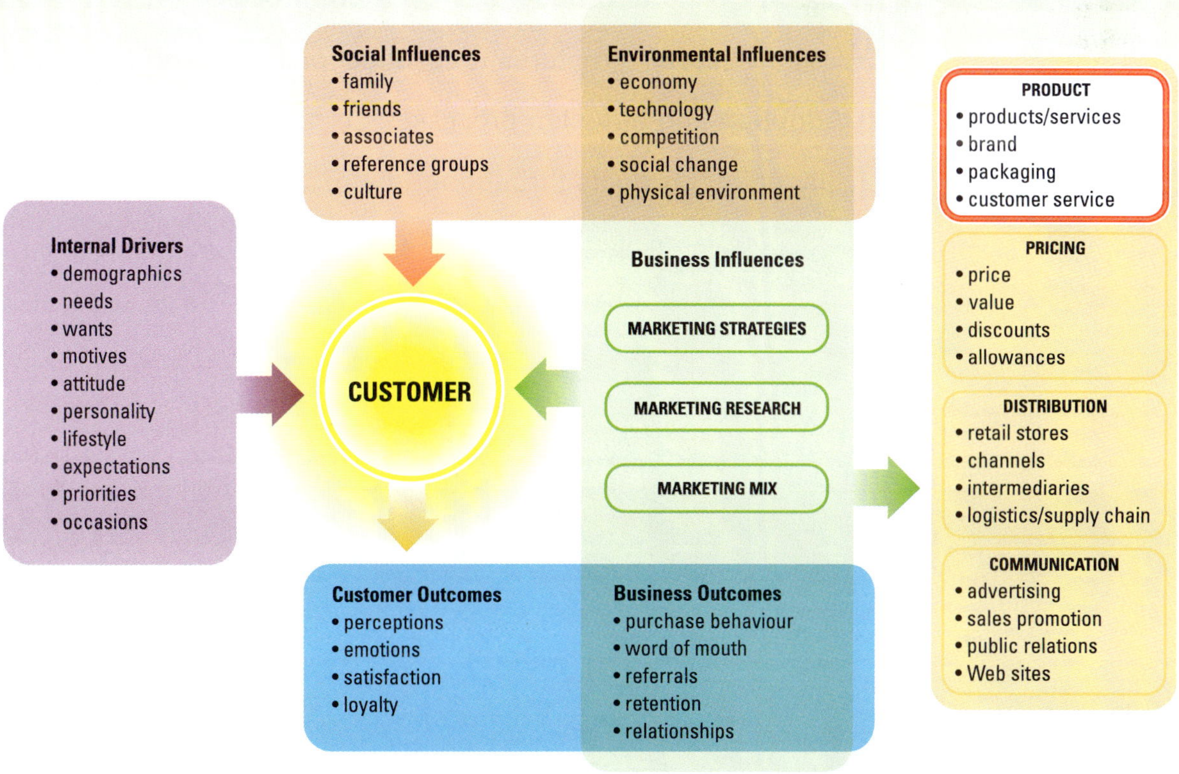

CHAPTER 7

Product Planning and Strategies

After studying this chapter, you should have an understanding of:

- The meaning of the word product in its fullest sense.
- The classification of consumer and business products.
- The major product-mix strategies.
- The importance of product innovation.
- The steps in the product-development process.
- Organizational structures for product planning and development.
- Adoption and diffusion processes for new products.
- Managing products throughout the product life cycle.

It's Like the Electronic Equivalent of a Swiss Army Knife

Are they new? Well, no, actually they are a decade old. Multifunction imaging peripherals — MFPs as they are called — machines that combine print, scan, copy and fax functions in one unit rather than four. When first introduced, they were targeted at home office customers who were mostly concerned with saving space, but the overall quality of their output was not as good as the individual units achieved. In recent years, however, continued product development has increased their ease of use, speed, reliability, cost of operation and quality of output.

This electronic equivalent of a Swiss Army knife, when it comes to moving information between computer and paper, took over the home desktop and is now carving out a place in professional offices across Canada. As performance and costs improved, so did the appeal of MFPs in a new market — small and medium-sized businesses. For such businesses, the improved product not only saves space, business and capital costs, but also increases employee ease of access to equipment and boosted productivity in surprising ways.

One such example comes from Vancouver-based North Shore Credit Union. To support a new customer-service strategy, desktop MFPs have replaced the centrally located printers, faxes, copiers and scanners. The result was that MFP equipped account managers had more face-to-face time with customers. They were able to discuss their clients' needs and at that same time, print and copy personalized colourful text and graphic materials without leaving their side. There is no more breaking the flow of customer interaction by having to run around the office building from machine to machine. Customers are impressed. "That's neat," they say — an important customer comment about the care and attention provided in such a business relationship.

This success of MFPs means the end of growth and the beginning of the decline of stand-alone printers and scanners. 2004 became the first year that unit sales declined in Canada. And as printer and scanner sales declined, MFP sales took off — by almost 50 percent. In 2005, MFPs held almost 40 percent of the printer market. Not bad for an older "new" product finally hitting a real growth stage in its life cycle by offering new benefits as a result of continued development.[1]

Remember the stars, cash cows, question marks, and dogs of the Boston Consulting Group matrix discussed in Chapter 3? Product strategy played a key role in the model. In this chapter, we review the major product strategies as well as their consumer behaviour foundations. But before we discuss strategy and approaches to new-product idea generation, we need to look at some basics — the meaning of the word product and the main product classification systems.

The Meaning of Product

What is a product? Most of us would probably use it to refer to physical, tangible items. In a narrow sense, a product is a set of attributes assembled in an identifiable form. Each product is identified by a commonly understood descriptive or generic name, such as "steel," "insurance," "tennis racquets," or "entertainment." But in the reality of the marketplace, we need a broader definition of product; essentially, it is the essence of what a company or organization is offering its customers. We need to indicate that consumers are not really buying a set of attributes (a production-centred concept) but rather the valuable benefits that those attributes provide (a customer-centred concept). Customers don't want a printer, a scanner, a copier and a fax machine — they want easily achieved useful and impressive output at a reasonable cost. They don't want a wireless hand-held personal digital assistant (PDA) — they want quick and convenient communication. And a product that provides the desired benefits, whether tangible or intangible, provides satisfaction.

product
A product can be a physical item or a service, place, person, or idea; it has a set of tangible attributes, including packaging, colour, price, quality, and brand, plus the services and reputation of the seller.

Marketers usually offer the consumer multiple versions of their products. Each offering is made up of a set of tangible and intangible attributes that combine to provide the benefits in which a target market segment is interested, benefits that will give the satisfaction consumers in that segment want. Figure 7-1 illustrates the range of attributes that comprise the benefits offered by a product. Competing marketers may offer a range of designs, colours, brands, quality levels, warranties, packaging, services, prices, and sellers' reputations. Each combination is designed to provide a somewhat different set of benefits. Just think of the variety of benefits that the different styles, features, formats and brands of cellular phones make available for different user groups.

What, then, is a **product**? It is a set of tangible and intangible attributes, including packaging, colour, price, quality, and brand, plus the seller's services and reputation, that provides a set of perceived consumer benefits. A product may be a tangible product, service, place, person, or idea. But consumers are buying much more than a set of physical attributes when they buy a product. They are buying want satisfaction in the form of the benefits they expect to receive from the product.

You should consider how different marketers develop the product they are promoting. In other words, what is the nature of the product for which they are responsible? As a manufacturer, you might be responsible for developing a product strategy for a new multimedia cellphone. What features should it have? Colours? Price? On the other hand, as a retailer you might be responsible for developing a product strategy for a chain of hardware stores. What new products should you introduce? Should you carry housewares? Electronics? High-end merchandise?

Figure 7-1:
Product Attributes

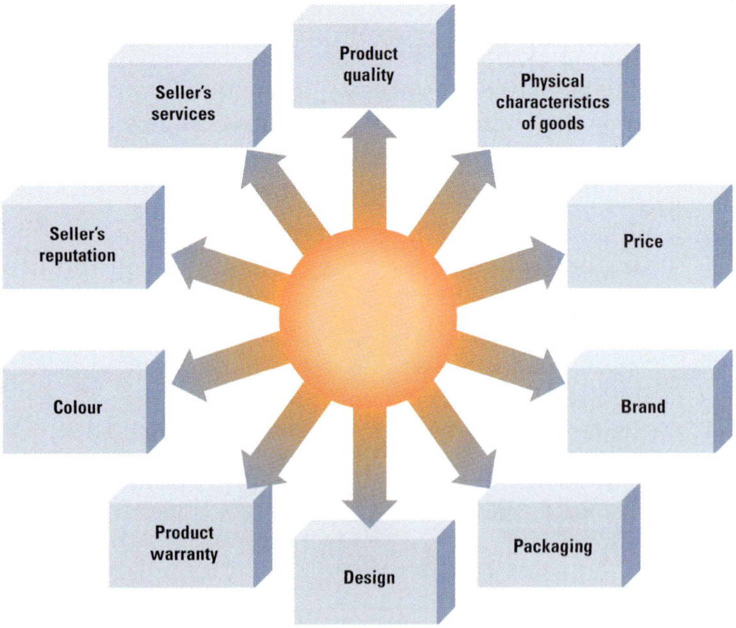

Product Classification Systems

To design effective marketing programs, firms must organize their approaches. First, we can divide all products into two categories — consumer and business products. Then, we will subdivide each category still further.

Consumer and business products

consumer product
A product that is intended for purchase and use by household consumers for non-business purposes.

business product
A product that is intended for purchase and use in producing other products or in rendering services in a business.

Consumer products are intended for use by household consumers for non-business purposes. **Business products** are intended for resale, for use in producing other products, or for providing services in an organization. The two types of products are distinguished on the basis of who will use them and how they will be used. Kellogg's Corn Flakes are categorized as consumer products if household consumers will use them in their existing form. However, when sold to restaurants and university dining halls, they are categorized as business products.

Often it is not possible to place a product in only one class or the other. Seats on an Air Canada flight from Regina to Vancouver may be considered a consumer product if purchased by students going on vacation or a business product if bought by a sales representative on a business trip. Air Canada, or any other company in a similar situation, recognizes that its product falls into both categories and therefore develops separate marketing programs for each market.

Classification of consumer goods

One method of classifying consumer goods is based not on the nature of the goods themselves, but on the nature of the buying process customers most commonly used in their acquisition. Table 7-1 shows three of the four categories of goods — convenience, shopping, and specialty — and the marketing considerations associated with each one. The fourth category, unsought goods, is explained later.

convenience goods
A class of consumer products of which the consumer has prior knowledge and purchases with minimum time and effort.

Convenience goods: Consumers know enough about them so they can be bought with minimum effort — a routine problem-solving approach or, sometimes, a very limited problem-solving approach. Convenience goods include many food items, inexpensive candy, drugstore sundries such as shampoo and toothpaste, and staple hardware items such as light bulbs and batteries; convenience services include such things as banking transactions, and scanning and copying services.

shopping goods
A class of consumer products purchased after the buyer has spent some time and effort comparing price, quality, colour, and/or other attributes of alternative products.

Shopping goods: Those for which customers want to compare quality, price, and perhaps style in several stores or on several Web sites before purchasing; the decision-making can be limited or extended problem solving. Clothing, furniture, major appliances, computer components, and automobiles fall into this category. The process of searching and comparing continues as long as the customer believes that the potential benefits from a better purchase more than offset the additional time and effort spent shopping.

specialty goods
A class of consumer products with perceived unique characteristics; consumers are willing to expend special effort to buy them.

Specialty goods: Those for which consumers have a strong brand preference and are willing to expend substantial time and effort in their acquisition. Customers forego more accessible substitutes to search for and purchase the desired brand given the strong relationship that exists. Examples include ultra-expensive clothing brands, sound equipment, health foods, photographic equipment, and, for many people, automobiles and certain home appliances. Various brands, such as Prada, Jaguar, and Nikon, have achieved specialty-good status in the minds of consumers around the globe.

unsought goods
A type of consumer product that consists of new products of which the consumer is not yet aware or products that the consumer does not yet want.

Unsought goods are different. They are so unlike the other three categories that we have not included them in Table 7-1. One form of unsought good is a newly developed product. Consumers are often not aware it exists or may not understand its function or purpose. Alternatively, unsought goods can be products that the consumer is aware of but does not want right now. Newly created products and innovations begin as unsought goods, because

TABLE 7-1 Categories of Consumer Goods: Characteristics and Marketing Considerations

	Type of Product*		
	Convenience	**Shopping**	**Specialty**
EXAMPLES:	Canned drink	Furniture	Expensive suits
Characteristics			
Time and effort devoted to shopping	Very little	Considerable	Cannot generalize; consumer may go to nearby store and buy with little effort or a distant store and spend much time and effort
Time spent planning purchase	Very little	Considerable	Considerable
How soon want is satisfied after arising	Immediately	Relatively long time	Relatively long time
Are price and quality compared?	No	Yes	No
Price	Usually low	High	High
Purchase frequency	Usually frequent	Infrequent	Infrequent
Marketing Considerations			
Length of channel	Long	Short	Short to very short
Retailer	Relatively unimportant	Important	Very important
Number of outlets	As many as possible	Few	Few; often only one in market
Stock turnover	High	Lower	Lower
Gross margin	Low	High	High
Responsibility for advertising	Producer's	Retailer's	Joint responsibility
Point-of-purchase display	Very important	Less important	Less important
Brand or store name important	Brand name	Store name	Both
Packaging	Very important	Less important	Less important

*Unsought products are not included. See text explanation.

it is difficult to look for a product if you don't know it exists. For that matter, some goods you may not really want to buy at all! Many new high-tech products and services may very well be unsought goods simply because, while they are technologically feasible, they do not offer consumer benefits that are easily recognized as having value. Traditional unsought goods include such things such as funeral services, gravestones, and life insurance.

Classification of business goods

BACK TO THE TOP

Business goods are separated into five categories with their characteristics and marketing considerations presented in Table 7-2. This classification is based on the product's broad uses, not the manner in which buyers shop for the goods. For example, a business good may be used in producing other products or in operating an organization. The multifunction imaging peripherals (MFPs) discussed in our chapter opener are clearly considered accessory equipment.

raw materials
Business goods that have not been processed in any way and that will become part of another product.

fabricating parts and materials
Materials that become part of other finished products, distinguished from raw materials in that they have already been processed and bought by manufacturers for assembly into their final products. Some undergo further processing and may be referred to as fabricating materials.

installations
In the business market, long-lived, expensive, major industrial capital goods that directly affect the scale of operation of an industrial firm.

accessory equipment
In the business market, capital goods used in the operation of a firm.

operating supplies
The "convenience goods" of the business market: short-lived, low-priced items purchased with a minimum of time and effort.

TABLE 7-2 Categories of Business Goods: Characteristics and Marketing Considerations

	Type of Product				
	Raw Materials	**Fabricating Parts and Materials**	**Installations**	**Accessory Equipment**	**Operating Supplies**
EXAMPLES	Iron ore	Engine blocks	Blast furnaces	Storage racks	Paper clips
Characteristics					
Unit price	Very low	Low	Very high	Medium	Low
Length of life	Very short	Depends on final product	Very long	Long	Short
Quantities purchased	Large	Large	Very small	Small	Small
Frequency of purchase	Frequent delivery; long-term purchase contract	Infrequent purchase, but frequent delivery	Very infrequent	Medium frequency	Frequent
Standardization of competitive products	Very much; grading is important	Very much	Very little; custom made	Little	Much
Quantity of supply	Limited; supply can be increased slowly or not at all	Usually no problem	No problem	Usually no problem	Usually no problem
Marketing Considerations					
Nature of channel	Short; no intermediaries	Short; intermediaries only for small buyers	Short; no intermediaries	Intermediaries used	Intermediaries used
Negotiation period	Hard to generalize	Medium	Long	Medium	Short
Price competition	Important	Important	Varies in importance	Not main factor	Important
Pre-sale/post-sale service	Not important	Important	Very important	Important	Very little
Promotional activity	Very little	Moderate	Salespeople very important	Important	Not too important
Brand preference	None	Generally low	High	High	Low
Advance buying contract	Important; long-term contracts	Important; long-term contracts	Not usual	Not usual	Not usual

PAGE UP!

1. To the marketer, what is a product?
2. ________________ products are intended for use by household consumers while ________________ products are intended for use by organizations.
3. What are the four types of consumer goods?

Product Strategies

product mix
All products offered for sale by a company.

breadth of product mix
The number of product lines offered for sale by a firm.

depth of product line
The assortment within a product line.

product line
A broad group of products intended for essentially similar uses and possessing reasonably similar physical characteristics.

Panasonic

At any given time, firms specializing in business or consumer products will be marketing some new products and some old ones, while other products are being planned and developed. In this section of the chapter, we'll cover the main strategic decisions pertaining to an organization's assortment of products and services.

Product-mix and product-line strategies

Few firms rely on a single product or service; most sell many. What each firm does is dictated by the product strategy it chooses to devise and implement. The set of all products offered for sale by a company is called a **product mix** or product portfolio. The structure of a product mix has both **breadth** and **depth**. The number of product lines carried is a measure of the breadth of the product mix. The depth is measured by the variety of sizes, colours, and models offered within each product line. A product-mix strategy is illustrated in Figure 7-2.

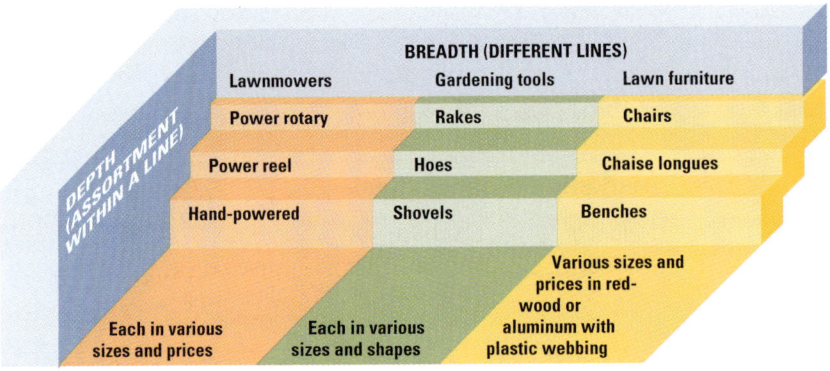

Figure 7-2: Product Mix — Breadth and Depth
Part of the product mix in a lawn and garden store

Panasonic lets you explore product mix, breadth, depth, and line at your leisure.

A broad group of products, intended for essentially similar uses and having similar physical characteristics, constitutes a **product line**. Panasonic's product lines (**www.panasonic.ca**) include televisions, DVD players, telephones, small home appliances, and several lines of audio components. To examine the depth of one particular product line, DVD players for example, we would count the various models that are connected to external screens, the number of portable models offered, and then include the in-dash model for cars.

Planned Product-Mix Strategies

Many firms offer a large number of products to consumers — Johnson & Johnson and Sony are prime examples. In service industries, firms such as Bell Canada (telephone, Internet, etc.) and Loblaws (groceries, dry-cleaning, photo services, financial services) offer customers many services and many ways to access them. These diverse assortments of goods and services did not develop by accident: They reflect a planned strategy by the company.

Product positioning

Management's ability to position a product appropriately in the market is a major determinant of company profitability. Equally important is the ability of management to reposition a product over the long run. In addition to the positioning strategies based on market segmentation discussed in Chapter 4, a variety of other positioning strategies are available.

MARKETING AT WORK — 7-1: STRATEGY

McCain and Kraft Take Different Tacks in Marketing Dogfight!

The original ad campaign for McCain Rising Crust Pizza wasn't just bad — it was so misguided that it actually boosted sales for its competitor!

From 1999 to 2004, McCain Foods Ltd. and Kraft Ltd. were advertising competing products with very similar campaigns. As a result, consumers were having a hard time telling the products apart! McCain's tagline was, "Who can tell it from takeout," while Kraft claimed "It's not delivery — It's Delissio."

McCain introduced the rising crust concept in early 1999, but Kraft became the brand leader shortly after when it introduced a similar product and has continued to gain market share ever since. McCain's was haemorrhaging market share. Then last year, McCain's market research suggested that consumers couldn't differentiate the ads for the two products and that it seemed Kraft owned the consumer mind space for a frozen substitute to pizzeria pizza.

McCain conducted focus groups to find a way of advertising that was different and discovered that teenagers greatly influenced mom's decisions about what frozen pizza to buy. Until now, McCain's rather folksy, unfussy ads have come to define the image of the brand, but no one can question the company's effectiveness: $6.4 billion in global sales in 2004 and undeniably high brand recognition among Canadians and its core target — moms 29- to 43-years old. What McCain needed, however, was a rebel in the brand family —someone to speak up. The Crescendo had to break out of the familiar and comfortable image that McCain had built its success on.

The outcome has been to position away from the Delissio brand by changing the product name and primarily targeting 13-to-17-year olds. The ads speak directly to teens without trying to be too cool. Using the "Nothing rises like a Crescendo" pitch, the commercials, called "tan lines," poke fun at teens and young adults so marvelled by watching the pizza crust as it bakes, that they walk away proudly sporting oven-window-shaped tans on their faces. While not loved by everyone, the ads are starting to show up in pop culture such as cartoons in the *Montreal Gazette* and with the *Toronto Star* asking scientists whether such a tan was possible through an oven door.

Kraft is planning to stick with its good-as-delivery brand positioning and, unlike McCain, will continue to target adults.

QUESTIONS:

1. What is McCain risking by differentiating in this fashion?
2. Is there potential here for product extension if the focus on this segment is successful?
3. Can McCain build a strong relationship with this target segment based on this type of product differentiation?

SOURCE: Adapted from Keith McArthur, "Teens, Moms Targeted in Oven-Ready Pizza War," *The Globe and Mail*, February 24, 2005, p. B4; Andrew Young, "Not your mom's pizza," *Marketing Magazine Online*, www.marketingmag.ca, January 17, 2005.

Positioning in relation to a competitor For some products (Coca-Cola and Pepsi-Cola, for example), the best position is directly against the competition. This is a particularly effective approach if a product has better features or some other differential advantage over the competition. While frozen pizza may not sound too exciting, it's actually a $2.5-billion-dollar industry and the competition is thawing as things heat up in the industry. While some brands have tried a sophisticated culinary image, others have tried to tell you it's the same as pizzeria pie – but, New Brunswick–based McCain's Crescendo line of frozen pizzas is now targeting 13-to-17-year olds and it's turning up the 'cool factor.' Traditionally McCain's has targeted moms, the main grocery shopper. As such, to young consumers the brand has no zip and is seen as a mainstream brand.

Next up to make the McCain brand appealing to younger consumers is the launch of Zwak (a name kids in focus groups associated with fun and action), a re-branding of the company's drinking boxes. The brand is aimed at 6-to-12-year-olds and competes in a market where there is a lot of price discounting and private labels. The Zwak Pack characters appear in online games and animated TV spots that will, hopefully, help McCain increase its 20 percent share of the $303 million juice pack market. Zwak is also reduced in sugar and has added vitamin C so that it attracts the attention of moms as well.[2]

Positioning in relation to a product class or attribute Sometimes a company's positioning strategy entails associating its product with (or dissociating it from) a product class or attribute. Both Rona and Home Depot lay claim to the DIY market. Some firms promote their wares as being in a desirable class, such as "Made in Canada," or having an attractive attribute, such as "low energy consumption," "all-natural," or "environmentally friendly." A survey of consumers' opinions of manufactured goods made in various countries revealed that Canadians rate their own manufactured goods more favourably than products produced in Japan, Germany, and other countries.[3] This is good news for Canadian firms that want to position their products on a "Made in Canada" basis, particularly since it seems that this positioning is also effective outside of Canada. Canada, as seen from abroad, is credited with expertise in everything to do with ice — from hockey to beverages — as evidenced by the success of Canadian beer, ice wine, ice vodka, and bottled water made from iceberg or glacial water.[4]

Mighty Ducks

Positioning works for services as well as for tangible products In an attempt to capture the attention of the lucrative teen and 'tween marketplace Family Channel has repositioned Family and The Movie Network (TMN), offering kids the chance to win trips to Vancouver to meet the cast of the hit Family Channel program, Radio Free Roscoe. It partnered with Nintendo to promote its new Donkey Kong Jungle Beat game — to the tune of 6,000 SMS entries and 30,000 paper entries. The channel is continuing forward, looking to partner with cereal companies, video games, toy manufacturers, and school supply companies.[5] Another successful service positioning was The Mighty Ducks of Anaheim (www.mightyducks.com). It has been positioned as the "fun" team of the National Hockey League. The team's logo and colour scheme were selected with merchandising in mind, to appeal not only to hockey's traditional audience — men — but also to women and children deciding on teal and purple for official team merchandise.[6]

The NHL's "fun" team.

Positioning in relation to a target market Regardless of which positioning strategy is used, the needs of the target market always must be considered. This positioning strategy doesn't suggest that the other strategies ignore target markets. Rather, with this strategy, the target market — rather than another factor, such as competition — is the focal point in positioning the product.

Day-Timer

Day-Timers, Inc. (**www.daytimer.com**), widely known for its daily planners and organizers targeted at businesspeople, has also developed a product for the home. This was the result of a realization by the company that there was a general untapped market of consumers looking for products to use for time management. The majority of this market was anticipated to be female. When researching the target market to design the product, the manufacturer learned that the proposed users wanted the planner to be basic; made of softer, leather-like material; with a closure such as a zipper or clasp. The product was introduced in a variety of colours, designs, and sizes, and sold at very low prices in comparison with the business products. To appeal to younger groups, the styles now offered include brighter colour schemes and more generic filler sheets that can be used for a variety of purposes.

Virgin Mobile had a cheeky plan to introduce itself to its 12-to-34-year old target market when it entered Canada in 2005. "More than 11 million Canadians have the Catch," stated Sir Richard Branson, Virgin founder. The symptoms? Monthly billing discomfort, unsightly hidden fees, irregular growth in rates, and paralyzing contractual obligations! Virgin was positioning itself as a prepaid cellular phone brand with nothing to hide — and no catch — trying to appeal to those jaded from earlier cellphone experiences. Transit ads exposed how customers are being "ripped off by the mobile industry" and teaser billboards promoted **www.curethecatch.ca** where visitors could determine if they too were suffering from the Catch. Service in the way of accessibility was another important part of this strategy — making Virgin phones available in more than 1,500 stores across Canada including HMV and 7-Eleven locations, and top-up cards available in 10,000 stores such as Shell and London Drugs. The 'fun brand' further demonstrated its irreverence with clever phone names like "hot little model" and "fully flipped out." Among their features a "ring rescue" to save users from bad dates, a list of tried-and-true pick-up lines, and a wake-up call featuring the vocals of an overly enthusiastic reggae singer.[7]

Cure the Catch

Positioning by price and quality Some retail stores are known for their high-quality merchandise and high prices (Harry Rosen, Birks, Holt Renfrew). Positioned at the other end of the price and quality scale are discount stores such as Wal-Mart and Zellers. This doesn't mean that such retailers position themselves as lacking quality, but rather that value for money and low price are stressed.

Four Seasons
Choice Hotels

In the hotel industry, positioning by price and quality is common. Canada's Four Seasons Hotels chain (**www.fourseasons.com**) is well known for its high standards in rooms and services. Luxurious furnishings and guest courtesies clearly differentiate this chain from others that target a lower-paying clientele. Choice Hotels International (Comfort Inn, Quality, Econo Lodge, Sleep Inn), on the other hand, has positioned itself as offering clean, comfortable rooms and economical prices (**www.choicehotels.com**).

product-mix expansion
Increasing the depth within a particular product line and/or the number of lines a firm offers to consumers.

line extension
One form of product-mix expansion in which a company adds a similar item to an existing product line with the same brand name.

Product-mix expansion

Product-mix expansion is accomplished by increasing the depth within a particular line and/or the number of lines a firm offers to consumers. Let's look at these options.

Line extension is the term used when a company adds a similar item to an existing product line with the same brand name. For examples, look at the coupons in your local newspaper or the ones that appear in your mailbox. You will probably see lots of examples of new products that are actually line extensions.

Gillette keeps extending the Mach 3 line, with help from Becks.

Gillette introduced the Mach3 Turbo for wet shaving and then extended it with the Mach3 Power Nitro that, with the aid of a battery in the handle, sends out micro-pulses ahead of the blades, raising facial hair for a closer shave. More extensions are on the way! Lever Brothers has experienced great success with its line of Dove soap products, causing it to introduce a successful line of hair care and then face care products marketed under the same master brand.[8] X marks the spot for Nissan's new SUV, the X-Trail — a Canada-only introduction to the Nissan line. Nissan's successful line-up of SUVs included the Pathfinder, X-Terra, and the really big Armada, but the company did not have a small SUV. The small SUV market in Canada comprises about 50 percent of the total volume, compared to only 20-25 percent in the United States. In order to make sure the company didn't lose customers it introduced, "The small SUV for your big life."[9]

The line-extension strategy is also used by service organizations. Universities and colleges are offering more and more programs to appeal to older and working students, such as distance courses and part-time programs. Some group medical practices and some hospitals have added nutrition counselling clinics and forms of exercise counselling to their services, acknowledging that an important part of their role is to keep people well.

The main reason for a line extension is that the firm wants to appeal to more market segments by offering a wider range of choices for a particular product. Another reason is that companies want to take advantage of the considerable functional and emotional relationship value that resides in their established brands. There is often a much lower risk involved in introducing a new product as an extension to an existing line under a recognized brand than there would be in launching a completely separate line with a new brand name. Marketers have found that a line extension has a greater chance of success than a totally new brand.

Another way to expand the product mix, referred to as **mix extension**, is to add a new product line to the company's current assortment. Sometimes this is an innovative new product never seen before, but more often it is simply something that the company has never offered previously. When Procter & Gamble introduced the Swiffer, it was doing both of these things. As a totally new and innovative product (to be discussed in the next section), it created a new category of product that other companies quickly tried to copy and add to their mixes. When P&G created SwifferWet, Mitt, Max, and WetJet, these were line extensions.

mix extension
A way of expanding the product mix by adding a new product line to the company's current assortment.

Under a mix-extension strategy, the new line may be related or unrelated to current products. Furthermore, it may carry one of the company's existing brand names or may be given an entirely new name. The following are examples of these four alternatives:

- ***Related product, same brand***: Tim Hortons added canned ground coffee and then introduced a line of Tim Hortons home coffee makers. McDonald's introduced its Lighter Choices Menu to entice health-conscious Baby Boomers with veggie burgers, new salads, and a fruit and yogurt parfait.
- ***Unrelated product, same brand***: Swiss Army Brands, the maker of the original Swiss Army knife, extended its mix by adding Swiss Army watches and sunglasses as well as travel gear and apparel. Other examples include the extension into home furnishing by clothing manufacturer Roots and into cosmetics and housewares by Club Monaco.

- ***Unrelated product, different brand***: When a company adds a new division in a different field. Companies today are more likely to eliminate unrelated product lines than to add unrelated ones. For example, Pepsi-Cola amassed a number of diversified companies such as Pizza Hut and KFC and then sold them.[10]

- ***Related product, different brand***: Procter & Gamble introduced Luvs to store shelves right beside its Pampers disposable diapers. Black & Decker produced a line of professional/industrial tools under the DeWalt brand; Panasonic produces some of its audio equipment under the Technics brand. DaimlerChrysler recently introduced the Smart brand of commuter car to Canada through its Mercedes-Benz dealerships.

Most often, a new line is related to the existing product mix, since the company wants to capitalize on its expertise, experience and the quality of customer-brand relationships. IKEA, which has been known for offering reasonably-priced, medium-quality Scandinavian home furnishings, expanded into a line of office furniture.[11] Thomson Minwax Ltd., an Ontario firm, is expanding beyond its line of wood stains and producing a new line of decorative paints.

MARKETING AT WORK 7-2: STRATEGY

iPod To The Rescue

As the digital audio market keeps growing, so does the overall strength of Apple Computers. One reason is Apple's iPod, the portable music player that can store hundreds and hundreds of songs and that has control of more than half the market among the 14-to-18-year-old group. Would you consider the iPod to be, well, sort of a computer? If so, would it make it a "related-product, same-brand" extension? If not, would it be considered an "unrelated-product, same-brand" extension? Then again, you could even argue for calling the iPod an "unrelated-product, different-brand" extension in that the iPod name has become so well-known that people usually don't use the Apple brand name when they refer to the product.

What is clear is that the music player's huge and rapid popularity has provided a piggyback opportunity for Apple marketing across its other newly developed products. In the last quarter of 2005, Apple sold over 14 million iPods; up 206 percent from the same period in 2004. And, of course, it doesn't hurt that iTunes, Apple's online music store and a service extension of the iPod, sells over 70 percent of all the downloaded music that is actually paid for online. Since Apple's marketers had hoped that its new Mac Mini, as well as its new iMac series, would appeal to Windows computer users who also use the iPod, they see the iPod as a "related-product, same-brand" extension. Would you agree?

Regardless of how we label the music player, it has caused Windows users to come into Apple stores and those of their channel partners by piquing their interest in Macs — something that has not been easily done by Apple prior to the iPod extension. And then there is the new Mac operating system product extension now launched. And, horror of horrors, the Mac machines that run Windows as well as the Apple OS.

QUESTIONS:

1. Will Apple come in from being on the fringe and become a more mainstream competitor? With what kind of product extension and innovation?
2. Which of the new products have the potential of alienating Apple's core market?

SOURCE: Adapted from John Heinzl, "Apple results expected to be sweet melody to investor's ears," *The Globe and Mail*, April 13, 2005, p. B16; "Apple tears up Street profit target as iPods account for 31% of sales", *The Globe and Mail,* April 14, 2005, pp. B1, B19; Stan Sutter, "Me and my iPod", *Marketing Magazine Online*, www.marketingmag.ca, January 23, 2006.

Trading up and trading down

trading up
A product-line strategy in which a company adds a higher-priced, prestige product to its line in order to increase sales of the existing lower-priced products in that line and attract a higher-income market.

The product strategies of trading up and trading down involve a change in product positioning and an expansion of product line. **Trading up** means adding a higher-priced product to a line to attract a broader market. The seller also intends that the new product's prestige will help the sale of its existing lower-priced products.

Consider some examples of trading up. Facing stiff competition in the middle-price market, Holiday Inns introduced the higher-price Crowne Plaza Hotels, with nicer surroundings and more amenities. To its line of inexpensive casual watches, Swatch added the higher-priced Chrono stopwatch, James Bond Collection, and other upgraded watches, as well as the SwatchTalk, the first watch with an integrated cellphone. Hyundai, which owns Kia, has tried to de-emphasize its position as an economy car manufacturer by continuing to offer more expensive and diversified products. These have recently included the Amanti sedan, intended to be the company's contribution to the entry-level luxury car segment as well as the Sedona minivan available in a wide variety of trim packages. The new models have helped attract a wider range of auto buyers and helped shift the image of the company to that of one that fills a wide variety of automotive needs.

trading down
A product-line strategy in which a company adds a lower-priced item to its line of prestige goods in order to reach a market that cannot afford the higher-priced items.

A company is said to be **trading down** when it adds a lower-priced item to its line of prestige products. The company expects that people who cannot afford the original product will want to buy the new one because it carries some of the status of the higher-priced product. Mont Blanc, the West German manufacturer of the "world's most famous fountain pen," introduced a lower-priced ballpoint pen, thereby allowing its purchasers to own a Mont Blanc without having to pay more than $400 for the top-of-the-line fountain pen. New for 2006, the Mercedes Benz B-Class Sports Tourer was introduced at about $30,000 while the Saab 9-2X comes in at just under $29,000 — these models, the most basic ever offered by these brands, are intended to recruit brand-loyal buyers at an earlier age now that the price tag for the sought-after marques now reside in their price neighbourhood.

Gap
Old Navy

Trading up and trading down are risky strategies because the new products may confuse buyers resulting in negligible net gain. It is equally undesirable if sales of the new item or line are generated at the expense of established products. When trading down, the new offering may permanently hurt the firm's reputation and that of its established high-quality product. To reduce this possibility, new lower-priced products may be given different brand names to distinguish them from the established brands. Gap (**www.gap.com**) chose Old Navy Clothing Co. (**www.oldnavy.com**) as the name for its lower-price outlets. Gap also owns two higher-priced brands, Banana Republic and in August 2005 opened Forth & Towne, geared toward the over-35-year-old female Boomer market.[12]

The Gap trades customers up to Banana Republic.

In trading up, on the other hand, the problem depends on whether the new product or line carries the established brand name or is given a new name. If the same brand name is used, the firm must change its image enough that new customers will accept the higher-priced product. At the same time, the seller does not want to lose its present customers. The new offering may present a cloudy image, not attracting new customers but driving away existing customers. If a different brand name is used, the company must create awareness for it and stimulate sales. The latter strategy means that the company will not be able to trade on the reputation of its existing brand.

Modifying existing products

product modification
Improvement of an established product as a less risky and more profitable alternative to developing a completely new product.

As an alternative to developing a completely new product, management should take a fresh look at the organization's existing products. Often, improving an established product — **product modification** — can be more profitable and less risky than developing a completely new one. The substitution of NutraSweet (**www.nutrasweet.com**) for saccharin in diet soft drinks increased sales of those drinks by improving flavour and reducing health-related concerns about saccharin. Similarly, the use of all-natural or organically grown products is popular with certain market segments. Product modification, however, is not without risks.

NutraSweet

For some products, redesigning is the key to relaunching or repositioning. Many companies frequently redesign or reformulate their products to give them fresh appeal. In recent years, disposable diapers have been redesigned to be less bulky and are now available in separate styles for girls and boys. To revitalize its brand, BMW hired a very controversial automobile designer to breathe new life into its model line. Polaroid developed less-expensive and funkier accessory-type cameras such as the I-Zone pocket camera and the JoyCam, with features such as sticky-back film and different-size photo options, for $25 to $35 each. Garnier, a division of L'Oreal, has tried to shed the image of hair colour for older people hiding their grey and instead position it as a trendy, fashion product for the 15 to 40 age group.[13] Sometimes the redesign might simply involve the addition of a new flavour, in which case the product becomes more of a line extension, as when General Mills launched Apple Cinnamon Cheerios.

Another example involves changing the shape or basic look of a product. Canada's own Polar Ice Vodka created a new look to distinguish its quadruple-distilled beverage with the exceptionally clean taste, as well as to support charging $30 per bottle in a very competitive category.

As a variation of this strategy, developing new uses for the existing product can be part of the relaunch and repositioning. Eagle Brand redesigned the labelling of its sweetened condensed milk and promoted its use in mocha and other specialty coffees, five-minute fondues, no-bake bars, and as an after-school beverage.[14]

BMW is constantly redesigning.

Alternatively, especially for consumer products, only the packaging is altered. Kraft Canada relaunched its Honey Toasted Shredded Wheat cereal with new packaging and a multimedia ad campaign. The line extension to Shredded Wheat debuted a year earlier, but sales quickly tailed off as it became lost in a sea of other cereals with yellow packaging. Made to look like a bee, the packaging communicated the flavour and created a striking image when stacked together on the store shelf. Tylenol introduced its products in red-capped bottles with ridges for ease of opening; Evian redesigned its bottle with ridges to improve its ability to be crushed for recycling. Packaging can be altered to enhance appearance or to improve a product's usefulness. Sometimes it also helps to attract new attention and reposition the image of the brand. In response to the tremendous growth in private-label products both Shoppers Drug Mart and Sobeys relaunched their own brands with new upscale packaging and, in some cases, new brand names.[15]

Product-mix contraction

product-mix contraction
The elimination of an entire line or simplification of the assortment within a line to weed out low-profit and unprofitable products.

Another product strategy, **product-mix contraction**, is carried out either by eliminating an entire line or by simplifying the assortment within a line. Thinner and/or shorter product lines or mixes can weed out low-profit and unprofitable products. The intended result of product-mix contraction is higher profits from fewer products. General Mills decided to concentrate on its food business and, consequently, sold its interest in Izod (the "alligator" apparel maker) and its lines of children's toys and games. In service fields, some travel agencies have shifted from selling all modes of travel to concentrating only on cruises or tours focused on certain destinations or tailored to certain age groups.

PAGE UP

1. The set of all products offered for sale by a company is called a ________________.
2. A company can expand its product mix in two ways. What are they?
3. What is the difference between trading up and trading down?

Developing New Products

Many of the strategies just discussed call for the development of new products. It is obvious that without a flow of new products, a company will have great difficulty surviving over the long run.

- Every company's current products eventually become obsolete, as their sales volume and market share are reduced by changing consumer needs and/or superior competing products.
- As a product ages, its profits generally decline. Introducing a new product at the right time can help maintain a company's profits.

Risks of new-product development

Typically, some 25,000 new consumer products are introduced each year in North America alone. And, just as typically, as many as 95 percent of them crash and burn, often within months (or even weeks) of their launch.[16] Why do new products fail? The single most important reason is that most new products are not perceived by consumers to be different from existing ones — regardless of what marketers think, say, or do. Some new products simply do not deliver what they imply or promise. Others do not have a large enough market, a fact missed because of faulty or insufficient market research. Other factors contributing to product failure include poor positioning and lack of marketing support. Another reason a new product can fail is that it is perceived as offering poor value in relation to its price.

What then is a "new" product?

Just what is a "new" product? Are the auto manufacturers' annual models new products? Is a new version of the Apple operating system software new? Sony's PSP? Nike's spring-loaded Shox shoe? Sanyo's MM-5600 camera-phone? Or must a product be revolutionary, never before thought of, before we can classify it as new?

How new a product is will affect how it should be marketed. There are numerous connotations of "new product," but we will focus our attention on three distinct categories:

Panasonic

- ***Products that are really innovative*** — truly unique. A recent example is a security device that electronically compares the shape of a person's hand with the image of a hand encoded on an identification card.[17] What about Honda's ASIMO, a human-shaped robot the company thinks will be serving as an assistant in homes and offices within 10 years?[18] A new model of a car is not a new product, but what if it's a hybrid gas-electric car that recharges itself and gets about 110 kpg on the highway, like the Honda Insight coupe? What about the Daimler-Benz fuel cell vehicle?[19] Products in this category satisfy a real need. Electric or hybrid vehicles are new since they provide new solutions to fossil fuel and pollution problems. Other models have quickly followed from Toyota and Honda. Still-to-be-developed products in this category would be a cancer cure and easily and inexpensively repaired automobiles.

Is this robot a true innovation or an extension to Honda's product line?

- ***Replacement products that are significantly different*** from existing products in form, function, and most important — benefits provided. Johnson & Johnson's Acuvue2 extended-wear, disposable contact lenses (**www.jnjvision.com**) and Panasonic's (**www.panasonic.com**) Viera PlasmaTV (110-cm screen, 9 cm thick, and only 32 kg) are both replacing traditional models. At times, even new fashions in clothing are different enough to fit into this category. The MFPs discussed in the chapter opener are actually new products for the companies that manufacture them, even though they incorporate the same functions as other stand-alone products. They address different needs for different target segments, and have to be marketed differently as a result.
- ***Imitative products that are new to a company but not new to the market:*** Usually, annual models of autos and new versions of cereals are appropriately placed in this category. In another situation, a firm may simply want to capture part of an existing market with a "me-too" product. To maximize company-wide sales, makers of cold and cough remedies routinely introduce imitative products, some of which compete with a nearly identical product from the same company. Computer manufacturers and assemblers do this all the time.

Ultimately, of course, whether a product is new or not depends on how the intended market perceives it. If buyers consider it to be significantly different from competitive products in some relevant characteristic (such as appearance or performance), then it is indeed a new product. As in other situations, perception is reality!

Criteria for new products

When should a company add a new product to its current assortment of products? The following are guidelines that some producers use in answering this question:

There must be adequate market demand. Too often management begins with the wrong questions: Can we use our present sales force? Will the new item fit into our production system? Can we just put it up on our Web site, since we get a lot of traffic? The necessary first question is: Do enough people really want this product?

Shoppers Drug Mart

Shoppers Drug Mart (**www.shoppersdrugmart.com**) made sure it knew what it was doing before it introduced a new private-label make-up line, Quo. Research indicated that the average Canadian woman visited Shoppers every eight days, and yet bought most cosmetics at department store brand-name cosmetic counters. No department store, however, can boast such a customer frequency. Shoppers' new private-label line was positioned between pricey high-end department store brands and inexpensive mass-market offerings, filling a very real gap in the marketplace. With no visible tie-in to Shoppers Drug Mart on the packaging and with a timeless quality design featuring clean, sleek lines and displayed in a special showcase in the cosmetics department, the product had the high-end brands in its sights.

The product must satisfy key financial criteria. At least three questions should be asked: Is adequate financing available? Will the new item reduce seasonal and cyclical fluctuations in the company's sales? And, most critical: Can we make sufficient profit with the product? Adequate financing means more than that required to produce the product; it must ensure that enough market research is carried out and that sufficient marketing support is provided to bring the product to the awareness of the targeted segments.

The product must be compatible with environmental standards. Key questions include: Do the production processes avoid polluting the air or water? Will the finished product, including its packaging, be friendly to the environment? And: After being used, does the product have recycling potential?

The product must fit into the company's present marketing structure. Benjamin Moore would probably find it quite difficult to add margarine to its line of paints. Specific questions related to whether a new product will fit the company's marketing expertise and experience include: Can the existing sales force be used? Can the present channels of distribution be used? To reduce risk, many firms rely on brand extensions. For example, Sunlight successfully moved out of the laundry room and into the kitchen with Sunlight dishwashing products. It seems that the idea of removing stubborn dirt and stains carried over well from clothing to greasy dishes. The name was less successful, however, when it came to hand soap, and its furniture polish never made it past the test market phase.[20]

Bayer

Besides these four issues, a proposed product must satisfy other criteria. For instance, it must be in keeping with the company's objectives and image. Bayer (**www.bayer.com**), to promote a new garden bug spray, used an aggressive marketing push that included television ads with animated insects choking and wheezing before their final demise. The question is: What image might come to parents' minds the next time that they give their children that little pink Bayer Aspirin?

The new-product strategy statement

It's clear that every new-product project or venture should have an explicit strategy statement identifying the role the new product is expected to play in achieving company and marketing goals. A new product might be designed to protect market share or maintain the company's reputation as an innovator. Or a new product's role might be to meet a specific return-on-investment goal or establish a position in a new market. With computer technology, the imperative is often to be the first to market.

As shown in the box below, given a stated company goal, specific product strategies — such as those discussed in the previous section — can be implemented to aid in achieving that goal. Thus, a line extension, product modification, or completely new product-development approach may be what is needed.

Goal	Strategy	Example
Defend market share	Introduce addition to existing line	Mike's Hard Lemonade's introduction of new flavours — orange, raspberry iced tea, etc.
Strengthen reputation as an innovator	Introduce significantly new product	Sony's introduction of the CLIÉ line of hand-held personal entertainment organizers that combine PDA capabilities with multimedia and remote-control capabilities for other home electronics.
Increase customer satisfaction	Develop mass customization to improve service	Johnson & Johnson's development of a contact lens system that can be fitted within 10 minutes and can be used for one-week extended wear.

new-product strategy
A plan that defines the role that new products are to play in helping the company achieve its corporate and marketing goals.

With the availability of new communication and information technology, firms are able to orient their **new-product strategies** toward mass customization in order to provide increased product value. Individual consumer preferences can be built into new products either by requiring that a modular strategy be used for product design or by positioning the final step of individual product differentiation at the last minute in the product creation process, the delivery or consumer "try-on" stage. Auto manufacturers allow consumers to custom-order their new cars via the Internet with the hope of reducing inventories held at dealerships by producing more on demand.

Stages in the development process

Guided by a company's new-product strategy, a new product is best developed through a series of six stages. Compared with unstructured development, the formal development of new products provides benefits such as higher success rates, increased customer satisfaction, and greater achievement of time, quality, and cost objectives.[21]

At each stage, management decides whether to proceed to the next stage, abandon the product, or seek additional information.[22] A brief description of what should happen at each stage of the new-product development process follows:

1. ***Generating new-product ideas***: New-product development starts with an idea or a concept. A system must be designed for stimulating new ideas within an organization and then acknowledging and reviewing them promptly. Customers should also be encouraged to propose innovations. In a research study, 80 percent of companies pointed to customers as their best source for new-product ideas.[23]

2. ***Screening:*** At this stage, new-product ideas are evaluated to determine which ones warrant further study.[24] Typically, a management team with representatives of various functions screens the pool of ideas.

business analysis
The stage of new-product development in which a surviving idea is expanded into a business proposal and management identifies product features; estimates market demand, competition, and profitability; establishes a development program; and assigns responsibility for further study.

market tests
The stage of new-product development that involves tests with actual consumers.

3. ***Business analysis:*** A surviving idea is expanded into a concrete business proposal. In the **business analysis**, management (a) identifies product features, (b) estimates market demand, competition, and the product's profitability, (c) establishes a program to develop the product, and (d) assigns responsibility for further study of the product's feasibility.

4. ***Prototype development:*** If the results of the business analysis are favourable, then a prototype or trial model of the product is developed. In the case of tangible products, a small quantity of the trial model is manufactured to designated specifications. Laboratory tests and other technical evaluations are carried out to determine whether it is practical to produce the product. A firm may be able to construct a prototype of a new type of cellular telephone but be unable to manufacture the new product in large quantities or at a cost low enough to stimulate sales and still yield a profit. In the case of services, the facilities and procedures necessary to produce and deliver the new product are designed and tested. That certainly is a necessary step in the development of a new roller-coaster ride at an amusement park!

5. ***Market tests:*** Unlike the internal tests conducted during prototype development, **market tests** involve actual consumers. A new tangible product may be given to a sample of people for use in their households (in the case of a consumer good) or their organizations (a business good). Beta versions of all types of software are made available free to those who will download and make use of it. Following this trial, consumers are asked to evaluate the product. Consumer-use tests are less practical for pure services, due to their intangible nature. If a service can be simulated on a computer, however, some form of trial can be achieved.

   This stage in new-product development often entails test marketing, in which the product is placed on sale in a limited geographic area. Results, including sales and repeat purchases, are monitored by the company that developed the product and perhaps also by competitors. In this stage, the product's design and production plans may have to be adjusted as a result of test findings. Following market tests, management must make a final "go" or "no-go" decision about introducing the product.

6. ***Commercialization:*** Finally, full-scale production and marketing programs are planned and implemented. Up to this point in development, management has virtually complete control over the product. Once the product is "born" and enters the introductory stage of its life cycle, however, the external competitive environment becomes a major determinant of its destiny.

In the six-stage process, the first three stages are particularly critical, because they deal with ideas and are therefore the least expensive. More importantly, many products fail because the idea or the timing is wrong — and the first three stages are intended to identify such situations. Each subsequent stage becomes more costly in terms of the budget and human resources necessary to carry out the required tasks.

Some companies, trying to bring new products to market faster than their competitors, skip stages in the development process. The most common omission is the fifth stage: market tests. Without this stage, however, the company lacks consumer reactions to the proposed product.

Historically, the marketing of goods has received more attention than the marketing of services, so it is not surprising that the new-product development process is not as advanced in services fields as it is in goods industries. However, on the positive side, this means that services firms have more flexibility to devise a new-product development process that suits their distinctive circumstances.

Organizing for Product Innovation

If new-product programs are to be successful, they must be supported by a strong, long-term commitment from top management. This commitment must be maintained even when some new products fail. To implement this commitment to innovation effectively, new-product programs must be soundly organized.

Types of organization

There is no "best" organizational structure for product planning and development. Many companies use more than one structure to manage these activities. Some widely used organizational structures for planning and developing new products are:

- **Product-planning committee**: Members include executives from major departments — marketing, production, finance, engineering, and research — and, especially in small firms, the president and/or another top-level executive.
- **New-product department**: These units are small, consisting of five or fewer people. The department head reports to the president (which, in a large firm, may be the president of a division).
- **Venture team**: A small group responsible for the development of new products, with representatives from engineering, production, finance, and marketing research, that operates like a separate small business. Typically, the team reports directly to top management and has a great deal of flexibility.
- **Product manager**: This individual is responsible for planning new products as well as managing established products. Although still effective in some firms, we'll discuss in the next section why this structure is being displaced in many firms by one of the other structures discussed above.

Which organizational structure is chosen is not the key point here — each has strengths and weaknesses. What's critical is to make sure that some person or group has the specific responsibility for new-product development and is backed by top management. To maximize the chances for successful new-product development, it is vital that employees responsible for product planning have the right skills, particularly the ability to work well with other people and operate in a supportive environment.

As the new product is completed, responsibility for marketing it usually is shifted either to an existing department or a new department established just for this new product. In some cases, the team that developed the product may continue as the management nucleus of the new unit.

Product and brand management

product-adoption process
The stages that an individual goes through in deciding whether to accept a new product or innovation.

product diffusion
The process by which a new product or innovation is spread through a market or social system over time.

Companies with many brands, such as Procter & Gamble and Kraft Foods, assign the responsibility for planning new products as well as co-ordinating the marketing efforts of existing ones to a product manager. Essentially, a product manager, sometimes called a brand manager, plans the complete marketing program for a brand or group of products. Specific tasks include setting marketing goals, preparing budgets, and developing plans for advertising and personal selling and service activities. Developing new products along with improving established products is usually part of the job description.

The likelihood of achieving success with a new product — especially a really innovative one — as well as an established one, is increased if management understands two natural processes: (1) product adoption and diffusion and (2) product evolution or product life cycle. Both will now be discussed and illustrated.

New-Product Adoption and Diffusion

The **product-adoption process** describes the set of successive decisions a customer makes before accepting a new product or innovation. **Product diffusion** is the process by which a new product or innovation spreads throughout a market or social system over time.[25] By

stages in the product-adoption process
The six stages a prospective user goes through in deciding whether to purchase something new, including awareness, interest, evaluation, trial, adoption, and confirmation.

understanding these processes, marketing and product managers gain insight into how a product is or is not accepted by consumers and which groups of consumers are likely to buy a product soon after it is introduced, later on, or never.

Stages in the product-adoption process

A prospective user goes through six **stages in the product-adoption process** — deciding whether to purchase something new. These stages are summarized in the box below.

Stage	Activity in That Stage
Awareness	Individual is exposed to the innovation; becomes a prospect.
Interest	Prospect is interested enough to seek information.
Evaluation	Prospect judges the advantages and disadvantages of a product.
Trial	Prospect adopts the innovation on a limited basis. A consumer buys a sample, if the product can be sampled.
Adoption	Prospect decides whether to use the innovation on a full-scale basis.
Confirmation	After adopting the innovation, prospect becomes a user who immediately seeks assurances that the decision to purchase the product was correct.

Adopter categories

innovation-adopter categories
Five categories, based on the point in time when individuals adopt a given innovation, comprising innovators, early adopters, early majority, late majority, and laggards.

innovators
The first group of people — a venturesome group — to adopt a new product or service.

early adopters
The second group (following innovators) to adopt something new. This group includes opinion leaders, is respected, and has much influence on its peers.

early majority
A more deliberate group of innovation adopters that adopts just before the "average" adopter.

late majority
The sceptical group of innovation adopters who adopt a new idea late in the game.

Some people will adopt an innovation soon after it is introduced. Others delay before accepting a new product, and still others may never adopt. Research has identified five general **innovation-adopter categories**, based on the point in time when individuals adopt a given innovation. Non-adopters are excluded. The characteristics of early and late adopters are summarized in Table 7-3.

Innovators, representing about 3 percent of the market for a specific product, comprise the small group of venturesome consumers who are the first to adopt an innovation. In relation to later adopters, they tend to be younger, have higher social status, and are in better financial shape. They also tend to have broad social relationships involving various groups of people inside and outside their local community. They are likely to rely more on non-personal sources of information, such as advertising and the Internet, rather than on salespeople or other personal sources.

Early adopters make up about 13 percent of the market and purchase a new product after innovators but sooner than others. Unlike innovators, early adopters tend to be involved socially within a local community. Notably, they are greatly respected in their social circles and communities, and other people are interested in and influenced by their opinions. The early-adopter category includes more opinion leaders than any other adopter group. Salespeople are probably used more as information sources by early adopters than by any other category.

The **early majority** group is large, representing about 34 percent of the market. It consists of those more deliberate consumers who accept an innovation just before the "average" adopter in a market segment or social system. This group is a bit above average in social and economic terms. Consumers in the early majority group rely quite a bit on ads, salespeople, and contact with and observation of early adopters.

The **late majority**, another 34 percent of the market, is a sceptical group of consumers who usually adopt an innovation to save money or in response to social pressure from their peers. They rely on their peers — late or early majority — as sources of information. Advertising and personal selling are less effective with this group than is word-of-mouth communication.

TABLE 7-3 Characteristics of Early and Late Adopters of Innovations

	Early Adopters	Late Adopters
Key Characteristics		
Venturesome	Innovators (3% of total adopters)	
Respected	Early adopters (13%)	
Deliberate	Early majority (34%)	
Sceptical		Late majority (34% of total adopters)
Tradition-bound		Laggards (16%)
Other Characteristics		
Age	Younger	Older
Education	Well educated	Less educated
Income	Higher	Lower
Social relationships: within or outside community	Innovators: outside Others: within	Totally local
Social status	Higher	Lower
Information sources	Wide variety; many media	Limited media exposure; limited reliance on outside media; reliance on local peer groups

laggards
Tradition-bound people who are the last to adopt an innovation.

Laggards are consumers who are bound by tradition and therefore are last to adopt an innovation. They make up about 16 percent of the market. Laggards are suspicious of innovations and innovators; they wonder why anyone would pay a lot more for a new kind of light bulb, for example. By the time laggards adopt something new, it may already have been discarded by the innovators in favour of a newer concept. Laggards are older and usually are at the low end of the social and economic scales.

non-adopters
Consumers who never adopt an innovation.

Keep in mind that we are discussing only adopters of an innovation. For most innovations, there are many people who are not included in our percentages. They are **non-adopters**, who never adopt the innovation.

How new-product characteristics affect adoption

A series of five product and service innovation characteristics have been found to affect the rate at which innovations are adopted. Firms would like their new product to be able to satisfy all five, but this can happen only if the characteristics and their affects are attended to in the product-development process. While some firms are careful about the characteristics that aid the adoption of an innovation, others are not.

3M

1. ***Relative Advantage***: The degree to which the new item is superior to existing ones. The new product may cost less, be safer, and be easier to use. Safest Stripper, a paint and varnish remover introduced by 3M (**www.3m.com**), scored much higher than existing ones on safety, since it contains no harmful chemicals, is odourless, and allows users to refinish furniture indoors rather than having to work outdoors.

2. ***Compatibility***: The degree to which the innovation is seen as coinciding with the values and predispositions of potential users. Since most North American consumers want to save time and satisfy their desires now rather than later, cellular phones eminently meet

this value and predisposition. Supermarkets cater to values by offering ethnic foods. The growth in the type and variety of frozen and fresh prepared meals caters to the importance of time to customers.

3. ***Complexity***: The degree of difficulty in understanding or using an innovation. The more complex a new item is, the more a consumer must learn to be able to use it and the less rapidly it will be adopted — if it is adopted at all. Combined shampoo-conditioners posed no challenge to consumers, but many forms of insurance and consumer electronics products are hard to understand and use for many consumers.

4. ***Trialability***: The degree to which an innovation may be sampled on some limited basis. The greater the trialability, the faster the adoption rate. New modular home air-conditioning systems are likely to have a slower adoption rate than an easily sampled new seed or fertilizer. Costly products will be adopted more slowly than less expensive ones; many services (such as financial instruments) are difficult to use on a trial basis, so they tend to be adopted rather slowly.

MARKETING AT WORK — 7-3: STRATEGY

HDTV — Now, Later or Never

Canadians are suddenly buying high definition television sets. The rate of adoption has increased so dramatically that, by 2007, 5.2 million sets will be sold and roughly 16 percent of us will be able to watch HDTV programming.

For years, a TV was a TV; it received an analog signal to deliver programming. With continuous product development, the quality of what you saw and heard was slowly improved. And you knew all you needed to know to buy and operate it — plug it in, hook up the cable connection, turn it on, turn it off.

Then along came digital technology that delivered much better quality picture and sound than you could get from a TV relying on an analog signal. And that meant new TVs that were equipped to receive and present digital signals as well as analog ones. But for customers increasingly interested in buying a new up-to-date TV, the purchase decision was anything but a simple replacement or limited problem-solving one. In shopping and deciding, customers could easily see and hear the product quality (observability test passed); picture sound and quality were really superior (relative advantage test passed); since everyone values better performance, the compatibility test was easily passed; but what about complexity and trialability?

As customers work to solve the TV buying decision, they find that, well, there are a lot of things to understand and decide about: There is a difference between SDTV and HDTV; while both are superior to analog TV, HDTV is better than SDTV. Connectors at the rear of the set — who cares? Well, you need lots of different types to give you superior quality as opposed to only ordinary quality. How many connections? Well, one for the cable box, one for the DVD, the old VCR needs another, external speakers for the new sound system — there is more! It takes a lot of work to pass the complexity test, or a customer can just do what the sales rep tells them.

Trialability? You can watch HDTV with your friends or neighbours or in the TV store. But real trialability starts with the purchase and installation. You need a digital box from your cable company — will that be SDTV or HDTV? If you install it yourself, good luck. Gone are the days of one or two remotes, add another one or two depending on your 'system.' Have to keep those straight! And then there is programming, what it was all about. Well, there is some high definition stuff available, but most of it is still analog based. So what do you get? Well, it depends — a better picture with standard digital, better still with HD. But your biggest problem is programming. There just isn't that much — but it's coming.

A 2005 survey revealed that over half the owners of HDTV sets do not have a set top box which allows them to receive HDTV signals; about 20 percent bought their set to watch DVDs in high definition; about 20 percent are waiting for more HDTV programming and are hopefully patiently waiting for the benefits they thought they were buying. Some are not pleased at having paid so much for so little. There are a lot of potential customers out there who may remain potential for quite a while and adoption may not take off much further until complexity and trialability issues are successfully dealt with.

QUESTIONS:

1. Is the technology at present too complex for the non-technical customer?
2. How important is trialability at the current stage of product life?
3. What strategy can you propose that would simplify this purchase decision?

SOURCE: Adapted from "Is the Future of Digital Television SDTV?" www.digitalhomecanada, April 8, 2005; Ruth O'Kelly-Lynch, "Canadians buy into High Definition Television," *NovaNewsNet,* www.ukings.ns.nova news, April 8, 2005; Richard Blackwell, "High-definition TV a bit fuzzy, poll finds," *The Globe and Mail,* May 2, 2005, p. B4.

5. ***Observability***: The degree to which an innovation actually can be seen to be effective. In general, the greater the observability, the more rapid the adoption rate. A new weed killer that works on existing weeds will be accepted sooner than a product that prevents weeds from sprouting. The latter product, even if highly effective, produces no dead weeds to show to prospective buyers.

Digital cameras are a good way to illustrate these characteristics. The relative advantage of the product is quite apparent considering the ability to store thousands of pictures on a memory card — especially for travellers. The cameras are compatible with the changing lifestyles of the potential users — busier people with less time to arrange pictures in photo albums. The increased use of home computers and the Internet amongst all age groups decreases the complexity of using the cameras and the associated software. The increase in the number of retailers selling digital cameras and the increased number of self-serve kiosks where the consumer can choose only those pictures which are desired, increase the trialability and observability of the product.

PAGE UP!

1. What percentage of new consumer products introduced each year in North America fail?
2. What are the three categories of new products?
3. In marketing, what is a laggard?

Product Life-Cycle Management

product life cycle
The stages a product goes through from its introduction, to its growth and maturity, to its eventual decline and death (withdrawal from the market or deletion from the company's offerings).

All consumer and business products, whatever their classifications, come to an end through obsolescence of one form or another. The life cycle of a product consists of four stages: introduction, growth, maturity, and decline. The concept of product life applies to a generic category of product (microwave ovens, for example). The category can consist of a number of product lines: high-powered and fully featured, medium-powered with standard features, or low-powered with basic features. The category thus consists of all brands of all lines being offered by competitors, not specific brands such as Sony or Braun. A **product life cycle** consists of the aggregate sales over an extended period of time for all brands making up a generic product category.

Stop at this point and think about the distinction being made between product category and brands of a product. Intuitively, this sounds simple, but a little more thought may be required to ensure that you understand what this cycle refers to. Many students assume they understand, but when asked for an example on an exam, often provide a brand of a product to illustrate a stage of the cycle.

A product life cycle is graphed by plotting aggregate sales volume for a generic product category over time, usually years. It is also worthwhile to accompany the sales-volume curve with the corresponding profit curve for the product category, as shown in Figure 7-3. After all, we are interested ultimately in profitability, not just sales.

The shapes of these two curves vary from one product category to another. Still, for most categories, the basic shapes and the relationship between the sales and the profit curves are as illustrated. In this typical life cycle, the profit curve for most new products is negative (signifying a loss) through much of the introductory stage.

In the latter part of the growth stage, the profit curve starts to decline, while sales volume is still rising. Profits decline because the companies in an industry usually must increase their advertising and selling efforts or cut their prices (or both) to sustain sales growth in the face of intensifying competition during the maturity stage. The length of time it takes a product to

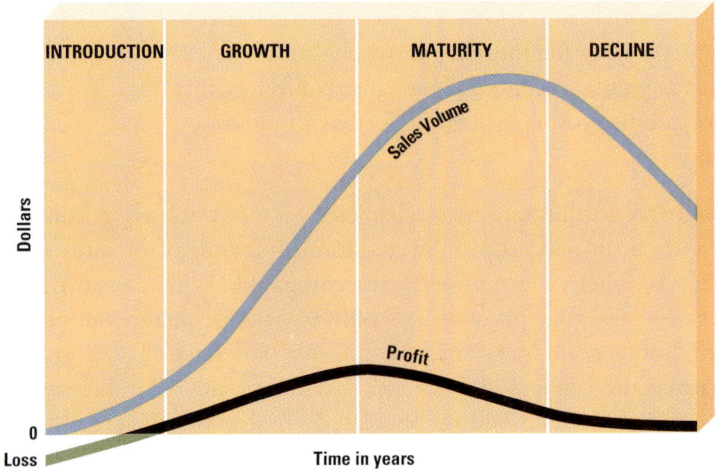

Figure 7-3:
Typical Life Cycle of a Product Category
During the introduction stage of a life cycle, a product category — and virtually all brands within it — is unprofitable. Profits are healthy during the growth stage, but then start to decline while a product's sales volume is still increasing.

reach maturity varies considerably, depending on the nature of the product. Some products remain in the maturity stage much longer than others. Electronic equipment, such as computers and cellular phones, have a very short maturity stage. Continuous new developments in technology cause the life cycle of these products to be quite short.

Introducing a new product at the proper time will help maintain a company's desired level of profit. Building on its original product lines, Kraft (**www.kraftcanada.com**) is constantly extending product life cycles with innovations. Kraft Dinner is a good example of a product that has been sustained in this way. Over the past 15 years, the company has introduced Alfredo, Rugrats, and Easy Mac versions. These products have all sold at premium prices. The Gillette Company (**www.gillette.com**) has had to constantly evolve to compete against the disposable variety of razors in the wet-shave market. The Sensor featured independently suspended blades and consumers were willing to pay a little more for the superior shave it provided. Trading up, Gillette produced the triple-blade Mach3, which is more expensive. Trading up again, the Mach3 Turbo was introduced, which allows the shaver to be pulled in any direction on the face without irritation and there is the Mach3 Nitro that sends out micro pulses stimulating facial hair so that it stands out and a closer shave is achieved.[26] In August of 2005, Gillette introduced two new products simultaneously, the Gillette Fusion and the Fusion Power. The Gillette Fusion Power is the first razor to use advanced electronics in wet shaving with an on-board micro-chip which optimizes the performance of the razor.[27] Will consumers continue to be convinced to spend more and more for such disposable products?

Kraft
Gillette

The product life-cycle concept is both straightforward and powerful, but it is too general to be useful in specific cases and therefore must be adapted to fit different circumstances. A company's marketing success can be affected considerably by its ability to determine and adapt to the life cycles of each of its product categories.

Characteristics of each stage

Management must be able to recognize in which part of the life cycle its product is at any given time. The competitive environment and marketing strategies that should be used ordinarily depend on the particular life-cycle stage. Table 7-4 contains a synopsis of all four stages, and each stage is discussed below.

introduction stage
The first part of a product life cycle, during which a generic product category is launched into the market in a full-scale marketing program.

BACK TO THE TOP

Introduction During the **introduction stage,** a product is launched into the market in a full-scale marketing program. It has gone through product development, including idea screening, prototype, and market tests. The entire product may be new, such as a substitute for fat in prepared foods. Or it may be well known but have significant new features that, in effect, create a new product category — multi-function printers and multimedia cellphones are examples. A total program would be designed to achieve awareness, arouse interest, elicit evaluation, promote adoption, and confirm that adoption. Prime target customers would be those who are considered innovators for the type of product being launched, followed by those who would be considered to be early adopters.

This introductory stage (sometimes called pioneering) is the most risky and expensive, because substantial amounts of money must be spent in seeking consumer adoption of the product. However, many products are not accepted by a sufficient number of buyers and

TABLE 7-4 Characteristics and Implications of Different Product Life-Cycle Stages

Each stage of a product's life cycle has different characteristics; as a result, marketing must be modified over the course of the cycle.

	Stage			
	Introduction	**Growth**	**Maturity**	**Decline**
Characteristics				
Customers	Innovators	Mass market	Mass market	Loyal customers
Competition	Little, if any	Increasing	Intense	Decreasing
Sales	Low levels, then rising	Rapid growth	Slow/no annual growth	Declining
Profits	None	Strong, then at a peak	Declining annually	Low/none
Marketing Implications				
Overall strategy	Market development	Market penetration	Defensive positioning	Efficiency or exit
Costs	High per unit	Declining	Stable or increasing	Low
Product strategy	Undifferentiated	Improved items	Differentiated	Pruned line
Pricing strategy	Most likely high	Lower over time	Lowest	Increasing
Distribution strategy	Scattered	Intensive	Intensive	Selective
Promotion strategy	Category awareness	Brand preference	Brand loyalty	Reinforcement

SOURCE: Adapted from material provided by Professor David Appel, University of Notre Dame, Notre Dame, IN.

therefore fail at this stage. For really new products, there is very little direct competition. Promotional programs designed to stimulate demand affect the entire product category, not just the seller's brand. Advertising and promotion should emphasize product features that aid in speeding up the rate of adoption.

growth stage
The second part of a product life cycle, during which the sales and profits of a generic product category rise and competitors enter the market; profits start to decline near the end of this part of the cycle.

Growth In the **growth stage**, sales and profits rise at a rapid rate as early majority, a portion of the late majority, and some of the laggard group of potential customers purchase the product. Competitors enter the market, often in large numbers if the profit outlook is particularly attractive. Mostly as a result of competition, profits start to decline near the end of the growth stage.

maturity stage
The third part of a product life cycle, during which sales of a generic product category continue to increase (but at a decreasing rate), profits decline largely due to price competition, and some firms leave the market.

Maturity During the first part of the **maturity stage**, sales continue to increase, but at a decreasing rate, as late majority and laggard groups become product users. When sales level off, profits of both producers and intermediaries decline. The primary reasons: intense price competition, as well as much demand being replacement sales rather than coming from new customers. Seeking to differentiate themselves, some firms extend their product lines with new models. During the latter part of this stage, marginal producers, those with high costs or without a differential advantage, are forced to drop out of the market. They do so because they lack sufficient customers and/or profits.

decline stage
The fourth, and final, part of a product life cycle, during which the sales of a generic product category drop and most competitors abandon the market.

Decline For most products, a **decline stage**, as gauged by sales volume for the total category, is inevitable for one or more of the following reasons:

- Very few or no new consumers are available in the market and almost all sales are replacement sales.

- The need for the product disappears, as when frozen orange juice generally eliminated the market for juice squeezers.
- A better or less expensive product is developed to fill the same need. DVDs are replacing VCR tapes, as well as CDs, that in turn replaced tapes and vinyl records because the sound, durability, and storage capability of the new product is far superior to that of the old product.
- People simply grow tired of a product (a clothing style, for instance), so it disappears from the market, goes out of favour or fashion.

Seeing little opportunity for revitalized sales or profits, most competitors abandon the market during the decline stage. However, a few firms may be able to develop a small market niche and remain moderately successful in this stage. Some manufacturers of wood-burning stoves have been able to do this. Whether a product at this stage has to be abandoned or can be continued on a profitable basis often depends on the skills and creativity of the marketing manager responsible for the product.

Length of product life cycle

The total length of the product life cycle — from the start of the introduction stage to the end of the decline stage — varies across product categories. It ranges from weeks or a short season (for a clothing fashion) to many decades (for cars). This varies because of differences in the length of individual stages from one product category to the next. Furthermore, although Figure 7-4 suggests that all four life cycle stages cover nearly equal periods of time, the stages in any given product's life cycle usually last for different periods.

Three variations on the typical life cycle are shown in Figure 7-4:

- In one variation, the product gains widespread consumer acceptance only after an extended introductory period (see Part A). The hand-held computer is an example of a current product that, for this category, has experienced a long introductory period with a relatively slow adoption rate after innovators and early adopters entered the market.
- In another variation, the entire life cycle begins and ends in a relatively short period of time (Part B). This variation depicts the life cycle for a fad, a product or style that becomes immensely popular nearly overnight and then falls out of favour with consumers almost as quickly. Beta format VCRs and videodisc players are examples of entertainment technology that did not survive very long in the consumer marketplace.
- In a third variation, the product's mature stage lasts almost indefinitely (Part C). This life cycle is illustrated by canned, carbonated soft drinks and also by the automobile with a gasoline-powered, internal-combustion engine.

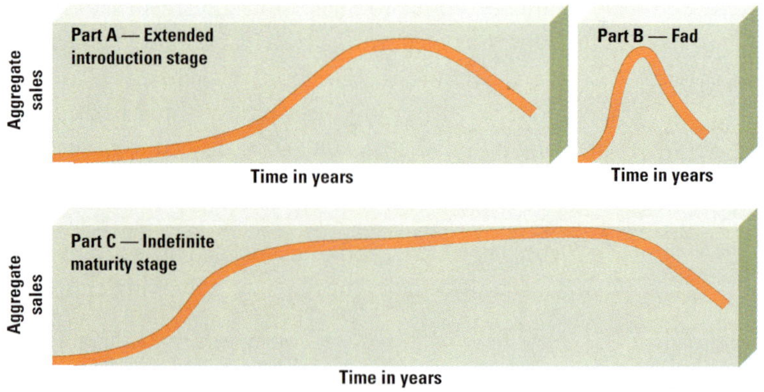

Figure 7-4:
Product Life Cycle Variations

Product life cycles are becoming shorter. If competitors can quickly introduce a "me-too" version of a popular product, it may move swiftly into the maturity stage — or rapid changes in technology can make a product obsolete virtually overnight. Some said that would occur in the audio field, with digital audiotapes replacing CDs, but that didn't happen. The latest forecast is that even newer formats, notably Super Audio CDs and DVD-Audio, will turn the CD into a dinosaur.[28] What possible impact will MP3 technology have on CDs in the long term?

Life cycle is related to a market

Ortho

When we say that a product is in a specific stage of its life cycle, implicitly we are referring to a specific market. A product may be well accepted (growth stage) in some markets (consisting of innovators and early adopters) but still be striving for acceptance in other markets consisting of early majority or even late adopters. At the time that Ortho Pharmaceuticals (**www.orthomcneil.com**) introduced Retin-A as a treatment for acne, existing products already served this purpose, so the acne-treatment category probably was in the maturity stage. However, it was then discovered that Retin-A might be effective in reducing facial wrinkles. In effect, this created a new product category, so Retin-A fit into both the acne-treatment category that was in the maturity stage among teenagers and into the wrinkle-remover category that was in the introductory or perhaps early-growth stage among the middle-aged. Rapid growth is now occurring in this category as many cosmetic firms rush to get products into the marketplace, greatly increasing the level of competition as Baby Boomers start to sag around the edges — or at least around the eyes! But not just those who are already starting to sag are being targeted: L'Oréal, for example, is targeting women in the 25 to 45 age range, with a skew toward the 30 to 35 category.[29]

Life-cycle management

To a surprising extent, the shape of the sales and profit curves for a product category can be controlled. The collective actions of firms offering competing products in the same category shape the curves, but even single companies can have an impact. A giant firm may be able to shorten the introductory stage by broadening the distribution or increasing the promotional effort supporting the new product.

Most firms, however, cannot substantially affect the sales and profit curves for a product category. Their task, therefore, is to determine how best to achieve success with their own brands within the life cycle for an entire product category. For an individual firm, successful life-cycle management depends on (1) predicting the shape of the proposed product's cycle even before it is introduced and (2) successfully adapting marketing strategies at each stage of the life cycle.

Entry strategies A firm entering a new market must decide whether to plunge in during the introductory stage. Or it can wait and make its entry during the early part of the growth stage, after innovating companies have proven that there is a viable market.

Perrier

The strategy of entering during the introductory stage is prompted by the desire to build a dominant market position right away and thus lessen the interest of potential competitors and the effectiveness of actual competitors. This strategy worked for Apple with the iPod, Perrier (**www.perrier.com**) with bottled sparkling water, and Nike with running shoes. The hurdles may be insurmountable when you enter with a "me-too" product or service and try to play catch-up — to grow market share against an entrenched competitor.

Sometimes, delaying entry until the market is proven can pay off. Pioneering requires a large investment and the risks are great — as demonstrated by the high failure rate among new products. Large companies with the marketing resources to overwhelm smaller innovating firms are most likely to be successful with a delayed-entry strategy. In one such case, Coca-Cola introduced Tab and Diet Coke, and Pepsi-Cola introduced Diet Pepsi — and the two giants surpassed Diet Rite Cola, an early pioneer. It's not clear-cut which is the better entry strategy. Each has its advantages and disadvantages, its successes and failures. As with nearly all marketing decisions, sound managerial judgement is critical.[30]

Managing on the rise When sales are growing strongly and profits are robust in a product category, you might think that a marketing manager has little to do except tally up an anticipated bonus. During the growth stage of the life cycle, a company has to devise the right strategies for its brand(s) and Web sites in that product category. Promotion that will cause consumers to desire the company's brand of product must be considered. Distribution must be expanded and made more efficient and rapid, and product improvements must be considered. Decisions made during the growth stage influence (a) how many competitors enter the market and (b) how well the company's brand does within a product category both in the near and distant future.

Home video games were introduced in the 1970s, but the more captivating (and perhaps addictive) Nintendo brand, in effect, created a new product category in the 1980s. As the 1990s began, this product appeared to be in the growth stage of its life cycle. However, in the mid-1990s, video games stagnated. To stimulate sales, Nintendo and its competitors Sega and Sony have been engaged in a game of "technological leapfrog." As revenue potential grew to about $700 million in Canada alone, Microsoft even entered the category with its first contender, the Xbox, in 2002. These firms are in a constant struggle to gain some sort of differential advantage, even if it's only temporary, by increasing the video, audio, or graphics capabilities of their systems. At the same time, they are trying to control prices. In November 2005, Microsoft introduced the Xbox 360, an entertainment hub linked to a PC, TV and digital camera, with greater capability and a sleeker look than the original.[31]

Managing during maturity Various strategies may be effective in maintaining or boosting sales of a product during the maturity stage of its life cycle. Of course, what works magnificently for one product may perform dismally for another. Common strategies during maturity include modifying the product, designing new promotions, and devising new uses for the product. The Campbell Soup Company recently celebrated its hundredth birthday and used this event as an opportunity to redesign its labels, giving a more mature look to the product.[32] Such steps may lead to added purchases by present customers and/or attract new customers. As sales in the North American cruise industry flattened out, some cruise lines modified their services by adding fitness programs and offering special theme cruises (sometimes in conjunction with a professional sports team or celebrity entertainers). Playskool, a division of Hasbro Canada Inc., has modified its mature product line of children's toys, equipment, and furniture. To make the products more competitive, the company has added an antibacterial agent to the plastic in the manufacturing stage.[33]

Surviving the decline stage Perhaps it is in the decline stage that a company finds its greatest challenges in life-cycle management. For instance, the advent of digital cameras and slim camera phones hint at the decline of photographic film as a product category. Kodak Canada is trying to prevent the decline of this product while keeping pace with competitors in examining bold new products. With one such product, which Kodak calls Photo CD, consumers take pictures as they normally have; the big difference comes at the time of film processing, when the prints can be stored on a compact disc. Then they can be shown on a TV, if you have a videodisc player. Kodak is also extending the life of the traditional film product by maintaining an aggressive research and development process to improve the overall performance of its films and processing services such as PerfectTouch processing that detects and reduces red eye as well as shadows while producing more detail and vibrant colours.

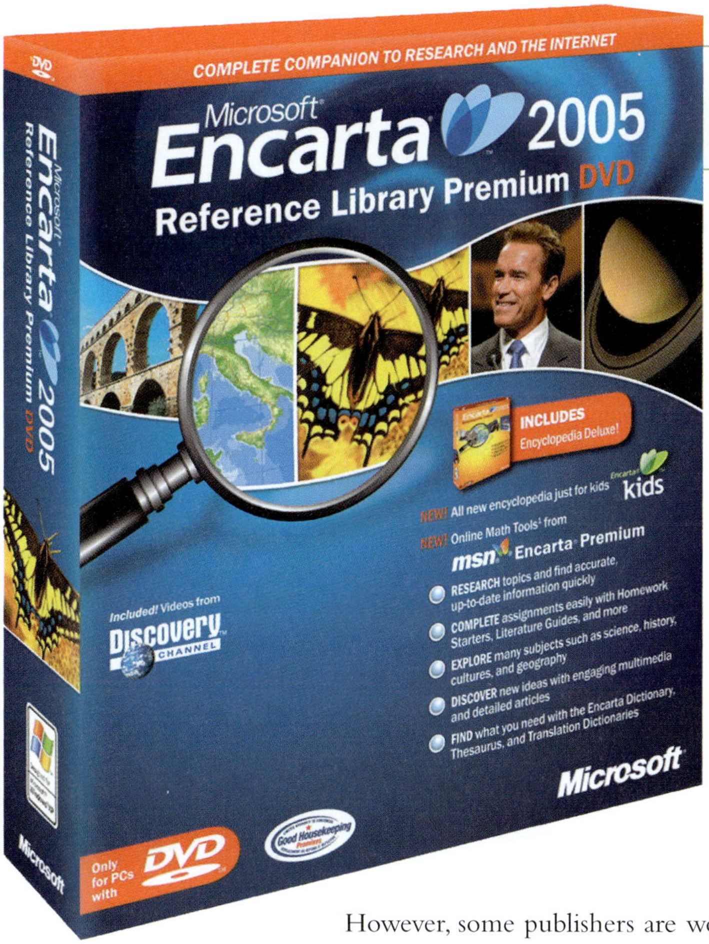

Extending the life cycle of a dictionary by adding lots of new forms of value.

When sales are declining, management has the following alternatives:

- Ensure that marketing and production programs are as efficient as possible.
- Prune unprofitable sizes and models. Frequently, this tactic will decrease sales but increase profits.
- "Run out" the product; that is, cut all costs to the bare minimum to maximize profitability over the limited remaining life of the product.
- Best (and toughest) of all, improve the product in a functional sense, or revitalize it in some manner. Some publishers of printed dictionaries have attempted to do this. Other reference materials, including dictionaries available on personal computers and online encyclopaedias, seemed to have pushed such traditional reference materials into — or at least toward — decline.

However, some publishers are working hard to maintain the appeal of the dictionary. St. Martin's Press has introduced a dictionary that includes workplace slang, 5,000 biographical references, geographical and cultural notes, and more than 4,000 illustrations. A collaboration with Microsoft, the Encarta World English Dictionary and Reference Library is available on CD-ROM as well as the traditional printed format. Also, MSN Encarta provides many of these same resources online as well as Homework Help sponsored by Sylvan Learning centres. Here visitors can get assistance with online tutoring in math and foreign languages.[34]

If, or when, such alternatives fail to capture the interest or fulfill the needs of consumers, management will have to consider product abandonment. The expense of carrying profitless products goes beyond what shows up on financial statements. For example, there is a very real cost for the managerial time and effort that is diverted to terminally ill products.

In the final analysis, the most compelling — but often painful — alternative may be product abandonment. Knowing when and how to abandon products successfully may be as important as knowing when and how to introduce new ones. Certainly, management should develop systematic procedures for phasing out weak products.

PAGE UP!

1. What are the four stages of the product life cycle?
2. During the ____________________ stage, sales and profits rise at a rapid rate.
3. The ____________________ stage is the most risky and expensive.

Key Terms and Concepts

accessory equipment 191
breadth of product mix 192
business analysis 204
business product 189
consumer product 189
convenience goods 189
decline stage 211
depth of product line 192
early adopters 206
early majority 206
fabricating parts and materials 191
growth stage 211
innovation-adopter categories 206
innovators 206
installations 191
introduction stage 210
laggards 207
late majority 206
line extension 195
market tests 204
maturity stage 211
mix extension 196
new-product strategy 203
non-adopters 207
operating supplies 191
product 188
product-adoption process 205
product diffusion 205
product life cycle 209
product line 192
product mix 192
product-mix contraction 200
product-mix expansion 195
product modification 199
raw materials 191
shopping goods 189
specialty goods 189
stages in the product-adoption process 206
trading down 198
trading up 198
unsought goods 189

Questions and Problems

1. What is a product? In answering this question select a product/service that you may have recently purchased and define the complete set of tangible and intangible attributes of this product/service. How can each of these influence a consumer's decision to buy?
2. What is a 'new' product? In what ways can a newly introduced product actually be considered 'new'?
3. Describe the depth and breadth of product mix for each of the following:
   a. Canadian Tire
   b. McCain Foods.
   c. Ford Motor Company Group.
4. In what respects are the products different in each of the following cases?
   a. A Whirlpool dishwasher sold at an appliance store and a similar dishwasher sold by Sears under its Kenmore brand name. Assume that Whirlpool makes both dishwashers.
   b. A Sunbeam Mixmaster sold by a leading department store and the same model sold by a discount house.
   c. An airline ticket purchased through a travel agent and an identical ticket purchased directly from the airline.
5. Compare the elements of a producer's marketing mix for a convenience good with those of the mix for a specialty good.
6. When a new product is truly innovative and the marketplace has never before been exposed to the innovation and/or technology, the marketing for that product must account for this unfamiliarity. Using examples of recent new innovations explain what is required of marketers to ensure success in the introduction stage of the product life cycle.
7. In developing new products, how can a firm make sure that it is being socially responsible with regard to scarce resources and the environment?
8. Assume that the following organizations are considering additions to their product lines. In each case, does the proposed product meet the criteria for adding a new product? Explain your decisions.
   a. McDonald's: salad bar.
   b. Safeway: automobile tires.
   c. Esso: personal computers.
   d. Banks: life insurance.
   e. General Motors Canada: outboard motors for boats.
9. Describe the kinds of people who are most likely to be found in (a) the innovator category of adopters and (b) the late-majority category.
10. "Trading up and trading down are product strategies closely related to the business cycle. Firms trade up during periods of prosperity and trade down during recessions." Do you agree? Why or why not?

11. Name one category of tangible products and one category of services that you believe are in the introductory stage of their life cycles. For each product, identify the market that would consider your examples to be truly new.

12. What are two products that are in the decline stage of the life cycle? In each case, point out whether you think the decline is permanent. What recommendations do you have for rejuvenating the demand for either of these products?

13. How might a company's advertising strategies differ, depending on whether its brand of a product is in the introduction stage or the maturity stage of its life cycle?

Hands-On Marketing

1. Arrange a meeting with the manager of a large retail outlet in your community. Discuss two topics with the manager:
   a. What recently introduced product has been a failure or seems destined to fail?
   b. Did this product, in retrospect, satisfy the criteria for adding a new product? (Remember to consider not just the intermediary's criteria but also applicable producer's criteria.)

2. Go to **www.bombardier.com** and discuss the depth and breadth of the company's product mix creating a diagram/chart for the company similar to that of Figure 7-2 of the text.

Back to the Top

Think about the example of new-product development described in the chapter opener. What are the obvious advantages that MFPs hold for both business and home-office customers? Consider the development of MFPs in the context of the evolution of office equipment as a product category. How is it similar to the evolution of home entertainment equipment and mobile telephone technology?

Online Learning Centre

Want to get better grades, tips on how to study more effectively, and up-to-date information on happenings in the world of marketing? Then, visit the Online Learning Centre for practice tests, Study Smart software, *Marketing Magazine*, and much more! **www.mcgrawhill.ca/olc/sommers**

CHAPTER 8

Services and Customer Relationships

This chapter focuses on the marketing of services and the role of customer service in marketing. It discusses the implications of an increased emphasis on service delivery and quality across all industries. The concept of service quality and the connection between quality and profit, the linkage between human resources and marketing, and the development and implications of a customer-relationship focus in marketing are key issues addressed in this chapter. After studying this chapter, you should have an understanding of:

- The nature of marketing in services companies.
- The characteristics of services and the marketing implications of these characteristics.
- The value proposition in services companies.
- Issues related to planning the marketing mix for services.
- The importance of supplementary services in all firms.
- The role of customer service in driving customer satisfaction.
- The importance of service in building customer relationships.
- The prospect for improved productivity in services.
- The impact of technology in the provision of services.

Hairstylist or Friend?

It was Saturday morning, just coming up to 10 o'clock, when Sandra walked into the Aveda salon, and was met by Melissa who welcomed her with, "Hi, Sandra. Nadia will be right with you."

Sandra started coming to this Aveda salon six years ago, just after finishing college and moving to Calgary. A friend at work had recommended the salon and she had found Nadia. During that time she has had her hair styled by only one other person, two years ago when she spent a month with her sister in Vancouver, and she wasn't really pleased with the result. When she got back to Calgary, she was certain that Nadia knew she had visited another salon, but neither of them mentioned it.

While she has never been disappointed with the way Nadia cuts her hair, and she enjoys the conversations they have, she is getting a little tired of her hair style — she's thinking, maybe something a little shorter.

This morning, Sandra is in a particularly good mood, as she and Jack leave tomorrow for a week in Hawaii. Nadia is also feeling great as she has just returned from a week-long training session at the Aveda Institute in New York, where she learned some new techniques for styling shorter hair; styles that she described as "funky." As soon as she sat in the chair, Sandra said, "Why don't we try something a little different this morning?" Nadia suggested a new colour as well, and Sandra said, "Why not?"

Just before noon, Sandra walked out of the Aveda salon carrying a bag with her usual Rosemary Mint shampoo and conditioner, and met Jack for lunch as planned. She was delighted when Jack said how much he liked her hair — he's not usually that quick to notice.

The services industry (of which Aveda and other hair salons are a part) is a prime example of how tangible and intangible elements combine to create customer value. While companies such as restaurants, airlines, hotels, banks, and others often provide tangible products, their main role is the provision of intangibles. In other words, their "core products" are actually services. They provide customers with an array of services from which to choose, and they deliver these primarily through their employees.

In this chapter, we will discuss the importance of getting the core service right — if Nadia gave terrible haircuts, chances are Sandra would not have remained a customer for six years. We also address the importance of quality service delivery, making sure opening hours are convenient, that they don't keep clients waiting, and call to remind them of their appointments. We also will discuss the interpersonal relationships that often develop between service providers and their clients, relationships built on conversation, trust, empathy and understanding. Customers often develop long-lasting relationships with providers of personal services such as hairstylists, message therapists, and mechanics.

Potentially, some confusion can arise in a discussion on services in marketing. So, let's clear up that confusion now. In this chapter, we will talk about services in three contexts. First, there are *services industries*, whose core offering to their customers is intangible — they don't manufacture things. Second, we often refer to services that all companies and organizations offer to their customers. We will refer to these in this chapter as *supplementary services*. In this sense, all businesses are services businesses, because they all potentially have to offer their customers credit terms, delivery, post-purchase service, billing, and so on. Finally, we will discuss "*service*" principally in the context of how the word is used by customers. We often hear customers comment on a business where service is excellent, or of another that they'll never go back to because of terrible service. The delivery of service in this sense is an integral part of marketing, dealing mainly with how customers interact with the business and how they are treated.

Nature and Importance of Services

More than three-quarters of working Canadians are employed in the services sector. Services industries currently account for more than two-thirds of Canada's gross domestic product, and represent the fastest-growing part of the Canadian economy. Virtually all growth in employment experienced in the past 20 years was due to growth in the services sector.

The rapid growth of this sector is attributable to major changes in the marketing environment as we discussed in Chapter 3. You will recall that these included such things as a technological advancement and massive communication changes, as well as changing workforce demographics. Demands for and the ability to provide services have increased. For example, an entire industry has grown up around servicing the Internet and mobile communications. Other examples include increased requirements for eating out, since both partners in many households are in the workforce; more interest in time-saving and convenience, through home cleaning services and Internet banking, for example; and the rapid growth in television networks and home entertainment products such as DVD rentals and direct-to-home television. All of these changes have placed greater emphasis on services and increasing demands on the quality of service delivery.

This discussion of the growth in the services sector tends to focus on the expansion of areas that traditionally have been classified as service industries. When we consider that the service sector includes retailing, transportation, entertainment, education, health care, government and financial services, it is no wonder that such a large portion of the Canadian economy is included. But it is not simply because of the critical importance of services industries that we focus on the marketing of services, we should not lose sight of the extremely important fact that service is an integral component of the marketing of any product, whether tangible or intangible.

Traditionally, services marketing has been thought to be different from the marketing of tangible products. In fact, however, the principles of marketing are essentially the same. In each

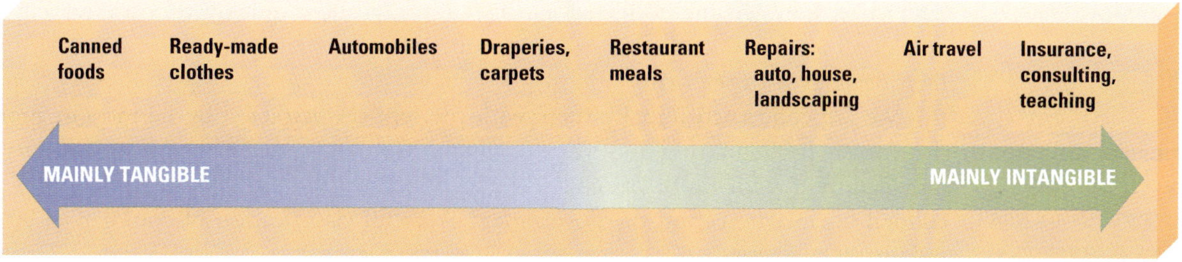

Figure 8-1: A Goods-Services Continuum

case, the marketer must select and analyze target markets. Then, a marketing program must be developed. There are characteristics of services that differentiate them from tangible products, and these must be considered in developing the marketing program. All tangible products have a service element, and consumers place considerable value on the services that accompany the purchase of such products. The distinctions between services marketing and tangible-goods marketing become much less important. As we see in Figure 8-1, no company is marketing a pure service or a tangible product that has no service component.

Definition and scope of services

We are talking about services in marketing, but do we have a clear understanding of what we mean by services? The term is potentially confusing because, in addition to being the core product in many organizations (such as in banking or education, where the core is intangible), services are also an important part of the marketing of tangible products. Services require supporting products (you need an airplane to provide air transportation services; hairstylists need scissors, combs and shampoo) and products require supporting services (delivery, credit, warranties, and repair services accompany the sale of a refrigerator). Furthermore, a company may sell a combination of goods and services. Thus, along with repair service for your car, you might buy spark plugs or an oil filter. It may be helpful to think of every offer or value proposition of a company as a mix of tangible products and intangible services located on a continuum ranging from mainly tangible to mainly intangible, as shown in Figure 8-1.

core services
Services that are the main purpose or object of a transaction — the intangible essence of the offer.

To move closer to a useful understanding of services, two classes of services can be identified. In the first group are services that are the main purpose or object of a transaction. These are known as **core services**. As an example, suppose you want to rent a car from Avis. The rental car company needs a car (tangible product) to provide the rental service. But you are buying the use of the car, not the car itself. The second group consists of **supplementary services** that support or facilitate the sale of a tangible product or another service. Thus, when you buy an Apple iPod, you may want technical information from a salesperson and the opportunity to pay with a credit card. Virtually every transaction involves both tangible and intangible elements. It is useful to distinguish between situations where the core of what is being exchanged is intangible — this is the situation that we refer to as the marketing of services — and the supplementary services and general level of customer service that accompanies the sale of everything that we buy.

supplementary services
Services that support or facilitate the sale of a tangible product or a core service.

services
Identifiable, intangible activities that are sometimes the main object of a transaction and at other times support the sale of tangible products or other services.

Consequently, our definition of services in this chapter is as follows: **Services** are identifiable, intangible activities that are sometimes the main object of a transaction and at other times support the sale of tangible products or other services. In the first part of the chapter, we will focus primarily on the marketing of services that are the principal objective of a transaction, as in retail, financial, entertainment, hotel, and transportation services. Then, we will turn our attention to the very important services associated with the marketing of every product, whether tangible or intangible. These include delivery, after-sale service, credit, and so on. Finally, marketers are realizing more and more that one of the most effective ways to compete and to differentiate one's company from the competition is to offer excellent service. This topic is approached principally from the view of the customer and addresses mainly the interaction between the company and its customers, how quickly they are served, whether employees are helpful, whether calls are returned, and generally how customers are treated in their dealings with the firm.

We are concerned initially, then, with the services marketed by business or professional firms with profit-making motives — **commercial services**. Other important services are provided by not-for-profit organizations, such as churches, universities and colleges, arts and cultural organizations, and the government. A useful classification of commercial services by industry is as follows:

commercial services
The services marketed by business or professional firms with profit-making motives, as compared with the services offered by public and not-for-profit organizations.

- ***Accommodations*** (includes rental of hotel rooms, condos, apartments, houses, and cottages).
- ***Household operations*** (includes utilities, home repairs, painting and decorating, appliance repairs, landscaping, and household cleaning).
- ***Recreation and entertainment*** (includes rental and repair of recreation equipment; admission to all entertainment, recreation, and amusement events, movies, concerts, golf).
- ***Food services*** (includes restaurants, fast-food outlets, university and college cafeterias, and catering services).
- ***Personal care*** (includes laundry, dry-cleaning, massage therapy, hair and beauty care).

MARKETING AT WORK 8-1: STRATEGY

Like a Virgin!

In 2005, Virgin Mobile Canada LLC entered the cellular telephone market dominated by Rogers Communications, Telus Mobility, and Bell Mobility Inc. Its aim? To attract "lots" of the 8 million people it estimated will sign up for cellular service in Canada in the next five years. The job would be challenging, as at the time Canadians couldn't take their cellphone numbers with them when they switch to a rival carrier.

Sir Richard Branson, rebel billionaire and owner of the Virgin empire which operates businesses ranging from an airline to cellphones to resorts to music stores, launched the new wireless service in Canada with characteristic flair. Dressed as a superhero out to rescue wireless customers, he whizzed 15 stories commando-style down a zip-line from a downtown Toronto building and rode a monster truck over a line-up of cars symbolizing competitors. And don't forget the buxom blondes in high-heeled boots and scanty nurse uniforms — to assist customers haemorrhaging heavy fees as a result of doing business with other wireless providers. These were all intended as visual metaphors for everything the company stands for: a new and irreverent alternative. This supported the other "No Catch" advertising which ran simultaneously on billboards and magazines promising a simple, honest, no gimmicks approach to wireless that didn't "rip off" customers like the competition.

Branson also had plans to push Canada's telecommunications regulator to introduce wireless number portability, something the government was already working on and later approved, to take effect in 2007. Branson's aim in Canada is to shake up the youth segment with Virgin's renowned brash style. The company offers only prepaid wireless services. Clients must buy phones that cost between $99 and $219.

In anticipation of Virgin's splashy entrance and branding efforts, competitors such as Bell Mobility had slashed prices for prepaid wireless services. The youth segment is a heavy user of wireless services and as more competitors crowd the playing field the play will get rougher and injuries are likely. Where did those nurses go just when we may need them?

QUESTIONS:

1. How would you describe Virgin Mobile's strategy for competing in the crowded Canadian wireless market?
2. How are they differentiating their brand from competing brands like Bell, Rogers and Telus?
3. For whom is the Virgin brand likely to have the greatest appeal?

SOURCE: Adapted from Catherine McLean, "Virgin's Sir Richard Makes Wireless Pitch," *The Globe and Mail,* March 10, 2005, p. B4.

- ***Medical and other health care*** (includes all medical services, dental, nursing, hospitalization, optometry, and other health care).
- ***Education*** (includes courses taken at a community college, university, or private college).
- ***Business and other professional services*** (includes legal, accounting, marketing research, management consulting, and computer services).
- ***Insurance, banking, and other financial services*** (includes personal and business insurance, credit and loan services, investment counselling, and tax services).
- ***Transportation*** (includes freight and passenger services on airplanes, trains, and ferries; automobile repairs and rentals).
- ***Communications*** (includes telephone, fax, Internet, e-mail, and other business communications services).

Characteristics of services

The special nature of services stems from a number of characteristics that distinguish services from tangible products. These features create special marketing challenges and opportunities for those companies whose core product is intangible. As a result, services firms often require marketing programs that are different from those found in the marketing of tangible goods.

intangibility
A characteristic of a service indicating that it has no physical attributes and, as a result, is impossible for customers to taste, feel, see, hear, or smell before buying.

Intangibility Because services are intangible, it is impossible for customers to sample a service before they buy it. As a result, there is often some degree of uncertainty or risk associated with a decision to eat at a restaurant, stay in a hotel or go to a hairstylist for the first time. Unlike a physical product such as a bicycle or DVD player, we can't examine or test-drive a service. As a result of the **intangibility** of services, a company's promotional program should portray the benefits to be derived from the service, rather than emphasizing the service itself, so prospective customers can have some idea of the service before deciding to buy. Four promotional strategies that may be used to suggest the benefits associated with services are as follows.[1]

- ***Visualization***: For example, banks that offer Internet banking services depict the convenience and freedom of 24-hour banking by showing clients at home late at night in their comfy clothes doing their banking or on holiday, sitting on the beach with their laptops.
- ***Association:*** Connect the service with a tangible object, person, or place. The Australian airline, Qantas, uses a cuddly koala in its advertising to project a warm, friendly image of Australia. Prudential Insurance suggests trust and security with its logo depicting the Rock of Gibraltar, a landmark often referred to as a symbol of stability and strength.
- ***Physical representation:*** GM Goodwrench uses the image of its service representatives. Ads show clean-cut employees in their familiar, freshly pressed black-and-red uniforms beaming a warm smile to communicate trustworthiness, dependability, and cleanliness.
- ***Documentation:*** Midas muffler shops have used the company's warranty in print advertisements. This represents the company's commitment to the customer and supports the claim of performance, dependability, and customer satisfaction.

inseparability
A characteristic of a service indicating that the service cannot be separated from the creator or seller of the service.

Inseparability There are two ways of looking at the concept of **inseparability**; both of which are pertinent for how we view services. First, services typically cannot be separated from the creator or seller of the service. In other words, when we buy a service, we often buy it from a specific service provider. A haircut from Nadia is not the same as a haircut from anyone else. This has a lot of implications for the building of customer relationships with specific individuals within firms.

Second, many services are created, delivered, and consumed simultaneously, so we can't separate production from consumption. For example, dentists and hairstylists create and dispense their services at the same time, and they require the presence of the consumer for the services to be performed. Nadia can't cut Sandra's hair unless Sandra is seated in her chair! Because of this inseparability, consumers are usually directly involved in production and marketing in services firms, and customers receive and consume services at the production site. Consequently, customers' opinions regarding a service frequently are formed through their contact with service personnel and their impressions of the physical surroundings of the company's premises.

BACK TO THE TOP

From a marketing standpoint, inseparability frequently means that direct sale is the only possible channel of distribution. Also, a seller's services cannot be sold in very many markets, because one person can repair only so many cars in a day or treat only so many patients. This characteristic limits the scale of operations in many firms whose services are delivered by its staff.

The inseparability of a service from the people providing it has important implications for companies that are operating in services businesses. This includes not only those companies in true "service" industries, such as financial services, entertainment, hotels, and restaurants, but also those that must pay particular attention to the services that support the marketing of their tangible products. For example, although Upper Canada Brewery is technically a manufacturer of beer, it is also in the business of making sure that its products are delivered on time, in the quantity and condition the customer ordered, and are conveniently available.

heterogeneity
A characteristic of a service indicating that the nature and quality of the service is different each time it is delivered.

Heterogeneity It is generally impossible for a services company to standardize output. Each "unit" of the service is somewhat different from other "units" of the same service. This is principally so because of the individualized approach that service providers take to the production and delivery of a service. Because most services are delivered by people, service delivery is prone to the differences that exist across human beings. Because we are all different and our interaction with other people is affected by personality, mood, and a number of other factors, service delivery and quality are bound to vary considerably. As a result, every haircut that Nadia does is different, as is every movie experience, even though you may be seeing the movie for a second time.

The hairstylist is the product and every product is different.

An added complication is the fact that it is often difficult to judge the quality of a service. It is particularly difficult to forecast quality in advance of buying a service. A person pays to see the Toronto Blue Jays play the Boston Red Sox at the Rogers Centre without knowing whether the game will be exciting or dull. Some companies are able to address this by allowing customers to sample a service before buying — for example, cable television companies will give new subscribers a free trial month's service on new channels. However, it is difficult for most services companies to provide samples. How can you sample a haircut, for example?

The **heterogeneity** of services is of concern to service providers, but the ability to deliver customer satisfaction is further complicated by the fact that customer expectations are not at all consistent. Although a student on a short lunch break may spend only 15 minutes grabbing a quick meal at a restaurant near campus, the same student may take more than an hour to enjoy a pizza with a friend after a Saturday night movie. In the first case, the customer wants to be served as quickly as possible; in the second, the customer is prepared to wait a little longer for service. Because service expectations differ across customers and even over time for the same customers, it is very difficult for service businesses to standardize their level of service.

In recent years, some services companies have turned to technology in an attempt to standardize the type and quality of service provided. Unfortunately, this is often at the expense of losing personal contact and the ability to respond to customers' questions or concerns. Nevertheless, some technology-delivered services, such as those provided by ATMs, Internet banking, and self-service gas stations, can become standardized and are accepted by a large number of customers. Canada's telephone companies have automated directory-assistance services and have introduced a voice-response system for handling collect calls.

While such technology-based services achieve standardization of service, in part by delegating much of the service provision or delivery to the customers themselves, some risks are inherent in their use. Some customers may resent having to do all of the work, especially when they are paying for the service. Also, some customers simply prefer to deal with real people and become confused or irritated when they encounter technology. Many customers are frustrated when they encounter difficult-to-navigate telephone voice response systems or what many call "voice mail." Finally, in some industries, management is faced with the dilemma of not being able to keep in touch with customers or to establish relationships with them, since the customers are dealing primarily with technology.

Perishability and fluctuating demand Services are highly perishable and they cannot be stored. Unused hotel rooms, empty seats in a stadium, and idle hairstylists waiting for customers all represent business that is lost forever — a seat at today's Blue Jays game can't be sold tomorrow. Furthermore, the market for services fluctuates considerably by season, by day of the week, and by hour of the day. Most ski lifts are idle all summer and golf courses go unused in the winter. The use of city buses fluctuates greatly during the day.

perishability
A characteristic of a service indicating that it disappears if not sold and cannot be placed in inventory as can tangible products.

There are notable exceptions to this generalization regarding the **perishability** and storage of services. In health and life insurance, for example, the service is purchased by a person or a company; then, it is held by the insurance company (the seller) until needed by the buyer or the beneficiary. This holding constitutes a type of storage — it is always there when the customer needs it. Similarly, many services generally considered "public utilities" are able to store services until they are needed. For example, telephone and electricity services are available on demand. We can access them whenever we need them. Because of this, there is a very real probability that consumers will take such services for granted, simply because they are always available. This causes potential problems for companies that are marketing such services, because it makes it difficult for them to interest their customers in buying more or in adopting new services. It certainly creates a challenge for the establishment of close customer relationships.

The combination of perishability and fluctuating demand offers planning, pricing, and promotion challenges to services marketing managers. Some organizations have developed new uses for idle capacity during off-seasons; for example, during the summer, several ski resorts operate their ski lifts for hikers and sightseers who want access to higher elevations. Advertising and creative pricing are also used to stimulate demand during slack periods. Hotels offer lower prices and family packages on weekends, for example, and telephone companies offer lower rates at nights and on weekends when circuits are less busy.

PAGE UP!

1. What is the difference between core services and supplementary services?
2. Education and insurance are both examples of ________________ services.
3. What are the principal characteristics of services?

The Value Proposition for Services

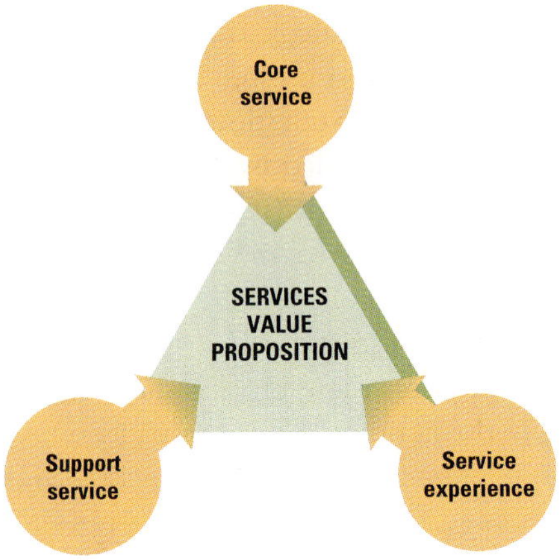

Figure 8-2:
The Services Value Proposition

services value proposition
The value proposition of a services company, which must include core and support elements of the service provided to customers and the service experience delivered to the customer.

For companies that operate in the services sector, the development of a **value proposition** that customers will find attractive is a challenge, made all the more so by the characteristics of services that we have just discussed. We think it is important at this stage to clarify the three components of the value proposition of services organizations. It is also important to note that this discussion is not only important in companies that have services as their core offer to customers. The concept of the services value proposition is also critically important for non-businesses, particularly organizations that operate in the not-for-profit sector, such as symphony orchestras, theatre companies, and colleges and universities, as these too provide services to their target segments.

The three components of the value proposition that pertain especially to companies and organizations that operate in the services and not-for-profit sectors are presented in Figure 8-2. We have been discussing characteristics of the core service that lies at the heart of the value proposition. This core service (and tangible products) must be delivered or presented to the customer using a number of support or supplementary services. Finally, the way in which the company interacts with, treats, or serves its customers is often referred to as the service experience and is what customers generally are referring to when they talk about "service." What is important, of course, is that each of these components of the value proposition is important in creating value for the customer and in contributing to customer satisfaction.

It is also important to remind ourselves that what principally distinguishes services companies from those that operate in a product-based environment is the intangibility of the core offering. While companies such as Burger King, Best Western, and Amazon.ca are considered services companies, companies that make things, such as Kraft Foods, Honda, and Burton Snowboards, are not. The businesses in this latter group are considered to be manufacturers, whose core products are tangible. But it is critical to appreciate that all companies must be aware of the implications of being successful at the second and third levels of our services value proposition. All companies and organizations must have effective supplementary services to surround and support their core offerings, and all must deliver a positive customer experience in order to achieve customer satisfaction.

The remainder of this chapter will be devoted to examining in greater detail each of these three components of the services value proposition.

Strategic Aspects of the Core

Because of the characteristics of services (notably, intangibility), the development of a marketing program in an organization that has services as its core offering is often challenging. Nevertheless, as we have observed before, the fundamental principles of marketing are the same, regardless of what is being marketed. Ultimately, we are interested in achieving long-term customer satisfaction. Let's consider some of the strategic implications of putting a marketing program together in the services sector.

Understanding the customers of services

Marketers of services should understand the customers who buy their services. What are their buying motives? Sellers must determine buying patterns for their services: When, where, and how do customers buy, who does the buying, and who makes the buying decisions? The psychological determinants of buying behaviour — attitudes, perceptions, and personality — become even more important when marketing services rather than tangible goods, because typically we cannot touch, smell, or taste a service offering. This has implications for how consumers buy and for the need to gain a complete understanding.

For consumers, the purchase of services may be more problematic and potentially risky than is the case for tangible products, which can be examined and even tested before purchase. As a result, customers of services tend to rely more on conversations with and referrals from other customers than they do when they are buying tangible products.

Planning core services

Introducing new services is just as important to a service company as the launch of new products is to a tangible-products firm. Similarly, the improvement of existing services and elimination of unwanted, unprofitable services are also key goals. Product planning and development has its counterpart in the marketing program of a services organization. Management must select appropriate strategies based on answers to these questions:

PetCare Insurance

- What services products will be offered?
- What will be the breadth and depth of the services mix?
- How will the services be positioned? What attributes will they have?

A product that meets the needs of pet lovers.

Services offering

Many firms have become successful by identifying a previously unsatisfied consumer need and then developing a service to address that need. Examples of this are everywhere. How about pet insurance covering 6,000 illnesses and all types of accidents? PetCare Insurance Brokers (**www.petcareinsurance.com**) offers a range of products that will cover the family's cat or dog from head to tail with prices to suit all budgets. In a society that is placing increased importance, and resources, on the family pet, many see this insurance as being well worth the money.

Service-mix strategies

Several of the product-mix strategies discussed in Chapter 7 can be employed effectively by services marketers. Consider the strategy of expanding or enhancing the line of services offered. This is often referred to as a process of adding value for the customer. In fact, one of the most effective ways of adding value to existing products and services is by adding new support services. Many hotel chains and even some "bed and breakfasts" have added desks, fax machines, and high-speed Internet connections to their rooms, and provide photocopier and printer services on request for business guests. Rental car companies offer no-smoking cars and GPS, and rent cellular telephones. Most now have computerized the process of returning rental cars at airports to speed travellers on their way.

Managing the life cycle of a service is another strategy that is being practised more and more by services marketers. Recognizing that the competitive credit card industry is in its maturity stage, Canadian banks have explored new ways of gaining consumer popularity. The result in many cases is that consumers now carry several credit cards when they had only one previously. One of the many variations on the VISA card is the CIBC HBC Rewards

VISA card, a co-branded, loyalty-based card from CIBC and Hudson's Bay Company that allows cardholders to earn 15 HBC reward points for every dollar spent using the card. Cardholders also get automatic HBC 'gold' status, allowing them to obtain rewards such as digital cameras, appliances and even holiday trips for 20 percent fewer points from Canada's number one loyalty program.

Service features In some respects, product planning is easier for services than for tangible products. Packaging and labelling play a much less important role in services marketing, although there are both packaging and labelling aspects to services. Other features, such as branding and quality management, for example, present greater challenges for services industries.

BACK TO THE TOP

Branding of services is a problem because maintaining consistent quality (a responsibility of brand ownership) is difficult. Also, a brand cannot be physically attached to a label or to the service itself — once Sandra leaves the salon, no-one can tell she has had an Aveda haircut. A services marketer's goal should be to create an effective brand image. In most successful services companies, the company or organization name is the brand name. Thus, customers become loyal to Tim Hortons or to WestJet or to Telus. Although there are some notable exceptions, most services companies have not been successful in creating strong brands for their individual service products.

The strategy to achieve a strong services brand image is to develop a total theme that includes more than just a good brand name. To implement this strategy, the following tactics may be used:

- Include a tangible component as part of the brand image — like the torn movie ticket for Blockbuster Video, the bright yellow price-cutting 'happy face' to represent Wal-Mart's everyday low price strategy, the maple leaf representing the Canadian Tire brand, or the koala of Qantas Airlines.
- Tie in a slogan with the brand — for instance, Ocean Spray's "Crave the Wave," or Hallmark's "When you care enough to send the very best."
- Use a distinctive colour scheme — such as the red-and-yellow signage and "golden arches" of McDonald's or the patriotic red and white colours for Canadian Tire.

The fresh fruit at this store tangibilizes the brand message.

Pricing of services

In the marketing of services, nowhere is there a greater need for managerial creativity and skill than in the area of pricing. Since services are intangible, perishable, usually cannot be stored, and often have a fluctuating demand, it is extremely difficult to demonstrate their value. To further complicate the situation, customers may perform some services themselves (auto and household repairs, for example).

Because of the heterogeneity and difficulty of standardizing quality, most services are highly differentiated. Also, it is virtually impossible to have complete market information; customers often have considerable difficulty assessing the quality of the service and, therefore, the perceived value that they have received. As an example, consider the issue of auto repairs. Many customers of auto dealers and repair shops do not understand how cars work, particularly with the on-board computer systems that are in most cars today. As a result, they are unable to assess whether they have received good value from a repair job.

Distribution of services

Traditionally, most services have been sold directly from producer to customer. No intermediaries are used when the service cannot be separated from the seller or when the service is created and marketed simultaneously. For example, medical care, auto repair, and other personal services are typically sold without intermediaries, simply because the service could not exist without the people who are providing it. Not using intermediaries does limit the geographic markets that service providers can reach, because they have to be there in person to provide the service. But it also enables sellers to personalize their services and get quick, detailed customer feedback.

Geeks on Call
Mad Science

The only other frequently used distribution channel for services involves one agent intermediary. Some type of agent or broker is often used in the marketing of securities, travel arrangements, entertainment, and housing rentals. Sometimes dealers are trained in production of the service and then are **franchised** to sell it. This is the case with Geeks on Call (www.callthegeeks.com), which supplies on-site computer services such as repairs, networking, and one-on-one training, or Mad Science (www.madscience.com), which offers over 1,000 hours of customized experiments for schools, parties, camps, and community events.

franchising
A type of contractual marketing system that involves a continuing relationship in which a franchiser (the parent company) provides the right to use a trademark plus management assistance in opening and operating a services business in return for financial considerations from a franchisee (the owner of the individual business unit).

In recent years, some firms have realized that the characteristic of inseparability is not an insurmountable limitation to a seller's distribution system. With a little imagination, a services marketer can broaden distribution considerably. Let's look at some examples.

The use of intermediaries is another way to expand distribution of services. Banks have arranged for companies to deposit employees' paycheques directly into their bank accounts. The employer thus becomes an intermediary in distributing the bank's service. Insurance firms have broadened distribution by setting up vending machines in airports. Canada Post now operates post offices in drugstores across Canada. Canada's lottery corporations sell their tickets through kiosks in shopping malls and through thousands of retail agents in convenience stores and gasoline stations across the country. Courier services such as Purolator and FedEx have made it convenient for their customers by installing drop boxes on street corners and in office buildings in the downtown business districts of major cities.

The characteristic of intangibility essentially eliminates physical-distribution problems for most service producers. For example, other than office and other supplies, accountants and consultants have no physical inventory to store or handle. However, not all service producers are free from physical-distribution headaches. Those who are unable to deliver their services without the support of tangible products still have to address issues relating to physical storage and logistics. Retailing, for example, is considered to be a service industry, but retailers certainly have to deal with inventory issues and questions relating to location.

Many companies have succeeded in separating some services from the people who provide them by delegating the delivery of their services to technology. While we normally associate the concept of a vending machine with the ones that supply chocolate bars and soft drinks, much of the equipment and technology that deliver services are essentially service vending machines. When we make a telephone call from a payphone, we are using a vending machine of sorts. Similarly, ATMs supply financial services in much the same way that "Coke machines" supply soft drinks. When you use a coin-operated photocopying machine in your college library, you are buying a service.

Promotion of services

Several forms of promotion are used extensively in services marketing, but because services are often inseparable from the people who provide them, personal selling and word of mouth play a dominant role. For example, any employee of a services firm who comes in contact with a customer is, in effect, part of that firm's sales force. In addition to a regular sales force, customer-contact personnel might include airline flight attendants, receptionists, couriers, bank tellers, and ushers at theatres. We use the term **service encounter** to describe a customer's interaction with any service employee or with any tangible element such as a service's physical surroundings (bank, ballpark, law office). Customers often form opinions of a company and its service on the basis of service encounters, and they talk with their friends and associates about those encounters. Consequently, it is essential that management recognize the strategic importance of service encounters and prepare contact personnel and physical surroundings accordingly. A key step in preparing to sell a service is to provide sales training and service information for contact personnel, impressing on them the importance of their role.

service encounter
In services marketing, a customer's interaction with any service employee or with any tangible element, such as a service's physical surroundings or through technology.

For years, of course, advertising has been used extensively in many service fields — hotels, transportation, and insurance, for example. What is newer is the use of advertising by professional-services firms, including legal, accounting, physiotherapy, and chiropractic. Previously, professional associations in such fields prohibited advertising on the grounds that it was unprofessional. While some associations still control the type of advertising that may be done, the promotion of professional services is much more open and accepted than ever before.

Support Services

All organizations, regardless of the nature of their core product or service, must offer a range of support or supplementary services. These are additional to the core and have a very important role to play in enhancing the customer's perception of the core and in contributing to customer satisfaction. They are support services that relate to the provision of information, the physical delivery and care of the core product, the processing of transactions, and generally to making it easy and less frustrating for the customer.

Such support services are essential in enabling the company to add value to its core product or service. There is little point in having a superbly crafted and excellent-quality product if the company is unable to deliver it to customers in a timely and convenient way. Essentially, the supplementary services that we are discussing in this section apply to all types of organizations, and they are essential to the successful management of the interaction with customers. In many cases, these support services are critical to achieving customer satisfaction, even more important than the core product itself. This is particularly true when the core product is in danger of becoming a commodity. For example, in financial services, virtually all banks offer approximately the same services. There is very little different in a mortgage or a savings account at the Royal Bank of Canada as compared with CIBC or Scotiabank. The support services made available are important in differentiating one from the other and in attracting customers.

We can divide the range of support services offered into a number of categories. The first of these relates to the provision and management of information. Today, many companies provide information to customers through their Web sites, including where to buy their products and how to order them or to make reservations. Organizations have to make it easy for customers and others to communicate and interact with them. Services relating to the company's Web site, telephone system, and e-mail are all critical in contributing to that ease of interaction. Accurate and timely billing systems, provision of credit, and customer feedback processes are also part of the communications-information component of support services.

Other support services relate to access and convenience; thus, the hours that a retailer's store is open and VIA Rail's train schedule are part of the services that surround the core. So, too, is FedEx's pick-up and delivery schedule, the location of its drop boxes, and the planning of routes. Auto dealers offer courtesy cars to deliver customers to their homes and offices after they have dropped off their cars for service. Airport hotels have shuttle buses that meet guests at the airport to bring them to the hotel.

Manufacturers in particular offer a range of support services that pertain to the physical products that they sell. Dell, for example, must have a distribution system that allows for the delivery and set-up of its computers. The company must also put into place post-purchase services, including repair and the provision of information to customers when things go wrong. Many companies now use the Internet to allow customers to troubleshoot problems themselves before calling a toll-free number for assistance. The call centre itself is, of course, a support service.

Choice and variety represent a large part of support services. Retailers and others must offer customers a wide enough range of options from which to choose or they will go to the competition. Honda must manage its inventory of new cars and parts to make sure that they are in the right place at the right time to meet customer demand.

FedEx

Support services also contribute to the reduction of risk and anxiety. Many manufacturers and some services companies offer their customers guarantees and warranties. Air Canada allows you to check its Web site to see if the flight you are planning to meet is on time. On its Web site (**www.fedex.com**), FedEx allows you to track a package that you have sent as it makes its way across Canada, and actually see the signature of the person who signs for it at the other end.

There are often physical aspects to the provision of supplementary services. Doctor's offices, airport gates, and bank branches must be designed and operated to make waiting tolerable or even enjoyable. Comfortable seating, current magazines, water coolers, and acceptable music are all part of the services, as are washroom facilities and parking. Movie theatres have expanded the range of services that surround the core (the movies) in recent years to include parking, games arcades, and food courts.

Support services should be viewed, therefore, as an essential component of the value proposition of a firm. Not only do they support and enhance the core, but also often become the factors that lead to a customer deciding on one company versus another. We often deal with the company that offers the best choice, that is more conveniently located, or that is open when we want to buy, and not necessarily the one that has the best core product.

PAGE UP!

1. What is meant by the services value proposition?
2. Why is pricing difficult in services marketing?
3. What does the term service encounter mean?

The Service Experience

Each time a customer or prospective customer interacts with a company, a service encounter takes place, regardless of whether that encounter is with an employee face to face or over the telephone, or one that involves interaction with an automated phone system or the company's Web site. Each interaction represents an opportunity for the company to create a positive or negative experience.

How often have you been impressed with the kind of service you have received from a company or one of its employees? — so much so that you told friends or family members how happy you were and how you will definitely go back again. On the other hand, you have likely also walked out or retail stores or hung up the phone or left a Web site simply because you were so frustrated with the way you were being treated or being kept waiting, to the point where you vowed never to go back. What is really interesting and important about such examples is that the satisfaction level of the customer and his or her decision to buy again or never go back has little or nothing to do with the quality or variety of the products being sold or the prices being charged or the company's advertising or store opening hours — it has everything to do with what customers generally refer to as "service."

When customers speak of "service," they are usually referring to how they are treated in their interaction with a business or to the processes to which they are exposed. So, while standing in a slow-moving queue on a busy day at the auto parts counter in the local Canadian Tire, one aspiring home mechanic might turn to the person waiting next to her in line and observe, "The service here is terrible!" Or, having looked without success for someone to offer advice on the various models of lawnmowers available at Sears, an impatient gardener might complain, "What do you have to do to get some service around here?" Conversely, when you encounter a retail salesperson who offers to check with another of the company's stores to see if she can locate that dress in your size and then arranges to have it delivered for you, your comment probably relates to the fact that you feel that you were treated well and received great service.

service experience
That part of the company's value proposition that addresses how the company interacts with its customers; the kind of experience the customer has during his or her encounters with the company.

We are dealing here with customer service, or more correctly with service as defined by the customer, with how that customer interacts with a company and its employees, and the processes, systems, and procedures that are encountered along the way — the **service experience**. Some people also refer to such encounters as "moments of truth," as they represent opportunities for a company to impress or disappoint the customer. These encounters represent the situation where the "rubber hits the road," in that the company's reputation is on the line and it either performs or it doesn't.

The service experience does not have to involve in-person meetings with employees, as companies are increasingly interacting with their customers through technology such as the Internet, banking machines, self-service gas pumps, and telephone-based interactive ordering systems for concert tickets. All of these are service encounters, as they involve the customer-service experience at the hands of the company.

service quality
The value that consumers perceive they are receiving from their purchase of services; generally very difficult to control and measure.

Service quality Quality, whether of tangible products or intangible services, is difficult to define, measure, control, and communicate. Yet, the quality of the service provided to customers is critical to a firm's success. Two airlines each fly an Airbus A345 on the Toronto–Hong Kong route for approximately the same fare, two auto repair shops each use Ford or Chrysler parts and charge the same price, and two banks each offer the same investment accounts at identical interest rates. Assuming similar times and locations, **service quality** is the only factor that differentiates the offerings in each of these situations because the core product or service being sold is, in the minds of customers, largely undifferentiated — a situation which we often refer to as commoditization.

However difficult it may be to define the concept of service quality, management must understand one thing: Quality is defined by the consumer and not by the company that provides the service. Your hairstylist may be delighted with the job she did on your hair, but if you think your hair looks terrible, then the service quality was poor. What counts is what customers think about a service. Service quality that does not meet customer expectations can result in lost sales from present customers and a failure to attract new ones. Consequently, it is imperative that management strives to maintain consistent service quality at or above the level of consumer expectations. Yet, it is sometimes virtually impossible to standardize service quality; that is, to maintain consistency in service output. No two service encounters are identical.

As part of managing service quality, many companies have implemented an ongoing quality-improvement program that monitors the level and consistency of service quality. They also measure the quality of the service they provide as perceived by their customers. Many businesses have existed for years under the assumption that management knew what customers wanted and how they wanted to be treated. The most successful companies have now abandoned that way of thinking and have subscribed to the idea that "Good service is whatever the customer says it is." A program to measure the perceived quality of a business's service therefore must start by defining the aspects of the contact with the company that the customer considers most important.

Let's illustrate the components of service by considering customers of Bell Canada and other telephone companies that are interested, first of all, in ensuring that their telephone systems work properly, that calls go through, and that reception is clear (the "core product" aspects of the service). In fact, as technology has improved in this industry, customers do not expect their telephone systems ever to fail — the core service in this industry is largely taken for granted by customers; they almost never think about it.

The next component of service relates to the processes and support services that the telephone company has in place to deliver and support the core service — telephone bills, installation of new lines, activation of cellphone service, telephone directories, directory-assistance services, and optional services such as voice mail and call forwarding.

Finally, we must also appreciate that the quality of service as perceived by customers is related to the way in which employees of the company interact with their customers — whether operators are courteous and polite, whether salespeople know the technology, and how complaints are resolved. This not only relates to such aspects of personal service as courtesy, politeness, and product knowledge, but also to the ultimate effect of service — how the customer is made to feel while dealing with the service provider.

It may be suggested that, as the nature of service moves farther away from the actual product or service and more toward the "people" aspects of service, the less control management has over the delivery and, therefore, the quality of the service offered. For example, WestJet can control the actual flight from Calgary to Vancouver (the core service, getting passengers from one city to another). Barring unforeseen circumstances, management can also control, to a greater or lesser extent, the services that support that core product: frequency of flights, departure and arrival times, the number of ticket agents at the counter, baggage-handling systems, and meal or beverage service.

Management loses much more control over the details of the service provided at the interface between customer and employee — how the passenger agent greets the customer at the check-in counter, whether the baggage handler puts the suitcase on the right plane, whether the flight attendants are pleasant and helpful. In fact, it is in this latter component of service that many companies feel their greatest potential lies to differentiate themselves from the competition.

internal marketing
The process of directing programs to staff members with the intention of encouraging them to deliver superior service to customers and generally to adopt a customer focus in all that they do.

The realization that employees have the greatest potential to influence service quality and ultimately customer satisfaction has led many companies to introduce **internal marketing** programs. These programs are intended to ensure that employees "buy in" to the concept of customer service and appreciate that every satisfied customer means a returning customer. Again, the more progressive companies, and those that are most committed to exceptional levels of customer service, have developed elaborate training and motivation programs that emphasize excellence in treating the customer and reward those employees who treat customers well. It is at this level that marketing and human resources divisions of a company must co-operate, as both are ultimately responsible for the quality of service delivered by their employees.

MARKETING AT WORK — 8-2: STRATEGY

In New Baseball Ads, the Fans Are the Stars

It used to be all about the players, but not any more! After all, who knows when a player will be traded? Who knows when the next player will be accused of using steroids? For that matter, who knows when they'll go on strike again?

For 2005, the celebratory campaign to kick off the baseball season was all about the fans, unlike campaigns from previous years that focused on players like Derek Jeter and Alex Rodriguez.

The theme of the campaign, "I live for this," remains, only now it is uttered not by people wearing uniforms but team-themed costumes and logos painted on their faces.

"As important as it is for us to celebrate players, the fans are an important part of the game because the depth and intensity of our schedule asks a lot of them," says Tim Brosnan, VP at Major League Baseball headquarters in New York referring to the length of the season and the number of games played. "So we want to give them the stage to express their avidity for the game." Focusing on the game and the people who are passionate about it is a smart way to promote baseball and avoid getting into hot water," says one advertising executive who has long tracked the value of professional athletes as endorsers.

Concentrating on the fans and not the players might make more sense for baseball than other sports. According to research conducted among more than 10,000 passionate fans of 25 sports, for baseball fans player admiration ranks fifth trailing team devotion, nostalgia, the social aspects of the sport, and personal indulgence (time for oneself). By contrast NASCAR fans say drivers "are 1,2,3" among the reasons to follow stock-car racing. The turmoil over steroid use, the lockouts and strikes have all had their impact and some time must pass before the tarnish wears off.

The light-hearted tone of the campaign, a contrast to others that have taken a reverential approach, reflects the belief of the McCann-Erickson advertising agency that, "baseball is entertainment, not something you wrap a flag in or have to go to Harvard to take a course in."

QUESTIONS:

1. How successful do you think Major League Baseball will be in shifting the emphasis of fans somewhat away from individual players and more toward the fans and the game itself?
2. Contrast this with the PGA's campaign, the theme of which is "these guys are good."

SOURCE: Adapted from Stuart Elliott, "In New Ads for Baseball, the Fans Are the Stars," *New York Times Online*, www.nytimes.com, March 14, 2005.

service failure
The failure of a service to meet customer expectations or standards, resulting in disappointment, frustration, or similar emotions.

service recovery
The process of correcting the situation when a customer is dissatisfied with service provided. A company may attempt to recover from a poor service experience by apologizing or by offering the customer a price reduction or other form of compensation.

Service failure and recovery No matter how diligent a company's employees and how well designed its service processes, **service failure** is inevitable. It may or may not be the fault of the company, but eventually something will go wrong. An important issue relating to customer satisfaction is how a company responds when service fails. The process of dealing with service failure to make amends with the customer is called **service recovery**, as discussed briefly in Chapter 1.

Service recovery may be necessary when the core service fails. When the electricity fails because of a powerful thunderstorm or because ice build-up causes the toppling of hydro towers, the electrical utility works around the clock to restore power. An error on a bill will prompt immediate correction and an apology from a manager. Failure of a flight to depart and arrive on time may prompt an airline to offer its best customers a bonus of 500 frequent-flyer points as compensation. In some situations, such as haircuts, it is not easy for the service provider to recover from a disappointing service experience.

The issue relating to service recovery is: What can and should the company do when something goes wrong? Certainly, the answer is not "Do nothing." In many companies in recent years, managers have been paying increasing attention to the development of procedures to deal with service problems as they arise, with a view to solving the customers' problems before they decide to take their business elsewhere. Therefore, service recovery becomes an important component in a company's program to establish and maintain customer relationships. Research has shown that a company taking the necessary steps to deal with customers' service problems efficiently and effectively will lead to those customers being satisfied, even to the point that they will be more loyal than they would have been if the service problem had never occurred!

Companies have to ask themselves to what lengths they should go to recover from service failures. The decision depends on many factors. The seriousness of the problem is undoubtedly one factor to be considered. Mixing up a family's dinner reservations when they are celebrating their grandparents' fiftieth wedding anniversary is a more serious service failure than losing a lunch reservation for two businesspeople when there are lots of empty tables available. In addition, the importance of the customer to the company is another factor to be considered. This is not an easy one to deal with, as defining the importance or value of a customer is not a simple task.

Finally, some companies are so committed to recovering from service failure that they even take remedial steps in situations that are not their fault. An employee at Tim Hortons may give a customer a replacement coffee free when he accidentally dropped his large double-double in the parking lot, even though the company was not responsible for the fact that the first cup of coffee slid off the roof of the car.

Some companies are so intent on dealing with customer service problems that they actually encourage their customers to complain if they have a problem. If a dissatisfied customer who encounters a service failure simply leaves, vowing never to return, the company has missed a chance to deal with the problem, management may never know that the problem exists, other customers may experience the same problem, and the exiting customer has the opportunity to spread the bad news. Complaints provide an opportunity to restore customer satisfaction and even to impress the customer.

Service drives customer satisfaction

It should be obvious that the quality and level of service provided by a company is an important determinant of the satisfaction level of its customers. In fact, business is often lost because of poor service, even though the quality of the core product is excellent. We saw this in the Chapter 1 opener, where Sarah bought her running shoes at the store that offered the best customer service, even though she could have purchased them at a lower price at another store.

There are a couple of important lessons here. First, excellent customer service is an important differentiator. It sets a company apart from its competitors and gives it an advantage. Second, providing excellent service often allows a company to command a price premium. That is, customers are often prepared to pay higher prices in order to receive superior service. They'll say, "I know I'm paying more, but it's worth it." They clearly place a value on receiving great service and being treated well.

Many things contribute to customer satisfaction. We observed in Chapter 1 that customers are more satisfied when they perceive value in what they are offered by a firm. Value is created through product quality, attractive pricing, the provision of support services, and how the customer is treated. Thus, a company can create high levels of perceived value among its customers by employing well-trained, helpful, and courteous employees, by having an efficient Web site and telephone system, and generally by making it easy for customers to deal with the company.

We also observed in Chapter 1 that satisfied customers will generally return to buy from a company again, while dissatisfied ones will not. Producing high levels of customer satisfaction is essential, therefore, if companies want to retain customers, to have them come back again and again. Think about the companies that you deal with, some of which you have probably being going back to for a number of years. What makes them different? Chances are, you could probably get just as good a product or service somewhere else. You go back because of how you are treated and, ultimately, how you are made to feel.

customer expectations
What customers expect to encounter when dealing with a company or buying a product or service, based on past experience and desired outcomes.

Another aspect of service delivery that is receiving a lot of attention in businesses today relates to the idea of exceeding **customer expectations**. As customers, we are most impressed when we encounter service that is better than we were expecting. Some companies offer such good service or recover from service problems so well that the only possible response from customers is "Wow!" Whenever a company succeeds in generating a "Wow!" response from customers, high levels of satisfaction have been achieved and the customers are likely to tell others about their favourable experiences.

Let's close this discussion of the service experience by returning to the question of what level of service is necessary and appropriate. Just as we asked what level of service recovery is necessary, so too it is important to ask what level of service in general a company should provide. The answer will depend to some extent on the company's positioning. Does it want to be known as a superior service provider, or is it content to deliver acceptable but not superb service and to compete on some other basis?

value of a customer
The categorization of customers based on their value to the firm.

The level of service provided to specific customers will depend to some extent on the value the firm places on each customer. Some customers are simply more valuable than others. Many companies have begun to develop information systems to allow them to measure or estimate the **value of a customer** to their firms. The question of the value of a customer is important when companies are trying to decide on the level of service to provide and which customers they should retain. The principle here is one that many firms and organizations often find difficult to accept — they may not want all of their customers! Typically, companies earn as much as 80 percent of their profits from as few as 20 percent of their customers. The issue is to decide which are the most valuable ones so that a company can deliver superior service and protect its relationships with these. Some larger companies collect information on customers and their purchases and utilize this database information to assess the value of each customer. By categorizing customers, for example, into A, B, C, and D categories based on their value to the firm, a company can ensure that its best customers receive the highest levels of service and that attempts are made to address their problems immediately.

Service builds customer relationships

There is no doubt that the provision of excellent service leads to customer loyalty and causes customers to return to do business again. If this happens often enough, there is a possibility of a customer relationship developing. As we observe throughout this book, achieving high levels of customer satisfaction, leading to the establishment of customer relationships, is the principal objective of marketing.

A company achieves the status of a relationship with a customer when it has succeeded in creating an emotional bond or attachment. There is a special feeling toward the firm on the part of the customer, who enjoys dealing with the company and its employees. A high level of trust exists and the customer may even feel a sense of ownership toward the company or service provider. This is reflected when the customer refers to the firm as "my bank," "my supermarket," or "my hairdresser." When the status of customer relationship is achieved, there is a high degree of loyalty toward the firm; these customers recommend the company to others and give it a large share of their business. So, how is such a status achieved?

functional value
The value that a company creates for its customers that is based on the quality of its products and the efficiency of its services.

emotional value
The value that an organization is able to create for its customers that addresses the feelings that the customer has toward the company or its brands.

Essentially, relationships are interpersonal and emotional concepts. When we speak of our relationships, they are usually with people, and we reserve the word for those people toward whom we feel particularly close. We feel closest to people we trust, those we feel we can rely on, those with whom we feel comfortable, and those with whom we share things — common backgrounds, shared interests, and values. Companies have begun to realize the importance of creating such an emotional bond with customers.

Many companies now realize that customer satisfaction depends on the creation of two different types of value for customers — **functional value** and **emotional value**. Functional value is related to the provision of quality products, delivering them in a timely and convenient manner, and making sure that they work well. These are things that customers expect of well-run companies, but they may not be enough to lead to the establishment of customer relationships. In fact, as customer confidence and expectations have increased in recent years, customers are increasingly intolerant of companies that fail to deliver functional value.

Emotional value, on the other hand, is created largely through the interaction between the company and its customers, by how the company and its employees treat them, and ultimately how they are made to feel as a result. There is, therefore, a direct connection between the delivery of what the customer perceives to be excellent service and the emotional value that the customer experiences as a result. When customers are treated well, when they enjoy dealing with companies, and when they are recognized when they call, positive emotions are created and negative ones removed. Customers say that they feel comfortable dealing with their preferred service providers; they are made to feel valued and important; they trust these companies and feel that they can rely on them. Frustration, anxiety, and other negative emotions are reduced.

We referred earlier to relationships as an emotional, largely interpersonal concept. Relationships are best developed when customers are able to interact easily and comfortably with employees of the firm and when those employees have been selected, trained, and motivated to provide superior service.

MARKETING AT WORK 8-3: RELATIONSHIPS

Going For a Tim's?

Tim Horton, the former Maple Leafs great, and Tim Hortons the fast-food chain may be icons in Canada — let's face it, you knew what the title referred to when you read it — but the franchise has a challenge to meet in places like Columbus, Ohio, and other parts of the United States where the chain has been aggressively pushing to reach the 500-location mark by 2007.

The chain is only half way to that goal but plans to keep the U.S. formula simple: Go slowly, run the operation as if it was just another region of Canada, and don't forget your unpretentious coffee shop roots. And that's the secret to the strong relationship the brand has with consumers here in Canada. The only difference is that Americans want larger cups and they don't like the dutchie! According to one franchisee, "It's a tough market, but no tougher than in Canada. The same principles of success apply in both countries. At the end of the day, if a store delivers on its promise, you'll go back. If it doesn't, you won't."

And deliver is what it does in Canada — there is now one location for every 12,000 Canadians with average sales of $1.7 million each. Not bad for a business where the average purchase is less than three dollars. According to Rob Wilson, professor of marketing at Toronto's Ryerson University, "People don't go for coffee at Tim Hortons, they go for a Tim's." Canadians have a close relationship with the 'brand' and what it represents — it's like your neighbourhood pub without the alcohol. "Tim Hortons is a local meeting place — it's just a place to go and feel comfortable," according to Dave Mullen, VP of regional marketing and national promotions.

The company's association with Canadiana and its down-home (and, yes, sometimes corny) advertising resonates with consumers with situations that are relatable, allowing customers to see themselves in the ads such as the "True Stories" campaign showing how the brand is a part of our everyday lives. For example, "Jeff" in Europe with a Tim's mug strapped to his backpack or Tim's coffee arriving for a lonely student in a Glasgow dorm. The chain's involvement in youth sports also strengthens these relationships through its sponsorship of hockey, soccer and more recently curling.

Can we teach Americans to say "double double" like they really mean it? Only time and many cups of coffee will tell.

QUESTIONS:

1. Do you honestly believe that many Canadians have a "relationship" with Tim Hortons?
2. Where did this relationship come from and how would you describe it?
3. What will Tim Hortons have to do to create a similar relationship with Americans?

SOURCE: Adapted from Barrie McKenna, "Tim Hortons Filling U.S. Doughnut Holes," *The Globe and Mail Online*, www.theglobeandmail.com, March 27, 2005; Rebecca Harris, "Down-Home Smarts," *Marketing Magazine Online*, www.marketingmag.ca, February 7, 2005.

Increasing Service Productivity

The increased attention being paid to services companies and to customer service in recent years has been accompanied by a significant increase in competition. This competition has been stimulated by several factors. One is the reduction in government regulation in many industries, such as airlines, telecommunications, and banking. Relaxed regulations of professional organizations now permit advertising by the medical, legal, and other professions. New techniques have opened new service fields, in solar and wind energy and information technology, for instance. Technological advances have also brought automation to service industries in which employees generally performed many manual tasks. Service chains and franchise systems are replacing the small-scale independent in many fields, including restaurants, auto repair, hair salons, and real estate.

Companies in virtually every industry still continue to face the challenges of becoming more efficient and productive. The pressure on businesses is to deliver greater returns to shareholders, while in public sector organizations, governments at all levels have been looking for new ways to produce better value for taxpayers. Because service industries are very labour-intensive compared with manufacturing, the pressure to become more efficient has led in some organizations to "downsizing": reducing costs by reducing the number of employees. Services firms are employing other strategies to improve productivity. One is to invest in employee education and training programs, not just to teach basic skills, but also to improve efficiency. Another strategy is to bring in new technology that has enhanced or even replaced labour in a wide range of service industries. As technology has become more efficient, industries such as financial services are able to operate with far fewer customer-contact employees than ever before.

Elimination of many routine tasks may also occur as simple transactions are passed down to the consumer. Many banking transactions can be conducted at ATMs or through the Internet. Consumers pump their own gas and pay for it without ever meeting an employee. We obtain our own information on the Internet and complete our own course registration through our university or college computerized registration system. We interact with automated telephone systems that allow us to reach individuals or to leave messages without ever talking to a receptionist or operator. We even check out and bag our own groceries. While this use of technology and the downloading of service tasks to the customer make for greater efficiency and lower per-transaction costs for the company that uses these systems, they are not without their disadvantages.

Moving forward

The basic premise of this service efficiency model is that technology is the primary key to increased productivity and successful operations. The people who deliver the services are less important — so goes the premise. But this premise simply no longer works in the competitive services environment of today. Instead, we need a model that puts customer-contact employees first and then designs the business operations around these people. Four key elements in this new model are:[2]

- Companies value investments in people at least as much as investments in technology.
- Firms use technology to support the work of customer-contact people, rather than using it to monitor or replace these workers.
- Companies make recruiting and training as important for customer-contact employees as for executives.
- Management ties compensation to performance for employees at every level, from bottom to top.

Impact of technology

One of the most important issues facing services companies relates to how technology affects the way services are delivered to customers and how it influences the quality of service provided to them. Certainly, we are unable to avoid technology today. Probably no other force has had the impact on services industries that technology has had in recent years and will continue to have in the future. Everywhere we turn, there is evidence of technology-delivered service, from the myriad ways we can access financial services from our banks, the increasing number of interactive digital channels, and mobile Internet services accessible through our cellular phones.[3]

Many advances in technology certainly make the life of the customer easier, even though the consumer may not even realize the role that technology is playing. Companies that operate call centres to receive incoming calls from customers use sophisticated number-recognition software to direct a customer's call to the person to whom the customer last spoke, thereby helping to build a more personal relationship between an employee and the customer. Manufacturers like Caterpillar use on-board computers to measure the wear on parts and to send a signal to a satellite, which prompts the nearest Caterpillar dealer to contact the customer to replace the part before the customer's equipment fails.

Such use of technology to deliver improved levels of customer service is impressive. But, in service industries, technology has the potential to be a two-edged sword, particularly when you consider the quality of service delivered. While most consumers are familiar with the technology, not all of them wish to use it to do their banking or when they phone a business to make an inquiry. Sure, some people are still not used to it, but others simply prefer not to use it — they don't like it, compared to dealing with actual people and employees of a company.

Sometimes the technology just isn't user-friendly, or just doesn't work reliably. In all of these cases technology gets in the way of good service as defined by the customer. And it is the customer's definition that ultimately matters. Some customers resent efforts by their banks to encourage them to use ATMs or interactive phone systems because they are used to dealing with their favourite bank employee. They are uncomfortable with the interactive voice-response system they encounter when they want to place a collect call. They don't enjoy dealing with voice mail. Encountering technology may discourage these customers from doing business with a company. This is an issue that some companies have begun to address, but many also seem to want to rush headlong into implementation of more technology, without giving much thought to its impact on customers and on their view of the firm.

PAGE UP!

1. What is service quality and why is it difficult to measure?
2. What is service recovery?
3. What is the difference between functional value and emotional value?

Key Terms and Concepts

commercial services 222
core services 221
customer expectations 236
emotional value 236
franchising 229
functional value 236
heterogeneity 224
inseparability 223
intangibility 223
internal marketing 233
perishability 225
service encounter 230
service experience 232
service failure 234
service quality 232
service recovery 234
services 221
services value proposition 226
supplementary services 221
value of a customer 236

Questions and Problems

1. Consider the trends and changes in Canadian life in recent decades as was discussed when you studied environmental scanning. What are these trends and how have these changes in different parts of our lives lead to the growth of services industries?

2. Explain the difference between a core service and a supplementary service. What has caused many marketers of tangible products to focus increasingly on supplementary services?

3. a. Explain the marketing challenges created by each of the characteristics of services discussed in the chapter.
   b. For each of these challenges suggest ways in which companies can try to offset these factors through their marketing.

4. Why have intermediaries been used only occasionally in the marketing programs of service firms? Discuss the role of customer contact centres (call centres) as intermediaries between companies and their customers.

5. Discuss how loyalty programs such as Shoppers Drug Mart Optimum, Delta Privilege, or HBC Rewards add value for customers. Do they lead to genuine loyalty? Why?

6. Present a brief analysis of the market for each of the following service firms. Make use of the components of a market discussed in earlier chapters.
   a. Expedia.ca.
   b. Sheraton Gateway Hotel at Toronto's Pearson airport.
   c. Indoor tennis club.
   d. Credit union.
   e. Avis car rental

7. What are some of the ways in which the following service firms might differentiate themselves? (**Hint:** How can they provide better service than their competitors?)
   a. DVD/video game rental store.
   b. Hairstyling salon.
   c. Internet service provider.
   d. Amazon.ca.

8. Services companies struggle to provide customers with a consistent 'product.' What are the reasons for this? How does the product of a services company differ from products marketed by manufacturers?

9. Develop a brief marketing program for each of the following services. Your presentation should start with a description of the target market you have selected for the service. Then, explain how you would plan, price, promote, and distribute the service.
   a. A clown service for children's birthday parties.
   b. A small vegetarian restaurant near your campus.
   c. A pre-paid cellular phone card company.
   d. An Internet-based dating service.

Hands-On Marketing

1. Consider the college or university that you are currently attending. Take a look at its Web page and by looking through its list of departments and services identify those that are service-related. Can you identify problem areas or potential problems areas when it comers to service provision? What recommendations could you make that might allow your school to deliver better core and supplementary services?

2. In a group of friends or classmates list the most memorable service experiences you have had in the past two weeks; make sure you consider experiences on the Internet. Then consider the following:
   a. List these encounters as core or supplementary services. Would you consider any of these services to actually be supplementary? Explain?
   b. Determine for each encounter if it was a positive, negative, or neutral service encounter. In other words, was the person in your group particularly pleased or displeased with the outcome of the experience — or is he/she pretty much indifferent about the encounter? Why or why not?
   c. Try to find commonalities between these experiences. In other words, are there common reasons that seem to be responsible for these feelings? Are these reasons product-related or people-related? Do any 'themes' exist?
   d. In what ways could service provision be enhanced in each of these cases?

Back to the Top

Think about the example in the chapter opener. Why do you suppose Sandra has been going back to Nadia to have her hair styled for six years? What evidence is there that she has developed a relationship? Is that relationship with Nadia or with the Aveda brand or with the salon? What is her perspective on customer service as it pertains to hair styling? What is important to her? What aspects of the service she receives have contributed to the relationship she has developed?

Online Learning Centre

Want to get better grades, tips on how to study more effectively, and up-to-date information on happenings in the world of marketing? Then, visit the Online Learning Centre for practice tests, Study Smart software, *Marketing Magazine,* and much more! **www.mcgrawhill.ca/olc/sommers**

CHAPTER 9

Branding, Packaging, and Other Product Features

As the example that opens this chapter illustrates, the success of a company depends to a very great extent on the image communicated by its brand. Otherwise, how do you account for some people driving out of their way for their daily trip to Tim Hortons, when there are perfectly acceptable coffee shops located closer to home or the office? Consumer choice is influenced not only by the brand but also by the package, warranty, design, and other features of the product or service. Because these features are important elements in a marketing program, we devote this chapter to them. After studying this chapter, you should have an understanding of:

- The meaning and relevance of brands in our lives.
- Developing brand equity, loyalty, and relationships.
- Characteristics of a successful brand.
- Branding strategies of producers and intermediaries.
- Strategies for branding services.
- The nature and importance of packaging and labelling.
- The marketing implications of other image-building features — design, quality, warranty, and post-purchase service — and how these can increase value for the customer.

Canada's Best Managed Brand

Tim Hortons® is one of Canada's best-known brands. Its very Canadian television commercials and connection to our most loved sport guarantees it a place in the hearts of Canadians. Now, Tim Hortons is considered Canada's best-managed brand as well. In the first annual Canada's Best and Worst Managed Brands Survey, 42 percent of the survey respondents identified Tim Hortons as the best managed brand for reasons such as strong customer service, popular products, prolific community involvement, large number of retail locations, and implementation of an effective business system to deliver its products. Another very important reason cited by the respondents is Tim Hortons' consistent delivery of its brand promise. In other words, Tim Hortons knows what its brand stands for and remains true to it — qualities Canadians seem to like and characteristics that lead to strong brand equity and long-term financial success.

Canadians are on a first- name basis with the brand — like an old friend — Tim Hortons is known to many of their most loyal customers as simply "Tim's." Phrases like "Meet you at Tim's" and "Can I pick you up a Tim's?" illustrate how this brand has become part of the Canadian culture. It's not a Starbucks; it's not even a Second Cup — it's Tim's — the well-known, trusted brand that has become a part of daily life for millions of Canadians. Tim Hortons knows where it is positioned in the minds and hearts of Canadians — just notice the posters for minor hockey that are proudly displayed in the Tim Hortons stores. For Timbits® hockey "The first goal is having fun"® — how Canadian.[1] This snapshot of Tim Hortons, a Canadian icon, illustrates some of this chapter's most important topics: the importance of branding, the characteristics of a successful brand, the importance of building relationships and the relevance of brands to people's lives. Tim Hortons is certainly a successful brand and there are many more good examples of branding in this chapter. As you read, think about the brands that are important to you. Are they brands that you trust because you have always used them? Are they brands that your parents used? Are they new brands that have somehow made an impact on you either through quality, service, or what they stand for?

Brands and Branding

When we think of brands, most of us tend to think of products that we use often and that we have been using, or at least have been familiar with, for many years. Certainly, many well-established brands have been part of our lives and the lives of our families for 50 years or more — Oreo cookies, Campbell's soup, Heinz ketchup, Gillette shaving products, and Wrigley's chewing gum, to name just a few. Other, newer brands have not been available for many years but have achieved near-icon status nonetheless — Swiffer, iPod and Intel are good examples. But brands are just as important in the marketing of services. A retail store name, such as Aldo and Cotton Ginny, is really a brand, as are such names as Yahoo!, eBay, and Google, although these are not applied to tangible products. As we will see in this chapter, some retailers' names have become so trusted and accepted by Canadians that they constitute widely regarded brands in their own right.

brand
The essence of a company; more than the products and services that it markets— how it is presented to customers; what the company stands for; its reputation and image; and what it means to customers.

branding
The process that leads to a company or product acquiring a certain meaning over time; it comes to stand for something in the minds of customers.

The word **brand** is a comprehensive term that has come to mean a great deal in marketing in recent years. In fact, many organizations today are very conscious of the importance and value of their brands and have made **branding** an important part of their management strategy. They pay a lot of attention to what their brands represent and what they mean to customers and prospective customers. The concept of branding refers to the management of the company's brand in such a way as to clarify its meaning, to protect it and to increase its perceived value in the minds of customers.

The application of branding in companies has taken on greater importance in recent years, as companies have come to realize that a brand is much more than a name, and that how it is presented to customers and prospective customers must involve much more than its logo and company colours. A brand is, in fact, one of a company's most valuable assets, and it must be managed as any other investment.

As customers of various companies, we recognize certain firms, products, and services as legitimate brands and others as mere names. Few would deny that Heinz is a major brand, but very few would consider Bob's Ketchup to be a recognizable brand. So, if Bob was to establish a ketchup company, it would take some time to reach the status of Heinz — a status where we would refer to Bob's Ketchup as a recognized brand. What is it, then, that distinguishes brands from mere names? What has to happen for a new company to achieve the status of a brand? Simply put, as some companies mature, their names take on a certain meaning, depending on how consistently they present themselves and position themselves in the marketplace. The most successful brands develop a consistent image and reputation; they come to mean something special to their customers, to occupy a special place in their lives.

As with many such concepts in marketing, brand is an intangible, perceptual concept that resides in the mind of the consumer. On hearing the name Heinz (or Nike, or Oakley, or Nickelback), most of us are able to conjure up images of what the name stands for. The company or brand may mean different things to different people, but there would be some agreement that there is a certain meaning behind the brand, that it stands for something. It is this consistency of brand meaning that companies strive for and that is the objective of their branding strategies. A brand, then, is a name that has over time acquired certain meaning and comes to stand for something in the minds of target customers. In many cases, customers have developed a strong emotional attachment to their favourite brands.

Not all brands have the same meaning for all consumers. In fact, few brands are universal. While the Harley-Davidson brand may mean a great deal to an avid middle-aged biker who enjoys weekend rallies, it may mean nothing at all to someone who has no interest in such pursuits.

The meaning associated with a particular brand is acquired over time as a result of how the brand performs and presents itself, and is very closely related to concepts such as reputation and image, both of which also are perceived by consumers. A company such as FedEx is a recognized and respected brand in the minds of many people because of how it performs. It is a brand that has a reputation for service and an image as a company that is trustworthy and reliable. FedEx doesn't only deliver packages efficiently, it delivers peace of mind — "Relax, It's FedEx."

We see this view of a brand when we consider some of the comments referred to in our chapter opener. Clearly, Tim Hortons is a recognized and respected Canadian brand. In 1997, Tim Hortons introduced its "True Stories" series of commercials. In these commercials, Canadians were introduced to other Canadians who loved their "Tim's." For example, there was Lillian, the older lady who would walk a long distance every day to get a cup of her favourite coffee. Then, there was Cape Breton fiddling sensation, Natalie McMaster, who also loved her "Tim's." From Shorty Jenkins, the ice maker to David Mole, the Canadian student who was studying in Scotland — young and old, at home and abroad, Canadians wanted their Tim Hortons coffee.

These commercials are evidence of the phenomenal brand relationship between real Canadians and Tim Hortons. Tim Hortons has reached out to Canadians by showing that they understand what is important to everyday people — family, friends, relationships and tradition. The advertisements have fostered a trust not only in the products, but in the brand overall. As a result, many Canadians speak of "Tim's" as they would speak of an old friend.

brand mark
The part of a brand that appears in the form of a symbol, picture, design, or distinctive colour or type of lettering.

brand name
The part of a brand that can be vocalized: words, letters, and/or numbers.

In addition to the perceptual side of brands, there are a number of more tangible aspects of branding. A brand is indeed a name, consisting of words, letters, and/or numbers that can be vocalized. But it is more, as we discussed above. A **brand mark** is the part of the brand that appears in the form of a symbol, design, or distinctive colouring or lettering. It is recognized by sight but may not be expressed when a person pronounces the **brand name**. Xerox, Bell Canada, Sony, and Maple Leaf are brand names. Brand marks are illustrated by the distinctive lettering and styling of the name: the Nike "swoosh," the picture of the little girl with pigtails on the Wendy's sign, and the Pillsbury Doughboy. These marks, logos, or designs are usually legally registered and may be used only by the company that owns the mark. In many cases, the company name is the brand, particularly for services companies such as Loblaws, Four Seasons, and eBay.

trademark
A brand that is legally protected.

A **trademark** is defined as a brand that is given legal protection because, under the law, it has been used for some time by one company or organization. A trademark is essentially a legal term. Trademark protection gives the legal owner of the brand the exclusive right to use that brand. All trademarks are brands and thus include words, letters, or numbers that can be pronounced. They may also include a pictorial design (brand mark).

national brands
Brands of tangible products that are generally owned by manufacturers.

private labels
Brands that are owned by retailers.

One major method of classifying brands is on the basis of who owns them — producers or retailers. Major brands such as Sony, Toshiba, Corona, Tide, Levis, and Dove are producers' brands, while Motomaster, President's Choice, Kenmore, Body Shop, and Life are all brands that are owned by retailers. The term **national brand** has been used for many years to describe producer-brand ownership, while brands owned by retailers are generally referred to as **private labels**.

How We View Brands — Building a Brand Strategy

brand awareness
The first stage in building an association between customers and a brand; they become aware of it.

brand recognition
The stage in a brand's association with customers where it is recognized and many customers are familiar with it.

Companies and other organizations may approach brands and branding in a number of different ways. As is generally the case when we discuss such concepts, some business people will view the concept very simplistically, while others will have a greater appreciation for the potential for the concept to add value to their organizations. Such is the case with brands. While some managers think of their brand as the name of the company or product, others will realize that the brand is much more than this and that it has the potential to bond the customer to the company. This is very much related to the role of brands in building customer loyalty and relationships. How marketers manage their brands will determine whether the brand reaches its potential.

The most basic thinking views the brand as the name of the company or product and has as its objective "getting the name out there." In other words, at this stage a company is interested in publicizing its brand, gaining exposure, leading to high levels of **brand awareness** and **brand recognition**. Companies at this stage of the evolution of branding make little distinction between a brand and a name. This is mostly the view of the brand that is held by companies that are launching new products. Their objective is to create brand awareness and gain exposure, often through the expenditure of large amounts on advertising. The thinking is that people are not likely to buy the product if they have never heard of it.

brand characteristics
The stage of the development of a brand relationship in which customers are able to associate certain characteristics with the brand.

A somewhat more sophisticated view of the brand requires that marketers think about what **brand characteristics** they want their product or company to possess. This is part of the brand positioning decision and addresses the question of what the company wants people to think of the brand. The positioning is then achieved through appropriate advertising, packaging, and other forms of communications that are intended to send consumers a message about the kind of product or company this is. At this level of sophistication, marketers would be deciding whether their brand gives the image or impression of being old or young, modern or old-fashioned, simple or complex, local or foreign, fun or boring, high priced or low priced, exclusive or ordinary, and so on.

brand personality
The acquisition by a brand of certain characteristics normally associated with people; reflects the people who are most likely to feel comfortable with and to buy the brand.

BACK TO THE TOP

As it becomes more advanced in its view of branding, a company may begin to think of its product or company as having a certain **brand personality**. At this stage, a company will address the age-old question often asked by marketing researchers: "If this brand was a person, what sort of person would it be?" Again, largely through its communications efforts, a company at this level of thinking would have a strategy to give its brand an appropriate personality. Should the brand be portrayed as friendly or distant, outgoing or reserved, confident or reticent, serious or fun, moody or bubbly? It this sense, the brand begins to take on the characteristics of a person, and marketers can ask themselves whether this is a person with whom a consumer would want to spend time.

brand values
The qualities that are inherent in a brand and that govern how a company or brand conducts itself.

Progressive marketers also talk of **brand values**; what the company or product stands for or represents in the minds of its customers and others. We know immediately that Volvo and Michelin stand for safety of families, and that FedEx stands for reliability and peace of mind. Other companies, Tim Hortons included, present values of community and responsible corporate citizenship through their support for children's camps and other charitable initiatives. Some of the best examples of brand values are to be found in the not-for-profit sector where organizations like the Salvation Army have been consistently delivering a valued service for generations.

brand relationship
The ultimate stage of association between customers and a brand: They have an emotional attachment to it.

This leads nicely into the final and most up-to-date thinking surrounding brands: the creation of **brand relationships**. Consumers develop relationships with brands in precisely the same way that they develop relationships with other people and with companies, as we discussed in Chapter 1. Most of us as consumers can name products and companies that we have been dealing with for many years that are important to our lives. For example, we use a certain shampoo, drive clear across town to get a haircut, and read certain magazines regularly. Consumers often view brands as old friends; they can rely on them. Certain brands contribute to consumers' definition of self and become central to their lives. They develop high levels of brand loyalty, a concept that we will address in the following section. A very important issue that marketers face is how to create a situation in which consumers have a genuine relationship with their brands.

Figure 9-1: The Brand Pyramid

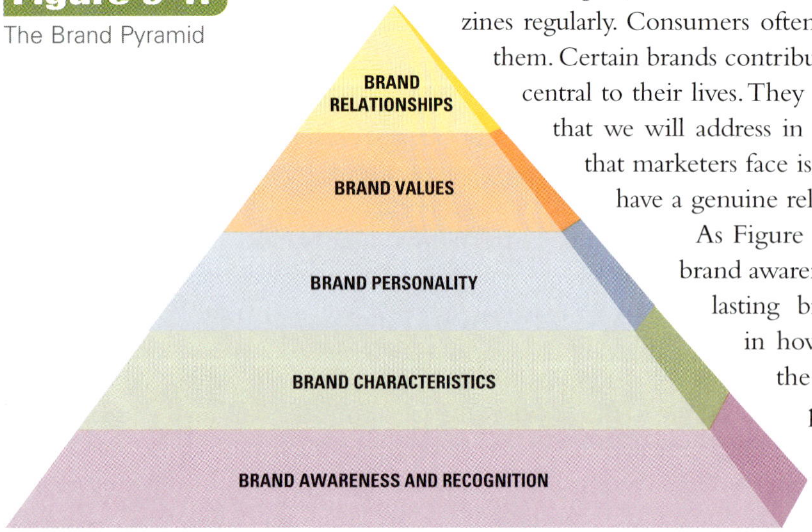

As Figure 9-1 suggests, the progression from a focus on brand awareness to an emphasis on cultivating strong, long-lasting brand relationships represents a development in how sophisticated managers are in their view of the role of brands. As they move up the "brand pyramid," they develop a much more complete view of what branding is all about.

Cultivating Brand Equity and Relationships

brand equity
The value that customers place on a company or brand; its value in their eyes. The higher the sense of loyalty, the greater the level of brand equity.

brand loyalty
The situation in which a customer buys a certain brand on a regular basis because of its performance and appeal.

Companies as diverse as Coca-Cola, Microsoft, Hallmark, Sony, and McCain recognize that the brands they own may be more valuable than physical assets such as buildings and equipment. What we are talking about here is **brand equity**, one of the hottest topics in marketing in recent years. Brand equity relates to the value of a brand as reflected in the loyalty that consumers feel toward it. Thus, Heinz Ketchup has much greater brand equity than Bob's Ketchup. Companies take some time to achieve high levels of brand equity, because it usually takes a long time to develop high levels of **brand loyalty** and relationships. These result from the ongoing provision of various forms of value by the firm to its customers.

Where does the equity in a brand originate? If, over time, large numbers of people enjoy using a particular product or shopping at a certain store, to the point where they buy that product or visit that store on a regular basis and are likely to recommend it to others, we can conclude that they have developed a loyalty to that brand. This loyalty represents a stream of earnings for the company in that the loyal customers keep coming back, buying more, and bringing in their friends or family members. It is the sum total of all such relationships that constitutes the equity in the brand.

A company will often realize the equity in its brands only when it decides to sell the company or one of its product lines to a competitor or a new investor. Ford Motor Company certainly would have paid a premium when it acquired such high-profiles brands as Volvo, Jaguar and Land Rover, as did Procter & Gamble when it bought Gillette.

Brand equity is also the value a brand adds to a product from the perspective of the customer. In the minds of many consumers, just having a brand name such as MEC, Swatch, Oakley, or New Balance on a product adds value to it. Beyond a product's value in its potential to do what it's supposed to do, a brand adds value to that product through its name awareness and its connotations of favourable attributes (such as quality or fashion). Many studies have confirmed that customers are willing to pay a premium price for products that carry recognized and respected brand names. As a result, products such as Heinz Ketchup, Bose and Chanel No. 5 are rarely discounted.

If you're not convinced that a brand name by itself can have much value, consider the results of two studies. In one, the proportion of subjects choosing Corn Flakes cereal jumped from 47 percent when the brand was not known to 59 percent when the brand was identified as Kellogg's. In another study, when a sample of computer buyers were asked how much more or less they would pay for particular brands than they would pay for the average computer brand, there was a range of \$364. Consumers said they would pay \$295 and \$232 more for the IBM and Compaq brands, respectively. Other brands commanding a premium include Apple, Starbucks, Rolex, and Prada.[2] It's evident that such brands have substantial equity.

Today, creating brand equity is about more than positioning, packaging, and imagery. It involves developing a relationship with customers. Customers want brands that they can trust and be happy to tell others about. Developing a brand is a process of creating loyal followers who provide word-of-mouth support and ultimately add equity to the brand and the company.[3] Substantial brand equity provides many benefits to the firm that owns the brand:

- The brand itself can become a differential advantage, influencing consumers to buy a particular product. Examples include Volvo, iPod, Godiva and Bose. Because it is expensive and time-consuming to build brand equity, a barrier is created against competing companies that want to enter the market with a similar product.
- The widespread recognition and favourable attitudes surrounding a brand with substantial brand equity can facilitate international expansion. For example, brands such as Pizza Hut, McDonald's, and Baskin-Robbins are now found literally all over the world. It also explains why new branches of companies such as Boston Pizza are often instant successes as soon as they open.

GUEST MARKETER

Kraft Dinner Macaroni & Cheese: Growing a Canadian Brand Icon

By Bruce Hunter

Bruce Hunter is the President of Lighthouse 360, a Toronto-based marketing and strategy consultancy. Prior to establishing this successful business, he served as VP of Marketing for Kraft Canada, GM of Kraft's Foodservice Division, and led the integration of Nabisco into Kraft. He has a B. Comm. from Queen's University.

The situation facing Brenda was daunting. Since she took over the Kraft Dinner Brand Manager spot, this Canadian icon brand faced increased competition from retail store private label brands. It is always a challenge to strike the right balance when your customer becomes a competitor. Several national chains had cut back the shelf facings for the national Kraft brand and reduced the amount of stock available. In addition, shelf position had been altered to favour the store's own brand. The net effect of this activity in the early 1990s was share of market and category declines for the Kraft Dinner brand. Brenda didn't know where to turn.

Brenda's concern was well founded. Kraft Dinner had grown from lowly beginnings in 1937 to become the number-one selling item in Canada's grocery stores and was a true brand icon. Everyone had a story about Kraft Dinner macaroni and cheese. The brand was introduced by J. L Kraft following his success in building his cheese business. Interestingly, the product had originally been introduced in order to sell more cheese and had grown to be a family favourite. At the time that Brenda had taken over responsibility for the brand in Canada, it had the leadership share of the category. In Canada, the brand sold over three times more than it sold in the entire United States! However, it now had a strong and good competitor.

What was Brenda to do?

The traditional response to competition in the grocery products business was to increase spending on trade promotions. While somewhat effective in the short term, the cost of these programs had to come from somewhere and that somewhere was the other elements of the marketing mix. The consumer-directed initiatives like advertising, consumer promotion, product innovation and product formulation were reduced to fund the increased focus on promoting to the retail trade. Consumer focus turned away from the power of the brand name.

Brenda looked at this situation and to her credit, chose to compete smarter with a broad array of marketing tactics across the total marketing mix directed toward reinforcing the credentials of the Kraft Dinner brand with the consumer. However, such pro-competitive activity comes at a significant cost! In fact, she presented her management with a plan that reduced the profitability of the brand in the short term. By the end of the decade, she would have re-established the place of Kraft Dinner with the Canadian consumer, driven significant new innovation and improved profitability of the brand. A tremendous turnaround — and here's how she did it.

The plan was comprehensive. From a product standpoint, Brenda observed that one of the key differentiators of the Kraft brand was its cheese. Consumers had often noted through focus groups and more stringent quantitative research that the Kraft Dinner cheese was a key piece of the brand's formulation. For consumers, the "cheesier" the better. After some initial consumer tests, the first thing Brenda did was to increase the quantity of the cheese flavour in Kraft Dinner. This meant a significant quality improvement and served to differentiate it from private-label competitors. In order to announce this change, she also redesigned the packaging graphics to contemporize the brand image and signal a change. The new package design reflected the strength and leadership position of the brand. Once the packaging was done for the base, she turned to the promotion, both advertising and consumer.

Advertising was a challenge. She wanted to break through with a leadership message and debated over a number of ways to go to market. The tough thing about advertising for a product as well known as Kraft Dinner is exactly that...it's already very well known, so there's not much you can tell consumers that they don't already know. She elected to go with a leadership, emotional feel for the advertising directed at moms with younger kids. As we'll see later, this advertising was not as effective as another campaign introduced subsequently. As she turned to consumer promotion, she directed her efforts to supporting the new news on the base brand and extended the sampling program. Consumers needed to taste the new formulation and experience its superiority to the new competitor.

Innovation was also critically important. The Kraft sales group contributed to a new idea. Why not sell multiple packages of Kraft Dinner as a promotion package? For very limited and discreet periods of time (initially only two times per year) Kraft would offer promotional packages of 18-packs of Kraft Dinner at a reduced price per box from the regular price. This encouraged multiple purchases and got the new quality-improved brand into consumers' hands. The tactic worked brilliantly and became a mainstay for the brand for a number of years.

The next decision Brenda made was to innovate and flank the base brand. For a number of years, Kraft had offered some flanking products. Products directed to children, like the Flintstones and others offering shapes like Kraft Spirals. She knew that her pro-competitive response to private label needed to include a revamp of these sub-lines as well. In order to do this, she quickly put into place an aggressive timetable for innovation and consumer testing of new products.

Over 100 ideas were generated and put into consumer testing. Of these ideas, several were identified as having significant potential and were then commercialized. With so many to choose from, Brenda created a staged plan that would see these new products introduced in sequence over the next few years. She had built an array of product innovations to capture consumers' attention.

To leverage the base Kraft Dinner brand, Brenda changed the look of the packaging. The packaging of the line was converted to base-brand blue so that the position and impact on shelf would be markedly improved. Over the next few years, the Canadian consumer would come to know new products such as White Cheddar, Extra Creamy, Three Cheese, Sharp, Cheese and Tomato, Easy Mac and even Kraft Spaghetti. (The latter was not successful; but it was a good thought.)

All of these products served to support the Kraft Dinner brand. But what about the advertising we had talked about earlier?

One of the real breakthroughs that led to further success for Kraft Dinner was a change of target audience. When the advertising that we referred to earlier proved to be relatively ineffective, a new round of consumer research was commissioned to determine why. The brand group threw out its previous conceptions about the brand and spent countless hours listening to consumers tell stories about Kraft Dinner. It soon became apparent that the brand group had missed the mark. Kraft Dinner was talked about in reverent terms. It was a rite of passage. Everyone had a story about how the brand had been an integral part of their lives. All the brand group had to do was to capture that relationship in its creative. It could move from a "Mom's brand" to "My brand." It could be edgy and alive. That was the breakthrough. The advertising reflected that feeling by capturing a universal consumer experience with the brand (university setting) and the results were staggering.

Brenda created a brilliant marketing program that played out over the ensuing years. She set in place a plan which touched all elements of the marketing mix and focused on creating consumer value. She reinvested in base brand product quality, revamped packaging, introduced new products and contemporized advertising and consumer promotion. To her credit, Kraft Dinner remains a growing and vibrant Canadian brand icon.

- Brand equity can help a product survive changes in the operating environment, such as a business crisis or a shift in consumer tastes. Although The Gap brand is undergoing some pressure to remain relevant as its target market matures, it probably has enough brand equity to allow it to transition to its next positioning.[4] In 2004, The Gap introduced clothes that would allow this maturing target market to dress up their wardrobes for work and social occasions. The introduction of Sarah Jessica Parker (of *Sex and the City* fame) and later Joss Stone as spokespersons for the brand helped celebrate the individual style around which The Gap had built its brand. Maintaining its casual weekend apparel while introducing more "grown-up" pieces has allowed The Gap to use its brand equity to change with target market needs.[5]

brand extensions
New products or services that are launched by a company under an existing brand name.

Brand equity is often valuable in allowing a company to expand a product line, especially to extend a brand into new varieties or even new products. A company will use a strategy of **brand extensions** when it has a very strong brand with lots of equity, bringing out new related products under the existing brand. The view is that the relationship consumers have with the original brand is so strong that it will allow the firm to transfer that confidence and trust to new products under the same name. In fact, it may be argued that brand extensions are not possible unless the parent brand has established considerable equity. Examples include a wide variety of Ocean Spray (**www.oceanspray.com**) products, including juices that extend far beyond the cranberry flavour the company is known for and Craisins, dried cranberries in assorted flavours usually found in the produce department.

Ocean Spray

A brand that developed a high level of brand equity very quickly is Swiffer, the dry mop from Procter & Gamble. Only six years after the launch of the brand, there are now many extensions to the Swiffer brand, including the Swiffer Wet, Swiffer Dusters, Swiffer Max, Swiffer WetJet and the new Swiffer CarpetFlick. Procter & Gamble has effectively used the brand relationship with the original Swiffer Dry and all subsequent products into a brand extension

MARKETING AT WORK — 9-1: STRATEGY

Chocolate is Still in Vogue

In 2005, Cadbury Adams Canada Inc. launched a "master brand" strategy with new products, rebranded packaging and marketing that included models wearing "chocolate couture." To start, Cadbury Adams developed eight new chocolate bars specifically for Canadians. One example is the new Cadbury Thins, a tiny 100-calorie chocolate bar targeted at women who want portion control.

The company also made changes to the packaging by adding its signature purple colour to all of its brands. It seems that many consumers did not recognize Crispy Crunch®, Crunchie® and Mr. Big® as Cadbury Adams products. By adding the purple to the packaging, Cadbury Adams hoped to build synergies between brands and promote new products based on the trust consumers have in established Cadbury® brands such as Cadbury Creme Egg® and Caramilk®.

Of course, there can be a negative impact with such a strategy. If there is a problem with one brand it can negatively impact other products.

To promote the new products and packaging, Cadbury Adams launched contests and held a chocolate couture fashion show. Lesya Lysyj, Senior Vice-President of Marketing, says that the fashion show, "was all about bringing together two things women love most, which is fashion and chocolate."

QUESTIONS:

1. What evidence is there that Cadbury® is more than a name, that is it indeed a brand?
2. Why is it important that consumers know that a chocolate bar is a Cadbury-branded product? Think about the role of colour in communicating brand positioning.

SOURCE: Adapted from Rebecca Harris, "Sweet rebranding," *Marketing Magazine*, November 7, 2005.

Swiffer has spawned many brand extensions in a relatively short time.

of seven products, with new extensions seeming to come along every month or so. The rationale for using an existing, strong brand name on a new item or line is that the brand's equity will convey a favourable impression of the product and increase the likelihood that consumers will at least try it.

Some retailer brands have succeeded in acquiring considerable brand equity, often in competition with long-established manufacturers' brands. Examples include President's Choice (Loblaws), Motomaster (Canadian Tire), and Life (Shoppers Drug Mart). In these cases, what started out as private-label brands have now, because of the trust that consumers place in them, evolved into full national brand status, because they have the strength of major retailers behind them. Some online retailers have succeeded in achieving a similar status, to the point where companies such as Lands' End, L.L. Bean, and Eddie Bauer stock only their own brands.

PAGE UP!

1. What is a brand? How is it different from a name?
2. Define brand equity.
3. When a company has a very strong brand, it will often bring out new, related products under the existing brand. This strategy is called ______________________.

What's in a Name?

The history of brand marketing shows that once a brand establishes a position of leadership in a product category, this position is often maintained over a very long period of time. Many of the leading brands that we buy today were purchased regularly by our parents and even our grandparents. Brands that continue to dominate their consumer product categories include General Electric, Kellogg, Levis, Kraft, Nabisco, Heinz, Tide, Crest, and Campbell.

Other brands have been around for a much shorter time, and have nevertheless succeeded in becoming brand leaders within their product or service category. Many of these are recognizable manufacturers of technology products, including Nokia, Intel, Samsung, Canon, BlackBerry and Apple. But, others are acknowledged leaders in service industries, including Starbucks, Yahoo!, the Running Room, and Chapters-Indigo. What distinguishes these relatively new companies from those that have been around a lot longer is that they have been particularly innovative in a new industry sector and have been largely responsible for the growth of that sector. In some cases they may be said to define and dominate the sector, or to practically "own" it.

NikeID

The development and protection of brand names has become a very important element of marketing management and one that demands increased attention all of the time. Companies such as Nike have made conscious decisions to manage their brand names in such a way that they dominate their product category. Nike defined itself early as a leader when it convinced several US marathoners to wear Nike shoes during the 1972 Olympic time trials in Eugene, Oregon. When some the athletes made the team, Nike wasted no time running an ad that said, "Nikes were worn by four of the top seven finishers." Nike has since ensured through product innovation, brand extensions and celebrity endorsements that it remains the dominant name in athletic equipment and apparel.[6] Today, NikeID (**www.nikeid.nike.com**) allows athletes to customize their own products online. A customer starts with a blank product, chooses design features such as colour and adds the ID. The customer can review the design, play around with it some more and choose whether or not to buy it.

A relatively new brand leader.

By stretching the original successful brand name to cover a number of brand extensions, the marketer is trading on the success of the original brand, but is also running some risk. Clearly, there may be some new products to which the original brand should not be applied. This raises the question of how far the successful brand can be extended before the marketer is stretching the credibility of the link between the brand and the product. Roots, the Canadian company once famous for its revolutionary leather footwear, has long sold leisure wear but has tried to extend the brand to include home furnishings and a remote forest getaway resort.[7] In January 2006, Roots and Sears announced that Roots furnishings and home décor items will be available at Sears Home Stores and sears.ca. This will give Roots a larger market for these items.[8]

Some natural brand extensions include the Tide to Go stain removal pen and Iams pet insurance. Nike has added fitness apparel, bags and new lines of shoes for skateboarding. These are all natural extensions of the Nike brand, but would consumers buy Nike kitchen appliances or electronics? Brand extensions that clearly didn't fit with the brand's core values and stretched the boundaries are the Harley Davidson cake decorating kit and the Evian water-filled bra!

Brands make it easy for consumers to identify goods and services. Brands also help to assure purchasers that they are getting comparable quality when they reorder. For sellers, brands can be advertised and recognized when displayed on shelves in a store. Branding also helps sellers control their markets, because buyers will not confuse one branded product with another. Branding reduces price comparisons because it is hard to compare prices on two items with different brands. Finally, for sellers, branding can add a measure of prestige to otherwise ordinary commodities (Sunkist oranges, Sifto salt, Lantic sugar, Highliner fish, Chiquita bananas).[9]

Selecting a good brand name

Some brand names are so good and so appropriate that they contribute to the sales success of the product or service; others are so poor or inappropriate that they appear to contribute little if anything to sales success and may even seem to be a factor in market failures. Some products appear to have been successful despite having names that may seem to add little to their appeal. Some brand names attain considerable value over time and remain customer favourites for many years. It takes some time for the name of a product, service, or company to achieve the status where it becomes a "brand." The word itself implies that customers recognize the name and attach some meaning to it.

The challenge Today, selecting a good name for a product or service is more challenging than ever. The reason is that we are running out of possibilities — many of the good names have already been used. Many thousands of new products are launched annually in North America, yet the standard desk-size dictionary contains only about 50,000 words. When you consider that a new brand can't be labelled Panasonic, Oreo, Esso, or Timex because these brands have been used successfully for many years, and that there are many other words you would not want to have associated with your product or service, it is no surprise that companies often resort to words that aren't really words, or that they bring out the new product as an extension of an already successful brand.

Many company and brand names have now achieved a certain status, but at one time they probably meant very little to consumers. Only over time have these names become recognizable and respected brands. Consider, for example, the names of companies such as Ford and Kraft. At one time, these were family names only — the name of the person who started the company. What if Henry Ford had been born Henry Murphy? Would many families all over the world now have Murphys parked in their driveways?

IKEA

Most people have shopped at IKEA (**www.ikea.com**) but many may not realize where the name came from. It is not a Scandinavian word for furnishings; rather, it is the fabrication of the guy who started the company, Ingvar Kamprad. It is easy to see where the I and the K come from. Since Ingvar grew up on a farm called Elmtaryd, we have I-K-E. Elmtaryd is in a town called Agunnaryd. I-K-E-A. And that's how this company got named. So, the IKEA name itself doesn't mean anything in particular to most people, but the brand certainly does.

The need for names and brands that are likely to contribute to a product's success has led to the establishment of companies that specialize in coming up with attractive and appealing brand names. These firms use database searches and rely on unusual sources to identify likely names. Some even employ qualified linguists on staff, often coming up with names that aren't part of any language: Pentium (Intel's microprocessor chip), Zoloft (a new pharmaceutical product), Lexus, Acura, and Compaq. Branding on the Internet through Web addresses has been approached in a similar manner, with sites such as fundu.com or imandi.com. The creation of a new brand name often involves research to determine whether consumers will react positively to the brand being proposed. It's an expensive process, as some branding firms will charge $25,000 or more for a new brand name.[10]

Desirable characteristics Five characteristics determine the desirability of a brand name for a product or service.[11] While it is difficult to think of one that has all five, a brand name should possess as many of these characteristics as possible:

- ***Suggest something about the product's characteristics (its benefits, use, or action):*** Some names that suggest desirable benefits include Beautyrest, Motomaster, and — perhaps best of all — DieHard. Product use and action are suggested by Hi-Liter, La-Z-Boy, Mr. Clean, and Easy-Off. Or Web site addresses such as GardenCrazy.com, or clickabid.com.

- ***Be easy to pronounce, spell, and remember:*** Simple, short, one-syllable names such as Tide, Ban, Aim, and Raid are helpful. Top-Cuts, Weed Man, and Speedy are other examples of brand names that are easy to remember. However, even some short names, such as nynex and Aetna, aren't easily pronounced by some customers.

- ***Be distinctive:*** Brands with names like National, Star, Ideal, or Standard fail on this point. Many services firms begin their brand names with adjectives connoting strength and then add a description of the business, creating brands such as Allied Van Lines and United Parcel Service. Some brand names play on patriotism as, for example, Maple Leaf food products, Air Canada, and Molson Canadian.
- ***Be adaptable to new products that may be added to the product line:*** An innocuous name such as Kellogg or Lipton may serve the purpose better than a highly distinctive name suggestive of product benefits. Frigidaire is an excellent name for a refrigerator and other cold-image products. But when the producer expanded its line of home appliances and added Frigidaire kitchen ranges, the name may have lost some of its sales appeal. Amazon.com suggests a huge selection and/or inventory of any product, but has come to be associated primarily with a huge choice of books and music.
- ***Be capable of being registered and legally protected under the Trade-marks Act and other statutory or common laws***: Names that are generic and in common usage in the English language would not meet this criterion. For example, the word "water" used as a name could not by itself be registered and legally protected. Names must also not already be registered or in use by other firms.

Protecting a brand name

Over a period of years, some brands have become so well accepted that the brand name is substituted for the generic name of the particular product. Examples of brand names that legally have become generic are linoleum, celluloid, cellophane, kerosene, shredded wheat, and nylon. Originally, these were trademarks limited to use by the owner. Current brands that have become synonymous with what they do are Google and BlackBerry. When a brand becomes a verb — as in "I must Google that" or "I think I'll Xerox that article," it is in danger of becoming generic.

A brand name can become generic in several ways. Sometimes the patent on a product expires. There is no simple generic name available, so the public continues to use the brand name as a generic name. This happened with shredded wheat, nylon, and cellophane. Sometimes a firm just does too good an advertising and selling job with an outstanding brand name. While not yet legally generic, names such as Xerox, Aspirin, Band-Aid, Scotch Tape, Ski-Doo, and Kleenex are on the borderline in Canada. Some of these brands have already lost their trademark protection in other countries. For example, in the United States and Great Britain, one can buy many brands of aspirin.

It is the responsibility of the trademark owner to assert the company's rights in order to prevent the loss of the distinctive character of the trademark. A number of strategies are employed to prevent the brand name from falling into generic usage. The most common strategy is to ensure that the word "trademark" or "TM®" appears adjacent to the brand name wherever it is used. A second strategy is to use two names — the brand name together with either the company's name or the generic name of the product such as HP Scanjet Scanner or Apple iPod. A third strategy for protecting a trademark involves the incorporation into the trademark of a distinctive signature or logo.

Branding Strategies

Both producers and intermediaries face strategic decisions regarding the branding of their goods or services. Whether a firm is branding a product or a service, some fundamental things need to be kept in mind. Branding is a means of creating and maintaining a perception of customer value.

There is an expectation on the part of the customer that the brand name stands for quality and other values and characteristics. Branding also provides the means of differentiating products and services from those of the competition. When consumers see the offerings as all being alike, there is a tendency to shop on the basis of price. Branding provides consumers with another reason to choose a product. When brands provide better quality in products and services, they tend to be remembered by the consumer.[12] This is brand differentiation.

BACK TO THE TOP

Product-branding strategies are often viewed differently than are services-branding strategies. Services branding is generally synonymous with the name of the company. The best example of services branding is franchising, in which companies such as Avis, Boston Pizza, and Tim Hortons sell the rights to their name and products to independent franchisees. The brand or name has come to stand for a service encompassing recognizable features. For example, McDonald's represents fast service, a children's focus, and consistent products. Other examples of services branding include hotel chains like Fairmont or Hilton, and professional-service companies, including consulting firms such as Accenture and Ernst & Young. Sometimes, service products are licensed for sale by intermediaries. An example of this is a training facility that delivers Microsoft training programs.

Producers' strategies

Manufacturers must decide whether to brand their products and whether to sell any or all of their output under intermediaries' brands.

Marketing entire output under manufacturers' own brands Companies that market their entire output under their own brands usually are very large, well financed, and well managed. Procter & Gamble, Maytag, and IBM are examples. They have broad product lines, well-established distribution systems, and large market share. They generally have enough demand for products branded with their own names that they have no need to make products for other companies.

MARKETING AT WORK — 9-2: ETHICS

Support for the Brand

A telephone research project conducted by Corbin Partners of Toronto involved trained interviewers calling more than 160 La Senza lingerie stores across Canada to enquire about a new line of IPEX bras. The results of the research showed that clerks in more than 60 percent of La Senza stores confirmed that the IPEX product was either in stock or expected to arrive soon.

No surprise so far, but the kicker is that La Senza does not manufacture or sell the IPEX brand. Who does? Actually, IPEX is a brand made and sold by La Senza's major U.S. competitor, Victoria's Secret, who just happened to be Corbin's client and had commissioned the research. Why was Victoria's Secret interested in knowing whether La Senza store clerks thought they stocked IPEX bras? It's all part of a legal battle between the two retailers concerning IPEX and a competing bra sold by La Senza branded ITEC, which not only has a similar name but is also marketed with a similar marketing campaign and model, leading to confusion, as Corbin's research revealed, even among La Senza employees.

Victoria's Secret, armed with the research results, hired a law firm to take the matter to court, alleging that La Senza was trying to divert some of Victoria's Secret's sales of its successful IPEX bra in Canada by using a confusing marketing campaign. The research, conducted with the public as well as with La Senza employees, confirmed the confusion between the two brands.

QUESTIONS:

1. What do the research results suggest is happening in the minds of consumers with respect to the two brands?
2. Why is it important to Victoria's Secret to protect its brand in this way?
3. What does this tell us about the value of brands?

SOURCE: Adapted from Jacquie McNish, "Lawyers provide support behind bra wars," *The Globe and Mail*, April 26, 2006, p. B9.

Some reasons for adopting this policy have already been covered in the section on the importance of branding to the seller. In addition, intermediaries often prefer to handle producers' brands, especially when the brands have high consumer acceptance.

co-branding
A branding strategy that involves two or more brands appearing on the same product. Both brands benefit because they are mutually supportive and a good "fit."

Co-branding of parts and ingredients Some producers of fabricating materials and parts (products used in the further manufacturing of other goods) brand those products along with the manufacturer's brand in a form of **co-branding** strategy. This strategy is used in the marketing of Fiberglas insulation, Pella windows, Dolby noise reduction, Intel processors, and many automotive parts — spark plugs, batteries, oil filters. DuPont has consistently and successfully used this strategy, notably with its Lycra Spandex fibre and Stainmaster stain repellent for carpets. Gore-Tex is another brand that is prominently featured in clothing and footwear.

Underlying this strategy is the seller's desire to develop a market preference for its branded part or material. For instance, G.D. Searle Ltd. wants to build a market situation in which customers will insist on food products sweetened with NutraSweet, so that food manufacturers will be convinced that their sales will be increased if their products contain NutraSweet. Similarly, a parts manufacturer wants to persuade a producer of a finished item that using its branded materials will help to sell the end-product. Intel has used this strategy by having its logo on computers made by a variety of manufacturers. Consumers have demanded the Intel microprocessor and have come to look for and rely on the Intel brand.

Certain product characteristics lend themselves to the effective use of this strategy. First, it helps if the product is also a consumer good that is bought for replacement purposes. This factor encourages the branding of Champion spark plugs and Fram oil filters, for example. Second, the seller's situation is improved if the item is a major part of the finished product — a microprocessor in a personal computer, for instance. Intel Corp. developed the slogan "Intel Inside" to strengthen its product's position. By having "Intel Inside" prominently displayed on the front of the laptop, Intel ensured that this component would be known by its brand name. Many people can tell you if their computer has Intel inside, but may not be able to remember the brand name of the computer. Computer manufacturers realize that consumers are looking for the Intel logo and that this increases consumer confidence in the product overall.

Marketing under intermediaries' brands A widespread strategy is for producers to brand part or all of their output with the brands of their intermediary customers. For example, a manufacturer of salad dressing makes products for Loblaw Companies Limited, and they are sold under the President's Choice label. For the manufacturer, this intermediary's brand business generates additional sales volume and profit. Orders typically are large, payment is prompt, and a producer's working-capital position is improved. Also, manufacturers may use their production resources more effectively, including their plant capacities. Furthermore, refusing to sell under a retailer's or wholesaler's brand will not eliminate competition from this source. Many intermediaries want to market under their own brands, so if one manufacturer refuses their business, they will simply go to another.

Intermediaries' strategies

The question of whether or not to brand the products they carry must also be answered by intermediaries. There are two strategies that are typically followed:

Carry only manufacturers' brands Most retailers and wholesalers follow this policy because they are not able to take on the dual burdens of promoting a brand and maintaining its quality. This is especially the case with smaller retailers, such as local shoe stores, whose volume of business is not sufficient to allow them to contract with a manufacturer for products labelled with the store's own brand.

Carry retailers' brands alone or with manufacturers' brands Many large retailers and some large wholesalers have their own brands. In fact, some of the most successful brands in recent years have been retailers' own brands, including President's Choice from Loblaw Companies Limited, Motomaster from Canadian Tire, and Life from Shoppers Drug Mart. Intermediaries may find it advantageous to market their own brands for several reasons. First, this strategy increases their control over their market. If customers prefer a given retailer's brand, they can get it only from that retailer's store. Furthermore, intermediaries can usually sell their brands at prices below those of producers' brands and still earn higher gross margins. This is possible because intermediaries can buy at lower prices. The costs may be lower because (1) manufacturers' advertising and selling costs are not included in their prices or (2) producers are anxious to get the extra business to keep their plants running in slack seasons.

Intermediaries have more freedom in pricing products sold under their own labels. Products carrying a retailer's brand become differentiated products, and this hinders price comparisons that might be unfavourable to that retailer. Also, prices on manufacturers' brands can be cut drastically by competing retail stores. This last point is what has been happening in recent years in the marketing of clothing with designer labels such as Calvin Klein, DKNY, Ralph Lauren, Fendi, and Hugo Boss. Some of the large retailers' upper-priced clothing departments have increased their stocks of apparel carrying the store's own brand. These stores have cut back on products with designer brands such as Calvin Klein and others. The reason for this brand-switching is that some designer-labelled products are now available at much lower prices in stores such as Wal-Mart, Zellers, and other "off-price" retailers.

The strategy of marketing as many products as possible under the retailer's own label has met with considerable success for such Canadian retailers as Loblaw Companies Limited and Canadian Tire. In fact, Loblaw Companies Limited is among the leading companies in the world in the private-label business, creating a situation where more than 30 percent of all Loblaw Companies Limited sales are accounted for by private-label products such as President's Choice Decadent cookies, Blue Menu natural and healthy products, and now Joe Fresh Style™ clothing. In fact, Loblaw Companies Limited has been so successful at developing the market for private-label products that the company has licensed the President's Choice brand to chains around the world. It has even extended the PC brand into financial services. Loblaw Companies Limited is an excellent example of how private-label products can replace national brands in the consumer's mind when the retailer develops products and value in which the consumer can be confident.[13]

Loblaws has entered the fashion world with Joe Fresh.

Another large Canadian grocery retailer, Sobeys has increased its private label presence by introducing lines of premium and seasonal products that consumers want but without the high price tag. The Compliments Seasonal Collections was introduced in Fall 2005 and included 30 products, and the Compliments Sensations line included 50 new premium products. Sobeys plans to carry its seasonal private label brand extensions into Easter and Thanksgiving.[14]

Strategies common to manufacturers and intermediaries

Manufacturers and intermediaries alike must adopt some strategy in relation to branding their product mix and branding for market saturation.

Branding a line of products/services At least four different strategies are widely used by firms that sell more than one product or service:

- The same "family" or "blanket" brand may be placed on all products. This policy is followed by Heinz, Catelli, Campbell, McCain, and others in the food industry. Other examples include the YM-YWCA and Pizza Hut.

- A separate name may be used for each product. This strategy is employed by Procter & Gamble and Unilever. Pampers are produced by Procter & Gamble; Dove soap is a Unilever product.
- A separate family brand may be applied to each grade of product or to each group of similar products or services. Sears groups its major home appliances under the Kenmore name, its paints and home furnishings under Harmony House, and its insurance under Allstate.
- The company trade name may be combined with an individual name for the product or service: Johnson's Pledge, Microsoft's Excel, Kellogg's Rice Krispies, Molson Export, the Royal Bank's VISA, and Ford Mustang.

family-brand strategy
A branding strategy in which a group of related products is given a single brand.

When used wisely, a **family-brand strategy** has considerable merit. This strategy makes it much simpler and less expensive to introduce new related products to a line. Also, the general prestige of a brand can be spread more easily if it appears on several products rather than on only one. A family brand is best suited for a marketing situation when the products are related in quality, use, or some other manner.

The success of major brands and families of brands certainly makes it easier for companies, whether manufacturers or intermediaries, to introduce new products under an established family brand or as brand extensions to well-established brands. This is obvious when one considers the number of varieties of Oreo cookies and Ritz crackers now produced by Nabisco and the wide array of products marketed under the Motomaster label by Canadian Tire. But the use of family brands and established brands to launch new products places a burden on the brand owner to maintain consistently high quality across all products marketed under that brand. One bad item can reflect unfavourably on other products that carry the brand and may even lead to the creation of a negative image for the overall brand.

multiple-brand strategy
A strategy in which a firm has more than one brand of essentially the same product, aimed either at the same target market or at distinct target markets.

Tide

Branding for market saturation

Frequently, to increase its degree of market saturation, a firm will employ a **multiple-brand strategy**. Suppose, for example, that a company has built one type of sales appeal around a given brand. To reach other segments of the market, the company can use other appeals with other brands. For example, Procter & Gamble markets a line of detergents that includes Tide, Bold, Cheer, and Ivory Snow. There may be some consumers who feel that Tide, even with its many varieties (phosphate-free, with bleach, unscented, liquid, regular, high-efficiency Tide, Tide with Febreze, Tide with a touch of Downy, and Tide Coldwater, to name a few), is not suitable for washing lingerie and other delicate clothing. For these people, Procter & Gamble offers Ivory Snow, a detergent whose image is gentler than that of Tide and trades on its association with the purity and gentleness of Ivory soap. With this brand line-up, Procter & Gamble is assured of having a brand or a brand variation to appeal to every segment of the detergent market.

Co-branding strategies

In addition to the strategies mentioned above, some companies carry brands of other producers in association with their own or even promote them together. This is another form of co-branding in which companies feature the brands of the products they serve or of companies with which they have partnership arrangements. For example, Air Canada entered into an agreement to serve in-flight food items made by Harvey's, Subway, Montana's and Swiss Chalet. McDonald's has an agreement with Wal-Mart to set up outlets inside its stores, and Starbucks has a similar arrangement with Chapters-Indigo. Many large hotel chains prominently display to conference delegates during coffee breaks that they "proudly serve Starbucks coffee." Extending the "Intel Inside" marketing approach is Chiquita which is branding the bananas in Ben and Jerry's 'Chunky Monkey' ice cream and Lexus is offering Mark Levinson audio systems in their cars.[15]

Some brands have even become "umbrella" brands or brand warehouses inside which other brands happily cooperate. For example, Aeroplan began in the 1980s as the frequent-flyer program of Air Canada. Today it has evolved into a major brand in its own right and has entered into partnerships with some of Canada's largest companies. The co-branded Aerogold card from CIBC is the most widely-carried credit card in Canada. But, American Experss now also offers an AeroplanPlus card. Imperial Oil, Hilton, Delta, Fairmont and most other major hotel chains, Future Shop, Avis, Hertz, Bell and Rogers are all Aeroplan partners whose brands appear alongside the Aeroplan brand, thereby benefiting from the association. (**www.aeroplan.com**)

Aeroplan

PAGE UP!

1. To be successful, a brand name should have many or all of five characteristics. What are they?
2. What are the dangers of a brand name becoming generic?
3. In what circumstances would a firm consider using a multiple-brand strategy? A co-branding strategy?

Packaging

packaging
For products, the activities in product planning that involve designing and producing the container or wrapper for a product; for services, bundling and promotion activities are involved.

Packaging is usually defined as all of the activities of designing and producing the container or wrapper for a physical product. Generally, we think of packaging in the context of physical products, and consumer products in particular — breakfast cereal, toothpaste, soft drinks — but services can also be packaged, even though they are not wrapped in brightly coloured boxes or displayed in containers.

Packaging involves making the appearance of the collection of goods or services more attractive to the consumer. There are three reasons for packaging:

- Packaging of tangible products often serves several safety and utilitarian purposes. It protects a product on its route from the producer to the final customer, and in some cases, even while it is being used by the customer. Effective packaging can help prevent product tampering. Some protection is provided by child-proof caps on containers of pharmaceutical products and others that are potentially harmful to children. Also, compared with bulk items, packaged goods generally are more convenient, cleaner, and less susceptible to losses from evaporation, spilling, and spoilage.

- Packaging may play an important promotional role in a company's marketing program. Packaging helps identify a product and so may prevent substitution of competitive products. At the point of purchase, the package can serve as a silent salesperson. Furthermore, the advertising messages on the package will last as long as the product is used in its packaged form. A package may be the only significant way in which a firm can differentiate its product. In the case of convenience goods or business operating supplies, for example, many buyers may feel that one well-known brand is about as good as another. The package may be designed in such a way as to set a largely undifferentiated core product apart from its competition. Altoids, "the curiously strong mints," are packaged in a metal tin — not because they have to be, but because it sets them apart from "ordinary" mints. The NikeTown retail stores could be considered as one big "package" for Nike products.

  Some feature of the package may add sales appeal — a reusable jar or a self-applicator (a bottle of shoe polish or glue with an applicator top, for example). Heinz Ketchup introduced squeezable no-drip bottles (contoured for little hands) that mothers love, which eliminate spills and that messy crust that used to form around the neck of the bottle. Colgate introduced 2-in-1 toothpaste and mouthwash in slim, easy-to-carry, flip-top bottles. Other marketers have been quick to duplicate these strategies. Concentrated formulations of cleaning solutions can be marketed as adding convenience by virtue of being smaller, lighter, and more environmentally friendly. Refill pouches for several household cleaning products serve this purpose.

  Packaging may even drive sales promotion initiatives, as in Tim Hortons' annual "R-R-Roll up the Rim to Win" promotion.

BACK TO THE TOP

- A firm can package its product in a way that increases profit and sales volume. A physical package that is easy to handle or minimizes damage losses will cut marketing costs, thus boosting profit. The previously discussed changes to several cleaning products helped to reduce transportation and storage costs, as well as attracting environmentally sensitive consumers. On the sales side, packaged goods typically are more attractive and therefore can be perceived as being better than items sold in bulk. Many companies have increased the sales volume of an article simply by redesigning its package. Diet Pepsi redesigned the look of its can a few years ago to revitalize its image in light of increasing competition from energy and health beverages. Sometimes, consumers just need a little nudge to remember that a product is still there. Gatorade also came to the realization that its packaging was not too child-friendly — it was hard for little hands to hold and there was too much product in the bottle. The result? The company offered identical but smaller plastic bottles, as well as freezer-friendly tetra packages.[16]

Importance of packaging in marketing

Historically, packaging was a production-oriented activity in most companies, performed mainly to obtain the benefits of protection and convenience. Today, however, the marketing significance of packaging is fully recognized, and packaging is truly a major competitive force in the marketer's attempt to attract consumers. The widespread use of self-service selling and automatic vending means that the package must do the selling job at the point of purchase. Shelf space is often at a premium, and it is no simple task for manufacturers even to get their products displayed in a retail outlet. Most retailers are more inclined to stock the products of producers that have used effective packaging.

In addition, the increased importance of branding and rising standards of public health and sanitation have contributed to a greater awareness of packaging. Safety in packaging has become a prominent marketing and social issue in recent years. Extensive consumer use of microwave ovens also has had a significant impact on packaging. Many food products are now packaged so that they can go straight from the shelf or freezer into a microwave oven.

New developments in packaging, occurring rapidly and in a seemingly endless flow, require management's constant attention. We see new packaging materials replacing traditional ones, new shapes, new closures, and other new features (measured portions, metered flow). These all increase convenience for consumers and selling points for marketers.

Packaging is an important marketing tool for companies that operate in international markets. Most countries have regulations governing the packaging of products and the wording that must appear on labels. A company that wants to export its product to another country must, therefore, be aware of the packaging laws of that country. For example, companies in other countries that export to Canada and the Canadian importers that represent them have to be aware of Canadian packaging regulations pertaining to metric package sizes, bilingual labelling, and the standard sizes of packages used in some industries. In addition to regulations, exporters must understand that packages that work in one country may not be accepted in another, because of design, illustration, or colour. Cultural differences as well as traditions and attitudes affect how consumers respond to brand colours and image, as well as situations and usage portrayed in advertisements.

Packaging strategies

Changing the package In general, management has three reasons for considering a package change: to combat a decrease in sales, to extend the brand's life cycle, and to expand a market by attracting new groups of customers. More specifically, a firm may want to correct a poor feature in the existing container or it may want to take advantage of new materials. Some companies change their containers to aid in promotional programs. A new package may be used as a major appeal in advertising copy or because the old container may not

This family package can be recognized instantly.

show up well in advertisements. A package change may be an important element in a brand repositioning strategy. It is also a way of breathing new life into a tired brand, thereby rekindling interest and extending the product's active life.

Packaging the product line A company must decide whether to develop a family resemblance in the packaging of its several products. Family packaging involves the use of identical packages for all products or the use of packaging with some common feature. Campbell's soup, for example, has used virtually identical packaging for its products for many years. As Campbell's introduced new products, including its Chunky products, the Gardennay line of boxed soups, and its Soup at Hand microwaveable product, they adopted new package designs, but always have retained the same Campbell's signature logo (visit **www.campbellsoup.ca** to see the entire range of Campbell's packaging). Management's philosophy concerning **family packaging** generally parallels its feelings about family branding. When new products are added to a line, promotional values associated with old products extend to the new ones. On the other hand, family packaging should be used only when the products are related in use and are of similar quality.

family packaging
A strategy of using similar packages for all products or packages with a common and clearly noticeable feature.

Campbells

Reuse packaging Another strategy to be considered is reuse packaging. Should the company design and promote a package that can serve other purposes after the original contents have been consumed? Decorative cookie tins can be used for any number of household functions, such as button boxes, containers for school supplies, or children's small-toy storage. Baby-food jars make great containers for small parts such as nuts, bolts, and screws. Reuse packaging also should stimulate repeat purchases, as the consumer attempts to acquire a matching set of containers.

multiple packaging
The placing of several units of the same product in one container or by physically wrapping them together.

Multiple packaging For many years, there has been a trend toward **multiple packaging**, the practice of placing several units in one container. Dehydrated soups, motor oil, beer, golf balls, building hardware, candy bars, yogurt, and countless other products are packaged in multiple units. Test after test has proved that multiple packaging increases total sales of a product.

Packaging of Services

bundling
The process of grouping together a number of services that are sold as a single unit.

There are two aspects of what is often referred to as the packaging of services. The first of these is **bundling**, which involves the marketer putting together an attractive "bundle" of services that can be bought as one unit but can include many elements. Financial services companies bundle many services with a credit card, so that the customer receives several of the services, including travel insurance and access to travel information, for example, for a single monthly fee. Tour operators do the same thing when they bundle air travel, car rental, and an all-inclusive stay at a resort for one total fee. Telecommunications companies are now able to bundle local and long-distance telephone service, cellular telephone service, Internet access, and cable TV for a single monthly fee.

The second aspect of services packaging relates to how the services are promoted. With services, the container is not the tangible package we associate with products, but it does represent a package of value for the consumer. Because of the intangibility of services, it is often difficult to communicate effectively about the quality of the service being provided. Services companies must "tangibilize" their offer through the production of point-of-sale displays, brochures, and other promotional materials that play the same promotional role as attractive product packages. These will be discussed in greater detail in Chapter 15.

Labelling

label
The part of a product that carries written information about the product or the seller.

Labelling is another product feature, primarily of tangible consumer products, that requires managerial attention. The **label** is the part of a product that carries information about the product or the seller. A label may be part of a package or it may be a tag attached directly to the product. Obviously, there is a close relationship among labelling, packaging, and branding.

Types of labels

brand label
The application of the brand name alone to a product or package.

grade label
Identification of the quality (grade) of a product by means of a letter, number, or word.

Typically, labels are classified as brand, grade, or descriptive. A **brand label** is simply the brand name alone applied to the product or to the package. Some oranges and bananas are brand-labelled (stamped) Sunkist or Dole, for example, and some clothes carry the brand label Sanforized. A **grade label** identifies the product quality with a letter, number, or word. Canadian beef is grade-labelled A, B, or C, and each grade is subdivided by a number from 1 to 4, indicating an increasing fat content.

Descriptive labels give objective information about the use, construction, care, performance, or other features of the product. On a descriptive label for a can of corn, there will be statements concerning the type of corn (golden sweet), the style (creamed or in kernels), and the can size, number of servings, other ingredients, and nutritional content.

eco-labelling
Seals of approval awarded by a government to encourage environmentally safe products.

Eco-labeling or environmental labeling indicates that a product meets standards of environmental soundness that are supported by extensive research into the product's impact on the environment. The Environmental Choice® Program (ECP) is Environment Canada's eco-labeling program. It provides access to a list of more environmentally responsible products and services that have received the EcoLogo certification.

Greening Government

The international symbol ENERGYSTAR® identifies products that are the most energy-efficient on the market. In Canada, ENERGYSTAR® includes several product categories: office equipment; appliances; heating, ventilating and cooling equipment; consumer electronics; lighting; signage and commercial and industrial equipment. (**www.greeninggovernment.gc.ca**)

Statutory labelling requirements

statutory labelling requirements
Federal and provincial laws regulating packaging and labelling.

The importance of packaging and labelling in its potential for influencing a consumer's purchasing decision is reflected in the large number of federal and provincial laws that contain **statutory labelling requirements** to regulate this marketing activity. At the federal level, the Competition Act[17] regulates the area of misleading advertising, and a number of companies have been convicted of misleading advertising for the false or deceptive statements that have appeared on their packages. In this case, the information that appears on a package or label has been considered to constitute an advertisement.

The Hazardous Products Act[18] gives the Government of Canada the power to regulate the sale, distribution, advertising, and labelling of certain consumer products that are considered dangerous. As such, cleaning substances, chemicals, and aerosol products must carry on their labels a series of symbols that indicate the danger associated with the product and the precautions that should be taken with its use.

Similarly, the federal Food and Drugs Act regulates the sale of food, drugs, cosmetics, and medical devices. Certain misleading and deceptive packaging and labelling practices are specifically prohibited. Without question, the strictest regulations applied to packaging in Canada pertain to the cigarette industry. Canadian regulations require that packaging used to sell these products in this country display health warnings that constitute 50 percent of the primary display surface of the package. Further, these warnings contain graphic depictions of the potential damage that can result from use of these products. This represents the largest and most graphic of such warnings required anywhere in the world.[19]

MARKETING AT WORK 9-3: STRATEGY

Debbie Travis' Branding Lessons

She has been called the master of paint and plaster by Oprah, and Regis has crowned her the reigning queen of renovation. She has even been described as the Canadian Martha Stewart. Debbie Travis certainly knows how to decorate. From her Montréal-based business, she has built a decorating empire with her HGTV show *Debbie Travis' Facelift*, along with decorating books and videos. Now Debbie has started her own line of branded products available exclusively in Canada at Canadian Tire.

The line starts with paints that are designed by Travis to capture moods — working off the design techniques she uses on *Facelift*. Following that was the introduction of storage items and then the rollout of items for bathrooms, kitchens and outdoor living.

Travis has been offered branding opportunities from Canadian retailers in the past but didn't bite until the deal from Canadian Tire came along. Travis has complete control over all items that bear her name. She says, "I don't want anybody putting my name on something that people would go 'that's not Debbie Travis.' It's got to look young, it's got to look hip, it's got to sell."

Canadian Tire carried the Martha Stewart line of branded items but dropped them due to poor sales. Why, then, would a deal with Debbie Travis be any different? After all, with so many comparisons to Stewart, one would think Canadian Tire would be wary of such a branded line. However, Canadian Tire was looking for somebody likeable and believable, who could inspire women to shop for home décor products at their stores. The fact that many young Canadians have grown up with Travis is an added benefit. Those same young people will soon start decorating — first dorm rooms and then apartments and homes. Canadian Tire and Travis are hoping to cash in on a still growing home décor market and that the new generation of amateur decorators will follow the Debbie Travis Canadian Tire line for many years.

QUESTIONS:

1. Is Debbie Travis a brand?
2. Is there a good "fit" between the Debbie Travis brand and the Canadian Tire brand?
3. What do they have in common?

SOURCE: Adapted from Eve Lazarus, "Mrs. Fix-it," *Marketing Magazine Online* , www.marketingmag.ca, November 28, 2005; Danny Kucharsky, "Debbie Does Branding," *Marketing Magazine Online*, www.marketingmag.ca, April 11, 2005.

The Textile Labelling Act requires that manufacturers label their products according to the fibre content of the product, with the percentage of each fibre in excess of 5 percent listed.

The Consumer Packaging and Labelling Act regulates all aspects of the packaging and labelling of consumer products in this country. The regulations that have been passed under this Act require that most products sold in Canada bear bilingual labels. The net quantity of the product must appear on the label in both metric and imperial units. This Act also makes provision for the standardization of container sizes.

The provinces have also moved into the field of regulating packaging and labelling. A number of provinces have passed legislation regarding misleading advertising, and any information that appears on a package or label is considered to be an advertisement. Many of the provincial and municipal governments across the country have established recycling programs and regulations about what packaging materials may be disposed of in public landfill sites.

We can expect to see further changes in the labels required on food and grocery items in the future, as consumers demand more information about the products they are consuming and using. The most likely changes relate to the listing of nutritional information on food products, brought about by the increasing interest of consumers in health and nutrition.

Other Image-Building Features

A very important part of a company's marketing initiative is the support of the brand and the cultivation of a reputation and image. The packaging and labelling used mainly by manufacturers of tangible products represent a major part of that image-building initiative. A well-rounded program for product and service planning and development includes a company policy on several other attributes intended to build a solid image for the brand: product design, colour, quality, warranty, and after-purchase service.

Product design and colour

One way to satisfy customers and gain a competitive advantage is through skilful product design. In fact, a distinctive design may be the only feature that significantly differentiates a product. Many firms feel that there is considerable glamour and general promotional appeal in product design and in the designer's name. In the field of business products, engineering design has long been recognized as being extremely important. Today, there is a realization of the marketing value of appearance design as well. Office machines and office furniture are examples of business products that reflect recent conscious attention to product design, often with good sales results. The marketing significance of design has been recognized for years in the field of consumer products, from major items such as automobiles and refrigerators to small products such as fountain pens and clothing.

Good design can improve the marketability of a product by making it easier to operate, upgrading its quality, improving its appearance, and/or reducing manufacturing costs. In October 2005, Apple introduced its iMac G5 which featured a built-in iSight™ video camera for out-of-the-box video conferencing and the debut of Apple's breakthrough Front Row media experience. Front Row gives users a simple way to enjoy music, movies, photoslideshows and television shows. The built-in iSight video camera allows users to have convenient access to video conferencing and to take quick snapshots. These new design features are available in a sleeker, lighter product that Apple hoped would make the product more marketable to users who wanted all of the features in a highly portable product.[20]

Product colour often is the determining factor in a customer's acceptance or rejection of a product, whether that product is a dress, a table, or an automobile. Colour by itself, however, has no selling advantage, because many competing firms offer colour. The marketing advantage comes in knowing the right colour and in knowing when to change colours. Sometimes just the presence of colour can be enough. When Apple introduced the iPod nano, the most fashionable and wearable iPod ever, it also introduced an optional set of iPod nano Tubes in pink, purple, blue, green and clear, which offer fashionable protection for the nano. As well, optional armbands which come in a variety of colours were introduced so that users could wear their iPod nano as a fashion and sports accessory.[21]

Product quality

The quality of a product is extremely significant, but it is probably the most difficult of all of the image-building features to define. Users frequently disagree on what constitutes quality in a product, whether it is a cut of meat or a work of art or music. Personal tastes are very much involved. One guideline in managing product quality is that the quality level should be compatible with the intended use of a product; the level need not be any higher. In fact, good and poor sometimes are misleading terms for quality. Correct and incorrect or right and wrong may be more appropriate. If a person is making a peach dessert, Grade B or C peaches are the correct quality. They are not necessarily the best quality, but they are right for the intended use. It is not necessary to pay Grade A prices for large, well-formed peaches when these features are destroyed in making the dessert. Another key to the successful management of quality is to maintain consistency of product output at the desired quality level.

Quality of output also is a primary consideration in the production and marketing of services. The quality of its service can determine whether a firm will be successful. Yet it is virtually impossible for a firm to standardize performance quality among its units of service output. We frequently experience differences in performance quality from the same organization in appliance repairs, haircuts, medical examinations, football games, or marketing courses. You might want to return to our discussion of service quality in Chapter 8.

To aid in determining and maintaining the desired level of quality in their products and services, many companies have established quality-improvement programs. Such a program should be an ongoing group effort of the design, production, marketing, and customer-service departments. A firm may then justifiably claim in its advertising that its product quality has improved or is better than the competition's. Of course, companies must live up to their claims of superior quality in products or services, or consumers simply won't believe these claims.

Warranties and guarantees

warranty
An assurance given to buyers that they will be compensated in case the product does not perform up to reasonable expectations.

express warranty
A statement in written or spoken words regarding restitution from seller to customer if the seller's product does not perform up to reasonable expectations.

implied warranty
An intended but unstated assurance regarding restitution from seller to customer if the seller's product does not perform up to reasonable expectations.

service guarantees
Guarantees that companies offer to their customers that attest to the quality of their service.

Warranties represent a promise from the manufacturer of a product that, if something goes wrong or if the customer is not satisfied with the performance of the product, it may be returned or repairs will be carried out at no cost to the consumer. Sometimes warranties are referred to by consumers as guarantees. The purpose of a **warranty** is to assure buyers they will be compensated in case the product does not perform up to reasonable expectations. In years past, courts seemed to recognize only **express warranties** — those that were stated in written or spoken words. Usually these were quite limited in their coverage and seemed mainly to protect the seller from buyers' claims. Some companies were reluctant to honour a warranty unless it had been formally provided in writing.

But times change! Courts and government agencies have broadened the scope of warranty coverage by recognizing **implied warranties.** This means that a customer can now assume that a warranty was intended, although not actually stated by the seller. In other words, a consumer today can assume that a warranty is in place even if the seller has not provided one in writing. Therefore, a consumer can assume a certain level of quality to be present and, if it is not, that the manufacturer or retailer will replace or repair the product. Furthermore, manufacturers are being held responsible even when the sales contract is between the retailer and the consumer.

In recent years, manufacturers have responded to legislation and consumer complaints by broadening and simplifying their warranties. Many sellers are using their warranties as promotional devices to stimulate purchase by reducing consumers' risks. Advertising may be designed around claims regarding the quality of the warranty. This has been popular with high-ticket items such as automobiles, claiming coverage for a certain number of years or kilometres. The effective handling of consumers' complaints related to warranties can be a significant factor in strengthening a company's marketing program.

Some companies have even extended the concept of warranties to the offering of **service guarantees**. They have essentially guaranteed the quality of service that the consumer will receive, often offering money-back guarantees if the customer is not satisfied. This has become a fairly common practice in very competitive industries such as hotels and airlines. But, it is also a practice that may be difficult to implement because of some of the characteristics of services discussed in Chapter 8. It is, of course, more difficult to control the quality of service than that of a manufactured product, so service quality is highly variable. Also, as we discussed in Chapter 8, quality of service is based to a very great extent on the perception of the customer. The customer decides whether service is of an acceptable quality, influenced by past experience, expectations, and other factors. As a result, companies that offer service guarantees must be extremely diligent in their training of employees and in other aspects of service delivery to ensure that the best possible quality is being provided to customers.[22]

Post-purchase service

Many companies have to provide post-purchase service, notably repairs, to fulfil the terms of their warranties. Other firms offer post-purchase services such as maintenance and repairs not only to satisfy their customers but also to augment their revenues. Companies that offer products such as automobiles and mechanical equipment, such as elevators or heating and ventilation systems, rely on their service contracts for a substantial portion of their sales and profits. With more complex products and increasingly demanding and vocal consumers, post-purchase service has become essential. A frequent consumer complaint is that manufacturers and retailers do not provide adequate repair service for the products they sell.

Many responsive companies have established toll-free telephone numbers that connect the customer directly with a customer-service representative. Many actually invite customers to complain, acting on the principle that if the customer doesn't complain, the company won't know there is a problem and can't take steps to correct it. This post-purchase service is also required for troubleshooting and assembly assistance for many products and services such as audio systems or Internet installation. Many companies post their toll-free customer-service numbers on the doors of their stores and feature them in their advertising. While it may not always be pleasant to listen to customer complaints, the alternative of customers taking their business elsewhere is much worse in the long run.

Post-purchase service has the potential to be either a differential advantage or a disadvantage for an organization. Therefore, it is an issue that managers must monitor on a regular basis.

PAGE UP!

1. In marketing, what is bundling?
2. What are three reasons why management would consider changing the packaging of its product?
3. What is the purpose of a warranty?

Key Terms and Concepts

brand 244
brand awareness 245
brand characteristics 246
brand equity 247
brand extensions 249
brand label 261
brand loyalty 247
brand mark 245
brand name 245
brand personality 246
brand recognition 245
brand relationship 246
brand values 246
branding 244
bundling 260
co-branding 255
eco-labelling 261
express warranty 264
family-brand strategy 257
family packaging 260
grade label 261
implied warranty 264
label 261
multiple-brand strategy 257
multiple packaging 260
national brands 245
packaging 258
private labels 245
service guarantees 264
statutory labelling requirements 261
trademark 245
warranty 264

Questions and Problems

1. Answer the following question to determine Heinz Ketchup's brand personality: If Heinz Ketchup was a person, what sort of person would it be? List five personality traits.

2. Evaluate each of the following brand names in light of the characteristics of a good brand, indicating the strong and weak points of each name.
   a. Xerox (office copiers).
   b. Lululemon (retailer).
   c. Holiday Inns (hotels).
   d. Moschino (clothing).
   e. Red Lobster (restaurant).
   f. Ecco (footwear).

3. When does a company or product name become a brand? What distinction do you make between a "name" and a "brand"? Does the term "brand" imply that the product or company has achieved a certain status?
4. Suggest some brands that are on the verge of becoming generic. What course of action should a company take to protect the separate identity of its brands?
5. Name some private-label products and determine which brand names compete with them. Which product do you prefer and why? (**Example:** President's Choice Decadent chocolate chip cookies versus Chips Ahoy!)
6. What examples can you identify of co-branding. What advantages are there for the companies involved for entering into such a branding strategy with other brands? Give examples of good co-branding strategies and others that may not work as well.
7. Why do some firms sell an identical product under more than one of their own brands?
8. What changes would you recommend in the typical packaging of these products?
   a. Soft drinks.
   b. Hairspray.
   c. Adventure vacation.
   d. Toothpaste.
9. Give examples of products for which the careful use of the colour of the package has increased sales. Can you give examples to show that poor use of colour may hurt a company's marketing program?
10. How would the warranty policies set by a manufacturer of skis differ from those adopted by an automobile manufacturer?

Hands-On Marketing

1. Consider the branding strategies of four "coffee shops," all of which are successful in the Canadian market — Second Cup, Timothy's, Tim Hortons and Starbucks. Check out their Web sites and other information that you may be able to gather and identify how you believe each has set out to build its brand strategy. How has each brand been able to create high levels of brand awareness and recognition? What are the most obvious characteristics of each brand?

   What would you say is each brand's personality? What are each brand's values? And, how does each succeed in creating brand relationships? Now, is it obvious to you why Tim Hortons is Canada's best managed brand?
2. Interview five students who are not taking this course or five friends and ask them to tell you about their favourite brands. Note what kinds of products and services they are most likely to associate with a "brand." Ask them for reasons why these are their favourite brands. Try to determine what these brands mean to them, what roles the brands play in their lives, and how they would feel if one of these brands was suddenly no longer available.

Back to the Top

Thinking back to the chapter opener, what do you think are the main reasons why Tim Hortons has become such a well-loved brand in Canada? Certainly, the coffee is not that different than other coffee shops and the remainder of the product line is not unique. If you think about the discussions in this chapter regarding what makes a brand successful, you will realize that it is more than the product, the name or the service. Brands relationships, brand equity and brand loyalty are important concepts for successful brand management. Consider the Tim Hortons brand in light of this chapter and decide for yourself why it has become a Canadian success story.

Online LearningCentre

Want to get better grades, tips on how to study more effectively, and up-to-date information on happenings in the world of marketing? Then, visit the Online Learning Centre for practice tests, Study Smart software, *Marketing Magazine*, and much more! **www.mcgrawhill.ca/olc/sommers**

CASE 3-1:

Multimedia

Yaris — Who's Your Favourite Uncle?

"My guess is it's a new music station," Brad said as Jesse approached the group of three of his friends deep in discussion. "What are you talking about?" Jesse asked. "We're talking about these TV ads about this guy named Uncle Yaris. Have you seen them?" Jesse shook his head. "I think it might be a new music station because I saw a poster about how Uncle Yaris knows his music," Brad continued. "I also saw a commercial with him scratching on what looked like 10 decks." Kyle interrupted, "No, I think you're wrong, because I saw one commercial with him riding like a crazy guy on an exercise bike — what does that have to do with music?" "Was there a telephone number or a Web site or something?" Jesse asked. "Yeah, I went to the site - it has music playing all the time. It looks pretty flashy to be just a home page of a person. I dug around to see who's behind it, but, there's nothing there."

An ad campaign with no company logo nor any mention of the product. Brilliant or just plain confusing?

Although known as a conservative, mainstream, family-oriented company, Toyota (Canada) was successful in launching an amusing campaign to attract a youthful demographic for its new Yaris subcompact car. Where did the name come from? It's actually a bizarre combination of the Greek goddess Charis, the city Paris, and the German word "ja." Toyota recognized the fact that you need to do things people will notice in an environment full of media clutter — even if it means taking a big risk.

The Tease

The campaign was aimed at people born in the late 1970s or early 1980s who are buying their first car and who tend to be into non-mainstream stuff. Market research indicated that uncles hit a positive nerve with the target, and hence Uncle Yaris was born. For the campaign's first 10 days, known as the "tease," the wordless and energetic Uncle Yaris, a long-haired guy wearing unfortunate looking tracksuits appeared in TV spots doing wacky things like carrying a bunch of fruit to a supermarket counter, frantically riding an exercise bike and DJ-ing, comically, on several outdoor turntables. But there was no mention of the car, nor of the company who made it! The spots advertised a Web site, **www.yaris.ca**, which motivated some people to visit, but again, it didn't tell you anything about the product. But at the very least Toyota had people wondering. It was kooky, odd and got people talking.

Uncle Yaris' Web site played music by Toronto buzz band, The Deadly Snakes, featuring Uncle Yaris, but, again, no outright connection to the automaker. The "Uncle Yaris" campaign continued, featuring five quirky TV commercials, a cinema commercial, billboards, newspapers and magazines. The ad where "Uncle Yaris was born in Europe," reflects the car's European styling, while "Uncle Yaris goes and goes," represents the fact that the Toyota Yaris is fuel-efficient. His face even appeared on pizza boxes and static-cling mirror pictures. Internet blogs and chat rooms buzzed about who Uncle Yaris was, and the mystery product he represented.

The Reveal

A second phase of the campaign, the "reveal," removed the obscurity and subtlety, and linked Uncle Yaris directly with the car it represented, a replacement for Toyota's Echo line. It created that buzz. People kept talking about it, especially because they could put the Uncle Yaris character together with the car. Toyota hopes that the Yaris can do what the Echo didn't quite achieve — appeal to a younger target market. But age isn't the only thing — the Yaris should appeal to people who step outside the mainstream in their activities, lifestyle, clothing, and music. Mainstream or not, there is no denying that almost every family has at least one member who never fails to surprise the adults and amuse the kids at family get-togethers. In the Toyota family, could this be Yaris?

In addition to the Uncle Yaris-themed commercials, there were commercials set in medieval times. The two commercials, available on video, reinforce that the Yaris is fun to drive and deceptively spacious. They are, however, very different from the Uncle Yaris launch ads. Furthermore, the Web sites, **www.yaris.ca** and **www.toyota.ca** provide another opportunity for would-be buyers to explore the features of the Yaris.

But are these campaigns too different for a Toyota built car? What about Toyota's loyal customers who have come to expect the dependable, family-oriented, no-nonsense advertising?

Questions:

1. Evaluate the launch of this new model in the Toyota lineup. Is this new car likely to appeal to the intended audience?
2. What should Toyota do to ensure that the Yaris campaign does not alienate more traditional, loyal Toyota customers? Is the Yaris brand positioned appropriately?
3. Suggest how Toyota can follow up this campaign for the next model year once the excitement and fun of the brand launch is completed.
4. View the video that accompanies this case and discuss the appeal of the Uncle Yaris campaign and the ads in the video. Why would Toyota choose these campaigns? How are they similar/different? As well, visit the Web site for Yaris and the Camry section of the Toyota site. Discuss the similarities and differences between the two. Suggest how Toyota may want to change the Yaris site to be more consistent with the ad campaign discussed in this case.

SOURCE: Adapted in part from, Shaun Ohler, "Would you buy a car from this man?" *The Edmonton Journal*, November 20, 2005.

CASE 3-2:

Multimedia

Europe's Best — Repositioning Frozen Fruit and Veg

In many parts of Canada and the U.S., there is limited access to affordable, fresh fruits and vegetables year round. As a result, many people do not get their recommended 5 to 10 servings of fruits and vegetables per day. Accessibility, coupled with changing lifestyles and household composition, prevent many consumers from having a variety of fresh fruits and vegetables in their diet.

You can probably relate. How many times have you shopped with all good intentions to eat healthier, only to find that the healthy foods were much more costly than the unhealthier choices? Even worse, many of us have bought the fresh fruits and vegetables only to find them a week later, in the bottom of the refrigerator, less than appetizing in the plastic produce bags.

Although frozen fruits and vegetables are not a new idea, many people are reluctant to choose frozen produce fearing inferior taste and nutrition. But frozen food can be good food. According to reports, freezing produce can actually lock in important vitamins and stop nutrient loss that can occur in fresh produce. These reports are causing consumers to take another look at just what is available behind those big glass doors in the freezer aisle!

In just three years, Europe's Best brand of frozen fruits and vegetables has become a top seller and is carried by retailers across Canada and has been introduced into the U.S. market. Products include traditional frozen vegetables such as peas, carrots and corn, as well as new offerings such as Romanesco Concerto, a combination of broccoflower romanesco, yellow carrots, orange carrots and cut green beans. While the Romanesco may not be your typical frozen vegetable, the idea of frozen vegetable medleys and fruit is nothing new. Producers such as McCain's, Green Giant and Bird's Eye Foods have been providing this convenience for consumers for some time.

So, what makes Europe's Best different? According to the company, Europe's Best has revolutionized the freezing, packaging and transportation of the food and "hand-picks" their producers. This makes Europe's Best the best, according to their Web site **www.europesbest.com** and their commercials. But, when you are standing in the freezer aisle at the supermarket, why would you choose Europe's Best over one of the better recognized brands mentioned above? Other producers will surely make the same claims about freshness, packaging and quality products in their ads. Note the visual appeal of the Europe's Best Web site and the product packaging. View the advertisements available in the Media section of the Web site. For each ad, note the messages and the appeal.

Europe's Best has entered a market with a category of products that have always been seen as second best compared to their fresh counterparts. While lifestyles and health reports would support consumers using frozen produce, many consumers still believe that nutritious food is time-consuming to prepare and that produce must be fresh to be nutritious and tasty. But when these fresh products double in price in January, or, are not available at all, why will consumers in Canada and the U.S. choose Europe's Best over other brands?

Questions:

1. Describe the brand positioning and target market segments for Europe's Best products. How has this company chosen to create value for these customers? Will this brand succeed in making the entire frozen fruit and vegetables category more appealing?
2. How believable are the product claims that Europe's Best is making? What's more important in the customers' decision, fresh or frozen, product or packaging?
3. Comment on the appeal of the various ads you have viewed at **www.europesbest.com**. Do you think these advertisements portray the right message for the brand? Why or why not?

CASE 3-3:

Multimedia

Everybody's Got Junk!!!

In 1989, Brian Scudamore started a full service junk removal business in Vancouver, British Columbia with $700 and a pick-up truck. Eighteen years later, Scudamore's 1-800-GOT-JUNK? business has grown to include Franchise Partners in Canada, the United States, Australia, and the U.K. The 1-800-GOT-JUNK? brand has been featured on Oprah and Dr. Phil and in *USA Today, The New York Times, The Wall Street Journal*, and the *Associated Press*. Accolades include numerous business and humanitarian awards, including the *Fortune Small Business* Best Boss Award, *Entrepreneur Magazine's* Franchise 500 and The Best Company To Work for award by *Watson Wyatt*.

How can a junk removal service generate such interest and success? Garbage removal is nothing new — it happens at least once a week on most city streets. However, junk removal is something very different. For one thing, unless things fit neatly into garbage bags, most community town and city garbage trucks won't take it from the curb on regular pickup days. In addition, most municipalities charge extra to take large items such as appliances, mattresses and other household junk. In addition to broken appliances and worn-out furniture, many homes have boxes and bags of junk — not necessarily garbage, but things that are no longer used — books, magazines, stereo systems and toys, to name a few. One of the primary differences between junk and garbage, however, seems to be people's emotional attachment to junk. Whether it's the stereo that belted out tunes in a college dorm or a child's first ride-on toy, people can be sentimental about junk!! Another primary difference is size — junk is often bigger, bulkier and more difficult to move than garbage.

When Scudamore first started his business, many smaller and unprofessional junk removal services existed across North America. Many home and business owners, however, are reluctant to invite these unprofessional Sanford and Son type of operators into their homes to remove their junk. At 1-800-GOT-JUNK? customers are treated to professional service whether they book by telephone or online. The operators show up on time in uniform, driving shiny blue trucks. Onsite, prices are quoted up-front before any loading begins. Operators finish the job by sweeping up the area that was cleared and the driveway, if necessary.

Review both the video advertisements that accompany this book and the Web site at **www.1800gotjunk.com** before proceeding to the discussion questions. As well, you should visit **http://www.cbc.ca/venture/millionairequiz/millionaire_scudamore.html** for more information on Brian Scudamore's view of the world and of his business.

Questions:

1. What has Brian Scudamore done to differentiate his junk removal service from other companies in the same business?
2. Why are people willing to pay more for professional-looking junk removal?
3. What is the appeal of the 1-800-Got-Junk? advertisements? Do you think the use of rats in advertisements for junk removal is a good idea? Why or why not?
4. Discuss some of the other marketing techniques described on the Web site, such as the Blue Wigs, the roadside signs and the community involvement. Do you think these same techniques will work in international markets? Explain your answers.

CASE 3-4:

GuestLink — Kraft Dinner

In Chapter 9, our Guest Marketer, Bruce Hunter, former Vice-President, Marketing at Kraft Canada outlined the strategy behind the relaunch of one of that company's most famous grocery products, Kraft Dinner. This brand, given its position in the Canadian grocery products industry, offers an excellent insight into brand strategy. It is interesting to trace the development of the KD brand through the various stages of brand strategy development from awareness and knowledge, to its characteristics, its personality, the values it represents, and on to the relationships it has established with Canadian consumers.

Questions:

1. Discuss with your class where KD is currently positioned at each of these stages — what level of awareness does it enjoy and with whom; what are the characteristics of the brand; what is its personality; what values does it represent; and what's the nature of the brand relationship that some Canadians have with KD?
2. To whom is the KD brand targeted? What are its primary and secondary target segments? What occasions do each of these segments associate with the brand?
3. Discuss the "Dorm" TV commercial for Kraft Dinner. What's the message? To whom is this commercial directed? How does this ad support KD's brand values?

PART 4

Pricing

The determination of the price for a product or service and its connection to the creation of value

In **Part 4**, we deal with the second component of the marketing mix, the price to be charged for the firm's products or services and the broader issue of how companies can create value for their customers.

Having developed and launched our product or service, selected a brand and decided on packaging and labelling, we turn now to pricing, where we face two tasks. First, we must understand the role of price as seen by the customer and appreciate its role as a tool to communicate value. Then, we must turn our attention to the task of setting price and implementing pricing strategies.

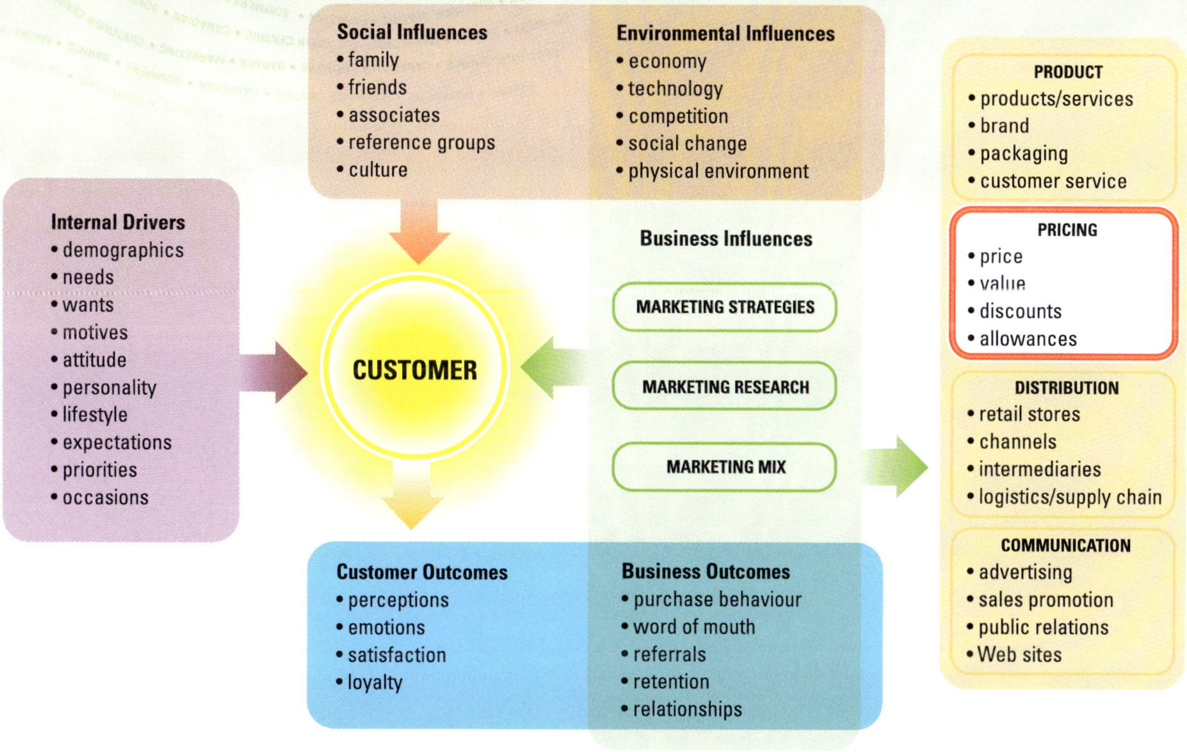

CHAPTER 10

Price and Value

In this chapter, we address the importance of price and the creation of value in the marketing of products and services — what price is, how it functions as a marketing tool, and how it is set. After studying this chapter, you should have an understanding of:

- How consumers think about price and the messages price can communicate.
- What makes up the price we pay for products and services.
- The concept of value and how it relates to price.
- Pricing objectives and goals.
- Factors influencing how price is set.
- The types of costs incurred in producing and marketing a product.
- Approaches to pricing and the role of break-even analysis.

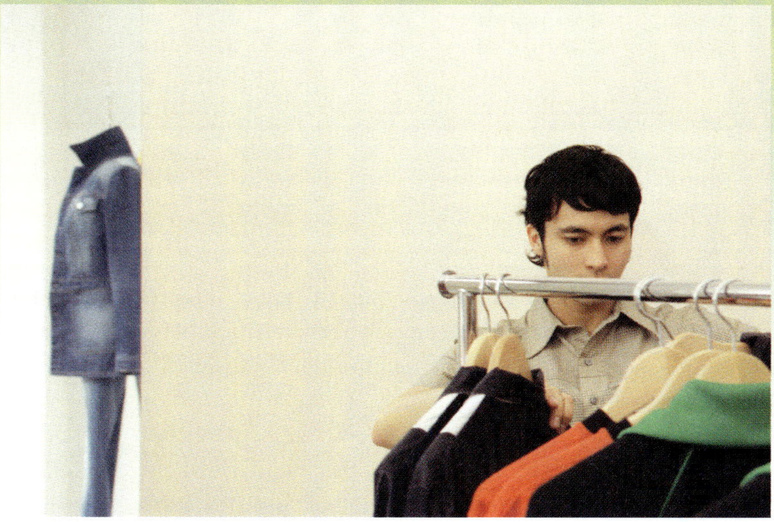

How Much Is That T-Shirt?

Like many young men, Rohan doesn't enjoy shopping for clothes. Generally, when he decides he needs new clothes he likes to make as few stops as possible to get as many items as he needs. One-stop shopping is his motto. One Saturday morning, Rohan decided to pick up a few things for a weekend he had been planning with friends. They were headed to Montréal in a couple of weeks and Rohan knew he needed some new clothes. One item on his short but specific list was a black t-shirt. Rohan figured he couldn't commit a fashion *faux pas* in a basic black t-shirt. Rohan headed for the mall and decided to check out a new men's clothing store his sister had recommended. He found a black t-shirt that looked basically the same as the one he owned (except not as faded). The Hugo Boss shirt was priced at $90. While shopping around wasn't his plan for Saturday, Rohan had planned to go to Sears to check out a great deal on golf balls that his friend, Ted, had told him about. So, he put the Boss shirt back on the shelf. At Sears, there was the usual collection of things Rohan could see himself wearing and a lot of things that he could buy for his father. He found a Calvin Klein t-shirt for $35 and a Tommy Hilfiger for $40. Then he spied a Point Zero black t-shirt for $18.75.

As Rohan was about to buy the $18.75 shirt, he noticed his friends Kate and Glenn coming down the aisle. Kate advised him to go to Winners where she had bought a Tommy Hilfiger shirt for Glenn for only $15. While going to yet another store was not sounding good to him — after all, Saturdays were for relaxing and this seemed more like work — Rohan had to admit that a Tommy shirt for $15 was a pretty good deal. In the meantime, he could save himself a trip to the other side of town if he just bought the shirt at Sears. After all, this shirt was costing Rohan his Saturday and that was a high price to pay. As Rohan headed out of the mall he had to question just how black t-shirts could be priced so differently. After all, it's just a t-shirt.

This chapter may help to make sense of the often-confusing world of pricing. The quandaries involved in making such a simple purchase as a t-shirt are not at all untypical, and the confusing array of prices in many product and service categories is equally common. So, what does a black t-shirt cost? The answer, of course, is that there is no single price. What a retailer charges for a shirt and what a customer is prepared to pay depend on many factors. The price obviously depends on the brand and on other factors. Does Rohan want to pay more for a Hugo Boss or Tommy Hilfiger shirt? What additional value is he getting for that price? Why is the Hilfiger shirt so much cheaper at Winners? We will address questions such as these in this chapter.

Deciding How Much to Charge

The issue of how much a company or organization should charge for its products and services involves many factors. As the chapter opener shows, the value that consumers perceive in a product or service is always a factor influencing the price that can be charged. And costs are always present and must be paid. As a result of technological advances and increased competition, lower costs generally will lead to lower prices. There are, of course, many other factors that must be taken into consideration, including the target segment for the product or service, the image and market positioning of the brand, and the prices being charged by competitors. These factors must be taken into account when a company introduces a new product or service or considers changing the price of an existing one. Pricing is about much more than how much money a firm can obtain from the consumer — it should be all about delivering value for money. Price is the most important and universally accepted indicator of value — price is used by consumers as a tool to reflect value.

In this chapter, we will discuss methods used by companies and other organizations to determine prices. Before being concerned with actual price setting, however, managers — and you — should understand the meaning and importance of price.

The Meaning of Price

price
The amount of money and/or other resources needed to acquire some combination of a product and its accompanying services.

Some pricing difficulties occur because of confusion about the meaning of **price**, even though the concept is easy to define in familiar terms. Simply, price is the amount of money and/or other resources that are needed to acquire a product or service.

Generally, we tend to think of price in strictly monetary terms: A sweater costs $100, a movie ticket costs $10. But how much does a trip to a doctor's office cost? Because of our health-care system, very few of us have any idea what a visit to a doctor costs because we don't pay for it, at least not directly. It may be useful to think of price as what it costs us to acquire something, whether that something is a tangible product or service. But, price is only part of what it costs the customer.

But, what it costs to acquire that sweater is actually more than $100. It involves shopping time and effort and it may involve other non-monetary considerations, such as having to find a parking space, or taking public transit, or having to visit several stores to find the size and other features you need. Viewing price as a monetary factor oversimplifies the buying process. When customers decide whether they are satisfied with a sweater or with a meal at a restaurant, they implicitly think about the value received. As a result, we often hear customers say, "I'll never go back there. It's just not worth the ____________." They may fill the blank with "money," but it's just as likely that they'll use words like "time," "hassle," or "aggravation." Some may also occasionally say, "I know I'm paying more, but it's worth it to me."

value of a product or service
The ratio of perceived benefits of a product or service to perceived costs, including price and other incurred costs.

Therefore, we need to consider the **value of a product or service** when we talk about price. A marketer who is interested in creating customer satisfaction will focus on creating value for the customer. There are many ways to create or add value, only one of which is to reduce price. But, because our economy utilizes money as the medium of exchange, we tend to state prices in monetary terms. As you read this chapter, however, it may be useful to think of the effect that price has in communicating value to customers.

Price is the most important way that marketers have of communicating value. It is an indicator to consumers of what a product or service is "worth." On seeing the price, the consumer must decide whether the product or service is worth it. A great deal of psychology is at work, as the consumer often makes an immediate and subconscious decision whether or not to buy. Some, on hearing a price, will respond with comments like "I'd never pay that kind of money for that," or "There's no way that's worth it." But, there are also circumstances in which customers are prepared to pay higher prices for what would appear to be very similar if not identical products and services. This is illustrated in our chapter opener where some customers will willingly pay $90 for a black Boss t-shirt while others will feel that's far too much to pay.

BACK TO THE TOP

Price, therefore, must be set in the context of what the customer is seen to be getting in return. It also must be viewed in light of what else the customer is expected to commit to its purchase. Customers will generally expect to pay less if they have to take the table home from IKEA and assemble it themselves. They will similarly expect to pay more for a table from another retailer that is fully assembled and delivered. Customers are generally prepared to pay more for products and services that are made available conveniently and with high levels of support services. Despite the opinion of many managers that customers are always looking for lower prices, many are often heard to comment that they would be prepared to pay higher prices "if the company would only ____________."

Practical problems also arise when we try to state simply the price of a product or service. There is no simple answer to a question like "what does a black t-shirt cost?" The answer is always "it depends." On what does price depend? Well, it depends on what the customer wishes to obtain in return and how much value the customer attaches to the various components of what he or she receives. As we see in Marketing at Work file 10-1, the cost of an airline ticket between two cities depends on many factors, including not only the class of service, but such things as whether the customer wishes to have some flexibility to change the flight time or date if needed, and how many seats are left to sell on a particular flight.

Price Is What You Pay for What You Get

Here are prices under various names:

- Tuition → Education.
- Interest → Use of money.
- Rent → Use of living quarters or a piece of equipment for a period of time.
- Fare → Taxi ride or airline flight.
- Rate → Price paid per hour, day or week.
- Fee → Services of an accountant or lawyer.
- Retainer → Lawyer's or consultant's services over a period of time.
- Toll → Long-distance phone call or travel on some highways.
- Salary → Services of an executive or other white-collar employee.
- Wage → Services of a blue-collar employee.
- Commission → Salesperson's services.
- Dues → Membership in a union or a club.

And in socially undesirable situations, there are prices called blackmail, ransom, or bribery.

SOURCE: Suggested in part by John T. Mentzer and David J. Schwartz, *Marketing Today*, 4th ed. (San Diego: Harcourt Brace Jovanovich, 1985), p. 599.

Our example of the black t-shirt indicates that the definition of price depends on determining exactly what is being purchased. A seller usually is pricing a combination of (1) the specific core product or service that is the object of the transaction, (2) several supplementary services (such as a warranty), and (3) in a very real sense, the need- or want-satisfying benefits provided by the product. Sometimes it is difficult to define even the price of the core product or service itself. The question of brand also complicates the pricing decision. What value does the Boss brand add that an unrecognizable brand may not? Is a Hilfiger shirt sold at Sears the "same" shirt as the one available at Winners? So, to know the real price of a product, you need to look at the identifiable tangible and intangible components that make up that product.

The price paid, therefore, will depend on various factors: the amount of planning that has gone into the purchase, how badly the customer needs the product, and how much the customer is prepared to put into the purchase — how much it is valued. If you absolutely have to have your favourite group's new CD right away, you'll pay more for the instant gratification and buy it at a retail store, even though you could have obtained it more cheaply on the Internet or you could simply download individual tracks. It all depends on how the customer defines the value associated with the purchase.

Price, from the customer's perspective at least, is very much related to what people are prepared to pay. While many will complain about prices, in almost all cases, the customer has the right not to buy at the price being charged. If a company sets its prices too high, its prod-

MARKETING AT WORK — 10-1: STRATEGY

Coffee, Tea or a Cheaper Seat?

Going to www.aircanada.ca to buy a ticket is fairly straightforward. The site is easy to navigate and the flight options are presented so that you can choose one-way, return or multi-city trips with ease. If you have ever booked a ticket online, however, you realize that there are a number of fare options available. For example, on flights from Montréal to Vancouver, Air Canada offers so many options it is mind-boggling. There may be as many as three non-stop and 17 connecting flights on a given day. For each of these flights there are five different fare options — Tango, Tango Plus, Latitude, Latitude Plus, and Executive Class. Of course, depending on the time of day and whether the flight is direct to Vancouver or has a connection in Toronto, Calgary, Ottawa or Edmonton, the fares change. On any particular day, there may be as many as 15 different fares for the one-way trip. Combine this with the return fares, which are equally as numerous, and a customer should have no problem choosing his or her flights.

Or, is that necessarily the case? Depending on the nature of the travel, the time of day the passenger wishes (or needs) to arrive in Vancouver, the amount he or she is willing to pay, and the flexibility required for last minute changes, the mix can become more complicated. For example, the Tango fare provides 50 percent non-status Aeroplan miles and one Aeroplan mile for every $3 spent online. In addition, customers must pay $15 for advance seat selection, a $30 flat fee to make unlimited changes (plus any difference in the fare) and $150 for same day airport changes. Tango Plus, as the name suggests, provides a 100 percent Aeroplan Status Miles, one Aeroplan mile for every $2 spent online and complimentary advance seat selection. In addition, the same-day airport change fee is reduced to $50 and the unlimited changes still cost $30.

So what does a return ticket from Montréal to Vancouver cost? With early morning Tango fares, the trip can be done for about $650 while the same time of day Tango Plus fares would be approximately $710. How about the Latitude flight which provides for more flexibility and 100 percent Aeroplan miles? That will cost about $1,600 while Latitude Plus, which includes complimentary access to the Maple Leaf Lounge will cost about $3,000. Of course, these fares will change depending on how far in advance you buy the ticket.

Air Canada is now offering Fight Passes which are prepaid one-way flight credits that customers can use to book online tickets. These flight passes are available in the North American Pass, which provides eight flight credits that can be used for any destination in North America, and the Small Business Pass that consists of 30 one-way flight credits that can be used by as many as eight employees of a firm over a three-month period. These passes promise the customer up to 30 percent in savings and more control to book, change, rebook and cancel.

QUESTIONS:

1. What does a flight from Montréal to Vancouver really cost?
2. Why are some of the factors mentioned so important in determining the price a passenger pays?
3. Think about what the customer is actually buying; the airline's value proposition.

ucts will not sell. Nowhere is the supply and demand nature of pricing more evident than on eBay, where the person who is prepared to pay more gets the product. So, it is an interesting question to ask what Rohan is actually getting when he eventually buys a black t-shirt. Is there more to this than the shirt?

It may be useful to view price in the context of an equation. If customers feel that what they have obtained for what they paid is somewhat in balance, there will be satisfaction with the price. The consumer will feel that what was obtained was "worth it." If there is an imbalance, however, the customer will either be delighted at having obtained a real deal or disappointed at having paid too much. When customers conclude that something isn't worth it, the price is not necessarily being questioned. What is being questioned is the value that is being offered for the price charged. Therefore, marketers should pay attention to making the value proposition as attractive as possible, rather than concentrating always on bringing prices down.

Importance of Price

Price is significant to an individual firm and in the minds of consumers. It is a very obvious component of a marketing program that determines whether a firm's offer is acceptable to the customer. Price epitomizes and makes tangible the notion of value that lies at the heart of the exchange process. Let's consider just how important price is for both customers and companies.

In the consumer's mind

price sensitivity
The extent to which a customer or a certain segment of customers will respond to price changes or is focused on price when buying.

At the retail level, a small segment of customers is interested primarily in low prices — they have a high level of **price sensitivity**. Another segment may be indifferent about price in making purchases. The majority of consumers are somewhat sensitive about price but are also concerned with other factors such as brand image, the nature of the shopping situation, store location, convenience, quality, and, ultimately, value. Consumers who utilize the Internet to comparison-shop and research prices are often much more price-sensitive about some goods because they can compare prices very easily — others are not as price-sensitive. Consumers' relative interest in price also can vary across demographic groups. Consumers with large families, single parents, and those on low incomes and/or fixed incomes are likely to be much more price-sensitive. But even customers in these situations will, on occasion, be prepared to pay more to get what they consider to be better value. Further, even those with a lot more money at their disposal may still seek value for their money, cautiously assessing benefits and features versus price before purchasing.

Economic conditions may dictate for some consumers that they focus mainly on low prices, but in today's increasingly hectic environment, other costs beyond the price, as previously discussed, are figuring into the calculation of what a customer is prepared to pay. We could think of this as cost-sensitivity, using cost in the broadest sense of that term. There will always be those who are not looking primarily for the lowest price. In the purchase of many routine products and services, the greatest cost to some consumers is the time required in an already hectic schedule and the mental effort involved. Time and psychological effort may be more expensive than money, so these consumers will be prepared to pay a higher price for convenience, expediency, or just to get exactly what they want. What they want may simply be a less hectic or pressured shopping environment, which is why some customers are prepared to pay more at a neighbourhood specialty store, rather than battle the crowds to get a "better deal" at Wal-Mart, Costco or Winners.

quality
The characteristics of a product or service in relation to the expectations of the customer.

Another consideration is that some consumers' perceptions of product and service **quality** vary directly with price. Typically, the higher the price, the better the quality is perceived to be. Have you ever questioned product quality — when you're looking at ads for MP3 players, for example — when the price shown was unexpectedly low? Or, at the other extreme, have you ever selected a restaurant for a special dinner because you heard it was fairly expensive, assuming this meant it would be very nice? Consumers' perceptions of quality are, of course, influenced by other factors, such as store reputation, product colour or texture, brand, advertising, or the nature of the service and sales encounter. Many consumers are prepared to pay more for good service.

Price is so central to the decision process and to perception of value that many consumers live by rules of thumb, many of them learned from their parents. How many of us have been berated by our parents when a low-priced item of clothing fell apart the first time it was washed? The rule of thumb invoked on this occasion may have been "You get what you pay for" — meaning had you paid more, you would have received better quality.

More and more customers, in both B2C and B2B markets, are demanding better value in the goods and services they purchase. Value is the ratio of perceived benefits to perceived costs, including price and other incurred costs. Time associated with shopping for the product, time spent on the Internet browsing to gather information, the cost of gasoline or bus fares incurred travelling in search of your purchase, and time (and perhaps aggravation) assembling the product are examples of these other incurred costs.

When we say a product has good value, we don't necessarily mean it is inexpensive. Rather, good value indicates that a particular product has the kinds and amounts of potential benefits — such as product quality, image, and purchase convenience — that consumers expect from that product at a particular price level.

value for money
A customer's perception of what is received for the price paid.

Many businesses are responding to consumers' calls for more value by devising new products and services. The intent is to improve value (or more correctly, **value for money**) — essentially, the ratio of benefits to price. And benefits, real or otherwise, have to be perceived. This can be thought of in the following way:

$$\text{value for money} = \frac{\text{perceived benefits}}{\text{price}}$$

Improving value can be accomplished by maintaining essential elements, adding new elements or features, dropping other elements to cut costs, lowering prices, or more effectively communicating benefits that already exist. In other words, by increasing what is in the numerator of our ratio.

Rogers

Some major retailers, such as Zellers and Wal-Mart, have essentially adopted a low-price strategy, offering their customers good value for money. Other businesses are striving for better value with existing products. Fast-food firms such as Wendy's, Burger King, and McDonald's, have reduced prices on basic items by taking a "combination meals" approach, which bundles several items for a lower price than if the items were purchased separately.[1]

Bundles increase perceived value.

A good example of service bundling is the Rogers™ Better Choice Bundles™ (www.rogers.com) that allow customers to choose two or more services they want from the variety of available

services. This allows customers to choose from wireless high-speed Internet, cable TV, and home phone services and save up to 15 percent on their monthly bills. Of course, the convenience of having one service provider and one bill is also promoted. This bundling of services allows Rogers to provide more of what a customer wants while enjoying savings and convenience.

In the individual firm

The price of a product or service is an important determinant of the level of demand for it. Price affects a firm's competitive position and its market share. But, more than anything, price has a considerable bearing on a company's sales revenues and net profits. Obviously, it is through prices that money comes into an organization.

Some businesses use higher prices to convey an image of superior quality, but this would make sense only to consumers who consider quality to be important or feel they can afford to pay for it. Differentiated product features, a favourite brand, high quality, convenience, or some combination of these and other factors may be more important to consumers than price.

As we saw in Chapter 9, one objective of branding is to decrease the effect of price on the demand for a product. Some brands have been so successful in creating a solid, high-value image that they rarely if ever have to reduce their prices. Heinz Ketchup is the "gold standard" in the ketchup category, and customer loyalty to the brand is so strong that the product is rarely discounted — consumers are prepared to pay regular price all of the time. The same is true with many fashion brands, such as Chanel, whose famous No. 5 fragrance is almost never discounted.

Hugo Boss
Issey Miyake
Prada

Price plays a very important role in positioning the firm and its brands. Many companies will use the price of their products and services to send a message to customers that they are prestige or discount brands. Thus, some hairstylists will cut your hair for $9, while a haircut at a fashionable salon could cost you $50 or more. You can eat lunch for $5.99 at a downtown diner, but lunch at a trendy cafe could set you back $40. What contributes to the price difference? Certainly, the cost of the materials used and the skills of the service provider will contribute to the difference, but some cynical observers will comment, "You're paying for the name." So, what's wrong with that? Many people are obviously prepared to pay more to wear Hugo Boss (**www.hugoboss.com**) or Issey Miyake (**www.isseymiyake.com**), or to be seen carrying a Prada bag (**www.prada.com**). This is an obvious part of a company's positioning strategy. For example, while both are well-recognized brand names, Prada's leather goods are not positioned in the same market space as Roots' leather goods; Wal-Mart is not considered to be a direct competitor of Harry Rosen. Boss t-shirts are not positioned to compete directly with Eddie Bauer or even Hilfiger shirts.

BACK TO THE TOP

The price that a company charges must also be part of a co-ordinated strategy, one that fits with other elements of the marketing mix. Price is only one of the elements of the mix, and it has to be consistent with the messages being sent by the other elements. Thus, it is difficult to charge higher prices when product quality is questionable or inconsistent, or when advertising messages suggest that prices are competitive, or when service is poor or the method of distribution is inconvenient. The price charged must reflect the value being offered and must be acceptable to consumers, considering the other elements of the marketing mix being offered — particularly quality, service and convenience.

value strategy
An overall strategy of a company to offer value to its customers; price is part of this strategy.

Price is, therefore, an important component of a firm's **value strategy**. The company must decide what it intends to mean to customers in terms of the value being offered, and how it will deliver that value. Ideally, a firm needs to achieve a position where customers believe its prices are reasonable and fair. To deliver on a high-price strategy, a company has to be seen to be delivering value in many ways to justify its higher prices. When a company stresses low prices, customers do not expect value to be added in other areas.

Pricing Objectives

pricing objective
The goals that management tries to reach with its pricing structure and strategies.

Every marketing activity — including pricing — should be directed toward a goal, so management should decide on its **pricing objective** as part of its overall value strategy before determining the actual price. Yet, as logical as this may sound, few firms consciously establish, or explicitly state, a pricing objective.[2]

To be useful, the pricing objective that management selects must be compatible with the overall goals set by the company and the goals for its marketing program. Let's assume that an established company's goal is to increase return on investment from its present level of 15 percent to 20 percent within three years. It follows that the pricing goal during this period must be to achieve some stated percentage return on investment. It would not be logical, in this case, to adopt the pricing goal of maintaining the company's market share or of stabilizing prices. We will discuss the following pricing objectives:

- **Profit-oriented:**
  - To achieve a target return.
  - To maximize profit.
- **Market-oriented:**
  - To achieve a certain image or market position.
  - To increase sales volume.
  - To maintain or increase market share.
- **Status quo-oriented:**
  - To stabilize prices.
  - To meet competition.

Profit-oriented goals

Profit goals may be set for the short or long run. A company may select one of two profit-oriented goals for its pricing policy.

target return
A pricing goal that involves setting prices to achieve a certain percentage return on investment or on net sales.

mark-up
The dollar amount that is added to the acquisition cost of a product to determine the selling price.

Achieve a target return A firm may price its product to achieve a **target return** — a specified percentage return on its sales or on its investment. Many established retailers and wholesalers use a target return on sales as a pricing objective for short periods, such as a year or a fashion season. They add an amount to the cost of the product, called a **mark-up**, to cover anticipated operating expenses and provide a desired profit for the period. A chain of men's clothing stores may have a target profit of 7 percent of sales, and price its products accordingly. Safeway or Loblaws, for example, may price to earn a net profit of 1.5 percent on a store's overall sales — in fact, one main reason why major supermarkets are now offering a wide selection of non-food products relates to their wish to achieve a higher profit level, based on the higher margins typically earned on non-food items.

This approach is not necessarily useful nor even easily used in fast-changing, high-technology industries. Cost and price structures, as well as competitive forces, change so rapidly these days that this method reduces effective forecasting — if forecasting can even be considered to be accurate in some of these industries. As well, advances in technology can be so rapid that prices must be quickly adapted to impending advancements.

profit maximization
The pricing objective of making as much money as possible in the short term.

Maximize profits The pricing objective of making as much money as possible — using a "what the market will bear" approach — is followed by some firms, particularly in industries in which there is relatively little competition. The trouble with this goal is that, to some people, **profit maximization** has an ugly connotation, suggesting profiteering, high prices, and monopoly situations. Sometimes, this description appears to be too close to the mark, if a firm attempting to maximize its revenues in this way is the only provider of a product or service. Alternatively, a firm may be trying to earn what it can before other providers enter the market, or a fad or trend passes, or the next technology arrives that lessens the market value of the current product.

Market-oriented goals

In some companies, management's pricing policy is focused on driving sales volume or on maintaining a certain market positioning. The pricing goal may be to increase sales volume, to increase the firm's market share, or to achieve a certain image.

Increase sales volume The pricing goal of increasing sales volume is typically adopted to achieve rapid growth or to discourage potential competitors from entering a market. The goal is usually stated as a percentage increase in sales volume over some period, perhaps one year or three years. Management may seek higher sales volume by discounting or by some other aggressive pricing strategy, perhaps even incurring a loss in the short run. Thus, clothing stores run end-of-season sales and auto dealers offer rebates and below-market financing rates on new cars to stimulate sales. Many vacation destinations, such as golf courses and resorts, reduce prices during off-seasons to increase sales volume.

market share targets
When a company sets a certain share of the market as its objective when setting prices.

Maintain or increase market share In some companies, both large and small, the pricing objective is to achieve certain **market share targets**. Why is market share protected or pursued so vigorously? In growing fields such as computers, information technology, and communications, companies want a large market share in order to gain leverage with vendors and to aid in driving down production costs and other costs that are sensitive to economies of scale.

Most other industries today are not growing much, if at all, and, if they have not yet rationalized their operations, have excess production and operations capacity. Since the size of the market "pie" isn't growing in most cases, businesses that need added volume have to grab a bigger "slice of the pie" — that is, greater market share. The North American auto and airline industries illustrate this situation.

Achieve market position As we observed briefly above, some firms use price strategically to present a particular image of their companies or brands, or to achieve a certain market position. In such cases, price plays a very important role in sending messages to customers about the position of the company against its competitors. Thus, some companies will want to be seen as the low-price leader that will not be undersold, while another will stake out a position in the market as the value leader — you will pay higher prices but it will be worth it.

Status quo goals

stabilizing prices
A pricing goal designed to achieve steady, non-volatile prices in an industry.

Two closely related goals — **stabilizing prices** and meeting competition — are the least aggressive of all pricing goals. They are intended simply to maintain the firm's current situation — the status quo. With either of these goals, a firm seeks to avoid price competition.

Price stabilization often is the goal in B2B markets in which the product is highly standardized (such as lumber products or bulk chemicals) and in which one large firm historically has acted as a leader in setting prices. Smaller firms in these industries tend to "follow the leader" when setting their prices. What is the reason for such pricing behaviour? A price cut by any one firm is likely to be matched by all other firms in order to remain competitive; therefore, no individual firm gains, but all may suffer smaller profits. Conversely, a price boost is unlikely to be matched, but the price-changing firm faces a differential disadvantage because other elements of a standardized product, such as gasoline, are perceived to be fairly similar.

MARKETING AT WORK 10-2: RELATIONSHIPS

No More Haggling

There was a time when buying a new car meant price haggling with the salesperson and negotiating the price as well as some add-ons which helped customers feel they had gotten better value. In recent years, car dealerships have moved from negotiable pricing to lowest price window stickers that tell just how much the car will cost — no negotiation possible.

While many may argue that this is the fairest pricing model — after all, customers do not negotiate the price of a shirt at Wal-Mart or a jug of milk at the supermarket — others would say that big ticket items should allow for negotiation. After all, isn't that part of the salesperson's job?

The move to no-haggle pricing is also related to some extent to how customers buy cars today as compared to ten years ago. With every make and model of car and virtually every purchase option available for review on the Internet, a very large percentage of Canadians now arrive at dealer showrooms having already decided what car they want to buy and how much they are prepared to pay for it.

The move to no-haggle pricing was in response to many customers having compared prices before sitting down with a salesperson, and salespeople wanting to offer value through service, customer relationship building and the buying experience, not through how low the monthly payments would be. This shift from a price focus to one of customer service may have been overdue in the automobile industry, but it can only work if customers feel they are getting greater value. One thing is for sure, comparison shopping on sticker price alone may be easier for the customer, but deciding who is giving better service and the closer relationship takes time. The customer usually has a price point in mind and unless there are some very obvious advantages, the higher priced vehicle may get left on the lot, even if the long-term service is better.

QUESTIONS:

1. What is the connection between no-haggle pricing in the auto industry and the building of customer relationships by both the manufacturer and the dealer?
2. How does a customer feel in a no-haggle dealership?

Future Shop
Staples

Even in industries in which there are no price leaders, countless firms deliberately price their products to meet the prevailing market price. This pricing policy gives management an easy means of avoiding difficult pricing decisions. Many stores have adopted a price-matching policy, such as Future Shop (**www.futureshop.ca**) and Staples/Business Depot (**www.staples.ca**). This allows the onus to be placed on the customer to present a lower price to be matched or beaten by a fixed percentage, while allowing the retailer to advertise having the lowest prices available.

non-price competition
A strategy in which a firm tries to compete based on some factor other than price; for example, promotion, product differentiation, or variety of services.

Firms that adopt status quo pricing goals to avoid price competition are not necessarily passive in their marketing. Quite the contrary! Typically, these companies compete aggressively, using other marketing-mix elements — product, distribution, customer service, and especially promotion. This approach is called **non-price competition**, and its objective is to provide the customer with reasons other than price for buying the firm's products or services. It is never desirable to depend on differentiation based only on price, as this will simply escalate price-matching and reduce profits all around. Some consumers will pay extra for better service, greater convenience, or other attributes that they believe offer incremental value. Non-price competition is discussed in more detail in the "Price Competition" section of this chapter.

PAGE UP!

1. What are some of the factors, other than cost, that a company must take into consideration when it sets the price for its product or service?
2. Value for money can be thought of as an equation. What does it equal?
3. Name three pricing objectives that a company can choose, depending on its overall goals and strategy.

Factors Influencing the Price to be Charged

base price
The price of one unit of the product at its point of production or resale; same as list price.

Knowing the objective of its pricing, a company then can move to the heart of price management: determining the base price of a product — how much it will charge its customers. **Base price**, or list price, refers to the price of one unit of the product or service at its point of production, resale, or delivery. This price does not reflect discounts or special allowances, delivery or freight charges, or any other modifications.

Estimating demand

In pricing, a company must estimate the total demand for the product or service. This is easier to do for an established product than for a new one. The steps in estimating demand are (1) determine whether there is a price that the market expects and (2) estimate what the sales volume might be at different prices.

expected price
The price at which customers consciously or unconsciously value a product; what they think the product is worth.

The **expected price** of a product is the price at which customers consciously or unconsciously value it — what they think the product is worth. Expected price usually is expressed as a range of prices rather than as a specific amount. Thus, the expected price might be "between $250 and $300" or "not over $20." The expected price will vary by circumstances and across individuals. One customer may expect not to pay more than $15 for a haircut, while another may expect to pay $40 or more in a certain salon. One may be prepared to pay $80 for a black t-shirt while another would never think of paying so much. The expected price also depends on the image of the company or brand, and on the situations in which customers find themselves. You will expect to pay more for a round of golf at 9 a.m. on a Saturday in July than you will at twilight in late-October. You would expect to pay more for that black t-shirt at Holt Renfrew than you would at American Eagle Outfitters.

BACK TO THE TOP

MAC Cosmetics
L'Oreal

It's possible to set a price too low. If the price is much lower than the market expects, sales may be lost. For example, it probably would be a mistake for MAC Cosmetics (**www.maccosmetics.com**), a trendy cosmetics maker, to put a $1.49 price tag on its lipstick or for L'Oréal (**www.lorealparis.ca**) to price its hair-colouring products at $5.99, well

You're prepared to pay more for these products, because you're worth it.

GUEST MARKETER

How Much is That Salad?

By Gregory Pope

Greg Pope is Vice-President — Finance of Boston Pizza International. He believes that in the intensely competitive restaurant industry, a superb customer experience every time is essential to capturing repeat business. A fresh menu offering customer value for selection, quantity, quality and price is a key component of that customer experience. Greg is a very customer-focused Chartered Accountant and has an MBA from Memorial University.

Developing menu pricing in a national franchised restaurant environment is a complex process, balancing the needs of both the franchisor and franchisee. The menu is one of the most important customer interfaces for any restaurant, so both the franchisor and the franchisee want as much control as possible over what is on the menu and at what price.

To develop the price of any given item on a restaurant's menu, the company has to consider both internal and external factors. The price of ingredients, exact quantities required for a given recipe, overhead operating costs, and desired return on investment are all internal components in the pricing equation. Externally, the competitive environment, local tax and wage regulations, and anticipated customer demand for the menu item are all very important components of the ultimate price charged.

In a national franchise environment such as Boston Pizza International, not only are the factors noted above part of the pricing equation, but the level of complexity grows exponentially. It is the basic tenet of the franchise concept that creates this challenge — the customer experience in any Boston Pizza from Victoria to St. John's must be the same. If a customer in the West tells his or her friend in the East to try the BBQ Chicken Pizza, then the two customers must receive the same product. To accomplish this, additional pricing considerations come into play such as:

- common recipes across the chain;
- common ingredients, and the buying power that comes with buying large quantities of ingredients;
- transportation costs. If we are going to ensure a common customer experience, then the nacho appetizer must use the same nachos everywhere. If our chosen supplier manufactures the product in Halifax then it will cost more to get that product to the western and northern regions of the country;
- when a franchise rolls out a new national menu, the pricing will typically be set for the upcoming year. Setting prices so far into the future requires analysis to ensure desired earnings margins are maintained despite cost shifts that are inevitable during the year.

Let's explore these external factors further, as it is these factors that separate the challenges faced by a national franchise restaurant from a local operation.

The basis for all cost inputs is the ingredients. To ensure we have common recipes across the Boston Pizza chain, our corporate chef is responsible for creating and testing new recipes, determining what ingredients produce the taste that our customers want, and testing menu items in various stores across the country in a program we call our "test features." We solicit customer feedback when they order these items and ultimately decide whether to include the items on our national menu and finalize the recipe and ingredients accordingly.

Knowing all of the ingredients for an individual recipe is still not sufficient to conclude the price of the item. Once the recipe is finalized, we then look at common ingredients across other products to determine the opportunity for buying power with the supplier. The supplier may sell one or more products that we need in our restaurants, and with well over 200 stores across the country, our buying power is significant. This is an area that allows us as the franchisor to benefit all of our franchisees by lowering their food input costs, which is a franchisee's largest expense next to labour. By being able to minimize franchisee costs, then we can help them be more successful.

Transportation cost is an area that makes it very difficult to maintain commonality across the franchise. We ultimately have two choices when faced with these cost challenges: we can price the menu so that the franchisee with the highest transportation input costs meets the desired return and price every other store accordingly, or allow pricing variations in different regions. The first alternative would create a competitive disadvantage in other markets, so the conclusion is to have varying prices in different parts of Canada. Like transportation, other costs such as more expensive rent in large urban centres

and varying wage and benefit regulations by province all make different pricing necessary. For Boston Pizza, our large cheese requirements for pizzas make milk prices and provincial milk marketing boards another important regional consideration.

Allowing different prices across the country can easily become a burden to the franchisee. Franchisees want to have a say in what is charged for their product offerings; after all, it is their business and their investment at risk. Conversely, if Boston Pizza allowed each restaurant to set prices individually then uniformity would be lost, violating the basic franchise principle previously noted. Customers would wonder why the same entrée is a different price between two restaurants on opposite sides of town. Boston Pizza concluded that it would have regional menus, ensuring that within a specific and relatively large area the pricing will remain the same. Transportation costs should be very similar to Regina and Saskatoon, for example, so the need for different pricing over that smaller area is negligible. Today we have a total of sixteen different pricing menus in Canada, with new franchisees opening a restaurant having to adopt the pricing scheme for their region. To ensure they still have the opportunity for input, each of those regions has a franchisee pricing group; a team of franchisees that conclude what will be charged for products. To help exercise some control as franchisor, we offer a range of pricing for each product to help ensure that pricing does not deviate too significantly between regions.

Setting menu pricing over a certain planning horizon is a challenge. It is very expensive to print menus, and franchisees do not want to bear additional costs unnecessarily. They also want to make sure that they do not have their costs escalate to the point that profit margins suffer with no ability to increase prices. As the franchisor, Boston Pizza determined that a one-year planning horizon is the right interval to review our pricing, thereby allowing for inflation considerations to be considered while not putting an unnecessary burden on franchisees. This time frame also allows us to consider product offering changes for items that may not be selling at the levels we expect, and adding successful test features on a permanent basis as described above.

Working with franchisees across Canada, dealing with suppliers, considering new menu offerings with the associated costs, and studying the competition in each of our markets is a full-time position in Boston Pizza. All of this just to determine a bunch of numbers on your local Boston Pizza menu.

below its competitors' prices. This would not be consistent with the image of the company that built its reputation on the slogan "Because you're worth it." In all likelihood, customers would be suspicious about product quality, or their self-concept would not let them buy such low-priced products.

Although many consumers know that a high price does not necessarily mean high quality, most believe that a low price is an indication of lower quality. The prices just discussed would be significantly lower than expected from these brands and would signal inconsistency with the traditional products and images of those cosmetics companies. After all, the well-known slogan "Because you're worth it" doesn't mean much if the hair colour is only $4.99. And most consumers know that a "Rolex" priced at $15 in a sidewalk vendor's jewellery tray is not likely to be the real thing.

inverse demand
A price-volume relationship: The higher the price, the greater the unit sales.

After raising a product's price, some organizations have experienced a considerable increase in sales. This situation is called **inverse demand** — the higher the price, the greater the unit sales. Inverse demand usually exists only within a given price range and only at lower price levels. Suppose a leading-edge electronics company such as Sony increased the prices of its line of DVD players. Would you wonder if perhaps this was the brand everyone was buying, or that the marketplace must recognize these as superior to other players? Perhaps you'd believe that it means they're in short supply and you should get one while you can. However, at some point, inverse demand ends and the usual pattern — declining demand as prices rise — becomes evident.

price elasticity of demand
The responsiveness of quantity purchased to price changes.

It is extremely helpful to estimate what the sales volume will be at several different prices. By doing this, the seller is in effect determining the demand curve for the product. Moreover, the seller is gauging **price elasticity of demand**, which refers to the responsiveness of quantity purchased to price changes. Estimates of sales at different prices also are useful in determining break-even points (we'll discuss this topic later in the chapter).

Do I go see my favourite band, or buy those new shoes I've been looking at?

Competitive reactions

Competition greatly influences base price. A new product is distinctive only until the inevitable arrival of competition. The threat of potential competition is greatest when the field is easy to enter and profit prospects are encouraging. This may provide a good opportunity for a firm to exercise its competitive intelligence skills. Competition can come from these sources:

- ***Directly similar products:*** Nike versus Adidas or Saucony running shoes.
- ***Available substitutes:*** Air freight versus truck shipping or rail freight.
- ***Unrelated products seeking the same consumer dollar:*** A Nokia camera phone, new sneakers, an iPod Shuffle or tickets to a concert.

In the case of directly similar products, a competitor may adjust its prices. In turn, other firms have to decide what price adjustments, if any, are necessary to retain their customers.

Other marketing-mix elements

A product's base price is influenced greatly by the other components of the marketing mix, such as the product itself, distribution, promotion, and service.

Product We have already observed that a product's price is affected by whether it is a new item or an established one. Over the course of the life of a product — its life cycle — price changes are necessary to keep the product competitive. The end-use of the product must also be considered. For instance, there is little price competition among manufacturers of packaging materials or producers of industrial gases, so their price structure is stable. These business products are only an incidental part of the final article, so customers will buy the least expensive product consistent with the required quality. The price of a product is also influenced by whether (1) the product may be leased as well as purchased outright, (2) the product may be returned to the seller, and (3) a trade-in is involved.

Distribution The channels and types of intermediaries selected will influence a producer's pricing. A firm selling both through wholesalers and directly to retailers often sets a different factory price for these two groups of customers. The price to wholesalers is lower because they perform services that the producer would have to perform otherwise — such as providing storage, granting credit to retailers, and selling to small retailers.

Also, in some cases, a more direct distribution channel may allow a firm to charge higher prices, because customers are generally prepared to pay more for convenience and speedy delivery. Insurance companies that sell direct, as opposed to using agents, illustrate how cost savings can be passed to customers because of a major change in a distribution channel.

Promotion The extent to which the product is promoted by the producer or intermediaries and the methods used are added considerations in pricing. If major promotional responsibility is placed on retailers, they ordinarily will be charged a lower price for a product than if the producer advertises it heavily. Even when a producer promotes heavily, it may want its retailers to use local advertising to tie in with national advertising. Such a decision must be reflected in the producer's price to these retailers. The promotional message must also be consistent with the pricing strategy of the company, so that customers know what to expect. Promotion is also important in establishing the market position of the brand, which is reinforced by its price.

Service The price being charged must be consistent with the level of service being offered to the customer and may reflect that level of service. Thus, customers expect to pay less to pump their own gas or to shop at supermarkets where they bag and carry out their own groceries. Most customers expect to pay less on the Internet because they are performing many of the functions that companies normally provide. Price also reflects the quality of service. We expect a "better" and more stylish haircut from a trendy downtown salon where we pay more, probably because we expect the stylist to have more experience or skill or we simply enjoy the feel of the place.

Cost-Based Pricing

Some companies today still attempt to establish their prices based on total cost plus a desired profit.

cost-based pricing
A company uses its costs as the basis for setting its prices and does not take the customer or market into account.

Let's discuss **cost-based pricing**, which means setting the price of a product or service mainly on the basis of the total cost of producing that product or service, plus some desired profit. Suppose that Regency Builders, a housing contractor, figures that the labour and materials required to build and sell 10 condominiums will cost $750,000, and other expenses (office rent, depreciation on equipment, management salaries, and so on) will be $150,000. The contractor wants to earn a profit of 10 percent on the total cost of $900,000. Cost plus desired profit is $990,000, so each of the 10 condos is priced at $99,000.

While it is an easily applied method, cost-based pricing has limitations. One is that it does not recognize various types of costs or the fact that these costs are affected differently by changes in level of output. What if the company is unable to sell all of the units and the price has to be reduced to sell the remaining ones? This changes the entire pricing structure.

A second and more important limitation of this pricing approach is that market demand is ignored (which might explain why we have unsold condos). That is, cost-based pricing assumes that all of the output will be produced and sold. If fewer units were produced, each would have to sell for a higher price to cover all costs and show a profit. But if the condominium market is becoming depressed or the location of the units is not that desirable, output must be cut, as it is not wise to raise the unit price. Another limitation

Figure 10-1:
Examples of Mark-Up Pricing by Retailers and Wholesalers

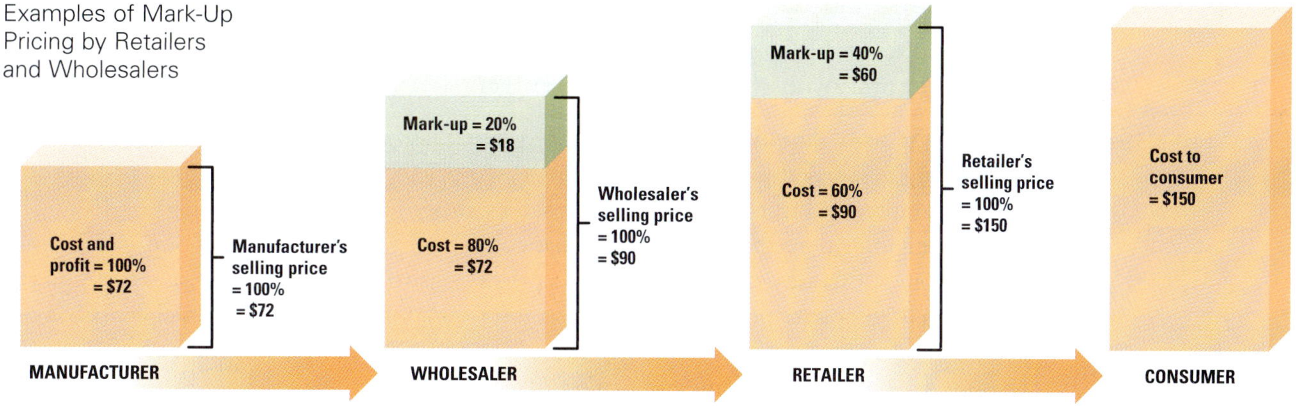

of this method is that it doesn't recognize that total unit-cost changes as output expands or contracts. However, a more sophisticated approach to cost-based pricing can take such changes into consideration.

One approach to cost-based pricing is to set prices based, at least, on variable costs only, not total costs. This is variable-cost pricing. Assume that a firm cannot obtain a price to cover its total costs because of, for example, extreme short-term competitive conditions — Air Canada may offer a seat sale on domestic and cross-border routes for a two-week period because of a downturn in demand and an oversupply of seats on competing airlines. If the firm can sell the product or service for any price in excess of its variable costs, the excess contributes to the payment of fixed costs. The firm can continue with this kind of pricing only if it has other sources of revenue to cover its total costs.

Pricing by intermediaries

At first glance, cost-based pricing appears to be widely used by retailing and wholesaling intermediaries. A retailer, for example, pays a certain amount to buy products and have them delivered to the store. Then the retailer adds an amount, a mark-up, to the acquisition cost. This mark-up is estimated to be sufficient to cover the store's expenses and provide a reasonable profit. Thus, a building materials outlet may buy a power drill for $30, including freight, and price the item at $50. The $50 price reflects a mark-up of 40 percent based on the selling price, or 66.7 percent based on the merchandise cost. Of course, in setting prices, intermediaries also should take into account the price expectations of their customers.

Various types of retailers require different percentage mark-ups because of the nature of the products handled and the services offered. A self-service supermarket has lower costs and thus can have a lower average mark-up than a full-service delicatessen. Figure 10-1 shows examples of mark-up pricing by intermediaries.

Is cost-based pricing really used by intermediaries? For the following reasons, it's safe to say that cost-based pricing is not widely used:

- Most retail prices are really only offers. If customers accept the offer, the price is fine. If they reject it, the price usually will be changed quickly, or the product may even be withdrawn from the market. Prices are always on trial.
- Many retailers don't use the same mark-up on all of the products they carry. A supermarket will have a mark-up of 6 to 8 percent on sugar and soap products, 15 to 18 percent on canned fruit and vegetables, and 25 to 30 percent on fresh meats and produce. These different mark-ups for distinctive products reflect competitive considerations and other aspects of market demand.
- The intermediary usually doesn't actually set a base price but only adds a percentage to the price already set by the producer. The producer's price is set to allow each intermediary to add a reasonable mark-up and still sell at a competitive retail price. The producer sets the key price with an eye on the final market.

Since a firm should be market-oriented and cater to consumers' needs, why are we considering cost-based pricing? Simply, cost-based pricing must be understood because it is referred to often in business. Further, it is used by many firms in the B2B market.

The traditional perspective has been that costs should be a determinant of prices, but not the only one. Costs are a floor under a firm's prices — particularly variable costs, as we pointed out earlier. If goods are priced under the cost floor for a long time, the firm will be forced out of business. But when it is used by itself, cost-based pricing is a weak and unrealistic method, because it ignores competition and market demand.

Break-Even Analysis

break-even point
The level of output at which revenues equal costs, assuming a certain selling price.

One way to consider both market demand and costs in price determination is to use break-even analysis to calculate break-even points. A break-even point is that quantity of output at which total revenue equals total costs, assuming a certain selling price. There is a different break-even point for each different selling price. Sales exceeding the **break-even point** result in a profit on each additional unit. The higher sales are above the break-even point, the higher will be the total and unit profits. Sales below the break-even point result in a loss to the seller.

Determining the break-even point

The method of determining a break-even point is illustrated in Table 10-1 and Figure 10-2. In our example, the Futon Factory's fixed costs are $25,000 and variable costs are assumed to be constant at $30 per unit.

The total cost of producing one unit is $25,030 — the Futon Factory obviously needs more volume to absorb its fixed costs! For 400 units, the total cost is $37,000 ($30 multiplied by 400, plus $25,000). In Figure 10-2, the selling price is $80 a unit, and variable costs of $30 per unit are incurred in producing each unit. Consequently, any revenue over $30 contributes to covering fixed costs (sometimes called overhead). When the price is $80, that contribution would be $50 per unit. At a price of $80, the break-even point is 500 units, because a $50 per-unit contribution will just cover the overhead of $25,000.

Stated another way, variable costs for 500 units are $15,000 and fixed costs are $25,000, for a total cost of $40,000. This amount equals the revenue from 500 units sold at $80 each. So, at an $80 selling price, the break-even volume is 500 units. Figure 10-2 shows a break-even point for an $80 price, but it is highly desirable to calculate break-even points for several different selling prices.

The break-even point can be found with this formula:

$$\text{break-even point in units} = \frac{\text{total fixed costs}}{\text{unit contribution to overhead}}$$

Because unit contribution to overhead equals selling price less the average variable cost, the working formula becomes:

$$\text{break-even point in units} = \frac{\text{total fixed costs}}{\text{selling price} - \text{average variable cost}}$$

TABLE 10-1 Futon Factory: Computation of Break-Even Point

At each of several prices, we wish to find out how many units must be sold to cover all costs. At a unit price of $100, the sale of each unit contributes $70 to cover overhead expenses. The Futon Factory must sell about 357 units to cover its $25,000 in fixed costs.

(1) Unit price	(2) Unit variable costs	(3) Contribution to overhead (1) – (2)	(4) Overhead (total fixed costs)	(5) Break-even point (rounded) (4) ÷ (3)
$60	$30	$30	$25,000	833 units
80	30	50	$25,000	500 units
100	30	70	$25,000	357 units
150	30	120	$25,000	208 units

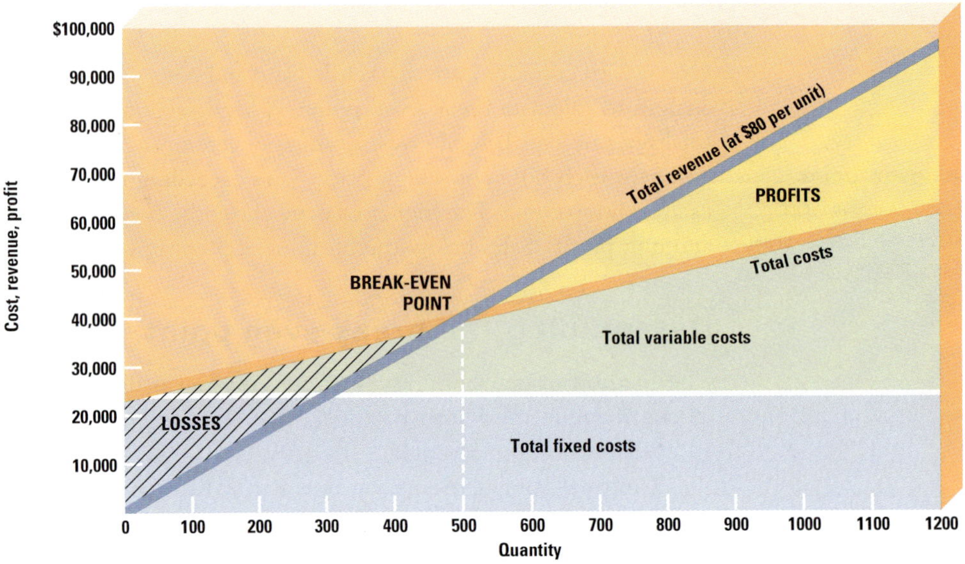

Figure 10-2:

Break-Even Chart for Futon Factory

Here the break-even point is reached when the company sells 500 units. Fixed costs, regardless of quantity produced and sold, are $25,000. The variable cost per unit is $30. If this company sells 500 units, total costs are $40,000 (variable cost of 500 × $30, or $15,000, plus fixed costs of $25,000). At a selling price of $80, the sale of 500 units will yield $40,000 revenue, and costs and revenue will equal each other. At the same price, the sale of each unit above 500 will yield a profit.

Evaluation of break-even analysis

Two basic assumptions underlie break-even analysis: Total fixed costs are constant and variable costs remain constant per unit of output. Actually, fixed costs may change, although not rapidly, and average variable costs normally fluctuate. Therefore, break-even analysis cannot be used conclusively in most companies, but it does provide some guidance.

Another drawback of break-even analysis is that it cannot tell marketers whether they can actually sell the break-even amount. Table 10-1, for example, shows what revenue will be at the different prices if the given number of units can be sold at these prices. The number the market will buy at a given price, however, could be below the break-even point. If that happens, the firm will not break even — it will show a loss.

Despite these limitations, management should not dismiss break-even analysis as a pricing tool. Even in its simplest form, break-even analysis is helpful because, in the short run, many firms experience reasonably stable cost-and-demand structures.[3] The break-even exercise tells marketers what they will have to sell at each price to cover costs. It assumes that the marketer's cost estimates are accurate, but does not give any indication whether the prices selected are reasonable in light of competitive activity or customer expectations. Nevertheless, it is a valuable exercise to force a company to focus on whether selling the break-even volume of units is a reasonable target.

Market-Based Pricing

Cost-based pricing is one extreme among pricing methods. At the other extreme are methods in which a firm's prices are set in relation to the market price. The seller's price may be set right at the market price to meet the competition, or it may be set above or below the market price.

Pricing to meet competition

Pricing to meet competition is simple to carry out. A firm ascertains what the market price is and, after allowing for customary mark-ups for intermediaries, arrives at its own selling price. To illustrate, let's take the high end of athletic shoes and a manufacturer like Nike. Nike's market research indicates that the Air Max 360 should be priced around $160 on the store shelf. Let's suppose that retailers want approximately a 40 percent average mark-up, based on their selling price. Consequently, after allowing $64 for the retailer's mark-up, Nike's price is $96. This manufacturer then has to decide whether $96 is enough to cover the associated costs and provide the desired level of profit. Sometimes, a producer faces a real squeeze if costs are rising but the market price is holding firm.

One situation in which management might price a product right at the market level is when competition is keen and the firm's product is not differentiated significantly from competing products: Product differentiation is absent, buyers and sellers are well informed, and the seller has no discernible control over the selling price. Most producers of agricultural products and small firms marketing well-known, standardized products use this pricing method. This describes the market condition known as **commoditization**, in which non-differentiated products are treated as commodities by customers.

commoditization
A situation in which consumers perceive little or no difference among the products of various companies and therefore focus on price as a differentiator.

Pricing below competition

A variation of market-based pricing is to set a price below the level charged by a firm's main competitors. Pricing below competition is done by discount retailers, such as Zellers, Costco and Wal-Mart that compete against conventional department stores such as Sears and The Bay. They stress low mark-up, high volume, and fewer customer services (including fewer salespeople). They price some heavily advertised, well-known brands below the suggested list price that is normally charged by full-service retailers. Even full-service retailers may price below the competitive level by eliminating specific services. Some gas stations offer a discount to customers who pay with cash instead of a credit card.

The risk in pricing below competition is that consumers begin to view the product as an undifferentiated commodity, such as coal and bulk salt, with all of the focus on price differences. If that happens, and some would say it already has in fields such as personal computers, then consumers choose the brand with the lowest price. In turn, competing firms are likely to wind up in a price war that diminishes or eliminates profits. One important problem faced by firms that consistently adopt a low-price strategy is that they have great difficulty ever raising their prices if they decide to adopt a different positioning strategy in the future.

BACK TO THE TOP

Think back to the chapter opener and Rohan's t-shirt dilemma. Rohan was perplexed as to why the prices of a basic black t-shirt would range from $18 to $90. After all, the product would be basically the same regardless of where he bought it. In reality he could get the Tommy shirt at Winners for much less than he could buy it at Sears. Why was it so much less at Winners?

Priced to communicate its prestige positioning.

Pricing above competition

Producers or retailers sometimes set their prices above the prevailing market level. Usually, pricing above competition works only when the product is distinctive or when the seller is staking out a prestige market position. Most communities have an elite clothing boutique and a prestigious jewellery store in which price tags are noticeably above the level set by other stores with seemingly similar products. However, a gas station that has a strong advantage based on a superior location (perhaps the only such station for many kilometres on the Trans-Canada Highway) may also be able to use above-market pricing.

Godiva
Purdys
Rogers
Crest

Above-market pricing often is used by manufacturers of prestige brands of high-cost products, such as automobiles (Porsche, Mercedes), clothing (Prada, Dolce & Gabbana), leather products (Gucci, Fendi), and watches (TAG Heuer, Rolex). Above-market pricing is sometimes found even among relatively low-cost products — chocolates, for example. Godiva (**www.godiva.com**), a brand of imported Belgian chocolates, follows this practice in Canada and the United States. Purdy's Chocolates (**www.purdyschocolates.ca**), based in Vancouver BC, provides premium chocolates at a premium price. Its Web site is designed so that customers can choose the products they want in quantities they desire. The site is attractive and provides pricing information in grams and ounces. The very popular Hedgehogs sell for $8.95 for 135 grams or 6 pieces. This is obviously a special buying situation and not your everyday chocolate fix! Similarly, Rogers Chocolates (**www.rogerschocolates.ca**) sells a 1 lb box of its Victoria Creams for $41.00 online.

Recently, even simple daily-use products have become premium-priced niche products. Mature, and highly competitive, product categories can provide some examples: Toothpaste has become a category where the old tried and true products with fluoride have had to give up shelf space to premium-priced products that deliver whitening solutions as well as a number of new flavours. Crest, for example, offers a line of products such as WhiteStrips, Night Effects Premium, Crest with Scope, Crest Pro-Health rinse and a full line of kid-friendly products. If you go to **www.crest.com** and open products there isn't a tube of plain old Crest in sight.

PAGE UP!

1. What are the factors that influence price determination?
2. Competition can come from similar products, available substitutes, or ______________ ______________.
3. What is the break-even point?

Price Competition

price competition
A strategy in which a firm regularly offers prices that are as low as possible, usually accompanied by a minimum of services.

In developing a marketing program, a firm decides on the positioning of its offerings and then manages the elements of its marketing mix to achieve and maintain the position — or reposition, if necessary. Some firms decide to compete primarily, but not exclusively, on the basis of price. Others use such non-price approaches as concentrating on quality of product or service and/or distribution, advertising, and promotion, but always with a compatible pricing policy.

A firm engages in **price competition** by:

1. Regularly offering products priced as low as possible and accompanied by a minimum of services. Zellers, Wal-Mart, and other discount houses and off-price retailers compete in this way.
2. Instigating changes in price that change the consumer's perception of product value without relying on other marketing factors. Supermarkets that rely on heavily discounted weekly specials to attract customers are an example of this practice. The "Bay Days" promotion regularly scheduled by The Bay department store is another such example.
3. Reacting to competitors' price changes with price changes of its own; for example, dropping prices to remain price-competitive.

Many companies today attempt to avoid price competition by striving to maintain prices and by attempting to protect or improve their market positions by emphasizing other aspects of their marketing programs. This does not mean that price setting is not an important component of the marketing mix. If the price of a product or service appears unreasonable in the marketplace, few consumers will buy it, regardless of how catchy the advertising jingle or how excellent the firm's reputation for service. In non-price competition, the seller is interested in creating value for the customer by offering something that will cause the customer not to focus on obtaining a lower price. When marketers are successful in adding such value, either through service or attractive features, the customer is often prepared to pay more.

In non-price competition, a manufacturer, retailer, or service provider will attempt to maintain or increase demand for its product by focusing on product differentiation, promotional activities, distribution, superior service, or some other technique. Some factor is chosen to distinguish this provider from others in the marketplace. This factor represents incremental value to the consumer beyond simply the cash price of the product or service, often proving to be a more enduring factor in consumer loyalty than is price. Price competition generally leads to customers switching brands in search of lower prices.

There are different ways to compete on a non-price basis, other than through the development of individual customer relationships previously discussed in this textbook. One similar way is through achieving mind share — clicking with customers on an emotional, non-price-related basis. Retailers such as The Gap, Old Navy, and Williams-Sonoma have achieved this. Forget about selling merchandise, sell the brand! Loblaws has done a good job of catering to and anticipating consumer needs, delivering a comprehensive array of products and services that forge a true brand connection.

Finding ways to deliver value unrelated to price is another method. It seems Canadian consumers have thumbed their noses at environmental concerns and embraced convenience as their mantra — offered by a wide variety of single-use, disposable products in the marketplace. Today, we have personal care wipes for face, toes, and virtually all regions in between, as well as household wipes for basically every cleaning need. Even a stodgy brand like Old Spice is getting in on the action with Cool Contact, Old Spice-scented deodorant body wipes targeted to college-aged men.[4]

Value pricing

value pricing
A strategy that is aimed at justifying a higher price based on offering the customer additional forms of value.

Earlier in this chapter, we discussed how more consumers are seeking better value in their purchases. In response, many companies in diverse industries are using what's called **value pricing**. This form of price competition aims to improve a product's perceived value — the ratio of its benefits to its price and related costs. Using value pricing:

- A firm may offer products with lower prices but the same, or perhaps added, benefits. Through bundling products or services, consumers may receive the benefit of reduced prices per item.
- At the same time, a firm may seek ways to reduce expenses so that profits do not suffer. If a company can manage to maintain costs or decrease them through increased efficiency, then there is a reduced need to increase prices as often and profit levels can be maintained.

It might be helpful to think of value pricing as a compromise or blend of price and non-price factors. Many things shape consumers' perception of value. Also, there is some variation among consumers as to what represents value. As discussed earlier, additional effort and cost must often be invested to enhance the offering, and yet there is an emphasis on reducing the final cash price to the customer. But, as also discussed, there are other components of total price beyond the cash that is exchanged between buyer and seller. A business can influence this by offering several value components at a number of levels — not just product features. Many times, if marketers can add value in some way, this will allow them to maintain price. If a competitive price gives the consumer greater flexibility and reduces risk or commitment, then this has provided more value to the consumer while not costing the seller a great deal.

Relationship pricing

Differentiated marketing is critical to attracting more loyal, longer-term customers. Companies have made advances in this area by discovering ways to reward their best customers for giving the companies their business. Many are developing value propositions for customers that correspond to their consumption patterns and value to the firm. In short, marketers are pricing in a way that encourages relationship-building, or at least customer retention.

relationship pricing
Related to the concept of value pricing, in which benefits are shared with customers to ensure that they receive better value and therefore remain loyal.

Relationship pricing is one of the elements of a broader customer-relationship strategy. You will recall that relationship marketing is about developing long-term, ongoing relationships with customers, the benefits of which include customer loyalty and reduced costs of doing business. In relationship pricing, some of these benefits are shared with customers to ensure that they receive better value and have another incentive to remain loyal. In other words, the firm gives a better price to its more valuable customers. In relationship pricing, customers are given a price incentive to encourage them to do all or most of their business with one supplier. For example, if you maintain a chequing account, savings account, mortgage account, and retirement fund with one bank, you will very likely be offered reduced interest rates on any borrowing or invited to join a plan that provides no-cost transactions. The bank is attempting to establish a relationship with you as a customer by offering you a preferred rate and is therefore encouraging you to do all of your business with it.[5] Insurance companies may offer a percentage discount based on the number of policies carried with the company.

Relationship pricing can be thought of as pricing based on bundling products or services over the longer term — sort of like a bulk purchase, but over time. It is pricing based on the long-term potential of the relationship determined on a discretionary one-to-one basis within a range of possible discount levels. Initially, relationship pricing is based on the perceived potential of future business to encourage a consumer to select this provider. Future exchanges may enhance the perception of a special relationship and express to customers their value to the firm, or combat the risk of defection. Beyond special pricing considerations, this approach might involve some free services or products and extra or discretionary services.

Leader pricing

leader pricing
Involves temporarily reducing the prices of well-known items; the price cuts are made with the idea that these "specials" (leaders) will attract customers to the store.

Many firms, primarily retailers, temporarily cut prices on a few items to attract customers. This price and promotional strategy is called **leader pricing** and items for which prices are reduced below the retailer's cost are often called loss leaders.

Items featured as leaders should be well known, heavily advertised articles that are purchased frequently. The idea is that customers will come to the store to buy the advertised leader items and then stay to buy other regularly priced merchandise. The net result, the firm hopes, will be increased total sales volume and net profit.

Market-Entry Pricing Strategies

In preparing to enter the market with a new product or service, management must decide whether to adopt a market-skimming or a market-penetration pricing strategy.

market-skimming pricing
A pricing strategy in which the initial price is set high in the target market's range of expected prices.

Market-skimming pricing

Setting a relatively high initial price for a new product is referred to as **market-skimming pricing**. Ordinarily, the price is set high in relation to the target market's range of expected prices. That is, the price is set at or close to the highest level that the most interested consumers will pay for the new product. This strategy assists in the recovery of research, development, and introductory costs as quickly as possible before decreasing the price to attract the next price-sensitive level of customers and to meet competitors who are likely to come into the market.

Further, lofty prices can be used to connote high quality and/or cutting-edge innovation and technology. Moreover, market-skimming pricing is likely to curtail demand to levels that do not outstrip the firm's production capacities. Finally, it provides the firm with flexibility, because it is much easier to lower an initial price that meets with consumer resistance than it is to raise an initial price that has proven to be too low to cover costs.

Market-skimming pricing is suitable under the following conditions:

- The new product has distinctive features strongly desired by consumers.
- Demand is fairly inelastic — most likely the case in the early stages of a product's life cycle. Under this condition, lower prices are unlikely to produce greater total revenues.
- The new product is protected from competition through one or more market-entry barriers, such as a patent.

Market-penetration pricing

market-penetration pricing
A pricing strategy in which a low initial price is set to reach the mass market immediately.

In **market-penetration pricing,** a relatively low initial price is established for a new product or service. The price is low in relation to the target market's range of expected prices. The primary aim of this strategy is to penetrate the mass market immediately and, in so doing, generate substantial sales volume and a large market share. At the same time, it is intended to discourage other firms from introducing competing products.

Market-penetration pricing makes the most sense under the following conditions:

- A large mass market exists for the product.
- Demand is highly elastic, typically in the later stages of the life cycle for a product category.
- Substantial reductions in unit costs can be achieved through large-scale operations. In other words, economies of scale are possible.
- Fierce competition already exists in the market for this product or can be expected to materialize soon after the product is introduced.

When computer firms introduced clones that imitated IBM or Apple models a number of years ago, they were relying on market-penetration pricing by undercutting the prices of the large, well-known producers. Now, a number of years later, pricing approaches have changed again. In an attempt to optimize price points, some manufacturers follow a pricing philosophy called "design to price." They figure out the price point consumers are willing to pay for a particular item, then they build the best product they can to meet that price point and achieve their profit objectives. In the case of Compaq, it determined that under $2,000 was a key price for personal computers. It designs its computers accordingly, cutting back on some options and specifications to meet that price point and capture that share of the market. Other PC manufacturers partner with software producers in order to equip their products with pre-installed, in-demand programs as part of the purchase price. Of course, Dell offers the ultimate in pricing — factory direct. Customers can buy a Dell directly from the manufacturer and cut out the associated intermediary costs. This, coupled with exceptional service and a quality product, has allowed Dell to take a commanding lead in the home computer market.

Discounts and Allowances

Discounts and allowances result in a deduction from the base (or list) price. The deduction may be in the form of a reduced price or some other concession, such as free merchandise or advertising allowances. Discounts and allowances are commonplace in business dealings.

quantity discount
A reduction of the list price when large quantities are purchased; offered to encourage buyers to purchase in large quantities.

Quantity discounts

Quantity discounts are deductions from the list price that are intended to encourage customers to buy in larger volumes or to buy most of what they need from the firm offering the discount. Such discounts are generally based on the size of the purchase, either in dollars or in units.

non-cumulative quantity discount
A quantity discount based on the size of an individual order of products.

A **non-cumulative quantity discount** is based on the size of an individual order of one or more products. A pro shop may sell golf balls at $2 each or at three for $5. Air Canada's Flight Pass program is an example of volume discounting. A manufacturer or wholesaler may set up a quantity discount schedule such as the following, used by a manufacturer of industrial adhesives:

Boxes purchased in single order	Percent discount from list price
1–5	None
6–12	2.0
13–25	3.5
Over 25	5.0

Non-cumulative quantity discounts are intended to encourage large orders. Many expenses, such as billing, order filling, and salaries of salespeople, are about the same whether the seller receives an order totalling $10 or one totalling $500. Consequently, selling expense as a percentage of sales decreases as orders grow in size. With a non-cumulative discount, a seller shares such savings with a purchaser of large quantities.

cumulative quantity discount
A quantity discount based on the total volume purchased over a specified period of time.

A **cumulative quantity discount** is based on the total volume purchased over a specified period. This type of discount is advantageous to a seller because it ties customers more closely to that firm. The more total business a buyer gives a seller, the greater the discount.

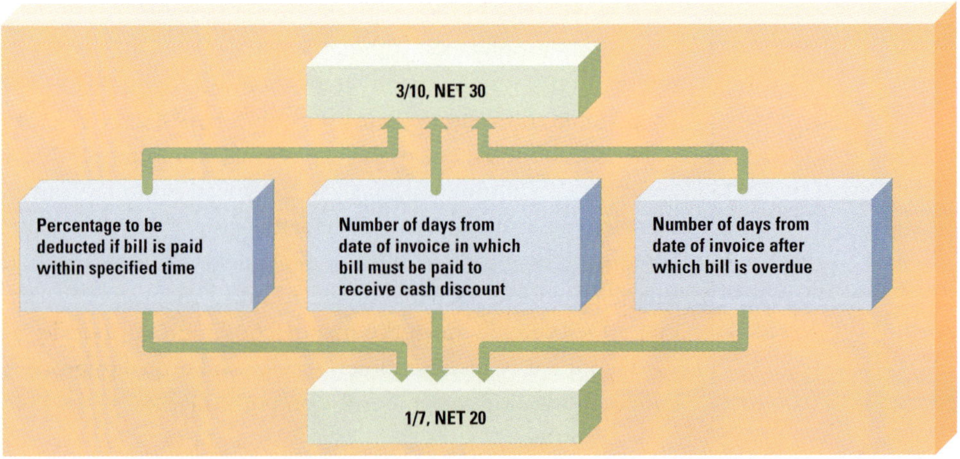

Figure 10-3: Parts of a Cash Discount

Airlines' frequent-flyer and hotels' frequent-guest programs are a form of cumulative discount. Cumulative discounts also are common in selling perishable products. These discounts encourage customers to buy fresh supplies frequently, so that merchandise will not become stale.

Trade discounts

Trade discounts, sometimes called functional discounts, are reductions from the list price offered to buyers in payment for marketing functions that the buyers perform, such as storing, promoting, and selling the product. A manufacturer may quote a retail price of $400 with trade discounts of 40 percent and 10 percent. The retailer pays the wholesaler $240 ($400 less 40 percent) and the wholesaler pays the manufacturer $216 ($240 less 10 percent). The wholesaler is given the 40 and 10 percent discounts. The wholesaler is expected to keep the 10 percent to cover the costs of the wholesaling functions and pass on the 40 percent discount to retailers.

Cash discounts

A cash discount is a deduction granted to buyers for paying their bills within a specified time period. The discount is computed on the net amount due after first deducting trade and quantity discounts from the base price. Every cash discount includes three elements, as indicated in Figure 10-3:

- The percentage discount.
- The time period during which the discount may be taken.
- The time when the bill becomes overdue.

Let's say that a buyer owes $360 after other discounts have been granted and is offered terms of 2/10, n/30 on an invoice dated November 8. This means that the buyer may deduct a discount of 2 percent ($7.20) if the bill is paid within 10 days of the invoice date — by November 18. Otherwise the entire (net) bill of $360 must be paid in 30 days — by December 8.

Most buyers are eager to pay bills in time to earn cash discounts. The discount in a 2/10, n/30 situation may not seem like very much, but this 2 percent is earned just for paying 20 days in advance of the date on which the entire bill is due. If buyers fail to take the cash discount in a 2/10, n/30 situation, they are, in effect, borrowing money at a 36-percent annual rate of interest.

seasonal discount
A discount for placing an order during the seller's slow season.

forward dating
A combination of a seasonal discount and a cash discount under which a buyer places an order and receives shipment during the off-season, but does not have to pay the bill until after the season has started and some sales revenue has been generated.

Other discounts and allowances

A manufacturer of goods such as air conditioners or snowmobiles purchased on a seasonal basis may consider granting a **seasonal discount**. This discount of, for example, 5, 10, or 20 percent is given to a customer who places an order during the slack season. Off-season orders enable manufacturers to better use their production facilities and/or avoid inventory carrying costs. Many services firms also offer seasonal discounts. For example, Sandals, other vacation resorts, and cruise lines lower their prices during the off-season.

Forward dating is a variation on both seasonal and cash discounts. A manufacturer of fishing tackle might seek and fill orders from wholesalers and retailers during the winter months, but the bills would be dated April 1, with terms of 2/10, n/30 offered as of that date. Orders filled in December and January help to maintain production during the slack season for more

MARKETING AT WORK 10-3: TECHNOLOGY

No-Contact Customers

RFID technology was introduced in the late 1980s and its initial applications were for tracking mobile assets and managing field operations. Now, radio frequency identification (RFID) is gaining ground in the customer service side of business. Customers can pay for gas, food and other items at the checkout counter with a wave of the hand. Texas Instruments provides wireless RFID technology that allows customers to use their mobile phones or a key chain to pay for purchases.

This technology allows customers to make quick purchases, but it also allows businesses to gather information about customer purchasing habits and to customize service for customers that can lead to greater customer loyalty, lower costs and increased profits.

Customers like the technology. Many feel that it is more secure than traditional monetary transactions. Additional applications for business include personnel access, ticketing, and PayTV. As well, there are applications for traditional loyalty programs as the consumer's purchases can be tracked using the RFID and the traditional loyalty stamp or swipe cards will no longer be needed.

QUESTIONS:

1. What are the implications of RFID technology for pricing?
2. Is the availability of such technology likely to cause customers to pay less attention to price?

SOURCE: Adapted from www.ti.com, accessed, February 10, 2006.

efficient operation. The forward-dated bills allow the wholesale or retail buyers to pay their bills after the season has started and they can generate some sales revenue from the products delivered earlier.

promotional allowance
A price reduction granted by the seller as payment for promotional services rendered by the buyer.

A **promotional allowance** is a price reduction granted by a seller as payment for promotional services performed by buyers. To illustrate, a producer of builders' hardware gives a certain quantity of free goods to dealers who prominently display its line. Or a clothing manufacturer pays one-half the cost of a retailer's ad featuring its product.

Regulation of Pricing

The discounts and allowances discussed in this section may result in different prices for different customers. When price differentials exist, there is price discrimination. In certain situations, price discrimination is prohibited by the Competition Act. This is one of the most important federal laws affecting a company's marketing program. Below are some excerpts from the Act (in italics) and their implications for common pricing strategies.

Price discrimination

Competition Act section 50 (1):

(a) Everyone engaged in a business who ... is a party or privy to, or assists in, any sale that discriminates to his knowledge, directly or indirectly, against competitors of a purchaser of articles from him in that any discount, rebate, allowance, price concession or other advantage that, at the time the articles are sold to such purchaser, is available to such competitors in respect of a sale of articles of like quality and quantity ... is guilty of an indictable offence and is liable to imprisonment of two years.

Predatory pricing

Competition Act section 50 (1):

(c) Everyone engaged in a business who engages in a policy of selling products at prices unreasonably low, having the effect or tendency of substantially lessening competition or eliminating a competitor, or designed to have such effect, is guilty of an indictable offence and is liable to imprisonment for two years.

Granting promotional allowances as an offence

Competition Act section 51 (1):

In this section, "allowance" means any discount, rebate, price concession or other advantage that is or purports to be offered or granted for advertising or display purposes and is collateral to a sale or sales of products but is not applied directly to the selling price.

The Act requires that promotional allowances be granted proportionately to all competing customers.

These provisions apply to the sale of both articles and services. Discrimination in the granting of promotional allowances is a per se offence, not requiring proof of the existence of either a practice of discrimination or a lessening of competition. A company that wishes to discriminate among its customers may do so through the legal practice of granting quantity discounts.

Resale price maintenance

Some manufacturers want control over the prices at which retailers resell the manufacturers' products. This is most often done in Canada by following a policy of providing manufacturers' suggested list prices, where the price is just a guide for retailers. It is a list price on which discounts may be computed. For others, the suggested price is "informally" enforced. Enforcement of a suggested price, termed resale price maintenance, has been illegal in Canada since 1951.

The Competition Act prohibits a manufacturer or supplier from requiring or inducing a retailer to sell a product at a particular price or not below a particular price. On occasion, a supplier may attempt to control retail prices through the use of a "suggested retail price." The use of suggested retail prices is permitted only if the supplier makes it clear to the retailer that the product may be sold at a price below the suggested price and that the retailer will not in any way be discriminated against if the product is sold at a lower price.

Geographic Pricing Strategies

In pricing, a marketer must consider the costs of shipping physical products to the buyer. These costs grow in importance as freight becomes a larger part of total variable costs. Pricing policies may be established under which the buyer pays all of the freight expense, the seller pays the entire cost, or the seller and buyer share this expense. The strategy chosen can influence the geographic limits of a firm's market, the locations of its production facilities, the sources of its raw materials, and its competitive strength in various geographic markets.

f.o.b. factory pricing
A geographic pricing strategy whereby the buyer pays all freight charges from the selling facility location to the destination.

Free on board (f.o.b.) point-of-production pricing

In one widely used geographic pricing strategy, the seller quotes the selling price at the factory or at some other point of production or origin. In this situation, the buyer pays the entire cost of transportation. This is usually referred to as **f.o.b. factory pricing**. Of the four strategies discussed in this section, this is the only one in which the seller does not pay any of the transport costs. The seller pays only the cost of loading the shipment aboard the carrier — hence the term f.o.b., or free on board.

uniform delivered pricing
A geographic pricing strategy whereby the same delivered price is quoted to all buyers, regardless of their location; same as postage-stamp pricing.

Uniform delivered pricing

Under the **uniform delivered pricing** strategy, the same delivered price is quoted to all buyers, regardless of their locations. This strategy is sometimes referred to as "postage-stamp pricing" because of its similarity to the pricing of first-class mail service. The net revenue to the seller varies, depending on the shipping cost involved in each sale.

A uniform delivered price is typically used where transportation costs are a small part of the seller's total costs. This strategy is also used by many retailers who feel that "free" delivery is an additional service that strengthens their market position.

Zone-delivered pricing

zone-delivered pricing
A geographic pricing strategy whereby the same delivered price is charged at any location within each geographic zone.

Under a **zone-delivered pricing** strategy, a seller would divide the Canadian market into a limited number of broad geographic zones. Then, a uniform delivered price is set within each zone. Zone-delivered pricing is similar to the system used in pricing parcel post services and long-distance telephone service.

Freight-absorption pricing

freight-absorption pricing
A geographic pricing strategy whereby the seller pays for (absorbs) some of the freight charges in order to penetrate more distant markets.

A **freight-absorption pricing** strategy may be adopted to offset some of the competitive disadvantages of f.o.b. factory pricing. With an f.o.b. factory price, a firm is at a price disadvantage when it tries to sell to buyers located in markets closer to competitors' plants. To penetrate more deeply into such markets, a seller may be willing to absorb some of the transportation costs. Thus, seller A will quote to the customer a delivered price equal to (1) A's factory price plus (2) the freight costs that would be charged by the competitive seller located closest to that customer.

Special Pricing Strategies

To set initial prices and evaluate existing prices, a firm needs to consider a number of distinctive strategies. It's likely that at least one, but probably not all, will apply to a particular pricing situation.

One-price and flexible-price strategies

one-price strategy
A strategy under which a seller charges the same price to all customers of the same type who buy the same quantity of goods.

flexible-price strategy
A pricing strategy under which a company sells similar quantities of merchandise to similar buyers at different prices; same as variable-price strategy.

Rather early in its pricing deliberations, management should decide whether to adopt a **one-price strategy** or a **flexible-price strategy**. Under a one-price strategy, a seller charges the same price to all similar customers who buy similar quantities of a product. Under a flexible-price strategy (also called a variable-price strategy), similar customers may each pay a different price when buying similar quantities of a product.

In Canada, a one-price strategy has been adopted more often than flexible pricing. Most retailers, for example, follow a one-price policy — except in cases in which trade-ins are involved, and then flexible pricing abounds. A one-price policy builds customer confidence in a seller, whether at the manufacturing, wholesaling, or retailing level. Weak bargainers need not feel that they are at a competitive disadvantage.

When a flexible-pricing policy is followed, the price often is set as a result of buyer-seller bargaining. In automobile retailing — with or without a trade-in — price negotiating (bargaining) is quite common, even though window-sticker prices may suggest a one-price policy. Variable pricing may be used to meet a competitor's price.

Psychological pricing

Considerations for final pricing decisions may often involve more than just calculations about covering costs and how much you can get the customer to pay: Thought is also given to how the price of an item or service can be used to communicate information to the

psychological pricing
Setting a price to have a special appeal to a particular segment of customers.

bait pricing
Attracting consumers with a low-priced feature item and then pointing out its weaknesses in order to sell a more expensive version.

prestige pricing
Raising prices above competitive levels.

price lining
Involves selecting a limited number of prices at which a business will sell related products.

consumer — to let the price tell the consumer (or let consumers think) something about the product. Price is used to communicate price level, of course, but the use of certain numbers influence the consumer's perception of that level and therefore the value received. Price also is used to connote quality, value, and up-to-date and cutting-edge innovation. While a high price does not mean high quality, it can be taken as an indication in many consumers' minds.

Psychological pricing means setting a price to have a special appeal to a particular segment of consumers. Loss-leader pricing (as discussed earlier) is intended to attract customers by selling some products at a very low price, perhaps at a loss, to get people into the store. This is often used for weekly supermarket sales. Or there is **bait pricing**, baiting consumers with a low-priced feature item but then pointing out its weaker details in order to sell a more expensive version. This approach also can work in the other direction — by raising prices above competitive levels, sometimes to such a degree that it is referred to as **prestige pricing**.

Price lining involves selecting a limited number of prices at which a business will sell related products. It is used extensively by clothing retailers. A sporting-goods store, for instance, may sell several styles of running shoes at $99.95 a pair, another group at $119.95, and a third at $149.95. For the consumer, the main benefit of price lining is that it simplifies buying decisions. For the retailer, price lining helps in planning purchases. The buyer for the sporting-goods store can go to market looking for shoes that can be retailed at one of its three prices.

odd pricing
A form of psychological pricing that consists of setting prices at odd amounts ($4.99 rather than $5.00, for example) in the belief that these seemingly low prices will result in larger sales volume.

Odd pricing, another psychological strategy, is commonly used in retailing. Odd pricing sets prices at uneven (or odd) amounts, such as 49 cents or $19.95, rather than at even amounts. Autos often are priced at $19,995 rather than $20,000, and houses sell for $189,500 instead of $190,000. Odd pricing is often avoided in prestige stores and on higher-priced luxury items. A man's suit at Holt Renfrew, for example, may be priced at $1,000, but not $999.95. While a cotton blouse at Zellers may be priced at $19.97, a cotton blouse at Aritzia may cost $131.

The rationale for odd pricing is that it suggests lower prices and, as a result, yields greater sales than even pricing. According to this reasoning, a price of 98 cents will bring in more revenue than a $1 price for the same product. Research indicates that odd pricing can be an effective strategy for a firm that emphasizes low prices.[6]

everyday low pricing (EDLP)
A pricing strategy that involves consistently low prices and few if any temporary price reductions.

Everyday low pricing (EDLP) may be trendy, but it certainly is not new. Basically, it involves consistently low prices and few if any temporary price reductions. Both Wal-Mart and Zellers have been extremely successful with this type of pricing, as have warehouse stores such as Costco and Staples/Business Depot. Some of these stores support this pricing policy with a guaranteed price-matching or price-beating policy. This feels like "insurance" to consumers and may reassure them that this particular store must offer the lowest prices in order to make this claim.

Many firms do not engage in EDLP but rather in high-low pricing, which involves charging relatively low prices for some products and higher prices for others. This strategy combines frequent price reductions and aggressive promotion to convey an image of very low prices. Many supermarkets and some department stores and chain drugstores rely on this approach.

PAGE UP!

1. What is non-price competition?
2. What is the difference between market-skimming and market-penetration pricing strategies?
3. Pricing very low to get people into a store or raising prices above the competition to make the product seem more prestigious are both examples of ______________ pricing.

Key Terms and Concepts

bait pricing 301
base price (list price) 283
break-even point 289
commoditization 291
cost-based pricing 287
cumulative quantity discount 296
everyday low pricing (EDLP) 301
expected price 283
flexible-price (variable-price) strategy 300
f.o.b. factory pricing 299
forward dating 297
freight-absorption pricing 300
inverse demand 285
leader pricing 294
market-penetration pricing 295
market share targets 281
market-skimming pricing 294
mark-up 280
non-cumulative quantity discount 296
non-price competition 282
odd pricing 301
one-price strategy 300
prestige pricing 301
price 274
price competition 292
price elasticity of demand 285
price lining 301
price sensitivity 277
pricing objective 280
profit maximization 280
promotional allowance 298
psychological pricing 301
quality 277
quantity discount 296
relationship pricing 294
seasonal discount 297
stabilizing prices 281
target return 280
uniform delivered pricing 299
value for money 278
value of a product/service 274
value pricing 293
value strategy 279
zone-delivered pricing 300

Questions and Problems

1. Explain how a firm's pricing objective may influence the promotional program for a product. Which of the six pricing goals involves the largest, most aggressive promotional campaign?
2. What marketing conditions might logically lead a company to set "meeting competition" as a pricing objective?
3. Name at least three products for which you think an inverse demand exists. For each product, within which price range does this inverse demand exist?
4. Why is the status quo goal of meeting the competition considered to be the least aggressive of all of the pricing goals?
5. A small manufacturer sold ballpoint pens to retailers at $8.40 per dozen. The manufacturing cost was 50 cents for each pen. Expenses, including all selling and administrative costs except advertising, were $19,200. How many dozens of pens must the manufacturer sell to cover these expenses and pay for an advertising campaign costing $6,000?
6. For each of the following products, should the seller adopt a market-skimming or a market-penetration pricing strategy? Support your decision in each instance.
   a. High-fashion dresses styled and manufactured by Lida Baday.
   b. An exterior house paint that wears twice as long as any competitive brand.
   c. A cigarette that is totally free of tar and nicotine.
   d. A tablet that converts a litre of water into a litre of automotive fuel.
7. A manufacturer of appliances quotes a list price of $800 per unit for a certain model of refrigerator and grants trade discounts of 35, 20, and 5 percent. What is the manufacturer's selling price? Who might get these various discounts?
8. The Craig Charles Company (CCC) sells to all of its customers at the same published price. One of its sales managers hears that Jamaican Enterprises is offering to sell to one of CCC's customers, Mountain Sports, at a lower price. CCC then cuts its price for Mountain Sports but maintains the original price for all other customers. Is CCC's price cut for Mountain Sports a violation of the Competition Act?
9. An eastern firm wants to compete in western markets, where it is at a significant disadvantage because of freight costs. What pricing alternatives can it adopt to overcome the freight cost differential?
10. Under what conditions is a company likely to use a flexible-price strategy? Can you name firms that use this strategy other than when a trade-in is involved?

Hands-On Marketing

1. Visit a local discount store such as Wal-Mart or Zellers. Note the prices of three products, including a child's toy, a piece of electronic equipment such as an MP3 player, and a small appliance. Check these prices at other outlets that sell on the basis of high-low pricing, such as Sears or The Bay. Determine whether there is a difference in price. Are the products selling at high or low prices in the non-discount outlets?

2. Karina's Pizza produces two products, 12-inch pizzas and 16-inch pizzas, with the following characteristics:

	12-Inch Pizza	16-Inch Pizza
Selling price	$500,000 ($5/unit)	$900,000 ($6/unit)
Variable cost	$300,000	$300,000
Expected sales (units)	100,000	150,000

The total fixed costs for the company are $700,000.

a. What is the anticipated level of profits for the expected sales volumes?
b. Assuming that the product mix in units would be the same as above at the break-even point, compute the break-even point in terms of number of units of each of the products.
c. If the product sales mix was to change to four 12-inch pizzas for each 16-inch pizza, what would be the new break-even volume for each of the products? Comment on the number of units required to break even for this sales mix, compared with the original sales mix.

Note: Question 2 was prepared by Associate Professor Judith A. Cumby, Faculty of Business Administration, Memorial University of Newfoundland, as a basis for class discussion and is not intended to reflect either an effective or an ineffective handling of a management problem.

Back to the Top

We'll never know what t-shirt Rohan eventually bought. If he was only interested in the lowest price, he might have taken that drive to Winners. If he wanted a mid-priced shirt he probably picked up the Calvin Klein or the Tommy Hilfiger at Sears. If he wanted to treat himself to a name brand product he may have returned to buy the Hugo Boss shirt that he saw first thing in the morning. Having read this chapter, we know that there is more to the cost of a product than the sticker price. Consumers may be convinced to buy for any number of reasons and may not choose the lowest priced alternative. So, what *is* the price of a basic black t-shirt?

Online LearningCentre

Want to get better grades, tips on how to study more effectively, and up-to-date information on happenings in the world of marketing? Then, visit the Online Learning Centre for practice tests, Study Smart software, *Marketing Magazine*, and much more! **www.mcgrawhill.ca/olc/sommers**

CASE 4-1:

Bay Day — How Much Are Those Pants?

Bob Jones was walking through the men's wear department of the downtown Bay department store, taking a shortcut to the restaurant where he was meeting Gail for lunch. As he neared the door, Bob noticed a rack of men's cotton pants, above which was a large sign announcing "Special! 50% off." Although Bob had not intended to buy pants that day, he was attracted by the sign and stopped to look at the goods.

As Bob examined the pants on the rack, he noticed that the brand was Izod and that the original price was $80. He thought, "I could use a pair of pants and this is a really good price." He had a couple of Izod golf shirts hanging in his closet, and he thought the sweater Gail had given him for his birthday may have been Izod as well. He picked out a dark green pair, size 32, and tried them on. They fit perfectly, so he decided to buy them.

"Will that be on your Bay account, sir?" asked the sales clerk. Bob replied that he would be paying cash and took a $50 bill from his wallet. The clerk then asked, "Do you have your Bay Day card?" Bob indicated that he wasn't familiar with a Bay Day card. The clerk explained that he should have been handed a Bay Day card as he entered the store and that, since this was Bay Day, he was entitled to scratch a certain part of the card to reveal the discount that he would receive on his purchase. As Bob didn't have a card, she reached under her counter and gave him one. Bob scratched the latex portion of the card and saw the words "30% off."

Bob was certain that he would not receive an extra 30 percent off pants that were already reduced by 50 percent. He didn't feel disappointed, though, because he thought that at 50 percent off the pants were already a good bargain. He showed the card to the sales clerk and commented, "Too bad I can't use this, the pants are already 50 percent off." The lady smiled at him and said, "Oh no, you get an additional 30 percent off the sale price. Let's see, that's another $12, so the price of the pants will be $28." Bob was delighted. He really hadn't expected to get the pants for such a low price. He had thought he was getting a good deal at $40. He paid the $28, plus tax, thanked the sales clerk, and rushed off to apologize to Gail for being late.

Questions:

1. What was the price of the pants that Bob bought?
2. What factors influenced his decision to buy?
3. What would Bob have done if he had seen a rack of pants at The Bay with a sign reading "cotton slacks $28" or a sign that said "cotton slacks $80"?

CASE 4-2:

Banking Fees — Pricing Financial Services

Richard Aucoin opened the chequing account statement for March and pored over the list of transactions. The usual ones were there — automatic deductions for the mortgage, the car payment, cable TV, RRSPs and RESPs; bill payments for electrical, telephone, credit cards and cellphones; transfers from savings to chequing (they rarely went the other way, Richard thought) and the many debit card purchases and ATM transactions. There were very few cheques written. After all, almost nobody wanted cheques any more. Only the daycare that Richard and Sarah's children attended still demanded payment by post-dated cheques. At the bottom of the three-page statement was the service charge fee for the month — a whopping $47.00. Richard was surprised. What service? After all, most of their banking was now done online or at ATMs — he served himself most of the time!!

When Sarah arrived home from work with the kids, Richard was ready to have the discussion about these fees. He had already pulled out the couple's bank statements for the past six months and had found that in December, they had paid $63.00 in service fees. Sarah admitted that she had paid little attention to the fees in the past. When she scanned the statement, she was only looking at the transactions to make sure no mistakes had been made. In a final tally, Richard found that they had paid over $500 in service fees in the past 12 months.

Richard decided to go online to do some investigation of the fees charged by their bank and others. It was surprisingly easy to find out which plans were available and which ones would be best for him and Sarah. Of course, Richard was not really interested in switching banks right now. After all, he had been with the same bank since he was a child, when his parents had opened an account for him. When he and Sarah married seven years ago, she had switched banks; as a grad student, her portfolio consisted of a chequing account and a student line of credit. Having grown up in Ireland and moved to Canada to study at the University of Toronto, Sarah had no real affiliation to any Canadian bank.

The Aucoins' bank offered a number of plans to choose from, based on the number and types of transactions that ran through an account each month. One plan offered additional services for travel — which would come in handy as Richard's new job would take him to the U.S. several times this year. This fee plan would cost only $25 per month — $22 less than they had paid in March.

Richard found that other banks offered similar plans that ranged in price from $25 to $35 monthly. With this new information, Richard decided he would go to his branch the next day to speak with a personal banker and sign up for the plan that was best for them. He was sure he wouldn't be paying almost $50 for bank fees each month. When he mentioned this to Sarah, she remarked that it was too bad that the bank hadn't made them aware that such plans were available — they could have saved a few hundred dollars last year. As Richard thought about this further, he realized that he had a few more questions for the personal banker; why were some people getting fees waived while others paid them? Why was this "fee sale" not advertised? Richard felt like he had been cheated out of fees simply because he hadn't asked the right questions or done his research.

Questions:

1. Does Richard have a right to feel cheated when the information, by his own admission, was easily accessible on the Web site?
2. How can banks justify offering fee plans to customers who ask for them, but charging individual transaction fees to those who don't?
3. Would Richard be justified in asking that their bank fees for the last six months be returned, less the monthly plan fee of $25?
4. Compare the banking fee plans with the variety of long distance and cellphone plans available. Are there similar issues? Explain.

CASE 4-3:

Sensational Video — Pricing a Rental Service

Nancy and Bill were discussing how they could increase their weekday customer traffic in their store — Sensational Video. They had done a limited amount of advertising during the past year and concluded that the slight improvement in store traffic did not justify the advertising costs. Now they were devoting their attention to the current pricing schedule for their products.

Sensational Video was a retail store that rented movies, DVD players and game systems like xbox and PlayStation 2. It was an independently-owned store, located in a shopping plaza in a town with a population of about 60,000. Bill's father had been the original owner; however, Bill took over the business about three years ago when his father became ill.

Sensational Video carried a rental stock of 3,500 movies, 10 DVD players, five xboxs and five PlayStation 2s. Products for sale included previously-viewed movies and games, blank CDs, disc cleaners, along with a number of convenience goods such as soft drinks and potato chips. Sensational Video purchased between 10 and 20 new titles per week, which included games, some in multiple copies, depending on the expected demand.

Nancy and Bill identified their market broadly as any person or family that owned a TV set. One segment of this market included people who owned a DVD player or a game system and rented DVDs or games, respectively. Another segment rented both the DVD player or the game system as well as the DVD or the games. The majority of the customers ranged in age from 15 to 50, but the most price conscious were certainly the students from the nearby community college. This group also seemed to be a lot less store-loyal than the older customers. The majority of customers resided in the immediate neighbourhoods surrounding the shopping plaza.

Sensational Video experienced considerable competition in the city. The biggest competitors were Jumbo Video and Blockbuster Video. Although both stores charged much higher prices and didn't provide the same level of personal customer service, they both had considerably more floor space, offered a wider selection of videos, which included more copies of the most popular videos, and provided different types of promotional guarantees. One store had recently started to offer a mail-in video rental option, which meant the customer didn't even have to leave home to rent a movie.

In Bill's opinion, the most serious difficulty facing the video store was the lack of store traffic during the week. Many days were extremely slow, and the problem seemed to be getting worse. Weekends didn't seem to be a problem, with their best night being Saturday.

Nancy and Bill had done a limited amount of advertising, mainly involving promotional flyers and coupons distributed in the neighbourhood. However, the slight improvement in customer traffic was not enough to justify the advertising costs.

As their focus started to drift away from their advertising effort, they began to focus on their current pricing structure, something that had been given little attention over the past couple of years. It was always assumed that as long as prices were kept somewhat lower than the biggest competitors, it should be fine. At the present time, the rental fee schedule was as follows:

For movies:
Monday, Tuesday, Thursday: 2 for $5 or $3 each.
Wednesday: 2 for 1 – additional movies $3 each.
Friday, Saturday, Sunday: $3 each with no quantity discount.

For games:
Monday, Tuesday, Thursday: 3 for $6 or $2.50 each.
Wednesday: 2 for 1 – additional games $2.50 each.
Friday, Saturday, Sunday: $2.75 each with no quantity discount.

For DVD players:
$12.95 per day, any day, including two "free" movie rentals.

For game systems:
$12.95 per day, any day, including one "free" game rental.

Sensational Video also had a frequent renter card, however, it could not be used with any other promotion. For instance, if customers rented two movies on a Wednesday night and got the 2 for 1 special, they did not receive a stamp. However, they would receive a stamp for any additional movies they rented. For every ten movies rented, customers receive one free rental.

As they reviewed their own pricing structure and compared it with competitors' prices, Bill raised the question of whether their pricing structure was too complicated and thus confusing to customers. He noted that some other video stores in town charged the same rental price every day of the week.

Questions:

1. What changes, if any, should Sensational Video make in its pricing schedule? Justify your answer.
2. How would you advise Nancy and Bill to develop a pricing plan that would appeal to different groups of customers? What factors should they take into consideration?
3. What options, other than price change, should Sensational Video consider to increase value and customer loyalty? What non-price things could they do to allow them to possibly maintain prices at a higher level?

CASE 4-4:

Multimedia

GuestLink — Boston Pizza

In Chapter 10, our Guest Marketer, Greg Pope, Vice-President — Finance at Boston Pizza International, outlined that company's pricing strategy to ensure as much uniformity as possible on menu items at the company's 200+ restaurants across Canada. We also learned a lot about Boston Pizza from Case 2-3 and the "Big Switcheroo" video from CBC *Venture* that accompanies that case. From these two exposures to the company, and possibly from your own personal experience, you have likely formed some impressions of the kind of company this is. We now have an opportunity to view some Boston Pizza TV advertising.

Take a look at the three TV commercials that accompany this GuestLink and discuss them in the context of the pricing strategy and general approach to business that Greg Pope has outlined.

Questions:

1. Discuss how the approach to advertising reflected in these three Boston Pizza commercials is consistent with the values of the company that you have identified in Case 2-3 and in Greg Pope's column.
2. Is there a connection between Boston Pizza's pricing and advertising strategies? How are they linked?
3. How would you describe the approach to advertising that Boston Pizza is taking in these three commercials? What's the message they are conveying and to whom is that message directed?

PART 5

Distribution

Systems for distributing products and services from producer to user, including channels and logistics

We are in the process of developing a marketing program to reach the firm's target markets and achieve the goals established in strategic marketing planning. So far, we have considered the product and pricing components in that marketing mix. In **Part 5**, we explore how companies get their products and services to the customer — the distribution channel and its various support components.

The system for getting products and services to customers is very complex. Consumers see and interact with one part of this system on a regular basis — the retailing system, which is presented in Chapter 11. In Chapter 12, we deal with more behind-the-scenes aspects of distribution, addressing the questions of how products and services get to the retailers and the various systems and processes that exist to ensure they do.

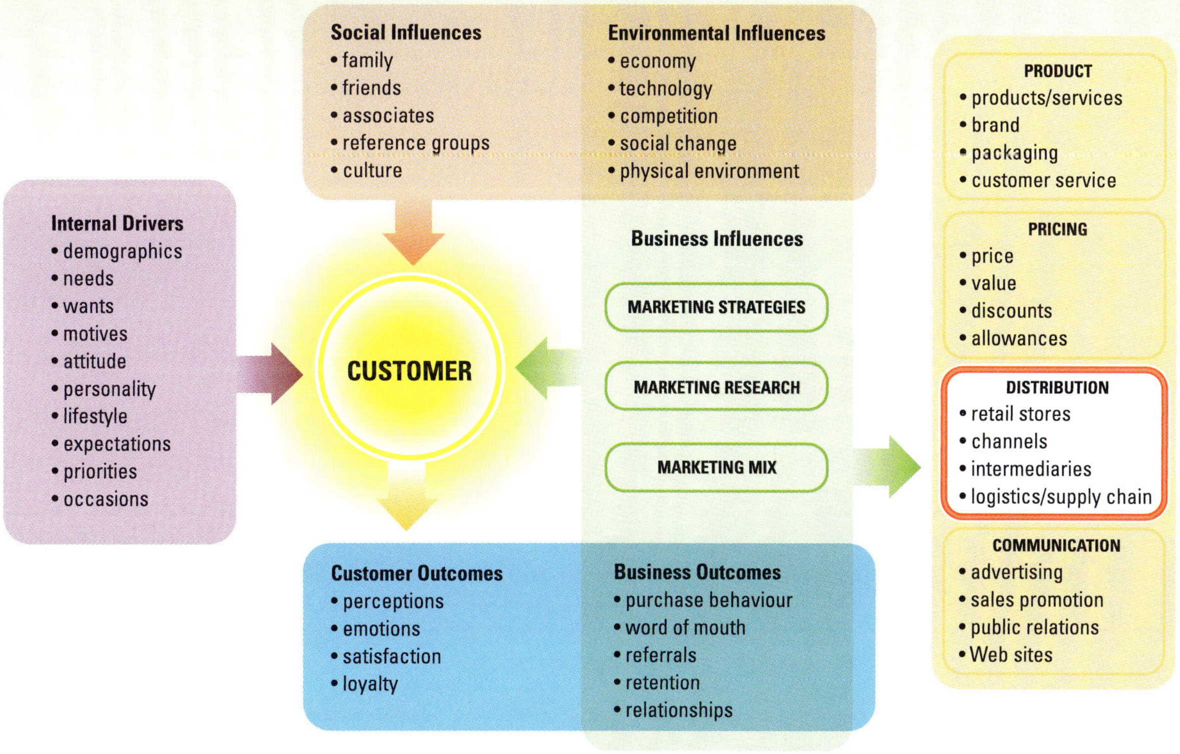

CHAPTER 11

Retailing

You have a great deal of experience with retailing — every day you are a customer. And perhaps you have worked in retailing. This chapter builds on that experience and provides insight into retail markets, different types of retailers, and key strategies and trends in retailing. After studying this chapter, you should have an understanding of:

- The nature of retailing.
- What a retailer is.
- Types of retailers.
- Retail marketing strategies.
- Forms of non-store retailing.
- Retailing on the Internet.
- Trends in retailing.

The Canadian Tire Five-Year Plan

Canadian Tire is in a constant competitive marketing war with the likes of Wal-Mart, Home Depot, RONA, Home Hardware, and now even Loblaws. Chief executive officer, Wayne Sales, wants to increase shareholder profit by 12 to 15 percent. He wants to attract more customers to the company's three chains of general merchandise, clothing, and auto parts stores. "We want to be the first choice of our customers not just for this week or this month but for a lifetime across all of our businesses." To achieve this, he has a five-year, $1.5 billion plan. The overall objective is to increase same-store sales by 3 to 4 percent in each of the next five years.

For Canadian Tire stores, this means increasing the number of major merchandise outlets by 24 to 481; replacing or refurbishing 251 stores using a newly developed design with 20 percent more retail space to hold wider product lines, as well as wider aisles for customer comfort and shopping convenience.

For the Mark's Work Wearhouse casual clothing stores, it means going from 333 to 400 stores over the five-year period. These stores generate over 70 percent of their sales from their store owned brands — Mark's, Wind River, Denver Hayes, and Dakota. And for Parts Source stores, which sell parts and components to professional auto installers and serious auto do-it-yourselfers, the five-year task is to expand from 47 to 130 stores.

Canadian Tire will also expand its Canadian Tire Petroleum gas bars by up to 35 new sites for a total of 254 outlets to reinforce its position as Canada's largest independent gas retailer. The firm is also testing new Q convenience stores at gas bar sites. Q is positioned as a premium retailer featuring brand name tenants such as Starbucks, Sobeys Express, and Richtree Market Restaurants. The goal is to have between five and eight of these ultimate convenience centres up and running by 2007, according to Peter Kilty, Toronto-based president of Canadian Tire Petroleum. This will be followed by an aggressive roll-out to other parts of the country in 2008.

There's much more in the plan: increasing the number of credit card holders, offering more financial services such as savings accounts, personal loans and lines of credit. Current financial services clients are existing store customers. "We are not unlike banks," says Mr. Sales. "Customers have a tendency to have a trust of products and services from a provider like Canadian Tire."

It's all retailing, all the time, at Canadian Tire.[1]

Nature and Importance of Retailing

For every far-reaching retail superstar like Canadian Tire, HMV, Best Buy, Wal-Mart, Chapters/Indigo, Loblaws, or maybe Amazon, there are thousands of small retailers serving consumers, some in very limited and simple ways, some in very expansive and sophisticated ways. Despite their differences, all of these firms have one thing in common: They are the first contact that consumers have with the supply chain that began with producers located all over the world.

Retailing and retailers

Safeway
Sobeys
Shell
Canadian Tire
Ticketmaster

First, let's be clear about what is and what is not a retailer. If Safeway (**www.safeway.com**) or Sobeys (**www.sobeys.ca**) sells some floor wax to a gift shop operator to polish the shop floor, is this a retail sale? When a Shell gas bar (**www.shell.com**) or Canadian Tire store (**www.canadiantire.ca**) advertises that tires are being sold at the wholesale price, is this retailing? Can a wholesaler or manufacturer engage in retailing? It's definition time.

retailing
The sale, and all activities directly related to the sale, of goods and services to end-consumers for personal, non-business use; same as retail trade.

Retailing (or retail trade) consists of the sale, and all activities directly related to the sale, of goods and services to customers for personal, non-business use. While most retailing occurs through retail stores, it may be done by any institution, whether down the street or in cyberspace. A manufacturer selling brushes or cosmetics door to door is engaged in retailing as is Amazon or eBay on the Internet or a farmer selling vegetables at a roadside stand. Any firm — manufacturer, wholesaler, or retailer — that sells something to customers who are end-users for their own non-business use is making a retail sale.

And what we say about products applies equally to services. While one of the characteristics of services relates to the inseparability of the service from the individual or company that provides it, the marketing of services is often delegated to retailers. Travel agents are really retailers who sell to end-consumers the services offered by airlines, hotels, railroads, and car rental companies; banks and other financial services companies retail Canada Savings Bonds, ticketmaster (**www.ticketmaster.ca**) retails theatre and concert tickets.

Characteristics of retailing

retailer
A firm engaged primarily in retailing.

All **retailers** — whether they are down-the-street bricks-and-mortar stores or the Web sites of Chapters/Indigo and Amazon — serve as purchasing agents for their customers and as sales specialists for their suppliers. To carry out these roles, retailers perform many activities, including anticipating customers' needs and wants, developing assortments of products, acquiring market information, and financing.

It is relatively easy to become a retailer. No large investment in production equipment is required, merchandise can often be purchased on credit, and store space can be leased with no down payment. Some retailers don't actually need to do this much; Internet retailers need only a virtual storefront and often Internet service providers will assist customers to set up shop. If not retailing a downloadable product such as software or information, there is still a requirement to have some sort of warehousing — but even this can be outsourced, eliminating the need for capital investment or expertise. This ease of entry results in fierce competition among retailers and better value for consumers.

If getting into retailing is easy, so is being forced out — and many small retailers do exit due to their inability, for a host of reasons, to adapt to market conditions and financial requirements. To survive, retailers must do at least a satisfactory job in their primary role — catering to customers — as well as their secondary role — serving suppliers, producers, and wholesalers. This dual responsibility is both the justification for retailing and the key to retail success.

Retail Trends

Since retailing is dynamic, even volatile, it isn't easy to see where it is heading in the future, but certain trends can be seen:

Entertainment—More on-site entertainment ("retailtainment"), which includes whatever stimulates the senses or emotions to make shoppers want to stay, tell others, and/or come back again. The comfy couches at Chapters and the listening posts at HMV were just the beginning. Even retailers such as Toys R Us entered into retailtainment agreements with such suppliers as Virtual Sports Systems.

Service and convenience — Time pressed customers are going to fewer stores, and spending less time in each. Retailers are responding with extended hours, drive-through windows, delivery — offering what they know customers want. Loblaws' new retailing strategy is to be "the supplier of consumers' everyday household needs." This is reflected in a broader range of housewares and kitchen goods, larger stores, and a push into children's clothing. It offers a wide range of services in many of its stores, including pharmacies, photo labs, financial services, travel agencies, nurseries, and cigar shops. The store has increased its natural food offerings and has also introduced a line of organic products.

Specialty and "big box" — More savvy consumers demand either more specialties or specials. A generalist approach may no longer be effective in today's competitive environment — specialize or offer low prices! Shoppers Drug Mart, in order to contend with increasing competition from stores such as Costco, Wal-Mart, and Zellers, is opening 20 to 25 big-box, stand-alone drugstores. Sears is developing specialty stores to compete with rivals such as Home Outfitters (owned by the Bay) and to cash in on the expanding home décor market.

Managing customers — Customer retention and loyalty are key to retail success. We continue to see the introduction, improvement, and reorganization of loyalty or customer-appreciation programs and other attempts at customer-relationship development. Customer-relationship management (CRM) software has made possible the organization of databases that contain client information and purchase history. While this software provides for one aspect of what is required to aid in developing relationships, appropriate staff recruiting and training supported by a consistent customer orientation helps build strong customer relationships.

Multi-channel retailing — More retailers use more channels than ever. The biggest change is the number of "traditional" retailers who place more and more emphasis on the Web to retail their products. Often the most successful are those companies that have already successfully established efficient distribution systems through a catalogue retail experience such as L.L. Bean, Lands' End, and Sears. We are also seeing retailers gaining additional penetration by allowing other retailers to sell their products, such as Sears offering selected Roots merchandise, and Lands' End merchandise.

SOURCE: Adapted from Lisa D'Innocenzo, "HMV Engages Customers with In-Store Displays," *Strategy*, March 12, 2001, p. B12; Sarah Smith, "Checking Out the New Loblaw," *Marketing Magazine*, April 29, 2002, pp. 10, 11; "Sears Mulls Martha Stewart Stores," *Marketing Magazine*, June 17, 2002, p. 3; www.visualsportssys.com, accessed February 2006.

Dimensions of the retail market

There are about 250,000 retail stores in Canada. The number varies with economic conditions; there is growth of net entries during periods of economic expansion and net declines during periods of contraction. Retail trade accounts for about 12 percent of all establishments, trailing far behind the services industry, which accounts for about 35 percent.

Most retail establishments are very small, with 15 to 20 percent of all retailers having annual sales of $100,000 or less. However, despite their numbers, such stores account for a very small percentage of total retail sales.

At the same time, there is a high degree of concentration in retailing. This becomes increasingly the case as large retailers merge and departments stores decline in number. A small

BACK TO THE TOP

Hudson's Bay Company

number of companies account for a substantial share of total retail trade. These companies, such as Wal-Mart, Canadian Tire, Loblaws, Sears Canada and the Hudson's Bay Company (the Bay and its sister store Zellers can both be found at **www.hbc.com**), own many individual stores and account for the considerable degree of concentration in the industry.

Stores of different sizes present different management challenges and opportunities. Buying, promotion, personnel relations, and expense control are influenced significantly by whether a store's sales volume is large or small. Store size brings with it certain advantages — see Table 11-1. Relatively large stores have a number of competitive advantages over small stores, but small retailers can and do still succeed:

contractual vertical market system
An arrangement in which independent firms (producers, wholesalers, and retailers) operate under a contract specifying how they will try to improve their distribution efficiency and effectiveness.

- Some are able to become part of a **contractual vertical marketing system** (VMS), in which independently owned firms join together under a contract specifying how they will operate (this is discussed in more detail later). These entities — called retailer co-operatives, voluntary chains, or franchise systems — give individual members certain advantages of large stores, such as specialized management, buying power, system owned brands, and a well-known store name.
- Many consumers seek benefits that small stores can often provide better than can large stores. A major one is accessibility and shopping convenience. Small outlets located near residential areas offer just that — and it is a valuable benefit.
- Other consumers want high levels of personal service. A small store's highly motivated owner-manager and well-supervised staff may easily surpass a large store on this important patronage dimension. Small retailers have a better opportunity to develop strong functional and emotional relationships (particularly the latter) than do large ones. Frequently, the emotional component of a relationship can compensate for occasional functional lapses, and keep consumers returning.

TABLE 11-1 Competitive Positions of Large and Small Retail Stores

Selected Bases for Evaluation	Who Has the Advantage?
Division of labour and specialization of management	Large-scale retailers — their biggest advantage.
Flexibility of operations — merchandise selection, services offered, store design, reflection of owner's personality	Small retailers — their biggest advantage.
Buying power	Large retailers buy in bigger quantities and thus get lower costs.
Access to desirable merchandise	Large retailers promise suppliers access to large numbers of customers, whereas a single small retailer may be viewed as insignificant.
Development and promotion of retailer's own brand	Large retailers.
Efficient use of advertising, especially in citywide media	Large retailers' markets match better with media circulation.
Ability to provide top-quality personal service	Small retailers, if owners pay personal attention to customers and also to selecting and supervising sales staff.
Opportunity to experiment with new products and selling methods	Large retailers can better afford the risks.
Financial strength	Large retailers have resources to gain some of the advantages noted above (such as private brands and experimentation).
Public image	Small retailers enjoy public support and sympathy. However, this same public often votes with its wallet by shopping at big stores.

Physical facilities

physical facilities
The location, design and layout of a retail store's site.

Some firms engage in non-store retailing — by selling through catalogues, the Internet, or door to door — but many more firms rely on retail stores. Firms that operate retail stores must consider three aspects of **physical facilities**:

1. ***Location:*** There are three keys to success in retailing: location, location, and location! Although overstated, this axiom does suggest the importance that retailers attach to location. A store's site should be the first decision made about facilities. Considerations such as surrounding population, traffic, and cost determine where a store should be located. For Internet retailers as well as other non-store retailers, location also matters, as they require warehousing and call centres. But instead of wanting to be located in highly populated areas, these retailers focus more on outlying areas, where property and labour costs are usually lower. This must, of course, also be balanced with an optimal location that provides for timely and low-cost shipping provisions.

2. ***Design:*** This factor refers to a store's appearance, both exterior and interior. This is important for attracting and retaining customers, as well as setting the image or tone for the location. Canadian Tire constantly reviews aspects of store design to assure customer appeal. For the non-store retailer, design is of little importance, except to ensure that the working environment is not a source of dissatisfaction for employees.

3. ***Layout:*** The amount of space allocated to various product lines, specific locations of products, and a floor plan of display tables and racks make up the store's layout. The layout should be convenient for customers (as discussed in the opening Canadian Tire vignette) while showcasing merchandise in the most prudent manner. For non-store retailers, the location's layout, like its design, is not to enhance the consumer's shopping experience but rather to facilitate the efficient, safe processing of customer orders.

As might be expected, retail store locations tend to follow the population. Consequently, the bulk of retail sales takes place in urban, rather than rural, areas. And suburban shopping areas and power centres continue to be popular, while many downtown areas have been weakened. However, some counter-trends can be seen in new city-centre condominium and retailing development. In many Canadian cities, professional couples and retired empty-nesters are reinhabiting city cores.

shopping centre
A planned grouping of retail stores in a multi-unit structure, with the physical structure usually owned by a single organization.

Shopping centres are the predominant type of retail location in most suburban areas. The traditional **shopping centre** consists of a planned grouping of retail stores that lease space in an enclosed structure that is typically owned by a single organization and can accommodate multiple tenants. With the growing popularity of catalogue and online shopping, as well as the strong competition from big box store specialists, many shopping mall owners have been trying to create more reasons for customers to come and stay longer — by increasing the number of services offered and the entertainment options available, from movie theatres to piano bars, improved food services, child care facilities and amusement parks. In the last few years, 80 percent of new retail development has been of the open air rather than the enclosed form (often called a 'power centre') and 30 percent of these have been populated by large specialty stores (commonly called big box stores) rather than enclosed ones.[2]

Some malls are going to great lengths to make the traditional mall more attractive to everyone. For example, the Richmond Centre in Vancouver now offers a play centre for children that includes a miniature Cathay Pacific plane. Since 45 percent of the shoppers at the centre are Asian, management thought that Cathy Pacific fit the brand better than Air Canada or WestJet.

Given that the average age of shoppers at Richmond Centre is 39, the mall decided to go for a more family-oriented and fun atmosphere. A playground aimed at 5-10 year olds is the first step to achieving that environment. If this works out, the mall will install more of these corporate-themed playgrounds in the future.[3]

Traditional shopping centres can be classified by size and market served:

- ***Convenience centre:*** Usually consists of 5 to 10 outlets, such as a dry-cleaner, bank branch, convenience grocery store, and video rental store.
- ***Neighbourhood centre:*** Has 10 to 25 tenants, including a large supermarket and perhaps a drugstore.
- ***Community centre:*** Includes 25 to 50 stores and features a discount house or junior department store. It may also include a supermarket. Given its composition of stores, a community centre draws shoppers from a larger area than does a neighbourhood centre.
- ***Regional centre:*** Anchored by one or more department stores and supermarkets and complemented by as many as 200 smaller retail outlets, a regional centre is typically enclosed in a climate-controlled mall. A variation on the regional centre, sometimes called a power centre, consists of a collection of highly specialized or big box retailers with very wide and deep inventories.

PAGE UP!

1. Define retailing.
2. What is multi-channel retailing?
3. What are the three aspects of physical facilities that retailers must consider?

Forms of Retailing

Different forms of retail ownership confer different strategic and operating advantages and disadvantages on owners and managers of retailing establishments. The major forms of ownership in retailing are independent, corporate chain, and the vertical marketing system. Within the VMS category are several types of organizations: wholesaler-sponsored voluntary chains, retailer-owned co-operatives, and franchise systems.

Independent stores

independent retailer A company with a single retail store that is not affiliated with any type of contractual VMS.

The most numerous of all retailers, an **independent retailer** is a company with a single retail store that is not affiliated with any type of contractual vertical marketing system. Most retailers are independents, and most independents are quite small. Of course, an independent department store or supermarket can have $10 million or more in annual sales, so it may have more economic power than small chains consisting of only a few stores. Still, independents usually have the characteristics of small retailers that were presented in Table 11-1.

Independents are typically viewed as having higher prices than chain stores. On the other hand, they are usually more accessible than any other retail form and, of great importance, they have the best opportunity of developing strong relationships with consumers, both functional and emotional. As for the question of prices, because of differences in merchandise and services, it is difficult to directly compare the prices of chains and independents. For instance, chains often have their own private brands that are not sold by independents. Also, the two types of retailers frequently provide customers with different levels — and perhaps quality — of services. Many customers are willing to pay extra for services that are valuable to them, such as credit, delivery, alterations, installation, a liberal returns policy, and friendly, knowledgeable personal service.[4]

Corporate chain stores

corporate chain
An organization of two or more centrally owned and managed stores that generally handle the same lines of products.

A **corporate chain**, sometimes called a chain store system, consists of two or more centrally owned and managed stores that generally handle the same lines of products. Three factors differentiate a chain from an independent store and a contractual VMS:

1. Technically, two or more units constitute a chain. Today, however, many small-scale merchants have opened two or three units in shopping centres and in newly populated areas. These retailers ordinarily do not think of themselves as chains. Having four or more units is a more valid basis for discussing chain stores.
2. Central ownership distinguishes corporate chains from contractual vertical marketing systems.
3. Because of their centralized management, individual units in a chain can have little autonomy. Strategic decisions are made at headquarters, and there is considerable standardization of operating policies for all of the units in a chain.

Corporate chains continue to play a major role in retail trade in Canada as chains with four or more stores do more than 35 percent of all retail business. The importance of chains varies considerably from one type of business to another. Chains account for 70 percent or more of total sales in the general merchandise, variety store, family clothing, and shoes categories. Among grocery stores, hardware stores, and pharmacies, however, chains account for 30 percent of sales or less. There are still a large number of independent food retailers in small towns and neighbourhoods throughout Canada.

Competitive strengths and weaknesses Chain store organizations are large-scale retailing institutions and are subject to the general advantages and limitations of all large retailers.

Lower selling prices Chain stores have traditionally been credited with selling at lower prices than do independents. But the claim of lower prices needs careful scrutiny, because it can be misleading. It was probably more justified in the past than it is today: Many independents have pooled their buying power so that, in many instances, they can buy products at the same price as the chains can. However, it is almost certainly true that chains have a cost advantage over independents.

It is very difficult to compare the prices of chains with those of independents. The merchandise is often not exactly comparable, because many chains sell items under their own brands — for example, it's difficult to compare the prices of a global brand with a Loblaws or Safeway brand. It is even more difficult to compare an item of apparel from Zellers with one from a "designer" store. The quality and durability of the fabric, the garment's construction, and other factors are almost impossible for the average person to knowledgeably compare. Also, it is not accurate to compare the price of a product sold in a cash-and-carry, no-customer-service store with the price of an identically branded product in a full-service store. The value of services should be included in the comparison.

Multi-store feature of chains Chain stores do not have all of their eggs in one basket (or in one store). Even large-scale independent department stores or supermarkets cannot match this advantage of the chains. A multi-unit operation has automatically spread its risks among

MARKETING AT WORK 11-1: GLOBAL

The Power of IKEA

IKEA Canada, with eleven stores countrywide, is now being run by Kerri Molinari, the first woman and foreigner to run IKEA'S 14 superstores in the home country of Sweden. She had worked in IKEA stores in Toronto and Chicago prior to going to Sweden to head the home store chain. In Toronto, she oversaw a 20 percent expansion of the North York store. In Chicago, she brought the first IKEA store to the U.S. Midwest — a unique three story octagonal open concept with a restaurant in the centre among the sofas. With Canadian and U.S. store design and operations management experience, she moved to Sweden where her five-year job was to remodel and expand the 14-store chain to appeal to a market and maintain relationships where almost everyone in the country had already been an IKEA customer.

In Canada, her job is to see that the right stock is on the shelves, improve store displays, and get customers into the stores and out smoothly — particularly on heavy shopping weekends. Strong merchandising, attractive and appealing product presentation and constant change to catch customers' attention is her focus.

IKEA stores are continually being shrewdly engineered and re-configured to appeal to customers. Consider the ambiance in the newest Toronto store. Mike Baker, the manager, fusses about the music as someone has messed up the music list. "The tunes are supposed to be upbeat in this area," he says, as a melancholy country song drifts overhead. "The point is to give people a lift, make them feel like opening their wallets. This is a hurtin' song." The store is so big, it has its own radio station used to transmit a stream of IKEA messages. Customers file past 9,500 products, ranging from particle-board shelves to leather sofas and stainless steel-clad appliances. The music, from 300 speakers, changes as customers move between areas of the store: Moroccan kasbah-sounding in the carpet area, happy tunes in the children's area, and, in the cash lanes, acoustic guitar solos — better to calm the customers as they reach for their wallets.

"You shop with more than your eyes," explains Hilde Abbleloos, Etobicoke's project manager. "If I could have introduced smells to the store, I would have. Cookies baking in the kitchen area, that sort of thing."

The company studies all of its markets with anthropological zeal — it knows most Canadian couples argue when buying furniture, so the staff is trained in conflict resolution. Also, Vancouverites are obsessed with storage space, so displays are set up accordingly. Québec residents demand a superior selection of cookware. Torontonians are in a work-at-home phase, so the emphasis is on home offices at this location. Room settings have been painstakingly designed to reflect local tastes, such as an emphasis on lofts. Gone are the cardboard display electronics and TV sets — real ones are used for authenticity.

QUESTIONS:

1. Do you think there are problems in importing retail strategies and tactics from abroad for use in a local culture?
2. What does IKEA do to adapt to local conditions?

SOURCE: Adapted from Marina Strauss, "Kerri Molinari shows IKEA a few things about running stores," *The Globe and Mail*, April 13, 2005, pp. B1, B19 and Brian Hutchinson, "IKEA: That's Swedish for BIG," *Financial Post*, October 17, 2001, p. FP1.

many units. Losses in one store can be offset by profits in other units. Multi-store organizations can experiment quite easily, trying a new store layout or a new type of merchandise in one store without committing the entire firm.

A chain can make more effective use of advertising than can even a giant, single-unit independent store. A grocery chain may have 15 medium-sized stores blanketing a city. An independent competitor may have one huge supermarket doing three to four times the business of any single unit of the chain. Yet the chain can use the metropolitan daily newspaper as an advertising medium, with much less waste in circulation, than the independent can. Many chains can also make effective use of national advertising media.

On the negative side Standardization, the hallmark of a chain store system and a major factor in its success, is a mixed blessing. Standardization, while it can reduce marketing and operating costs, can also mean inflexibility. Often a chain cannot adjust rapidly to a local market situation. Chains are well aware of this weakness and have consequently given local store managers greater freedom to act in various situations. Also, with improved information systems, chains can better tailor their merchandising efforts to their specific local markets. Implementing a relationship strategy is much more difficult in a chain operation than in an independent store or, sometimes, in a vertical marketing system.

Contractual vertical marketing systems

In a contractual vertical marketing system, independently owned firms join together under a contract specifying how they will operate. Three types of contractual VMSs are common:

Retailer co-operatives and voluntary chains These exist to increase the competitiveness of members and to provide members with management and administrative systems and assistance. The difference lies in how they are organized. A retailer co-operative is formed by a group of small retailers that agree to establish and operate a wholesale warehouse. In contrast, a voluntary chain is sponsored by a wholesaler that enters into individual supply contracts with interested retailers.

Historically, these two forms of contractual VMSs have been organized for defensive reasons — to enable independent retailers to compete effectively with larger chains. They are able to do this by creating volume-buying power for members. Assistance is also provided with store layout, training programs, promotion, accounting, and inventory-control systems. While retailer co-operatives are declining, there is still strong representation in groceries and hardware, such as True Value Hardware. Voluntary chains have been common in the grocery sector, but are also found in hardware and auto supply operations.

Franchise systems Franchising involves a continuing relationship in which a parent company provides the right to use a trademark and management assistance in return for payments from the owner of the individual business unit. The parent company is called a *franchiser,* and the owners of the individual business units are called *franchisees.* The combination of these individuals is called the *franchise system.* This type of contractual VMS continues to grow.

There are two kinds of franchising:

- ***Product and trade name franchising:*** Historically, the dominant type of franchising, product and trade name, is most prevalent in the automobile (Ford, Honda) and petroleum (Esso, Petro-Canada) industries. It is a distribution agreement in which a franchiser authorizes a franchisee-dealer to sell a product line, using the parent company's trade name for promotional purposes. The franchisee agrees to buy from the franchiser-supplier and also to abide by specified policies. The focus in product and trade name franchising is on what is sold.
- ***Business-format franchising:*** Much of franchising's growth and publicity over the past two decades has been associated with business-format franchising (including names such as KFC, Tim Hortons, Midas, and H&R Block, as can be seen in Table 11-2). This kind of franchising covers an entire format for operating a business. A firm with a successful retail business sells the right to operate the same business in different geographic areas. Quite simply, the franchisee expects to receive a proven business format from the parent company; in return, the franchiser receives payments from the individual business owner, as well as conformance to policies and standards. The focus here is on how the business is run — and the business must be run according to the format provided.

  What the franchiser provides to franchisees in this format is management assistance, especially marketing expertise. There is also a great deal of proven brand equity in the brand name of the organization, so the franchisee has a head start at further developing a functional relationship with customers, as well as being able to focus on the emotional relationship.

Retailers such as Winners specialize in offering the lowest prices.

TABLE 11-2 Numerous Products Reach Consumer Markets through Business-Format Franchises

Product/Service Category	Sample Franchises
Fast food	McDonald's, Tim Hortons, Harvey's, Druxy's, Pizza Hut, Treats, A.L. Van Houtte
Auto rental	National, Avis, Thrifty, Budget, Hertz
Auto repair	Ziebart, Midas, Speedy, Thruway Muffler, Jiffy Lube, Mister Transmission
Personal care/services	Regis, H&R Block, Money Concepts, Nautilus Fitness, Body Shop
Home décor/services	Color Your World, Bathtub Doctor, Molly Maid, Weed Man, Servicemaster, College Pro Painters
Printing/photography	Kwik-Kopy, Japan Camera, U Frame It, Kinko's
Clothing	Sportchek, Benetton, Rodier
Computers and video	Compucentres, Computerland, Jumbo Video
Health and personal care	Nutri/System, Shoppers Drug Mart, Optical Factory, Tridont Health Centre
Convenience stores	7-Eleven, Mike's, Mac's, Green Gables, Red & White

MARKETING AT WORK 11-2: STRATEGY

Coffee Pub, Fast-Casual, New Franchise Category?

The Williams Coffee Pub chain is not large or nationally visible yet, but it has pioneered 'fast-casual dining'— a new food service category in Canada. The founders ..."didn't want to be a coffee house... we also didn't want to be bistro. We thought of a pub as a place where people go to meet." Today, while coffee is still the main element at the Coffee Pub, the chain stresses healthy breakfast, lunch, and dessert; this keeps the restaurant busy from early morning until late evening.

What happens in a Williams Coffee Pub that doesn't happen in rivals Tim Hortons or Starbucks? Customers order, take a number and then proceed to their table with their coffee. A waitress (no tipping allowed) then brings their food order to them. The whole experience takes longer than ordering coffee at a fast food outlet but much less time than at a conventional eat-in chain.

Why does this work? "People come here because they are not rushed out and they like the quality of the product," says Bill Giannakopoulos, one of the chain's founders. Williams is able to offer customers authentic European coffee selections without compromising quality — something fast-food chains seem to have difficulty doing. Customers seem to want to meet in comfortable surroundings unlike those of a fast food culture, order quickly, eat and drink at leisure. The concept works so well that there are now 48 Williams' locations and the plan is to expand to 100 locations in the next two to three years. Even McDonald's Canada likes the concept and has invited Williams to open two small outlets in two traditional golden-arches locations. While McDonald's does not usually work with potential rivals, it sees Williams as complementary since it has not been successful in the coffee market and wants to improve its offerings and the customer experience.

Williams Coffee Pub is now working on its 'systems,' ranging from customer handling to the buying, storing and handling of supplies. Such improvements should help cut costs and appeal to franchise holders and prospective franchise buyers. Franchises are sold for $35,000; franchise holders must invest between $250,000 and $600,000 to build their locations. Franchises regularly produce more than $1 million in annual revenue and a 10 to 20 percent return on the franchisee's investment. With growth will come large increases in marketing and advertising budgets.

QUESTIONS:

1. What is unique about the Williams approach?
2. Can competitors easily imitate it?

SOURCE: Adapted from Robert Thompson, "Breakfast, lunch, dessert," *National Post,* April 28, 2005, p. FP 8.

Retail Marketing Strategies

Whatever its form of ownership, a retailer must develop marketing-mix strategies to succeed in its chosen target markets. In retailing, the marketing mix emphasizes product assortment, price, location, promotion, and customer services.

Let's look at retail strategies by examining the major types of retail stores, paying particular attention to three elements of their marketing mixes (see Table 11-3):

1. Breadth and depth of product assortment.
2. Price level.
3. Number of customer services.

Department stores

department store
A large-scale retailing institution that has a broad and deep product assortment, prefers not to compete on the basis of price, and offers a wide array of customer services.

Still a mainstay of retailing in Canada (but somewhat troubled) is the **department store**, a large-scale retailing institution that has a very broad and deep product assortment, tries not to compete on the basis of price, and provides a wide array of customer services. Familiar department store names that can be found across the country include Sears and the Bay.

Traditional department stores offer a greater variety of merchandise and services than any other type of retail store. They feature both "soft goods" (such as apparel, sheets, towels, and bedding) and "hard goods" (including furniture, appliances, and consumer electronics). Department stores also attract — and satisfy — consumers by offering many customer services. The combination of distinctive, appealing merchandise and numerous customer services is designed to allow the stores to maintain the manufacturers' suggested retail prices. That is, department stores strive, and sometimes even succeed, to charge full, or non-discounted, prices.

TABLE 11-3 Retail Store Types and Key Marketing Strategies

Type of Store	Breadth and Depth of Assortment	Price Level	Number of Customer Services
Department store	Very broad, deep	Avoids price competition	Wide array
Discount house	Broad, shallow	Emphasizes low prices	Relatively few
Limited-line store	Narrow, deep	Traditional types avoid price competition; newer kinds emphasize low prices	Vary by type
Specialty store	Very narrow, deep	Avoids price competition	At least standard and extensive in some
Off-price retailer	Narrow, deep	Emphasizes low prices	Few
Category-killer store	Narrow, very deep	Emphasizes low prices	Few to moderate
Supermarket	Broad, deep	Some emphasize low prices; others avoid price disadvantages	Few
Convenience store	Narrow, shallow	High prices	Few
Warehouse club	Very broad, very shallow	Emphasizes very low prices	Few (open only to members)

However, department stores face mounting problems. Mostly because of their prime locations and customer services, their operating expenses are considerably higher than those of most other kinds of retail business. Many manufacturers' brands that used to be available exclusively through department stores are now widely distributed and often carry discounted prices in other outlets. Also, the quality of personal service, especially knowledgeable sales help, has deteriorated in some department stores.

Intense horizontal competition is also hurting. Other types of retailers aim at consumers who have long supported department stores. Specialty stores, off-price retailers, and even some discount houses (all of which will be discussed later) have been particularly aggressive in trying to lure shoppers away from department stores. To varying degrees, retail chains such as Wal-Mart and Zellers compete directly against the conventional department stores.

In order to gain a competitive advantage in a market increasingly dominated by the large discounters and big box category-killer stores (discussed later in this chapter), the more conventional department stores have had to adopt new ways of doing business. For example, Sears (**www.sears.ca**), Canada's leading department store chain, is striving to establish its trademark as a statement of quality and value. Other strategies being used include redesigning stores, dropping or moving entire product lines, launching new ad campaigns, and stepping up sales and promotions. Sears is trying to increase strength in products such as apparel and home furnishings. The store has focused on building the brands of its own private-label apparel and has developed the Whole Home brand of furnishings and accessories for the entire home. In some markets, it has opened furniture stores under this name.

Sears

Discount houses

Discount retailing uses price as a major selling point by combining comparatively low prices and reduced costs of doing business. Several institutions, including off-price retailers and warehouse clubs, rely on discount retailing as their main marketing strategy.

discount retailing
A retailing approach that uses price as a major selling point by combining comparatively low prices and reduced costs of doing business.

discount house
A large-scale retailing institution that has a broad and shallow product assortment, emphasizes low prices, and offers relatively few customer services.

Not surprisingly, the prime example of discount retailing is the **discount house**, a large-scale retailing institution that has a broad, shallow product assortment, emphasizes low prices, and offers relatively few customer services. A discount house normally carries a broad assortment of soft goods (particularly apparel) and grocery items, and may carry well-known brands of hard goods (including appliances and home furnishings). It also advertises extensively. Zellers and Wal-Mart are leading discount-house chains in Canada. Some observers believe that Amazon is a fledgling discount retailer. Do you think it fits into this category?

The success of discount houses can be attributed to two factors. First, other types of retailers traditionally had large mark-ups on appliances and other merchandise, thereby providing discount houses with the opportunity to set smaller margins and charge lower prices. Second, consumers were receptive to a low-price, limited-service format. Discount houses have had a major impact on retailing, prompting many retailers to lower their prices.

Wal-Mart (**www.walmart.com**) has experienced tremendous success in Canada built on the image of lowest prices, a position that has been promoted extensively by the chain. It also maintains state-of-the-art distribution technology, which builds on strong supplier relationships, behind-the-scenes ordering, and inventory management systems.

Wal-mart

While Zellers continues to feel the strong competitive impact of Wal-Mart despite amending its low-price strategy and complementing it with broader assortments, Canadian Tire has protected itself and grown as discussed in previous pages. In its competitive battle, Zellers added the private label Truly line, consistent with the company's positioning as being truly Canadian. The line was selected by the U.S. trade magazine Private Label as being one of the top five brands of its type. Zellers has changed its practice of featuring a large number of weekly specials in favour of an everyday low-pricing policy similar to Wal-Mart. It has also expanded its loyalty program to include purchases made at sister retailer, the Bay.[5]

BACK TO THE TOP

Limited-line stores

limited-line store
A type of retailing institution that has a narrow but deep product assortment; its customer services tend to vary from store to store.

Much of the action in retailing in recent years has been in **limited-line stores**. This type of institution has a narrow but deep product assortment and customer services that vary from store to store. Traditionally, limited-line stores strived for full or non-discounted prices. Currently, however, new types of limited-line retailers have grown by emphasizing low prices.

Breadth of assortment varies somewhat across limited-line stores. A store may choose to concentrate on:

- Several related product lines (shoes, sportswear, and accessories).
- A single product line (shoes).
- Part of one product line (athletic footwear).

We classify limited-line stores by primary product line — furniture store, hardware store, clothing store. Some retailers such as grocery stores and drugstores (which used to be limited-line stores) now carry a much broader assortment.

specialty store
A type of retail institution that concentrates on a specialized product line or even part of a specialized product line.

off-price retailing
A strategy of selling well-known brands below the manufacturer's recommended retail price.

Specialty stores

Specialty stores have very narrow and deep product assortments, often concentrating on a specialized product line (baked goods) or even part of a specialized product line (cookies). Examples of specialty stores are bake shops, furriers, athletic footwear stores, meat markets, and dress shops. (Specialty stores may carry any category of consumer goods, not just specialty goods.)

Most specialty retailers strive to maintain manufacturers' suggested prices and provide at least standard customer services. Some, such as the Running Room, emphasize extensive customer services and particularly knowledgeable and friendly sales help. Their success depends on the ability to attract and serve well the customers whose two primary concerns are deep assortments and extensive, top-quality services. They excel at functional and emotional relationship-building. In general, they are successful because they have clear strategies with a narrow focus, rather than the broad approach of department stores.[6]

Some specialty retailers are broadening their reach with what has been termed lifestyle retailing. These retailers realize that their store "is the brand" and they leverage their brands by selling a lifestyle concept that goes far beyond just clothing. The cachet of their labels has allowed once very limited-line retailers such as Club Monaco, Roots, La Senza, La Vie en Rose, and Northern Getaway to label products as varied as fragrances, household goods, furniture, massage oil, and feather-applied edible powder![7]

Specialty retailers such as Diesel cater to specific target segments

Off-price retailers

Positioning themselves below discount houses, with lower prices on selected product lines, **off-price retailers** are most in evidence in the areas of clothing and consumer electronics. They offer a narrow, deep product assortment; emphasize low prices; and offer few customer services. Store names such as Labels and Winners are now well known to consumers in many cities in Canada. A number of chains of off-price retailers now operate in various regions of the country.

Some off-price retailers buy manufacturers' excess output, inventory remaining at the end of a fashion season, or irregular merchandise at lower-than-normal wholesale costs. In turn, their retail prices are much lower than those for regular, in-season merchandise sold in other stores. Customers are attracted by the low prices and fairly current fashions.

factory outlet
A special type of off-price retail institution that is owned by a manufacturer and usually sells only that manufacturer's clearance items, regular merchandise, and perhaps even otherwise unavailable items.

Factory outlets A special type of off-price retailer, **factory outlets** are often owned by manufacturers and usually sell a single manufacturer's clearance items, regular merchandise, and perhaps even otherwise unavailable items. Canadian retailers such as Danier Leather, Club Monaco, Parasuco, and Roots all operate factory outlets. As well, many other famous brands offer off-price locations in Canada, including Esprit, Guess, Liz Claiborne, and Mexx. Some large fashion retailers, such as Harry Rosen and Holt Renfrew, also operate discount outlets.

category-killer store
A type of retail institution that has a narrow but very deep assortment, emphasizes low prices, and offers few-to-moderate customer services; it is designed to "destroy" all competition in a specific product category.

IKEA
HMV

Category-killer stores Featuring a narrow but very deep assortment, emphasizing low prices, and offering few-to-moderate customer services, **category-killer stores** (also called big box) are so-named because they are designed to destroy all competition in a specific product category. Highly successful category killers include IKEA (**www.ikea.ca**) with its broad assortment of assemble-it-yourself furniture and Future Shop and Best Buy in consumer electronics. Other product areas where category killers tend to operate include office supplies, sporting goods, housewares, and records, tapes, and compact discs.

This form of retail institution concentrates on a single product line or several closely related lines. The distinguishing feature of a category killer is a combination of many different sizes, models, styles, and colours of the product, coupled with low prices. For example, IKEA stocks literally thousands of furniture and home furnishing items. Music retailers such as the major stores of HMV (**www.hmv.ca**) carry such an assortment that consumers need to make only one stop to ensure that they can find particular CDs or DVDs.

The category killer's marketing goal is to dominate in such a way that the consumer believes this is the first store to visit and that the value will be better there. Although the major category killers tend to be found in large metropolitan markets, it is in fact easier for a major retailer to dominate a category in a smaller market, where the competition is not likely to be as fierce and where competitors tend to be smaller, local independents. However, most kinds of merchandise as well as many geographic areas will not generate the large sales levels that permit low prices through high-volume buying power. Existing category killers are not without problems — they face a major challenge in maintaining inventories that are large enough to satisfy customer demand but not so large as to result in excess inventories, requiring significant markdowns.

supermarket retailing
A retailing method that features several related product lines, a high degree of self-service, largely centralized checkout, and competitive prices.

supermarket
A type of retailing institution that has a moderately broad and moderately deep product assortment, spanning groceries and some non-food lines, that offers relatively few customer services and ordinarily emphasizes price in either an offensive or defensive way.

Supermarkets

As a method, **supermarket retailing** features several related product lines, a high degree of self-service, largely centralized checkout, and competitive prices. The supermarket approach to retailing is used to sell various kinds of merchandise, including building materials, office products, and — of course — groceries.

The term supermarket usually refers to an institution in the grocery-retailing field. In this context, a **supermarket** is a retailing institution that has a moderately broad, moderately deep product assortment, spanning groceries and some non-food lines, and offers relatively few customer services. Most supermarkets emphasize price. Some use price offensively by featuring low prices in order to attract customers. Other supermarkets use price more defensively by relying on leader pricing to avoid a price disadvantage. Since supermarkets typically have very thin gross margins, they need high levels of inventory turnover to achieve satisfactory returns on invested capital. In recent years, supermarkets have added a variety of non-food lines to provide customers with one-stop shopping convenience and to improve overall gross margins.

Today, stores using the supermarket method of retailing are dominant in grocery retailing. However, different names are used to distinguish these institutions by size and assortment:

- A superstore is a larger version of the supermarket. It offers more grocery and non-food items than a conventional supermarket does. Many supermarket chains are emphasizing superstores in their new construction.
- Combination stores are usually even larger than superstores. They, too, offer more groceries and non-foods than does a supermarket, but also offer most product lines found in a large drugstore.

For many years the supermarket has been under attack from numerous competitors. For example, a grocery shopper can not only choose among many brands of supermarkets (Loblaws, Safeway, Provigo, and Sobeys) but also various types of institutions (warehouse clubs, gourmet shops, meat and fish markets, and convenience stores). Supermarkets have reacted to competitive pressures primarily in one of two ways: Some cut costs and stress low prices by offering more private brands and generic products and few customer services. Others expanded their store size and assortments by adding more non-food lines (especially products found in drugstores), groceries attuned to a particular market area (foods that appeal to a specific ethnic group, for example), and various service departments (including video rentals, restaurants, delicatessens, financial institutions, and pharmacies).

The trend toward eating out more often has cut into the profits of supermarkets. As well, the days of "made from scratch" are a thing of the past. Consumers today are looking for a 20/20 solution — that is, 20 minutes to get the shopping done and then just as quickly to prepare most meals. Supermarkets have responded by expanding home-meal replacement (HMR) offerings. An HMR is any frozen or fresh meal prepared in-store for immediate consumption at home. Some supermarkets provide café areas where many of the products can be consumed on-site.

From bagged salads to frozen lasagna, the trend has reshaped supermarkets across the country. It has become a battle to recapture food dollars that time-strapped Canadians have been shelling out to restaurants and fast-food outlets. In southern Ontario, Fortino's has added a sushi bar, along with a wine shop and a cigar counter. And Pete (otherwise known as the Fresh Prince of Papaya) of Pete's Frootiques in Bedford, Nova Scotia, has a power-juice bar and a professional piano player positioned over the grapes.[8]

Convenience stores

This retailing institution concentrates on convenience groceries and non-foods, has higher prices than most other grocery stores, and offers few customer services. Gasoline, fast foods, and selected services (such as car washes and automated banking machines) can also be found at many **convenience stores**.

convenience store
A type of retailing institution that concentrates on convenience-oriented groceries and non-foods, has higher prices than found at most grocery stores, and offers few customer services.

Convenience stores are typically located near residential areas and are open extended hours; some never close. Hence, the reputation for being convenient! Examples of convenience store chains are 7-Eleven (originally open from 7 a.m. to 11 p.m. but now always open in most locations), Mac's, Mike's, and Beckers. Couche-Tard, based in Laval, Québec, which operates these last three convenience chains and is the largest convenience store operator in Canada, has recognized the same trends as the supermarkets. The company has adapted by targeting the meal-replacement market, hoping to allow the stores to expand their customer base and lessen their reliance on tobacco sales. Aside from increasing fresh and frozen meal offerings, these stores have also added branded products such as Subway, Taco Bell, and Timothy's coffee. Through these diversified offerings and store renovations, the chains have increased their appeal beyond the typical 18- to 34-year-old market and are attracting more women and 35-plus customers.[9]

Convenience stores compete to some extent with both supermarkets and fast-food restaurants. Furthermore, gasoline companies have almost phased out all auto repairs and supplies and added a convenience store section. This has evolved as the convenience store has — Chevron in B.C. advertises the White Spot fresh-baked bread products it carries in its convenience stores, while Couche-Tard plans to steal market share away from Tim Hortons and Dunkin' Donuts with its freshly brewed coffee and fresh sandwiches, doughnuts, and muffins.[10]

BACK TO THE TOP

Canadian Tire is making a big leap into convenience retailing with its new Q stores. These stores will be much more than the small gas bar outlets we now associate with them. The Q stores will offer a wide assortment of items ranging from fresh produce and bakery items, to gift wrap and cards, to Starbucks coffee. Do you think this is a good strategy for Canadian Tire?

Warehouse clubs

warehouse club
A combined retailing and wholesaling institution that has a very broad but very shallow product assortment; offers very low prices but few customer services, and is open only to members (same as wholesale club).

Another institution that has mushroomed is the **warehouse club**, sometimes called a wholesale club. A combined retailing and wholesaling institution, it has very broad but very shallow product assortments, extremely low prices, few customer services, and is open only to members. Costco (**www.costco.com**) is the major warehouse club chain in Canada.

A warehouse club carries about the same breadth of assortment as a large discount house but in much less depth. For each item, the club stocks only one or two brands and a limited number of sizes and models. Many products are sold in larger, bulk sizes. It is housed in a warehouse-type building, with tall metal racks that display merchandise at ground level and store it at higher levels. Customers pay cash (debit cards are ok in some areas but credit cards are generally not accepted) and handle their own merchandise — even bulky, heavy items.

Costco
Electrolux
Amway

PAGE UP!

1. What are the three major forms of ownership in retailing?
2. Name the different types of retail stores.
3. What is the difference between discount houses and category killers?

Non-Store Retailing

non-store retailing
Retailing activities resulting in transactions that occur away from a retail store.

A large majority — over 80 percent — of retail transactions are carried out in stores. However, a growing volume of sales are taking place away from stores. Retailing activities resulting in transactions that occur away from a retail store are termed **non-store retailing**. In this section, we review the four types of "traditional" non-store retailing: direct selling, telemarketing, direct marketing, and automatic vending. Then, in the next section, we will discuss the newest form — Internet retailing.

Direct selling

direct selling
A form of non-store retailing in which personal contact between a salesperson and a consumer occurs away from a retail store.

Canadian consumers are increasingly turning to non-store retailers for the purchase of many products. **Direct selling** is the retail marketing of consumer goods to household consumers by other than a regular retail store outlet. We can expect the impact of non-store retailers on traditional retailers to continue to increase as customers demand the convenience of shopping at locations and times that are convenient for them.

Among the many well-known direct-selling companies are Avon, Mary Kay, Tupperware, Amway (**www.amway.com**), Electrolux (**www.electrolux.com**), and The Pampered Chef. Many diverse products are sold through the direct-selling route, most of which require some form of testing or demonstration (cosmetics, water purifiers, vacuum cleaners). Essentially, the

Creating a friendly "party" atmosphere.

direct-selling approach involves a salesperson contacting potential customers outside of a conventional retail store environment.

The two major kinds of direct selling are door to door and party plan. Sometimes **door-to-door selling** simply involves "cold canvassing," without any advance selection of prospects. The use of door-to-door techniques has declined considerably as both adult partners increasingly work outside the home. More often, there is an initial contact in a store, by telephone, or by a mailed-in coupon.

Today, even traditional retailers are trying the direct-selling route. Jockey International and the Body Shop have started direct sales units with some of the products that are identical to those sold in stores. As well, direct sales representatives are becoming more strategic in their sales tactics. Some use the Internet to "meet" potential customers and recommend products.

With **party-plan selling**, a host or hostess invites some friends to a party. These guests understand that a salesperson — for a cosmetic or a housewares company, for example — will make a sales presentation. The sales rep has a larger prospective market and more favourable selling conditions than if these people were approached individually or door to door, and the guests get to shop in a friendly, social atmosphere. The Pampered Chef (www.pamperedchef.com) "parties" involve food preparation using the company's products, with gifts of the firm's merchandise for the person who hosts the gathering and the food preparation. Tupperware (www.tupperware.ca), the best known of the party-plan retailers, continues to market its extensive range of plastic houseware products primarily through in-home parties, involving 374,000 dealers in more than 100 countries as well as through catalogues, office parties, shopping mall kiosks, television infomercials, and the Internet.[11] Party-plan selling continues to expand as more companies see the advantage of selling in this relaxed social environment. For example, Fantasia hosts about 10,000 parties across Canada each year, demonstrating its lingerie and erotic products.[12]

door-to-door selling
A kind of direct selling with the personal contact between a salesperson and an individual prospect occurring at the prospective customer's residence or business.

party-plan selling
A type of direct selling in which a host or hostess invites some friends to a party at which a salesperson makes a sales presentation.

Telemarketing

Sometimes called telephone selling, **telemarketing** refers to a salesperson initiating contact with a shopper and also closing a sale over the telephone. As with door-to-door selling, telemarketing may mean cold canvassing from the telephone directory or it may rely on prospects who have requested information from the company or whose demographics match those of the firm's target market. This information may be obtained by purchasing client lists from other organizations.

With the development of computerized mailing or calling lists and auto-dialing technology, literally hundreds of calls can be made during a day by a single telemarketer. Many products that can be bought without being seen are sold over the telephone. Examples include home cleaning and pest-control services, magazine subscriptions, credit card and other financial services, telephone and energy services, and athletic club memberships. Not-for-profit organizations thrive, if not depend, on direct-marketing channels such as mail and telemarketing because they are efficient and accountable.[13]

This form of selling is not without its concerns. Few sales representatives last very long in this job — encountering hostile responses on the other end of the phone, receiving more rejections than closed sales, and often working under high-pressure conditions, it's not uncommon for these centres to be referred to as "boiler rooms." Annual turnover rates often average

Pampered Chef
Tupperware

telemarketing
A form of non-store retailing in which a salesperson initiates contact with a prospect and attempts to close the sale over the telephone. Usually involves outbound calls from a company to prospective customers.

100 percent. Telemarketing's reputation has also been damaged by the unethical sales practices of some firms. These firms tell consumers that they are conducting marketing research and "are not selling anything." Such unethical procedures hurt other telemarketing companies as well as legitimate research firms that conduct telephone surveys. Such practices are known as "sugging" — selling under the guise of research.

It is anticipated that some of the negative outcomes of telemarketing will be reduced as privacy regulations are enacted and fine-tuned at both the national and provincial levels in the next couple of years. The Canadian Marketing Association (CMA) (**www.the-cma.org**) has been involved in national and international forums discussing privacy issues and the protection of personal information. The CMA Privacy Code allows individuals the right to obtain the source of their names on marketing lists and to have their names removed from direct mailing lists, amongst other things. The federal, territorial and provincial privacy regulations will give all Canadians increased privacy protection. For more information, go to **www.the-cma.org** and **www.privcom.gc.ca**.

The approaches used by some telemarketing companies, coupled with a desire on the part of many consumers not to be bothered at home, has led to a consumer backlash against telemarketing in some areas. Despite this problem, telemarketing sales have been increasing for several reasons. Certain consumers appreciate the convenience of making a purchase by telephone. The truly effective telemarketing programs are being run by companies that have adopted an approach to telemarketing that involves doing a better job of targeting those customers who are most likely to be interested in the product or service being offered, and conveying their sales message to the consumer in a polite, caring manner without pressuring the listener.

The Canadian Marketing Association
Tilley
Canadian Tire

Direct marketing

direct marketing
A form of non-store retailing that uses non-personal media to contact consumers who, in turn, purchase products without visiting a retail store.

There is no consensus on the exact nature of direct marketing; in a sense, it comprises all types of non-store retailing other than the three already discussed. We define **direct marketing** as the use of non-personal media to contact consumers who, in turn, purchase products without visiting a retail store. (Be sure to distinguish among the terms direct marketing, direct selling, and direct distribution.)

To contact consumers, direct marketers use one or more of the following media: radio, TV, newspapers, magazines, catalogues, and direct mail. Consumers typically place orders by telephone or mail. Direct marketing is big business. Everywhere we go today, we are exposed to direct-marketing efforts. We see advertisements for recordings and exercise aids on television from direct-marketing retailers, and we are encouraged to call a toll-free number, with our VISA or MasterCard number handy, of course. "Bill stuffers" are included with our monthly gasoline bills, retail store invoices, and credit card statements. We order clothing and other items from mail-order catalogues, by either mailing back an order form or, more likely, calling a toll-free number. A large volume of direct-marketing effort is rarely seen by end-consumers because it is directed at the business-to-business market, where direct marketers have relied on catalogues and mailing pieces for many years.

direct mail
An advertising medium in which the advertiser contacts prospective customers by sending some form of advertisement through the mail.

Given its broad definition, there are many forms of direct marketing. The major types are as follows:

catalogue retailing
One form of direct marketing, in which companies mail catalogues to consumers or make them available at retail stores, and consumers make their purchases from the catalogues, often ordering online.

- ***Direct mail:*** Music and book clubs, magazine clearing houses, and credit card companies make wide use of **direct mail**. Store retailers, such as Holt Renfrew, also use this approach — mailing out postcards to remind customers of their semi-annual sales or new product arrivals.
- ***Catalogue retailing:*** In **catalogue retailing**, companies mail catalogues to consumers and to businesses or make them available at retail stores. Examples of the latter include Tilley Endurables (**www.tilley.com**) and Canadian Tire (**www.canadiantire.ca**). Catalogue

retailers appear well suited to operating on the Internet, as they have the systems and distribution experience required for such an undertaking. In fact, according to one research firm, two catalogue retailers (Lands' End and L.L. Bean) quickly earned the top ratings in online apparel retailing.[14]

television shopping
A form of direct marketing in which TV channels show consumer electronics, jewellery, and other products for sale at relatively low prices.

- *Television shopping:* There are basically two approaches to providing **television shopping**. We have mentioned one above, in which individual products are advertised and the consumer places an order by calling a toll-free number and providing a credit card number. The second involves the use of a dedicated television channel such as The Shopping Channel (**www.TheShoppingChannel.com**), which provides continuous advertisements for a variety of products such as housewares, jewellery, and other items that can be sold without the need for demonstration or trial.

Internet shopping
Use of the Internet to offer products for sale, providing information that can assist in sales being made elsewhere, but also offering an alternative way to purchase products.

- *Internet shopping:* Stated simply, **Internet shopping** is the use of the Internet to offer products for sale. While this may be considered the newest form of direct marketing, its impact and nature is so broad that it is considered separately later in this chapter. It is a form of marketing that almost every type of retailer has exploited — whether simply to advertise and provide information regarding products and services, or to actually provide an alternative way to purchase products.

The Shopping Channel

Direct marketing has been a major growth area in retailing. Its advantages relate particularly to its ability to direct the marketing effort to those consumers who are most likely to respond positively. Also, it offers products and services in a way that is most convenient for the consumer. A company that uses catalogues and direct mail to reach its target customers maximizes the effectiveness of its marketing programs by having the most accurate and complete mailing list possible. In fact, the success of most direct-marketing programs lies to a very great extent in the preparation and maintenance of an accurate mailing list.

Technology has kept pace with (or even led to) developments in the direct-marketing field, as companies are now developing sophisticated computer databases of customers and prospective customers. These databases contain not only mailing addresses, but also other data on the characteristics of consumers and their households, and a history of purchases that these consumers have made. Companies such as VISA and American Express make very effective use of such databases for direct mailings to cardholders in their monthly statements. The types of advertisements that are sent to certain customers are determined to an extent by an analysis of their purchasing history using the credit card.[15]

Like other types of non-store retailing, direct marketing provides consumers with shopping convenience. Direct marketers often benefit from relatively low operating expenses because they do not have the overhead of retail stores. However, there are drawbacks to direct marketing. Consumers must place orders without seeing or trying on the actual merchandise (although they may see a picture of it). To offset this limitation, direct marketers must offer liberal return policies. Furthermore, catalogues (and, to some extent, direct-mail pieces) are costly and must be prepared long before they are issued. Price changes and new products can be announced only through supplementary catalogues or brochures. The biggest drawback is that some consumers react negatively to receiving unsolicited mailing pieces at their homes, spam in their e-mail, and telemarketing solicitations.

Automatic vending

automatic vending
A form of non-store retailing in which the products are sold through a machine, with no personal contact between the buyer and seller; same as automated merchandising.

The sale of products through a machine, with no personal contact between buyer and seller, is called **automatic vending** (or automated merchandising). Most products sold by automatic vending are convenience-oriented or are purchased on impulse. They are usually well-known brands with a high rate of turnover. For years, the bulk of automatic vending sales has come from three main product categories: coffee, soft drinks, and confectionery items.

You can get just about anything from a vending machine!

Vending machines can expand a firm's market by reaching customers where and when it is not feasible for stores to do so. Thus, they are found virtually everywhere, particularly in schools, workplaces, and public facilities. Automatic vending has to overcome major challenges, however: Operating costs are high because of the need to continually replenish inventories, and the machines require occasional maintenance and repairs.

Technology can allow these machines to be monitored from a distance, thereby reducing the number of out-of-stock and out-of-order machines and increasing revenue. Coca-Cola is testing a machine with two-way communication ability that would allow long-distance price changes based on supply and demand considerations. However, these technological advances are costly.[16]

While sales through vending machines have been somewhat volatile in recent years, there is reason to believe that we can expect to see more products sold through this form of non-store retailing in the future. The reason for this optimism relates to changes in vending machine technology and the continual flow of new products for these machines. As well, they can be set up to accept credit and debit cards. New product offerings include movie soundtracks (sold in theatre lobbies), freshly squeezed orange juice, prepaid calling cards, reheatable dinners, office supplies, and even live bait for fishing.

Of course, vending machines have come under close scrutiny in recent years. Linked to the latest statistics showing the obesity rates in children, school boards, parent committees, dieticians and provincial governments have called for less junk and more nutrition in school vending machines. In October 2004, the Ontario government (**www.edu.gov.on.ca**) released a plan to make the schools in that province healthier learning environments by requiring that the stock in vending machines give children healthy choices.

Online Retailing

When a firm uses a Web site to offer products and services for sale, and individuals or organizations use their computers to make purchases from this company, these parties are engaging in electronic transactions. While online retailing has grown substantially in recent years, and there is much interest and attention paid to it, it still represents less than 1 percent of the total operating revenue of private businesses as the vast majority of online transactions take place between businesses.[17] In this section, we focus on sales by firms to end-consumers.

Online retailing is being carried out by an almost countless number of firms — both new companies as well as many existing retailers. New retailers that have chosen the Web include Chapters.Indigo.ca and Buy.com, while familiar retailers such as Sears Canda and Lands' End have also found their way onto the Internet. Traditional retailers either operate on their own or in alliance with an Internet firm — see Marketing at Work 11-3. Some sites feature broad assortments, such as those of general merchandiser Wal-Mart. However, most e-tailers concentrate on limited product lines or categories that are obvious from their names, which usually are also the Internet locations where they can be found — garden.com, 1-800-flowers.com, or furniture.com, to name a few of the more obvious.

In December 2005, Canada's online retailers experienced significantly greater traffic than in the same time in 2004. "An analysis of select retail entities found significant increases among online-only retailers, multi-channel players, and many of Canada's key retailers," reported, *Click! Weekly* (**www.dmn.ca/click**). The retail categories with the most growth were flowers/gifts/

greetings, home furnishings, and tickets. This is good news for retailers who, just a few years ago, were struggling with profitability on the Web.

For those that are both "bricks and clicks" (multi-channel approach) in their structure, this doesn't mean that the company is unprofitable, but sometimes the cyber-component is not profitable. There are substantial expenses in establishing an online operation, many of which do not diminish once the site is set up — marketing costs continue to be high, as new start-ups as well as established sites must continually remind consumers that they are actually there to serve customers' needs. Without a physical presence of some sort, it is difficult to remain in consumers' minds. While organizations are still struggling to turn a profit on the Internet, many have discovered that the secret may lie in controlling costs and developing a streamlined logistics system that efficiently fills and distributes orders, while minimizing inventories held.

The Boston Consulting Group (BCG) has reported that the typical pure-play e-tailers spend US $82 to land each new customer, while the bricks-with-clicks spend $12. While pure-play Web retailers have fallen by the wayside, established stores have moved ahead. Only e-tailers who carve out a niche or strike a partnership to get purchasing deals are going to make it in the face of competition from giants such as Sears Canada and Future Shop.[18]

Despite this, it is anticipated that online retail sales in Canada will grow tenfold in the next couple of years — and were estimated at $24 billion in 2006, according to Forrester Research, Inc. That will represent about 8 percent of retail transactions in the country. However, in this same time period, the Internet is expected to influence another $59 billion in offline purchases, as consumers use the Web to research products and prices before buying. Therefore, it should be appreciated that the Internet will become one of the most important places to interact with customers in the future.[19]

MARKETING AT WORK — 11-3: STRATEGY

Putting the Experts to Work Online

Sears Canada is getting more serious about online marketing in the face of big box retail competition, particularly Wal-Mart. General merchandising business sales are not growing well and catalogue sales, even at $1.2 billion, have been slipping as customers have continued to move to Internet transactions. Although Sears is Canada's leading online retailer, it needs help in this area. It has teamed up with Amazon.com in order to improve its Web site by using the firm's technological and online marketing skills as well as to explore cross-selling opportunities. Amazon has been trying to market its online skills for a few years; now it will be able to re-tool and operate the Sears Web site. Amazon is also eyeing the potential of using the Sears Canada distribution and transportation network to aid in delivering product rapidly into their customers' hands.

Online retailing has become more important for Sears since in the last few years Internet sales have increased almost 20 percent annually and now represent about 15 percent of Sears' catalogue business. Sears would like to see online sales increasing to 25 percent of catalogue sales within 5 years.

To achieve this goal, the Sears site needs expert work: increase the amount of product information, reduce the number of menus, track customers' preferences by monitoring their 'clicking behaviour,' and add more personal messages for customers based on their previous purchasing patterns. In other words, increasing satisfaction with the online experience and building stronger, effective Internet relationships with more customers.

While Sears and Amazon work out the Internet business, Sears' management continues to focus on increasing sales in its 122 department stores by improving the customer experience in its men's wear, women's wear, bed and bath, major appliance and cosmetics departments. And moving from 'clicks' back to 'bricks,' based on the results at a one floor off-mall experimental store in Charlottetown, Sears has concluded that the best bricks and mortar store for today's customer is a single floor model.

QUESTIONS:

1. What do you think of the Sears strategy of collaborating with Amazon?
2. Does using one collaborator hamper Sears as far as getting the best technology is concerned?

SOURCE: Adapted from Holie Shaw, "Amazon signs deal to run Sears' Web site," *The Globe and Mail*, April 28, 2005, p. FP 4, and Marina Strauss, "Sears drafts Amazon.com to beef up e-sales," *The Globe and Mail*, April 28, 2005, p. B4.

Turning browsers into buyers is one of the challenges of Internet retailing — beyond those consumers with security issues. Online shopping-cart abandonment rates can be quite high — from 60 to 90 percent in some cases. One additional reason offered for cart abandonment is the cost of delivery. Web customers often find that once shipping/delivery costs are added to purchase costs, perceived value has been reduced too much. In addition, the buying process is often long and unwieldy, with user-unfriendly navigation through what can seem like a maze. Ways to help convince browsers to take the plunge include providing complete product information and description, with clear graphics illustrating product features; reducing the number of steps in the buying process; and prominently displaying security features and guarantees.[20]

Retail on the Internet is difficult to classify by country: By its very nature, marketers are not bound by geographical marketplaces. Firms may be based anywhere and have orders from anywhere, creating one truly global marketplace. Like most other trends in Canada, we frequently adopt behaviours that "catch on" in the United States. There is a lag effect, however, with regard to retail shopping on the Internet. While Canadians seem to welcome this opportunity, there is a relatively delayed acceptance. It is not clear yet whether this is because we are a more leery of Internet commerce. After all, our rate of household high-speed Internet access is greater than that in the U.S.

Which product categories are consumers buying on the Internet? Well, this doesn't seem to vary much by geography. At the top of the list: books, music, and videos; computer hardware and software; travel; and apparel. What will they be most likely to buy on the Internet in the future? Given the speed of change in cyberspace, these categories may soon be surpassed by others — perhaps groceries, toys, health and beauty aids, auto supplies, or pet supplies.[21]

Retailing Management

Fundamental to managing a retailing firm is the planning of sound strategies. Central to strategic planning are the selection of target markets and product lines, and the development of customer relationships. Also, in the future, a factor called retail positioning will probably be even more critical.

Retail positioning

retail positioning
A retailer's strategies and actions designed to favourably distinguish itself from competitors in the minds (and hearts) of targeted groups of consumers.

Retailers are increasingly thinking about positioning as they develop marketing plans. **Retail positioning** refers to a retailer's strategies and actions designed to favourably distinguish itself from competitors in the minds (and hearts) of targeted groups of consumers. Such positioning centres on three variables: product assortment, price, and customer services.

Let's briefly examine several positioning strategies.[22] When only price and service levels are considered, two strategies that have potential value are high price–high service and low price–low service. The former is difficult to implement because it requires skilled, motivated employees (especially salespeople); the latter necessitates careful management of operating expenses because gross margins are small.

When all three variables — product assortment, price, and customer services — are considered, two new options emerge. One is product differentiation, in which a retailer offers brands or styles different from those sold in competing stores. The second is service and personality augmentation, in which a retailer offers similar products but sets itself apart by providing special services and creating a distinctive personality or atmosphere for its stores.

A retailer's positioning strategy may include one or a combination of these options. Retail executives need to exhibit creativity and skill in selecting positioning strategies and implementing them.

Managing retail assortments: keep an eye on fashion

Not all retail assortments are subject to seasonal or fashion cycles, but many are. A strategic approach to making retail product line decisions is based on how consumers view newness, styles, and fashions. Consumers seem to be constantly searching for "what's new" but not "too new" in products, styles, and colours. Often, consumers satisfy their hunger for newness through fashion, and retailers supply the fashions in various ways as part of their positioning strategy in relation to assortments.

style
A distinctive presentation or construction of any art, product, or activity.

fashion
A style that is popularly accepted by groups of people over a reasonably long period of time.

Nature of style and fashion

A **style** is a distinctive manner of construction or presentation of any art, product, or endeavour. Thus, we have styles in automobiles (sedans, compacts, SUVs), in most clothing items (bathing suits can be one-piece, string bikini, or thong), in furniture (old Canadian pine, Mission, French Provincial), and in dance (waltz, salsa, hip hop). Ethnic foods represent styles of food preparation.

A **fashion** is any style that is popularly accepted and purchased by successive groups of people over a reasonably long period of time. Not every style becomes a fashion. To be considered a fashion, or to be deemed fashionable, a style must be accepted by many people. All of the styles listed in the preceding paragraph, except perhaps for hip hop, qualify as fashions. Fashion is rooted in sociological and psychological factors and furnishes us, as individuals, with the opportunity for self-expression.

fashion-adoption process
The process by which a style becomes popular in a market; similar to diffusion of an innovation.

Fashion-adoption process

The **fashion-adoption process** reflects the concepts of (1) large-group and small-group influences on consumer buying behaviour and (2) the diffusion of innovation. People usually try to imitate others at the same or the next higher status or socio-economic level by purchasing a product or using a service that is fashionable in the group they want to be like.

Thus, the fashion-adoption process is a series of buying waves that arise as a particular style is popularly accepted by one group, then another group, and then another, until it finally falls out of fashion. This movement, representing the introduction, rise, popular culmination, and decline of the market's acceptance of a style, is referred to as the fashion cycle.

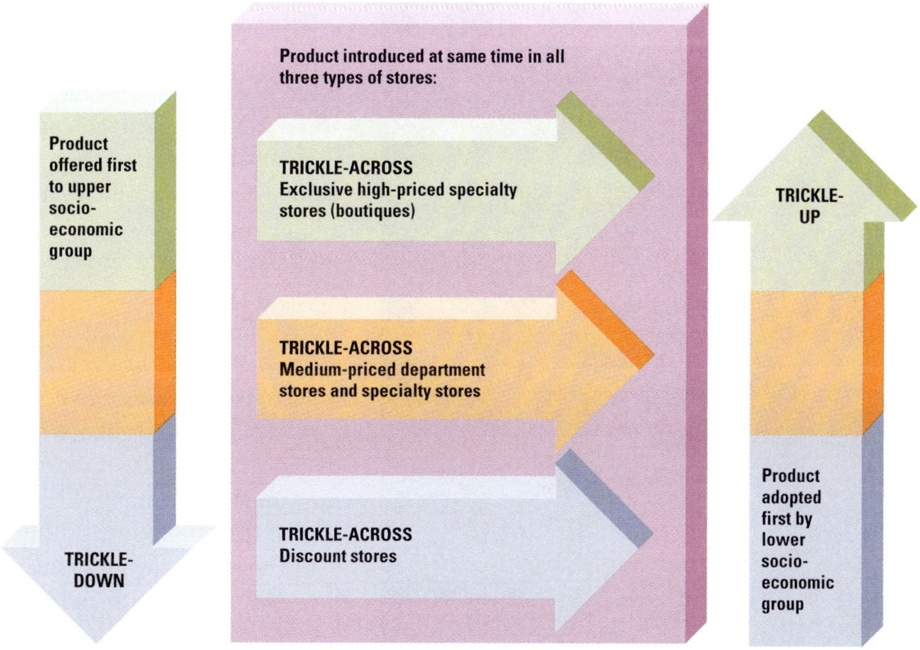

Figure 11-1: Fashion-Adoption Processes

There are three theories of fashion adoption (see Figure 11-1 on the previous page): the trickle-down, trickle-across, and trickle-up theories.

1. ***Trickle-down***: A given fashion cycle flows downward through several status or socio-economic levels.
2. ***Trickle-across***: The cycle moves horizontally and simultaneously within several status or socio-economic levels.
3. ***Trickle-up***: A style first becomes popular at lower status or socio-economic levels and then flows upward to become popular among higher levels.

Traditionally, the trickle-down theory has been used to explain the fashion-adoption process. As an example, designers of women's apparel first introduce a style — through fashion houses or boutiques — to opinion leaders in the upper socio-economic groups. If they accept the style, it quickly appears in leading specialty clothing or fashion stores. Soon, the middle-income and then the lower-income markets want to emulate the leaders, and the style is mass-marketed in department and related stores. As its popularity wanes, the style appears in bargain-price stores and finally, when it is no longer considered fashionable, appears in second-time-around clothing shops.

Today, the trickle-across theory best explains the adoption process for most fashions. It's true that there is some flow downward and obviously there is an upward flow, but, by means of high-speed production, communication, and transportation, style information and products can be disseminated so rapidly that all social levels can be reached at about the same time. For example, within a few weeks of the beginning of the fall season, the same style of dress (but at different quality levels) appears (1) in small, exclusive dress shops appealing to the upper social class, (2) in large department stores appealing to the middle social class, and (3) in discount houses and low-price women's ready-to-wear chain stores, where the appeal is to the portion of the lower social class that has some disposable income.

Look closely. Mountain gear specialist or fashion retailer?

Consider the popularity of mountain gear-inspired clothing for casual wear. Functional in design, these items were available at specialty stores for climbers and campers. Very durable and weather-resistant, such items were carefully constructed from special materials. They then became available in most sports stores, as people adopted them for various purposes. As they became a street fashion, clothing and department stores offered indoor and outdoor wear based on these styles. Although these durable fabrics have become cheaper with time, many lower-price outlets utilize common fabrics as this style becomes all about fashion and much less about function. Who by now doesn't have all-terrain sneakers, pants with pockets like pouches, and perhaps even zip-out leg bottoms or all-weather coats with a zillion zippers, drawstrings, and compartments? And how many members of the Mountain Equipment Co-op do you think are actually climbing mountains on the weekends?

Within each group, for example, clothing is purchased early in the season by the opinion leaders — the innovators. If a style is accepted, its sales curve rises as it becomes popular with the early adopters and then with the late adopters. Eventually, sales decline as the style loses popularity. This cycle is a horizontal movement, occurring virtually simultaneously within each of several socio-economic levels.

The trickle-up process also explains some product-adoption processes. Consider how styles of music such as jazz and rap became popular. Also look at acid-wash denim, T-shirts, Blacktop athletic footwear, boxer shorts peeking out over low-slung baggy pants, and even pasta in the 1990s. They all have one thing in common — they were popular first with lower socio-economic and inner-city groups. Only later did their popularity "trickle up" to higher-income markets.

Marketing considerations in fashion When a retailer's product lines are subject to the fashion cycle, retail management and buyers must know what stage the cycle is in at all times. Managers must decide at what point to get into the cycle and when to get out, and remain consistent with the agreed positioning strategy. Accurate forecasting is critical to success in fashion merchandising but it is extremely difficult, because the forecaster must deal with complex sociological and psychological factors and their effects on target markets. Frequently, a retailer operates not only with large databases but also with intuition and inspiration, tempered by considerable experience.

Ordinarily, a retailer cannot participate successfully in all stages of the fashion cycle at the same time. Thus, a specialty apparel store — whose stocks are displayed in limited numbers without price tags — should get in at the start of a fashion trend. And a department store appealing to the middle-income market should plan to enter the cycle in time to mass-market the style as it is climbing to its peak of popularity. Fundamentally, retail executives must keep in mind the product's target market in deciding at which stage or stages of the life cycle its stores should offer fashionable apparel.

Customer retention

customer-retention strategy
The measures that a company uses to retain current customers and have them make repeat purchases; includes getting to know customers in as much detail as possible in order to communicate effectively, and rewarding those who are loyal and continue to give the company their business.

In recent years, marketers in many businesses, especially in retailing, have begun to subscribe in increasing numbers to the philosophy that it makes considerably greater sense to retain the customers they have than to compete vigorously in order to attract new ones. This viewpoint acknowledges what should have been obvious to all marketers — that a company's most valuable assets are loyal customers. While not denying the importance of working to attract new customers, this approach to doing business places at least equal emphasis on keeping existing customers happy.

Two elements of a **customer-retention strategy** involve getting to know customers in as much detail as possible and rewarding those who are loyal and continue to give a company their business. The former implies the development and maintenance of a customer database and the latter often involves the establishment of a bonus or loyalty program for frequent shoppers. Air Canada's Aeroplan program is a Canadian classic and Shoppers Drug Mart has its Optimum card. Some of the most effective customer-retention programs combine these elements.

Other retailers have had or have recently established similar programs to encourage shopper loyalty. High-end retailer Holt Renfrew has its Club Select and Canadian Tire has issued its well-known Canadian Tire money for many years, essentially giving customers discounts of up to 5 percent on purchases made in the store. Sears Canada relaunched its Sears Club, a frequent-shopper program that rewards users of the Sears credit card with savings of up to 4 percent on purchases. Even Tim Hortons found a way to reward faithful customers through its R-R-Roll Up the Rim to Win promotion.

BACK TO THE TOP

PAGE UP!

1. What are the four types of "traditional" non-store retailing?
2. What is the difference between direct marketing and direct sales?
3. In retailing, to what does "bricks and clicks" refer?

Key Terms and Concepts

automatic vending 327
catalogue retailing 326
category-killer store 322
contractual vertical marketing system 312
convenience store 323
corporate chain 315
customer-retention strategy 333
department store 319
direct mail 326
direct marketing 326
direct selling 324
discount house 320
discount retailing 320
door-to-door selling 325
factory outlet 322
fashion 331
fashion-adoption process 331
independent retailer 314
Internet shopping 327
limited-line store 321
non-store retailing 324
off-price retailing 321
party-plan selling 325
physical facilities 313
retailer 310
retailing (retail trade) 310
retail positioning 330
shopping centre 313
specialty store 321
style 331
supermarket 322
supermarket retailing 322
telemarketing 325
television shopping 327
warehouse club (wholesale club) 324

Questions and Problems

1. Explain the terms *retailing*, *retail sale*, and *retailer* in light of the following situations:
   a. Avon cosmetics salesperson selling in offices.
   b. Farmer selling produce door to door.
   c. Farmer selling produce at a roadside stand.
   d. Sporting-goods store selling uniforms to a semi-professional baseball team.
   e. Chapters/Indigo selling books and music through its Web site.
2. What recommendations do you have for reducing retailing costs?
3. Reconcile the following statements, using facts and statistics where appropriate:
   a. "Retailing is typically small-scale business."
   b. "There is a high degree of concentration in retailing today; the giants control the field."
4. Of the criteria given in this chapter for evaluating the competitive positions of large-scale and small-scale retailers, which ones show small stores to be in a stronger position than large-scale retailers? Do your findings conflict with the fact that most retail firms are quite small?
5. What course of action might a small retailer take to improve its competitive position?
6. What could a department store do to strengthen its competitive position?
7. "The supermarket, with its operating expense ratio of 20 percent, is the most efficient institution in retailing today." Do you agree with this statement? In what ways might supermarkets further reduce their expenses?
8. "Door-to-door selling is the most efficient form of retailing because it eliminates wholesalers and retail stores." Discuss.

Hands-On Marketing

1. Arrange an interview with a representative of a small retailer. Discuss with this person the general positions of small and large retailers, as covered in this chapter. With which, if any, of these points does the small retailer's representative disagree, and why? Also ask what courses of action the company takes to achieve or maintain a viable competitive position. Interview a representative of another small retailer, ask the same questions, and compare the answers you received from both.
2. Go to a local independent bookstore that sells new or used books and think about the services offered by the bookstore and its competitive advantages in relation to online booksellers. Then, go to **www.amazon.ca** and examine the services offered to its customers. What are Amazon's competitive advantages relative to the small independent bookstore?

Back to the Top

When we think about retailing, we often think about traditional stores and outlets where we frequently buy goods and services. Retailers are facing new demands from consumers for increased convenience, increased selection and improved service. Given that Canadians are now making more purchases on the Internet and that retailers are moving away from traditional shopping malls to more power centres, direct selling and online retailing, what types of changes do you foresee in retailing in the coming years? Do you think traditional retailers like Canadian Tire, Sears, and Wal-Mart will be able to keep up with the new trends in retailing?

Online Learning Centre

Want to get better grades, tips on how to study more effectively, and up-to-date information on happenings in the world of marketing? Then, visit the Online Learning Centre for practice tests, Study Smart software, *Marketing Magazine*, and much more! **www.mcgrawhill.ca/olc/sommers**

CHAPTER 12

Supply Systems

This chapter will provide you with insight into the supply systems that lie behind retailers. We look at channels of distribution from raw materials producers to manufacturers and retailers. After studying this chapter, you should have an understanding of:

- The nature of wholesaling and the role of wholesalers.
- What a distribution channel is and how it is designed to supply producers and retailers.
- Channel arrangements to distribute to international markets.
- The nature of conflicts and control within distribution channels.
- How logistics and supply chain management help firms achieve their marketing goals, strengthen marketing programs and help keep customers satisfied.

What To Do When Your Product Lasts Longer Than Your Customer

There was a time when Padinox Inc. of Charlottetown, P.E.I., was almost bankrupt. The Paderno cookware "that it produced was so well made, and so high in quality that people could pass it on to their children," according to Tim Casey who bought the company when it was about to expire. "Customers loved what we produced. They were loyal. But too much quality meant that once customers bought a complete set, that was the end of it."

When Tim Casey took over Padinox, unit costs were high and sales volume was low — the result of making a product with no replacement sales and having a distrubution system made up of a few large retailers. The problem with the retailers was they put the Paderno product line on sale twice a year at a 40 percent discount; the rest of the year, sales were very slow. Something had to be done.

Faced with this pattern of concentrated distribution and the behavour of the retailers handling the product, Mr. Casey made some strategic decisions: He would go for market expansion by expanding his product lines and revising his distribution system. He decided to grow his market by getting more control over how Paderno was marketed at the retail level and to get more access to more customers than the 3 or 4 retail chains could provide.

In order to reach a broader market, he enlisted as retail distributors small retailers who would pay more attention to Paderno. The cookware was offered to them on consignment which meant that Padinox took all the inventory risk until the retailer sold the product. While the arrangement meant lower margins for the retailer, it also meant no inventory costs — an enticing incentive to carry the line and work with it. About 300 specialty boutique retailers now carry the lines. At the same time, Mr. Casey grew a chain of 21 retail outlets, some company owned and some franchised.

With this change in the distribution system, the large retailers also changed their behaviour; they began to market Paderno lines with more care and attention. Sears Canada stocks 22 Paderno items across the country and Canadian Tire carries a 10 piece set that was specially designed for the chain. In addition, Padinox does regular promotions with Loblaws. In 1998, the company launched one of the first Internet stores in the world; in its first week, sales were $15,000. Also, an annual Paderno catalogue was developed and distributed to customers.

On the product development front, the company launched the Chaudier line of cookware targeted specifically at professional cooks and chefs. Both the Paderno and Chaudier lines were produced in the Charlottetown factory in a seven-step process starting with sheet steel and ending with polished ready to ship cookware.

In addition to the changes in distribution, Paderno added utensils and kitchen items including nylon utensils, bakeware, tableware, cutting boards, and teapots. These lines further expanded retail offerings, broadened the retail market as retailers had much more product to work with and allowed Paderno collectors to keep collecting — even when their pots and pans lasted a lifetime.[1]

Although you shop regularly at retail stores, you rarely see or hear of the variety of wholesalers and channel arrangements that take place behind the retailer level. Also, beyond seeing company names on trucks and trains, you have little exposure to the logistics of product flow from the point of production to the point of final sale and consumption — through the channels of distribution. And you know pretty well nothing about the supplier networks that provide raw materials, components, processed goods to manufacturers and other producers. As a result, the role of wholesalers and other suppliers and the logistics involved in their distribution activities are often a mystery.

To de-mystify the behind-the-retailer operations, we will first discuss the nature of wholesaling and wholesalers. We can then proceed to examine how channels of distribution can be designed, and to compete our discussion we will review the principles of logistics and supply chain management.

Nature of Wholesaling

Wholesaling enables goods to be purchased for consumption. We already know that retailing involves sales to end-consumers for their personal use. Wholesaling has a different role in the marketing system.

wholesaling
All activities directly related to the sale of goods and services to parties for resale, use in producing other goods and services, or operating an organization.

Wholesaling (or the wholesale trade) is the sale, and all activities directly related to the sale of goods and services to businesses and other organizations for (1) resale, (2) use in producing other goods or services, or (3) operating an organization. When a business sells shirts and blouses to a clothing store that intends to resell them to final consumers, this is wholesaling. When a mill sells sheet steel to an industrial wholesaler who then supplies it to the Paderno factory for fabrication into cookware, this is also a wholesale transaction.

Sales made by one producer to another are wholesale transactions taking place at some point in the supply chain, and the selling producer is engaged in wholesaling. Similarly, a discount house is involved in wholesaling when it sells software, laser printers, calculators, and office supplies to a business firm. Thus, wholesaling includes sales by any firm to any customer except an end-consumer who is buying for personal, non-business use. From this perspective, all sales are either wholesale or retail transactions — distinguished only by the purchaser's intended use of the good or service.

In this part of the chapter, we focus on firms engaged primarily in wholesaling — the wholesaling intermediaries.

The rationale for wholesaling

At the customer end of the distribution channel, most retailers and final users buy in small quantities and have only a limited knowledge of the market and sources of supply. Thus, there is often a gap between the buyer (retailer or final user) and the seller (manufacturer or raw materials producer).

Most manufacturing firms are small and specialized and isolated from their customers. They don't have the capital to maintain a sales force to contact the many retailers or the final users that are (or could be) their customers. Even for large manufacturers with sufficient capital, some of their products or lines generate such a small volume of sales that it would not be cost-effective for them to establish a sales force to sell directly to consumers.

A variety of wholesalers thus exist to fill this gap by providing services of value to retailers, manufacturers and producers. Wholesalers can pool the orders of many retailers and/or final users, thereby creating a market for a small producer. At the same time, a wholesaler selects various items from among many alternatives to form its product mix, thereby acting as a buying service for small retailers. Essentially, the activities of wholesalers create time, place, and/or possession or ownership value.

From a broad point of view, the various wholesaling organizations bring to the total supply system the economies of skill, scale, and transactions:

- Wholesaling *skills* are efficiently concentrated in a relatively few hands. This saves the duplication of effort that would occur if many producers had to perform wholesaling functions themselves.
- *Economies of scale* result from the specialization of wholesalers performing functions that might otherwise require several small departments run by producing firms. Wholesalers typically can perform wholesaling functions more efficiently than can most manufacturers.
- *Transaction economies* come into play when wholesalers are introduced between producers and their retailers and other customers. Let's assume that four manufacturers want to sell to six retailers. Without a wholesaler, there are 24 transactions; with one wholesaler, the number of transactions is cut to 10. Four transactions occur when all of the producers sell to the wholesaler, and another six occur when the wholesaler sells to all of the retailers.

Profiling Wholesalers

There are more than 54,000 wholesaling locations in Canada. They are usually grouped into four major categories based on the services they offer to retailers and manufacturers as shown in Figure 12-1.

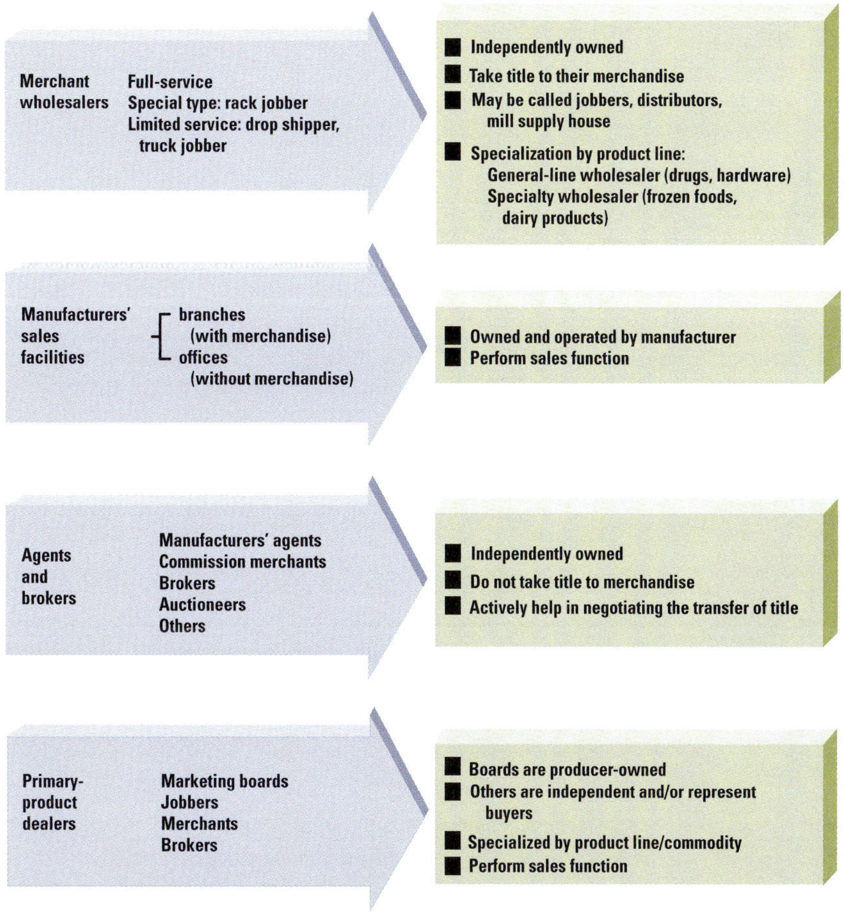

Figure 12-1: Types of Wholesaling Institutions

Merchant Wholesalers

Merchant wholesalers take title to — buy in their own names and therefore own — the products they handle, and account for the largest segment of wholesale trade. They generally provide the full array of services needed by a retailer or manufacturer.

Agent Wholesalers

merchant wholesaler
An independently owned firm that primarily engages in wholesaling and ordinarily takes title to the products being distributed; same as *wholesaler*.

agent wholesaler
An independent firm that primarily engages in wholesaling and does not take title to the products being distributed, but does actively negotiate their sale or purchase on behalf of other firms.

manufacturer's agent
An independent agent and wholesaler that sells part or all of a manufacturer's product mix in an assigned geographic territory.

As distinguished from merchant wholesalers who own the goods they supply, **agent wholesalers** (1) do not take title to products and (2) typically perform fewer services. Agent wholesalers receive a commission intended to cover their expenses and to provide a profit. Commission rates vary greatly, ranging from about 3 to 10 percent, depending mainly on the nature of the product and the services performed.

Agent wholesalers have lost market share to merchant wholesalers or direct distribution from producers. In the case of agricultural products and manufactured goods, agents are being replaced by merchant wholesalers or by direct sales to food-processing companies and grocery stores. As shown in Table 12-2, product characteristics and market conditions determine whether a distribution channel should favour an agent or merchant wholesaler.

On the basis of sales volume, the most significant types of agent wholesalers are manufacturers' agents, brokers, and commission merchants. These three types as well as several special types of agent wholesalers are described next.

Manufacturers' agents

An independent agent is not an employee of the manufacturer being represented — the agency is an independent business firm. Such agents have little or no control over prices and terms of sale since these are established by the manufacturers they represent.

TABLE 12-1 Full-Service Wholesalers' Typical Services to Customers and Producers

Service	Description
Buying	Act as purchasing agent for customers.
Creating assortments	Buy from many suppliers to develop an inventory matching needs of customers.
Subdividing	Buy in large quantities (such as a truckload) and then resell in smaller quantities (such as a dozen).
Selling	Provide a sales force for producers to reach small retailers and other businesses, at a lower cost than producers would incur by having their own sales forces.
Transportation	Make quick, frequent deliveries to customers, reducing customers' risks and investment in inventory.
Warehousing	Store products in facilities that are nearer customers' locations than are manufacturing plants.
Financing	Grant credit to customers, reducing their capital requirements. Aid producers by ordering and paying for products before purchase by customers.
Risk-taking	Reduce a producer's risk by taking title to products.
Market information	Supply information to customers about new products and producers' special offers and to producer suppliers about customers' needs and competitors' activities.
Management	Assist customers, especially small retailers, in areas such as inventory control, allocation assistance of shelf space, and financial management.

TABLE 12-2 Factors Suggesting Which Type of Wholesaling Intermediary Should Be Used in a Channel

	Favouring Agent	Favouring Merchant
Nature of product	Non standard, perhaps made to order	Standard
Technicality of product	Simple	Complex
Product's gross margin	Small	Relatively large
Number of customers	Few	Many
Concentration of customers	Concentrated geographically and in a few industries	Dispersed geographically and in many industries
Frequency of ordering	Relatively infrequently	Frequently
Time between order and receipt of shipment	Customer satisfied with relatively long lead time	Customer requires shorter lead time

SOURCE: Adapted from Donald M. Jackson and Michael F. d'Amico, "Products and Markets Served by Distributors and Agents," *Industrial Marketing Management*, February 1989, pp. 27–33.

Manufacturers' reps have continuing, year-round relationships with the companies (often called principals) that they represent. Each agent usually serves several non-competing manufacturers of related products and may specialize in toys and carry an assortment of non-competing lines in board games, dolls, learning materials, and outdoor play equipment.

When a manufacturer finds that it is not feasible to have its own sales force, a manufacturers' agent is often practical. An agent can be cost-effective because its major expenses (travel and lodging) are spread over a number of product lines. Also, producers pay agents a commission, which is a percentage of sales volume, so agents are paid only for what they actually sell — an average of 5.5 percent of sales.

An agent's main service to manufacturers is selling. Because a manufacturers' agent does not carry nearly as many lines as a full-service wholesaler, the agent can be expected to provide knowledgeable, aggressive selling — an important advantage. They are most helpful when:

- A small firm has a limited number of products and no sales force.
- A business wants to add a new and possibly unrelated line to its existing product mix, but the present sales force either is not experienced in the new line or cannot reach the new market.
- A firm wants to enter a new market that is not yet sufficiently developed to warrant the use of its own sales force.

There are limitations to what manufacturers' agents do. Agents do not carry an inventory of merchandise and typically are not equipped to furnish customers with extensive technical advice or repair service.

Brokers

broker
An independent agent wholesaler that brings buyers and sellers together and provides market information to either party.

Brokers ordinarily neither physically handle products being distributed nor work on a continuing basis with sellers or buyers. The broker furnishes information on many topics, including prices, products, and general market conditions.

Most brokers work for sellers, they do not set prices. They simply negotiate a sale and leave it up to the seller to accept or reject the buyer's offer. They are used in selling real estate and securities, but they are most prevalent in the food field. For example, a seafood broker handles the output from a salmon cannery, which operates only about three months each year. The canner employs a broker to find buyers among retail stores, wholesalers, and other outlets. Brokers provide limited services and, as a result, incur fairly low expenses, about 3 percent of sales. Likewise, they receive relatively small commissions — normally less than 5 percent.

primary-product agents
Intermediaries who trade in primary products as opposed to manufactured goods.

commission merchant
An independent agent wholesaler, used primarily in the marketing of agricultural products, that may physically handle the seller's products in central markets and has authority regarding prices and terms of sale.

auction company
An agent wholesaler that provides (1) auctioneers who do the selling and (2) physical facilities for displaying the sellers' products.

Primary-product and other agent wholesalers

Two other types of agent wholesalers account for smaller shares of the wholesale trade but provide valuable services in the distribution of primary products such as agricultural commodities. These **primary-product agents** are:

- **Commission merchants** set prices and terms of sale, sell the product, and perhaps physically handle it, but do not take title.
- **Auction companies** help assembled buyers and sellers complete their transactions. They are extremely important in the wholesaling of used cars and certain agricultural products (such as tobacco, livestock, and fruit).
- **Selling agents** act as a substitute for a marketing department by marketing a manufacturer's entire output. They play a key role in the distribution of textile products, coal, and, to a lesser extent, apparel, food, lumber, and metal products.
- **Import-export agents** bring together sellers and buyers in different countries. Export agents work in the country in which the product is made; import agents are based in the country where the product will be sold.

Channel Design: Putting Retailers, Wholesalers, and Producers Together

selling agent
A type of independent intermediary that essentially takes the place of a manufacturer's marketing department, marketing the manufacturer's entire output and often influencing the design and/or pricing of the products.

import-export agent
An agent wholesaler that arranges for distribution of goods in a foreign country.

To this point, we have discussed the various types of wholesaling organizations. We now turn to the question of how retailers, the producers of goods and services, and the wholesalers who supply producers, can be organized to form a supply chain.

What is a distribution channel?

A distribution channel consists of the set of wholesalers, facilitators, and retailers involved in moving and transferring the title to a product as it moves from a producer to end-consumer or business user. A channel of distribution always includes both the producer and the final customer for the product in its present form, as well as any retailers and wholesalers that are involved. In the case of services, the producer and the retailer are often one and the same.

The channel for a product extends only to the last person or organization that buys it without making any significant change to its form. When its form is altered and another product emerges, a new channel is started. When lumber is milled and then made into furniture, two separate channels are involved. The channel for the lumber might be lumber mill → broker → furniture manufacturer. The channel for the finished furniture might be furniture manufacturer → retail furniture store → consumer.

Besides the producer, wholesaler, retailer, and the final customer, other institutions facilitate the distribution process. Among these are banks, insurance companies, storage firms, voice- and data-transmission service providers, and transportation companies. However, because they do not take title to the products and are not actively involved in purchase or sales activities, these organizations are not formally included in the distribution channel.

PAGE UP!

1. What is wholesaling?
2. What is the difference between merchant wholesalers, agent wholesalers, and brokers?
3. The ______________________ is the set of wholesalers, facilitators, and retailers involved in moving products from producer to the end-consumer or business user.

Designing distribution channels

Companies that appear to be similar often have very dissimilar channels of distribution. For example, Tupperware sells its housewares primarily through a party-plan arrangement in which customers buy products at Tupperware "parties" held in the homes of friends and neighbours. Rubbermaid, on the other hand, sells its similar line of housewares through conventional department and variety stores. Some companies use multiple channels of distribution: Westin Hotels sell their products and services directly to walk-in customers, through travel agents, by mail, fax, telephone, through their Web sites, or even through Internet-based hotel room brokers.

Why do seemingly similar firms or the same firm wind up with such different channels? One reason is that there are numerous types of channels from which to choose. Also, a variety of factors related to the market, product, wholesalers and retailers, and the company itself, influence the choice of channels actually used by a firm.

The Internet is important in Westin Hotels' multi-channel distribution strategy.

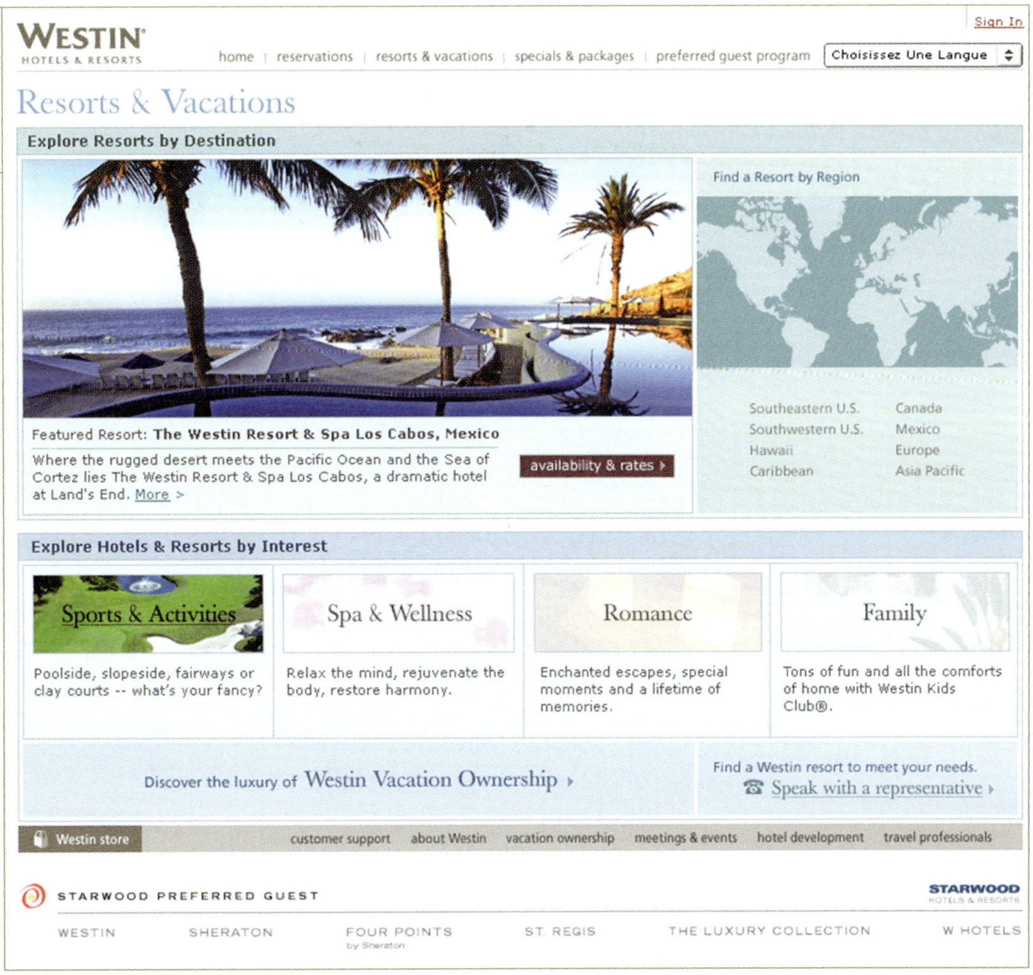

A company wants a distribution channel that not only meets customers' needs but also provides an edge on the competition. Some firms, such as Dell, gain a differential advantage with their direct as opposed to indirect distribution channel. Major corporations such as Caterpillar in construction equipment and John Deere in farm equipment, use dealers to provide many important services, ranging from advice about financing programs to rapid filling of orders for repair parts.

To design channels that satisfy customers and outdo the competition, an organized approach is required.[2] As shown in Figure 12-1, a sequence of four decisions is needed:

1. ***Specifying the role of distribution:*** A channel strategy should be designed within the context of the entire marketing mix. First, the firm's marketing objectives are reviewed. Next, the roles assigned to product, price, promotion and service are specified. Each element may have a distinct role, or two elements may share an assignment. For example, a manufacturer of pressure gauges may use both traditional wholesalers and retailers and direct marketing via mail and Internet advertising to convince prospective customers that it is committed to servicing the product following the sale.

   In services marketing, the role of distribution is generally related to accessibility. Because the consumer is often involved during the process of service provision, as, for example, in legal services, the ability to access the service directly is crucial to its saleability. Determining the role of distribution in the marketing plan includes consideration of the human resources that will be applied to the delivery of the service. While more and more services are being delivered over the Internet (financial and travel information, and entertainment, for example) most cannot be delivered by e-mail or the post office, stored on a shelf and passed over a counter, or delivered through indirect systems. The producer must be able to meet face to face with the buyer.

   A company must decide whether distribution will be used defensively or offensively. Under a defensive approach, a firm will strive for distribution that is as good as, but not necessarily better than, other firms' distribution. With an offensive strategy, a firm uses distribution to gain an advantage over competitors. Canadian banks provide a good example of the use of offensive strategies — they are world leaders in moving rapidly to get the jump on their competitors with the use of telephone service options and secure online services.

2. ***Selecting the type of channel:*** Once distribution's role in the overall marketing program has been agreed on, the most suitable type of channel for the company's tangible product or service must be determined. To illustrate the wide array of institutions available, as well as the difficulty of channel selection, consider a manufacturer of compact disc players. If the firm decides to use retailers to reach target markets, it must choose among many different types. At the retail level, the range of institutions includes specialty audio-video outlets, department stores, discount houses, mail-order firms, and Internet retail services. Sony, for example, utilizes all of these for their various lines of CD players. Another choice must be made if the firm decides to also use wholesalers to supply the retailers.

3. ***Determining intensity of distribution:*** The next decision relates to intensity of distribution, or the number of firms used at the wholesale and retail levels in a particular territory. The target market's buying behaviour and the product's nature have a direct bearing on this decision, as we will see later.

4. ***Choosing specific channel members:*** The last decision is selecting specific firms to distribute the product. For each type of institution, there are usually numerous companies from which to choose.

Using our CD player example again, assume that the manufacturer prefers two types of retailers: department stores and specialty outlets. If the CD players will be sold in Toronto, the producer must decide which department stores and audio retail outlets — Sears, the Bay, Bay Bloor Radio, Toronto Music Super Store — will be asked to distribute its product line. Also,

Figure 12-2:
Sequence of Decisions to Design a Distribution Channel

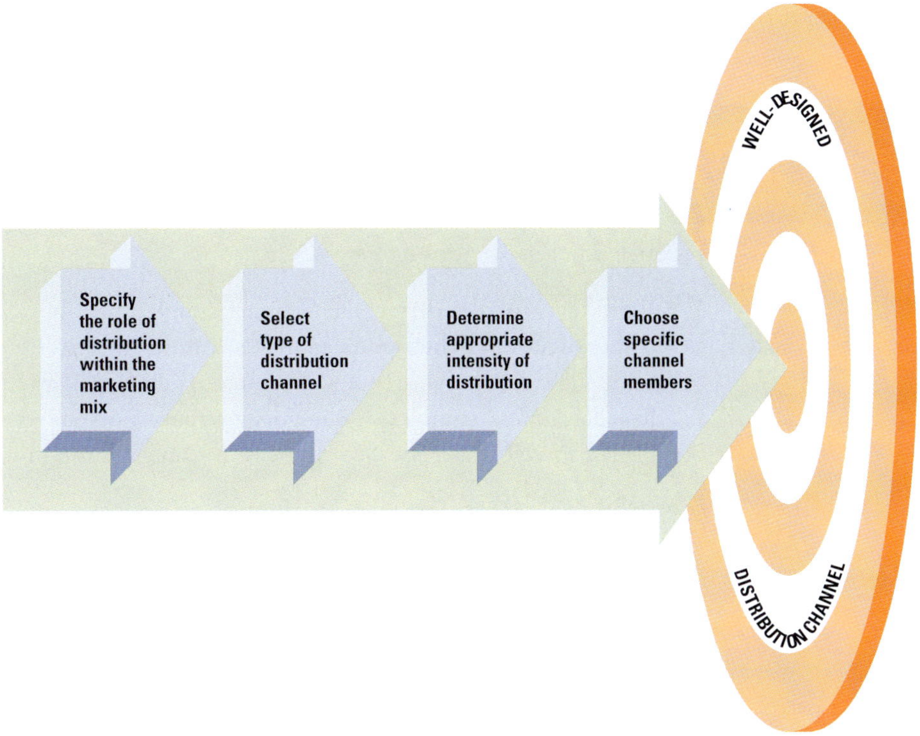

one or more audio Internet distributors — including, among others, GetPlugged.com and the Microsoft Network — may need to be considered. Similar decisions may be required for each territory in the firm's market.

When selecting specific firms to be part of a channel, a producer should assess factors related to the market, the product, its own company, and the nature of the wholesaler and retailer. Two additional factors are whether the intermediary sells to the market that the manufacturer wants to reach and whether the intermediary's product mix, pricing structure, promotion, and customer service are all compatible with the manufacturer's needs.

BACK TO THE TOP

When Padinox, Inc. decided to revamp its distribution, the decision was made to enlist large and small retailers as well as develop a retail chain. Added to this mix was an Internet store. While this may seem like a bold move, the line expansions, including the professional quality Chaudier line, dictated that Paderno be found in a number of outlets because of the variety. Providing the cookware on consignment to smaller retailers minimized the retailer's risk of carrying the line and ensured that Paderno products would be placed alongside the competition. Consumers would not have to seek out Paderno products from a small number of select retailers.

Selecting the Type of Channel

direct distribution
A channel consisting only of producer and final customer, with no intermediaries providing assistance.

indirect distribution
A channel consisting of producer, final customer, and at least one level of intermediary.

Most goods-distribution channels include retailers and wholesalers, but some do not. A channel consisting only of producer and final customer, with no others providing assistance, is called **direct distribution**. ServiceMaster uses a direct approach to sell its cleaning and property maintenance services to both residential and commercial customers. Schwan's sells a wide range of frozen food products from refrigerated trucks by door-to-door salespeople. Services are generally distributed directly because production and consumption usually occur simultaneously. Swiss Chalet restaurants, for example, produce the food they sell and distribute it directly to the consumer.

In contrast, a channel of producer, final customer, and at least one level of retailer or wholesaler represents **indirect distribution**. Air Canada and other airlines, while selling directly to consumers through offices and over the Internet, still rely on an indirect approach, through both travel agents and Internet-based travel services.

Major channels of distribution

The most common channels for consumer goods, business goods, and services are summarized in Figures 12-3, 12-4, and 12-5. In viewing these figures, keep in mind that the producer and/or any one or more wholesalers and retailers can be located in Canada or any other national market.

Distribution of consumer goods Five channels are widely used in marketing tangible products to ultimate consumers:

1. **Producer → consumer**: The shortest, simplest distribution channel for consumer goods is the direct one. The producer may sell from door to door, by mail, or on the Internet from Canada or another country, frequently the United States. For example, Arcuri Jewellers offers complete catalogue jewellery sales direct to the consumer through its Canadian Web page, and J. Crew sells in Canada through its U.S. Web site.

2. **Producer → retailer → consumer**: Many large retailers buy directly from manufacturers and agricultural producers. Companies such as Loblaws and Wal-Mart maintain direct dealings with producers in a number of countries.

3. **Producer → wholesaler → retailer → consumer**: If there is a traditional channel for consumer goods, this is it. Small retailers and manufacturers by the thousands find this channel the only economically feasible choice. For imported goods, a foreign-based producer may use this channel as well.

4. **Producer → agent → retailer → consumer**: Instead of using wholesalers, many producers prefer to use agents to reach the retail market, especially large-scale retailers. For example, a manufacturer of a glass cleaner selected a food broker to reach the grocery store market, including large chains.

5. **Producer → agent → wholesaler → retailer → consumer**: To reach small retailers, producers often use agents, who in turn call on wholesalers that sell to large retail chains and/or small retail stores.

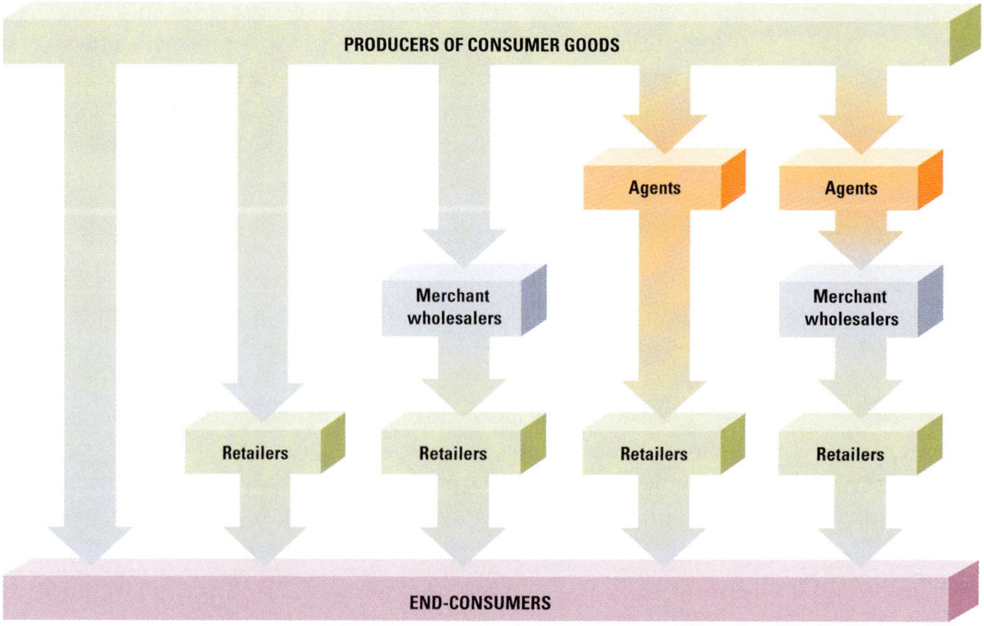

Figure 12-3:
Major Marketing Channels for Consumer Goods

Distribution of business products A variety of channels are available to reach organizations that incorporate the products into their manufacturing process or use them in their operations.[3] In the distribution of business products, the terms industrial distributor and merchant wholesaler are synonymous. The five common channels for business goods are:

1. **Producer → user**: This direct channel accounts for a greater dollar volume of business products than does any other distribution structure. Manufacturers of large installations, such as airplanes, generators, and heating plants, usually sell directly to users. Companies also allow direct consumer purchases of items such as computers and other electronic items, although they do offer retail networks through other channels.
2. **Producer → industrial distributor → user**: Producers of operating supplies and small accessory equipment frequently use industrial distributors to reach their markets. Paderno buys sheet steel to fabricate into cookware from an industrial distributor. Manufacturers of building materials and air-conditioning equipment are two examples of firms that make heavy use of industrial distributors.
3. **Producer → industrial distributor → industrial distributor → user**: This channel has been common for computer products and related high-technology items. The initial industrial distributor, usually a large firm, buys products from various manufacturers and then bundles them with related products for resale. These are often called value-added resellers. These firms then sell directly to the user as above or sell to smaller local firms, working closely with end-users to meet their needs for computer or communication system equipment and system design.
4. **Producer → agent → user**: Firms without their own sales departments find this a desirable channel. Also, a company that wants to introduce a new product or enter a new market may prefer to use agents rather than its own sales force. Producers in a growing number of industrial sectors are using Internet-based agents who create a virtual marketplace for them and buyers.
5. **Producer → agent → industrial distributor → user**: This channel is similar to the preceding one. It is used when, for some reason, it is not feasible to sell through agents directly to the business user. The unit sale may be too small for direct selling or decentralized inventory may be needed to supply users rapidly, in which case, the storage services of an industrial distributor are required.

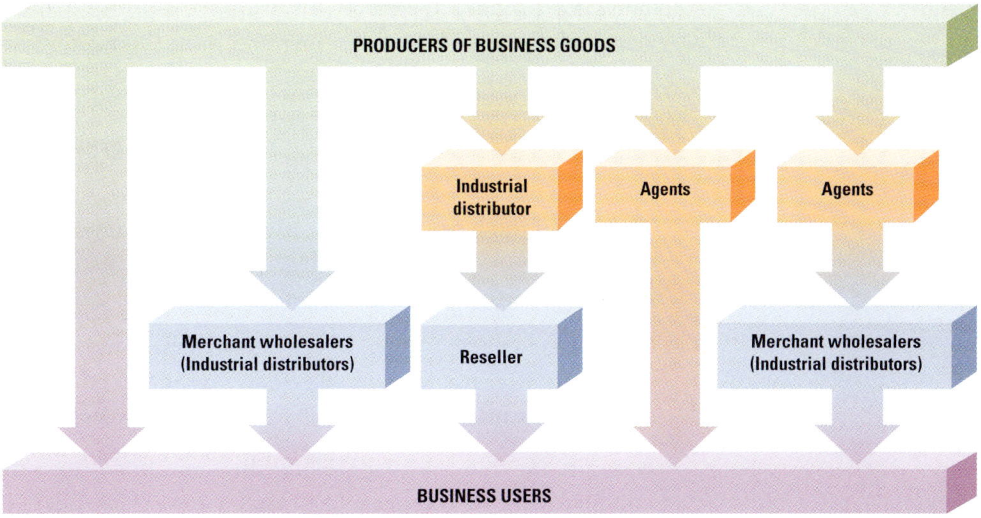

Figure 12-4: Major Marketing Channels for Business Goods

Figure 12-5: Major Marketing Channels for Services

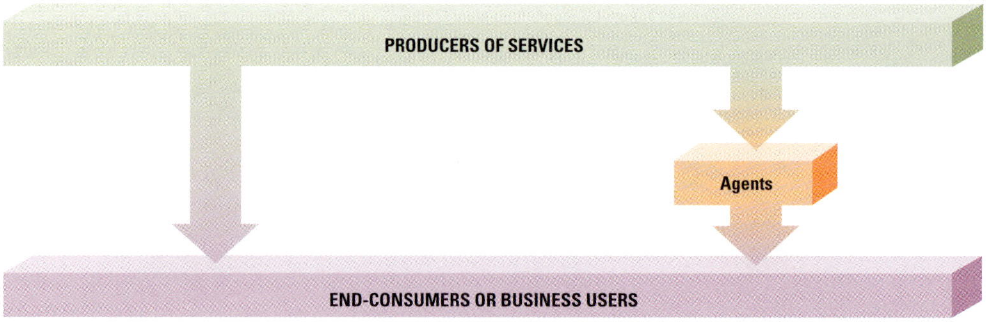

Distribution of services The intangible nature of services creates special distribution requirements. There are only two common channels for services:[4]

1. **Producer → consumer**: Because a service is intangible, the production process and/or sales activity often require personal contact between producer and consumer. Direct distribution is typical for many professional services, such as health care and legal advice, and personal services, such as haircutting and weight-loss counselling. Other services, including travel, insurance, and entertainment, also rely on direct distribution.
2. **Producer → agent → consumer**: While direct distribution is often necessary for a service to be performed, producer-consumer contact may not be required for distribution activities. Agents frequently assist a services producer with transfer of ownership (a sales task) or related tasks. Many services, notably travel, lodging, advertising media, entertainment, and insurance, are sold through agents. For example, how often have you purchased tickets to a concert, sports event, or theatre production that were labelled Ticketmaster? This firm is an agent that handles the logistics of selling admission to different venues. It doesn't know anything about organizing concert tours, directing plays, or running a circus or sports arena — its expertise is in ticket sales and distribution.

Multiple distribution channels

Many, perhaps most, producers are not content with only a single distribution channel. Instead, for reasons such as achieving broad market coverage, avoiding total dependence on a single arrangement, or entering a foreign market, they employ multiple distribution channels. The use of multiple channels, sometimes called dual distribution, occurs when:[5]

- The same product or service (for example, sporting goods or adventure tour packages) is being marketed to both consumer and business markets.[6]
- Unrelated products are being sold (margarine and paint; rubber products and plastics).

Multiple channels are also used to reach different segments within a single national market when:

- The size of the buyers varies greatly. An airline may sell directly to the travel departments of large corporations but use selected travel agents with physical outlets and Web-based solutions to reach small businesses and individual consumers.
- Geographic concentration differs across parts of the market. A manufacturer of industrial machinery may use its own sales force to sell directly to customers that are located close together, but may employ agents in sparsely populated markets.

A significant trend involves selling the same brand to a single market through channels that compete with each other. Nike shoes, Guess jeans, Levi's jeans, Maytag appliances, Sony electronics, Sherwin-Williams paints are distributed through the manufacturers' own retail stores as well as through wholesalers, independent retailers, and large retail chains. Producers such as Paderno Cookware may open their own stores, thereby creating dual distribution, when they are not satisfied with the market coverage provided by existing retail outlets. They also may establish their own stores primarily as testing grounds for new products and marketing techniques.[7]

BACK TO THE TOP

Although multiple distribution channels provide benefits to the producer, they can annoy existing channel members. Home Depot became so concerned with this increasing trend toward using the Internet as a cyber-intermediary that it wrote to many of its key suppliers advising them that it would view any attempt to sell directly to consumers in a very negative way. It implicitly threatened suppliers — such as toolmaker Black & Decker — that it might drop their products from stores if they chose to sell directly through the Web.

Vertical marketing systems

vertical marketing system (VMS)
A tightly co-ordinated distribution channel designed to achieve operating efficiencies and marketing effectiveness.

corporate vertical marketing system
An arrangement under which a firm at one level of a distribution channel owns the firms at the next level or owns the entire channel.

While in the past distribution channels stressed the independence of individual channel members, currently, the highly interdependent vertical marketing system has become perhaps the dominant form of distribution channel. A **vertical marketing system (VMS)** is a tightly co-ordinated distribution channel designed specifically to improve operating efficiency and marketing effectiveness. In a VMS, no marketing function is sacred to a particular level or firm in the channel. Instead, each function is performed at the most advantageous position in the channel. A vertical system obviously requires a great deal of trust among channel members and very strong relationships.

The high degree of co-ordination or control characterizing a VMS is formally achieved through one of three means: common ownership of successive levels of a channel, contracts between channel members, or the market power of one or more members. Loblaws, for example, is owned by George Weston Inc., which also owns a full range of bakery facilities, an ice cream production facility, and a soft drink bottling plant. As shown in Table 12-3, there are three distinct forms of vertical marketing systems: corporate, contractual, and administered.

In a **corporate vertical marketing system**, a firm at one level of a channel owns the firms at the next level or owns the entire channel. Sherwin-Williams and Goodyear, for example,

TABLE 12-3 Types of Vertical Marketing Systems

Type of System	Control Maintained By	Examples
Corporate	Ownership	Singer (sewing machines), Goodyear (tires), Radio Shack (electronics), Bata (shoes)
Contractual:		
Wholesaler-sponsored voluntary chain	Contract	IDA and Guardian Drugs, IGA stores
Retailer-owned co-operative	Stock ownership by retailers	Canadian Tire stores
Franchise systems:	Contract	
Manufacturer-sponsored retailers		Ford, Chrysler, and other auto dealers
Manufacturer-sponsored wholesalers		Coca-Cola and other soft-drink bottlers
Marketers of services		Wendy's, Speedy Muffler, Harvey's, Holiday Inn, Tilden car rentals
Administered	Economic power	Samsonite luggage, General Electric, Labatt

own retail outlets. Also, a growing number of apparel makers, such as Roots and Ralph Lauren, have retail stores to feature their brands of clothing. Some grocery chains own food-processing facilities, such as dairies, which supply their stores. In addition, some large retailers, including Sears, own all or part of the manufacturing facilities that supply their stores with many products.

contractual vertical marketing system
An arrangement in which independent firms (producers, wholesalers, and retailers) operate under a contract specifying how they will try to improve their distribution efficiency and effectiveness.

administered vertical marketing system
A distribution system in which channel control is maintained through the economic power of one firm in the channel.

In a **contractual vertical marketing system**, independent producers, wholesalers, and retailers operate under contracts specifying how they will try to improve the effectiveness and efficiency of their distribution. Three kinds of contractual systems have developed: wholesaler-sponsored voluntary chains (for example, IGA grocery stores), retailer-owned co-operatives (Canadian Tire), and franchise systems (Pizza Delight and Midas automotive maintenance and repairs).

An **administered vertical marketing system** co-ordinates distribution activities through the market and/or economic power of one channel member or the shared power of two channel members. This is illustrated by Corning in ovenware, Rolex in watches, and Kraft Foods in food products. Sometimes a producer's brand equity and market position are strong enough to gain the voluntary co-operation of retailers in matters such as inventory levels, advertising, and store display. However, retailers — especially giant ones such as Loblaws and the Bay — are more likely to dominate channel relationships now than in prior years.

Factors affecting choice of channels

If a firm is customer-oriented, its channels are determined by consumer buying patterns and preferences: The nature of the target market should be the key factor in management's choice of channels. Other considerations are the product or service being marketed, the types of retailers and wholesalers available, and the company itself.

Market considerations A logical starting point is to consider the target market — its needs, structure, and buying behaviour.

- ***Type of market:*** Because end-consumers behave differently from business users, they are reached through different channels. Retailers, by definition, serve end-consumers, so they are not in the channels for business goods.
- ***Number of potential customers:*** A manufacturer with few potential customers (firms or industries) may use its own sales force to sell directly to ultimate consumers or business users. Canadair uses this approach in selling its jet aircraft. For a large number of customers, the manufacturer would probably use other firms. Tim Hortons relies on numerous franchisee outlets to reach the large number of consumers buying coffee. A firm using others does not need as large a sales force as a company selling directly to final consumers.
- ***Geographic concentration of the market:*** When most of a firm's prospective customers are concentrated in a few geographic areas, direct sale is practical. This is the situation in the textile and garment manufacturing industries. When customers are geographically dispersed, direct sale is likely to be impractical due to high travel costs. Sellers may establish sales branches in densely populated markets and use intermediaries in less concentrated markets.
- ***Order size:*** When either order size or total volume of business is large, direct distribution is economical. Thus, a food-products manufacturer would sell directly to large grocery chains. The same manufacturer, however, would use wholesalers to reach small grocery stores, whose orders are usually too small to justify direct sale.[8]

Product considerations While there are numerous product-related factors to consider, we will highlight three.

1. ***Unit value:*** The price attached to each unit of a product affects the amount of funds available for distribution. For example, a company can afford to use its own employee to sell a large aircraft engine part that costs more than $10,000. But it would not make sense for a company salesperson to call on a household or a business firm to sell a $2 ballpoint pen. Consequently, products with low unit value usually are distributed through indirect channels. There are exceptions, however. For instance, if order size is large because the customer buys many products at the same time from the company, then a direct channel may be economically feasible.
2. ***Perishability:*** Some goods, including many agricultural products, physically deteriorate fairly quickly. Other products, such as services, can be consumed only in the presence of the producer. Legal advice, for example, is only available directly from a law firm. Perishable products require direct or very short channels.
3. ***Technical nature:*** A business product that is highly technical is often distributed directly to business users. The producer's sales force must provide considerable pre-purchase and post-purchase service; wholesalers normally cannot do this. Consumer products of a technical nature pose a real distribution challenge for manufacturers. Ordinarily, manufacturers cannot sell the goods directly to the consumer. However, the Internet has made it much easier for products to be distributed directly from the manufacturer, with substantial amounts of technical support being provided on sellers' Web sites.

Channel member considerations Here we begin to see that a company may not be able to arrange exactly the channels it desires.

- ***Services provided:*** Each producer should select firms that will provide those marketing services that the producer either is unable to provide or cannot economically perform. Foreign producers seeking to gain market share in Canada will utilize industrial distributors or importers.
- ***Availability:*** The potential channel members preferred by a producer may not be available. They may be carrying competitive products and may not want to add another line.
- ***Producer's policies:*** Sometimes manufacturers' choices of channels are limited because their marketing policies are not acceptable to certain types of firms. Some retailers or wholesalers, for example, are interested in carrying a line only if they receive assurance that no competing firms will carry the line in the same territory.
- ***Channel position:*** In some cases, a firm has achieved such a strong or even dominant position in the market that a manufacturer cannot afford not to distribute through them. For example, Staples/Business Depot and Chapters/Indigo occupy these types of positions.

Company considerations Before choosing a distribution channel for a product, a company should consider its own situation:

- ***Desire for channel control:*** Some producers establish direct channels because they want to control their product's distribution, even though a direct channel may be more costly than an indirect channel. By controlling the channel, producers can achieve more aggressive promotion and can better control both the freshness of merchandise stocks and their products' and services' retail prices. Dell Computer became extremely successful with direct distribution systems via the Internet and mail order.

MARKETING AT WORK 12-1: STRATEGY

Can Estée Lauder Improve Shoppers' Image and Profits?

Shoppers Drug Mart, Canada's largest drugstore retailer, covers the country with 935 stores. It carries many of its own private labels in many product categories, as well as well known national and international brands. Shoppers private label business is very profitable since it rings in 15 percent more profit than comparable national brands even though they are priced about 25 percent lower.

Shoppers wants to increase its very profitable high-end cosmetic business. The chain currently holds about 7 percent of this market, which translated into about $1.5 billion in annual sales; it has a 40 percent share of the lower-priced cosmetic market, also worth about $1.5 billion in current sales. More high-end sales are what Shoppers wants. Its sales of high-end labels such as Lancome and Dior are increasing at a faster rate than are those of lower–end national brands or its own Quo private label.

To achieve its goals for high-end cosmetics, Shoppers wants the Estée Lauder labels on the shelves of its cosmetics boutiques. Estée Lauder is the last prestige brand cosmetics company to hold out against agreeing to distribute cosmetics to drugstores rather than to traditional department store retailers. In making the case for getting the Estée Lauder brand, Shoppers' chief executive officer, Glenn Murphy, says, "Convenience is important to the prestige cosmetics buyer — we have more locations than department stores. We have better hours. Today's cosmetics buyer wants the freedom of choice." To further persuade Estée Lauder, Shoppers can point to its 30 newly created in-store beauty boutiques with another 30 on the way within the year.

The value of being a retail distributor of Estée Lauder products is clear to Shoppers — would it be clear to Estée Lauder? Or would there be some serious complaints from Canadian department stores. An interesting channel selection calculation!

QUESTIONS:

1. What do the Shoppers Drug Mart and Estée Lauder brands have in common?
2. Is there a conflict between Estée Lauder's brand positioning and the positioning of Shoppers Drug Mart among Canadian retailers?
3. Why do you suppose Estée Lauder has resisted a move to sell through drugstores as well as department stores?

SOURCE: Adapted from Marina Strauss, "Shoppers Wooing Estée Lauder," *The Globe and Mail*, May 12, 2005, p. B4.

- ***Services provided by seller:*** Some producers make decisions about their channels based on the distribution functions desired and occasionally demanded. Numerous retail chains will not stock a product unless it is pre-sold through heavy advertising by the producer.
- ***Ability of management:*** The marketing experience and managerial capabilities of a producer influence decisions about which channel to use. Many companies lacking marketing know-how turn the distribution job over to others.
- ***Financial resources:*** A business with adequate finances can establish its own sales force, grant credit to its customers, and/or warehouse its own products. A financially weak firm uses other firms to provide these services.

In a few cases, virtually all factors point to a particular length and type of channel. In most cases, however, the factors send mixed signals. Several factors may point to the desirability of direct channels, others to the use of wholesalers and/or retailers. Or the company may find that the channel it wants is unavailable. If a company with an unproven product that has low profit potential cannot place its product with wholesalers, it may have no other option but to try to distribute the product directly to its target market.

Distribution to Foreign Markets

Even Paderno distributes to a foreign market through a Boston-based retail store. In deciding to market in a foreign country, management must select an appropriate channel and organizational relationship in the same manner that it does for Canadian markets. There is a range of channels for distributing in foreign markets (see Table 12-4), representing successively greater levels of market involvement. While the basic considerations for distribution to foreign markets are the same as those for the Canadian market, the details of these markets are different. They exist in a different context, and differences range from economic, governmental, legal, and social systems to the specific trade practices of wholesalers and retailers and the channels that are available.

exporting
The activities by which a firm sells its product in another country, either directly to foreign importers or through import-export intermediaries.

export merchant
An intermediary operating in a manufacturer's country that buys goods and exports them.

export agent
An intermediary that operates either in a manufacturer's country or in the destination country, negotiating the sale of a product in another country; may provide additional services such as arranging for international financing, shipping, and insurance on behalf of the manufacturer.

company sales branch
A sales facility that carries a stock of the product being sold.

Exporting

The simplest way of distributing goods to foreign markets is by **exporting**, either directly to foreign importers or through import-export intermediaries. In international markets, just as in domestic markets, there are both merchant and agent wholesalers.

An **export merchant** operates in the manufacturer's country, buying goods and exporting them. Very little risk or investment is involved. Also, minimal time and effort are required on the part of the exporting producer. However, the exporter has little or no control over merchant wholesalers.

An **export agent** may be located in either the manufacturer's country or in the destination country. The agent negotiates the sale of the product and may provide additional services, such as arranging for international financing, shipping, and insurance on behalf of the manufacturer. Greater risk is involved, since the manufacturer retains title to the goods. These types of organizations are generally not aggressive marketers, nor do they generate a large sales volume.

To counteract some of these deficiencies, management can export through its own **company sales branches** in foreign markets. Operating a sales branch enables a company to (1) promote its products more aggressively, (2) develop its foreign markets more effectively, and (3) control its sales effort more completely.

Because it is the easiest way to distribute to international markets, exporting is popular with small firms.

Contracting Contracting involves a legal relationship that allows a firm to enter a foreign market indirectly, quickly establish a market presence, and experience a limited amount of risk. One form of contracting is a licensing arrangement: granting to another producer — for a fee or royalty payment — the right to use one's production process, patents, trademarks, or other assets. For example, the Suntory brewery in Japan is licensed by Anheuser-Busch to produce Budweiser beer. La Senza of Montréal has licensed its successful lingerie brand for use in Saudi Arabia.

Franchising Franchising has allowed Canadian service retailers, such as Pizza Pizza, Swiss Chalet, and Uniglobe Travel, to expand overseas. Franchising combines a proven operating formula with local knowledge and entrepreneurial initiative.

TABLE 12-4 The Range of Channels and Structures for Distributing in International Markets

Exporting directly or through import-export intermediaries	Company sales branches	Licensing foreign producers	Contract manufacturing by foreign producers
Low involvement abroad ←			→ High involvement abroad

MARKETING AT WORK — 12-2: GLOBAL

MEGA Bloks: Happy Customers in 100 Countries

MEGA Bloks is a winner of a 2005 Canada Export Award, repeating its 2003 Award performance as well as being named Exporter of the Year that year. MEGA Bloks? Think Lego. The Montréal company employs over 1,000 people and manufactures 75 percent of its product there; a broad range of construction toys that feature the company's interlocking plastic blocks. "No matter where kids live, they love to build, create, learn." So says Marc Bertrand, President and CEO, and the firm's global success attests to his view. His firm produces a core product with constant and universal appeal with an affordable rice range. Some 90 percent of MEGA's US$ 250 million sales involve distribution to more than 100 countries.

In most countries MEGA Bloks sells directly to recognized mass market retailers such as Wal-Mart and Toys R Us in the U.S., and in Europe to Carrefour and Tesco. "Our approach is to have our own people on the ground selling directly to those major brands," says Brahm Segal, Vice President of Corporate Affairs. Local representatives help tailor retailers' stocks and marketing programs to suit local culture and product preferences. They visit stores often to see that product is well displayed and even help retailers in foreign country markets translate and adapt store advertising for local consumption. Segal says, "Retailers feel they are getting an international brand but are dealing with someone local who is looking after their needs." As these large international retailers expand into more country markets, MEGA Bloks follows, having established such solid relationships.

In Latin America, the Middle East, and Africa, where some mega chains have not yet penetrated, MEGA Bloks goes to market through agents and distributors. To identify potential channel members in such markets, the firm consults independent researchers to identify prospective distributors and then makes in-person visits to assess potential partners. Those that are growing, are financially sound, and are well respected in their trade become prime candidates to be part of the supply chain. Qualifying partners is crucial to MEGA Bloks and is not seen as a really expensive effort — primarily the price of a plane ticket and long-distance calls.

While MEGA does not normally adapt its products for the local market, it has made an exception in the case of Japan where it entered into a joint-venture agreement with a Tokyo-based manufacturer. The German market has just been opened up to Mega after a German court struck down a 40-year-old law that protected Lego's market control. The new countries in the European Community are next on the list for market development after Germany.

In January 2006, Mega acquired "The Board Dudes," a privately held company based in Corona, California. The President and CEO of MEGA Bloks, Marc Bertrand, said that the acquisition would offer retailers and consumers a "compelling value proposition in all our product categories." "The Board Dudes" products are sold in mass and specialty channels in the U.S. and throughout Canada. This will add depth to MEGA's already well developed distribution channels, especially in the stationery and back-to-school product offerings. By acquiring the company, retaining its executives, and using the already developed distribution channel, MEGA Bloks is building on its distribution networks in North America. With channels in Europe and Japan already developed, MEGA can begin to market "The Board Dudes" lines in those markets as well.

QUESTIONS:

1. What is the role of the local sales representatives who call on MEGA Bloks' major retail accounts? Where do they fit in the company's distribution strategy?
2. Why is it so important for MEGA Bloks to "qualify" prospective agents and distributors in new markets?
3. How should MEGA Bloks integrate the distribution channel for its own products with the channel used to distribute the products of The Board Dudes?

SOURCE: Adapted from infoexport.gc.ca, accessed May 6, 2005; PROFITguide.com, accessed May 6, 2005; Bertrand Marotte, "MEGA bloks building up global push," *The Globe and Mail*, May 6, 2005, p. B 6; www.megabloks.com.

PAGE UP!

1. Describe the sequence of four decisions that need to be made when designing a channel.
2. When choosing channel members, what are some of the considerations companies should keep in mind?
3. ________________ is the simplest way of distributing goods to foreign markets.

Determining Intensity of Distribution

intensity of distribution
The number of intermediaries used by a producer at the retailing and wholesaling levels of distribution.

At this point in designing a channel, a firm knows what role has been assigned to distribution within the marketing mix, whether direct or indirect distribution is better, and which types of wholesalers and retailers will be used (assuming indirect distribution is appropriate). Next, the company must decide on the **intensity of distribution** — that is, how many firms will be used at the wholesale and retail levels in a particular territory.

There are many possible degrees of intensity. As shown in Figure 12-6, we consider the three major categories — intensive, selective, and exclusive. Different degrees of intensity may be appropriate at successive levels of distribution. A manufacturer can often achieve intensive retail coverage with selective, rather than intensive, wholesale distribution. Or selective intensity at the retail level may be gained through exclusive intensity at the wholesale level. Of course, the wholesaling firm or firms will determine which retail outlets actually receive the product. Despite this lack of control, a producer should plan the levels of intensity needed at both the wholesale and retail levels.

Intensive distribution

intensive distribution
A strategy in which a producer sells its product in every available outlet where a consumer might reasonably look for it.

Under **intensive distribution**, a producer sells its product through every available outlet in a market where a consumer might reasonably look for it. Manufacturers of convenience goods use intensive distribution. Retailers often control whether a strategy of intensive distribution actually can be implemented. For example, a new manufacturer of toothpaste or a small producer of potato chips may want distribution in all supermarkets, but these retailers may limit their assortments to four best-selling brands.

Selective distribution

selective distribution
A strategy in which a producer sells its product through multiple, but not all, wholesalers and/or retailers in a market where a consumer might reasonably look for it.

In **selective distribution**, a producer sells through multiple — but not all possible — wholesalers and retailers in a market where a consumer might reasonably look for it. Selective distribution is appropriate for consumer shopping goods, such as various types of clothing and appliances, and for business accessory equipment, such as office equipment and handheld tools.

A company may shift to a selective distribution strategy after some experience with intensive distribution. The decision to change usually hinges on the high cost of intensive distribution or the unsatisfactory performance of current channel members. Some firms perennially order in small, unprofitable amounts; others may be poor credit risks. Eliminating marginal channel members may reduce the number of outlets but increase a company's sales volume. Companies have found that they were able to do a more thorough selling job with a smaller number of accounts.

A firm may move toward more selective distribution to enhance the image of its products, strengthen customer service, and/or improve quality control. The Italian firm Gucci concluded that its brand was on too many leather goods and fashion accessories and was carried by too many retailers. As part of a new marketing strategy, Gucci slashed both its product line and the number of outlets carrying its goods.

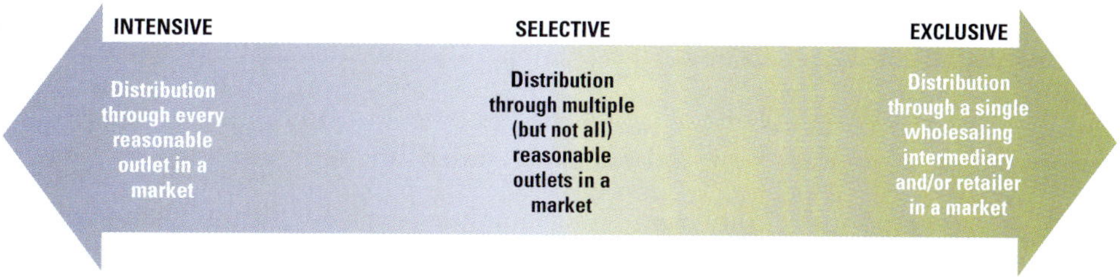

Figure 12-6: The Intensity-of-Distribution Continuum

Exclusive distribution

exclusive distribution
A strategy in which a producer agrees to sell its product to only one wholesaling intermediary and/or retailer in a given market.

Under **exclusive distribution**, the supplier agrees to sell its product only to a single wholesaler and/or retailer in a given market. At the wholesale level, such an arrangement is normally called an exclusive distributorship; at the retail level, an exclusive dealership. A manufacturer may prohibit a firm that holds an exclusive distributorship or dealership from handling a directly competing product line.

Producers often adopt an exclusive distribution strategy when it is essential that the retailer carry a large inventory. Exclusive dealerships are frequently used in marketing consumer specialty products such as expensive suits. This strategy is also desirable when the dealer or distributor must furnish installation and repair service. For this reason, manufacturers of farm machinery and large construction equipment grant exclusive distributorships.

Exclusive distribution helps a manufacturer control the last level of supply before the final customer. A retailer or wholesaler with exclusive rights is usually willing to promote the product aggressively. Why? Interested customers will have to purchase the product from this firm because no other outlets in the area carry the same brand. However, a producer suffers if its exclusive retailers in various markets do not serve customers well. Essentially a manufacturer has "all of its eggs in one basket."

An exclusive dealer or distributor has the opportunity to reap all of the benefits of the producer's marketing activities in a particular area. On the other hand, a wholesaler or retailer may become too dependent on the manufacturer. If the manufacturer fails, the firm also fails (at least for that product). Another risk is that once sales volume has been built up in a market, the producer may add other dealers or, worse yet, drop all dealers and establish its own sales force.

Conflict and Control in Channels

Distribution is occasionally characterized by goals shared by suppliers and customers and by co-operative actions. But conflicts as well as struggles for control are more typical, whether the channel is a domestic or international one. To manage distribution channels effectively requires an understanding of both conflict and control, including techniques to (1) decrease conflict, or at least its negative effects, and (2) increase a firm's control within a channel.

channel conflict
A situation in which one channel member perceives another channel member to be acting in a way that prevents the first member from achieving its distribution objectives.

Channel conflict exists when one channel member perceives another channel member to be acting in a way that prevents the first member from achieving its distribution objectives. Firms in one channel often compete vigorously with firms in other channels; this represents horizontal conflict. Even within the same channel, firms might argue about operating practices and try to gain control over other members' actions — this illustrates vertical conflict.

Horizontal conflict

horizontal conflict
A form of channel conflict occurring between firms on the same level of distribution, between intermediaries of the same type, or between different types of intermediaries.

Horizontal conflict occurs among firms on the same level of distribution. The cellphone field provides an excellent example. Cellphones and services can be purchased at a multitude of places — office supply outlets, department stores, warehouse clubs, consumer electronics retailers, and through telecommunications providers such as Telus and Bell Canada, via their own stores, toll-free lines, and Web sites.

Horizontal conflict may occur between:

- Firms of the same type: Maryvale Home Hardware versus Fred's Friendly Hardware, for example.
- Different types of firms on the same level: Maryvale Home Hardware versus St. Clair Paint and Wallpaper versus Wal-Mart.

The main source of horizontal conflict is scrambled merchandising, in which competitors diversify by adding product lines not traditionally carried by their type of business.

Supermarkets, for instance, expanded beyond groceries by adding health and beauty aids, small appliances, recordings, and various services such as snack bars. Retailers that originally sold these product lines became irritated — both at supermarkets for diversifying and at producers for using multiple distribution channels.

Vertical conflict

vertical conflict
A form of channel conflict occurring between firms at different levels of the same channel, typically producer versus wholesaler or producer versus retailer.

Perhaps the most severe conflicts in distribution involve firms at different levels of the same channel. **Vertical conflict** typically occurs between producer and wholesaler or producer and retailer.

Producer versus wholesaler Tensions occasionally arise between producers and wholesalers. A producer and wholesaler may disagree about aspects of their business relationship. For instance, John Deere has argued with distributors about whether they should sell farm equipment made by other companies or if they should restrict their efforts to the Deere brand.

Why do conflicts arise? Manufacturers and wholesalers have differing points of view. On the one hand, manufacturers think that wholesalers neither promote products aggressively nor provide sufficient storage services, and that wholesalers' services cost too much. On the other hand, wholesalers believe producers either expect too much or do not understand the wholesalers' primary obligation to customers.

Channel conflict typically stems from a manufacturer's attempts to bypass wholesalers and deal directly with retailers or consumers. The presence of the Internet makes this much easier to do. Direct sale occurs because (1) producers are dissatisfied with wholesalers' services or (2) market conditions call for direct sale. Ordinarily, battles about direct sale are fought in consumer goods channels. Such conflicts rarely arise in channels for business goods, because a tradition of direct sale to end-customers in business markets already exists.

To bypass wholesalers, a producer has two alternatives:

1. ***Sell directly to consumers:*** Producers may employ Internet, house-to-house, or mail-order catalogue selling. Producers may also establish their own distribution centres in different areas or even their own retail stores in major markets.

2. ***Sell directly to retailers:*** Under certain market and product conditions, selling directly to retailers is feasible and advisable. An ideal retail market for this option consists of retailers that buy large quantities of a limited line of products.

Direct distribution — a short channel — is advantageous when the product (1) is subject to physical or fashion perishability, (2) carries a high unit price, (3) is custom-made, or (4) requires installation and technical service. Direct distribution, however, places a financial and managerial burden on the producer. Not only must the manufacturer operate its own sales force and handle the physical distribution of its products, but a direct-selling manufacturer also faces competition from its former wholesalers, who no doubt now sell competitive products.

Wholesalers also can improve their competitive position and thereby reduce channel conflict. Their options include:

- ***Improve internal management*** by modernizing operations, upgrading the calibre of their management, and building new, low-operating-cost facilities.

- ***Provide management assistance to retailers*** by helping to meet certain retailers' needs and providing assistance with functions such as store layout, merchandise selection, promotion, and inventory control.

- ***Form voluntary chains*** (discussed in Chapter 11) by agreeing to furnish a group of retailers with management services and volume buying power. In turn, retailers promise to buy all, or almost all, of their merchandise from the wholesaler. IGA supermarkets are an example of this approach.
- ***Develop private brands***, since a voluntary chain of retailers provides a built-in market for the wholesaler's brand.

Producer versus retailer Another struggle for channel control takes place between manufacturers and retailers. Conflict can arise over terms or conditions of the relationship between any two parties, or producers may compete with retailers by selling direct via the Internet, by catalogue, or through producer-owned stores. A number of apparel makers — including Ralph Lauren, Levi Strauss, and Liz Claiborne — have opened retail outlets. In doing so, they have annoyed department stores and specialty retailers that also carry their brands.

Producer and retailer may also disagree about terms of sale or conditions of the relationship between themselves. Large retail outlets continually demand lower prices as well as more service from suppliers. Some retailers demand a so-called **slotting allowance** to place a manufacturer's product on store shelves. This is most evident in the grocery products field. In some cases, companies with new products are required to pay a fee ranging from $100 to more than $1,000 per store for each version of the product, or payment may be in the form of free products. Of course, not all manufacturers are paying all of these fees, and some small producers cannot afford them. Manufacturers criticize slotting allowances, claiming they stifle the introduction of new products, particularly those developed by small companies. Retailers defend them as a way to recoup the costs of reviewing the flood of new products, stocking some of them, and removing failures.

slotting allowance
A fee that some retailers demand from manufacturers to place manufacturers' products on store shelves.

Producers and retailers both have methods to gain more control. Manufacturers can:

- **Build strong consumer brand loyalty**. Creative and aggressive promotion is a key to creating such loyalty.
- **Establish one or more forms of a vertical marketing system**.
- **Refuse to sell to unco-operative retailers**. This tactic has to be defensible from a legal standpoint.

Effective marketing weapons are also available to retailers. They can:

- **Develop strong consumer relationships** with skilful advertising, strong store brands, and good service and customer handling.
- **Improve computerized information systems** to be able to determine what sells and how fast it sells and use such information in negotiating with suppliers.
- **Form a retailer co-operative** by having a group of retailers (usually fairly small ones) band together to establish and operate a wholesale warehouse and gain lower merchandise costs through volume buying power.[9]

Who controls channels?

Traditionally, manufacturers have been viewed as having **channel control** — making the decisions regarding types and number of outlets, participation of individual firms, and business practices to be followed by a channel. But this is a one-sided, outdated point of view. In many lines of trade, power has shifted to the big-box store brands and the category-killer retailers because of the volume of sales they control. Other strong retailers have gained much control because of the strong relationships they have developed with their customers.

channel control
The ability to influence the behaviour of other channel members.

MARKETING AT WORK 12-3: RELATIONSHIPS

What To Do When You Lose a Big Account? Compete With It!

In early 2007, Browns Shoe Shops will no longer operate the 15 shoe departments in the nine Holt Renfrew stores. Over the more than 14 years of their relationship, Browns taught Holt's how to sell shoes to its carriage trade market and Holt's, having learned the lessons well, will take over the departments and operate them on their own. This means that Browns and Holt's will become direct competitors for the same style conscious women who like to wear Manolo Blahnik, Prada, and other very expensive designer brands.

From 1992 to date, Browns helped Holt's raise its annual shoe sales more than five-fold. But the relationship was not always a smooth one. Holt's and Browns disagreed over what proportion of designer shoes were to be carried in the Holt's departments; Holt's wanted a higher proportion of designer brands while Browns wanted to maintain a good proportion of its less expensive private label shoes which represented half the department sales. Browns found that it could not sell the higher proportion of designer shoes at full price; such stock could only be moved with significant price markdowns, thus reducing the department's profitability. While the shoe department relationship was being played out, Holt's kept moving to more expensive merchandise in its various other departments. The gap between the Browns approach and the Holt's store approach widened.

With Browns and Holt's becoming direct competitors in the high fashion shoe business, Browns is now changing, making new plans. Browns will launch 10 new stores in the next few years and enlarge its existing locations. It has plans to open new B2 stores — it already has five that carry 'funky' styles. Browns operates eight shoe boutiques in seven Hudson's Bay stores and is in discussions to move into more of the chain's outlets. Browns also plans three flagship locations, all close to Holt Renfrew stores in Vancouver, Toronto and Montréal. The company is also in talks with other retailers hoping to establish shoe boutiques in their locations.

Meanwhile, Browns' buyers continue to scour fashion markets looking for trends; travelling to Europe for style shows, watching celebrity antics, and at all times, keeping an eye on feet.

QUESTIONS:

1. Over the years, do you suppose customers thought they were buying their shoes from Browns Shoes or from Holt Renfrew? Why is this an important question for Browns to be addressing?
2. What does this scenario tell us about the dynamics of retail partnerships?
3. Given the fact that their partnership with Holt Renfrew is coming to a close, why would Browns Shoes continue to look for opportunities to operate shoe departments in other retailers' stores? What do you suppose they may have learned from their experience in dealing with Holt Renfrew?

SOURCE: Adapted from Marina Strauss, "Browns get ready to walk away from Holt's," *The Globe and Mail*, April 12, 2005, p. B5.

Certainly the names Safeway, Loblaws, and Sears Canada mean more to consumers than the names of most brands sold in these stores. Large retailers are challenging producers for channel control, just as many manufacturers seized control from wholesalers years ago. Even small retailers can be influential in local markets, because their prestige may be greater than their suppliers' prestige.

A channel viewed as a partnership

Sometimes, members see a channel as a fragmented collection of independent, competing firms. The reality is that a channel is not something to "command and control," but rather it is a partnership aimed at satisfying end-users' needs.[10] Thus, co-ordination and relationship-building is needed throughout a distribution channel.

When Paderno decided to open retail stores — corporate owned and franchises — the company took greater control of its distribution channel by making decisions about how and where products would be sold. By entering into agreements with Canadian Tire and Loblaws, Paderno cemented relationships with these large retailers by providing products and configurations that fit with their existing lines. This increased coordination and improved relationships in the channel helped Paderno get its products to consumers using new and existing channels of distribution.

BACK TO THE TOP

GUEST MARKETER

How Do Those Fries Get To Your Favourite Restaurant?

By John Gardner

John Gardner is Chairman and CEO of Genesis Worldwide. He has had many years experience in the senior management ranks of Canadian food distribution companies, including Sobeys, Serca and SYSCO Canada. He is a Chartered Accountant and has an MBA from Memorial University.

Eating dinner at your college dining hall, getting that coffee and donut at Tim Hortons, that sizzling steak from The Keg, or the meal served to your grandmother at the retirement home all have something in common. The supply of these products in a timely and cost-effective manner is all part of the foodservice industry which has its own unique supply chain, distinct from that which serves your local supermarket.

The food service industry is all about food that is prepared away from home. Restaurants, hotels, university and college dining halls and cafeterias, hospitals and catering companies provide most of its customer base. The supply chain in this industry can be summarized with the phrase "from the farmer's field to the dinner plate."

To understand the supply chain initiatives necessary in this industry, one must first understand the customer as distinct from the end consumer. The foodservice industry involves business-to-business marketing. The common characteristics of a typical foodservice customer are:

- The customer has very little safety stock, probably no more than enough to last a week.
- 50 percent of the products used are fresh products, such as meat, poultry, seafood, fruits and vegetables. These products have a very short shelf life.
- Each chef has his or her own special recipes and favourite ingredients.
- Storage capacity at the kitchen is very limited.
- Forecasting models used by chefs are very basic; while most meals are planned, it is not unusual for large events to be scheduled with little notice.
- Consumers generally arrive at most establishments within a very narrow timeframe (mealtimes).
- Products must be handled in three different temperature environments: frozen, chilled, and ambient temperature.

To respond to this environment, an efficient foodservice distributor must:

- provide frequent and small deliveries
- carry a wide variety of products

- fill orders completely and error free
- provide delivery within a tight time window (certainly not at mealtimes)

How is all this accomplished profitably within a very competitive industry? It is best to work backwards. In other words, from the plate to the farmer's field.

The first important step is the relationship that the foodservice company has with the chef, who is usually responsible for placing orders for food. The relationship is normally established between the chef and the sales associate of the foodservice distributor. Many sales associates have a culinary background; some are trained chefs themselves. This relationship allows the sales associate to know intimately the menu at the establishment, and the normal work flows and consumer patterns that the establishment experiences. From this, the sales associate can determine what products are required, in what quantities and the physical delivery requirements. This relationship also allows the sales associate to respond to emergency situations that frequently occur, such as an unexpected event.

In today's foodservice industry, sales associates are technically advanced. They have real time access to inventory levels at the distributor's warehouse; plus, they are armed with all the data necessary for all product offerings.

The next part of the chain involves the foodservice distributors themselves. The most important task involves their inventory management and outbound delivery systems.

Most food distributors will have an inventory management system that manages expected demand, based upon sales history and seasonality. They will use a forecasting model to determine their own economic order quantity, which would incorporate expected demand, forecasts, lead time from the various manufacturing facilities, the shelf life of the product, safety stock, and any minimum that they must meet from the manufacturer.

Supply chain interaction with the manufacturer requires a thorough understanding of their cycles of production and logistical capabilities. Electronic Data Interchange (EDI) is a standard in the industry. The interchange allows for the timely and accurate exchange of information between the distributor and the manufacturer, such as order quantity, supply quantity, cost changes, product changes, product availability, etc. A typical foodservice distributor would deal with over 700 different suppliers, located in many different countries: shrimp from Vietnam, olive oils from Italy and Spain, tomatoes from Mexico, and cheese from France, just as an example.

The distributor's outbound delivery system is critical to efficient supply chain management. They must be able to receive orders from their customer, select the order error free, and then ship to the customer in good condition and within the expected time delivery window. Typically this is done within a 24-hour window: ordered today, received tomorrow. Distributors will use a warehouse management system to manage the selection of products. Newest technology utilizes scanning to communicate the customer's need to the order selector. Scanning technology dramatically reduces errors in product selection. The distributor will also use delivery software to route the deliveries to customers efficiently. All deliveries are made in temperature-controlled vehicles.

That part of the supply chain from the farm to the manufacturer involves more than simply harvesting product and shipping to the manufacturing plant. Issues such as product quality, product size and harvest cycles must be considered. Natural disasters such as hurricanes and low rainfall disrupt the supply chain and alternative supply must be quickly put in place. It is vital that the supply chain is never broken.

What is in the future? The future is focused on two things: eliminating cost in product handling and food safety. Major foodservice companies such as SYSCO are opening redistribution centres. This concept is based upon economies of scale. It is less costly to ship larger quantities to a central warehouse than to ship smaller quantities to multiple warehouses. RFID (Radio Frequency Identification) is another initiative that will be implemented by many companies in the next few years. RFID involves tagging each case of product with its own scannable label that contains important product data, such as best before date, temperature tracking information, product identification, etc. Food safety and product handling will be greatly enhanced with RFID.

What seems simple — ordering a coffee and a donut at Tim Hortons, getting that pizza from the university cafeteria, or ordering your favourite pasta dish at your local restaurant — is all supported by a sophisticated supply chain system that ensures that customers can get their favourite food items in a safe, timely and cost-effective manner.

Logistics and Supply Chain Management

logistics
Activities involved in the flow of products as they move physically from producer to consumer or industrial user.

logistics management
The cost efficient organizing and managing of the flow of raw materials, in-process inventory, finished goods and related information from point of origin to point of consumption to satisfy customer requirements.

Designing a channel of distribution doesn't get goods and services into the hands of customers. There is the matter of operating the channel — creating the flow. Channel members of all types, be they retailers, wholesalers, manufacturers and other goods and materials producers, must arrange for the actual activities involved in getting the right products to their customers in the right places at the right times. Flow activities are the actual **logistics** of the channels. The logistical activities to be managed normally include inventory location and warehousing, materials handling, inventory control, order processing, and transportation. In its full scope, **logistics management** means the cost efficient organizing and managing of the flow of raw materials, in-process inventory, finished goods and related information from point of origin to point of consumption to satisfy customer requirements.[11]

Two key components of logistics management must be kept in mind:

- Logistics management deals with decisions concerned with the total flow or movement of product, starting with constituent raw materials and ending with customer use.
- Logistics management decisions must be cost effective within the limits of providing the levels of service and satisfaction that customers require, not just the lowest costs possible.

The first point tells us that the scope for logistics management is all encompassing. The second underscores the need for a company to establish what customer needs are in terms of having the right product at the right time in the right place. Having established these needs, it is then that logistics costs can be efficiently managed. Without establishing the levels of service associated with having the right product available at the right time and the right place, low logistics costs can be achieved, but it is not likely that customer requirements can also be achieved.

The classic early success story of logistics management is the Procter & Gamble experience beginning in the 1990s. At the time, P&G was facing growing complaints from retailers, large and small, about their logistical services and costs. Purely and simply, retail sales and profits were being lost because product was not being made available on store shelves to the satisfaction of retailers and most importantly, customers. The company embarked on a major logistics management program that consisted of working much more closely than in the past with P&G suppliers as well as retailers. A key part of the program was the sharing of product movement information and collaborating and partnering with suppliers and retailers in logistics decision-making. Within 18 months, P&G had succeeded in saving itself, suppliers, and retailers a great deal of money in logistics costs while increasing sales as a result of much better product availability. Very importantly, the firm succeeded in greatly strengthening supplier, retailer, and customer relationships.[12]

The lesson of the P&G example is that to have satisfied customers, channel members, and suppliers, you need to build a system of relationships among all the organizations involved in getting product into customers' hands. This resulting system of relationships we now call a **supply chain**.

supply chain
The sequence of organizations that perform the logistics and related activities required to create and deliver a product to consumers or industrial users.

Referring back to the SYSCO supply chain mentioned by our Guest Marketer, it is evident that there are some key steps in managing the supply chain effectively. The relationship with the chef is the first key step — so important that many of SYSCO's sales associates are licensed chefs. This allows the associates to make suggestions for substitutions if an item is not immediately available. Knowing the customer's menu is also important so that demand forecasting and product variety can be well established.

Technology is also important to effective supply chain management. All SYSCO orders are electronically communicated each day. Truck loading and delivery routing are also managed electronically.

Of course, interaction with manufacturers and processors, and understanding their production cycles are important elements of the supply chain. SYSCO ensures effective supply chain management through developing relationships with the customers, using technology to maintain inventory levels and understanding processors' logistical capabilities.

Supply Chain and Logistics Management

All companies are members of a supply chain. In Figure 12-7, we show the relationships between channels of distribution and supply chains as well as the scope of logistics and **supply chain management**. A supply chain differs from a marketing channel in terms of the firms involved. First, the scope of a supply chain is all encompassing. It includes suppliers of raw materials and components to manufacturers as well as the various wholesalers and retailers who deliver products to customers. Secondly, what is to be managed is different. Supply chain management deals with the development of relationships among those in the system. Management's focus is to build trust and confidence with and among system units so that information about logistical matters and related decision-making can be communicated and shared. Logistics management has a narrower focus — it deals with the coordination and flow of products.

supply chain management
The integration and organization of information and logistics activities across firms in a supply chain to create and deliver goods and services that have customer value.

The growth and success of a supply chain management perspective is based in large part on increasingly sophisticated information technology in general, as well as the flood of handheld equipment which can be deployed almost anywhere needed in a distribution channel and supply

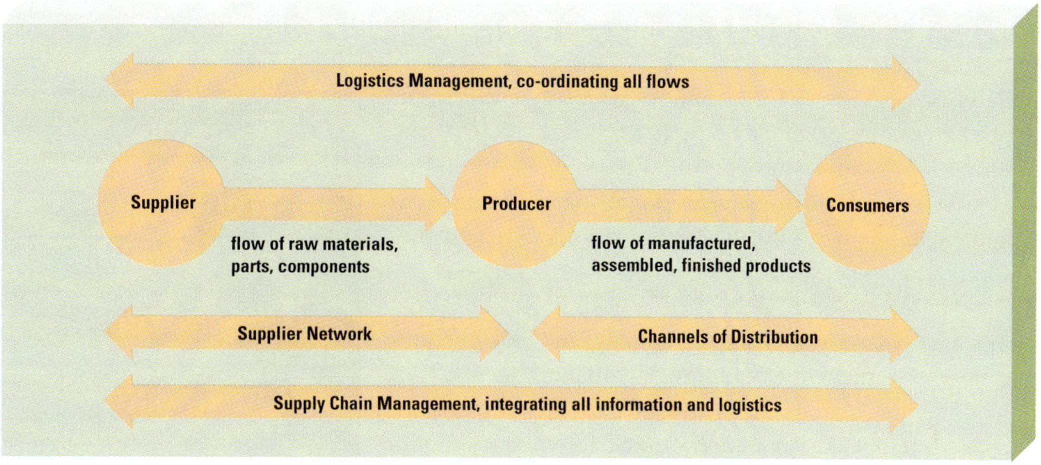

Figure 12-7: Scope of Channels of Distribution, Supply Chains, Logistics, and Supply Chain Management

system. The digital technology allows companies to share information and operate systems for order processing, transportation scheduling, and inventory and facilities management in a much more rapid manner than ever before.

Marketing Strategy and Supply Chain Management

Supply chains can range from very simple to very complex with either the supplier network being very simple or complex or the channel of distribution being simple or complex, or both can be complex. Paderno cookware may have a simple supply network for its Charlottetown factory, but its channels would be more complex — ranging from catalogues and the Internet to Sears and Canadian Tire warehouses, Paderno retail outlets and a large number of specialty retailers. The configuration of a supply chain flows from a company's marketing strategy and is based on understanding its customers, understanding what a supply chain can and cannot accomplish, and being able to co-ordinate a supply chain with the marketing strategy for a particular product or related line. There are three steps in aligning a supply chain with a firm's marketing strategy:

- **Understanding the customer:** The company needs to be clear as to the customer segment(s) being served; it must know the needs and expectations of each segment (low price, convenience, easy access to retailers) so it can determine the relative importance of chain cost efficiency versus chain customer responsiveness.
- **Understanding the supply chain:** There should be an understanding of what a particular supply chain can do well and not do so well; every chain will have some inflexibilites built into it due to channel, partnering, and information exchange arrangements which may lead to not being able to emphasize either lowest delivered cost or a high degree of responsiveness to customer requirements.
- **Making the chain consistent with marketing strategy:** If a chain as designed is not capable of delivering what is required by target segments in terms of the required degree of cost efficiency or customer needs and service, then appropriate changes should be made in terms of either information flows, the nature of relationships in the chain, or with respect to the various logistical activities being performed. It is sometimes the case that a problem may exist with elements of the marketing strategy. The box on the next page illustrates how an acknowledged leader in supply chain management has harmonized key marketing strategies with approaches to supply chain management.

Nygard International Designs Clothing and Supply Chains

Peter Nygard runs a $300-million company, with almost 3,000 employees in Winnipeg, Montréal, New York, Hong Kong, and Europe. Still others work in joint-venture manufacturing operations in Mexico and Asia and in more than 200 retail stores in Canada and the United States.

His company is positioned as being on the leading edge of supply chain technology and information systems. At the same time, quality manufacturing and clothing design are his hallmarks. Nygard believes, "that as apparel manufacturers develop quick response methods, a limiting factor to the overall supply chain can be the textile industry. Integrated strategies must be established between the textile supplier, apparel manufacturer [the supply network], retailer, and ultimately the customer [the channels of distribution] to ensure rapid delivery of fabrics to coincide with the time of need."

Nygard International manages a textile supply network within the U.S. market and other key markets including Europe, Korea, Japan, and Indonesia. Within North America, the company supply network strategy is to use a small number of textile makers. Developing and maintaining strong relationships and constant co-ordination via EDI links has allowed all the suppliers in the chain to respond rapidly to changing consumer fashion tastes and preferences.

The firm has spent well over $30 million to automate the entire organization.

An internal system called Continuous Replenishment, shortens the time between order entry from the retail level and delivery. Retail buyers can enter their orders and trigger a chain reaction of supply that begins with the fabric and component suppliers and ends with the billing department. As a bonus, customers are guaranteed delivery of the quantity in the time required. On some styles, Nygard guarantees 100 percent correct orders delivered within 24 hours or the merchandise is free. Most of Nygard's retailers are already connected to the supply system, thanks to the firm's decision to cover the cost of the equipment and training for each retailer.

The ability to respond rapidly to orders and manufacture quickly is backed by newly installed modular manufacturing operations in some of the Winnipeg plants. Fabric can be unloaded in the cutting room and reordered, using EDI.

In order to better control transportation, costs and distribution logistics in the supply chain, Nygard International is establishing cut and sew operations closer to the fabric sources, particularly in the North American market. Another quick response method used to shorten and speed the supply chain has been to rent warehouse space within its own facilities to its suppliers.

Ever-ambitious to make technology work for his firm, Nygard is banking on the Internet to improve both the service and convenience aspects of doing business with his company. Buyers are able to see garments (via the Internet) any time, particularly when they have sample fabrics in their hands. The Web site used is intended to be primarily for B2B — allowing retailers anywhere in the world to track down the exact model, colour, and size of articles they want — and once ordered, articles will be shipped within 24 hours.

End-consumers are also served through this channel. According to Bianca, Nygard's daughter and appointed Web chief, customers will be able to enter such personal information as type of clothes preferred and lifestyle preferences and interests, and the system will generate personalized fashion suggestions. With that input, Nygard can micro-market to customers.

Although fashion is perhaps the hardest product to sell to consumers directly on the Internet, this obstacle has not fazed Nygard. Confident that no other clothing brand enjoys the same trust and loyalty that Nygard does, he is certain his cyber-time will come.

SOURCE: Adapted from, "Managing the Supply Chain," Nygard.com, May 13, 2005; Denise DeVeau, "Clear Challenge: Be Easy on the Eyes and Budget," *Computing Canada*, July 2002, p. 13; Martin Slofstra, "The Web and Fashion: Not Just a Pretty Face," *eBusiness Journal*, July 2001, p. 11; Serena French, "In the Company of Women," *National Post*, May 4, 2000, p. B1.

The new approach to supply chains has been enormously successful. Specialists in manufacturing, purchasing and distribution as well as financial, information and customer service personnel all become involved in the process. As usual, without support from senior managers and their internal and external efforts at relationship building, supply chain improvements would be much harder to achieve.

While high speed and low cost are seen as the hallmarks of successful supply chains, research has shown that the most successful supply chain managers, Amazon.com, Wal-Mart, and Dell Computers, have been not only fast and cost effective, but are also agile, adaptable and aligned. It is these three characteristics which make them stand out:

- **Agile:** They exhibit quick responses to supply and demand changes; handle disruptions smoothly, recover quickly from natural disasters and computer viruses and other shocks to the chain while maintaining good cost control. They continuously provide partners with data, collaborate with customers and suppliers to redesign processes and products, and finish products only when they have information on customer preferences.
- **Adaptable:** They change and evolve over time with economic, political, demographic and technological changes in their environment; they are not caught asleep. They constantly track events, use intermediaries in unfamiliar markets, create flexibility by ensuring different products, and use the same components and processes.
- **Aligned:** They align the interests of all firms in the supply chain with their own so that each firm can not only maximize its own interests but also the chain's as well. They provide partners with clear incentives and clear cost and reward information for their efforts, equal access to sales data, forecasts and plans, and clarify partner roles and responsibilities to avoid conflict (remember Browns Shoes and Holt Renfrew).[13]

order processing
Consists of the set of procedures for receiving, handling, and filling orders.

The Basic Logistics Activities

Regardless of whether a firm is part of a logistics alliance or handles these activities using a supply chain management approach, five interrelated sets of logistics activities are involved. These are order processing, inventory control, inventory location and warehousing, materials handling, and transportation.

electronic data interchange (EDI)
Digital transmission of orders, invoices, or other business information.

inventory control
Involves maintaining control over the size and composition of inventories in order to fill customers' orders promptly, completely, and accurately while minimizing both the investment and fluctuations in inventories.

economic order quantity (EOQ)
The optimal quantity for reorder when replenishing inventory stocks, as indicated by the volume at which the inventory carrying cost plus the order-processing cost are at a minimum.

Order processing

The starting point for logistics is **order processing** — a set of procedures for receiving, handling, and filling orders promptly and accurately. This activity should include provisions for billing, granting credit, preparing invoices, and collecting past-due accounts.

Most order processing makes use of digital technology advances, notably **electronic data interchange (EDI)**. Under EDI, orders, invoices, and other business information are transmitted in high-speed digital formats, thus speeding up the total process.

Inventory control

Maintaining control over the size and composition of inventories, which represent a sizeable investment for most companies, is an essential part to any physical-distribution system. The goal of **inventory control** is to fill customers' orders promptly, completely, and accurately, while minimizing both the investment and fluctuations in inventories. Two factors play a key role in inventory control:

- ***Customer-service requirements***: Inventory size is determined by balancing costs and desired levels of customer service. That is, what percentage of orders does the company expect to fill promptly from inventory on hand? Out-of-stock conditions result in lost sales, loss of goodwill, and even loss of customers. Generally speaking, about 80 percent more inventory is required to fill 95 percent of the orders than to fill only 80 percent.
- ***Economic order quantity***: Management must establish the optimal quantity for reorder when it is time to replenish inventory stocks. The **economic order quantity (EOQ)** is the

volume at which the sum of inventory carrying costs and order-processing costs are at a minimum. Typically, as order size increases, (1) inventory carrying cost goes up (because the average inventory is larger) and (2) order-processing cost declines (because there are fewer orders).

just-in-time (JIT) inventory control
An inventory-control system that involves buying parts and supplies in small quantities just in time for use in production and then producing in quantities just in time for sale.

A popular form of inventory control, purchasing, and production scheduling is the **just-in-time (JIT)** concept. The idea of JIT is that a producer buys in small quantities that arrive just in time for production and then produces in quantities just in time for sale. In a well managed system, the producer carries very little inventory.

The focus of JIT inventory control tends to be on production and the relationship between the producer and its suppliers. A parallel trend involves producers or distributors of finished goods and their customers. We refer to this counterpart of JIT as a **market response system**, or quick response system. The central idea is that a purchase by a final customer, one who intends to consume the product, should activate a process to produce and deliver a replacement item to inventory. In this way, a product is pulled through a channel on the basis of demand rather than being pushed through on the basis of short-term price reductions or other inducements that often result in excessive inventory costs.

market response system
A form of inventory control in which a purchase by a final customer activates a process to produce and deliver a replacement item to inventory.

The intent of a market response system is similar to that of JIT — to have the right volume of goods to satisfy consumers and to replenish exhausted stocks rapidly. By resulting in better inventory control, a market response system can both reduce stock carrying and operating costs.

Inventory location and warehousing Management must make critical decisions about the size, location, and transporting of inventories. These areas are interrelated in often quite complex ways. The number and location of inventory sites, for example, influence the inventory size and transportation method. One important consideration in managing inventories is **warehousing**, which embraces a range of functions, such as assembling, doing any necessary repacking, storing products, and then preparing them for reshipping.

warehousing
A broad range of logistics activities that include assembling, doing any necessary repacking, storing products, and then preparing them for reshipping.

- ***Public and Private Warehouses:*** Any producer, wholesaler, or retailer has the option of operating its own private warehouse or using the services of a public warehouse. A private warehouse is more likely to be an advantage if (1) a company moves a large volume of products through a warehouse, (2) there is very little, if any, seasonal fluctuation in this flow, and (3) the goods have special handling or storage requirements. A public warehouse offers storage and handling facilities to individuals or companies. Public warehousing costs are a variable expense. Customers pay only for the space they use, and only when they use it. Public warehouses can also provide office and product display spaces, and accept and fill orders for sellers.

distribution centre
A concept in warehousing that develops under one roof an efficient, fully integrated system for the flow of products, taking orders, filling them, and delivering them to customers.

- ***Distribution Centres:*** These are planned around markets rather than transportation requirements. The idea is to develop under one roof an efficient, fully integrated system for the flow of products — taking orders, filling them, and preparing them for delivery to customers. Initially, IKEA expanded very slowly in Canada and the United States because the company wanted to find locations and facilities that effectively met the needs of its **distribution centres**.

Materials handling Selecting the proper equipment to physically handle products, including the warehouse building itself, is the **materials-handling** subsystem of physical-distribution management. Equipment that is well matched to the task can minimize losses from breakage, spoilage, and theft. Efficient equipment can reduce handling costs as well as the time required for handling.

materials handling
The subsystem of logistics management that involves selecting and operating the equipment and warehouse building used in physically handling products.

- ***Containerization*** is a cargo-handling system that is standard practice in materials handling. Shipments of products are enclosed in large metal or wooden containers. The containers are then transported unopened from the time they leave the customer's facilities (such as a manufacturer's plant) until they reach their destination (such as a wholesaler's warehouse). Containerization minimizes physical handling, thereby reducing damage, lessening the risk of theft, and allowing for more efficient transportation.

Transportation A major logistics function in many companies is transportation — shipping products to customers. Management must decide on both the **mode of transportation** and the particular carriers.

mode of transportation
The manner in which the movement of goods is carried out; leading modes of transportation are railroads, trucks, ships, and airplanes.

- ***Major modes*** of transportation are railways, trucks, ships, and airplanes. Selecting the best modes involves considerations of speed, cost, reliability, delivery schedules available, and accessibility. Working through available options and considering the rate or change in tariffs can make selecting a mode daunting.
- ***Intermodal transportation***: When two or more modes of transportation are used to move freight, this is called intermodal transportation. The intent of intermodal transportation is to take advantage of multiple forms of transportation. One type of intermodal transportation, piggy back service, involves carrying truck trailers on railroad flatcars. This type of intermodal transportation provides (1) more flexibility than railroads alone can offer, (2) lower freight costs than trucks alone, and (3) less handling of goods.
- ***Freight forwarders***: A specialized marketing institution serving firms that ship in less-than-carload quantities. Its main function is to consolidate less-than-carload or less-than-truckload shipments from several shippers into carload and truckload quantities. The freight forwarder picks up the merchandise at the shipper's place of business and arranges for delivery at the buyer's door. A small shipper benefits from the speed and minimum handling associated with large shipments.
- ***Package-delivery firms***: Companies that deliver small shipments of packages and high-priority mail, such as United Parcel Service (UPS), Federal Express (FedEx), and Loomis, compete directly with Canada Post. These commercial package-delivery giants attempt to position themselves more favourably than their competition by trying to surpass each other in relation to delivery times, technology that allows customers to prepare and track their shipments, and — of course — low prices.[14] In many respects, these companies offer the same services as freight forwarders. However, whereas the typical freight forwarder does not have its own transportation equipment, package-delivery firms do. Companies such as UPS and FedEx are essentially integrated as cargo airlines and trucking companies.

All of the logistics activities in channels of distribution and supplier networks have become more efficient as new digital drivers appear, almost on a daily basis. And while technology has enabled most of these efficiencies, the application of logistics and supply chain management concepts has been key to the success of the hardware and software. But even more important than the enabling technology has been the continuing work of personal co-ordination between supply chain members and the building and maintaining of strong personal relationships. As the technical complexities increase, keeping personal contact to maintain trust becomes even more important. Recall Chapter 6, since distribution is about B2B relationships.

PAGE UP!

1. In distribution, what is the difference between horizontal conflict and vertical conflict?
2. What are four methods used by suppliers when they want to exercise control?
3. What is meant by logistics?
4. What is meant by supply chain management?

Key Terms and Concepts

administered vertical marketing system 350
agent wholesaler 340
auction company 342
broker 341
channel conflict 356
channel control 358
commission merchant 342
company sales branch 353
contractual vertical marketing system 350
corporate vertical marketing system 349
direct distribution 345
distribution centre 366
economic order quantity (EOQ) 365
electronic data interchange (EDI) 365
exclusive distribution 356
export agent 353
export merchant 353
exporting 353
horizontal conflict 356
import-export agent 342
indirect distribution 345
intensity of distribution 355
intensive distribution 355
inventory control 365
just-in-time (JIT) inventory control 366
logistics 361
logistics management 361
manufacturers' agent (manufacturers' representative) 340
market response system 366
materials handling 366
merchant wholesaler 340
mode of transportation 367
order processing 365
primary-product agents 342
selective distribution 355
selling agent 342
slotting allowance 358
supply chain 362
supply chain management 362
vertical conflict 357
vertical marketing system (VMS) 349
warehousing 366
wholesaling 338

Questions and Problems

1. Which of the following institutions are intermediaries? Explain.
   a. Avon salesperson.
   b. Electrical wholesaler.
   c. Real estate broker.
   d. Railroad.
   e. Auctioneer.
   f. Advertising agency.
   g. Grocery store.
   h. Stockbroker.
   i. Bank.
   j. Radio station.
2. "The great majority of business sales are made directly from producer to business user." Explain the reason for this, first in relation to the nature of the market and then in relation to the product.
3. Is a policy of intensive distribution consistent with consumer buying habits for convenience goods? For shopping goods? Is intensive distribution normally used in the marketing of any type of business goods?
4. From a producer's viewpoint, what are the competitive advantages of exclusive distribution?
5. What are the drawbacks to exclusive distribution from a retailer's point of view? To what extent are these alleviated if the retailer controls the channel for the particular brand?
6. What role is the Internet playing in changing distribution networks? Provide examples to illustrate the changes that are occurring.
7. Which of the following are wholesaling transactions?
   a. Colour Tile sells wallpaper to an apartment building contractor and also to the contractor's family for its home.
   b. General Electric sells motors to Whirlpool for its washing machines.
   c. A fish "farmer" sells fish to a local restaurant.
   d. A family orders carpet from a friend, who is a home decorating consultant, at 50 percent off the suggested retail price. The carpet is delivered directly to the home.
   e. Weber Supply sells nails to Home Hardware.
   f. A local bakery delivers goods to Sobeys.

8. Which type of wholesaling intermediary, if any, is most likely to be used by each of the following firms? Explain your choice in each instance.
   a. A small manufacturer of a liquid glass cleaner to be sold through supermarkets.
   b. A small canner in Nova Scotia that packs a high-quality, unbranded fruit product.
   c. A small-tools manufacturing firm that has its own sales force selling to the business market and now wants to add backyard barbecue equipment to its product mix.
   d. A Québec textile mill producing unbranded towels, sheets, pillowcases, and blankets.
   e. A virtual bookstore that has no existing physical infrastructure other than its call centre for receiving orders.
   f. A software e-tailer that features only downloadable products.
9. Looking to the future, which types of intermediaries do you think will increase in importance and which ones will decline? What continuing impact, if any, will Internet technology have on the role of intermediaries in distribution? Explain.
10. Name some products for which you think the cost of physical distribution constitutes at least one-half of the total price of the goods at the wholesale level. Can you suggest ways of decreasing the physical-distribution cost of these products?

Hands-On Marketing

1. A manufacturer of precision lenses used in medical and hospital equipment wants to ship a 5-kg box of these lenses from your town to a laboratory in Stockholm, Sweden. The lab wants delivery in five days or less. The manufacturer wants to use a package-delivery service but is undecided as to which shipper to choose. Compile and compare the types of services provided and prices charged by Federal Express, United Parcel Service, and one other package-delivery firm.
2. Arrange an interview with either the owner or a top-level manager of a small manufacturing firm. Inquire about (a) what distribution channel(s) the company uses for its primary product, (b) what factors were the greatest influences in choosing the channel(s), and (c) whether the company would prefer some other channel(s).

Back to the Top

Why was distribution so important to Padinox when Tim Casey took over? Think about the chapter opener and how Paderno products have been made available to Canadian consumers. As well, think about the way in which SYSCO manages its supply chain. What are the common factors in effective distribution and supply chain management?

Online Learning Centre

Want to get better grades, tips on how to study more effectively, and up-to-date information on happenings in the world of marketing? Then, visit the Online Learning Centre for practice tests, Study Smart software, *Marketing Magazine,* and much more! **www.mcgrawhill.ca/olc/sommers**

CASE 5-1:

Multimedia

Running Room: More Than a Place to Buy Shoes

Elena Lee is a senior account executive at a Toronto ad agency. She and Peter Taylor met when her agency made a pitch for a promotional campaign to the Toronto Raptors more than ten years ago, not long after Peter had moved from Ottawa to Toronto and the Raptors were struggling in their first season in the NBA. Peter had realized his dream of working in sports-related marketing after completing his MBA.

Elena and Peter have now been married for almost six years and, with two kids and an even more senior role in the agency, she's finding life to be extremely busy. Soon after they were married, Elena and Peter bought their first house on Ranleigh Avenue, just north of Lawrence; a location that allows either she or Peter to drop the children off at daycare and hop on the subway at the end of the street.

Typical of many young women in her situation, Elena was finding that there seemed to be little time in her life for herself. Everything revolved around the children and her job. She and Peter rarely went out with friends, and she can't remember the last time she went shopping on her own. And, she was not happy with the fact that she simply felt out of shape. Over a late dinner on a Tuesday evening in late April, after the children were in bed, Peter brought up the fact that they had not run together since Colin was born, almost four years ago. Elena decided then and there that she was going to get back into running, even if she could only get out a couple of times a week.

The following Saturday morning, pushing 16-month-old Emily in her stroller, Elena walked the few blocks south on Yonge Street to Running Room. Who better to advise her on what shoes to buy than a company with "Running" in its name? She was impressed with the level of service and with the fact that the guy, Todd, who served her, looked like a runner. He asked how much running she planned to do and whether she planned to train for any races.

When Elena explained that she was just getting back into running after a few years, Todd suggested that she might want to attend one of the clinics offered at the store or to train with the running group that runs every Wednesday evening at 6:30 and on Sunday mornings. He indicated that she could check out all the details on the Web site (**www.runningroom.com**). Elena thanked him as he rang in her purchase, but said that it would probably be some time before she was ready to run a race.

Elena tried a couple of runs on her own, but was having trouble fitting it into her schedule. She decided that she needed some discipline if this running idea was going to work. So, recalling her conversation with Todd, she turned to the Running Room Web site. She found a clinic that was just for women. She talked it over with Peter and thought she might like to go. He was very supportive, indicating that she really should do it.

Elena went along to the first clinic and felt she learned a lot about how she should gradually get back into running. She met a number of other women who live in the area. After a couple of weeks, she had formed a close friendship on the after-clinic runs with Beth, who lived just a couple of blocks away and also had a young family.

Eventually, she and Beth decided to go along to some of the group runs that started from the Running Room store on Wednesday evenings and Sunday mornings. She and Beth usually jogged a couple of blocks north to the Starbucks on Yonge Street to have coffee after the Sunday morning run. Elena was really enjoying the company of the other runners and was already feeling more healthy. The group had become so close-knit that, on one Wednesday evening after the group run, they all went back to the store on Yonge Street and had a potluck dinner, seated in a circle on the floor of the store. Elena had brought a three-bean salad.

As she and Beth began to feel more comfortable with running three or four times a week, they progressed to 5k and 7k runs by the end of June. Just before she and Peter left for two weeks at his parents' cottage near Peterborough, she and Beth had decided to run in the Don River 10k Run at the end of August.

As she crossed the finish line, met by Peter and the kids, Elena had such a great feeling of accomplishment. She thought, "if anyone had asked me in March whether I'd be running a 10k race by the end of August, I would have laughed at them."

Visit **www.runningroom.com** and navigate through the site before proceeding with these questions.

Questions:

1. What is the Running Room's value proposition? What differentiates it from other sporting goods stores?

2. To view John Stanton's training videos go to the Resources section of the Running Room Web site and visit the Running Tips area. As well, enter the Members' area of the site. Why does Running Room refer to their customers as "members"? What is the advantage of the Web site for current and potential "members" such as Elena?
3. What do you think is the brand relationship that some of its customers have with Running Room? How would you describe this relationship?
4. Having read this case and viewed the Web site, explain why the recruitment, selection and retention of store personnel are key elements in Running Room's marketing strategy.

CASE 5-2:

Thrift Stores and Winners: The Bargain Experience

When you think of "thrift store," what comes to mind? A bright purple pair of velour pants? A moth-eaten tweed jacket? Apparently perceptions change. Since when has second-hand clothing become trendy? Aren't those stores reserved for the needy? Somehow it hasn't stopped those who aren't needy from shopping there! People of all ages and socio-economic levels now shop at Value Village and other used clothing stores, some of them run by religious and charitable organizations, such as the Salvation Army and the SPCA. It has become chic to be cheap and the trend has spread quickly. As Canadians become more value-conscious, many refuse to pay exorbitant prices for clothing they can find elsewhere at much lower prices. But this doesn't mean that they will settle for low quality. Consumers want to pay less, but still expect a certain level of quality. In other words, there is a new generation of Canadians that are demanding more bang for their buck. So far, they've managed to find quite a lot of bang at Value Village for very low prices.

The popularity of thrift stores has been driven by more than just cheap prices. In recent years, retro styles and vintage clothing have become trendy, bringing new prestige to bargain hunting and used clothing — or, as it is often referred to today, pre-owned, previously-loved, gently-used, or second-time-round items. It is not uncommon to hear someone bragging about how little he paid for a really cool pair of pants or how she can't believe how lucky she is to have found such a funky sweater. The best part about used-clothing stores: You don't have to worry about showing up at a party and finding someone else wearing the same shirt!

The popularity of Value Village and other similar stores has been infectious. They attract so many Canadians that they actually present a threat to other mainstream retailers such as Le Chateau, whose clothing tends to be more funky in nature. But why would you pay $80 for hip huggers when you can get the real thing at a thrift store? This may explain why Value Village is showered with so many awards including "Best Thrift Store" and "Best Used Clothing Store" in cities across Canada!

Thrift stores were once viewed as drab stores that couldn't hold a candle to many of the retailers around town. For that matter, they didn't really try to compete with other retailers at all. Donations of clothing and other items were revitalized and presented as attractively as possible, with the hope that these items would meet the needs of the less advantaged who would buy the clothes at low prices. But as Canadians flock to these stores in record numbers, the whole feel of the store has changed. Now, one finds teenagers and young adults sorting through racks in search of a good find. As they say, one person's junk is another person's treasure. Value Village has become a bargain hunter's mecca. The low price increases the value of the treasure, making it more difficult for traditional clothing retailers to sell retro clothes at steep prices. Customers who shop at thrift stores are looking for more than just bargains. It is often the unknown and the "thrill of the hunt" that attracts people to the thrift stores.

Many of the same observations may be made about the experience of shopping at Winners. This retailer provides fashions and home décor items at 20-60 percent off the department store and specialty store prices. While it is certainly not a thrift store, it shares some of the same characteristics. Winners provides a customer with an experience that may be comparable to the thrift store if the customer wants unique items at discounted prices. While the atmosphere at Winners may not provide for an outstanding shopping experience, the bargains just might — Jones New York pants, Kenneth Cole purses and Tommy Hilfiger shirts at a fraction of the original prices. And, oh the thrill of finding your size and your colour on one of those lucky days when the hunt pays off!! It's certainly not the experience for everyone — just like no-frills airlines, Winners and Value Village are not for everyone. But, for people who shop at Winners, the experience is very personal — the store doesn't pre-manufacture the experience with décor, music and service — it's up to the customer to make the experience her own, whether by finding just the right thing today, or in anticipating the next visit.

Questions:

1. Do Winners and Value Village appeal to the same target market segments? Who do you feel represent the main target segments for each? Prepare a detailed profile of a regular Value Village shopper and a regular Winners shopper.
2. What factors (social, psychological, etc.) other than price influence a consumer's decision to buy at Value Village and Winners? Do different factors motivate a loyal Value Village shopper as compared with a loyal Winners shopper?
3. Do you think customers who frequently shop at "dollar stores" are looking for the same experience as those who shop at Value Village and Winners? Why or why not? Is this yet another bargain experience? What differences are there in customers' reasons for shopping at dollar stores versus discount and thrift stores?
4. Visit **www.valuevillage.com** and **www.winners.ca**. After you have visited each site, suggest ways each site can be modified to have more appeal to their potential and current customers. Explain your suggestions.

SOURCE: Adapted in part from Karl Moor and Matt Hertz, "Welcome to the experience economy," *The Globe and Mail Online*, www.globeandmail.com, December 27, 2005.

CASE 5-3:

CBC

Mystery Shoppers

John has worked part-time at Roots for almost a year. While he generally enjoys his job, he wasn't enjoying himself on this particular Tuesday evening. The 21-year-old student was unable to concentrate. All he had on his mind was his biology mid-term at 9 o'clock the following morning. He had tried to switch shifts but none of his co-workers was able to work for him that night. So, he was stuck with his shift and completely stressed about it. He would have to stay up half the night studying if he wanted to pass that exam. He had just handed in two papers for other courses that day and was hoping to have the rest of the day and evening to study. Here he was, exhausted from staying up the night before to write his papers and only four hours into an eight-hour shift. Besides that, he had to close the store that night which meant at least an extra 20 minutes. At this rate, he wouldn't get home before 10 pm.

John was stressed. Several times in the last month, he had thought about quitting his job, but he needed the money to supplement his student loan. He was only making slightly more than minimum wage, but the salary was just enough to allow him a little spending money. And, with his employee discount, John could afford some nice clothing. That night, John had brought his biology book to work. He knew Tuesdays were slow and that he'd be able to put in a bit of time studying. Besides, Mike was working with him that night and told him he'd take care of customers while John studied.

No sooner had John opened his book when a lady walked into the store. She looked around the store, seemed to go through every single rack, picked out some items and walked up to Mike to ask him questions. John was focused on the chapter he was reading and didn't hear the conversation. After what seemed like 10 minutes, the woman walked up to John and started asking him detailed questions about the clothing, the material it was made of, the available sizes, and the washing instructions. Mike walked over to the counter looking helpless. The woman had clearly not been satisfied by his answers and now she was waiting for John to be more helpful. She explained to him that they didn't have her size. John apologized and, while he knew he could have phoned another store and had them send it over, he did not want to make Mike look incompetent. He simply shrugged his shoulders. The woman put the clothes down on the counter and left the store.

Mike turned to John and said, "She seemed awfully curious. Do you think she was one of those mystery shoppers?" John looked puzzled. "A what?" Mike explained to him what he had seen on television the night before. The program had shown a segment on mystery shoppers, people hired by stores to examine service quality, among other things. Mystery shoppers look like ordinary customers and, as such, employees don't know they are secretly being evaluated. John shook his head. "No man, you're just paranoid." But, as he said it, he wasn't convinced. Maybe the company had hired someone to check up on them.

Questions

1. If the woman was indeed a mystery shopper, was it fair to evaluate John when he was having a bad day?
2. Is it ethical to spy on your staff? How would you feel if you worked in a clothing store and knew that management hired mystery shoppers?
3. Do managers have other options for evaluating staff and making sure they are delivering high-quality service to customers?

SOURCE: CBC *Marketplace*, "Mystery Shoppers."

CASE 5-4:

GuestLink — Safeway: Ingredients for Life

Multimedia

This case is reproduced with the permission of the Radio Marketing Bureau. It provides background on an award-winning radio campaign for Safeway, a major food retailer.

For more than 20 years, radio has been the centrepiece of one of Canada's largest food and drug retailers' advertising programs. Radio has helped Safeway grow in individual Canadian communities, build and establish its brand, and successfully drive product promotions.

Background

Safeway is a significant brand in Canada, particularly in the western provinces. With 214 stores in B.C., Alberta, Manitoba, Saskatchewan, as well as in Northern Ontario, today it is one of the largest food and drug retailers in the country.

Over the years, Safeway has established itself as a sought-after brand. A key ingredient of this success is a strong private label program, which offers more than 2,500 products under the Safeway and Lucerne banners, and 1,250 premium products under the award-winning Safeway Select label.

Today, the marketplace is changing, along with the modern family and its habits, and so is grocery shopping. Two-income households are the norm; this means more frequent shopping and less volume spending per visit.

Needs and tastes are also shifting. More active lifestyles, time constraints, and increased nutrition awareness have stimulated the growth of the prepared foods category as consumers demand fast, easy, healthy substitutes for home-cooked meals. Established companies and new players are focusing on these new opportunities.

The grocery retailers' world of high volumes and small margins was already highly competitive. Now, with an influx of niche and non-traditional grocers raiding the marketplace in response to changing consumer habits and lifestyle demands, it's more competitive than ever.

Marketing Objectives

Safeway's strategy has always been to offer the highest quality produce, meat, bakery and deli products, private-label brands, prepared meals, and superior customer service. In today's retail climate, the chain's objective is to differentiate itself by offering the customer an enjoyable, productive, one-stop shopping experience.

Safeway has been aggressively opening new stores and remodelling existing stores in a new "lifestyle" format. This features inviting décor, a warm ambiance and subdued lighting to highlight top quality, freshness and enhance the overall Safeway shopping experience. Many of these stores also offer full-service meat counters and bakeries, floral design centres, and unique products such as natural and organic foods, sushi bars, and olive bars.

In April 2005, Safeway unveiled new brand positioning to showcase its efforts to be the grocery store of choice for today's active consumers. The focus is Safeway's uniquely superior quality of perishable and proprietary brands, the new format, and the chain's outstanding customer service. With this campaign, Safeway positions itself as more than a supermarket that sells ingredients for meals — it offers "Ingredients for Life."

Radio's Role Within The Media Strategy

The intimate, personal nature and community strength of radio is ideal for building the Safeway brand. In an industry that relies heavily on newspaper inserts and flyers, for 20 years Safeway has stood out as a 52-week-a-year radio advertiser. Radio is a vital and versatile component of its media mix, which includes print, Internet, and television.

With its consistent radio schedule, Safeway ensures a high-frequency, top-of-mind presence throughout the year. Continuous radio use also allows Safeway to support customer retention and reinforce the brand: price, product innovation, and quality presented in an environment reflective of the target market's lifestyle.

Safeway has tested and experimented with different mixes of media and is now satisfied it has found exactly the right blend for an effective overall buy. Radio station selection for Safeway is constantly reviewed, and formats are custom selected to best fit each store location.

While Safeway has found radio as an excellent brand-building medium, it also uses the flexibility of the medium for fast, tactical advertising of last-minute specials or changes. Radio offers the advantage of quick production of new spots. It's also ideal for events such as Grand Openings through the use of radio remotes; pre-promotion spots that can run four to five days before an event; and live cut-ins with well-known station personalities to create excitement around the event. Safeway's overwhelmingly positive experiences with radio include noticeable traffic lifts from these remotes.

Results

Radio has been an integral part of Safeway advertising for over 20 years. Safeway's 52-week-per-year investment in radio has been an effective strategy for reaching all its objectives: building the brand, driving sales, and making the chain an integral part of the customer's everyday life.

Questions:

Answer the following questions after reading the case, listening to the two radio spots and reading John Gardner's Guest Marketer column, "How do those fries get to your favourite restaurant?"

1. How must suppliers respond to the trend of supermarkets entering the foodservice industry with freshly prepared meals such as the soup described in the Safeway advertisement? How do you think this will impact the relationship supermarkets already have with their suppliers?
2. Using John Gardner's article as a guide, identify the differences between providing fresh ingredients for cafeterias, restaurants and institutions and providing these same types of products for supermarkets. What modifications may need to be made to satisfy the needs of the supermarkets? Provide the rationale for your answer.
3. Do you think the radio ads featured in the Safeway case communicate the brand positioning they have described? Explain your answer. Do you think that radio is the best medium for Safeway to communicate this positioning to its current and potential customers? Why or why not?
4. In the advertisements, the tagline "Ingredients for Life" is used. Why is it important for Safeway to communicate back through the distribution channel its commitment to providing fresh foods for active consumers?

PART 6

Marketing Communications

Informing, persuading, and reminding current and prospective customers

In **Part 6**, we examine how companies communicate with their customers, including the various tools used to get information and messages to them.

Chapter 13 presents an overview of integrated marketing communications, including the various types of marketing communications, how marketing communications work, and the management issues involved in developing marketing communications programs. Chapter 14 looks at advertising, the most obvious and public form of marketing communications. The selling process, sales promotion, public relations, and publicity are the subjects of Chapter 15.

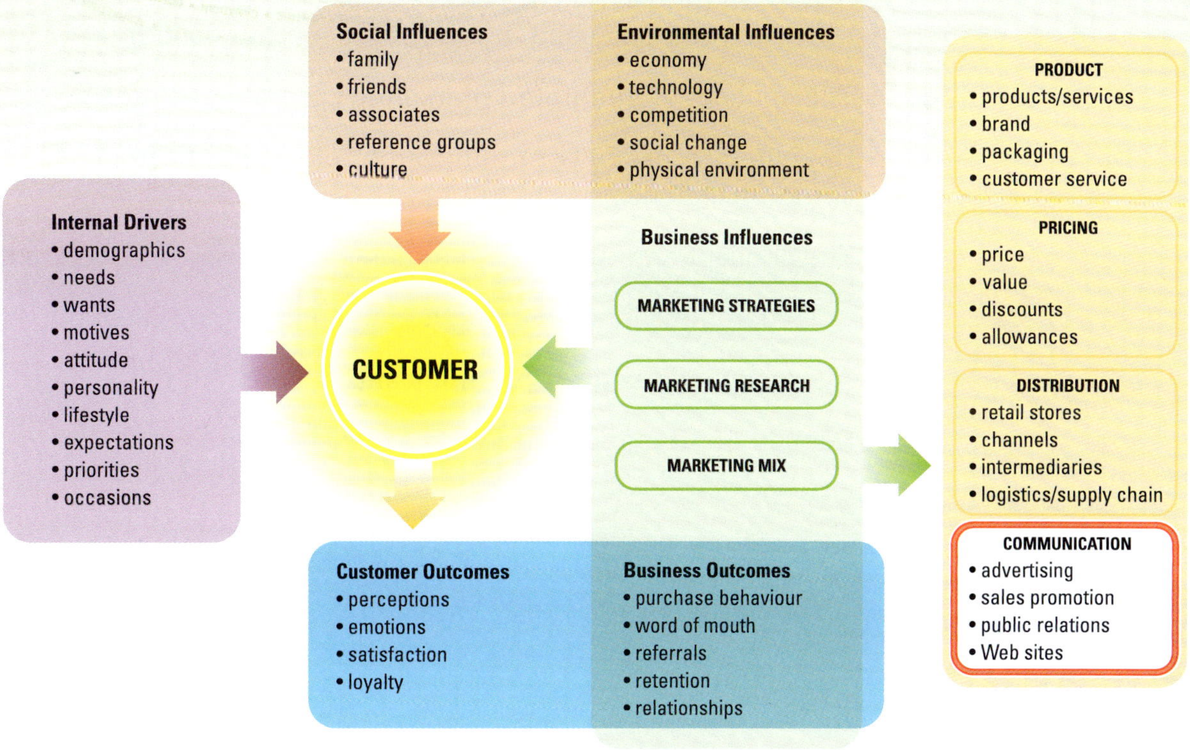

CHAPTER 13

Marketing Communications Programs

This chapter will help you to understand how marketing communications decisions are made by describing what marketing communications is and how it fits into a firm's total marketing program. After studying this chapter, you should have an understanding of:

- The role of marketing communications.
- Different methods used in marketing communications.
- The concept of integrated marketing communications.
- How the process of communicating relates to effective marketing communications.
- The concept and design of the marketing communications mix.
- Considerations in developing a marketing communications program.
- Alternative marketing communications budgeting methods.
- Regulation of marketing communications.

The New World of Communicating About Movies

Movie studios are up against it. In the past, big studios threw millions of dollars into mass North American TV campaigns to reach as wide an audience as possible and get it into theatre seats. But there is plenty of competition for the attention of the public, as well as for its entertainment dollars. One result of this intensified competition is that traditional network TV continues to lose viewers in the face of the inexorable growth of cable TV specialty channels, DVD players, video games, digital sound, and image delivery of almost everything by cellphone, MP3, and iPod. Movie marketing needed to change and it has. Large and small studios and film distribution companies have revamped their communications strategies and means of delivering movie entertainment messages to target audiences.

Enter The Disney Studio, with the launch of *The Chronicles of Narnia*, a $150-million movie based on the C.S. Lewis book about four British children who discover a world of mythical creatures and talking animals where they must help good battle evil. Disney is the first big studio to go after a number of movie market segments — as opposed to a single target — all at the same time. With its partner Walden Media, it pulled a variety of themes from the story line of the movie and built the communications program around them. Included were the World War II historical background, the fantasy element of the story, the religious references of the characters and sub-plots, as well as the basic movie themes of loyalty, family, courage and good versus evil.

The overall communications strategy was to deliver relevant *Narnia*-related messages to every segment with an interest in one or more of the above themes. So, yes, schools and young peoples' organizations were targeted, Ronald McDonald Houses, a large variety of church groups, veteran's groups, Boy Scout and Girl Guide organizations, YM-YWCAs, child agencies, and other groups with an interest in family, family values, and family loyalty.

The communications campaign started with the pre-movie release goal of getting kids to read the C. S. Lewis book, *The Lion, the Witch and the Wardrobe* (first published in 1950), and then to see the *Narnia* movie. Disney and Walden worked closely with the book's publishers to get copies of the book (upon which the movie is based) into the right hands. Teachers and librarians were approached at their professional conferences to find out how they might use the story for school purposes and organize class trips to attend showings. *Narnia* materials consisting of posters, study guides, and copies of the novel were sent to every elementary and middle school in the U.S., as well as to selected schools in English-speaking markets around the world where the Lewis book had been known for years. Libraries at 200 sites were given new copies of the novel to replace reader-worn ones. Librarians were encouraged to design *Narnia* events and were provided with sophisticated wardrobe displays.

As a result of this grass roots marketing, classes of teenagers held mock trials and debated whether Edmund, a character in the movie version, had betrayed his family. In other venues, such as Los Angeles Probation Department centres, the book was read, crumpets were made in cooking classes, and movie sets were built in construction classes. Similar activities were undertaken in the U.K., Canada, Australia, India and other markets. And, of course, the movie was seen after all this interest-group activity.

The grass roots marketing was further supported by Disney recruiting a large number of promotional partners to offer *Narnia*-related goods and services, estimated to have a value of $150 million. Kids and families at malls were faced with movie clips, exhibits, movie scenes, and a variety of products.

A major Disney challenge was developing an approach to the Christian fan segment — estimated to be more than 5 percent of the total expected customer base. While the movie contains Christian religious symbolism, too much emphasis on such could upset segments who had no interest in religious symbolism, while inappropriate emphasis could upset those Christian communities which could comprise a valuable market segment. Disney employed consultants to work with church groups in helping to convince them of the faithfulness of the film adaptation.

Having done all of this, Disney, of course, put a big traditional blockbuster budget to work in TV, newspapers, and a variety of Internet advertisements and promotions.[1]

The Role of Marketing Communications

One of the main functions of marketing communications is to differentiate the offerings of a company from those of its competitors. In the absence of effective differentiation, consumers will likely perceive no differences and make their purchase decisions based largely on brand image or price. Therefore, you see differences emphasized when President's Choice bottled water and Banff Ice Vodka focus on being made from iceberg and glacial water, or Becel margarine focuses on being the best margarine for heart health because it "takes your health to heart." Becel shows how it can make a difference.

A firm also hopes that marketing communications will create a strong consumer relationship with the firm or its brand to affect consumer responses to price increases and decreases (demand elasticity). This means that when prices go up, demand will decrease very little and when prices go down, demand will actually increase. Management wants marketing communications to create an image and to send certain messages that will give the consumer a number of non-price reasons to acquire and use the product. In fact, one of the main roles of marketing communications is to create non-price value — to communicate sufficient value for the company and its products and services to take the customer's mind off price to a certain extent. It provides many other reasons to buy, over and above an attractive price.

Fido

There are also many products and services that would appear to be the same across providers — and the companies that market them want to provide a little "personality" to their offering or company through communications. Although available nationally, in Québec, people may say, "Call me on my Fido" — referring to a cellphone from Fido Microcell Solutions of Montréal (**www.fido.ca**), a personal communications services provider. The canine term

Becel communicates a strong health differentiation.

How many "factors" is Fido communicating here?

has come to be used generically in this marketplace, in much the same way that people use brand names such as Xerox, Kleenex or Band-Aid to refer to a product category. The marketing communications program has successfully branded a service that has been fraught with price competition and has now come to be perceived as a commodity.

Communications in the context of marketing

Marketing communications serves three essential roles: It informs, persuades, and reminds prospective customers about a company and its products. The relative importance of these roles varies according to the circumstances faced by a firm.

marketing communications
All of the elements of an organization's marketing (usually advertising, publicity, public relations, personal sales, and sales promotion) that serve to inform existing and potential customers.

Communicating to inform The most attractive product or brand will be a failure if no one knows it is available! Because distribution channels are often long, a product may pass through many hands between its producer and consumers. Therefore, a producer must inform wholesalers as well as end-consumers or business users. Wholesalers, in turn, must inform retailers, and retailers must inform consumers. As the number of prospective customers grows and as markets become global, the problems and cost of informing target customers increase. Simply making available a well-designed or useful product is not enough. A communications program must be designed to reach different groups — and to reach them effectively through word and imagery. Imagery transfers a great deal of information rapidly and often remains after words have been forgotten.

Since consumers are exposed to thousands of marketing communications messages each day, and the average grocery shopper spends slightly more than 20 minutes buying a product, covers less than a quarter of the supermarket in the process, and looks at a typical product for just 2.5 seconds before buying, marketers can't rely on the idea that, once a product is packaged and on the store shelf, all has been done. A communications program is needed that will cause consumers to not only understand a product and recognize its features and demand it, but also keep coming back for more.

When Panasonic wanted to launch the new line of Power Activator (PA) batteries aimed at the battery-eating electronics of today's youth markets, it knew it had to be "cool" about it, but without looking as if it was trying too hard. The solution was to employ "guerrilla" tactics aimed at building grassroots awareness in the target market's own environment and culture. First, the product's logo was circulated without product identification through underground channels — posters were used in and around dance clubs, showing blown-out electronics and just the PA logo. Then the logo was emblazoned on T-shirts, hats, and stickers that were distributed at more than 30 events in major Canadian cities. Club DJs were also enlisted to assist by wearing the PA T-shirts at their clubs. Eventually, this merchandising was replaced with similar gear, but this time revealing the product itself in addition to the logo. The campaign was then tied in with MuchMusic and a MuchDance CD release. Also, a contest mini-site was connected to the MuchMusic Web site (**www.muchmusic.com**), with prizes of Panasonic electronics and, of course, PA batteries.[2]

MuchMusic

Campbells

Communicating to persuade Another purpose of marketing communications is persuasion. The intense competition among different industries, as well as among different firms in the same industry, puts tremendous pressure on the communications programs of marketers. Campbell (**www.campbellsoup.com**) has been selling soup for more than 120 years and has annual soup sales of close to $2 billion. Studies show that 96 percent of Canadian households have canned soup in their kitchen cupboards. Yet the firm spends more than $60 million each year advertising soup, since there is still room to "win more stomachs for Campbell's." To increase its share of the fast-growing, home-prepared soup market, Campbell continues to innovate in order to persuade non-Campbell users to switch brands. It does this by launching new varieties of canned, boxed, freeze-dried, and fresh-frozen soups with new features. All of these new products have to be advertised to non-users so as to create awareness of their features and benefits and indicate how they meet existing consumer needs better than the soup brands now being used. Of course, they also have to be advertised to current users to persuade them to stay with the Campbell brand and to try new offerings.[3] To encourage current users to increase their consumption of Campbell's soups, the Campbell's Centre for Nutrition and Wellness (**www.campbellwellness.com**) provides information about the benefits of eating soup every day as part of a "lifeplan" or a diet plan.

Persuading consumers to buy a company's offering also includes the packaging appearance and style — whether it's sitting on the shelf or making an impression in advertising, packaging says something. All communication uses "visual vocabulary" — more than 40 percent of communication is visual. And what is more visual than packaging? Further, 80 percent of this visual communication is driven by colour and shape — words tell and pictures sell! Text most often is forgotten, so marketers must rely on images, colours, and shapes to elicit a positive emotional response, while remaining true to brand character. Colour, for example, can make a package something it isn't: Black and dark colours impart visual weight, while light colours make packages appear to be less heavy. Dark colours can make them look compact, while light ones can make them look larger.[4]

Persuasion is also about positioning the product in consumers' minds. "Being a guy just got better" according to Corby Distilleries' new multi-million dollar campaign for CC&G — which apparently is just for guys! Targeting men in their 20s and 30s, it was "especially made for guys who like the taste of rye and aren't satisfied with vodka or rum coolers," according to the company. The ready-to-drink blend of Canadian Club and ginger ale is intended as a response to market research indicating that young men are looking for a refreshing alternative to beer.[5]

Music plays an important role in persuasion. It not only soothes but also keeps consumers from tuning out an advertiser's message. According to a recent woman's magazine survey, nearly 47 percent of women 45 to 54 cited music as a key element in holding their attention during television commercials. Also, 43 percent of women 18 to 34 gave music as a top reason for why they watch commercials.[6] This doesn't mean spending a fortune for the rights to a rock and roll classic; simply matching the music to the product or market is all that's necessary. But sometimes a classic might be just what is needed. Popular musicians often license their music to be used with or without lyrics. For example, Madonna's "Ray of Light" was used for the launch campaign for Windows XP, while Moby's "Porcelain" was used for Toyota's "You Belong Outside" campaign promoting its SUV. The Gap has always made music a key element in their ad campaigns. In July 2005, The Gap announced that it was adding Alanis Morrisette, Jason Mraz and Michelle Williams, amongst others, to its TV commercials. Having dropped Sarah Jessica Parker as its spokesperson, the clothing retailer decided to have singing stars performing their favourite songs (a classic by another performer) while wearing their favourite jeans. The combination of fashion, music, and celebrities is not a new phenomenon in advertising; however, introducing a different star and a different song for each jean style takes this promotional idea to a new level.

Communicating to remind Because of competitive clutter, consumers must be reminded about the availability of a product or brand and its potential to satisfy. In addition, they need to be reminded on occasion of broader messages that are related to the image of companies and not-for-profit organizations. Advertisers expose the marketplace to thousands of messages every day in the hope of attracting new consumers and reinforcing their relationships with existing customers. Even an established firm must constantly remind people about its brand to retain a place in their minds. It is unlikely that a day goes by, for example, in which you don't see some form of marketing communications (an ad, in-store display, counter sign, billboard, or imprinted T-shirt) for Pepsi or Coke. Wrigley gums — Juicy Fruit, Doublemint — have been around for a long time but the company still spends millions of dollars each year on "reminder" advertising.

Older brands often need to remind you that they're still out there and to keep their image current. Campbell, in addition to attempting to persuade non-users to switch soup brands, makes sure that it reminds users of the benefits of their brand loyalty. The makers of Kahlua liqueur (**www.corby.ca**), in order to keep up with trends in alcoholic beverages, has run vibrant ads with recipes to reflect the popularity of ready-to-drink cocktails such as the Mudslide and the White Russian.

Corby

Marketing Communications Methods

Marketing communications takes five basic forms: personal selling, advertising, sales promotion, public relations, and publicity. Each has distinct features that determine the role that it can play in a communications program.

- ***Personal selling,*** or just plain "selling" or "sales," is the direct presentation of a product or service to a prospective customer by a representative of the organization that is marketing it. These days, it covers many different kinds of sales positions from retail salespeople to pharmaceutical sales reps to telemarketers. Personal selling takes place face to face, over the telephone, or by means of an Internet "chat," and it may be directed to a business or a final consumer. More money is spent on personal selling than on any other form of marketing communications.

- ***Advertising*** is non-personal mass communication that the sponsor has paid for and in which the sponsor is clearly identified. The most familiar forms of ads are found in the broadcast (TV and radio) and print (newspapers and magazines) media, as well as on the Internet. Other advertising alternatives include direct mail, billboards, and directories — both printed and online. Product placement in movies, television shows, and video games is another, more subtle and growing way of getting a brand in front of the consumer.

- ***Sales promotion*** is demand-stimulating activity designed to supplement advertising and facilitate personal selling. It is paid for by the sponsor and frequently involves a temporary incentive to encourage a purchase. Many sales promotions are directed at consumers, including the coupons that arrive in the mail and the contest that allows you to win tickets to a Barenaked Ladies concert. Many sales promotions, however, are designed to encourage a company's sales force or other members of its distribution channel to sell its products more aggressively. This latter category is called trade promotion. Included in sales promotion is a wide spectrum of activities, such as contests, trade shows, in-store displays, rebates, samples, premiums, discounts, and coupons.

MARKETING AT WORK — 13-1: STRATEGY

Creative Communications

With the launch of 15 products in 2005, Procter & Gamble used all kinds of marketing to reach consumers. The new launches included Tide Coldwater, Tide to Go, Old Spice Red Zone After Hours, Pringles Prints, and Olay Quench. Procter & Gamble Canada's president, Tim Penner, said that they would lead the charge into using marketing communication tools that go beyond television spots.

To stand out and retain its top position in the $70-billion food and consumer products industry, P&G Canada used new local marketing initiatives that differed from those used in the U.S. As well, they tripled their in-store event marketing expenditures in 2005, with improved demonstrations for really new products like the Mr. Clean Magic Reach.

In addition, P&G increased its use of PR, event marketing, and the Internet to increase awareness. But perhaps its most innovative new initiative was for Cover Girl lipstick. Mirrored posters with a built-in motion–activated sound chip were hung in women's washrooms. This "Is your lipstick still on?" campaign intercepted women to inform them of a new lipstick during a "moment of vanity."

QUESTIONS:

1. Why is P&G broadening its use of marketing communications tools?
2. Why was it felt necessary to break away from the American strategy?

SOURCE: Adapted from *Marketing Magazine Online*, www.marketingmag.ca, December 12, 2005.

- ***Public relations*** encompasses a wide variety of communications efforts to contribute to generally favourable attitudes and opinions toward an organization and its products. Unlike most advertising and personal selling, it does not include a specific sales message. The targets may be customers, shareholders, a government agency, or a special-interest group. Public relations can take many forms, including newsletters, annual reports, Web sites, lobbying, and sponsorship of charitable or civic events. Many large companies, such as the Royal Bank of Canada and Air Canada, gain national attention through their sponsorship of organizations and events such as symphony orchestras and the Special Olympics.
- ***Publicity*** is a special form of public relations that involves creating and placing a news story, editorial, or announcement about an organization or its products or services. Like advertising, it involves a non-personal message that reaches a mass audience through the media. But several things distinguish publicity from advertising: It is not paid for, the organization that is the subject of the publicity has little control over it, and it appears as news and therefore may have greater credibility or "legitimacy" than advertising. Organizations seek good publicity and frequently provide the material for it in the form of news releases, photographs, and press conferences. Publicity is not always positive — as in cases when a firm has lower than expected sales or earnings or when it lays off a large number of employees.

Is this public relations or publicity?

PAGE UP!

1. Name the three essential roles that marketing communications plays.
2. What are the five basic forms of marketing communications?
3. What are the essential differences between advertising and public relations?

Integrated Marketing Communications

BACK TO THE TOP

While marketers have a variety of communications tools at their disposal, making effective use of them means that a company's personal selling, advertising, and other communications activities should form a co-ordinated program within its total marketing plan. Again, the *Narnia* communications program illustrates how this can be done.

In many firms, communications activities are not well co-ordinated, with potentially damaging consequences. For example, advertising directors and sales force managers sometimes come into conflict over resources, or the sales force may not be adequately informed about the details of a sales promotion effort. This wouldn't happen if the elements comprising the marketing communications program were part of an **integrated marketing communications (IMC)** effort. IMC is a strategic business process used to plan, develop, execute, and evaluate co-ordinated communication with an organization's customers and the general public.[7]

integrated marketing communications (IMC)
A strategic business process used to plan, develop, execute, and evaluate co-ordinated communication with an organization's customers and the general public.

IMC begins with a strategic planning effort designed to co-ordinate marketing communications with product planning, pricing, and distribution — the other marketing mix elements. The communications program is influenced, for example, by how distinctive a product is and whether its planned price is above or below that of the competition. A manufacturer or intermediary must also consider its promotional links with other firms in the distribution channel. Ford recognizes that its success is closely tied to the performance of dealers. In addition to advertising Ford products directly to consumers, the company has developed dealer certification processes to train sales and service personnel in how to provide the best experience possible for the customer. Ford's Blue Oval Certified program uses a thumbprint in Ford's trademark blue colour to indicate certification status. According to one employee, the logo is "A symbol to show customers we've done everything in our power to make sure that their stay at the dealership was the best it could be."[8] Such programs also offer cash incentives to dealers with high customer-satisfaction scores. IMC efforts such as these often incorporate what is referred to as an internal marketing component. That is, marketing messages that inform, persuade, and remind employees — educating and helping employees to do their jobs well, thereby enhancing their employment experience and providing better product quality and customer service.

An audience perspective

An IMC approach adopts the position that a customer or prospect is exposed to many bits and pieces of information about a company or brand. Certainly, some of these bits are designed and presented by marketers but others, possibly the majority, come from other sources. These sources can include personal experience, the opinions of others, and comparisons made by competitors in their advertising. Based on all of this information, individuals make evaluations and form judgements. With so little control over what information consumers can use, a marketer's efforts must be highly co-ordinated and complementary to have a useful impact. That means anticipating the opportunities when the target audience will be exposed to information about the company or brand, and effectively communicating the appropriate message in those "windows of opportunity." Usually, this involves using several different communications methods and requires a high degree of co-ordination.

IMC elements

The use of the IMC approach to marketing communications is reflected in how managers think about the information needs of the message recipients. Organizations that have adopted an IMC philosophy tend to share several characteristics:

- An awareness of the target groups' information sources, as well as their media habits and preferences.
- An understanding of what such groups know and believe that relates to the desired response.
- The use of a mix of communications tools, each with specific objectives but all linked to a common overall goal.
- A concerted effort in which personal selling, advertising, sales promotion, public relations, and publicity are co-ordinated in order to communicate a consistent and continuous flow of information adapted to the audience's needs.
- A long-term perspective that focuses on continuing co-ordination and integration to contribute to the building of brand equity.

Implementing IMC

In developing integrated communications, a company co-ordinates its advertising, personal selling, sales promotion, public relations, and publicity to accomplish specific objectives. For example, IBM's communications efforts had become highly fragmented a few years ago. The company was using more than 80 advertising agencies around the world, and its ads were sending mixed messages. To take care of the problem and co-ordinate efforts:

- The 80 agencies were replaced by one.
- All packaging, brochures, and trade show booths were standardized to present a unified image.
- Sports sponsorships were consolidated into a few big events (such as the Olympics) to better showcase IBM technology.
- Internet home pages with a consistent look and content were developed for 77 countries in their native languages. Some differences were accommodated due to differences in technology and infrastructure, but the Web pages otherwise were consistent. Good comparisons can be seen by looking at the U.S. (**www.ibm.com**), Canadian (**www.ibm.ca**), and German (**www.de.ibm.com**) IBM Web pages.

IBM

Communications at IBM is now built around the theme and content of being a technology innovator that is accessible and responsive.[9]

An IMC program may incorporate several different communications campaigns, with some even running concurrently. Depending on objectives and available funds, a firm may undertake simultaneous local, regional, national, and international programs as was done with the *Narnia* program. Moreover, a firm may have one campaign aimed at consumers and another at wholesalers and retailers.

We have discussed how, with so many products available, companies must go beyond designing an attractive product, to actually communicating with and attracting the attention of the marketplace. This includes those in the supply chains that make decisions regarding carrying a product and reordering.

Can you tell that this is Coke's Far Coast brand?

Coca-Cola (www.cocacola.com) continues to be the best example of a truly global product — around the world, "It's the real thing." The company uses this phrase, which it owns, as a part of its global message — or, at least as close to it as can be literally and culturally communicated and translated. The "Coke" part of the "Vanilla Coke" campaign was extremely important in the international roll-out of this flavour. These global programs are designed to be easily tailored to specific markets. Coca-Cola also acts nationally, regionally, and locally, to bolster individual markets.

Coke has always initiated a variety of programs unique to Canada (such as the Coke Card promotion) but also uses programs with regional "flavouring," such as the hockey-themed campaign featuring a young girl singing the Canadian anthem. To show that it's still "the real thing," in Atlantic Canada, the company produced an advertisement that showcased a series of well-known and familiar sites throughout the Atlantic provinces, in which Atlantic Canadians were shown enjoying the product.[10] Coke also chose Canada as the first country in which to launch their new Far Coast line of premium brewed beverages. "Toronto is an ideal location for the launch because it is a multicultural city that fits the cultural exploration brand positioning of Far Coast and is in a country that has a highly developed brewed beverage market," stated Silvio Annosantini, who leads this project in Canada. To help build awareness and trial of the Far Coast brand, the company has created a Far Coast Concept Store in Toronto. The Concept Store will provide a venue for consumers to taste and explore the wide range of premium Far Coast blends.

Evaluating IMC

The final step in IMC is evaluation. A program can be evaluated in a number of ways. One approach is to examine how it is implemented. For example, if the communications program of a large manufacturer of consumer goods is being carried out in a manner consistent with the notion of IMC, we would expect to find:

- An advertising program consisting of a series of related, well-timed, carefully placed ads that reinforce personal selling and sales promotional efforts.
- A personal selling effort that is co-ordinated with the advertising program. The firm's sales force and distribution channel members would be fully informed about the advertising portion of the campaign — the theme, media used, and the schedule for appearance of the ads. The salespeople would be able to explain and demonstrate the product benefits emphasized in the ads and would be prepared to transmit the promotional message and supporting material to intermediaries so that they could take part in the campaign.

- Sales promotional devices such as point-of-purchase display materials that are co-ordinated with other aspects of the program. Incentives for intermediaries would be clearly communicated and understood. Retailers would be briefed about consumer promotions and adequate inventories would be in place.
- Public relations efforts scheduled to coincide with the other mix components and emphasizing the same theme.
- Publicity activities that "make" news for the advertiser.

More rigorous evaluation examines the results of the program. The outcome of each component is compared with the objectives set for it to determine if the effort was successful. Below are some typical objectives and some common measures associated with each of them.[11]

- ***Awareness of a company or brand:*** Competitive brand position studies; focus groups with distributors at trade shows; Web site "hits."
- ***Interest in a product or brand:*** Number of brochures or other company publications distributed; attendance at company-sponsored seminars; Web site traffic — number of pages viewed, time spent at the site, requests for company and product information.
- ***Action:*** Usage of and results from support tools provided to distributors and retailers; responses to direct mail; customer enquiries or store visits; sales.

To be meaningful, most of these measures need to be taken both before and after the communications effort, with the difference between the two measures indicating its effect.

Barriers to IMC

Despite its attractiveness, an IMC approach is not universally supported. In some organizations, the communications functions are managed by different departments. The sales force may be in a unit separate from where advertising decisions are made. The result is a lack of internal communication and co-ordination. In other firms, there is a belief that communications activities are so imprecise that efforts to carefully design objectives and co-ordinate efforts would be unproductive. In still other firms, there is a history of relying on particular forms of communications and a resistance to consider alternatives.

Fully utilizing an IMC approach would probably require a firm to make several changes. One involves restructuring internal communications to ensure that all relevant parties involved in communications work together. Some firms have approached this by creating a marketing communications manager who oversees the planning and co-ordination of all promotional and communications efforts. A second change involves conducting research to gather the necessary information about the target audience. Firms utilize extensive databases for this purpose, but these are costly to create and expensive to maintain. Finally, and most importantly, senior management must support the effort to integrate marketing communications efforts. Strong leadership is essential to break down barriers and help create co-operative situations.

Next, we will examine how basic communication, the core of all marketing communications, actually works. We will then move on to key managerial issues in the marketing communications program.

communication
Verbal or non-verbal transmission of information, through a medium or media, between a sender and a receiver.

The Communication Process

Let's now turn to the basic elements of the communication process. **Communication** is the verbal or non-verbal transmission of information between someone wanting to express an idea and someone else expected or expecting to understand that idea. Because the components of marketing communications are examples of communication between two or more parties, much can be learned about structuring effective marketing messages by examining the communication process.

Fundamentally, communication requires only four elements: a message, a source of the message, a communication channel, and a receiver. In practice, however, important additional components come into play:

- The information that the sending source wants to share must first be encoded into a transmittable form. Encoding is the conversion of an idea into words, pictures, symbols in an advertisement, or some other form, such as a product display in a supermarket, a coupon, or a "hot button" on a Web site.
- Once the encoded message has been transmitted through some communication channel, the symbols must be decoded — perceived, or given meaning, by the receiver. The perceived message may be what the sender intended, or something else, depending on the receiver's knowledge and experience.
- If the message has been transmitted successfully, there is some change in the receiver's knowledge, beliefs, or feelings. As a result of this change, the receiver formulates a **response**. The response could be non-verbal (a positive reaction, as indicated by a smile while watching an ad), verbal (suggesting to a friend that she try an advertised product), or behavioural (purchasing the advertised product).

response
The reaction (non-verbal, verbal, or behavioural) of an information receiver that serves as feedback to the sender of a communication.

- The response serves as feedback, telling the sender whether the message was received and how it was perceived by the recipient. Through feedback, the sender can learn why a communication failed and how to improve future communication.
- All stages of the process can be affected by noise — any external event or factor that interferes with successful communication, such as a competitive ad. Noise occurs when a television viewer sees ads for both Speedy and Midas within a short time period or when your system crashes while filling your shopping cart at a retail Web site.

Figure 13-1 illustrates these components of a communication process and relates them to marketing communications activities.

What does the communication process tell us about producing effective marketing communications programs? First, the act of encoding reminds us that messages can take many forms. Messages can be physical (a sample, a premium) or symbolic (verbal, visual), and there are many options within each of these categories. For example, a verbal message can be factual, humorous, or even threatening.

Second, the number of channels or methods of transmitting a message are limited only by the imagination and creativity of the sender. Most marketing communications messages are transmitted by familiar channels, such as the voice of a salesperson, the airwaves of radio, a Web site, the side of a bus, or the lead-in to a feature film in a movie theatre. Each channel has its own characteristics in terms of audience reach, flexibility, permanence, credibility, and cost. In selecting a channel, a marketer must have clearly defined objectives and a familiarity with the features of the many alternatives.

Third, how the message is decoded or interpreted depends on its form (encoding and transmission) and the capability and interest of the recipient. In designing and sending messages, marketers must be sensitive to the audience. What is the vocabulary and level of verbal sophistication of audience members? What other messages have they received? What experiences have they had? What will get and hold their attention?

Finally, every component of the marketing communications program should have a measurable objective that can be determined from the response and feedback provided by the

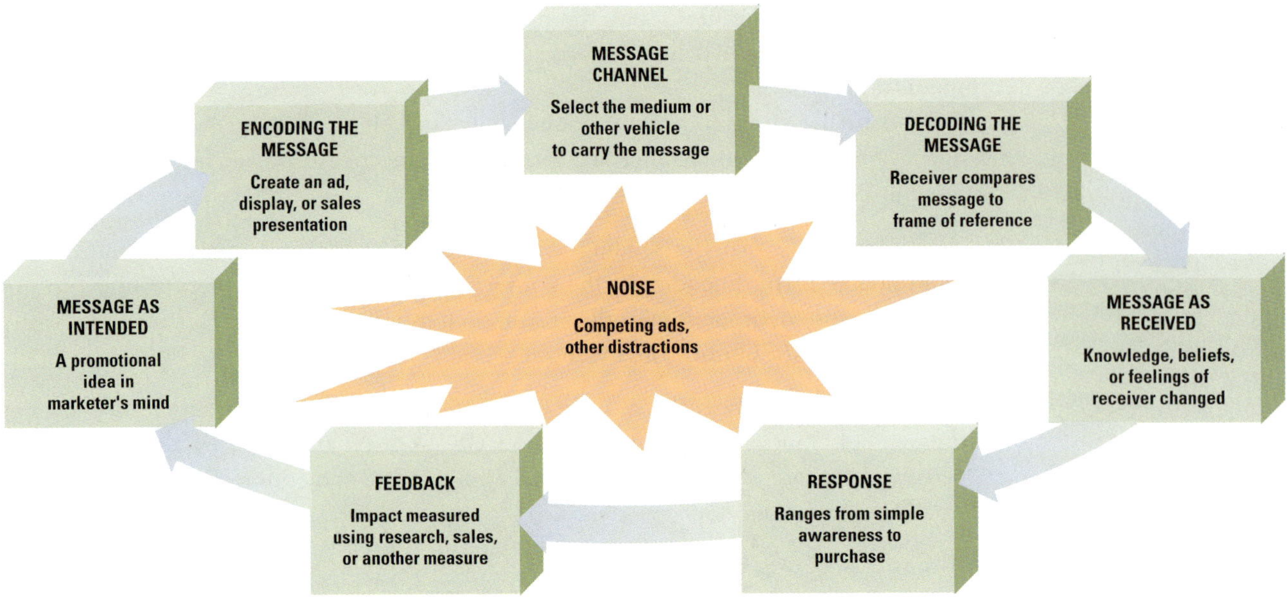

Figure 13-1: The Communication Process in Marketing Communications

recipients. Feedback may be collected in many forms — changes in sales, recall of advertising messages, more favourable attitudes, increased awareness of a brand or an organization — depending on the objective of the marketing communications message. For some promotional activities, the objective may be modest; for example, an increase in the audience's awareness of a brand or stimulating trial of a new product. For others, such as a direct-mail solicitation, the objective would be a particular level of sales. Without objectives, the effectiveness of a message cannot be evaluated.

MARKETING AT WORK 13-2: TECHNOLOGY

Text Sells!!

Marketers are increasingly looking for ways to integrate technology into their marketing communications plans. It is necessary to reach consumers on their own terms. The Toronto-based online classifieds site, Tradepoint.ca, decided to run a promotion that integrates text messaging (SMS) and ads on interactive LCD units in the back of taxicabs in the Greater Toronto Area.

The touch screens will run ads for Tradepoint.ca that invite viewers to text in to win a trip. The 1,500 cab drivers whose cars are fitted with the screens will keep a record of how many passengers ride with them, which will allow Tradepoint.ca to track exactly how many people saw the ad and compare that with the number of people who responded. Because cab drivers will have to supply passengers with a SMS number, Tradepoint.ca will also know which areas of the city provide the best responses.

The plans are to expand the advertising from just Tradepoint.ca ads to city information, news, weather, and sports. Tradepoint.ca expects to reach 10,000 passengers each day.

Lancome, a division of L'Oreal Canada, also decided to run a text messaging campaign for its new line of eye makeup, Color Design. The campaign consisted of putting 155 ads in women's washrooms in restaurants and bars in Montréal, Ottawa, Toronto, Calgary and Vancouver in February 2006. The ads invited consumers to text message to a six-digit code and receive an instant message with a toll-free number they can call to book a free Lancome Eye Design makeup session at The Bay. The text messaging campaign was supported by an ad in *Nightlife* magazine in Montréal and point of sale materials in Bay stores, in addition to the washroom ads.

QUESTIONS:

1. Does using a text messaging-based campaign restrict these sponsors' ability to reach their target markets?
2. "Reaching customers on their own terms" means what for Tradepoint.ca and L'Oreal? Can technology do this in these cases?

SOURCE: Michelle Halpern, "Tradepoint text campaign targets cab drivers," *Marketing Magazine Online*, www.marketingmag.ca, February 13, 2006; "Lancome runs texty campaign for eye shadow," *Marketing Magazine Online*, www.marketingmag.ca, February 13, 2006.

PAGE UP!

1. What is the purpose of IMC?
2. What are some of the barriers to IMC?
3. Define communication.

Determining the Marketing Communications Mix

BACK TO THE TOP

A **marketing communications mix** is a company's combination of personal selling, advertising, sales promotion, public relations, and publicity. An effective mix is a critical part of virtually all marketing communications strategies and the *Narnia* illustration is a prime example of just such a mix.

marketing communications mix
The combination of personal selling, advertising, sales promotion, publicity, and public relations that is intended to help an organization achieve its marketing objectives.

Product differentiation, market segmentation, trading up and trading down, and branding all require effective communications with target audiences. Designing an effective marketing communications mix requires a number of strategic decisions, as we will now see.

Factors influencing the marketing communications mix

Five factors should be taken into account when determining the marketing communications mix: (1) the target market; (2) the objective of the communications effort; (3) the nature of the product or service being promoted; (4) the stage in the life cycle of the product or service; and (5) the amount of money available for marketing communications.

Target market As in most areas of marketing, decisions on the marketing communications mix will be greatly influenced by the target market segments that are of principal interest to the company. At least four variables affect the choice of an approach to communicating with a particular market segment:

- ***Readiness to buy***: A target segment may be in any one of six stages of buying readiness. These stages — awareness, knowledge, liking, preference, conviction, and purchase — are called the hierarchy of effects, because they represent stages that a buyer goes through in moving toward a purchase, and each defines a possible goal or effect of marketing communications.

awareness
Stage 1 of buying readiness: The customer gains information about the product and the brand name.

At the **awareness** stage, the marketer's task is to let buyers know that the product or brand exists. Here the objective is to build familiarity with the product and the brand name. In the 2006 *Sports Illustrated* Swimsuit Issue, GMC ran three ads showing models wearing swimsuits printed with graffiti. The one line of text that stood out was "beyond the drawing board.com." When readers went to the URL, they were taken to gmc.com where they viewed an ad for the new 2007 GMC Yukon. The placement of the URL on the models' swimsuits attracted attention and the simplicity of the text would be intriguing to readers. Just how many people put down their magazines to log on is unknown!

Does this image succeed in creating "awareness"?

knowledge
Stage 2 of buying readiness: A customer learns about a product's features and how it can meet a need.

Knowledge goes beyond awareness to learning about a product's features: The provider has to tell or show you what it is and what it can do for you. For example, what exactly can the new generation of cellphones do to make my life easier? What exactly is a personal VCR? How will seeing the *Narnia* movie reinforce family values?

BACK TO THE TOP

liking
Stage 3 of buying readiness: The knowledgeable customer moves from being indifferent about the brand to having positive feelings about it.

Liking refers to how the market feels about the product or brand. Marketing communications can be used to move a knowledgeable audience from being indifferent to actually liking a brand. A common technique is to associate the item with an attractive symbol or person. Buick, historically the choice of older customers, as part of an integrated effort to lower the average age of its buyers, has redesigned some products and engaged a celebrity spokesperson, as well as using a little humour in its advertising. The result? Ads featuring Tiger Woods have attracted new, younger buyers, never before seen in Buick showrooms. Buick has also staked its territory as the official vehicle for the Professional Golf Association tour and the title sponsor of its four major events. By doing this, the company has tried to balance its popularity with younger and older age segments.[12] For the 2006 tour, Buick offered golfers a chance to win Tiger's game car and a trip for two to the next tournament, each time Tiger wins. This will, hopefully, keep the consumers interested in Buick products and increase traffic to the Web site to check out the features on Tiger's car and others.

preference
Stage 4 of buying readiness: The customer distinguishes among brands and prefers yours.

Creating **preference** involves distinguishing among brands, so that the market prefers yours. It is not uncommon for consumers to like several brands in the same product category, but the customer can't make a decision until one brand is preferred over the alternatives. The Internet has recently provided one of the best venues for a type of marketing that focuses on creating preference, allowing manufacturers the opportunity to present side-by-side comparisons of their products and those of the nearest competitors, often down to the smallest detail. This has become particularly popular with automotive and high-technology products such as personal computers and digital cameras. Ads that make direct comparisons with the competition are intended to create a preference.

conviction
Stage 5 of buying readiness: The customer makes an actual decision or commitment to purchase.

Conviction entails the customer's actual decision or commitment to purchase. The marketing communications objective here is to increase the strength of the buyer's need. Trying a product and experiencing the benefits that come from using it are very effective in strengthening the conviction to own it. Consider how video game, WebTV, and CD systems are set up ready to use in stores and how sites such as CDNOW (**www.cdnow.com**) provide sampling on the Internet.

purchase
Stage 6, the last stage of buying readiness: The customer overcomes any inhibitors that might delay or postpone purchase and buys the product.

Purchase can be delayed or postponed indefinitely, even for customers who are convinced that they should buy a product. The inhibitor might be a situational factor, such as not having enough money at the moment or a natural resistance to change. Action may be triggered through a marketing communications price discount or offering additional incentives. Postponement or cancellation can also be a challenge for Internet retailers, as e-shoppers will often abandon their cybercarts containing merchandise before submitting their orders. E-tailers try to encourage follow-up of this purchase intent by holding these items in the customers' cart until the customers remove the products themselves. On each return to the site, customers are also reminded that there are items in their shopping carts.

CDNOW

- ***Geographic scope of the market:*** Personal selling may be adequate in a small local market, but as the market broadens geographically, greater emphasis must be placed on advertising, using a variety of media. The exception would be a firm that sells to concentrated pockets of customers scattered around the country. For example, the market for certain plastics is heaviest in Ontario and Québec, because these plastics are used by component suppliers to the auto industry. In this case, emphasis on personal selling may be appropriate, because spending on advertising that is widely distributed would be wasteful.

This retailer has to advertise to both B2B customers and end consumers.

- ***Type of customer:*** Marketing communications strategy depends in part on the level of the distribution channel that the organization hopes to influence. Final consumers and resellers sometimes buy the same product, but they require different marketing communications. This is common among computer products that are targeted toward business and personal applications. To illustrate, Staples/Business Depot (**www.staples.ca**) serves both consumer and business markets. Aside from other differences utilized, the company designs TV advertisements that communicate to both audiences.

Staples

- ***Concentration of the market:*** The total number of prospective buyers is another consideration. The fewer potential buyers there are, the more effective personal selling is, compared with advertising. For example, in Canada, there are only a handful of manufacturers of household vacuum cleaners. Clearly, for a firm selling a component part for vacuum cleaners, personal selling would be the best way to reach this market.

Nature of the product Several product attributes influence marketing communications strategy. The most important are:

- ***Unit value:*** A product with a low unit value is usually relatively uncomplicated, involves little risk for the buyer, and must appeal to a mass market to survive. As a result, advertising would be the primary marketing communications tool. In contrast, high-unit-value products often are complex and expensive. These features suggest the need for personal selling. BMW dealers are being encouraged to have salespeople get out of the showroom and call on prospects. By increasing the personal selling effort through techniques such as delivering cars to potential customers for test-drives, BMW hopes to stimulate North American sales. Such a component to the program would be consistent with the service ideology of such a high-end product offering.

- ***Degree of customization:*** If a product must be adapted to the individual customer's needs, personal selling and service (or sometimes a technology-based equivalent such as a highly sophisticated Web site) are necessary, so you would expect to find an emphasis on personal selling for something like home remodelling or an expensive suit. However, the benefits of most standardized products can be effectively communicated in advertising. The increasing number of firms making use of advanced production techniques and information management (such as data warehousing and electronic communication), has made it possible to customize some products for large markets without a great deal of personal service.

- ***Pre-purchase and post-purchase service:*** Products that must be demonstrated, for which there are trade-ins, or that require frequent servicing to keep them in good working order lend themselves to personal selling, sometimes combined with Internet-based demonstrations, video cassettes, and displays of product performance. Typical examples are riding lawnmowers, powerboats, and personal computers. For example, Bombardier would want to show its Ski-Doo (**www.ski-doo.com**) and Sea-Doo (**www.sea-doo.com**) machines in action.

Ski-Doo
Sea-Doo

Stage of product life cycle Marketing communications strategies are influenced by a product's life-cycle stage. When a new product is introduced, prospective consumers must be informed about its existence and its benefits, and wholesalers and retailers must be convinced to carry it. Both advertising (to consumers) and personal selling (to channel members) are therefore critical in a product's introductory stage. At introduction, a new product may also be something of a novelty, offering excellent opportunities for publicity. Later, if a product becomes successful, competition intensifies and more emphasis is placed on persuasive advertising. Table 13-1 shows how marketing communications strategies change as a product moves through its life cycle.

Funds available Regardless of what may be the most desirable marketing communications mix, the amount of money available for marketing communications is the ultimate determinant of the mix. A business with ample funds can make more effective use of advertising than can a firm with limited financial resources. Small or regionally based companies are likely to rely on personal selling, dealer displays, or joint manufacturer-retailer promotions.

Lack of money may limit the options a firm has for its marketing communications effort. For example, television advertising can carry a particular message to far more people and at a lower cost per person than can most other media. Yet a firm may have to rely on less expensive media, such as Yellow Pages advertising, because it lacks the funds to take advantage of television's broad coverage.

Choosing a push or a pull strategy

push strategy
A communications program aimed primarily at wholesalers and retailers.

pull strategy
A communications program aimed primarily at end-users.

As we have seen, producers aim their marketing communications mix at both channel members and customers, both B2B and end consumers. A communications program aimed primarily at wholesalers and retailers is called a **push strategy**, and a program directed primarily at customers is called a **pull strategy**. It is not unusual for firms to use both types of strategies for the same brand. Figure 13-2 contrasts these two strategies.

When using a push strategy, a marketer directs its message primarily to the firms that are the next link forward in the distribution channel. The product is "pushed" through the channel. Take the case of a hardware manufacturer such as Stanley tools, which sells its products to household customers through wholesalers and retailers such as True Value (**www.truevalue.com**) and Home Hardware (**www.homehardwaredealers.com**). The producer promotes heavily to wholesalers, which then also use a push strategy to retailers. In turn, the retailers promote to consumers. A push strategy usually involves a lot of personal

True Value
Home Hardware

TABLE 13-1 Communications Strategies for Different Product Life-Cycle Stages

Market Situation	Promotional Strategy
	Introduction Stage
Customers are not aware of the product's features, nor do they understand how it will benefit them.	Inform and educate potential customers that the product exists, how it might be used, and what want-satisfying benefits it provides. In this stage, a seller must stimulate primary demand — the demand for a type of product — as contrasted with selective demand — the demand for a particular brand. For example, producers had to sell consumers on the value of compact discs in general before it was feasible to promote a particular brand. Normally, heavy emphasis must be placed on personal selling. Exhibits at trade shows are also used extensively in the communications mix. A trade show gives a new product broad exposure to many intermediaries. Manufacturers also rely heavily on personal selling to attract intermediaries to handle a new product.
	Growth Stage
Customers are aware of product's benefits. The product is selling well, and intermediaries want to handle it.	Stimulate selective (brand) demand as competition grows. Increase emphasis on persuasive advertising. Intermediaries share more of the total communications effort.
	Maturity Stage
Competition intensifies and sales level off.	Advertising is used more to remind and persuade rather than only to provide information. Intense competition forces sellers to devote larger sums to advertising and thus contributes to the declining profits experienced in this stage.
	Decline Stage
Sales and profits are declining. New and better products are coming into market.	All communications efforts are cut back substantially. The focus becomes reminding remaining customers.

selling and sales promotion, including contests for salespeople and displays at trade shows. Also, awards and prizes are promoted, based on the volume of product sold through individual outlets. Attractive display cases to showcase products may also serve as an incentive if space is available, as in large hardware stores and other warehouse-sized outlets. Discounting may also be used to encourage carrying a new product or buying larger quantities. This marketing communications strategy is appropriate for many manufacturers of business products, as well as for various consumer goods.

Procter & Gamble

With a pull strategy, marketing communications messages are directed at end-users — usually the public. The intention is to motivate end-consumers to ask retailers for the product. The retailers, in turn, will request the product from wholesalers, and wholesalers will order it from the producer. In effect, marketing communications to consumers is designed to "pull" the product through the channel. This strategy relies on heavy advertising and various forms of consumer-directed sales promotions, such as coupons, samples in consumers' mailboxes, or in-store demonstrations. To promote its new Olay collection of cosmetics, Procter & Gamble (**www.pg.com**) mailed more than 1.5 million tiny lipstick samples in a first-ever campaign of this type. The cosmetics, aimed at women 25 and older, were sent to let consumers actually

Figure 13-2:
Push and Pull Strategies of Marketing Communications

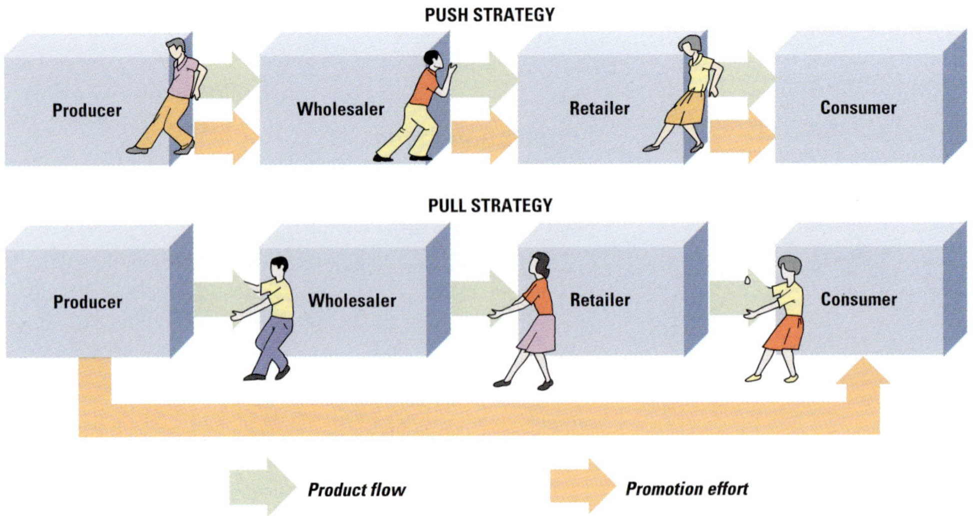

Sunny Delight

try the product and see the benefits.[13] Sunny Delight (**www.sunnydelight.com**) sent out small bottles of juice to consumers (using the same unique bottle shape as the large bottles) packaged in cardboard refrigerators with doors that open to reveal the product and coupons for future purchases. These are obviously expensive to produce and distribute, but they get the product into the consumer's hands — or, well, consumer's mouths in these examples.

The Marketing Communications Budget

Establishing marketing communications budgets is extremely challenging, because management generally lacks reliable standards for determining how much to spend altogether on advertising or personal selling and determining how much of the total budget to allocate to each element of the marketing communications mix. A firm may have the alternative of adding seven salespeople or increasing its trade show budget by $700,000 per year, but frequently it cannot accurately determine precisely the increase in sales or profits it could expect from either expenditure. As a result, rather than one generally accepted approach to setting budgets, there are four common marketing communications budgeting methods: percentage of sales, all available funds, following the competition, and budgeting by task or objective. These methods are frequently discussed in connection with the advertising budget, but they may also be applied to any communications activity to determine the total marketing communications budget.

Percentage of sales

The marketing communications budget may be related in some way to company income, as a percentage of either past or anticipated sales. A common approach for determining the sales base is to compute an average of the previous year's actual sales and expected sales for the coming year. Some businesses prefer to budget a fixed amount of money per unit of past or expected future sales. Manufacturers of products with a high unit value and a low rate of turnover (automobiles or appliances, for example) frequently use the per-unit approach to setting budgets.

Because the percentage-of-sales method is simple to calculate, it is probably the most widely used budgeting method. Moreover, it sets the cost of marketing communications in relation to sales income, making it a variable rather than a fixed expense.

Two things must be noted about basing marketing communications expenditures on past sales. First, management is effectively making marketing communications a result of sales when, in fact, it is a cause of sales. Second, a percentage-of-past-sales method reduces marketing communications expenditures when sales are declining — just when advertising and other forms of communications usually are most needed.

All available funds

A new company or a firm introducing a new product or service frequently ploughs all available funds into its marketing communications program. The objective is to build sales and market share as rapidly as possible during those early, critical months and years. We have seen many Internet start-ups spending all of their funds in an effort to create awareness and Web site traffic — a few successfully, many not so successfully. After a time, management generally finds it necessary to invest in other things, such as new equipment or expanded production or distribution capacity, so the method of setting the marketing communications budget is changed.

Follow the competition

A weak method of determining the marketing communications budget, but one that is used occasionally, is to match the marketing communications expenditures of competitors or to spend in proportion to market share. Sometimes, only one competitor is followed. In other cases, if management has access to industry average expenditures on marketing communications through a trade association, these become company benchmarks.

This approach has at least two problems. First, the firm's competitors may be just as much in the dark regarding how to set a marketing communications budget. Second, a company's goals may be quite different from those of its competitors because of differences in the marketing strategies being followed.

Task or objective

The best approach for establishing the marketing communications budget is to determine the tasks or objectives that the communications program must accomplish and then decide what they will cost. The task method forces management to define realistically the goals of its marketing communications program. Sometimes, it may be defined as straightforwardly as wanting to increase revenue by 10 percent or unit sales by 5 percent, or increasing the price while maintaining a particular level of sales.

Sometimes this is called the build-up method because of the way it is constructed. For example, a company may decide to enter a new geographic market. Management determines this venture will require 10 additional salespeople. The compensation and expenses of these people will cost a total of $1,000,000 per year. Salary for an additional sales supervisor and expenses for an extra office and administrative needs will cost $170,000. Hence, in the personal-selling component of the marketing communications mix, an extra $1,170,000 per year must be budgeted. Similar estimates can be made for the anticipated costs of advertising, sales promotion, and other communications tools. The budget is developed by adding up the costs of the individual marketing communications tasks needed to reach the goal of entering a new territory.

A few years ago, British Columbia Hydro decided to alter the goals of its communications plan and its budget accordingly. Instead of focusing on warm-and-fuzzy images and messages to promote the brand in the newly deregulated industry, management decided on a more task-oriented approach. To deal with the tight labour market situation in the province, it was decided that $1 million needed to be directed toward employee recruitment. Another $2 million would be split roughly evenly between public relations activities and advertising dealing with tenders, water flow levels, and community-impact activities. The decision that $3 million was required to achieve the goals of the plan meant that the company would actually spend $2 million less than in the previous year.[14]

Regulation of Marketing Communications Activities

Because the primary objective of marketing communications is to sell something by communicating with a market, marketing communications activities attract attention. Consequently, abuses by individual firms are easily and quickly noted by the public. In turn, this situation soon leads to (1) public demand for correction of the abuses, (2) assurances that they will not be repeated, and (3) general restraints on marketing communications activities. To answer public demand, laws and regulations have been enacted by the federal government and by most provincial governments. In addition, many private business organizations have established voluntary codes of advertising standards to guide their own marketing communications activities. The advertising industry itself, through the Advertising Advisory Board and its Advertising Standards Councils, does a considerable amount of self-regulation.

The federal role

A number of federal government departments administer legislation aimed at controlling various aspects of marketing communications, particularly advertising. The Broadcasting Act established the Canadian Radio-television and Telecommunications Commission (CRTC) and provided for sweeping powers of advertising regulation. The CRTC may make regulations concerning the character of broadcast advertising and the amount of time that may be devoted to it. While the potential for substantial control exists, the CRTC does not in reality approve each radio and television commercial — it has delegated authority in certain fields to other federal departments, such as Health Canada and Industry Canada.

Health Canada deals with advertising in the fields of drugs, cosmetics, and devices (officialese for birth control products), and it has sweeping powers to limit, control, rewrite, or ban certain communications for the products under its authority. The department deals with general types of prohibition aimed at preventing the treatment, processing, packaging, labelling, advertising, and selling of foods, drugs, and devices in such a manner as to mislead or deceive, or even to be likely to create an erroneous impression concerning the nature of the products. It also prohibits the advertising of whole classes of drugs and diseases or conditions for which a cure may not be advertised under any circumstances. This prohibition stands even if a professionally accepted cure exists. The logic for the prohibition of advertising, in spite of the existence of a cure, is that Health Canada does not want members of the general public to engage in self-diagnosis of a condition that can be treated.

Health Canada has been delegated (by the CRTC) absolute control over radio and television advertisements for the products under its jurisdiction. All such advertisements must be submitted to it at least 15 days prior to airing, and no radio or television station can air an ad without its having been approved by the department and, therefore, by the CRTC.

In contrast to the delegated review powers that Health Canada has over advertisements using the broadcast media, its position in relation to the print media is weak. Its formal control is over alleged Food and Drugs Act violations, which must be prosecuted in court. Given the lack of jurisprudence in this area, the department is loath to go to court in case it loses and thus sets a precedent, or in case its regulations (many of which have not been tested in court) are found to be illegal. What the department does is advise advertisers of its opinion of advertisements that are

MARKETING AT WORK — 13-3: STRATEGY

Wyeth-Ayerst Looks for the Better Way

In Canada, pharmaceutical companies may advertise their drugs as long as they provide viewers with only the name, quantity, and price of their products. The rationale is that this is the bare minimum required for manufacturers to promote their products in a pharmacy. Manufacturers are also free to produce informational TV shots that make no mention of any specific product, but rather discuss the disease or condition that a product treats. The strategy is to motivate consumers to seek more information from their doctors, who will be able to list all available treatments, including (hopefully) the advertiser's.

Wyeth-Ayerst Canada Inc., the pharmaceutical company that makes Alesse birth control pills decided to find a better way to advertise their product and not run afoul of the wording of the advertising regulations. They wanted to communicate effectively on national television with ads geared specifically to young people.

Wyeth-Ayerst Canada Inc. did not develop commercials that named the drug and talk about what it does. The company developed two commercials: One talking about birth control options, the other providing a "lesson learned" feature and staying within Health Canada's guidelines of name, price, and quantity. Two 15-second TV spots advertise the Alesse brand (there is also a 60-second cinema ad) and one 30-second informational TV spot discusses the importance of birth control in general. With a 10-week run on Canada's MuchMusic network, the commercials were destined to hit its target market of "with-it" young women. In fact, all of the commercials featured such women talking about men and relationships. Each woman discusses "a lesson," such as a lesson in relationship break-ups: "Don't lend him anything you ever expect to get back," and a lesson in guys: "Never play hard to get. Be hard to get."

While the 15-second commercials identify the brand name and show a package of Alesse pills, the 30-second infomercial reveals neither. It did, however, wind up with a woman saying, "Talk to your doctor about your birth control options," to which another woman adds, "Less could make sense for you." Although the line refers to the pill's low-dose formula, it also sounds coincidentally like "Alesse could make sense for you." Come to think of it, all those "a lessons" sound coincidentally like "Alesse," too.

Wyeth-Ayerst's integrated advertising strategy — along with the TV and cinema commercials, posters appeared throughout city transit systems — is a classic device. Sending similar messages about a product through multiple media channels so that the consumer associates one with another and then combines them all into a unique, more complex message, is nothing new. What was new was Wyeth-Ayerst's take on the integrated advertising approach. The information commercial and the branded commercial are not run at the same time. The firm has spaced these commercials according to Advertising Standards Canada (ASC) guidelines. After all, the similarity in the casting, copy, and overall look and feel of the ads ensured there would be overlap between the various Alesse "lessons." The fact that the ads ran during the same time period made the overlap even more pronounced. The deciding factor would be: How much of an overlap is too much?

If, for example, Wyeth-Ayerst placed the two kinds of ads in the same media time and space, where a consumer who saw one and then the other was likely to make a connection between birth control and Alesse, Health Canada would be forced to make a fuss. Or would it? Health Canada doesn't prescreen prescription drug ads. That role is performed by the ASC, the ad industry's self-regulating organization. And the ASC has given the Alesse campaign a thumbs-up.

QUESTIONS:

1. Do you think the Alesse campaign was too smart by half or OK?
2. Does making use of an integrated program as a strategy help or hinder the sending of ambiguous messages? Who does it help or hinder in this case?

SOURCE: Adapted, in part, from Patrick Allossery, "Health Canada Challenge," *Financial Post*, May 15, 2000, p. C5; John Heinzl, "A lesson in drug advertising," *The Globe and Mail*, May 5, 2000, p. M1; Shawna Cohen, "The Pill Is Controversial Once Again," *Marketing Magazine Online*, www.marketingmag.ca, May 15, 2000; "Study measures influence of direct-to-consumer drug ads," accessed at www.cbc.ca, March 8, 2006.

prepared for the print media. This opinion is not a ruling, and ads submitted, as well as those that are not, are still subject to the regulations for which the department has responsibility. This does not mean that the department does not monitor the print media: Newspapers and magazines are sampled and advertisements are examined.

What is actually on the product package is also a part of the marketing communications package — and is subject to regulation. Aside from legalities about the labelling of contents, size, etc., there are also regulations about what else you can say about your product. In recent years, the health dimension of a product has become a very popular marketing focus for many foods, from Becel margarine to Sun-Rype Fruit & Veggie bars to So Good soya beverages.

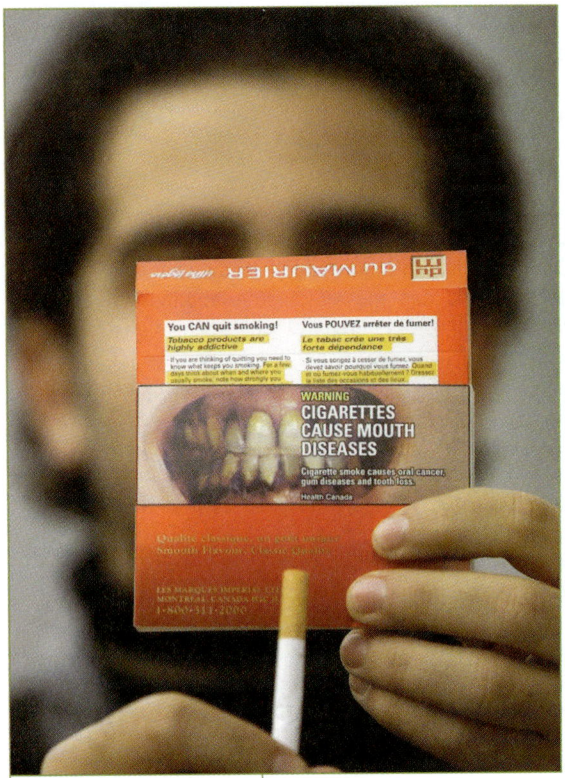

Do you think grotesque images work?

Legislation that became effective in January 2001 made Canada the first country to require cigarette manufacturers selling their products in this country to carry warnings accompanied by grotesque images depicting the potential damage that may result from using the product. One of the warnings (there are 16 different ones, in total) has to take up the top half of the front and back of each package. These messages are significantly more graphic than those required by the 1995 Supreme Court ruling.

Industry Canada has substantial responsibility in the area of regulating marketing communications. The Acts administered include: (1) the Precious Metals Marking Act (definitions of sterling and carat weight), (2) the Trade-marks Act, (3) the Consumer Packaging and Labelling Act, and (4) of greatest significance, the Competition Act. In the **Competition Act**, a number of sections pertain directly to the regulation of the following types of advertising and marketing communications activities:

- Manufacturers or wholesalers who offer marketing communications allowances to retailers must offer such allowances on proportionate terms to all competing purchasers.
- In general, misleading advertising is prohibited.
- "Bait and switch" advertising is not allowed.[15]
- The making of any false or misleading statement in relation to warranties is banned.
- When a retailer promotes a product at two different prices or when two prices appear on a product at the point of sale, the retailer must sell the product at the lower of the prices.
- An advertiser who promotes a product at a "sale" price must have sufficient quantities of the product on hand to satisfy reasonable market demand.
- Selling a "sale" item at a price higher than the advertised "sale" price is prohibited.
- Advertisers who promote contests must disclose the number and value of the prizes and the geographical areas in which prizes are to be distributed, and the prizes must be distributed on the basis of skill or random selection.

Competition Act
The major federal legislation in Canada that governs the marketing and advertising activities of companies and organizations operating in Canada.

The provisions of the Competition Act relating to misleading advertising do not apply to publishers and broadcasters who actually distribute the advertising in question to the general public, provided that these publishers have accepted the contents of the advertising in good faith. In essence, this means that a newspaper cannot be prosecuted for misleading advertising if it accepted the advertising on the assumption that its contents were not misleading.

The provincial role

In each of the provinces, a considerable variety of legislation exists that is aimed at controlling various marketing communications practices. For instance, in Ontario, various degrees of control are exercised by the Liquor Control Board of Ontario, the Ontario Superintendent of Insurance, the Ontario Human Rights Commission, the Ontario Securities Commission, the Ontario Crime Control Commission, the Ontario Racing Commission, various ministries of the Ontario government responsible for financial, commercial, consumer, and transportation functions and services, and more. Most of the provinces have similar sets of legislation, regulatory bodies, and provincial departments. Each of the provinces, for example, regulates various aspects of the promotion of alcoholic beverages.[16] While much of the federal regulation must, in the end, result in argument and prosecution in a courtroom, the provincial machinery would appear to be much more flexible and potentially regulatory in nature, and if pursued, may have a more substantial effect on undesirable practices.

The powers of provincial governments in relation to the regulation of misleading advertising have been increased considerably in recent years. A number of provinces have legislation in place dealing with unfair and unconscionable trade practices. The trade practices legislation of British Columbia, Alberta, and Ontario, for example, contain "shopping lists" of practices that are illegal in those provinces. In reality, these pieces of legislation write into law practices that have been considered illegal by federal prosecutors for a number of years.

Relating to advertising, these Acts prohibit such practices as advertising a product as new when it is in fact used; advertising that fails to state a material fact, thereby deceiving the consumer; and advertising that gives greater prominence to low down payments or monthly payments rather than to the actual price of the product. The Alberta Fair Trading Act also contains a provision for corrective advertising. This provision means that a court, on convicting an advertiser for misleading advertising, can order that advertiser to devote some or all of its advertising (for a certain period) to informing customers that the advertiser had been advertising falsely in the past and to correcting the misleading information that had been communicated in the offending advertisements.

The Province of Québec has a section in its Consumer Protection Act that regulates advertising directed at children. This section forbids the use of exaggeration, endorsements, cartoon characters, and statements that urge children to buy. Québec's Charter of the French Language also contains a number of sections that govern the use of French and English in advertising in that province.

Regulation by private organizations

Several types of private organizations also exert considerable control over the marketing communications practices of businesses. Magazines, newspapers, and radio and television stations regularly refuse to accept advertisements that they feel are false, misleading, or generally in bad taste. In so doing they are being "reasonable" in the ordinary course of doing business. Some trade associations have established codes of ethics that include points pertaining to sales force and advertising activities, and regularly censor advertising appearing in their trade or professional journals. Better Business Bureaus located in major cities across the country are working to control some very difficult situations. Advertising Standards Canada administers the Canadian Code of Advertising Standards; a number of other advertising codes, including the Broadcast Code for Advertising to Children (on behalf of the Canadian Association of Broadcasters); and a code regulating the advertising of over-the-counter drugs, which was developed in co-operation with drug firms and Health Canada.

PAGE UP!

1. Five factors must be considered when determining the marketing communications mix. What are they?
2. What are the six stages of buying readiness?
3. What is the difference between a push strategy and a pull strategy?

Key Terms and Concepts

awareness 389
communication 386
Competition Act 398
conviction 390
integrated marketing communications (IMC) 383
knowledge 390
liking 390
marketing communications 379
marketing communications mix 389
preference 390
pull strategy 392
purchase 390
push strategy 392
response 387

Questions and Problems

1. Describe and explain the components of the marketing communications process in the following situations:
   a. A college student trying to convince her parents to buy her a used car.
   b. A salesperson trying to sell a car to a college student.
2. Explain how the nature of the market affects the marketing communications mix for the following products:
   a. Auto insurance.
   b. Golf balls.
   c. Plywood.
   d. Aircraft maintenance.
   e. Compact discs.
   f. Computers used as servers.
3. Describe how classifying consumer goods as convenience, shopping, or specialty goods helps determine the best marketing communications mix (refer to Chapter 7 for information on the classification of goods).
4. Explain whether personal selling is likely to be the main ingredient in the marketing communications mix for each of the following products:
   a. Chequing accounts.
   b. Home swimming pools.
   c. Liquid laundry detergent.
   d. A large order of fries at McDonald's.
5. Explain whether retailer trade promotion efforts should be stressed in the marketing communications mix for the following:
   a. Levi jeans.
   b. Sunkist oranges.
   c. Canada Saving Bonds.
   d. VISA card.
6. Identify the central idea — the core or basic theme — in three current marketing communications campaigns.
7. Assume that you are marketing a liquid that removes creosote (and the danger of fire) from chimneys used for wood-burning stoves. Briefly describe the roles you would assign to advertising, personal selling, sales promotion, and publicity in your marketing communications campaign.
8. Do you think we need additional legislation to regulate advertising? To regulate personal selling? If so, explain what you would recommend.

Hands-On Marketing

1. An advertisement should have a particular objective that would be apparent to a careful observer. For each of the following marketing communications objectives, find an example of a print ad:
   a. Primarily designed to inform.
   b. Primarily designed to persuade.
   c. Primarily designed to remind.
2. An IMC program or campaign is a co-ordinated series of marketing communications efforts built around a single theme and designed to reach a predetermined goal. It often includes advertising, sales promotion, personal selling, public relations, and publicity. For an important event at your school (such as homecoming, recruiting new students, and fund raising), describe the marketing communications tools used in the campaign and evaluate their appropriateness based on the criteria in the chapter for designing a marketing communications mix.

Back to the Top

Think about the program used by Disney and its partners to launch *Narnia*. It used many of the components of an integrated marketing communications program. Identify those components and think about how useful each could be to pique interest and communicate the different appeals and themes in the film. Which component could do the best overall job? Would there be any reason to use any of the other components to reinforce the objectives that Disney has for the film?

Online LearningCentre

Want to get better grades, tips on how to study more effectively, and up-to-date information on happenings in the world of marketing? Then, visit the Online Learning Centre for practice tests, Study Smart software, *Marketing Magazine,* and much more! **www.mcgrawhill.ca/olc/sommers**

CHAPTER 14

Management of Advertising

This chapter examines the major non-personal, mass-communications promotional tool — advertising. After studying this chapter, you should have an understanding of:

- The nature, purpose, and scope of advertising and what it means to the individual firm.
- The characteristics of the major types of advertising.
- How advertising campaigns are developed and advertising media are selected.

Going After Millions of Eyeballs

The Olympic Games! Are they really the single biggest mass event left for companies to flaunt their wares in this age of continuing audience fragmentation?

Seems to be the case. Large global companies pay hundreds of million of dollars for the rights to use the Olympic rings in their advertising and to be known as proud sponsors of the Games! Others, like Kraft Canada and Tim Hortons, advertise on the broadcasts of the Games themselves without being sponsors. Still others, like Roots and Esso, spend their promotional budgets on the sports federations that back up the athletes as they develop their skills and train for the Games. According to sports marketing expert Keith McIntyre, getting involved at a number of levels — buying Olympic rights, supporting sports federations and sponsoring individual athletes — is the most successful approach. He believes that while being a Games sponsor and having the rights to use the golden rings can be successful in getting attention and helping build a brand image, being associated with a sports governing body adds credibility to a communication and sponsoring individual athletes adds reality and personalization to a mass message. Other Canadian firms have gone farther: McDonald's has created an online community for Canadian fans of the games, Bell Canada is taking mock medal podiums to shopping malls to bring home their beaver games mascots and their message.

Competition for Olympic sponsorship is intense as only one company can have exclusive 'ring rights' in each designated industry. This means that industry competitors must bid higher and higher for exclusive rights or use other approaches to gain association with the Olympics. Since the Royal Bank of Canada became an official sponsor, competing CIBC put its budget behind Alpine Canada, (the skiing sports federation) and then went one step further by sponsoring skier Thomas Grandi.

Companies who have won the bidding for 'ring rights' in their industry watch their competitors very closely to see if their rights are being infringed upon by those who take other approaches to gaining the reflected marketing glory of the Olympics and rings association. Rights holders expect that the Olympic officials who sold them rights will make sure that competing brands do not piggyback on their dearly paid for advertising and promotional turf. During the 2002 Salt Lake City Games, Olympic sponsor Labatt complained about Molson advertisements portraying hockey teams who were to play Team Canada cowering in various corners in fear. During the 2004 Athens Games, the Canadian Olympic Committee asked LG Electronics, Air Canada, Volkswagen, and the Toronto Stock Exchange, among others, to modify their CBC-carried commercials so as not to infringe on rights holders. Sponsors seemed to be much more careful during the 2006 Winter Games as there was less disciplinary activity evident.[1]

advertising
All activities involved in presenting to a group a non-personal, sponsor-identified message regarding a product or organization.

Advertising is the main mass-communications tool available to marketers with the Games being the largest mass. And, as the terminology suggests, the mass in mass communications means using the same message for everyone in an audience. The mass communicator trades off the advantage of personal interaction (the opportunity to tailor a message to each prospective customer on a face-to-face basis) for the advantage of reaching many people at a lower cost per person. However, as the emergence of interactive television advertising and the use of the Internet illustrate, mass communications is becoming less mass and more closely targeted. Advertisers are constantly seeking ways to present their messages to more clearly defined audiences.

Nature and Scope of Advertising

All advertisements have four features: a verbal and/or visual message; a sponsor who is identified; message delivery through at least one medium; and payment by the sponsor to the media carrying the message.

Advertising, then, consists of all of the activities involved in presenting to an audience a non-personal, sponsor-identified, paid-for message about a product or organization. And one of the most vital changes taking place in advertising is the vastly increased ability of marketers to reach specific audiences with tailor-made messages. As a result, we see advertising moving rapidly in the direction of becoming 'near personal' as specialty channels, print and digital publications, and other media continue to innovate and flourish. Viewers are able to program individual entertainment preferences, database marketing continues to be refined and based on actual individual consumption behaviour, and technological advances continue to push towards the 'near personal' goal.

TABLE 14-1 Net Canadian Advertising Revenues by Medium (in millions of Canadian dollars)

Medium		2003	%	2004	%
Television	Total	$2380	27	$2957	27
	Network	$507	5	$323	5
	Selective	$1716	16	$1908	17
	Infomercial	$17	0*	$18	0*
Radio		$1170	11	$1207	11
Weeklies/community newspapers		$788	9	$820	9
Consumer magazines		$601	6	$647	6
Outdoor and transit		$284	3	$303	3
Internet		$237	2	$295	3
Other		$3782	36	$3970	36
	Yellow Pages	$1121	11	$1162	10
	Direct mail	$1399	13	$1,499	13
	Other print	$1269	12	$1309	12
TOTAL ALL MEDIA		$10,620		$11,131	

*Less than 0.5 percent.

SOURCE: *2006, Media Digest.* Published by *Marketing Magazine* as compiled by TVB from Statistics Canada, CRTC, CNA, CCNA/Les Hebos du Québec, Magazines Canada, CARD, CAN, Tele-Direct, Canada Post, IAB, and industry estimates.

Types of advertising

Advertising can be classified according to (1) the target audience, either consumers or businesses; (2) what is being advertised, a product or service versus an organization or company; and (3) the objective sought, the stimulation of primary or selective demand.

TYPE:
Consumer and business-to-business advertising

DEFINITIONS:

Consumer advertising: Advertisements directed to consumers.
Business-to-business advertising: Advertisements directed to businesses rather than consumers.

EXPLANATION:

Most retailers by definition sell only to end-consumers, so they are not faced with the choice of whether to target a consumer or a business audience. There are exceptions — such as Staples/Business Depot — that target both. The publishers of *The Globe and Mail* and similar newspapers and magazines must decide what portion of their advertising budgets will be used to attract advertisers (called trade advertising) and what portion will go toward gaining subscribers and selling magazines, newspapers and access to specialized Web sites.

TYPE:
Product and institutional advertising

All advertising may be classified as product (or service) or institutional (or corporate).

DEFINITIONS:

Product advertising focuses on a particular product or service brand, and is subdivided into direct-action and indirect-action advertising.

- **Direct-action advertising**: Product advertising that seeks a quick response.
- **Indirect-action advertising:** Product advertising that is intended to inform or remind consumers about a product and its benefits.

Institutional or corporate advertising presents information about the advertiser's business or tries to make a good impression. It is intended to create a positive image of the company and its brands in the eyes of customers, prospective customers, and the general public. Two forms of corporate advertising are:

- **Customer-service advertising:** Advertising that presents information about the advertiser's operations.
- **Public service advertising [PSA]:** Advertising designed to improve the quality of life and indicate that the advertiser is a responsible member of the community.

EXPLANATIONS:

Direct-action advertising seeks a quick response — for instance, a magazine ad containing a coupon, a URL or a toll-free number urges the reader to redeem the coupon, visit the Web site or call immediately for a free sample, or a supermarket ad in a local newspaper stresses this week's specials. Indirect-action advertising is designed to stimulate and hold customer interest and demand for a company's products or services over a longer period of time. It informs

Life Fitness wants communication — by telephone, by clicks, or at bricks.

Indirect-action or institutional advertising? No matter which, a special place to visit.

or reminds that a product exists and points out its benefits. Most television advertising is of this type — working to build awareness and recognition of a brand. Customer-service advertising presents information about the advertiser's operations. Advertisements describing the level of personal service available at Ford dealerships are an example. Public service advertising (PSA) is designed to show that the advertiser is a responsible member of the community. Such ads may urge the audience to avoid drugs or to support a local anti-pollution campaign, or may show how the advertiser is making a contribution by supporting worthwhile projects and community activities.

Public service advertising by CIBC for the Run for the Cure

TYPE: Primary-demand and selective-demand advertising

DEFINITIONS:

Primary-demand advertising is designed to stimulate demand for a generic category of a product. **Selective-demand advertising** is intended to stimulate demand for individual brands. Primary-demand advertising that is done in the introductory stage of the product life cycle is known as **pioneering advertising**. **Comparative advertising** is a type of selective-demand advertising in which the advertiser — either directly (by naming a rival brand) or indirectly (through inference) — points out how the advertised brand is better.

EXPLANATIONS:
Primary-demand advertising is used in either of two situations. The first is when the product is in the introductory stage of its life cycle. This is called pioneering advertising. A firm may run an ad about its new product, explaining the product's benefits but not emphasizing the brand name. The objective of pioneering primary-demand advertising is to inform, not to persuade, the target market. The second use of primary-demand advertising occurs throughout the product life cycle. It is usually done by trade associations, trying to stimulate demand for their industry's product. The Dairy Farmers of Canada's ads (**www.dairybureau.org**) urge us to drink more milk. They don't really care what brand of milk and dairy products we buy, just that we use more of them.

Selective-demand advertising essentially is competitive advertising — it pits one brand against another — Ford against GM in terms of which brand is the North American best seller. This type of advertising typically is used when a product has gone beyond the introductory life-cycle stage. The product is reasonably well known and in competition for market share with several brands. The objective of selective-demand advertising is to increase the demand for a brand. To accomplish this goal, it emphasizes the particular benefits — the **differential competitive advantages** — of the brand being advertised.

TYPE:
Co-operative advertising
This type of advertising may be vertical or horizontal.

DEFINITIONS:
Co-operative advertising is advertising for which two or more firms share the cost. **Vertical co-operative** advertising is advertising for which firms at different levels of the distribution channel share the cost. **Horizontal co-operative** advertising involves firms on the same level of distribution sharing the cost.

EXPLANATIONS:
Co-operative advertising promotes products of two or more firms that share the cost of the advertising. There are two types — vertical and horizontal. Vertical co-operative advertising involves firms on different levels of distribution. For example, a manufacturer and a retailer share the cost of the retailer's advertising of that manufacturer's product. Cannondale, Honda, or Kawasaki, for example, would share with their dealers across the country the cost of advertising their bikes or all-terrain vehicles in local newspapers and sometimes on television. Frequently, the manufacturer pays for the preparation of the actual ad, leaving space for the retailer's name and location. Then the manufacturer and retailer share the media cost of placing the ad. Many retail ads in newspapers are co-operative ads.

Another type of vertical co-operative advertising uses an **advertising allowance**, or cash discount offered by a manufacturer to a retailer, to encourage the retailer to advertise or prominently display a product. This approach is often used in retail advertising of grocery products and other household items. Major retailers such as Loblaws, Canadian Tire, and Wal-Mart Canada have much of the cost of preparing their flyers covered by the advertising allowances provided by the manufacturers whose products are featured in the flyers. The difference between co-operative advertising and allowances is the amount of control exerted by the manufacturer over how the money is actually spent.

Horizontal co-operative advertising is undertaken by firms on the same level of distribution — such as a group of retailers — that share the costs of advertising. For example, all stores in a suburban shopping centre may run a joint newspaper ad. The principal benefit is that by pooling their funds, the firms can achieve much greater exposure than if they advertised individually.

Creating selective demand for a commodity

Cost of advertising

The significance of advertising is indicated by the amount of money spent on it. In 2004, expenditures on advertising in Canada totalled over $10 billion. Table 14-1 shows the estimated total revenue by medium. For many years, daily newspapers have been the most widely used medium, but the percentage of total expenditures accounted for by newspapers has been declining steadily, from approximately 30 percent in the mid-1970s to 16 percent in 2004. In fact, the percentage of total advertising expenditures going to the traditional mass media — radio, television, newspapers, and magazines — has been declining steadily, as many advertisers have been switching at least part of their advertising budgets to established media such as direct mail, directories, and weekly newspapers, and to new media such as the Internet and CD-ROMs.

Another change in advertising expenditures includes that now expended on Internet advertising. According to an Internet Advertising Bureau of Canada (IAB) and Ernst and Young survey, online advertising expenditures for 2004 totalled $295 million, up from the projected $250 million. It is also estimated that spending on Internet advertising in Canada would hit $400 million, a growth of 36 percent from 2004. According to another study by the IAB, the Internet is the third most time-consuming media among Canadian adults, accounting for 16 percent of per capita share. Television accounted for 35 percent and radio for 31 percent.[2]

Advertising expenditures Some industries in Canada spend a lot more money than others on advertising. The retail industry spent over $950 million on advertising in 1998 — much more than the $750 million spent by automobile manufacturers. This pattern of spending has been relatively consistent in recent years. Retailers represent a very large proportion of this spending because there are so many of them and some are very large. Some of the advertisers who spend a large amount of money on advertising each year actually devote a very small percentage of their total sales to advertising. Data collected by Statistics Canada indicate that the largest percentage of sales spent on advertising is by companies that manufacture health and beauty aids, soaps, and cleaning products. In general, companies in the consumer-products field spend a higher percentage of sales on advertising than do manufacturers of industrial products. Major companies spend an average of about 2 percent of total sales on advertising, while companies that manufacture consumer products spend approximately 3 percent on average.

Advertising cost versus personal selling cost While we do not have accurate totals for the costs of personal selling, we do know that they far surpass advertising expenditures. In manufacturing, only a few industries (such as drugs, toiletries, cleaning products, tobacco, and beverages) spend more on advertising than on personal selling. Advertising runs from 1 to 3 percent of net sales in many firms, whereas the expenses of recruiting and operating a sales force are typically 8 to 15 percent of sales.

At the wholesale level, advertising costs are very low. Personal selling expenses, however, may run 10 to 15 times as high. Even among retailers in total — and this includes those with self-service operations — the cost of personal selling is substantially higher than that of advertising.

PAGE UP!

1. What are the four features of all advertisements?
2. ______________ consists of all of the activities involved in presenting to an audience a non-personal, sponsor-identified, paid-for message about a product or organization.
3. What is the difference between direct-action advertising and indirect-action advertising?

Developing an Advertising Campaign

advertising campaign
The total advertising program for a product or brand that involves co-ordination, a central theme, and specific goals.

Buckleys

An **advertising campaign** consists of all of the tasks involved in transforming a theme into a co-ordinated advertising program to accomplish a specific goal for a product or brand. For example, everyone has seen the now-infamous advertising for Buckley's Mixture, the famous cough remedy from W.K. Buckley Limited (**www.buckleys.com**), which uses the tag line "It tastes awful. And it works." Of course it tastes awful, it's made from Canada balsam, menthol, camphor, and pine needle oil — it should taste awful! This campaign has been running successfully for many years and has now been extended to include recent additions to the Buckley's line. It relies on a blend of humour and trust in the grandfatherly figure of the company's president, Frank Buckley as well as Buckley employees and 'sufferers' like you and me. The campaign has been very effective and has transferred successfully to international markets as the company has extended distribution. Most products are not this fortunate — but a taste this bad is truly a global thing.

An advertising campaign is planned within the framework of the overall strategic marketing program and the marketing communications campaign. Before designing an advertising campaign, management must:

- Know who the target audience is.
- Establish the overall promotional goals.
- Set the total promotional budget.
- Determine the overall promotional theme.

MARKETING AT WORK 14-1: STRATEGY

Your Favourite Uncle

When Toyota Canada decided to launch the Yaris — the model designed to replace the Echo — it knew something unusual would be needed. The Yaris, although popular in Europe, was virtually unknown in North America; the Echo enjoyed strong brand equity; but the perhaps the greatest obstacle of all was the perception of sub-compacts as boring econo-boxes. To disrupt this perception and quickly build name awareness, Toyota ran zany ads that featured a hip, slightly offbeat character who served as a metaphor for the new Yaris. Since research had shown that uncles struck a chord with the target market, this quirky, likeable individual was dubbed Uncle Yaris. Toyota's other goal — to reach the young male demographic — was accomplished by building a strong personality for the Yaris (giving it a dominating presence in the category) and by challenging male buyers to consider Yaris as being different from the usual, rather feminine sub-compact.

The online video for the Yaris featured young people text-messaging their friends and showing the generous amounts of cargo space the Yaris offered. The obviously "cool crowd" and upbeat music was attractive to younger car buyers. The micro-site **yaris.ca** also featured an online journal to further engage the target market.

The TV, print, online, and out-of home advertising seemed to have raised considerable awareness since the microsite **yaris.ca** received almost 72,000 unique visitors in its first 14 days. Yaris sales were so brisk in the first month that it allowed Toyota to achieve 11.9 percent market share in October 2005. Even more impressive, Toyota sales were up 6.2 percent in October 2005 in a market that was down 3.8 percent!

Toyota ran ads in *Exclaim! Magazine* whose 400,000 readers consist mostly of 18-34 year olds. Since attracting first-time car buyers was another of Toyota's goals, the magazine seemed to be the perfect fit. The launch campaign included a CD compilation of 19 of Uncle Yaris' favourite tunes. In late September 2005, 10,000 of these free CDs were distributed in 20 different venues in Toronto — before most people even knew that the Yaris was a car.

The quirky Uncle Yaris and the appeal of the print and TV advertising captured the attention of the target audience for Yaris. The plan is to hold that attention for the long term.

QUESTIONS:

1. Do you think that the quirkiness of the Uncle Yaris character, together with the appeal of the print and video advertising, got the attention of the target audience for the Yaris?
2. Do you believe that this approach can hold that attention for the longer term?

SOURCES: "Outstanding new campaigns" by Annette Bourdeau, *Strategy Magazine*, November 2005, p. 24; "Annette Bourdeau, Retail: man on a mission — David Brimson, Toyota Canada's national manager, PR and advertising," *Strategy*, December 2005, p.19; "Sarah Dobson, Toyota pushes Yaris to first-time buyers," *Marketing Magazine Online*, marketingmag.ca, October 26, 2005; www.yaris.ca.

With these tasks completed, the firm can begin formulating an advertising campaign. The steps in developing a campaign are: defining objectives; establishing a budget; creating a message; selecting media; and evaluating the campaign's effectiveness.

Defining objectives

The purpose of advertising is to sell something — product, service, idea, person, or place — either now or later. This goal is reached by setting specific objectives that can be expressed in individual ads that are incorporated into an advertising campaign. Recall again from the buying-decision process discussed in Chapter 2 that buyers go through a series of stages from unawareness to purchase. Therefore, the immediate objective of an ad may be to move target customers to the next stage in the hierarchy, from awareness to interest, for example. Note also that advertising seldom is the only communications tool used by a firm. Rather, it is typically one part of a strategy that may also include personal selling, sales promotion, a company Web site, and other tools. Therefore, the objective of advertising may be to "open doors" for the sales force.

Specific advertising objectives will be dictated by the firm's overall marketing strategy. Typical objectives are:

- ***Support personal selling:*** Acquaint prospects with the seller's company and products, easing the way for the sales force.
- ***Improve dealer relations:*** Wholesalers and retailers like to see a manufacturer support its products.
- ***Introduce a new product:*** As well as being made aware of new products, consumers need to be informed about line extensions that make use of familiar brand names.
- ***Expand the use of a product category:*** Attempt to lengthen the season for a product (as Lipton did for iced tea); increase the frequency of replacement (as Fram and Purolator did for oil filters); or increase the variety of product uses (as Arm & Hammer and Cow Brand did for baking soda). Sometimes, it's really the same use but for a different group. Repackaging a product can also alter the advertising message.
- ***Counteract substitution:*** Reinforce the decisions of existing customers and reduce the likelihood that they will switch to alternative brands.

Establishing a budget

Once a marketing communications budget has been established (as discussed in Chapter 13), it must be allocated among the various activities making up the overall program. In the case of a particular brand, a firm may wish to have several ads, as well as sales promotion and public relations activities (directed at different target audiences) all under way at the same time.

The great dot-com boom and bust of the late 1990s illustrated what can happen to communications budgets when some fundamentals are not handled well. Many start-ups at the time ran into great budgeting difficulties, since many were unknown and spent heavily to gain attention and build market share. For example, Vancouver-based Savingumoney.com was launched as a new firm with a new concept: Instead of sending out promotional coupons to consumers, consumers would be asked to surf to the company's Internet site to select and print coupons in which they were interested. The firm, being completely unknown, set a number of communications goals, starting with selection of the company name, Savingumoney.com, as one way of introducing the concept of an electronic coupon.

Next, awareness and interest had to be generated to attract companies to supply coupons and consumers to use the coupons. The conundrum was that attracting each required the presence of the other. The company had to promote and position itself effectively and this

Frito Lay Targets Asian and South Asian Snackers

The Problem

Canada's salty snack food market is worth $1.1 billion, and 50 percent of that market is accounted for by potato chips. Market research firm NPD says that 32 percent of Canadians eat potato chips at least once a week and over half the sales are regular or plain flavoured chips. But there is growing evidence that all Canadians are seeking out more exotic flavours — particularly the "heavy user" potato chip consumer, 18-24 year olds. Frito Lay Canada wants a bigger share of the market and developed a unique way to get it.

The Primary Target

The initial approach taken was to target Canada's Asian and South Asian population, 6.6 percent of Canada's total population, and half of the total visible minority population (13.4 percent) for new product development. According to Dale Hooper, vice-president in charge of brand marketing at Frito Lay Canada, "...(in Asia)...they have a plethora of different snacking options — nuts, meats, those kinds of things are much bigger from an Asian perspective. So the challenge for us was to find the perfect intersection between the flavours and tastes they like and something Western, which is the potato chip."

The Product

Frito Lay created and tested 40 different potato chip recipes with flavours ranging from seaweed, cucumber, and green tea to wasabi and spicy curry, and settled on the latter two.

The Primary Objective

To launch the two new flavours in the Vancouver and Toronto markets where they expect good acceptance from the Asian and South Asian communities since both communities are "heavy snackers" and underserved by mainstream food companies.

The Secondary Objective

Since both cities are ethnically cosmopolitan and accustomed to a variety of "ethnic food" flavours, Frito Lay hopes to convert mainstream Canadian chip snackers to these two new flavours. Success in meeting this objective would then allow Frito Lay to take the products to the national market.

The Advertising Task

Prior to launching the new flavour lines, Frito Lay began running TV and print ads in Mandarin in order to get the attention of Chinese consumers. The ads featured Frito Lay regular and Stax chips, and resulted in a greater awareness of the product category and the Frito Lay brands as well as increased sales.

Following up on these ads, the new flavours were introduced. An important objective of the new ads was to educate consumers in general about the flavours. Mr. Hooper understands that the average Canadian has straightforward tastes and that "...there are Canadians who don't know what wasabi is, so we'll teach them."

SOURCE: Adapted from Andy Hoffman, "Frito Lay plans to spice up life with new chips," *The Globe and Mail*, February 21, 2006, p. B3.

requires a little more consideration than creating banner ads on a couple of Web sites. The target for electronic coupons, however, didn't appear to be a very good match with the typical Web-savvy shopper. The new coupons, which were essentially the already familiar and widely distributed ones used for traditional everyday products, differed only in their mode of delivery. The clippers of such coupons were largely female and skewed to a mature age category (45 to 54) — hardly the typical Web shopper.

A $6 million campaign was designed to convey the essence of Savingumoney.com's positioning — "Coupons online for just about anything." The campaign was also aimed at cultivating an engaging brand image: friendly, helpful, and just a little on the clever side. This budget was about a hundred times the original budget used when the site was quietly launched the previous year. Aside from some online advertising, the linchpin for the campaign was newspapers — this allowed a broad reach (very critical), flexibility, and fast turnaround times. Television was used in some U.S. markets where significant coupon offerings were available. Ads were designed to look like a coupon — with the depiction of a dotted line and scissors. Images included a completely bare room with an offer for "free burglar alarm installation." Another showed a seagull and the tag line "20% off dry-cleaning."[3]

We see here a set of objectives, tasks defined, and a $6 million budget drawn up and spent on the various media selected to carry out these tasks. Sorry that we can't report happy results, or any results — Savingumoney.com is no longer in business. While the budgeting process followed was reasonable, it was based on flawed assumptions, flawed research, or both. Perhaps the concept offered no consumer value, or the wrong target market was chosen, or the budget was too small, or the media plan was flawed, or the execution was faulty. Many dot-com firms suffered the same fate at the time with much larger budgets. Perhaps the budget was not the essential problem.

Many firms, particularly smaller ones, find the establishment of an advertising budget to be a very difficult exercise. This is because many businesspeople find it difficult to measure the payback from advertising and therefore don't feel that they are in a position to decide where to place their advertising dollars to get the greatest return. The result is that a lot of advertising money is wasted, and many companies probably pay much more than they should for effective advertising.

Creating a message

attention
Getting people to notice your message.

influence
The ability to cause a change in a person's beliefs, attitudes, or intentions.

Whatever the objective of an advertising campaign, the individual ads must accomplish two things: get and hold the **attention** of the intended audience, and **influence** that audience in the desired way. Remember that the ultimate purpose of advertising is to sell something and that the ad itself is a sales message. The ad may be a fast-paced sales talk, as in a direct-action TV ad by a car dealership. It may be a very long-range, low-key message, as are many institutional ads. Whatever the method, the goal is to sell something sooner or later.

Attention, getting people to notice your message, can be achieved in many ways (recall the discussion of perception in Chapter 2). The most common approach is to present material in an unexpected or surprising way or to use an unconventional technique to capture the attention of the audience. Thus, a print ad may be mostly white space or a television commercial might show the product in an unusual setting or address a topic from a new perspective. Quizno's Subs gets attention when it features Don Cherry in its TV and print ads. A well-known Canadian sports personality like Cherry can have huge appeal to a target audience who has grown up with him. Some advertising for social programs, such as anti-smoking campaigns and appeals against drinking and driving, uses dramatic emotional content to shock viewers and get their attention.

BACK TO THE TOP

Those companies that are sponsors of the Vancouver Winter Olympics will develop a special Olympic advertising strategy that will be reflected in the appearance and content of their advertising that leads up to and runs during the Olympics.

appeal
The reason, justification, or argument presented in an advertisement to cause a message receiver to be influenced.

If the ad succeeds in getting the audience's attention, the advertiser has a few seconds to communicate a message intended to influence beliefs and/or behaviour. The message has two elements: the **appeal** and the execution. The appeal in an ad is the reason or justification for believing or behaving. It is the benefit that the individual will receive as a result of accepting the message.

Some advertisers mistakenly focus their appeal on product features or attributes. They either confuse attributes with benefits or assume that if they present the product's attributes, the audience will infer the correct benefits. Telling customers that a cereal contains fibre (an attribute) is much less meaningful than telling them that, because it contains fibre, consuming it reduces the possibility of colon cancer (the benefit). Common appeals or benefits and examples of product categories in which they are frequently used include:

- Health (food, non-prescription drugs).
- Social acceptance (cosmetics, health and beauty aids).

- Material success (automobiles, investments).
- Recognition (clothing, jewellery).
- Sensory pleasure (movies, candy).
- Saving time (prepared foods, convenience stores).
- Peace of mind (insurance, tires).

Execution means to combine in a convincing, compatible way the feature or device that gets attention with the appeal. An appeal can be executed in different ways. Consider the ways you could communicate the benefit of reliable performance in a home appliance — presenting operating statistics, obtaining the endorsement of a respected person or organization, collecting testimonials from satisfied owners, or describing the meticulous manufacturing process. Rather than doing any of these, Maytag opted for "the lonely repairman," an amusing and memorable execution that gets attention and conveys the benefit of reliability.

Creating an advertisement involves writing the copy, selecting the illustration (for visual media), preparing the visual or verbal layout, and reproducing the ad for the selected media. The copy in an ad is all of the written or spoken material in it — it's the words. Copy in a print ad includes the headline, coupons, advertiser's identification, and the main body of the message. In a broadcast ad, the copy is the script.

advertising media
The communications vehicles (such as newspapers, radio, and television) that carry advertising.

For visual ads, the illustration is a powerful feature. The main points to consider about illustrations are (1) whether they are totally appropriate to the product advertised and (2) despite the adage "A picture is worth a thousand words," whether the illustration represents the best use of the space. The layout is the physical arrangement of all of the elements in an advertisement. In print ads, it is the appearance of the page. For television, the layout is the set, as well as the positioning of actors and props. The layout of a radio ad is the sequence in which information is presented. A good layout can hold interest as well as attract attention. It should lead the audience through the entire ad in an orderly fashion.

The cost of creating an ad can vary from almost nothing for a local radio spot written by the staff at a radio station to as much as $500,000 or even more for a complex television commercial. In recent years, production costs for network TV ads have escalated dramatically. As a result, fewer commercials are being made, and they are kept on the air longer or are modified to create a number of variations.

Does the appeal of these ads capture your attention?

Selecting media

In describing the steps in developing an advertising campaign, we discussed creating an advertising message before describing the selection of **advertising media** in which to place the ad. In reality, these decisions are made simultaneously. The appeal and the target audience determine both the message and the choice of media. The following discussion focuses on selecting appropriate media in which to place advertising.

Advertisers need to make decisions at each of three successive levels to determine which specific advertising medium to use:

1. Which type of medium will be used — newspaper, television, radio, magazine, or direct contact through mail or the Internet? What about the prominent media such as billboards, specialty items, and blog and podcast sites?

2. Which category of the selected medium will be used? Television has network and cable and a host of different channels; magazines include general-interest (*Maclean's*, *Time*) and special-interest (*Chatelaine*, *Ski Canada*, *Wallpaper**) categories; and there are national as well as local newspapers. On the Internet, there are e-magazines, news sites, and a variety of retail and general-purpose portals from which to choose.

3. Which specific media vehicles will be used? An advertiser who decides first on radio and then on local stations must determine which stations to use in each city.

Here are some general factors that influence media choice:

- ***Objectives of the ad:*** The purpose of a particular ad and the goals of the entire campaign influence the choice of which media to use. If the campaign goal is to generate appointments for salespeople, the company may rely on direct mail or telephone contact. If an advertiser wants to produce quick action, newspaper or radio may be the medium to use.
- ***Audience coverage:*** The audience reached by the medium should match the geographic area in which the product is distributed. Furthermore, the selected medium should reach the desired types of prospects with a minimum of wasted coverage. Wasted coverage occurs when an ad reaches people who are not prospects for the product. Many media — even national and other large-market media — can be targeted at small, specialized market segments. *Maclean's* magazine publishes regional editions with different ads in its Atlantic, Ontario, and Western editions, as well as a French-language edition for Québec. As well, many U.S. magazines print "split-runs" to allow for some separate editorial content and advertising specifically for Canadian audiences.
- ***Requirements of the message:*** The medium should fit the message. Food products, floor coverings, and apparel are best presented visually. If the advertiser can use a very brief message (the rule of thumb is six words or less), as is common with reminder advertising, billboards may be a suitable medium — provided, of course, that the preferred audience includes people who are likely to drive or walk by the billboards.
- ***Time and location of the buying decision:*** The medium should reach prospective customers when and where they are about to make their buying decisions. Research shows that radio scores the highest in immediacy of exposure: More than 50 percent of adults were last exposed to radio within one hour of making their largest purchase of the day. This factor highlights one of the strengths of place-based advertising such as in-store ads (on shopping carts and in the aisles of supermarkets) — reaching consumers at the actual time of purchase.
- ***Media cost:*** The cost of each medium should be considered in relation to the budget available to pay for it and its reach or circulation. For example, the cost of network television exceeds the available funds of many advertisers.

cost per thousand (CPM)
The media cost of gaining exposure to one thousand people with an ad.

The **cost per thousand (CPM)** people reached ("M" is the Roman numeral for a thousand) is a standard measure routinely provided to prospective advertisers by all media. It allows an advertiser to compare costs across media. The CPM is computed as follows:

$$\text{CPM} = \frac{(\text{ad cost} \times 1{,}000)}{\text{circulation}}$$

For example, let's assume that the advertising rate for a full-colour, one-page ad in *Holiday Getaways*, a magazine with an international circulation, is \$42,000 and the circulation is 1,200,000. Therefore, the CPM for the magazine is:

$$\text{CPM} = \frac{(\$42{,}200 \times 1{,}000)}{1{,}200{,}000} = \$35$$

Of course, it's essential to estimate what proportion of all people reached are truly prospects for the advertiser's product. If an advertiser is interested only in females over 50 years of age, we might find that there are 650,000 *Holiday Getaways* readers in this category. Therefore, we would have to calculate a weighted CPM:

$$\text{Weighted CPM} = \frac{(\$42{,}200 \times 1{,}000)}{650{,}000} = \$64.62$$

PAGE UP!

1. What tasks must management complete before designing an advertising campaign?
2. What are the five steps in developing an ad campaign?
3. Name the different types of media used to advertise products and services.

Beyond these general factors, management must evaluate the advertising characteristics of each medium it is considering. We have chosen the term characteristics instead of advantages and disadvantages, because a medium that works well for one product is not necessarily the best choice for another product. To illustrate, a characteristic of radio is that it makes its impressions through sound and imagination. The roar of a crowd, running water, the rumbling of thunder, or screeching tires can be used to create mental images quickly and easily. But radio will not do the job for products that benefit from colour photography. Let's examine the characteristics of the major media.

MARKETING AT WORK — 14-2: STRATEGY

New Media, New Ways to Connect?

With 67 percent of Canadians now accessing the Internet through high speed, and with over 13 million wireless subscribers in Canada, advertisers have to think about how they will reach their audiences. It's not even a matter of new media taking over from old formats. Canadians still watch TV, listen to the radio and read magazines. Advertisers will have to use combinations of traditional and new media to reach Canadians who are on the move and adopting new technologies at an increasing rate.

Enter the blog and the podcast. Blogs were originally thought of as a place for people devoted to the Internet. However, blogs have gained momentum, and, due to their informal nature and low publishing barriers, blog information tends to be particularly timely. However, there are concerns about advertising on blogs since the content is not moderated. Podcasting is a way of publishing sound files to the Internet, allowing subscribers to feed and receive new content automatically. There are increasing numbers of podcasts on the Web with Canadian radio stations like CHUM and Corus launching beta versions. Since 67 percent of Canadians access the Internet via high speed and with the increasing number of MP3 players, podcasting will become even more popular with Canadian audiences and offers up new advertising opportunities.

Cellphones are used for more than just talking — the popularity of camera phones is a testament to that. Text messaging is popular amongst 15- to-19-year-olds and advertisers are finding ways to use text messaging in their campaigns. One of the most common ways is to have a text message code on print advertising that the consumer can use to download coupons and other promotional offers.

QUESTIONS:

1. Can communication strategies be the same or different given these technological developments? Do marketers still need to choose the right media for their message and audience?
2. Will these new channels of communication and, surely, more on the way as technology develops, change the challenge or just make it more complex?

SOURCE: *2006, Media Digest.* Published by *Marketing Magazine* as compiled by TVB from Statistics Canada, CRTC, CNA, CCNA/Les Hebos du Québec, Magazines Canada, CARD, CAN, Tele-Direct, Canada Post, IAB, and industry estimates.

Newspapers As an advertising medium, newspapers are flexible and timely. They account for the largest portion of total advertising dollars spent in Canada and can be used to cover a single city or a number of urban centres. The daily *National Post* and *The Globe and Mail*, while headquartered in Toronto, are printed regionally and distributed nationally.

While newspapers are attractive to a national advertiser, they remain the principal advertising vehicle for local advertisers, particularly when they are used as the distribution vehicle for advertising flyers. Ads usually can be inserted on one day's notice and can be cancelled on a few days' notice. Newspapers can give an advertiser intense coverage of a local market because a very large percentage of consumers read newspapers. Also, because they're produced locally, the ads can be adapted to local audiences and to social and economic conditions. Circulation costs per prospect are low. On the other hand, the life of a newspaper advertisement is very short. High-quality colour printing has improved the visual impact of this medium, allowing for more appealing graphic representations.

Television Television is probably the most versatile and the most rapidly changing of all media. It makes its appeal through both the eye and the ear — products can be demonstrated as well as explained. It offers considerable flexibility in the geographic market covered and the time of message presentation. By making part of its impression through the ear, television can take advantage of the personal, dramatic impact of the spoken word. Because the Olympics is one of the most-watched events on television, sponsors of the Vancouver Olympics will invest large amounts of money in television advertising.

But television can be an extremely expensive medium. The message is not permanently recorded for the message receiver. The prospect who is not reached the first time is lost forever, as far as a particular message is concerned. Television does not lend itself to long advertising copy, nor does it present pictures as clearly as magazines do. As with direct mail and radio, television advertisers must create their own audiences.

Cable has also changed television as an advertising medium. Canada is still among the most heavily "cabled" nations in the world, with more than 90 percent of homes in many urban areas wired for cable. Having cable television often allows Canadians access to upward of a hundred channels, many of which are American. Some "local" channels also carry ethnic-language programming appealing to very specific markets. Many channels carry specialized programming, including sports, weather, movies, youth programs, country music, arts and entertainment, and popular music formats. This increased access to television channels has resulted in a dramatic change in the nature and effect of television as an advertising medium.

fragmentation
The break-up of the mass audience for television or other media into smaller audiences as the result of technological innovations, such as the proliferation of channels, channel-zapping, skip devices, use of VCRs and DVD players.

In households with cable, television is now a much more focused medium. The sheer variety of channels has led to a situation described as **fragmentation**: Not only are fewer viewers tuned to a given channel compared with the past, but viewers regularly "zap" their way through the range of channels available, often when a commercial appears. This proliferation of channels through cable, coupled with the use of VCRs and DVD players, remote-control devices, commercial-skip devices, video games, and the Internet, has meant that the audience likely to be exposed to a television commercial is reduced, thereby limiting the effectiveness of television in reaching a mass market. As a result, some advertisers have begun to use shorter, more attention-getting commercials, or have moved some of their advertising budgets away from television to other media.

In the cluttered world of television, advertisers are constantly looking for ways to reach targeted audiences and to make their advertising messages stand out. Some large advertisers are experimenting with interactive television, which many feel will become a major element of media advertising in the near future. Others are developing infomercials, which are intended to stand out from other forms of advertising on television. Finally, some companies have moved their advertising from the mainstream television networks to specialty channels in order to increase the likelihood of reaching their targeted audiences. Advertising on such specialty cable channels as CBC Newsworld, The Weather Network, MétéoMédia, TSN, Outdoor Life Network, CMT, MuchMusic, MusiquePlus, YTV, Bravo, Showcase, and Vision TV reaches millions of viewers every day in Canada. The result is that television is fast becoming much more of a targeted medium and less of a mass medium to reach mass audiences.[4]

Television audiences have become more fragmented and broadcasters have more competition than ever before. With the latest generation of wireless devices, regular TV programs, and some specialized for these portable receivers and players — as well as some advertising — are beginning to become available and popular in certain market segments.

Concern about television viewing also arises from increasing Internet usage. While many are using the Internet for more reasons, this concern arises over increasing usage by 12- to 17-year-olds. This age group spends considerable amounts of time on the Web for entertainment purposes. Since this is an important consumer group, and if group members are spending more time somewhere on the Internet, then they are not watching TV advertisers' carefully designed ads placed just for them! While Nielsen Media Research says that levels have remained the same since 1996 — at about 16 hours per week — other youth-oriented research groups (Youth Culture and Corus Entertainment) believe there is cause for concern. Some suggest multi-tasking is the answer, but if the teen target is using the computer while watching TV, is the advertising message getting through?[5]

Magazines Magazines are an excellent medium when high-quality printing and colour are desired in an ad. Magazines can reach a national market at a relatively low cost per reader. Through special-interest or regional editions of general-interest magazines, an advertiser can reach a selected audience with a minimum of waste circulation. Magazines are usually read in a leisurely fashion, in contrast to the haste with which other print media are read. This feature is especially valuable to the advertiser with a lengthy or complicated message. Magazines have a relatively long life, anywhere from a week to a month, and a high pass-along readership.

BACK TO THE TOP

With less flexible production schedules than newspapers, magazines require ads to be submitted several weeks before publication. In addition, because they are published weekly or

MARKETING AT WORK 14-3: STRATEGY

Supporting TV with New Tools

Let's look at the Olympics again — after all, the Winter Games in Vancouver aren't until 2010. While TV used to be a primary media vehicle in general and particularly for large events like the Super Bowl and the Olympic Games, it is now one medium in a portfolio in which other media are gaining more and more attention and being used more and more strategically.

The Vancouver Organizing Committee of the 2010 Winter Games has already picked up $500 million selling Games rights to a handful of Canadian sponsors including HBC, Bell Canada, and the Royal Bank. These sponsors plan to use their Games platform in a varied number of ways. Experts calculate that for every dollar a sponsor pays for Olympic rights, it must spend another $4 to make that sponsorship investment pay off.

General Motors Canada, while it will be relying on traditional advertising to draw attention to its sponsorship, will use more and more unconventional tools as the 2010 games draw closer. Tom Laurie of GM Canada says that, "...television certainly delivers the biggest audience over a short period of time... however, things like the Internet are going to be there on a consistent basis and are going to deliver the message every day. I think you have to exercise every one of your communications channels because they all contribute something different."

Bell Canada is using its beaver "icons" in all its advertising media. It is running online contests, hosting events in Whistler, sending 'street teams' to malls where they install Olympic medal presentation platforms and take mall visitors' photos. According to Bell's VP of corporate marketing, "as mobility and cellphones give more bandwidth to do different things, it's [advertising] going to become much more experiential."

QUESTIONS:

1. What do you think is the reason for the strategy change referred to here?
2. Is it possible that the 'new tools' will begin to result in message overkill?

SOURCE: Adapted from Keith MacArthur, "Sponsors expand efforts to market Olympic cachet," *The Globe and Mail*, February 21, 2006, p. B7.

monthly, it is more difficult to use topical messages. Magazines are often read at times or in places — on planes and in doctors' offices, for instance — far removed from where a buying impulse can be acted on.

Direct contact Direct mail and direct e-mail has probably become the most personal and selective of all of the media and, if properly used, can do much to develop strong consumer and customer relationships. Because direct mail reaches only the market that the advertiser wants to contact, there is little waste circulation. Articles or other editorial matter does not accompany direct mail unless the advertiser provides it. That is, most direct mail is pure advertising. As a result, a direct-mail ad creates its own circulation and attracts its own readers. The cost of direct mail per prospect reached is quite high, compared with that of other media, but other media reach many people who are not real prospects and thus have higher waste-circulation costs. A severe limitation of direct mail is the difficulty of getting and maintaining good mailing lists. Direct-mail advertising also suffers from the stigma of being classed as "junk mail."

The effectiveness of direct mail has been increased in recent years through the application of technology to the process of identifying prospects to whom advertising materials are to be mailed. Highly specialized mailing lists can be purchased from mailing-list brokers, but many firms are now able to produce their own highly targeted mailing and contact lists from their own databases. Buying lists can be expensive, but they do offer advertisers the ability to target precisely the groups in which they are interested. Many companies have developed their own mailing lists through an effective design of their internal information systems. For example, by capturing sales data in an appropriate way, a travel agency can produce a list of all of the clients who made business trips to Europe in the past year, or took vacations in the southern United States, or made more than 15 business trips. These individuals then represent target segments for special-interest mailings. Wastage is dramatically reduced, because the advertising reaches precisely those people who are most likely to be interested.

Technology, the Internet, and the development of databases have made many contributions to furthering direct-mail effectiveness. The refinement of database software, along with a better understanding of how to meaningfully combine demographic or customer data, has led many firms, both store and non-store retailers, to tailor it into a mix that works for their organizations. Customer relationship and loyalty programs allow retailers to maintain a lot of information on regular customers. These programs also allow a company to maintain a link or "personalized" connection to the consumer — not unlike cookie programs used by Internet retailers. Maintaining information on past consumers (those who have responded by mailing in cards, calling toll-free numbers, or visiting the company's Web site) provides a valuable target list for information regarding new products, services, or other information changes. These databanks can also be generated from delivery information, or simply by asking for name and postal code information at the cash register, which can be keyed into the terminal at the time of sale. This information can be used to generate a mailing list for flyers and other promotional information.

Bank of Montreal

The Bank of Montréal's First Canadian Funds (**www.bankofmontreal.com**) developed an interactive program on a disk to position its Intuition fund as the most appropriate education savings plan. In a few minutes, recipients could quickly calculate the funds required for their children's education and how they could get these funds. The program was a success, generating a response three-and-a-half times greater than was expected.[6]

While direct mail is widely regarded as one of the most cost-effective of advertising media, it is also one that must be managed very carefully. The effectiveness of a direct-mail advertising program is very heavily dependent on the accuracy of the mailing list being used. Some users of direct mail spend too little time on ensuring the accuracy of the mailing list, with the result that many people on the list may not be at all interested in the product or service (sound familiar?), while some will receive two or three mailing pieces because their names appear on the list in a number of different forms. When this occurs, people develop

GUEST MARKETER

RADIOlogy™

by Ralph van Dijk

Ralph van Dijk is co-founder of Eardrum, the U.K.'s most awarded radio specialist agency with offices in London and Sydney. Ralph has written and produced numerous campaigns for the world's largest advertisers, including Levis, Mastercard, Toyota, and Red Bull, as well as branding campaigns for the British, Australian and New Zealand radio industries. Formerly an agency copywriter in New Zealand, Ralph began specializing in radio advertising and moved to the U.K. to set up Eardrum in 1990. He recently moved to Sydney to set up Eardrum Australia.

"Watch Where You Point That Thing. It's Loaded!"

Oh, the glamour of Radio Advertising. The exotic locations, the flirty models, no wonder you got into advertising. But ignore it at your peril, because it's powerful stuff. The media rationale is very clear. Radio is well targeted, cost effective, portable and offers unique speed-to-market advantages. But that's nothing compared to radio's ability to illicit an emotional response in the consumer.

Listeners already have a close relationship with their favourite radio station. It's in tune with their lives and goes pretty much wherever they go. They aren't as suspicious of the content as they are of, say, TV and they accept that the ads are a part of the landscape.

Understanding the way listeners listen is fundamental in harnessing radio's power. Carl Jung, that famous Dutch footballer, believed that 3 percent of the human mind is made up of conscious thought and 97 percent subconscious thought. Most decisions and thoughts are derived from our subconscious. We act and react because we feel something, not because we think something.

This explains why — in the right hands — **RADIO** is so powerful as an advertising medium. More than any other medium, it is regarded as a friend and is therefore close to the listener's emotions. It gets under their skin and you reach the 97 percent of the listener that responds to feelings. At Eardrum, we call this understanding RADIOlogy, and it gives us an enormous opportunity to use radio to achieve all manner of marketing objectives.

Role of the Writers

E.T.A Hoffman, the 18th century writer/composer, said, "Hearing is seeing from the inside." When you think of radio in this way, you realize there is so much more to say than "great service and free parking!!"

Good, experienced creatives love working on radio — it's a very liberating medium. But so often, their ideas are not realized to their fullest extent. Creatives need to defend their ideas and insist on the best cast, musicians, and directors to realize them. Radio offers so much opportunity to stand out (and win awards), that teams should be fighting over the radio briefs.

The Script

The script is the key to getting your message into the hearts and minds of the listener. It needs to concentrate on the consumer's needs and aspirations, and not that of the advertiser. Then it should show them graphically and convincingly what the brand can do for them. Once you know **WHAT** you're saying, it's down to the copywriter to create **HOW** it's said — an idea that comes straight out of product or proposition and stands out from the surrounding ads.

Radio delivers a world of opportunity in scenes and characters. Every emotion is available, from hate to suspicion, love to hysteria. Despite this, 70 percent of all radio ads are comedy based. One reason we default to comedy so often is that humour equals entertainment and, with the line between advertising and programming blurred, there is a pressure for advertising to no longer feel like advertising.

It should be a form of entertainment, or even part of everyday life. What gives radio advertising such a bad name is that so much of it is "interruption marketing." Those days are over and we are now in an era of "permission" marketing, where consumers invite the message in. For that to be reality, our messages need to entertain as well as inform. So if you're going to run a funny ad, make sure it's really funny — because listeners will hear it again and again and again. Create three-dimensional characters; use a radio director to help you find extra layers, and **KEEP IT REAL**.

The Cast

The fact that the ears are sensitive to honesty fits with what consumers sometimes say about bad radio advertising — that the voices sound "artificial" or that the actors are "pretending." We need to be more genuine in our ads. If you ask your announcer to be unbelievably enthusiastic about your product, then, sure enough, people are unlikely to believe him/her. If we want the listener to believe our characters enough to zone in on what they're saying, we need to cast good actors, give good direction, and allow enough studio time to find out what works.

Why is casting so important to the success of your campaign? You have no pictures, so the voice conveys corporate image and personality, as well as all the information. Remember, radio is an intimate medium, get it right and it's like talking to a trusted friend. The commercial will draw the listener into a conversation and be more open and receptive than they would be toward any other medium. Get it wrong and it's like having an unwelcome guest at a party.

Too much radio ad-land is filled with bland, over-used voices. In the real world, no one speaks like Mr. & Mrs. Voice-Over Person. They are too false and intrusive for a personal medium like radio and you run the risk of cheapening the brand. We need calm, REAL-sounding voices that listeners can trust and relate to. Remember, your ad is up against the station's programming, which is full of people and music with real attitude. Reality TV has also tuned the nation's ears to real dialogue.

As George Burns famously said, "The secret to great acting is sincerity. Fake that and you got it made."

Brand Impression

Every radio ad influences the listener's impression of a brand, regardless of whether this is intended by the advertiser or not. Radio is "the word of mouth" medium, so you had better watch what you say and how you say it.

Brand Image vs. Brand Character

It's a subtle difference, and both image and character represent different ways of knowing the brand. Radio is good at brand character because it doesn't speak the language of image (which is largely a visual concept). It doesn't use glossy, aspirational imagery, and it speaks with a human voice. Consumers will be more inclined to form a relationship with a brand when they get to know its *character*.

So, how can brands connect with consumers better in this new model of the marketing universe? In his book *The New Marketing Manifesto*, John Grant explores some key principles to help encourage consumers to engage with brands and pull them into their world:

- Be **intimate** — get as close as possible to people's lives.
- Be **relevant** — tap into the needs, changing lives and mentality of your audience.
- Be **participative** — allow the active and media-literate audience to get involved in interesting ways.
- Be **consensual** — put the audience at the centre of your activities and make word of mouth your main medium.

Overall, these principles reflect a need to involve people in brand ideas that are relevant in their lives — a clear step forward from the traditionally one-dimensional approach of most image-based advertising.

"You Talkin' to Me?"

Reality TV, mobile phones, instant messaging — there is a global resurgence in dialogue. We've regained our interest in conversation. No other advertising medium does one-to-one word of mouth better than radio. Use it to connect individuals to your brand, and be rewarded with their custom.

a low opinion of the medium. In a study conducted for National Public Relations, 7 out of 10 respondents considered direct mail to be the least credible way for them to learn about a company's new product or service.

Radio During the last decades of the twentieth century, radio made a real comeback. Today, local radio (as contrasted with national networks) is especially strong. The medium accounts for just over 10 percent of all advertising revenues in Canada, attracting almost $840 million in sales annually.

Radio's big advantage is its relatively low cost. It also has tremendous reach — the ability to get to almost everybody. At the same time, with special-interest, targeted programming, certain radio stations can do a very effective job of reaching specific target market segments. In recent years, a number of Canadian stations began to pay more attention to the growing segment of the market in the 30- to 50-year-old age group. The result is that the top three formats in Canadian radio stations are country and western, adult contemporary, and news/talk. Specialty stations have emerged in many of the larger radio markets in Canada, ranging from Toronto's 680News news/talk, to Saskatoon's CFMC-FM adult contemporary, to Alberta's aboriginal station (CFWE).

Although radio is one of the more targeted of the mass media and can deliver an audience at a fairly low CPM, it does have its limitations. On the one hand, it makes only an audio impression, so it is of limited value when visual impact is needed. On the other hand, some advertisers who believe in the value of radio consider this to be one of radio's strong points — it is able to stimulate the imagination of the listener. Radio also does not have a captive audience, in that many people listen to the radio for "background" entertainment while they are working around the house, driving in their cars, or doing homework! The exposure life of a radio commercial is quite short, resulting in a need to deliver multiple exposures to gain impact.

Out-of-home advertising Out-of-home advertising, which includes billboards, posters, bus shelter ads, and electronic digital billboards, has a low cost per exposure and is able to reach a large percentage of the population. But, because it is typically seen by people "on the go," this category of advertising is appropriate only for brief messages. It is excellent for reminder advertising, and it carries the impact of large size and colour. Motion and three-dimensional figures can be incorporated into a billboard's design for increased attention-getting ability. Billboards provide flexibility in geographic coverage and intensity of market coverage within an area. However, unless the advertised product or service is widely used, considerable waste circulation will occur. Although the cost of reaching an individual person is low, the total cost of a national billboard campaign can be quite high. Finally, the landscape-defacing aspect of outdoor advertising has aroused considerable public criticism. Another issue is that posters and billboards have to be maintained by the companies that erected them if they are going to appeal to passing consumers.[7]

What Are Your Customers Reading?

RAZOR Magazine (**www.razormagazine.com**) is for men prepared to move beyond frat-house magazines such as Maxim, but not quite ready for their Esquire years. It offers cutting-edge articles, interviews, music, sports, extreme fitness, beautiful women, and depth.

RAZOR Media claims its readers are 80 percent male and 20 percent female, with a median household income of about $56,000 ($US) and median age of 26.

A one-third page spread runs, in U.S. dollars, $6,500; a full page, $14,500; and a two-page spread. $23,000. Premium options such as inside and back covers go for between $20,000 and $26,000. North American circulation is 300,000, with a readership of more than one million. *RAZOR* also has an online edition.

What would the average reader of *RAZOR Magazine* look like to marketers?

Architectural Digest (**www.archdigest.com**) is a global magazine that offers an exclusive look at the homes of influential men and women in the fields of entertainment, business and finance, fashion, literature, and the arts. Its distinctive brand of design journalism spans a wide range of styles from contemporary to traditional. Topics regularly include travel, shopping, automobiles, and technology.

Full-colour rates range, in U.S. dollars, from about $28,000 for a third of a page to more than $62,000 for a full page, and for covers, between $65,000 and almost $90,000. With a circulation of more than 800,000 (over 600,000 of those paid subscribers), advertisers can be sure their messages will be seen in a wide variety of upscale households. As well, professionals in the design industry would also represent many readers of such a publication. Most readers are in the United States, with fewer than 30,000 magazines sold in Canada and about 35,000 internationally. Online advertising opportunities are also available.

What products or services would benefit from advertising in *Architectural Digest*?

Wired magazine (**www.wired.com**) is the journal of record for the future. It speaks not just to high-tech professionals and the business-savvy, but also to the forward-looking, the culturally astute, and the simply curious. Each month, *Wired* covers the people, companies, and ideas that are transforming the way we live. It delivers incisive and resonant storytelling from some of the world's most provocative writers.

With a circulation of over half a million in North America, *Wired* magazine charges (in U.S. dollars) between $16,900 for a third of a page, $37,720 for a full page, and for full-colour advertising with covers, between $39,600 and $47,140. As with the others discussed, discount rates are available: An advertiser agrees to purchase space in multiple issues, earning a "bulk" price.

What types of variables would influence the different rates charged by *Wired* and the other publications discussed?

Specialty advertising An item of merchandise imprinted with the advertiser's name, message, or logo and given away free is specialty advertising. According to the Specialty Advertising Association International, more than 15,000 different items (from pens and baseball caps to coffee cups and calendars) are used in specialty advertising, and annual expenditures are more than $5 billion in North America. Specialty advertising is usually used in conjunction with other promotional activities, although it is sometimes used alone by firms with very small advertising budgets. Its greatest strength is its long life. Every time the specialty item is used, the advertising message is repeated.

The Internet and other emerging media Many advertisers are shifting budgets to Internet advertising to complement television, radio, newspaper as well as lesser-known media. But in these days of audience fragmentation, new media combinations, rather than the use of a single medium, are what savvy advertisers are aiming for.

- ***Internet:*** While it is pervasive and growing in all directions, it is really still emerging as shown in Table 14-1. Internet advertising growth continues and there is ample evidence that in addition to books, travel, music, and many small items, consumers are beginning to order large items such as appliances and large screen television sets from Web sites. Yahoo!, Google, and MSN portals generate much traffic and earn steadily increasing revenues from online advertising of all types. Canadian companies continue to launch and refine their Web sites but they are not keeping pace with their U.S. counterparts. The high cost of shipping across Canada and the lower population density of the Canadian marketplace make it more difficult for Canadian electronic retailers. Traditional retailers such as Canadian Tire and Sears have an advantage over pure Internet firms in maximizing their e-commerce potential, since they have established distribution networks. These companies send e-flyers that allow consumers to receive selective promotional information at their individual e-mail addresses.[8]

E-mail, whether permission based (recipients agree to contacts) or otherwise (mainly spam and unsolicited), continues to grow as an effective marketing and communication tool. While permission-based e-mail marketing has matured significantly, it is still experiencing some growing pains. Yet it is a fraction of the cost of direct mail and is credited with having response rates anywhere from 2 percent to 20 percent — well above the industry direct-mail norm. The numbers probably move toward the upper end of this when, instead of being used in isolation (and viewed as spam by recipients), it is used as part of an integrated marketing campaign in concert with direct mail.[9]

- ***Infomercials:*** Infomercials, which have been around for a while, are the lengthy television advertisements that generally run for up to 60 minutes and combine information with entertainment and product promotions. They have been popular in the United States for many years, and many have been beamed into Canada on U.S. channels. Infomercials often feature well-known presenters such as Cher, George Foreman, Suzanne Somers, and motivational speaker Tony Robbins, promoting everything from diet plans and personal-improvement programs to baldness remedies and the "Lean, Mean, Fat-Reducing Grilling Machine." While infomercials are not as widely used in Canada as they are in the United States, a number of companies, including the Royal Bank of Canada, have utilized this format.
- ***Place-based media:*** Some attractive target market segments, such as young professionals, teenagers, and dual-career families, have become increasingly difficult to reach through traditional advertising media. The solution is to place the advertising where the people are. Consequently, we have seen an increase in advertising in airports, shopping malls, waiting rooms, supermarkets, telephone booths, and even public washrooms. One approach to entertaining a captive audience has been the use of video screens in office building elevators.

Captivate Network

This can allow some segmentation, based on where the elevator is located. The Captivate Network (**www.captivate.com**) claims to have video screens located in the elevators of the most prestigious office towers in Canada and the United States, affording access to affluent, sophisticated consumers. Olympic sponsors will often have billboards and signage at prominent locations (such as at the bottom of ski hills) featuring their brands.

BACK TO THE TOP

Evaluating the advertising effort

In managing its advertising program, a company should carefully evaluate the effectiveness of previous ads and use the results to improve the quality of future ads. Shrinking profit margins and increasing competition — both foreign and domestic — force management to appraise all expenditures. Top executives want proof that advertising is worthwhile. They want to know whether dollars spent on advertising are producing as many sales as could be reaped from the same dollars spent on other marketing activities.

Difficulty of evaluation It is hard to measure the sales effectiveness of advertising. By the very nature of the marketing mix, all elements — including advertising — are so intertwined that it is nearly impossible to measure the effect of any individual element. Factors that contribute to the difficulty of measuring the sales impact of advertising are:

- ***Ads have different objectives:*** Although all advertising is ultimately intended to increase sales, individual ads may not be aimed at producing immediate results. Some ads simply announce new store hours or service policies. Other ads build goodwill or contribute to a company's image.
- ***Ads can have an effect over time:*** Even an ad designed to have immediate sales impact may produce results weeks or months after it appears. A consumer may be influenced by an ad but may not be able to act on it immediately. Or an ad may plant in the consumer's mind a seed that doesn't blossom into a sale for several weeks. It is very difficult to determine (with the exception of mail-order advertising) when a particular ad or campaign produced specific results.
- ***Measurement problems:*** Consumers usually can't say when or if a specific ad influenced their behaviour, let alone if it caused them to buy. At any rate, a consumer decision is rarely explained by a single factor.

Regardless of these problems, advertisers try to measure advertising effectiveness because they must — and some knowledge is better than none at all. An ad's effectiveness may be tested before it is presented to the target audience, while it is being presented, or after it has completed its run.

direct tests
Measures of the sales volume produced by an ad or an entire advertising campaign.

indirect tests
Measures of advertising effects that use something other than sales volume.

advertising recall
A measure of advertising effectiveness based on the premise that an ad can have an effect only if it is perceived and remembered.

Methods used to measure effectiveness Ad effectiveness can be measured directly or indirectly. **Direct tests**, which measure or predict the sales volume attributable to an ad or a campaign, can be used only with a few types of ads. Tabulating the number of redemptions of a reduced-price coupon incorporated in an ad will indicate its effectiveness. Coupons frequently are coded so that they can also be traced to the publications from which they came. Another direct test used to predict sales measures the number of enquiries received from an ad that offers additional information to prospects who call or write in.

Most other types of measures are **indirect tests** of effectiveness, or measures of something other than actual purchase behaviour. One of the most frequently used measures is **advertising recall.** Recall tests are based on the premise that an ad can have an effect only if it is perceived and remembered. Three common recall tests are:

- ***Recognition:*** Showing people an ad and asking if they have seen it before.

MARKETING AT WORK 14-4: TECHNOLOGY

Using Your Brain to Measure Effectiveness

Super Bowl football games have turned into advertising contests—not football contests. The Super Bowl has huge audiences and interest in the TV commercials (which also appear on assorted Web sites and are discussed on endless blogs and around endless water coolers) is rampant. Is it any wonder advertisers pay through the nose for a 30-second spot: In the U.S., about $2.5 million in 2006, up from $2.4 in 2005; in Canada, on the CanWest Global simulcast, $95,000 in 2006, up from $92,000 in 2005. In both countries, advertisers pay these prices to reach a large live audience, very valuable in the face of fragmentation, personal video recorders and remotes that enable 'commercial bypass.' Pepsi Cola Canada ran its 60-second spot for both countries in 2006; Labatt advertised Alexander Keith and six different Budweiser ads.

And what do the Super Bowl advertisers get besides the glory? There is usually a host of opinions from marketing experts and focus groups about which ads were most effective. But in 2006, the UCLA Ahmanson-Lovelace Brain Mapping Centre, with FKF Applied Research, a marketing firm, used functional magnetic resonance brain imaging on a sample that watched the ads to determine real underlying brain activity as opposed to what people say they like about an ad. On the assumption that a 'successful' ad should engage areas of the brain that deal with reward and empathy, two winning ads were the 'I'm going to Disney' ad and the Bud 'office' ad. Big flops were the Burger King and FedEx ads.

Aside from the ads themselves, which you can't see as you read this piece, what really stands out is the difference between what people say and what their brain activity seems to suggest. Some people lauded ads that showed little brain response in emotional, reward-related and empathy-related brain areas. People tend to tell you what they think you want to hear. Secondly, when ads are shown for a second time to the same subjects, the commercial elicits much weaker responses. The effects of repetition are not so straightforward. Thirdly, you will hear more about brain responses to communications as the cost of imaging is reduced and the cost of advertising increases.

QUESTIONS:

1. Is it important to know that people may not be telling you what they really think about an ad?
2. Do you think that pursuing this kind of research can result in better message design?

SOURCE: Adapted from Keith McArthur, "Super Bowl ad spots reach new pricing plateau," *The Globe and Mail*, February. 2, 2006 p. B4; Marco Iacoboni, "Who Really Won the Super Bowl?" *Edge, The Third Culture*, February 15, 2006.

- ***Aided recall:*** Asking people if they can recall seeing any ads for a particular brand.
- ***Unaided recall:*** Asking people if they can remember seeing any ads within an identified product category.

For broadcast media, this kind of testing can be conducted using a telephone survey, calling people at home within a few hours after an ad is aired, or after a campaign has been running for several weeks.

pre-test
An activity in which commercials in finished or nearly finished form are presented to panels of consumers in order to gauge their reactions.

Television ads are often tested before they are presented to the general public in what are called **pre-tests**. Commercials in finished or nearly finished form (to save production costs) are presented to panels of consumers for their reactions. This is often done in theatre settings, with the test ad shown along with other ads in the context of a regular TV program. After viewing the program and the ads, the viewers are quizzed about the commercial being tested.

A criticism of pre-tests is that the testing situation is unrealistic. The ads are often not in the final forms that the actual target audience would see, the research respondents have been invited to a theatre to participate, and the respondents are usually given an incentive for their involvement. The testers argue that since these factors exist across all commercials tested, they in effect "wash out," and the scores provide useful comparative information.

Refinements are constantly being made in advertising testing, and developments in areas such as laboratory test markets and computer simulations show promise. However, the complexity of decision-making, combined with the multitude of influences on the buyer, will continue to make measuring the effectiveness of advertising a difficult task.

Organizing for Advertising

A firm can manage its advertising in three ways:

- Develop an internal advertising department.
- Use an outside advertising agency.
- Use a combination of an internal department and an outside advertising agency.

Regardless of which alternative is selected, basically the same specialized skills are necessary to do the advertising job. Creative people are needed to prepare the copy, generate illustrative material, and design the layouts. Media experts are required to select the appropriate media, buy the time or space, and arrange for the scheduled appearance of the ads. Managerial skills also are essential to plan and administer the entire advertising program.

Internal departments

All of the advertising tasks, some of them, or just the overall direction, can be performed by an internal department. A company whose advertising is a substantial part of its marketing mix will usually have its own advertising department. Large retailers, for example, have their own advertising departments and many do not use advertising agencies at all.

Advertising agencies

advertising agency An independent company rendering specialized services in advertising in particular and in marketing in general.

Many companies, especially manufacturers of consumer products, use advertising agencies to carry out some or all of their advertising activities. An **advertising agency** is an independent company that provides specialized advertising services and may also offer more general marketing assistance, including public relations and media relations.

Advertising agencies plan and execute entire advertising and communications campaigns. They employ more advertising specialists than their clients do, because they spread the cost over many client accounts. A client company can benefit from an agency's experience gained from other products and clients. Many large agencies offer "full services," which include sales promotion and public relations, and they are frequently called on to assist in new-product development, package design, and selection of product names. In fact, some have become integrated agencies, offering services from strategic planning to market research and Web page design that previously were performed by other outside specialists or by the advertisers themselves.

Internal department and outside agency

Many firms have their own advertising department and also use an advertising agency. The internal advertising department acts as a liaison with the agency, giving the company greater control over this major expenditure. The advertising department approves the agency's plans and ads, is responsible for preparing and administering the advertising budget, and co-ordinates advertising with personal selling. It may also handle direct marketing, dealer displays, and other promotional activities if they are not handled by the agency.

PAGE UP!

1. Name some of the general factors affecting the choice of media for a company that wants to advertise.
2. Which medium is used most frequently by local advertisers?
3. What do advertising agencies do?

Key Terms and Concepts

advertising 404
advertising agency 425
advertising allowance 407
advertising campaign 409
advertising media 413
advertising recall 423
appeal 412
attention 412
business-to-business advertising 405
comparative advertising 406
consumer advertising 405
co-operative advertising 407
cost per thousand (CPM) 414
customer-service advertising 405
differential competitive advantage 407
direct-action advertising 405
direct tests 423
fragmentation 416
horizontal co-operative advertising 407
indirect-action advertising 405
indirect tests 423
influence 412
institutional (corporate) advertising 405
pioneering advertising 406
pre-tests 424
primary-demand advertising 406
public service advertising (PSA) 405
selective-demand advertising 406
vertical co-operative advertising 407

Questions and Problems

1. Businesses in different industries demonstrate quite different patterns in their advertising expenditures. Some are heavy advertisers on television, while others use no television at all. Some advertise heavily in daily newspapers, while others rely on magazines. Some firms, such as those in the consumer-products field, spend as much as 15 percent of sales on advertising, while others, including many industrial marketers, spend less than 1 percent. How do you account for such variations in advertising expenditures?
2. Which advertising medium would you recommend as the best one for each of these products?
   a. Park benches.
   b. Pantyhose.
   c. Tax-preparation service.
   d. A Web-based bookseller.
   e. Funeral services.
   f. Toys for young children.
   g. Plastic clothespins.
   h. Internet-based investment services.
   i. Pet grooming services
3. Many grocery product and chocolate bar manufacturers earmark a good portion of their advertising budgets for use in magazines. Is this a wise choice of media for these firms? Explain.
4. Why do department stores use newspapers more than local radio stations as an advertising medium?
5. Why is it worthwhile to pre-test advertisements before they appear in the media? How could a test market be used to pre-test an ad? (You may want to refresh your memory with a review of test marketing in Chapter 6.)
6. What procedures can a firm use to determine the level of sales that resulted from a direct-mail ad?
7. If a manufacturing firm hires an advertising agency, should it close its own advertising department? Should it consider any changes?

Hands-On Marketing

1. Bring to class four print ads or describe four radio or television ads that illustrate at least four of the specific advertising objectives outlined early in the chapter. As an alternative, find and describe two ads for the same brand that appear to be directed at different objectives.
2. Choose a brand that you like and perform a search on the Internet to find the brand's Web page. Then, flip through a magazine that you know advertises this brand and compare the two advertisements. What is different? The same? Discuss some of the challenges associated with advertising on the Web.

Back to the Top

Thinking back to the chapter opener, will Olympic advertising change for the 2010 Olympics in Vancouver? How should advertisers take advantage of the new and emerging media to get the most from their advertising efforts? What do you predict will be the biggest changes to advertising in 2010? What is it about the Olympics that garners such tough competition for sponsorships? Do you think this will change for future games as new communications options develop? Given the short time span of an Olympic Games — two weeks — what strategies can advertisers use to make the most of the mega bucks they spend for sponsorship rights? What can non-sponsors do to offset the exposure of their sponsoring competitors during this time?

Online *Learning* Centre

Want to get better grades, tips on how to study more effectively, and up-to-date information on happenings in the world of marketing? Then, visit the Online Learning Centre for practice tests, Study Smart software, *Marketing Magazine,* and much more! **www.mcgrawhill.ca/olc/sommers**

CHAPTER 15

Selling, Sales Promotion, and Public Relations

This chapter examines the selling function within an organization — what is involved in what is classically referred to as "sales." We will explore how the role of salespeople is changing in light of the changing customer and marketplace, as well as the technological environment in which most companies work. We will also examine the role of the sales function in contributing to the establishment of successful relationships with customers. Finally, we will explore two related functions that are important components of the broader marketing communications program of a firm: sales promotion and public relations. After studying this chapter, you should have an understanding of:

- The nature and advantages of the sales function in an organization.
- The variety and nature of sales positions.
- The new focus and changing patterns in professional selling.
- The sales process.
- Key issues in operating and evaluating sales force performance.
- The scope and management of sales promotions.
- The role of public relations and publicity in the marketing communications program.

Is This Selling?

Oscar Hornyik walked out of Ray Murphy's office, just a little bit confused. Oscar is a sales representative with Aliant, Atlantic Canada's largest telecommunications company, and he and his vice president, Alfred Whiffen, had just spent an hour talking with Ray Murphy and Paul Evoy, controller of Ray's company. Ray is the founder and CEO of Murphy's Pharmacies, Prince Edward Island's largest chain of independent drug stores.

Oscar had made a number of sales calls to Paul over the past year, but had never been able to get to see Ray. During his conversations with Paul, it became obvious that the existing telephone system that served Murphy's six stores was outdated and not capable of handling many new services that are available. But Oscar had not been successful in closing a deal for a new system.

As Alfred was making one of his regular visits to Aliant's office in Charlottetown, Oscar asked Paul a week or so ago if he could arrange a meeting when Alfred might meet Ray. That meeting was quickly arranged for 9 a.m. Tuesday.

After the usual introductions had been made, Alfred first commented on the attractive décor in the Murphy's stores and asked Ray what he tries to accomplish with this look. Alfred went on to ask, "What exactly would you say Murphy's stands for in the P.E.I. marketplace?" Obviously, this gave Ray an opening to comment on his view of a pharmacy and of Murphy's in particular. He talked about his passion for health education and the fact that society today is far too focused on a cure and not nearly enough on keeping healthy. To use his words, "We want to make people feel as well as they can feel."

The conversation went back and forth for more than 30 minutes as Ray expounded on the importance of health education, his plans for his business, and how his kids would take over some day. To Oscar's surprise, Alfred had not yet raised the important issue of the new phone system — when was he going to try to sell them that new system?

As the conversation wound down and Ray reminded them that he had another meeting at 10 a.m., Alfred got up to thank Ray and Paul for their time. Oscar was astounded when, shaking Alfred's hand, Ray turned to Paul and said, "About that new phone system, let's make that happen." Alfred's response was, "And we'll make sure that it supports your goal of making your customers feel as well as they can feel."

In this chapter, we will examine the sales function in Canadian companies, how it operates, and its role in the building of customer relationships. Selling is undergoing a dramatic change as customers increasingly take greater control of the interaction that they have with businesses. In fact, you may be surprised at the nature of the selling function in some firms. We will also look at two related marketing communications functions: sales promotion and public relations. These are important components in an integrated marketing communications program.

Nature of the Sales Function

sales function
The part of a company that is responsible for sales.

sales
The process of selling products and services to customers; usually involves sales personnel who interact with customers.

selling
The communication of information to persuade a prospective customer to buy a product, service, or idea. Increasingly being seen to include the offering of advice and the creation of solutions for customers.

The goal of all marketing efforts within a company or other organization is to increase profitable sales by satisfying consumers over the long run. The activity of sales personnel represents by far the major communications method used to reach this goal. The number of people employed in advertising is a small fraction of the number employed in sales. In many companies, sales salaries and expenses represent the largest single operating expense, often 8 to 15 percent of a company's total sales revenue. In contrast, advertising costs average 1 to 3 percent of revenue.

Let's make sure that we are clear on what we mean when we refer to the **sales function** in a firm. The word **sales** is used very widely within marketing, most often in an accounting sense to refer to the revenue that a company receives when it sells something. We also refer to making a sale, and we are going to talk about sales promotion later in this chapter. We refer to what salespeople do within a company as **selling**, or occasionally personal selling. This is the process of representing the company and its products and services to prospective customers. It is the part of a company or organization that is most in contact with the customer. We meet salespeople every day when we deal with companies, often face to face in a retail setting or on the telephone and through the Internet.

There is much discussion in many businesses these days concerning the role of sales or selling within marketing. As customers have access to more and more information, there is some suggestion that the role of sales persons is changing, that there is actually less selling to be done. In fact, there is good research evidence that many customers are actually rebelling against aggressive selling practices, opting to walk out of stores where the only interest of employees appears to be to try to sell something.[1]

As we will see in this chapter, sales or selling is a varied function, including such different jobs as retail furniture salespeople, pharmaceutical sales reps, and sales engineers for a chemical company. Sales personnel are very important in B2B marketing where they are selling to other companies and organizations. You and some of your friends may go into sales when you graduate. You could be working for a wide variety of companies and organizations, and you may or may not be engaged in actually trying to sell something; that is, in trying to convince customers to buy. The salesperson who serves you at a clothing store may not actually offer you assistance or advice, and may simply ring up the sale, but it is still considered a sales job. Similarly, many sales personnel today are called **customer-service representatives** and work in call centres.

customer-service representatives
Employees who represent the company to customers, usually providing advice and service over the telephone from call centres.

In Chapter 13, we discussed five factors that influence an organization's marketing communications mix — the target market, the objective, the nature of the product or service being promoted, the life-cycle stage of the product or service, and the budget available for promotion. Of the five factors, the sales function is likely to be responsible for a large portion of the marketing communications load when:

- The market is concentrated geographically, in a few industries, or in a few large customers. In this scenario, it is easier to contact people and actually meet them.
- The value of the product is not readily apparent to prospective customers. In other words, there are a lot of hidden factors to point out to them.

- The product has a high unit value, is quite technical in nature, or requires demonstration. Such products need the personal input of a salesperson to explain them, and they also are sufficiently high-priced that money can be spent on employing salespeople.
- The product must be fitted to an individual customer's need, as in the case of securities or insurance. In such a situation, the salesperson is needed to interpret the customer's need and to devise the right solution.
- The sale involves a trade-in. A salesperson is needed in this case to make an assessment of the value of the trade-in and to apply the value to the price of the item being bought. This is common in automobile sales.
- The product is in the introductory stage of its life cycle. Since the customer is often not familiar with the product and its features, a salesperson is needed to explain it.
- The organization does not have enough money for an adequate advertising campaign. Since mass advertising is costly, many start-up firms have to rely on the efforts of salespeople (often the owners) until they reach a stage of their development when they can afford to advertise widely. This is gradually becoming less important as the Internet provides companies with the ability to reach large numbers of customers at lower costs.

Advantages of selling

Selling involves the direct personal communication of information. This means that the sales effort can be more flexible than other communications tools. Salespeople can tailor their presentations to fit the needs and behaviour of individual customers. They can see their customers' reaction to a particular sales approach and make adjustments on the spot.

Also, selling usually can be focused on prospective customers, thus minimizing wasted effort. In contrast, advertising messages are usually directed at much larger audiences that contain many who are not realistic prospects.

Another advantage of selling is that its goal usually is to actually secure a sale. Other forms of promotion are designed to move a prospect closer to a sale. Advertising, for example, often has the less-ambitious goal of attracting attention, providing information, and arousing desire. Aside from retail and direct-response advertising, it is rarely the sole factor responsible for stimulating buying action or completing the sale or transaction.

Products like these usually require a salesperson to explain features.

On the other hand, a full-fledged sales effort is costly. Even though a well-organized selling function can minimize wasted effort, the cost of developing and operating a sales force is high. Another disadvantage is that a company may often find it difficult to attract and retain the quality of salespeople needed to do the job. A successful career in sales requires a certain personality; otherwise, the person most often does not enjoy the job — and customers often don't enjoy the interaction either! At the retail level, many firms have abandoned the use of sales staff and shifted to self-service for this very reason. More recently, many firms have adopted an e-commerce approach to dealing with customers, delegating the sales function to a Web site, call centre, or some combination of the two.

Scope of the sales function

inside selling
The kind of selling in which customers come to the salespeople; primarily face-to-face retail selling, but also includes phone-in ordering.

proactive selling
A situation in which the selling effort is initiated by the salesperson, who actively tries to interest the customer in buying.

reactive selling
A situation in which the sales process is initiated by the customer and the salesperson simply processes the sale.

outside selling
The kind of personal selling in which salespeople go to the customers, making contact by mail, telephone, or face to face.

outside sales force
A group of sales reps engaged in field selling; that is, selling in person at a customer's place of business or home.

Elements of selling can be found in almost every human interaction: When a recent marketing graduate tries to convince a human resources specialist at Research in Motion to recruit her, we often suggest that she has to "sell" herself; when a junior manager tries to convince a senior executive to change the company's approach to advertising, we observe that he is trying to "sell" the idea up the line; when your friends try to convince you to attend a movie with them, they are trying to "sell" you on the idea.

There are two kinds of sales roles, as shown in Figure 15-1. One is where customers come to the salespeople. Called **inside selling**, it primarily involves retail selling. In this kind of selling, we also include the thousands of employees who work in call centres across the country and who take orders over the telephone. This, too, is retail selling because it involves sales to the end-consumer. By far, most salespeople in Canada fall into this first category.

Regardless of whether face-to-face or technology-based interaction occurs between the customer and the salesperson, there are two distinct categorizations of inside selling, the first of which may be termed **proactive selling.** This involves an overt attempt on the part of the salesperson to convince the customer to buy. In such a situation, the selling effort is usually initiated by the salesperson and a creative process is followed to interest the customer in buying. This is the kind of selling that is often associated with automobile, furniture, and higher-end clothing sales. In situations in which the salesperson has to tailor the sales initiative to address specific customer needs and characteristics, creative selling is at work. Advice and information is often conveyed as the salesperson attempts to convince the customer to buy the product or service.

In many other cases, however, customers already know what they want to buy, or the purchase is so uncomplicated that little or no input is needed from salespeople. This is the situation in much of retail today, particularly in self-service environments such as supermarkets. We label this kind of selling **reactive selling**, as the salesperson does not actively have to sell, but simply processes the sale once the customer has decided.

In the other kind of selling situation, known as **outside selling**, salespeople go to the customer, as illustrated in our chapter opener where Oscar and Alfred called on Murphy's Pharmacies in their offices. Most sales forces operate outside the firm and usually represent producers, wholesalers or service companies that are selling to business customers and not to end consumers. Thus, we tend to associate the concept of an **outside sales force** with B2B marketing, as in the case of the telecommunications salesperson in our chapter opener or the

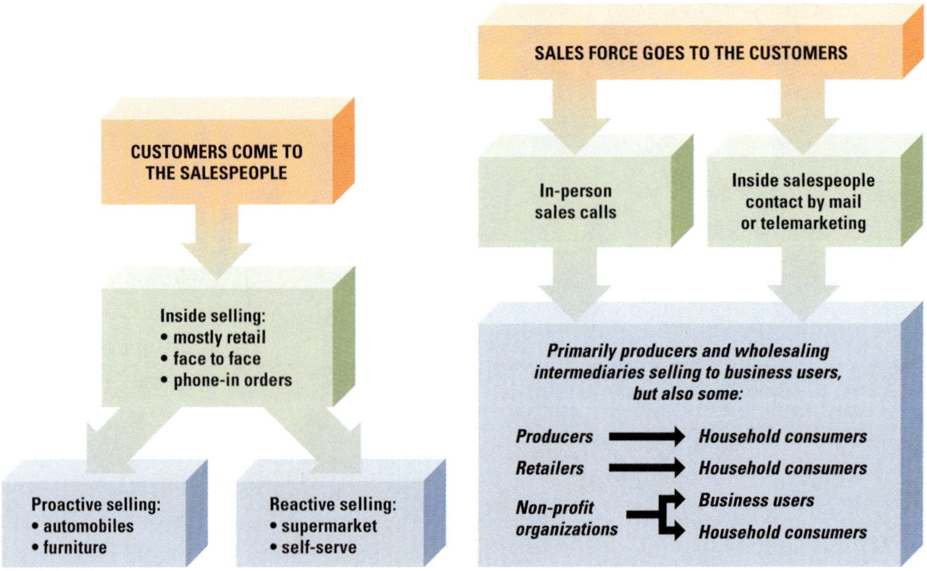

Figure 15-1: Scope of the Sales Function

sales reps for food manufacturing companies who sell to buyers at Loblaws, Overwaitea and Sobeys. However, in our definition of an outside sales force we also include: (1) producers whose representatives sell directly to household as well as business customers, for example, insurance companies such as Great-West Life, and in-home sellers, often called Consultants, such as those for Pampered Chef Products (**www.pamperedchef.ca**), Avon (**www.avon.ca**) or Mary Kay cosmetics (**www.marykay.com**); (2) representatives of retail organizations, such as those from home heating, home decorating, and renovations contractors, and also vacuum cleaner companies; and (3) representatives of non-profit organizations, for example, charity fund-raisers and workers for political candidates. Although this latter group is not typically thought to be in sales, their employees and volunteers who solicit donations are actually fulfilling a sales role.

BACK TO THE TOP

Pampered Chef
Avon
Mary Kay

A telephone-based sales function lies somewhere between inside and outside selling. It may also involve either proactive or reactive selling. The practice of **telemarketing** usually has salespeople engaged in proactive selling, because it involves outbound calling to prospective customers. Outbound telemarketing involves telephone sales representatives who call customers and attempt to interest them in the purchase of a product or service. Such an approach to selling became very popular in recent years, at least with sellers, based on the existence of large customer databases that are used to generate customer names. But, it is becoming very difficult for telemarketers to reach customers in their homes as many screen calls or do not have landline telephones. Telemarketing has also become increasingly unattractive to customers as calls are usually unsolicited and are considered by many to be intrusive or an invasion of their privacy.

telemarketing
A form of non-store retailing in which a salesperson initiates contact with a prospect and attempts to close a sale over the telephone. Usually involves outbound calls from a company to prospective customers.

Most call centres in Canada do not engage in outbound telemarketing, but rather serve as order desks and customer-service centres. These centres receive toll-free inbound calls from customers who wish to order a product or service or to obtain information from customer-service representatives. These salespeople engage in reactive selling in that they respond to calls placed by customers.

With advances in telecommunication systems as integrated components of overall management information systems, the use of call centres and telemarketing representatives has

Call-centre personnel take orders by telephone, but they are also in sales.

Dell
Gateway
Canadian Marketing Association

grown exponentially in recent years. This practice became particularly popular with financial service providers and other companies with mass appeal. This sales approach works particularly well in combination with a significant Internet presence. Dell (**www.dell.ca**) and Gateway (**www.gateway.com**) computer companies have both become specialists in selling equipment and accessories through these channels.

Many of Canada's largest companies have embarked on a telephone-based sales function in recent years as technology became more readily available and more sophisticated. But, all is not rosy on the telemarketing front. In November 2005, the Canadian government passed do-not-call legislation that is meant to put a stop to unwanted telemarketing calls. The legislation provides the Canadian Radio-television and Telecommunications Commission (CRTC) with the ability to establish a national do-not-call list which telemarketers must regularly download and respect. This will greatly reduce the number of unwanted telemarketing calls that Canadians receive at home.

The CRTC now has the right to impose fines on those telemarketers who break the rules — fines range from $1,500 to $15,000 per offending call. The Canadian Marketing Association (CMA) is pleased with the legislation; however, the telemarketing industry may face layoffs and increased fees for service when the list is up and running by 2007. The CMA (**www.the-cma.org/consumer/donotcontact.cfm**) also offers a do-not-contact service on its own Web site that allows customers to register to have their names removed from marketing lists held by members of the Canadian Marketing Association.[2]

Given this new legislation, companies will have to find new ways to reach their target customers. As customers add their names to the do-not-call list, telemarketing will become even less effective and, as a result, fewer companies will opt for this approach. Given the increasing use of text messaging, podcasts, and blogs, marketers should be able to create new ways to communicate with customers.

The new focus of selling

Consistent with the changes that have been taking place in marketing generally in recent years, the selling function within organizations is also being transformed by the shifting focus toward a longer-term emphasis on the building of relationships. Salespeople in companies are no longer being motivated merely to sell something, but rather are being given increasing responsibility to build relationships with customers. This is, of course, a natural extension of the sales role, as it is the salesperson who very often is the only point of personal contact between the company and the customer.

Customers rarely meet a company's chief executive officer or the vice-president of marketing. The impressions that customers receive of a company are often based on their interaction with salespeople, whether retail sales staff or B2B sales representatives. To customers, the salesperson is the company, as impressions of the firm are based largely on interactions with sales personnel. All other employees are usually behind the scenes. Consequently, companies today seek to employ individuals in sales positions who are capable of developing relationships with customers, so that those customers will come back to do business with them (and the company) again. They want to hire salespeople who are outgoing, helpful, and friendly, people who can be trusted and on whom customers feel they can rely. They should be people with whom customers enjoy dealing.

Companies today, particularly in a B2B setting, want to employ sales reps who can become accepted as part of the customer's team. In an ideal relationship, the customer calls the sales rep with questions, to seek advice, and to request special services, and not simply to place an order. Many companies want to move beyond the status of "supplier" to become a trusted partner in the exchange relationship. In that regard, therefore, the sales rep becomes more than a salesperson and increasingly is viewed as a problem solver and solutions provider.

To play such a role, a sales rep has to be a special kind of person. In some industries, there is a high turnover rate in sales positions, because some people are very good at it and others are not. Successful salespeople are not only good at selling things, but also are good at gaining the confidence of customers and in building loyalty to them and their company. They have to be able to cope with rejection and with complaints from customers, because they are the first line of contact with customers.

Selling to Different Types of Customers

There are essentially three types of customers, each of which requires a different approach to selling: (1) intrinsic value customers; (2) extrinsic value customers; and, (3) strategic value customers.[3]

Intrinsic value customers see value in the product itself. These customers already understand the product, and may view the product or service as a commodity. For them, sales people can add little or nothing to the value of the product. Extrinsic value customers focus on how the product is used to derive value. Because they are interested in solutions and applications, the sales force can add a great deal of value by providing advice and help. Strategic value customers want more than just products and advice, they want an ongoing relationship with the firm so that they can work together to create even greater value.

Of course, for each customer value type there is a corresponding selling type that best suits the customer's needs. Transactional selling is best suited for intrinsic value customers since, in the customer's opinion, the sales force can bring little added value to the customer. As intrinsic value buyers become better informed of their choices by obtaining information from sources other than the sales force, they are demanding transactional sales. Extrinsic value customers, on the other hand, are more likely to benefit from consultative selling, which focuses on helping customers understand their own needs, and on finding creative ways to solve problems. Enterprise selling is directed at strategic value customers and requires a unique set of skills, strategies and processes that are linked to the customer's strategic direction. It is not a one-on-one salesperson to customer relationship; rather, many people from each side work together to ensure the customer's success and, ultimately, the seller's success.

Nature of sales jobs

The sales job of today is quite different from the stereotype of the past. The images of high pressure, false friendship, and fast talk are largely outdated. As more companies focus on hiring salespeople who can look beyond making the sale to the development of successful relationships with customers, the kind of people who are hired for sales jobs has changed.

The professional salesperson A new type of sales rep has emerged: the professional salesperson. Today, these salespeople are managers of a market area: their territories or a customer category. They engage in a total selling job — serving their customers, building goodwill, selling their products, and training their customers' salespeople. Today's sales representatives act as a source of feedback on the market by relaying information back to the firm. They organize much of their own time and effort. They often take part in recruiting new salespeople, sales planning in their territories, and other managerial activities.

Humpty Dumpty
IBM

Wide variety of sales jobs The types of selling jobs and the activities involved in them cover a wide range. Consider the job of a Humpty Dumpty (**www.humptydumpty.com**) driver-salesperson who calls routinely on a group of retail stores. That job is completely different from that of the IBM (**www.ibm.ca**) systems consultant who sells a computer

MARKETING AT WORK 15-1: RELATIONSHIPS

What Does It Take To Be a Champion?

People who excel in sales have some unique characteristics. In the book, *Champion Selling*, five distinct, perspective-related traits are discussed. The authors, Tom Blake, Tom Hudson and Tony Enrico studied high-performing salespeople and developed the following list of five winning characteristics:

1. The desire to help others succeed. The definition of success is broadly defined from the customer's perspective.
2. The ability to help shape others' thinking. Skills such as strategic thinking, persuasive communication and creative problem-solving help customers accomplish their long-term strategic goals.
3. Risk-taking. The best salespeople go to the customer and put themselves in the customer's environments.
4. Adaptability. Top salespeople will adapt to the needs and style of the customer so that the customer is comfortable. This will allow for a stronger relationship between customer and seller since the customer will feel at ease with the seller.
5. Follow-through. Top salespeople are in it for the long-term and will work through problems with the customer, since success only happens when both parties are satisfied with the outcomes.

QUESTIONS:

1. Think about sales people with whom you have dealt in recent months. What differentiated those you enjoyed dealing with from those you didn't?
2. Which of them exhibited the characteristics described in this Marketing at Work file?

SOURCE: Adapted from "Characteristics of Champion Sellers," Profitguide.com, October 20, 2005.

driver-salesperson
A selling job in which the job is primarily to deliver the product; selling responsibilities, if any, are secondary to seeing that orders are filled correctly and on time.

inside order taker
A selling job in which the primary function of the salesperson is to take orders in person or by telephone inside a store or other type of business.

outside order taker
A selling job in which salespeople primarily go to customers in the field.

missionary salesperson
A selling job in which the salespeople are not expected to solicit orders but rather to influence decision makers by building goodwill, performing promotional activities, and providing service to customers; called a detail salesperson in pharmaceuticals marketing.

system for managing hotel reservations to major hotel chains such as Fairmont or Four Seasons. Similarly, Oscar, the sales representative for Aliant in our chapter opener, has a job only remotely related to that of the Mary Kay sales consultant who calls on customers in their homes. Likewise, the salesperson who works at The Gap has a very different selling role than either of these.

One way to classify sales jobs is on the basis of the creative selling skills required, from the simple to the complex. The classification that follows is updated and adapted from several classification schemes developed over time.[4]

1. **Driver-salesperson**: In this job, the salesperson primarily delivers the product, soft drinks or fuel oil, for example. Selling responsibilities are secondary, although most of these salespeople are encouraged to identify new business and are rewarded for finding opportunities to increase sales to existing accounts.
2. **Inside order taker**: This is a position in which the salesperson takes orders at the seller's place of business; for example, a retail clerk standing behind the counter at a Bay store or a telephone representative of the Eddie Bauer catalogue retail operation. Most customers have already decided to buy. The salesperson's job is to serve them efficiently and courteously.
3. **Outside order taker**: In this position, the salesperson goes to the customer in the field and prepares an order. An example is a sales representative for Benjamin-Moore Paints who calls on a building supplies store. Most of the sales made by outside order takers are repeat orders to established customers, and much of the salesperson's time is devoted to support activities such as assisting with promotion and helping train the account's salespeople.
4. **Missionary salesperson**: The job of a missionary salesperson is not to solicit orders but to build goodwill, perform promotional activities, and provide information and other support services for customers. These people may also be called merchandisers or detail salespeople. An example of this job is a missionary sales rep for Procter & Gamble

Procter & Gamble

(www.pg.com) who visits retailers regularly and may offer presentation suggestions, as well as assist in setting it up. They also help with special promotions. Also, there are "drug reps" who work for companies such as Merck or Eli Lilly, calling on doctors to introduce new products, provide information, and leave professional samples to be distributed to patients.

sales engineer
A selling job that often involves technically trained individuals selling sophisticated equipment; the emphasis is on the salesperson's ability to explain the product to the prospect and perhaps to adapt it to the customer's particular needs.

5. **Sales engineer**: In this position, the major emphasis is on the salesperson's ability to explain a complex product to a prospective customer and also to tailor the product to the customer's particular needs. The products involved are typically complex, technically sophisticated items. A sales engineer often works with another sales rep who regularly calls on an account. Examples include producers of industrial equipment that develop manufacturing systems according to a client's requirements.

consultative salesperson
A selling job in which the person engages in the creative selling of goods and services by addressing customer needs that are often not obvious, and then offering advice and solutions to those needs.

6. **Consultative salesperson**: This type of salesperson engages in the creative selling of products, services and solutions. This approach to selling is extremely complex because it generally involves a salesperson identifying customer needs that the customer may not be aware of. Consultative selling requires that a relationship of trust be established with the customer, because it usually involves a salesperson getting to know the customer's business in great detail. There is a sharing of information, so that the salesperson can uncover needs of the customer to which he or she may be able to offer a solution. This is a very creative form of selling in that the salesperson may address needs that are not necessarily obvious to the customer. Ideally, the salesperson wants to be able to say to the customer "we can look after that for you."

Consultative selling does not have to involve highly technical outside selling. Some degree of consultation is also involved in certain retail situations where the customer is buying complex or tailored products that require the advice and opinion of a salesperson. For example, when most people are buying electronic equipment, computers, and certain items of clothing, they want to receive good advice from knowledgeable salespeople.

TABLE 15-1 Why Sales Jobs are Different

- Salespeople deal most directly with customers and are seen as spokespersons for the firm and guardians of its relationships and reputation.
- Salespeople represent their company to customers and to society in general; they are on the front line and have to be effective, personable, and easy to deal with.
- Sales personnel often operate with limited direct supervision; they must be creative and show considerable initiative.
- Salespeople must have good people skills; they have to be empathetic and appear genuinely concerned about customers.
- Salespeople, particularly those who "cold-call" customers in an attempt to sell to them, must have a high tolerance for rejection.
- Some sales jobs involve considerable travelling and time away from home; they require mental toughness and physical stamina.

PAGE UP!

1. ________________________ involves the direct personal communication of information, in contrast to the impersonal communication of sales promotion and other marketing communications tools.
2. Name the two kinds of sales roles.
3. What is a consultative salesperson?

Changing Patterns in Sales

Traditionally, selling was a face-to-face, one-on-one situation between a salesperson and a buyer, in both retail B2C sales and B2B transactions. In recent years, however, some very different selling patterns have emerged. These new patterns reflect a growing expertise among consumers and business buyers, which in turn has fostered a growing professionalism in selling. They also reflect certain changes in the selling environment, including the always-important impact of technology. These changing approaches to selling are discussed below.

Team selling

team selling
Use of a number of sales personnel to represent a company, often calling on several people in the same account.

To match the expertise of the buying centre in business markets, a growing number of firms have adopted the organizational concept of a selling centre, or **team selling**. Team selling involves a group of people representing a sales department as well as other functional areas in a firm. This is also sometimes called a sales team.

Team selling is expensive and is used only when there is a potential for a high sales volume and profit. Procter & Gamble, for example, would have selling teams comprising salespeople and representatives from finance, distribution, and manufacturing assigned to cover a large retailer such as Wal-Mart. As an international retailer for most of P&G's products, the two firms work so closely together that Wal-Mart's scanner and inventory system is directly linked to P&G, allowing the company to perform inventory-control functions. The P&G sales team works closely with the retailer to develop, promote, and deliver products.

Systems selling

Xerox
Magna International

The concept of systems selling means selling a total package of related products and services — a system — to solve a customer's problem. The idea is that the system will satisfy the buyer's needs more effectively than selling individual products separately. Xerox (**www.xerox.ca**), for example, originally sold individual products, using a separate sales force for each major product line. Today, using a systems-selling approach, Xerox studies a customer's office information and operating problems, and then provides a total automated system of equipment and accompanying services to solve that customer's office problems.

Global sales teams

As companies expand their operations to various corners of the world, they expect their suppliers to do the same. Having products readily available and providing speedy service is essential to maintaining global customers, so many larger firms have established sales offices or distribution centres in some foreign locations to serve these customers. Now, to service their largest and most profitable customers, companies such as Bombardier, Magna International (**www.magna.ca**), and IBM form global sales teams. A global sales team is responsible for all of a client's requirements, for any of their locations, around the world.

Relationship Selling

Relationship selling means developing a mutually beneficial relationship with selected customers over time. Relationship selling can be a natural outcome from team selling or it can be developed by individual sales representatives in their continued dealings with customers. Relationship selling is based on the idea that instead of maximizing the number and size of individual transactions, the seller works to develop a deeper, longer-lasting relationship built on trust and mutual benefit. The salesperson must work with the client to identify needs and to determine what is in the best interest of the client. This may mean taking the time and effort to understand the needs and goals of the client's firm. The salesperson must place as much emphasis on the buyer-seller relationship as on the immediate sale during transactions and sales efforts. Sales representatives must receive the full support of the firm in these efforts in that their performance must be evaluated on longer-term relationship measures as well as sales performance.

In the face of all the hype about what technology can do, it's still people who form business relationships, understand customer needs, and fulfil them in a timely, cost-effective manner. The VP of strategic marketing for Best Buy Canada, Mike Nedelec, understands this. Nedelec often puts on a trainee badge to go on the floor at a Future Shop location to learn from the associates who work with customers daily. Associates know what customers are asking for and many promotional ideas come from the front-line people. In the fall of 2005, Best Buy and Future Shop increased their focus on customer-service initiatives that came from in-store insights. The no-commission policy of Best Buy helps put customers at ease with the customer-service representative and increases the information flow since customers have no fear of aggressive sales pitches.[5]

BACK TO THE TOP

The sales call that is described in our chapter opener is a good example of relationship selling, in which Alfred Whiffen clearly demonstrated a broader interest in the operation of the client's business and was not simply interested in selling a new phone system.

Telephone and Internet selling

The innovative use of telecommunications systems and the Internet is an important part of a company's "going to the customer" approach to selling. While telemarketing usually involves outbound telephone calling, ongoing contact by telephone reduces the time salespeople spend on routine order-taking. Redirecting routine reorders to a telephone ordering system or the Internet allows the field sales force to devote more time to creative selling, major account selling, and other more profitable selling activities. Some examples of selling activities that lend themselves nicely to such an approach are:

John Deere

- Outbound calls to generate leads to new accounts and identify prospective customers that sales reps can follow up with in-person calls.
- Processing orders for standardized products: Often the buyer's computer talks with the seller's computer to place orders and determine shipping dates.

Always connected to customers and their data.

- Dealing with small-order customers, especially those with whom the seller would lose money if field sales calls were used: Routine orders may be placed over the telephone or through the supplier's Web site.
- Improving relations with intermediaries: The John Deere farm equipment company (www. deere.com) "talks" via computers with its dealers about inventories, service, and financial management.
- Improving communications with intermediaries in foreign countries and competing better against manufacturers in those countries.

Sales force automation

Many firms are equipping their salespeople with laptop computers, wireless mobile phones, PDAs, fax machines, and pagers in order to give them access to databases, the Internet, e-mail, and other information and communication tools. The concept is quite simple, since a wide range of software has been developed to help salespeople manage information about their accounts and prospects, generate proposals, submit reports, and manage their time and territories more efficiently. By arming sales representatives with the appropriate technology, a firm can increase a salesperson's productivity and efficiency. By reducing time spent on routine administrative tasks, more time is free for pursuing new clients, following up on existing clients, and strengthening relationships. Sales reps can, therefore, provide a higher level of service.

Experiences with sales force automation have been mixed. As is often the case when new technology is implemented, many systems fail to meet expectations. However, a significant number of the problems that crop up seem to result from inadequate planning or implementation. Despite these difficulties, more and more sales forces are being automated.

The Sales Process

The sales process (see Figure 15-2) is a logical sequence of four steps that a salesperson takes in dealing with a prospective buyer. This process is designed to lead to customer action and ends with a follow-up to ensure customer satisfaction. The desired action usually is to get the customer to buy a product or a service, but it may be to get the company on a preferred supplier list or to encourage a customer to engage in promotional activity for the supplier's brand.

Prospecting

prospecting
The stage in the personal-selling process that involves developing a list of potential customers.

The first step in the sales process is called **prospecting**. It consists of two activities — identifying prospects and then qualifying them, that is, determining whether they have the necessary willingness, purchasing power, and authority to buy.

Identifying prospects The identification process is an application of market segmentation. By analyzing the firm's database of past and current customers, a sales representative may determine the characteristics of the ideal prospect. Comparing this profile to a list of prospective customers produces a set of target prospects.

Many other sources can be used to build the list of prospects. The representative's sales manager may prepare a list, current customers may suggest new leads, trade association and industry directories can be a good source, and leads can come from people responding to the firm's advertising. These responses include customers mailing in coupons, calling a toll-free number given in an advertisement, or responding to a Web address.

A little thought often will suggest logical prospects. Most salespeople will attend trade shows and conferences where they will meet potential clients. As well, there are numerous networking opportunities through Chambers of Commerce and professional organizations that reveal new prospects.

Qualifying the prospects After identifying prospective customers, a salesperson should qualify them — that is, determine whether they have the necessary willingness, purchasing power, and authority to buy. To determine willingness to buy, a company can seek information about

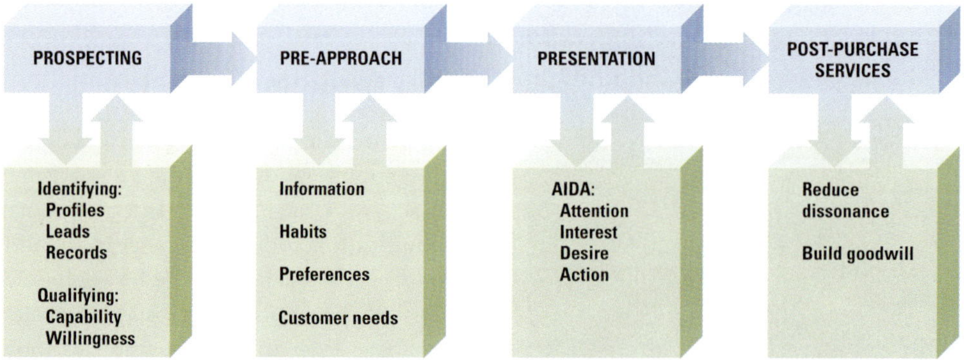

Figure 15-2: The Personal Selling Process

a prospect's relationship with its present suppliers. For example, a business firm or a household consumer may have had a long, satisfying relationship with a competing auto insurance company. In this case, there would seem to be little chance that an Allstate salesperson could get that prospect's business, so the salesperson may be better advised to target other customers.

Dun & Bradstreet

To determine a prospect's ability to pay, a marketer may refer to credit-rating services such as Dun & Bradstreet (**www.dnbcorp.com**). For household consumers or small businesses in an area, a seller may obtain credit information from a local credit bureau. Identifying the person who has the authority to buy for a business or a household can be difficult, as we saw in Chapter 6. In a business, the buying authority may rest with a committee or a senior manager at a distant location. Besides determining the buying authority, a seller also should identify the people who influence the buying decision. A purchasing agent may have buying authority, but the actual purchase may depend on the recommendation of office staff, factory engineers, or senior managers.

Pre-approach to individual prospects

Before calling on prospects, salespeople should learn as much as possible about them. This could mean finding out what products and services the prospects are now using and their reactions to them. In B2B selling, a salesperson or selling team should find out how buying decisions are made in the customer's organization. (Remember, in Chapter 6, we discussed the various roles played in the buying-decision process in business firms.) The right people can be targeted if the salesperson knows who the information gatekeeper is, who influences and/or makes the buying decision, and who actually makes the purchase.

An important component of the pre-approach is the determination of customer needs. This may involve a certain amount of intelligence gathering from the customers themselves or from employees of the firm who have dealt with similar customers in the past. It is important at this stage to define needs very broadly to include various issues and problems that the customer may be facing. If needs are defined narrowly or simply in terms of the customer's need for the product, it is likely that the sales rep will miss opportunities to address problems or to offer solutions that the customer may not have been expecting.

Information about prospects also allows salespeople to tailor their presentations to individual buyers. That information extends to issues and problems that the prospective client is facing. By approaching the sales situation appearing to be well informed and having done their homework, sales reps are in a better position to propose solutions and to appear knowledgeable and helpful. Demonstrating such expertise and commitment often prompts a customer to observe that the sales rep "really understands my business."

Presenting the sales message

With the appropriate pre-approach information, a salesperson can design a sales presentation that will attract the prospect's attention. The salesperson then tries to hold the prospect's interest while building a desire for the product and, when the time is right, attempt to stimulate action by closing the sale. This approach, called AIDA (an acronym formed by the first letters of attention, interest, desire, and action), is used by many organizations.

Attract attention — the approach The first task in a sales presentation is to attract the prospect's attention and to generate interest. When the prospect is aware of a need and is seeking a solution, simply outlining the capabilities of the product may be enough. However, more creativity is often required.

For instance, if a customer referred the salesperson to the prospect, the right approach might be to start out by mentioning this common acquaintance. Or a salesperson might suggest the product benefits by making some startling statement. One sales training consultant

MARKETING AT WORK 15-2: TECHNOLOGY

Making the Sales Force Smarter

Many companies have incorporated new technologies into their everyday sales functions which allow sales staff to keep in touch with suppliers, customers and the corporate office. The use of technology improves information flow and allows salespeople to have information available that was traditionally carried in folders and binders. Dakis Decision Systems, based in Montréal, has developed an interactive digital sales force technology that uses artificial intelligence to provide product and cross-selling recommendations for sales-staff and/or customers.

The workers at Brolisport in St-Hyacinthe, Quebec are the pilot group for the technology, known as the Humanized Expert, which uses a detailed questionnaire to determine the best sales processes for certain products. The information is accessed through a handheld PDA and at an in-store kiosk. Salespeople use the questionnaires to help customers make purchase decisions for complex and expensive pieces of sporting equipment. Sales of products programmed into the Humanized Expert have increased an estimated 12 percent.

Another user of the Dakis technology is the Centre du Pave et Jardin RDP in Montréal. This family-owned business uses the technology on its computer system to assist sales staff in pricing landscaping work. The owners hope for an increase of $30,000 to $50,000 a year in sales and they say that training time will decrease by one week per person.

Since salespeople will have more information available, literally at their fingertips, it is likely that customers will be more satisfied with the information they receive and will make better choices as a result. This may translate into increased value for the customer, repeat purchases, and better relationships in the long-term.

QUESTIONS:

1. What kinds of information do you think would make salespeople more effective in their jobs?
2. Where have you encountered salespeople who use technology to serve you better?
3. What exactly did they do and did it impress you?

SOURCE: Adapted from: Denise J. Deveau, "New digital technology smartens up the sales force," *The Globe and Mail*, May 12, 2005, p. B10.

often greets a prospect with the question, "If I can cut your selling costs in half and at the same time double your sales volume, are you interested?"

Hold interest and arouse desire After attracting the prospect's attention, the sales representative can hold it and stimulate further interest in the product with a sales talk. There is no common pattern here. Usually, however, a product demonstration is invaluable. Whatever pattern is followed in the talk, the salesperson must always show how the product will benefit the prospect. Increasingly, salespeople are using technology (often sales presentations on a laptop) to deliver a consistent sales message.

Meet objections and close the sale After explaining the product and its benefits, a salesperson should try closing the sale — obtaining the customer's agreement to buy. As part of the presentation, the salesperson may periodically venture a trial close to test the prospect's willingness to buy. By posing some "either/or" questions, a salesperson can bring the presentation to a positive result. For example, "Would you like the installation to begin next Monday or shall we book another time later in the week?"

The trial close is important because it gives the salesperson an indication of how close the prospect is to a decision or what objections the prospect has. If objections are stated, the salesperson then has an opportunity to handle them and clarify additional product or service benefits and to reinforce those that have already been presented.

Post-purchase service

An effective selling job does not end when the order is written up. The final stage of a selling process is a series of post-purchase activities that can build customer goodwill and lay the groundwork for future business. An alert salesperson will follow up sales to ensure that no problems occur in delivery, financing, installation, employee training, and other areas that are important to customer satisfaction. Many companies now have formalized customer contact after the sale to ensure that the product or service is meeting the customer's expectations. If it isn't, appropriate steps can be taken to restore that satisfaction by changing the product or offering needed information.

Post-purchase service reduces the anxiety that usually occurs after a person makes a buying decision and ensures that the customer perceives ongoing value. In this final stage of the selling process, a salesperson can reduce any concerns the customer may have about whether he or she has made the right decision by (1) reviewing the product's benefits; (2) repeating why the product is better than alternatives not chosen, and (3) addressing any questions the customer may have.

Managing a Sales Force

Most sales managers spend their time in staffing and supervising a sales force. Since selling involves people dealing with people, it should come as no surprise that most of the activities we'll discuss in this section are, in fact, more closely related to human resources than they are to the traditional definition of marketing. We now turn our attention to these activities, as shown in Figure 15-3.

Recruitment and selection

Personnel selection is the most important management activity in any organization. Consequently, the key to success in managing a sales force is selecting the right people. Even when a company has noticeable product advantages, if a sales force is distinctly inferior to that of a competitor, the competitor will win.

Sales force selection includes three tasks:

1. Determining the characteristics of the people to be hired.
2. Recruiting an adequate number of applicants.
3. Selecting the most qualified persons from among the applicants.

Determining hiring specifications The first step is to establish the proper hiring specifications, just as if the company was purchasing equipment or supplies. To establish these specifications, management must first know what the particular sales job entails. Then, a detailed job analysis and a written job description can be developed. This description will later be invaluable in training, compensation, and supervision decisions. Determining the qualifications needed to fill the job is the most difficult part of the selection function. We still don't really know all of the characteristics that make a good salesperson, nor can we measure to what degree each characteristic should be present. Most companies now opt for a combination of product knowledge, sales experience, and desired personality traits.

Figure 15-3: Staffing and Operating a Sales Force

Recruiting applicants A planned system for recruiting a sufficient number of applicants is the next step in selection. A good recruiting system:

- Operates continuously, not only when sales force vacancies occur.
- Is systematic in reaching all appropriate sources of applicants.
- Provides a flow of more qualified applicants than immediately needed.

To identify recruits, large organizations often use placement services on university and college campuses or professional employment agencies or "head-hunters," some of which specialize in locating applicants for marketing and sales positions. Smaller firms that need fewer new salespeople may place employment ads in trade publications and daily newspapers. Many firms solicit recommendations from company employees, customers, or suppliers.

Matching applicants with specifications Sales managers use a variety of techniques to determine which applicants possess the desired qualifications, including application forms, interviews, references, credit reports, psychological tests, aptitude tests, and physical examinations. Virtually all companies ask candidates to fill out application forms. In addition to providing basic screening information, the application form can indicate areas that should be explored in an interview. An interview helps an employer to determine (1) the applicant's degree of interest in the job, (2) the match between the requirements of the job and the applicant's skills, and (3) the applicant's motivation to work hard. The individuals involved in the selection process should be aware of the various provincial laws against discrimination to avoid inadvertent violations.

Training

Both new and experienced salespeople need an effective sales training program to improve their selling skills, learn about new products, and improve their time- and territory-management practices. Most large companies have a well-developed sales training program that exposes new salespeople to company policies and the details of the product line. In addition to product knowledge, sales employees must also receive training in how the company wishes to present itself to its customers. Most companies realize that its salespeople represent the front line and are the face of the company to its customers. Therefore they must be trained to represent the company properly. Some training programs, particularly for complex products and services, will last several weeks.

Motivation

Because salespeople often work independently, without supervision and guidance from management, motivation is often a challenge. People differ in what motivates them, and motivations change over time. A young person may be more motivated by monetary rewards alone, while older salespeople may be more interested in intrinsic motivation, such as receiving recognition for building long-term relationships with important customers.

Sales executives can draw from a wide assortment of specific motivational tools. Financial incentives — compensation plans, bonuses, fringe benefits — are frequently effective. Non-financial rewards — job enrichment; good, consistent feedback from management; recognition and honour awards (pins, trophies, or certificates) — may be appropriate. Many firms provide cruises, resort trips, and other incentives as rewards for sales reps who meet or exceed various qualitative and quantitative sales goals.

As many companies have broadened their view of the role of sales personnel to include the development and maintenance of customer relationships, compensation systems have changed as a result. Rather than simply relying on sales-based commissions to motivate salespeople, many firms now motivate them to build solid customer relationships by including a component in the compensation program that encourages such behaviour.

Compensation

Financial rewards are still the most widely used tool for motivating salespeople. Consequently, designing and administering an effective sales compensation plan is a large part of a sales manager's job. Financial rewards may be direct monetary payments (salary, commission, bonuses) or indirect monetary compensation (paid vacations, pensions, insurance plans).

Establishing a compensation system calls for decisions concerning the level of compensation, as well as the method of compensation and the kind of behaviour for which the salesperson will be compensated and rewarded. The level refers to the total dollar income that a salesperson may earn over a period of time. The method is the system or plan by which the salesperson will reach the intended level. The behaviour to be encouraged refers to whether the salesperson is to be rewarded only for making sales or whether there are other expectations.

Three widely used methods of compensating a sales force that are tied to sales are straight salary, straight commission, and a combination plan. A salary is a fixed payment for a period of time during which the salesperson is working. A salary-only plan (called a straight salary) provides security and stability of earnings for a salesperson. This plan gives management control over the selling efforts of the salesperson, and the sales representatives themselves are likely to cater to the customer's best interests. The main drawback of a straight salary is that it may not offer adequate incentive for some salespeople to increase their sales volume.

A commission is a payment tied to a specific unit of accomplishment; for example, a sales representative may be paid 5 percent of gross sales or 8 percent of gross margin. A commission-only plan (straight commission) tends to have just the opposite merits and limitations of a straight salary. A straight commission provides considerable incentive for salespeople, and it is a variable cost related directly to a representative's sales volume or gross margin. On the other hand, it is difficult to get salespeople who are paid only by commission to perform tasks for which no commission is paid. The straight-commission plan is most often used in retail selling situations and is based on the assumption that short-term sales results alone drive business success. It may have an unintended negative effect. The incentive behind such a system is to encourage salespeople to sell as much as possible. Many consumers do not like what they perceive to be the high-pressure approach that is often associated with commission-based selling.

Today, many companies are building into their compensation programs some component that rewards salespeople for achieving high levels of customer service, customer satisfaction, and customer relationships. To be able to reward salespeople for achieving these goals, a company must be able to measure such outcomes.

Evaluating Performance

evaluating sales performance
The process of determining whether sales personnel have achieved objectives; important for building customer loyalty and for compensation.

Managing a sales force includes **evaluating sales performance**. Sales managers must know what the salespeople are doing in order to know how well they are serving customers, to be able to reward them or to make constructive proposals for improvement. By establishing performance standards and studying salespeople's activities, management can develop new training programs for upgrading the sales force's efforts. And, performance evaluation should be the basis for compensation decisions and for other incentives and rewards.

Both quantitative and qualitative factors should be used as bases for performance evaluation. These are often referred to as "hard" and "soft" measures. The "hard" quantitative measures of sales performance generally have the advantage of being specific and objective, and usually involve financial and other data that the firm collects through its information system. The "soft" qualitative performance measures, although reflecting broader dimensions of desirable behaviour, are often limited by the subjective judgement of evaluators. For either type of appraisal, however, management faces the difficult task of measuring the desired outcomes and of setting standards against which a salesperson's performance may be measured.

Quantitative bases Sales performance may be evaluated quantitatively in terms of inputs (efforts) and outputs (results). Together, inputs (such as number of sales calls per day, number of proposals presented, or training sessions for dealers) and outputs (such as sales volume or gross margin, average order size, closing rate, or new accounts opened) provide a measure of selling effectiveness. These have the advantage of being fairly easily measured, and with sophisticated information systems today, such measures can be tracked directly to each individual salesperson by the company's information system. It is precisely because such measures are easily obtained that many companies have continued to use them exclusively.

An increasing number of firms, realizing the limitations of using an evaluation program that is tied only to quantitative measures, are incorporating measures of customer satisfaction or of service quality as a performance indicator. Satisfaction is measured a number of different ways, from detailed questionnaires that customers complete to counting the number of complaints received per customer. Assessing satisfaction reflects recognition by companies that there is more to selling than making a sale and it also allows salespeople more scope in working with new and established customers.

Qualitative bases Performance evaluation would be much easier if it could be based only on quantitative criteria, which would minimize the subjectivity and personal bias of the evaluators. However, many qualitative factors must be considered because they influence a salesperson's performance. The most important of these today relate to the objective of many firms to have sales representatives work at the development of customer relationships. While assessment of the quality of such relationships has been quite subjective in the past, today many progressive firms are beginning to quantify such previously qualitative variables. They have devised programs to actually measure the quality of customer relationships and are building such assessments into performance-evaluation programs. Some factors that have been considered to be qualitative but of considerable importance are:

- Knowledge of products, company policies, and competitors.
- Time management and preparation for sales calls.
- Customer relationships.

Historically, in evaluating the performance of salespeople, companies have tended to focus on short-term, historic, financial information relating mainly to sales and other variables measured within the company. Increasingly, companies are developing performance measures that are future-looking, non-financial, longer term, and collected from customers.

PAGE UP!

1. What is a selling centre?
2. ______________________ refers to selling a total package of related goods and services to solve a customer's problems.
3. What has been the most widely used tool for motivating salespeople?

Sales Promotion

sales promotion
Activities intended to stimulate short-term interest and purchasing, including contests for salespeople and consumers, trade shows, in-store displays, samples, premiums, and coupons; designed to supplement advertising and co-ordinate selling efforts.

Sales promotion is one of the most loosely used terms in the marketing vocabulary. We define sales promotion as tools and techniques used to stimulate customer interest and sales in the short term, to supplement advertising, and to support the sales effort. Examples of sales-promotion devices are coupons, premiums, in-store displays and demonstrations, trade shows, samples, and contests.

Manufacturers and intermediaries both conduct sales promotions. The target for manufacturers' sales promotions may be intermediaries, end-users — households or business users — or the manufacturer's own sales force. Intermediaries direct sales promotions to their salespeople or prospects further down the distribution channel.

Nature and scope of sales promotion

Sales promotion is distinct from advertising or selling, but these three forms of promotion are often used together in a co-ordinated fashion. For example, an in-store display (sales promotion) furnished by Michelin to dealers selling its tires may feature a slogan and illustrations (including, of course, the Michelin Man) from Michelin's current advertising campaign. This display, which helps retailers sell tires, also makes them more receptive to talking with Michelin salespeople. Or, as another example, prospective customers may be generated from people who enter a contest at the Canon copier exhibit at an office equipment trade show. These prospects might be sent some direct-mail advertising and then be contacted by a salesperson.

trade promotions
Sales promotion that is directed to members of a distribution channel.

consumer promotions
Sales promotion that is aimed at end consumers.

There are two categories of sales promotion: **trade promotions**, directed to the members of the distribution channel; and **consumer promotions**, aimed at consumers. Manufacturers as a group spend about twice as much on trade promotion as they do on advertising, and an amount about equal to their advertising on consumer promotions.

As consumer demands for convenience increase and marketers respond with products and services that meet these demands, it is also important to develop sales promotions that respond to the customer's expectations. Consumers are willing to take advantage of savings typically offered by promotions if it is easy and convenient to do so. Consumer promotions such as coupons, mail-in rebates, premiums and contests must be easy to use and provide value for the consumer. Consumer promotions can work to increase sales, however, they must provide a real incentive to attract users who are looking for value. For example, coupons must be redeemable at the place where consumers shop and where the product is sold. As with product and service selection, today's consumers are looking for value when they participate in promotions. Complex promotions which involve multi-brand purchases and/or collection of proofs of purchase can actually turn a consumer from the brand unless the incentive is very high.[6]

This consumer promotion will drive short-term sales.

Several factors in the marketing environment contribute to the surging popularity of sales promotion:

- ***Short-term results:*** Sales promotions such as sampling, couponing and trade allowances produce quicker, more measurable sales results. They are generally intended to stimulate trial of a new product or to give sales a short-term boost. However, critics of this strategy argue that these immediate benefits come at the expense of building brand loyalty. They feel that an overemphasis on sales promotion may undermine a brand's future. While the intent (for the longer term) is to stimulate trial of a product, it is thought that as much as half of coupon redemption, for example, is from existing users.[7]

- ***Competitive pressure:*** If competitors are offering buyers price reductions, contests, or other incentives, a firm may feel forced to retaliate with its own sales promotions. In the end, a "promotion war" may result.
- ***Buyers' expectations:*** Once they are offered purchase incentives, consumers and distribution channel members may get used to them and begin to expect them. Some companies seem to be offering continuous sales promotions, most of which offer customers reduced prices. In such cases, consumers often "catch on" and simply wait for the next promotion before buying.
- ***Low levels of retail selling:*** Many retailers use inadequately trained sales clerks or have switched to self-service. For these outlets, sales-promotion devices such as product displays and samples often are the only effective promotional tools available at the point of purchase.
- ***Door openers:*** When contact with salespeople is minimal, sales promotions often open the door to closer customer contact. When customers respond to a promotion, it provides a salesperson with an opportunity to make contact and to begin to establish a relationship.

Management of sales promotion

Sales promotion should be included in a company's marketing communications plans, along with advertising and selling. This means setting sales-promotion objectives and strategies, determining a budget, selecting appropriate techniques, and evaluating the performance of sales-promotion activities.

One problem management faces is that many sales-promotion techniques are short-run, tactical actions. Coupons, premiums, and contests, for example, are designed to produce imme-

MARKETING AT WORK — 15-3: STRATEGY

Connecting With the Target

To generate awareness and excitement about new X-Factor, Gatorade decided to run a text-based summer promotion. Beginning in July (when Gatorade sales would be high) consumers would receive an instant-win game card when they purchased two bottles of the beverage at convenience stores and gas stations. Players would scratch to reveal a code and PIN that they would then enter into their cellphones. The PIN could also be used online. Instant prizes consisted of ringtones, wallpaper and celebrity athlete voicemail, as well as bigger prizes such as a Sidney Crosby-autographed Team Canada jersey or a Nokia phone with the X-Factor logo on it. This promotion was aimed at males aged 13- to-18 but really reached up to 24 years of age. The athlete-inspired prizes and the instant win made this a great promotion for the demographic segment with whom Gatorade was trying to raise awareness.

Sales promotions have to be meaningful and accessible for the target market. This promotion was launched in the summer when the target group would be playing sports outdoors, on summer vacations, taking road trips (hence the gas station placement of the instant win cards), and getting excited about the return of hockey in a couple of months with the next "Great One" Sidney Crosby.

QUESTIONS:

1. What makes this an attractive promotion and for whom?
2. Why would this promotion work for Gatorade and possibly not for other brands?

SOURCE: Adapted from Lisa d'Innocenzo, "Dial "C" for clever," *Strategy*, May 2005, p. 34.

diate (but possibly short-lived) responses. As a result, they tend to be used as stopgap measures to reverse unexpected sales declines, rather than as integrated parts of a marketing strategy.

Determining objectives and strategies Three broad objectives of sales promotion are:

- Stimulating business-user or household demand for a product.
- Improving the marketing performance of intermediaries and salespeople.
- Supplementing advertising and supporting the activities of salespeople.

More specific objectives of sales promotion are much like those for advertising and personal selling. Examples are:

- ***Encourage customers to try a new or improved product:*** The companies that make Tetley tea or Neutrogena shampoo might send free samples through the mail.
- ***Disrupt existing buying habits:*** A coupon offering a large discount might cause a consumer to switch brands of a product that is viewed as generic, such as orange juice or motor oil.
- ***Attract new customers:*** Financial institutions have offered small appliances and other premiums to encourage consumers to open accounts.
- ***Encourage greater use by existing customers:*** Most major airlines have frequent-flyer programs to encourage travellers to use their airlines more often. Other businesses have established similar loyalty programs, including the popular Air Miles program to which a number of major retailers belong.
- ***Combat a competitor's promotional activity:*** For example, one supermarket chain runs a lottery or game to attract shoppers, and a competitor retaliates by offering triple-value coupons.
- ***Stimulate multiple purchases and volume buying:*** A company that offers a buy-two-get-one-free promotion is trying to get customers to buy more than they would have done.
- ***Increase impulse buying:*** End-of-aisle and island displays in supermarkets can increase sales of a product by as much as 50 percent.
- ***Inspire greater retailer co-operation:*** A sporting-goods manufacturer gets additional shelf space by setting up excellent point-of-purchase displays, training the retailers' salespeople, and providing tote bags to be given away with purchases.

The choice of sales-promotion tools is directly related to the objectives of the total marketing program. Consider the following situations and the different strategies available:

- A firm's objective is to increase sales, which calls for entering new geographic markets using a pull strategy. To encourage product trial and attract consumers away from familiar brands, possible sales-promotion tactics are coupons, cash rebates, free samples, and premiums.
- A firm's objective is to protect market share in the face of intense competition. This goal suggests a push strategy to improve retailer performance and goodwill. Training the retailers' sales forces, supplying effective point-of-purchase displays, and granting advertising allowances would be appropriate sales-promotion options.

Determining budgets The sales-promotion budget should be established as a specific part of the budget for the total marketing communications mix. Including sales promotion in an advertising or public relations budget is not likely to foster the development of a separate sales-promotion strategy, and as a result, sales promotion may be overlooked or poorly integrated with the other components of marketing communications. Setting a separate budget for sales promotion forces a company to recognize and manage it.

Within the concept of developing an integrated marketing communications strategy, the amount budgeted for sales promotion should be determined by the task method. This forces management to consider specific objectives and the sales-promotion techniques that will be used to accomplish them.

Selecting the appropriate techniques Common sales-promotion techniques are shown in Table 15-2, where they are divided into three categories based on the target audience:

- ***Sales promotion directed at final consumers:*** Many of the tools in Table 15-2 probably are quite familiar to you, but a brief discussion of some of them will give you a better sense of their significance.

  Since the development of electronic systems for distributing coupons, the number of paper coupons distributed in Canada has plummeted. While more than 22 billion coupons were distributed annually in the early 1990s, today fewer than 5 billion are sent out, as retailers continue the trend away from in-ad and on-package couponing to other strategies, such as everyday low pricing and loyalty programs. There has also been a steady decline in redemption rates, from 5 percent in the 1970s to less than 1 percent today.

  New distribution methods and formats have also been explored, ranging from Web sites, wireless cellphones, and targeted e-mail distribution, to cash register tapes and parking meters that dispense coupons when you insert your parking fee.

  save.ca

  Billed as Canada's first electronic-coupon magazine for packaged goods, save.ca (**www.save.ca**) guarantees clients a minimum of 250,000 visitors a month. Visitors click on the coupons they want, fill in their addresses, and indicate if they want to receive promotional offers, via e-mail, directly from the manufacturer. The coupons are then printed on high-gloss paper and mailed out the next business day. The challenge remains to keep visitors returning by continually offering new products and deals.[8]

  In keeping with the theme of convenience for consumers, MyThum Interactive and Givex Corporation have launched a program called Mx-Coupon. Cellphone users who sign up for the service can have a Givex coupon number delivered to their cellphone and redeem the coupon at participating retailers. The applications for this high-tech couponing may also extend to fast food restaurants offering discounts and be used as a reminder from a hairdresser that it is time to drop by, with a discount if the consumer does so by a certain date.[9]

  Whether these new forms of couponing will result in an increase in their use (redemption) or increase their success in encouraging product trial remains to be seen, but for now they do offer unique promotion opportunities for firms as the technology that makes them possible becomes available and remains novel to consumers.

  "Advertising specialties" is a miscellaneous category of small, usually inexpensive items imprinted with a company's name or logo that are given or sold by producers or intermediaries to customers and prospects. Examples are pens, calendars, key rings, paperweights, coffee cups, hats, and jackets.

- ***Sales promotion directed at intermediaries:*** Some of the tools just discussed may also be directed at intermediaries and their sales forces. In addition, trade associations in industries as diverse as shoes, travel, and furniture sponsor trade shows that are open only to wholesalers and retailers. Many producers also spend considerable time and money to train the sales forces of their wholesalers and retailers.

- ***Sales promotion directed at a producer's own sales force:*** Again, there is an overlap between the tools directed at intermediaries and those designed for the producer's own sales force. Sales contests are probably the most significant of these tools, with many firms offering one type or another. The most common incentive is cash, used in over half of all contests. Other incentives include merchandise, plaques, jewellery, and travel. Visual sales aids (flip charts, slides) are prepared for salespeople, and brochures are developed to reinforce sales presentations.

A key step in sales-promotion management is deciding which devices will help the organization reach its promotional goals. Factors that influence the choice of promotional devices include:

- ***Nature of the target audience***: Is the target group loyal to a competing brand? If so, a high-value coupon may be necessary to disrupt customers' purchase patterns. Is the product bought on impulse? If so, an eye-catching point-of-purchase display may be enough to generate sales.
- ***The organization's marketing communications objectives***: Does a pull strategy or a push strategy best complement the rest of the marketing communications program?
- ***Nature of the product***: Does the product lend itself to sampling, demonstration, or multiple-item purchases?
- ***Cost of the device***: Sampling to a large market may be prohibitively expensive.
- ***Current economic conditions***: Coupons, premiums, and rebates are good options during periods of recession or inflation, when consumers are particularly price-conscious.

Evaluating sales promotion Evaluating the effectiveness of sales promotions is much easier and the results are more accurate than is evaluation of the effectiveness of advertising. For example, responses to a premium offer or a coupon with a specified closing date can be counted and compared with a similar period when no premiums or coupons were offered. It is easier to measure sales promotion because:

- Most sales promotions have definite starting and ending points. Coupons must be redeemed by a certain date. Contest entries must be submitted before a particular deadline. Contests for the sales force include only the sales made during a specified period. This is quite different from advertising, where there can be significant residual effects and the results of one campaign may overlap with those of another.
- Most sales promotions are designed to drive sales directly. It is more difficult to measure a change in attitude or an increase in information about a product or brand than it is to count sales.

TABLE 15-2 Major Sales Promotional Tools, Grouped by Target Audience

End-Users (Consumer or Business)	Intermediaries and Their Sales Forces	Producers' Own Sales Force
Coupons	Trade shows and exhibitions	Sales contests
Cash rebates	Point-of-purchase displays	Sales training manuals
Premiums (gifts)	Free goods	Sales meetings
Free samples	Advertising allowances	Packets with promotional materials
Contests and sweepstakes	Contests for salespeople	Demonstration model of product
Point-of-purchase displays	Training intermediaries' sales forces	
Product demonstrations	Product demonstrations	
Trade shows and exhibitions	Advertising specialties	
Advertising specialties		

However, there are some pitfalls in measuring sales-promotion effects. First, not all sales promotions meet the conditions just mentioned. For instance, training given to a distributor's sales force may be valuable but may not produce immediate results. Second, current sales-promotion results may be inflated by sales "stolen" from the future. That is, a sales promotion may get buyers to act now, but they might have bought the product in the future anyway. An indication of this "cannibalizing" effect is a lower level of sales after the promotion ends, compared with the level before the sales promotion began. Third, any attempt at measurement must take into consideration external conditions, such as the behaviour of competitors and the state of the economy. A firm's market share may not increase following an expensive sales promotion, for example, but the promotion may have offset the potentially damaging impact of a competitor's promotional activity.

Public Relations

Public relations is a management tool designed to build favourable attitudes toward an organization, its products, and its policies. It is an often-overlooked form of promotion, relegated far behind sales, advertising, and sales promotion. It is also often ignored until the company is facing a crisis or a problem that brings it into the public eye. In this sense, it is often viewed as a defensive tool. On the other hand, many companies today are realizing the role of public relations in supporting the reputation-building activities of the firm and in protecting its brand image.

public relations
A broad communications effort designed to build or maintain a favourable image for an organization with its various publics.

In most companies, **public relations** is not the responsibility of the marketing department. If there is an organized effort, it is usually handled by a small public relations department that reports directly to the CEO. Only recently have many organizations come to appreciate the value of a solid public relations program. As the cost of marketing communications has gone up, firms are realizing that positive exposure through the media or as a result of community involvement can produce a high return on the investment of time and effort.

Nature and scope of public relations

Public relations activities typically are designed to build or maintain a favourable reputation and image for an organization and a favourable relationship with its various publics — customers, prospects, shareholders, employees, labour unions, the local community, and government.

Unlike advertising, public relations need not use the media to communicate its message. Good public relations can be achieved by supporting charitable projects (by supplying volunteer labour or other resources), participating in community service events, sponsoring athletic teams, funding the arts, producing an employee or customer newsletter, and disseminating information through exhibits, displays, and tours. Major companies often sponsor public events or special programs on television as part of their public relations efforts. Cultural organizations such as ballet companies and symphony orchestras would not survive without the support they receive from major corporations.

Publicity as a form of public relations

publicity
Media presentations about a product or organization that are not paid for and have the credibility of editorial material.

Publicity is any communication about an organization, its products, or policies through the media that is not paid for by the organization. Publicity usually takes the form of a news story appearing in a mass medium or an endorsement provided by an individual, either informally or in a speech or interview. This is good publicity.

There is also, of course, bad publicity — a negative story about a firm or its product appearing in the media. In a society that is increasingly sensitive about the environment and in which news media are quick to report mistakes, organizations tend to focus on this negative dimension of publicity. As a result, managers are so concerned with avoiding bad publicity that they overlook the potential of good publicity.

There are three approaches to gaining good publicity:

press release
News from a company sent to the media for publication.

1. ***Prepare a story and circulate it to the media:*** The intention of such a story, called a **press release**, is for the selected newspapers, television stations, or other media to report the information as news.
2. ***Communicate personally with a group:*** A press conference will draw media representatives if they feel the subject or speaker has news value. Company tours and speeches to civic or professional groups are other forms of individual-to-group communications.
3. ***Engage in one-on-one personal communication, or lobbying:*** Companies lobby legislators and other powerful people in an attempt to influence their opinions and, subsequently, their decisions.

Publicity can help to accomplish any communications objective. It can be used to announce new products, publicize new policies, recognize employees, describe research breakthroughs, or report financial performance — if the message, person, group, or event is viewed by the media as newsworthy. This is what distinguishes publicity from advertising: Publicity is not "forced" on the audience. This is also the source of its primary benefit. The credibility of publicity typically is much higher than that of advertising. If we tell you our product is great, you may well be sceptical, but if an independent, objective third party says on the evening news that our product is great, you are more likely to believe it.

Other benefits of publicity are:

- ***Costs less than advertising or personal selling:*** Publicity usually costs less because there are no media space or time costs for conveying the message and no salespeople to support.
- ***Increased readership:*** Many consumers are conditioned to ignore advertising or at least pay it little attention. Publicity is presented as editorial material or news, so it gets greater readership.
- ***More information:*** Because it is presented as editorial material, publicity can contain greater detail than the usual ad. More information and persuasive content can be included in the message.
- ***Timeliness:*** A company can put out a news release very quickly when some unexpected event occurs.

Opportunities to promote and enhance a brand come in a variety of ways. West49, based in Burlington, Ontario, is riding the skateboard wave. From one store in 1996, there are now 49 in Canada and three in the United States. The company has its own 1,860-square-metre skate park in St. Catharines, allowing it direct and virtually unlimited opportunities to connect with its market. The West49 World Cup of Skateboarding is held there each year and is eastern North America's largest skateboarding event, with a cash purse of $70,000. The retailer also has its own skate team, consisting of professional boarder Pierre-Luc Gagnon and six amateurs, which tours locations, providing demonstrations and autographs.[10]

Absolut Vodka

Absolut Vodka sponsors a Web site that corresponds nicely with the brand's ongoing association with the art world. The site (**www.absolutdigitalart.com**) welcomes submissions from digital and non-digital artists who, if chosen, are featured online. The portal is often featured in universities and colleges that offer digital art courses, as well as at art events across Canada, exposing and building the brand with an important demographic. Absolut refers to these efforts not as sponsorships, but as partnerships, where art is the key driver, and includes associations with painters, sculptors, jewellery designers, and even architects.[11]

MARKETING AT WORK — 15-4: STRATEGY

Public Relations Idol!

Public relations is an integral part of any integrated marketing communications plan and L'Oreal Canada has certainly ramped up its sponsorship presence in the past few years with its support of the Canadian Idol series on CTV. L'Oreal was trying to reach a younger demographic since L'Oreal Paris had traditionally been popular among women 30 and over. As well, the show gave L'Oreal an opportunity to expand into English Canada (L'Oreal Paris had always concentrated its efforts in Québec).

The sponsorship consisted of 30-second spots throughout the show, opening and closing billboards and a huge presence on the Idol Web site. The real value-added came from the inclusion of L'Oreal products in segments aired during each show. The segments showed the young women and men (L'Oreal sees men as its "last frontier" target group) being taught how to bring out their true Idol qualities by the L'Oreal professional team.

With millions of viewers each week tuning in to the show, L'Oreal had a captive audience since viewers wanted to see their favourite idols being pampered at the L'Oreal mansion!! L'Oreal Canada's sponsorship of Canadian Idol was such a success that L'Oreal Australia decided to sponsor Australian Idol.

QUESTIONS:

1. Why should sponsorship be an important part of the communications strategy of brands like L'Oreal?
2. What does sponsorship and other public relations tools offer the brand that basic media advertising does not?

SOURCE: Adapted from Danny Kucharsky, "Because you're worth it, L'Oreal," *Marketing Magazine Online*, www.marketingmag.ca, February 9, 2004.

Evaluating public relations

Although few executives would argue that having a good image and staying in touch with an organization's publics are unimportant, evaluating public relations and publicity is difficult. In the past, evaluation usually involved a report of activities, rather than of results. Public relations departments maintained "scrapbooks" to show management how many stories were written and published, the number of employees who volunteered for civic projects, and similar information. These days, to justify expenditures, more organizations are requiring publicity departments to provide specific public relations objectives and show measurable results. Because it is impossible to relate public relations and publicity directly to sales, other measures must be used. One is research to show, for example, increased awareness of a product or brand name, or changes in attitudes and beliefs about a firm.

More companies today are taking a scientific approach to the evaluation of public relations activities and opportunities. For example, before deciding to sponsor a particular group or event, or to associate with a particular business partner or spokesperson, some firms will conduct research to determine the "fit" between the firm and its brand on the one hand, and the event or organization or spokesperson on the other. If the fit (as perceived by the target audience) is not a good one, sponsorship money will be wasted and, more importantly, damage may be done to the firm and its brands.

PAGE UP!

1. Define sales promotion.
2. What are the three broad objectives of sales promotion?
3. ______________________ is a management tool designed to build favourable attitudes toward an organization.

Key Terms and Concepts

consultative salesperson 437
consumer promotion 447
customer-service representatives 430
driver-salesperson 436
evaluating sales performance 445
inside order taker 436
inside selling 432
missionary salesperson 436
outside order taker 436
outside sales force 432
outside selling 432
press release 453
proactive selling 432
prospecting 440
public relations 452
publicity 452
reactive selling 432
sales 430
sales engineer 437
sales function 430
sales promotion 447
selling 430
team selling 438
telemarketing 433
trade promotion 447

Questions and Problems

1. The cost of a full-page, four-colour advertisement in one issue of a national magazine is higher than the cost of employing two salespeople for a full year. A sales manager is urging her company to eliminate a few of these ads and, instead, hire a few more salespeople. This executive believes that one good salesperson working for an entire year can sell more than one ad in one issue of a magazine. How would you respond?
2. If you were preparing a sales presentation for the following products and services, what information about a prospect would you seek as part of your preparation?
   a. Two-bedroom condominium.
   b. New automobile.
   c. Carpeting for a home redecorating project.
   d. Marketing research project for a local department store.
   e. Building cleaning service.
3. How would you go about recruiting sales applicants for each of the following firms? Explain your choice in each case.
   a. Hilton Hotel Saint John.
   b. IBM, for sales of mainframe (large) computers.
   c. Mount Pleasant Cemetery.
   d. A tobacco company.
   e. A manufacturer of remote sensing devices.
4. Compare the merits of straight-salary and straight-commission sales compensation. What are two types of sales jobs in which each plan might be desirable?
5. How might a firm determine whether a salesperson is developing relationships with customers?
6. Scan a current issue of a local or national newspaper and note the sales-promotion tools that appear in the advertisements. Which one do you consider to be particularly effective?
7. Explain how sales promotion might be used to offset weak personal selling in retail stores.
8. Can a well-implemented company Web site help to offset weak or inconsistent selling in a company's retail outlets?
9. Describe a recent public relations event in your community. How did it benefit the sponsor?
10. How does publicity differ from advertising?

Hands-On Marketing

1. Review your activities of the past few days and identify those in which:
   a. You did some personal selling.
   b. People tried to sell something to you.

   Select one situation in each category where you thought the selling was particularly effective, and explain why it was so.

2. Visit a supermarket, drugstore, or hardware store and make a list of all of the sales-promotion tools that you observe. Describe how each one relates to the sales-promotion objectives described in the chapter. Which are particularly effective? Why?

Back to the Top

Now that you have studied more about the sales function in companies, consider what was happening during the sales visit that Oscar and his VP-sales made to Murphy's Pharmacies in our chapter opener. Do you think that Oscar's objectives and Alfred's were different? Why might this be the case? How do you explain Ray's decision to buy the new phone system at the end of the visit, when the system had not even been discussed? Why might this "sales" technique have worked in this situation, but possibly not in other situations?

Online Learning Centre

Want to get better grades, tips on how to study more effectively, and up-to-date information on happenings in the world of marketing? Then, visit the Online Learning Centre for practice tests, Study Smart software, *Marketing Magazine,* and much more! **www.mcgrawhill.ca/olc/sommers**

CASE 6-1:

Dove: The Campaign for Real Beauty

"Did you hear that Heidi Klum is the spokesperson for McDonalds?" Julie said as she ate her Big Mac. "Julie, are you serious? As if she eats McDonalds!" Donna said in a frustrated tone. "I'm so sick of supermodels appearing in commercials for things like wrinkle creams, when we all know they don't have a wrinkle in sight. Or commercials for cellulite cream, and we all know most of them probably don't even know the meaning of cellulite."

While perfect (and imperfect) human bodies are getting more and more media attention, there is also more concern about the effects that the images portrayed in the media are having on women of all ages. Fact is, there are only about a dozen supermodels in the world and billions of women with some sort of physical "flaw." Women (and men) are now speaking out about the impact of the unrealistic images of beauty that are promoted by fashion and cosmetics companies. And, somebody is finally listening. Unilever's Dove brand is doing away with the traditional marketing messages that tell women and girls that, if they buy a particular health or beauty product, they can look like the supermodel in the ad. How can "normal" women relate? The point is, most can't. So, if their target markets can't relate to the advertising message, why would anyone expect women to buy the products?

Instead of images of long locks, longer legs and incredibly lean bodies, Dove is promoting its products with a message of "real beauty." The campaign encourages women and girls to celebrate themselves as they are. The sentiment is articulated quite strongly through their slogan "real women have curves."

The Campaign for Real Beauty appeals to women on national and local levels. Print and TV ads feature candid and confident images of curvy, full-bodied, real women, not traditional models. The "six real women" appear in panties and bras in their natural, un-retouched glory. The women proudly show off their wrinkles, curves and bumps. National television and magazine advertising, as well as interactive billboards, transit station signage and city bus ads have been used to portray the message. The campaign is intended to challenge women's notions of beauty with communication in high-profile downtown locations and along high-traffic roads in major cities.

The ads promote Dove skin products such as Intensive Firming Cream, Intensive Firming Lotion and Firming Body Wash. Containing blends of glycerin, seaweed extract and elastin peptides, these products claim to have skin-firming properties and to reduce the appearance of cellulite. It tries to reach women who might be self-conscious about their bodies, but are also willing to accept being somewhat "imperfect." It would be a little difficult to believe that a size 0 supermodel needs that kind of product.

The campaign in Canada focuses entirely on body image. The second phase launched with a television and cinema advertisement, aired during Super Bowl XL, which featured Canadian girls and adolescents, aged five through fourteen. The girls share what they believe to be their own personal flaws. One dark-haired girl "wishes she were blonde." Another "thinks she's ugly." A red-haired girl "hates her freckles." You should view this ad at **www.camapignforrealbeauty.com**, at the "inside the campaign" section.

Wrinkled or wonderful? Flawed or flawless? Fat or fabulous? Whether this approach to beauty will take hold and replace traditional images remains to be seen. It won't be easy to compete with the perfect images portrayed in magazines, movies and TV. But, is it even a competition? Perhaps Unilever, the maker of Dove, is simply providing an alternative for real women. You decide.

Questions:

1. How is Dove positioning itself? Is this strategy too risky?
2. Could there be any negative repercussions for a campaign like this? (You should visit the Web site if you are unfamiliar with the campaign.) If so, what are they and how should Dove deal with these?
3. At **www.campaignforrealbeauty.com** read the articles pertaining to the campaign. Do you think Unilever can change stereotypes with print and TV ads? Comment on the effectiveness of the Web site.
4. Having viewed the ad discussed in the case, what do you think is its appeal?

SOURCES: Adapted from Rebecca Traister, "Real beauty? – or real smart marketing?" Salon.com, http://dir.salon.com/story/mwt/feature/2005/07/22/dove/index.html; July, 22, 2005. Retrieved on March 24, 2006; Alicia Clegg, "Dove Gets Real," Brandchannel.com, http://www.brandchannel.com/features_effect.asp?pf_id=259, April 8, 2005. Retrieved on March 24, 2006. "Dove's campaign for Real Beauty," Media Awareness Network, http://www.media-awareness.ca/english/resources/educational/teachable_moments/campaignrealbeauty.cfm. Retrieved on March 24, 2006.

CASE 6-2:

Basketball Buzz

Roberto has been playing basketball since he was very young. Every day after school, a couple of his buddies would come over to shoot some hoops. Roberto was never the top player, but he was always pretty good. When he was old enough to join the school's basketball team, he signed up right away. His passion for basketball extended beyond the court. His room was plastered with Detroit Pistons posters. As soon as an NBA game came on, Roberto was glued to the television.

For his twelfth birthday, Roberto's father bought him tickets to go see Atlanta play the Pistons in Detroit. Roberto can still recall the excitement he felt as his father drove over the Ambassador Bridge from Windsor into Detroit. That night, as he cheered from the stands, he dreamed of one day playing in the NBA, a dream no doubt shared by many boys his age.

Now sixteen, Roberto takes basketball very seriously. He doesn't mind that his basketball coach is very demanding. After all, their chances of making it to the finals this year are great; especially with Sam on the team. The team's 6'3" captain has been the top scorer this season. Whenever they play, a large crowd comes to watch the games. It has been rumoured that NBA scouts have been in the stands to watch Sam. Why, just the other day, a stranger approached Sam after the game and pulled him aside. Later, when asked about it, Sam wouldn't say who the man was.

Yesterday at practice, Roberto noticed that Sam was wearing a new pair of Adidas shoes. He hadn't seen that model before. During the practice, a couple of team members went up to Sam to ask him about his shoes. "Cool shoes, where'd you get them?" Sam mumbled the name of a sports store in the local mall. After practice, Roberto headed for the mall to see if he could find the shoes. As he walked into the store, he spotted them right away. He looked at the price tag. They weren't cheap. He wondered how he could convince his parents to buy him a pair.

What Roberto doesn't know is that the stranger in the audience was in fact a "product seeder" sent by Adidas to scout out the best player, or trendsetter, on his team to give him their latest shoes. The idea behind "buzz marketing," as it is called, is that friends and peers will notice the trendsetter's shoes and start talking about them. As word spreads and more kids buy the shoes, the benefits to the company are numerous. Brand awareness is heightened by the buzz. And the best thing about buzz marketing: people don't know they are being advertised to. But if Roberto found out how Sam got his shoes, would they have the same appeal to him?

Questions

1. Should "buzz marketing" be considered a marketing activity?
2. Why does Roberto want to get the same shoes as Sam? What value does he perceive in those shoes?
3. What do you think would be Roberto's reaction if he were to find out that what he thought was an NBA scout was in fact an Adidas rep, whose purpose was to get people talking about the shoes?
4. Do you see any ethical concerns in the practice of buzz marketing? How is it different from advertising in terms of how it might influence prospective customers?

SOURCE: Adapted from CBC *Venture*, "Buzz Marketing."

CASE 6-3:

Gamers

Multimedia

"Honey, it's dinner time — can you please stop playing that game?" "Just a second, I'll be right up!" After 20 minutes had passed, Lori proceeded down the stairs of their two-story house to physically collect her boyfriend. "Roger, I'm sick and tired of always having to drag you away from that computer game!" "Lori, it's not a computer game, it's a PlayStation 2." "Whatever it is, you're always on it." Not taking his eyes away from it, Roger asked, "Lori, why don't you come and play, you'll like it." As sceptical as Lori was, she proceeded to sit next to her boyfriend in front of their big-screen TV. "Okay, what kind of game is this?" she asked. "It's called *NHL 2006* — it's a hockey game." Still sceptical, she asked, "Okay, what do I have to do?" "Well, the first thing you have to do is pick your equipment. First pick your skates. Do you want CCM? Nike?" Lori looked surprised, "You can actually pick the brand name you want?" Roger laughed, "Yeah, I know — a lot of the games are doing it now — it makes it look so real. I played this game the other day called *Crazy Taxi*. You have to go around dropping people off to places like Pizza Hut, Levis, and KFC — it's really cool."

In *Perfect Dark Zero*, secret agent Joanna Dark communicates through her Samsung PDA device. In the latest version of *Splinter Cell*, lead character Sam Fisher carries a Sony Ericsson PDA. Monkeys roll around in giant balls and collect Dole bananas in *Super Monkey Ball*, while *Pikmin* players search for treasures that include Dr. Pepper bottle caps and Duracell batteries.

Welcome to the world of in-game advertising. But while product placement is a fixture in the game, new technology allows ads to run in games much like they do in television. Temporary ads are now appearing everywhere from in-game rink boards to logos on characters' shirts. The changing ads are delivered to gamers' systems via the Web connection, and they can run for specified periods of time, in hand-picked geographic areas and even change depending on the time of day.

A possibly-irritating situation for Lori is an opportunity for advertisers who are paying attention. The wonderful thing about it is that it's not just on the traditional gaming systems where gamers are immersed for hours in a game of *Halo 2* that this is cropping up. Players are playing games on their cellphones while riding the bus, and playing games like *Diner Dash* on their PCs. Is it the answer for all of the perplexed advertisers?

The typical "gamer" is not the stereotypical 14-year-old pimple-faced boy that has nothing better to do with his time than to play games. The statistics may be surprising. The average age of a gamer is 30. Thirty-six percent of Canadian households have a video game system, 38 percent of households play games online, and 8 percent use their cellphones to pay for, download and play games.

Marketers are continually complaining about how hard it is to hone their advertising efforts in on a particular group of target consumers — either because they have a TiVo or are serial channel-flickers or because every piece of 'junk mail' that arrives is quickly thrown in the garbage. According to Nielsen Interactive Entertainment, there is a 27 to 35 percent unaided recall of in-game advertising with one-third of respondents saying in-game ads influenced product purchases. In fact, over 50 percent of heavy gamers said they liked the games to contain real products. What better environment to capture this large market than in a place where they're finally paying attention? It is a great way for advertisers to connect with an audience to reveal the brand that understands them in a manner that is not invasive but part of the game experience.

Questions

1. What are the implications of this type of product placement for traditional media such as radio and TV? Identify the advantages and disadvantages of the type of advertising described in this case. Do you think product placement influences individual purchase decisions?

2. View the advertisement for Sony Entertainment that accompanies this case. What target market(s) do you think Sony had in mind when this ad was created?

3. What are the ethical considerations, if any, that game producers and advertisers should be aware of when placing products and brands in video games?

4. In addition to product placement in video games, advertisers are inserting virtual or digital products into movies and TV shows after scenes have been shot. In effect, the Kellogg's box on a kitchen table or the Diet Coke can on a coffee table may have not been in the original shot of a sitcom, a movie or even a music video. In your opinion, what does virtual and real product placement mean for traditional advertising like the Sony ad in the video? Do you think traditional advertising methods will cease to exist in the near future? Explain your answer.

SOURCE: Adapted in part from Eve Lazarus, "Keep it Real," *Marketing Magazine Online*, www.marketingmag.ca, March 13, 2006.

CASE 6-4:

Multimedia

GuestLink – Great Radio

In Chapter 14, Ralph van Dijk, an internationally-known producer of radio advertising provided his thoughts on the power of radio in his Guest Marketer column. Let's now listen to four award-winning commercials that Ralph has produced for clients in the United Kingdom. Think about how he brings the principles that he discussed in his column into the production of these ads.

Here are his brief notes on the four commercials:

Topic Bar — Primary School

Cadbury's Topic bars are milk chocolate, hazelnuts, soft nougat with a smooth caramel centre. This is one of fifteen ads in this campaign and all were recorded in a kind of Dogma style — no script, no actors, no studio — four 'extras' around a real dining table, given the outline of a scene and direction on where to start and where to finish. The rest was up to them. I edited a 10-minute conversation down to this 40-second ad.

Mastercard — Helium

The key for this script was to make the reactions sound completely real and spontaneous. So I took the actress to a different room, and told her just to play along when we called. I kept the helium part as a surprise and her reaction was beautiful.

Radio Advertising Bureau — Psychologist

This is part of an ongoing branding campaign for the British radio industry itself. They get played quite a lot, so it's important the script had new layers to pick up on each time you hear it.

Sega — Virtua Cop

The brief was to find an actor who sounded like an underworld criminal. There are plenty of Lock Stock type actors around, but when all you have is the voice, I was never convinced. We took a long shot and asked a local prison if we could interview an inmate. Why they agreed I'll never know, but it made for truly arresting radio.

Questions

1. Discuss these four commercials and what makes them different from much of the advertising we hear on radio (and on TV, for that matter).
2. Just from these four commercials, how would you describe Ralph Van Dijk's approach to advertising?
3. How are the principles that Ralph outlined in his Guest Marketer column reflected in these four commercials?
4. Put yourself in the shoes of Ralph's client in each of these cases and discuss your initial reaction to the commercials. How do you think they reinforce the brand strategy in each case?

PART 7

Tying Marketing Together

An overview of marketing in the modern customer-centric organization; its role in society, and considering where marketing is heading in the future

Up to this point, we have dealt separately with how a firm determines its positioning, how it selects its target market segments, and then develops and manages the elements of its marketing strategy for those target customers — all in the name of building a base of loyal customers. In the final part of the book, we return to the fact that the customer lies at the centre of all marketing in a company and that all marketing decisions of the firm are made with the goal of long-term customer stisfaction in mind.

At the beginning of **Part 7**, we present an overview of the role of marketing within an organization, proposing a very holistic view of what is involved in the practice of marketing. We reinforce our view that marketing starts with the customer. This is followed by a discussion of marketing evaluation — how marketing responds to its critics. Then, we review the current position of marketing in our society, examine how various organizations have responded to the changing face of marketing, and consider where marketing is headed in the future — what the keys are to marketing success.

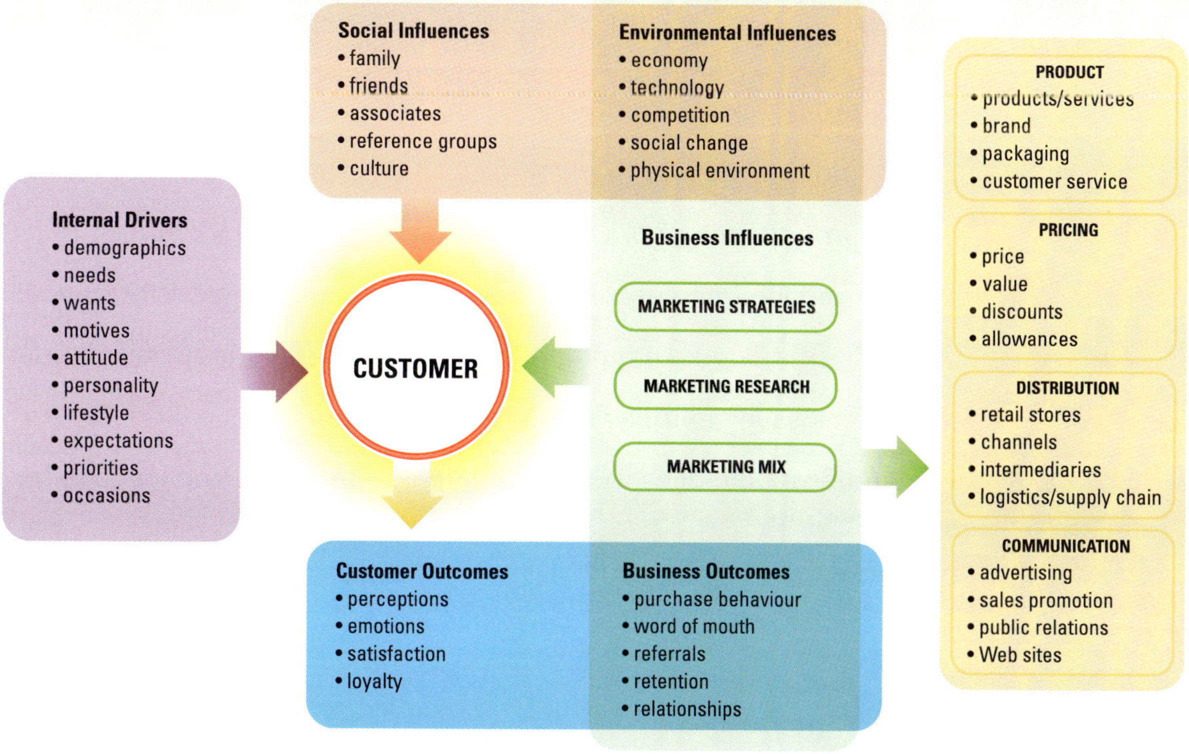

CHAPTER 16

Marketing: A Customer-Centric View

In this chapter, we discuss an holistic (all-inclusive) view of marketing in an attempt to communicate how marketing is evolving in progressive firms, whether they are retail, service, or not-for-profit organizations. Strategic management of the marketing function is becoming increasingly important in today's global marketplace. The planning, implementation, and evaluation of marketing programs are critical to this end. Management must periodically assess the appropriateness of its goals and its performance in reaching them.

This final chapter also addresses a number of criticisms of marketing, as well as ethical issues and current responses to these. Finally, we will peer into a crystal ball and consider some of the prospects for the future of marketing. After studying this chapter, you should have an understanding of:

- The holistic view of marketing.
- The importance of practising customer-centric marketing.
- A broadened perspective for evaluating marketing performance.
- Criticisms of marketing and the responses of various stakeholders.
- Ethical issues in today's marketing environment.
- Significant changes in the marketplace and their implications for marketing.

Looking After the Kids is Marketing Too

Saturday mornings are usually a time for the newspaper and cartoons at the Ferguson home, but not today. Anne, James and their two sons Jacob, 5, and Joshua, 3, are headed out for a morning of shopping. But this is no ordinary trip to the store. They are headed to IKEA to buy some much-needed furniture for the new multipurpose room they recently added to their house. With two small children, the renovating did not go as quickly as they had hoped. James is a do-it-yourselfer and completed the extension with some help from a few friends and family. The room adds much needed space to the family's home, but now they need functional, family-friendly furniture that won't break the budget.

Anne usually refuses to shop with both children — she compares the experience to a battleground. Because of this, she and James rarely get to pick things out together. They usually go through catalogues and flyers at home, decide on what they like and then one of them goes out to do the actual shopping. Internet shopping has also become a favourite way for this family to make purchases.

Today is different, however, because Anne knows that IKEA offers a supervised play area where Jacob and Joshua will be safe and happy while she and James shop. There's even a restaurant where the boys love to eat. The Fergusons are not going to IKEA without having done their homework, however. They have searched IKEA's online store and chosen some things they think will work. But the outing is necessary since they really want to see the furniture before making their final selections.

It's almost 3 o'clock when the Fergusons arrive home, their minivan stacked with boxes of furniture with names such as Ektorp, Leksvik and Bonde and the two boys sleeping in their car seats. Of course, Anne and James know that they have hours of assembling ahead of them before their room comes to life. Better hope for more cartoons on TV!

Throughout this book, we have tried to present a new and different view of marketing, one that is focused on the customer and on the building of relationships with customers. We have suggested that marketing is as much about how business deals with and treats customers as it is about a set of tools that are used to market a company and its products and brands. We have suggested that the term marketing is appropriately defined as virtually any aspect of an organization that has the potential to affect long-term customer satisfaction. This is a different view of marketing than has been practised by many companies and organizations in the past, and many are just now coming around to accepting it. While Joshua and Jacob are not too fond of shopping, especially when it replaces Saturday morning cartoons, they have been persuaded by the promise of the play area and lunch in the restaurant when their parents are finished. IKEA realizes that shopping is about more than buying furniture; it is also an experience for the customer and, in this case, the family. The more IKEA can do to make that experience enjoyable, the more often customers will return.

Marketing: The Holistic View

holistic view of marketing
The view that virtually everything a company does has an impact on long-term customer satisfaction and is, therefore, part of marketing.

We have proposed what we call an **holistic view of marketing.** This means that we need a "big picture" perspective of all of the things that should be included in marketing. We suggested earlier that marketing now extends well beyond the areas that have traditionally been considered the responsibility of the marketing department. In the past, these have generally been referred to as the four components of the marketing mix — the product, communications, distribution, and price. While we have suggested the broadest possible definitions of these areas and we have devoted several chapters of this book to explaining how each of these contributes, we have also encouraged you to think about lots of other things that have the potential to make customers satisfied or dissatisfied.

We suggest that marketing is essentially how the firm views its dealings with customers. If the prevailing view is one of how to sell them more products and services, we suggest that this firm has a sales emphasis, rather than a modern marketing emphasis. What's interesting is that this company may feel it is customer-focused, and indeed it is! It is focused on figuring out how to sell more to its customers, but that's not marketing — at least not how we view it.

customer-centric
Focused on customers and on achieving long-term customer satisfaction; the customer is at the centre of management thinking.

Today, it has become fashionable for companies and other organizations to portray themselves as customer-focused or **customer-centric.** The implication is that such firms are concentrating on their customers and doing things that will be considered attractive by those customers. While more and more companies are moving toward this customer-centric positioning, others are only part-way along the road. To be truly customer-centric means that a company not only must understand its customers intimately, but also must appreciate that many different things that are under the control of the company have the potential to contribute to the satisfaction of those customers, not only the things that have been considered to be part of the marketing department's responsibility.

It may be useful to think about the factors that we discussed in Chapter 1 that contribute to customer satisfaction. We suggested then that it's not enough to have great products at attractive prices and to advertise and distribute them effectively. It is also important to think about the many ways that a company can, on the one hand, make a customer feel important and valued or, on the other hand, angry and frustrated. We have suggested throughout this book that there is an important emotional side to what a company offers its customer — its value proposition — and that the emotional is at least as important as the so-called functional side of the offer in driving customer satisfaction. Thus, having great products and great prices is not enough if the customer is constantly frustrated in trying to deal with the company or encounters rude and unhelpful employees.

Again, IKEA has a very clear view of the kinds of customers to whom the company appeals. It understands its target customer segments and tailors its value proposition to them.

It markets to the entire family — in fact, family is a major focus of IKEA's marketing efforts. In that company, marketing is as much about how the customer feels when shopping as it is about conventional marketing mix components.

The most effective companies today understand that many things have the potential to create customer satisfaction and dissatisfaction, and they also realize that it is critically important that customers enjoy dealing with them. This kind of thinking is a result of the tremendous changes that have taken place in the marketplace in recent years. It has caused many companies and organizations to rethink how they view and define marketing. While it is acknowledged that the marketing function within a company continues to have responsibility for the components of the traditional marketing mix, there is also a view that suggests that all other aspects of how a business interacts with customers should be considered part of a broader definition of "marketing."

Should marketing have responsibility for all of the things that "touch" the customer? Should we conclude, as suggested in Marketing at Work file 16-1, that "marketing is everything?" Is IKEA's decision to offer a children's play area and a restaurant as elements of its value proposition part of their marketing strategy, or is it part of a broader customer strategy?

corporate culture
The atmosphere that prevails within a company, which contributes to employees' satisfaction and influences how they treat customers.

The firm and the brand

Our holistic view of marketing must be extended even beyond the relationships that customers have with retailers and brands to address the fact that how the firm is managed and its role in the broader community are also important. The extent to which employees buy into this view of marketing and feel themselves to be an important part of how its customers feel toward the firm will depend to a very large extent on how they are treated and whether they enjoy working for the firm. Therefore, we should include a discussion of the **corporate culture** in our definition of marketing. Happy employees generally create happy customers. It is easy for customers to know when an employee is unhappy working for a firm, because it is often reflected in the employee's attitude and behaviour toward customers.

The atmosphere within a firm and its culture — whether it is a pleasant place to work — is a function of the leadership of the firm and how the firm treats its people. That leadership rests with the CEO or general manager. It is not uncommon today in more progressive companies to hear the observation that the CEO is the main marketing executive of the company, or that the "CEO owns the customer."

Finally, we should look outside the doors of the firm and beyond its obvious marketing activities to examine its role within the broader community. How a company conducts itself in its dealings with customers, suppliers, its employees, and other groups, and how it demonstrates its role as a member of the community in which it operates will influence its reputation in that community. Its reputation is an important element in how the company is viewed by prospective customers and employees. If that reputation is a positive one, customers and others are more likely to want to

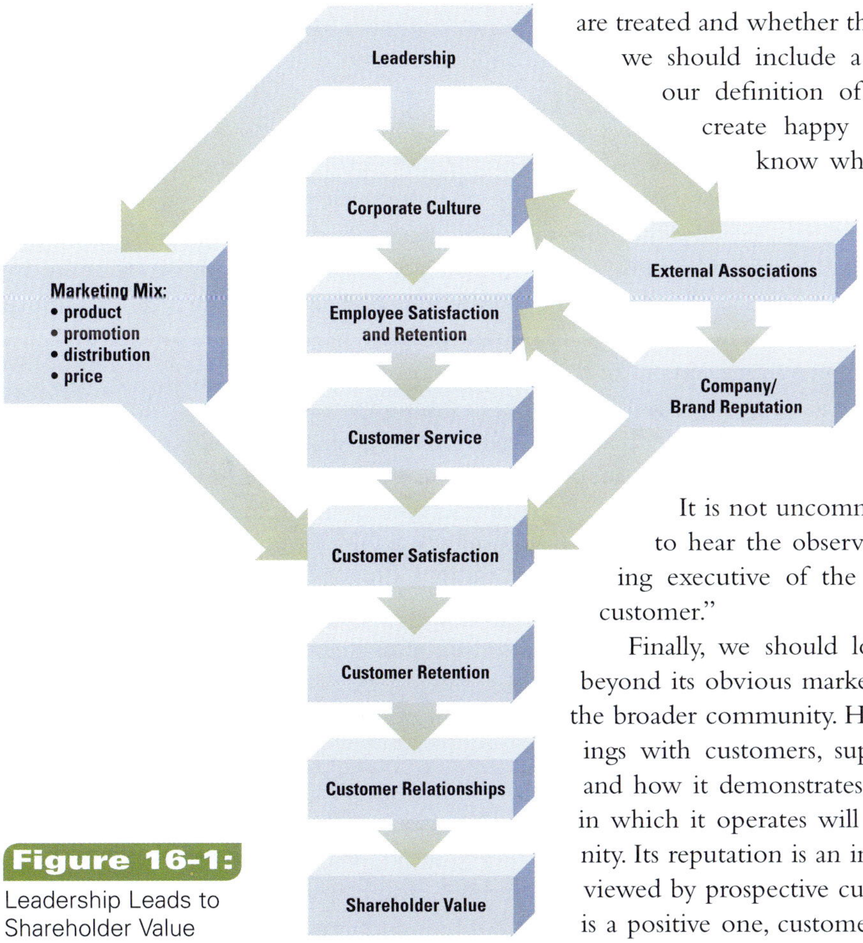

Figure 16-1: Leadership Leads to Shareholder Value

One of the best organizations at creating value for its stakeholders

deal with the company. Managing that reputation is of critical importance and again is the responsibility of senior executives. This is why public relations, sponsorships and related subjects are considered such important components of marketing, as we discussed in Chapter 15.

Therefore, in the broadest possible definition, we could argue that how a company behaves as a member of a community — the charities it supports, the events it sponsors, and the other businesses with which it associates; in other words, its reputation and image — is also part of its marketing program, because these can have an important impact on whether customers will want to deal with the company.

In Figure 16-1, we summarize the many facets of the new view of marketing, one that is focused on creating high levels of customer satisfaction that lead to customer retention and solid relationships. We suggest in this illustration that a firm's ability to create an environment leading to such results rests with the leadership of the company as provided by the senior management team, led by the CEO or equivalent. With the right kind of enlightened leadership, a culture will be created within the firm that will be conducive to employee satisfaction and to the employees treating customers well.

When customers experience excellent service and excellent treatment at the hands of the employees of a firm, they will be satisfied and will tend to return to do business again, leading to higher levels of customer retention. Once customers establish a pattern of repeat business, there is an opportunity for a customer relationship to be established. If a company enjoys high levels of positive relationships with large numbers of customers, that enhances the value of the company to its owners. Thus, we have a fairly direct link between the leadership provided by a CEO and the value that is created for the shareholders.

It is important to point out that the service provided by employees of the firm is only one component of the factors that drive customer satisfaction. At the same time, the four components of the conventional marketing mix — product, promotion, distribution, and price — are at work and must succeed in creating the right value for customers. Also, decisions that management makes in portraying the company to the general public and the community are important in influencing the image and reputation of the company and its brands, and in turn how they are viewed by customers. The important message here is that marketing is much more than getting the four elements of the marketing mix right.

BACK TO THE TOP

As we see in the chapter opener, IKEA offers its customer much more than great products at great prices, in conveniently located stores, and quirky advertising. This company thinks "outside the box." They think a lot about having great furniture at reasonable prices, but it goes well beyond this to address how they can make an emotional connection with customers. As IKEA marketing managers in Europe once told one of the authors of this book, IKEA's best customers are "those who like us the most." IKEA is not really in the childcare or restaurant business, but they see how enhancing the value proposition through the addition of these services adds to the value perceived by the customer and to the customer experience.

How Marketing is Changing

You are studying marketing at a time when the field is undergoing the most dramatic change of the past 50 years. Leading companies are not practising marketing today as they did even five years ago. They are responding to the changes in the environment that we have discussed earlier in this book. In fact, the leading companies that have been successful in earning customer loyalty have accepted the fact that marketing must be more than great products, nice stores, attractive prices, and eye-catching advertising. Jim Stengel, Global Marketing Officer of Procter & Gamble, told the American Association of Advertising Agencies' conference that, "The traditional marketing model is obsolete." He suggested that holistic marketing is driving the business at P&G.[1]

What Mr. Stengel and others are now suggesting is that marketing must change if it is to be responsive to the changes that businesses are experiencing in every product and service category and every country.

It is simply a different marketing environment that companies are facing today. It is an environment where the customer is very much in charge of the relationship. No longer are customers satisfied being the target of a company's advertising campaign or sales promotion. They have the confidence to make their own decisions, armed with more information than they have ever had before, most of it provided by independent sources through the Internet. Power has swung over to the customer, and companies are realizing that their future success depends on their ability to establish a long-term relationship with customers.

Customers are also less tolerant. Their expectations are higher than ever before, driven in part by the fact that some of the best companies are doing things really well. And there is a lot more choice available to them. Again, the Internet has made it possible for customers to access and buy products from around the world. This has changed the definition of competition for companies. No longer are they competing with the firm down the street; customers are buying the same products and services from companies in other countries and having them delivered electronically or by overnight courier.

To complicate things further, it is increasingly difficult for marketers to reach their customers and prospective customers with marketing messages. The mass media have fragmented and are no longer mass as a result. Customers in many segments are spending far more time online these days than they spend in front of a television set. Even when they are "watching" TV, they are likely to be media-multitasking; listening to their iPods, surfing the Internet, and texting friends on their cellphones.

Essentially, the world of marketing has changed and marketers are becoming aware that having great products and services, conveniently available at attractive prices is not enough.

Beyond Borders and Business

It is important to note that the principles we have been discussing in this book and the view of marketing that we have described in the preceding sections of this chapter are equally applicable in international markets and in non-business settings. Understanding the principles is important.

Today, many companies are exposed to international marketplaces and international competitors. In fact, it is difficult to think of an organization that does not interact with an international factor that has the potential to influence its success. Because consumers have so many options today as a result of technology, firms and other organizations often find that their competitors are no longer down the street, in the next town or even in Canada. Customers have the option, through the Internet and other channels, to buy products and services from companies that don't even operate in Canada. In that sense, a very large percentage of firms operate in a global marketplace, possibly without even realizing it.

At the same time, many firms have chosen to compete directly in foreign markets, exporting their products and services to other countries. Whenever these organizations venture into other markets, they are exposed to different customs and customer values and different ways of doing business. All of the concepts that we examined in Chapter 2 pertaining to customer behaviour also apply in other countries, but may not be at all similar to the situation in Canada. It is important, therefore, that companies get to know the marketplaces in which they plan to compete, because these are almost certainly different in some respects from the

Customer Relationship Management: More Than an Application of Technology

Over the past ten years or so, many companies have turned to Customer Relationship Management (CRM) as a means to build increased customer retention, loyalty and relationships. But the field of CRM is very confusing, and different companies tend to practise CRM in different ways. It is useful to take a more detailed look at what CRM means in different firms and how CRM can be made part of a holistic marketing initiative.

CRM as the Application of Technology

When the label Customer Relationship Management became popular in the mid-1990s, it was generally applied to the use of software and other forms of technology to enable a company to collect and manage customer data and to use the data to facilitate and improve customer interaction. In many companies and many countries, that continues to be the principal way that CRM is applied.

In many firms, CRM is associated with the management of customer databases, and the integration of data across divisions of a company, making sure that customer information is available to the sales force, at the point of sale, in call centres, and so on, and is integrated into systems for data capture. A company that takes this approach to CRM will make a major investment in CRM computer systems and software. They will typically employ sophisticated CRM software, sold by "vendors" that include Microsoft, Siebel, Salesforce.com, and SAP. Smaller companies will content themselves with creating and maintaining a less-sophisticated customer database employing spreadsheet software such as Microsoft Excel. In either case, the existence of a customer database is central to a technology approach to CRM.

Building the Customer Database

CRM applications or "solutions" provide for the collection or capture of customer data, usually through automatic data capture systems, such as scanner-equipped checkouts at retail stores, and the systems used by banks, telephone companies, and Internet service providers to capture every interaction with their customers. Thus, some companies have available, stored in "data warehouses," literally billions of pieces of information on their customers. Such detailed databases contain information on every item purchased, every telephone call made, every ATM, debit card and credit card transaction, and every Web site visited.

Where companies do not have access to automatically-collected customer data, they must create their databases "from scratch." It is a challenge to create customer databases in situations where the companies do not have "customer accounts" such as telephone companies and banks will have. In these cases, which include restaurants, movie theatres, and others who serve mainly "anonymous" customers, the companies involved must turn to getting customers to register on their Web sites, enter contests, provide their contact information at events such as concerts, or when they purchase tickets.

In such situations, companies will not have access to detailed customer purchase data and must obtain permission from customers to include them in the database and to send them information and offers from time to time. In these cases, companies will ask customers to provide certain demographic information and a list of products or activities in which they are interested. Some companies ask customers at the point of sale whether they would like to join the database, often referred to as a customer "club" or frequent shopper program. For example, Running Room (**www.runningroom.com**) asks "members" to "join" by registering and completing an online profile. Members can then use the Running Room site to log their daily workouts.

Some also incorporate data from customer surveys and from Statistics Canada and other databases that may provide information about the neighbourhood where the customer lives. This is why such massive databases are referred to as integrated or relational databases because they integrate data from several sources, and allow for the relating of one form of data to another. So, the company will be able to conclude that people with certain demographic profiles are more likely to buy certain products and can then direct marketing materials and campaigns to them.

Supporting Customer Contact

CRM systems also drive customer-contact programs by providing information online to better inform employees at the point of contact, thereby improving the interaction with customers. Contact centres have technology that recognizes the customer's incoming telephone number and provides a "screen pop" containing the customer's data, including products owned, credit history, last calls made, and other pertinent data that the call centre agent may need to know. The software may be "intelligent" enough to be able to route the customer's call to the last agent she talked with. Such CRM software applications are intended to address problems that customers often associate with contacting companies. They want their problem solved without them being handed off from agent to agent, and they like to be able to hear a "familiar voice."

CRM systems that provide employees with detailed customer account information on a screen in front of them also facilitate the employees engaging in "cross-selling" and "up-selling," suggesting additional or upgraded products and services they may like to buy, offering price bundles on services, or informing them of special offers on products they do not currently own.

One main advantage is that the CRM system allows employees to be better informed concerning the customer standing in front of them or to whom they are talking. The technology allows for the tailoring of information and guides how the customer should be handled. It permits special messages to be displayed concerning the customer's value to the firm or that he or she does not want to receive certain information.

CRM technology also allows a firm to send its customers pertinent information automatically. At its most crude and simple level, a car dealer may use its database to send birthday cards to customers, simply because the "system" captures the customers' birth dates from their driver's licences at the time of purchase. We also see this application at work when we buy a book from Amazon.ca, and the system informs us that other customers who bought *The Da Vinci Code* also bought *Holy Blood, Holy Grail*. Such software employs an algorithm that recognizes what you bought and even what books you last looked at on the site, and then suggests that you may also be interested in other titles — a form of electronic cross-selling.

Improving Customer Service

Integrated CRM software systems allow firms to implement various forms of self-service delivery of customer service. For example, Air Canada allows a customer to go to **www.aircanada.ca** and not only check the status of her flight, but also leave a message for the "system" to contact her by e-mail or by text message to her cellphone when the flight is more than 15 minutes delayed.

Automated customer contact turns over to the CRM system the collection of information and management of the customer contact. For example, *The Globe and Mail* offers an automated service that allows subscribers to call a toll-free number to register a "vacation stop" so that they can suspend delivery of their daily newspaper when they are away from home on vacation or business. Using a voice-activated system, the subscriber never talks to a "real person."

Frequent-shopper and frequent-guest programs (also known as "loyalty" or "rewards" programs) not only allow the company to capture information on their customers and to build customer retention through the awarding of "points," but it also provides the firm with the ability to send special offers from time to time that are personalized based on the customer's profile and recent purchase history.

Segmentation and Rewarding Loyalty

Some CRM installations use a technique known as descriptive modelling to create what some firms refer to as customer value segments, dividing the customer base into A, B, C, and D (or platinum, gold, silver, and bronze) segments based on some estimate of their value to the firm, such as total purchases or profitability. These applications group similar customers together into segments. Then, these classifications are used to drive customer contact and treatment, with A or platinum customers receiving special service.

For example, Air Canada's Aeroplan frequent-flyer program tracks the number of flights taken by members and uses this data to classify members into Super Elite, Elite, and Prestige categories of membership. Super Elite flyers, each of whom accumulates more than 100,000 points annually, are entitled to benefits that are not extended to Elite and Prestige members, thereby allowing Air Canada to reward them for their business.

For some firms, loyalty or rewards programs are the central component of their database and CRM systems. These drive data capture and allow the companies not only to know more about their customers' purchase patterns but to keep in touch with them on a regular basis. In addition to the frequent-flyer programs of the major airlines, other examples include Shoppers Drug Mart's *Optimum* program, *HBCRewards* from The Bay, and Delta Hotels' *Delta Privilege* program.

What the System Does with the Data...

In addition to ensuring that customer contact employees are as informed as possible about a customer and his or her history with the firm, and supporting improved interaction between the company and its customers, the CRM system also allows for the development of more efficient marketing programs. Through a process known as data mining, the CRM system applies complex data analysis techniques to identify patterns in the data and the characteristics of groups of customers that are related to certain purchase and other behaviour. Through this process, a firm is able to identify those customers in the database who are most likely to react positively to a marketing initiative. By so doing, it is able to dramatically reduce waste in the marketing budget.

An application known as predictive modelling allows the CRM installation to analyse the behaviour and characteristics of hundreds of thousands of customers in the database and predict what certain segments of customers are likely to buy next. By using data already collected, the system is able to predict what groups of customers are likely to respond positively to a certain direct marketing offer or which are most vulnerable and likely to leave for a competitor. The result is to make outbound direct marketing programs more efficient as the messages and offers are much more likely to end up in the mailboxes of people who are likely to be interested.

CRM systems also enable companies to better manage their outbound marketing campaigns and communications with customers. Not only will such systems co-ordinate which messages and offers should be directed to specific groups of customers, but they can also be used to evaluate the success of each campaign by tracking sales, responses, coupon redemptions, enquiries, and visits to Web sites. The CRM system also co-ordinates web site, e-commerce and e-mail activity. For example, customers who place an online order on **www.staples.ca** will receive confirmation of the order, information about shipping date and directions on how the shipment may be tracked. The Staples Web site can also be used to register manufacturer's rebates and customers receive regular e-mail messages concerning special offers.

A Softer View of CRM

Despite the obvious efficiencies associated with CRM software and systems, in terms of better directing information and offers to customers, there are also benefits to be derived in terms of building customer relationships. Some CRM applications are actually designed to contribute to an emotional connection with the customer. Through interactive technology and the creation of membership "clubs," many marketers utilize variations on CRM to get closer to their customers. The Home Depot (**www.homedepot.ca**) offers tips on how to lay ceramic tile or to install an underground sprinkler system. Kraft Canada (**www.kraftcanada.com**) offers a "Healthy Living" site on its Web page that offers tips on living a healthy lifestyle, as well as mouth-watering recipes. Running Room will help a new runner train for her first 10k race. Companies like these build brand relationships in part through their use of technology.

Others will argue that most CRM systems are actually intended to influence short-term customer behaviour and to make marketing initiatives more efficient. They ensure that employees are better informed about customers and that direct marketing initiatives are more efficient and better targeted. There is less wastage of time and money — an acknowledged good thing.

There are aspects of a technological approach to CRM that do have the potential to strengthen an emotional connection with customers, which is the basis for developing genuine customer relationships. Will customers appreciate the fact that employees appear to be more knowledgeable? Will they react more positively to offers for products and brands that seem to contain more things in which they are interested? The answer is likely to be "yes, but." Yes, customers may notice such things, but they will not necessarily drive genuine customer relationships.

There is a school of thought around CRM that maintains that customer relationships, if they are to be solid and lasting, require much more than technological solutions, that relationships are emotional and that most CRM initiatives do not necessarily drive positive emotional connections. Such proponents of a "softer" view of CRM acknowledge the role of technology in making customer contact more efficient and employees better informed, but argue that relationships are more likely to be built by employees in face-to-face situations and by how staff talk with and interact with customers.

Customer relationships are driven by the nature of the customer's interaction with the firm, by the total experience the customer has in dealing with the company and its employees. A firm that wants to build a solid relationship with its customers must ensure that the customer feels good about his or her dealings with the company and its employees. To build the kind of customer relationship that is characterized by customers feeling good about the firm requires more than data warehouses, data mining, and predictive modelling.

Customer Relationship Management, to be effective in creating loyal customers, must involve a combination of the application of technology solutions and an appreciation by the firm for the "softer" aspects of interaction that are more likely to drive an emotional connection with customers.

Canadian marketplace. Even marketing in the United States, a country that is right next door and one that many Canadians know quite well, presents numerous challenges as a result of marketplace and customer differences.

Having said that, the principles of marketing that we have been discussing in this book apply as well in international marketing as they do at home. The goal of the marketer is still to create high levels of customer satisfaction, leading to repeat business, positive word of mouth, and eventually to relationships with customers. IKEA, a Swedish company, is a great example of a firm that has worldwide appeal, simply because its business model and value proposition are relevant for customers in many countries. It is almost certainly true, however, that the route to achieving this satisfaction may be different in other countries.

BACK TO THE TOP

The same may be said about not-for-profit organizations. These entities do not operate in a classic business context, but rather offer their "customers" intangible services as diverse as police protection, symphony performances, food bank assistance, and religion. Thus, the definition of not-for-profit organizations is very broad and includes governments at all levels,

MARKETING AT WORK 16-1: STRATEGY

Is Marketing Really Everything?

There exists a school of thought that suggests that literally everything that a company does should be considered marketing, in that everything seems to have the potential to affect the company's image and how it is perceived by customers, and ultimately customer decisions.

Consider the following scenarios:

You are driving down the highway and in the distance in front of you is a large delivery truck, spewing plumes of thick, black smoke. As you get closer, you can see on the back of the truck the logo of the Pure Springs Bottled Water Company, and the slogan "nature's gift to you." Are you confused? Pure natural spring water from a company that is spoiling nature with its toxic fumes? What do you now think of this brand of bottled water? Who's responsible? Is the company's truck maintenance department part of marketing?

You are looking for a nice restaurant where you and your partner can enjoy a dinner to celebrate your birthday. A friend has recommended a new restaurant on the other side of town. As you drive down the street toward the restaurant, you see its sign. It is a flat, translucent plastic panel with an amateurish one-colour logo — the kind of sign that you would see on a cheque-cashing operation in a seedy strip mall. It certainly doesn't scream "fine dining." AND, you notice that "dining" is mis-spelled "DINNING." So, you drive right on by. Is the guy who orders the signs in marketing? Is spelling now a necessary marketing skill?

Finally, you are going to have your hair cut on Saturday morning. As you enter the salon, you trip on a torn corner of the carpet in the reception area. You remember that you have tripped on this torn carpet every time you have come here in the past year. You think, "I could have fallen and injured myself. Why can't they see that this should be fixed?" Is the torn carpet an irritant or more? Should you mention it? How do you really feel about the salon? Is the person responsible for building maintenance also in marketing?

QUESTIONS:

1. Just how far should we stretch the definition of marketing?
2. How has your definition of marketing changed in the past few months?
3. Is it important to get everyone in the company to realize that he or she is in marketing? How do we do that?

SOURCE: Adapted from Steve McKee, "All Together Now: Marketing is Everything," *Business Week Online*, www.businessweek.com, February 10, 2006.

charities such as the Canadian Cancer Society, cultural groups such as Symphony Nova Scotia and the Stratford Festival, religious bodies such as the Salvation Army, public transit organizations such as the la Société de transport de Montréal and the Toronto Transit Commission, and educational institutions such as your college or university.

Again, while the objectives and motivations of such organizations are not exactly the same as those of Provigo, or WestJet, or Toyota Canada, the principles of marketing still apply. It is important that not-for-profit organizations also strive for customer satisfaction, even though they may refer to their customers as members, taxpayers, donors, patrons, or passengers. In many cases, they don't want people to buy things from them as much as they want their donations, patronage, or simply support. To achieve that, not-for-profit organizations have to present an attractive value proposition, just as a retailer or a bank does. It has to appreciate the fact that it is operating in a competitive marketplace, where it is competing for the attention of its target audience in the same way that American Eagle Outfitters competes with The Gap.

One of the problems associated with not-for-profit organizations is that their leaders or executive members often are reluctant to practise marketing because the term is associated in their minds with commercial applications. They may respond that they can't be seen to be competing in the same way that Loblaws or Wal-Mart competes. However, the fact is that such organizations do compete. They compete for donations, for the time of volunteers, for public service announcements on radio, and for the hearts and minds of supporters. To be successful, there must be a realization that what they offer their target audience must be seen to be attractive and to offer value.

PAGE UP!

1. What does IKEA offer its customers beyond the product? How would you describe its value proposition?
2. What does it mean for a company to be "customer-centric"?
3. Why is marketing more than the conventional marketing mix? What do we mean by a holistic view?

Evaluating Marketing

Soon after a firm's plans have been put into operation, the process of evaluation should begin. Without evaluation, management cannot tell whether a plan is working and what factors are contributing to its success or failure. Evaluation logically follows planning and implementation. A circular relationship exists, as illustrated in Figure 16-2. Plans are made and put into action, the results of those actions are evaluated, and new plans are prepared on the basis of this evaluation.

Previously we discussed evaluation as it relates to individual parts of a marketing program — the product-planning process, the performance of the sales force, and the effectiveness of the advertising program, for instance. Now let's look at evaluation of the total marketing effort.

Before we can begin to appraise marketing, we have to agree on a basis for evaluating performance — what the objective of marketing should be. In our discussion of the marketing concept, we said that an organization's objective is to determine consumers' needs or wants and satisfy them. Thus, from the point of view of the individual company, if the target market is satisfied and the firm's objectives are being met, the marketing effort can be judged to be successful.

However, this standard makes no distinction between firms whose behaviour is detrimental to society and those whose activities are socially acceptable. Firms that pollute the environment or stimulate demand for harmful products or services would qualify as good marketers

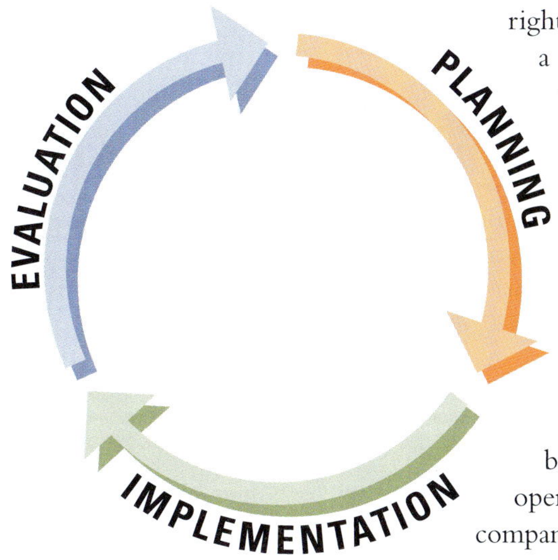

Figure 16-2:
The Circular Relationship among Management Tasks

right along with firms that behave responsibly. Therefore, we should take a broader, societal view that incorporates the best interests of others as well as the desires of a particular target market and the objectives of the marketer to satisfy that market. Marketing must balance the needs and wants of consumers, the objectives of the organization, and the welfare of society.

Marketing cannot, and certainly does not, exist in a vacuum. Practically speaking, consideration must be given to the cost-effectiveness of marketing efforts. In other words, how much does marketing contribute to the revenue of the firm or to the shareholders? Corporate performance is evaluated as a means of measuring the performance of management and the decisions they have made. Various means are used, but one method is through measurement of shareholder value. Have the operations of the firm over a particular period increased the value of the company for its shareholders? Unfortunately, these are often taken as short-term measurements when many marketing efforts take some time to yield results.

The principal objective of management, particularly in publicly-traded companies, is the creation of shareholder value. By this measure, the firm is assessed according to easily measured financial indicators. However, marketing results are often less easily measured. Marketing, today, is much more about developing long-term customer relationships, about building an emotional connection with customers. Organizations must recognize that relationships are required to establish long-term shareholder value through accumulative effects that provide future streams of value. Such intangibles are difficult to measure in the short term, yet customer relationships must be assessed for the long-term health of the firm.

Relationships, like marketing, require an understanding of what the customer wants, how to provide it, and where the firm is strong and where it is weak. Measures include customer value created, service quality, and customer satisfaction. To develop a sustainable stream of shareholder value a wider group of stakeholders should be considered, aside from shareholders. These include employees, suppliers, and customers.

Real shareholder value is created by guaranteeing the long-term viability and growth of the company. Value creation, therefore, is intimately tied to customer loyalty. Loyal customers deliver a stream of revenues as long as they are satisfied. Satisfaction drives customer relationships. Relationships are aided and influenced through well-planned and integrated marketing efforts.[7]

Evidence of the interrelationship of these three criteria is all around us. If a product does not meet the needs of consumers or if a firm is unable to provide the level of service that customers want, the consumer will not buy that product or service. The world is littered with companies that have gone out of business because they were unable to satisfy their customers. Likewise, if a firm behaves in a fashion that is viewed by consumers or the public to be detrimental to society, government will probably intervene, as it does in regulating the advertising, pricing and distribution of alcohol, tobacco, and other products judged to be potentially damaging to the health and safety of consumers.

Criticisms of Marketing

Criticisms of marketing tend to focus on the interaction between companies and customers and to the trade-off between the objectives of the firm and the needs and expectations of customers and/or the well-being of society. These issues can be categorized as follows:

- ***Exploitation:*** Marketers are sometimes accused of taking unfair advantage of a consumer or of a situation. Such criticisms relate to examples such as price increases during a shortage and misleading consumers with false or incomplete information. These behaviours are clearly in conflict with marketing's goal of long-term customer satisfaction.

- ***Pervasiveness:*** Marketing is everywhere. Or, more correctly, what many people associate with marketing is everywhere. For many people, marketing is advertising, promotions and other outward evidence of marketing in action. Some people are becoming tired of the fact that, everywhere they turn, they encounter advertising, flyers, contests, and other tools of marketing.

- ***Inefficiency:*** Some critics feel that marketing uses more resources than necessary. Accusations include inefficient promotional activity, unnecessary packaging, and excessive numbers of brands in many product categories. Inefficiency results in higher costs to companies, higher prices to consumers, and a waste of society's resources.

- ***Demand stimulation:*** A number of marketers have been accused of encouraging consumers or businesses to purchase products that are harmful in some way. For example, debate has raged throughout the Western world for the past 25 years or more concerning the marketing of cigarettes. The issue tends to revolve around the fact that tobacco is a legal product, although there are regulations in Canada that prohibit the sale of tobacco products to teens and children. Although the marketing of such products may meet the needs of some consumers and satisfy the objectives of the firms that produce and sell them, the marketing of tobacco products is controversial because society generally agrees that the product is detrimental to people's health.

- ***Inappropriate values:*** Related to the concept of unwholesome demand is that of the promotion of inappropriate values. The use of sexual imagery has often been criticized in advertising as well as the association of alcohol consumption and tobacco products with images of the "good life." This refers to images of "successful" or "popular" individuals that infer to viewers that the product has a role in delivering such desirable attributes.

- ***Illegal behaviour:*** Laws are passed to protect individuals, organizations, and society in general. Marketers are expected to abide by these laws, even when violating a law might benefit consumers or an organization. Price collusion, for instance, is detrimental to competitors of the colluding firms. Therefore, since the behaviour is unfair to others in society, it is unacceptable.

- ***Poor service:*** Some of the most vocal criticisms of marketing in recent years have been reserved for the way service is delivered to customers when they come into contact with marketing, particularly at the retail level. It seems everyone has a "terrible service" story to tell. There is no doubt that some companies and organizations have made great strides and have developed well-deserved reputations for providing superior service; others have not. Some companies, such as FedEx and Delta Hotels have made it a conscious strategy to set themselves apart from their competitors on the basis of the level of service they provide. Customers' expectations with regard to how they want to be treated have increased, and many organizations have simply not met the challenge. The result is considerable consumer dissatisfaction with service. The problem is that many firms and employees do not realize this.

- ***Reliance on technology:*** Many firms rely on database marketing and e-mail marketing systems as their principal basis for customer interaction. Efforts at relationship marketing have been jeopardized in some cases by this reliance on technology to manage customer contact. It has contributed to the image of direct-mail programs as "junk mail" or "spam." Companies are also accused of placing technology between them and their customers. For example, one of the most frequently heard criticisms deals with the use of IVR (Interactive Voice-Response) telephone systems to handle customers' calls. You know the kind; those that ask you to "press 1 for sales; press 2 for customer service; press 3 for billing, etc." and then tell you to stay on the line, because "your call is very important to us." Customers don't believe such claims. They know that if the call was truly important, it would have been answered by a live person.

Responses to Marketing Criticism

Efforts to address the issues that arise from marketing activities have come from consumers, the government, and business organizations. We will discuss some of these responses to marketing-related issues.

Consumer responses

One response that individual consumers have adopted to address criticisms that they may have of marketing activities or individual companies is to establish a "blog." Weblogs, or "blogs," have appeared out of nowhere in recent years as individuals with a story to tell have been able to post those stories on the Web for all to see. Although individuals who write blogs have a variety of objectives, some have used this technology to send information, often negative, to anyone who cares to know concerning the products and services of individual companies. The online capability allows disgruntled customers to voice their opinions not just to their close friends and family members but also to the whole world.

Some companies have started their own blogs to address such initiatives and to allow them to have open conversations with customers, shareholders and staff in an open forum, with nothing to hide. Blogs have become a source of customer feedback and input for many companies, and some senior executives, including Bill Gates, are joining in with their own blogs.[3]

Another response to marketing misdeeds, both actual and alleged, has come over the years not from average consumers, but from consumer activists. The Consumers' Association of Canada has been the leading national organization acting on behalf of customers for many years. The term **consumerism** was popularized just over 30 years ago when, in response to increasing consumer protests against a variety of business practices, Canada became the first country in the world to establish a government department at the federal level to be responsible for the rights of consumers (Industry Canada, Office of Consumer Affairs: **www.strategis.ic.gc.ca**; click on "Consumer Information"). The emphasis has been on protecting consumers from harmful products and from false and misleading advertising.

consumerism
Initiatives by consumers to identify unfairness and inefficiency in marketing, and the efforts to remedy these injustices.

Government responses

Strategis

Interest in consumer issues is not likely to disappear, mainly because today it is politically popular to support various consumer, social, and environmental causes. All of the provinces have legislation and consumer protection programs in place. A significant number of these laws were designed to protect the consumer's right to safety — especially in situations when consumers cannot judge for themselves the risk involved in the purchase and use of particular products. Legislation such as the Food and Drugs Act regulates and controls the manufacture, distribution, and sale of food, drugs, and cosmetic products. The Hazardous Products Act establishes standards for the manufacture of consumer products designed for household, garden, personal, or recreational usages, or for use by children.

One controversial area of product safety legislation is the paternalistic type of law that is intended to protect consumers — whether or not they want that protection. Thus, it is illegal to operate an automobile unless seat belts are fastened. In many cities, bicycle riders are required to wear helmets. In effect, somebody else is forcing a consumer to accept what the other person feels is in the consumer's best interests — truly a new and broadening approach to consumer legislation.

Another series of laws and government programs support the consumer's right to be informed. These measures help in such areas as reducing confusion and deception in packaging and labelling, identifying the ingredients and nutritional content of food products, advising consumers of the length of life of certain packaged food products, providing instructions and assistance related to the care of various textile products, and determining the true rate of interest in financial transactions.

Business responses

An increasing number of businesses are making substantive responses to consumer concerns and complaints, thereby addressing many of the criticisms of marketing. Here are a few examples:

- ***Better communications with and information for customers:*** Toll-free telephone numbers now appear on many manufacturers' packages, in their advertising and on their Web sites. Increasingly, advertisers are including their Web addresses in advertisements and are encouraging consumers to contact them via e-mail. Manufacturers' instruction manuals on the use and care of their products are more detailed and easier to read. Package labels are more informative than they were in the past. Many companies have call centres that are staffed around the clock, allowing consumers to call toll-free with questions or problems. The vast majority of larger companies now have Web sites that contain much more information than was available to the public in the past and in a much more accessible form.
- ***Product improvements:*** More marketers are making a concerted effort to incorporate feedback from consumers in the designs of their products. Some operate customer panels, and as a result of consumer input or complaints, have made improvements in their products. For example, detergent manufacturers have produced concentrated products that are more environmentally safe and scent-free products that contain no perfumes that might irritate people with allergies.
- ***Service quality measurement:*** Many companies have realized that it is becoming increasingly difficult to gain a competitive advantage through product design and that the key to success is to offer the customer the best possible service. Realizing also that they need feedback so that they know how well they are doing, many have developed and introduced programs that allow them to measure consumers' perceptions of the level of service they are receiving.
- ***More carefully prepared advertising:*** Many advertisers are extremely cautious in approving ads prepared by their advertising agencies, in sharp contrast to past practices. Advertisers also are involving their legal departments in the approval process.
- ***Customer-service departments:*** A growing number of companies have established departments to handle consumer enquiries and complaints. In addition to dealing with complaints, customer-service departments also gauge consumer tastes, act as sounding boards for new ideas, and often gain consumer feedback on new products.

PAGE UP!

1. What is shareholder value? What does it measure? How is it achieved?
2. What are some of the main criticisms that are occasionally levelled at marketing?
3. How have some companies responded to such criticisms?

Ethics and Marketing

ethics
The rules and standards of moral behaviour that are generally accepted by a society.

Ethics are standards of conduct. To act in an ethical fashion is to conform to an accepted standard of moral behaviour. Undoubtedly, virtually everyone prefers to act ethically. It is easy to be ethical when no hardship is involved — when a person is winning and life is going well. The test comes when things are not going so well — when pressures build up. These pressures arise in all walks of life, and marketing is no exception.

Marketing executives face the challenge of balancing the best interests of consumers, their organizations, and society into a workable guide for their daily activities. In any situation, they must be able to distinguish what is ethical from what is unethical and act accordingly, regardless of the possible consequences. However, there are many circumstances in which determining ethical behaviour is far from straightforward.[4]

Setting ethical guidelines

Avon

Many organizations have formal codes of ethics that identify specific acts (bribery, accepting gifts) as unethical and describe the standards by which employees are expected to live their business lives. A large percentage of major corporations have ethics codes, as do many smaller businesses. These guidelines lessen the chance that an employee will knowingly or unknowingly violate a company's standards. In addition, ethics codes strengthen a company's hand in dealing with customers or prospective customers who encourage unethical behaviour. For inexperienced managers, these codes can be valuable guides, helping them to resist pressure to compromise personal ethics in order to move up in the firm.

social responsibility
The commitment on the part of a company to improving the well-being of society.

However, every decision cannot be taken out of the hands of the manager. Furthermore, determining what is right and what is wrong can be extremely difficult. When faced with an ethical problem, honest answers to the following questions help to indicate which route a manager could follow:

- Would I do this to a friend?
- Would I be willing to have this done to me?
- Would I be embarrassed if this action was publicized nationally?

Many companies support worthy social causes.

Socially responsible behaviour

Ethical behaviour goes beyond avoiding wrongdoing. Ethical marketers recognize that the position they hold in society carries with it certain obligations. This **social responsibility** involves improving the well-being of society. Besides obeying the law and meeting the normal and reasonable expectations of the public, socially responsible organizations and individuals lead the way in setting standards of business and community performance. Some companies encourage their employees to join volunteer groups and will pay the fees for staff to join service clubs that are involved in community projects. Many companies donate money raised from the sale of certain items to charitable organizations. Since 1993, Avon Canada (www.avon.ca) has raised millions of dollars for breast cancer research, prevention, and education through the sale of its Avon Flame Crusade products. CIBC and Ford are major sponsors of the "Run For The Cure" and promote breast cancer research, education, diagnosis, and treatment year-round on their Web sites. Dove, a product of Procter & Gamble, has based much of its brand positioning in recent years on its Campaign for Real Beauty, an initiative to help young girls address issues of self-esteem. Such companies wisely choose social causes that may best identify with core or expanding target groups of consumers.

Protecting the customer's right to privacy

One of the most troublesome issues facing marketers relates to behaviour that threatens the customer's right to privacy. This is especially important today, because more and more companies are collecting information on customers from a number of sources and storing the data on databases to be used for marketing purposes. Some consumers object to businesses having the information in the first place and to their use of it to sell them things. The point is that the technology is available to permit the integration of databases, making it possible to obtain information about the characteristics of consumers and their households and to match that information with data about purchases, credit card usage, and other consumption behaviour.

Nowhere is the issue of privacy more pertinent than in the area of telemarketing. As the use of the telephone has increased to contact people in their homes for the purpose of marketing products and services, so too has the public outcry against such a practice. Many members of the public object to being telephoned at home, so they have installed answering machines or a call-management service provided by a telephone company that will allow them to screen

MARKETING AT WORK 16-2: RELATIONSHIPS

Is This Your Bank?

Coast Capital Savings in British Columbia unveiled a new look at its newest branch in Pitt Meadows in June 2005. On the bright blue wall the words "How can we help you?" are written in large white letters. There's a concierge to greet guests, help towers and a kids' room with video games. Along with new products and longer hours, this bank is trying to carve out a leadership position in the financial services industry.

Lawrie Ferguson, the senior vice-president of marketing for Coast Capital Savings, says the challenge was to give the "I've-heard-it-all-before" customers a reason to switch. It was important to know what the customer valued in a financial services institution and to then follow through on that. Instead of pouring the usual $1.3 million into the RRSP marketing campaign, Ferguson launched a Free Chequing, Free Debit and More account in January 2005. In September, Coast Capital launched an e-mail campaign aimed at 18- to 24-year olds that offered free debit. The campaign resulted in a 46 percent increase in online account openings.

Coast Capital Savings is attempting to distinguish itself from other financial institutions by knowing what is important to its customer and then offering products and services that the customer really wants. They have encouraged people to switch financial institutions based on their "helpfulness" and their "no fees" products. Together, the service and the products create a value proposition that is hard to ignore. With a 325 percent increase in annual membership growth during 2005, Coast Capital is clearly an attractive alternative to other financial institutions.

QUESTIONS:

1. Is it a good strategy for Coast Capital to stop behaving like a bank? Why?
2. Could any of Canada's major banks stop acting like a bank?
3. Why is this approach likely to work for some customers and not for others?

SOURCE: Adapted from Eve Lazarus, "Refreshingly Unbank-like," *Marketing Magazine Online*, www.marketingmag.ca, December 12, 2005.

calls or have paid extra for unlisted telephone numbers. The issue has now also found its way onto the Internet, as many consumers object to the amount of unsolicited advertising that appears each day in their e-mail inboxes.

Canadian Marketing Association

The direct-marketing industry has taken steps to police itself with regard to offering protection to consumers against invasion of privacy. The industry association, the Canadian Marketing Association (**www.the-cma.org**), has adopted a code of standards that regulates its members, who account for about 80 percent of all direct marketers in Canada.

As discussed previously, regulation of the use of customer information has begun. The Privacy Act changed the nature of how companies are allowed to handle client information. Companies have to be able to secure, dispose of, and disseminate this information in a controlled manner. The foundation for this legislation rests on the Canadian Standards Association's Moral Code and provides for three levels of consent regarding personal information collected by Web site operators who may attempt to use the information for purposes other than that for which it was collected. It is hoped that such practices, if enforced by law, will reduce consumers' fears about conducting transactions online and about how their personal information stored in company databases may be used.

What Lies Ahead for Marketing?

Let's now consider what lies ahead for marketing. It can be seen that the scope of marketing has been broadening recently to include everything that has the potential to affect the consumer. It is possible to infer that this trend will continue as consumers themselves change, as the technology that reaches into our homes becomes more pervasive, and as competition in the marketplace continues to intensify.

In the future, in order to be more effective and efficient, and to increase levels of customer satisfaction, what do marketers need to know and what do they need to do?

What's going on out there?

We discussed numerous aspects of the external environment in Chapter 3. In this section, we focus on the implications for marketing of four areas: demographic changes, shifts in consumer values and attitudes, the impact of technology, and the growth of information.

Consumer demographics Changes in demographics — the population's age distribution, income, education, ethnic composition, and household structure — all affect marketers' activities. For example, the population is getting older, and senior citizens are the fastest-growing age group. This shift creates expanded marketing opportunities in such areas as travel, tourism, health, and medical care. Another demographic change is the greater ethnic diversity in Canada's major cities, resulting primarily from increases in the level of immigration from Asia and other areas. These groups are large enough to attract the attention of marketers, but they present interesting challenges.

Values and attitudes Values — the widely held beliefs in a society — change slowly, as do consumers' attitudes. When they do change, however, the impact on existing institutions and the opportunities for innovative marketers can be great. Value shifts often accompany demographic changes. As the Canadian population ages and changes in other ways, we can expect some adjustments in values. For example, we are seeing:

- ***Increased scepticism:*** Education is at its highest level ever. Consumers have more confidence in their ability to make judgements and are less willing to accept unsubstantiated claims. Authority is subject to challenge. Consumers demand information and are willing to question traditions. The concerns of Canadians about social programs, including health care and education, are causing considerable scepticism about the leadership of elected officials. Some people are becoming quite jaded and tired of the pace of life and materialism that seem to dominate society.

- ***Balanced lifestyles:*** From a society that focused on work to produce a richer lifestyle, we are moving to a society that wants to balance work and leisure to enjoy life. This will mean increasing concern with wellness in the form of nutrition and exercise; the allocation of more time to home, family, and leisure; and a desire to become involved in activities viewed as worthwhile and fulfilling. Younger Canadians in particular do not appear to be driven to succeed nearly as much as their parents were.

- ***Greater self-confidence***: In part because of their higher levels of education but also in part because of their greater knowledge of the world around them, consumers today have more self-confidence and are more decisive. They understand how the marketplace works and are not at all reluctant to take their business elsewhere if they are not satisfied. As a result, many companies are experiencing high levels of customer churn.

- ***Demands for good service:*** The success of businesses such as Four Seasons Hotels, FedEx, and IKEA makes it clear that consumers reward good service. It is also apparent that many firms recognize this opportunity. Recognizing the need to offer good service is often easier than finding and training employees to provide it. A major challenge for organizations in the future will be to design and implement systems that provide consumers with high-calibre service. There is increasing evidence that the offering of superior customer service represents a strategic competitive advantage for successful companies.

BACK TO THE TOP

- ***Technology adoption:*** Technology has been used for some time in the supply chain, now more consumers are using technology to help them acquire and share information. With the introduction of iPods, TiVO, PVRs, satellite radio, podcasts and blogs, consumers are deciding what they hear and see. The customer is in control. The challenge for marketers is to communicate with customers on the customers' terms. Consumers are increasingly knowledgeable about the choices that are available to them and seek out information from a variety of sources. This is the key; marketers must ensure that their messages are available where the customers are seeking information.

- ***Consumer interaction:*** There is very good evidence that customers have become quite tired of a hard-sell approach to marketing. Recent studies indicate that 55 percent of all consumers would be willing to pay more to get only the kinds of marketing they prefer, and nearly 70 percent say they are interested in products that help them block out advertising that they do not want to see. Consumers want marketing that is short and to the point, marketing they can choose to see when it is convenient for them, and more personal communication of the message.[5]

- ***Polarization of the market:*** Consumers are shopping, in the same day, at dollar stores and high end boutiques. This polarization of retail has some people puzzled but it's hard to dismiss that dollar stores are the fastest growing sector in retail. For example, a customer will purchase a gift at Holt Renfrew and stop at the dollar store for a gift bag! Or, consumers are purchasing candle holders at a boutique, but stopping by the dollar store for the candles. Dollar stores are providing consumers with an alternative to buy those things which are consumable, or are seen as being undifferentiated.

What do these changes mean for marketing? We are likely to see increasing emphasis on quality over quantity in consumption and a more careful evaluation of the value of product features that seem to add more to style than to substance. One area in which values are evident is a heightened interest in the future quality of life. International concern over the dissipation of the atmosphere's ozone layer, the disappearance of rainforests, increases in acid rain, and the greenhouse effect is obvious. Other environmental issues of interest to consumers are waste disposal and landfills, air and water pollution, and biodegradability.

Technology There can be little doubt that marketing has been revolutionized in recent years because of the impact of technology. The development of advanced technology has been so rapid that it has created both opportunities and problems that have serious implications for how marketing is carried out in just about every organization. The developments in technology are so vast that we can provide only a brief overview here, but we will touch on a number of key areas where marketing has been affected.

- ***Internet marketing and e-commerce:*** One opportunity that is obvious from the advances in technology in recent years is the use of the Internet to market products and services to prospective customers around the world. Every major company and many smaller ones have created Web sites, and many of these are designed to sell things. Customers are becoming increasingly confident in the use of credit cards to buy things online and we can expect a dramatic increase in the volume of e-commerce transactions in the future.
- ***Fragmentation and customization of the electronic media:*** Technology is revolutionizing the media to which consumers are exposed. Not only are there many more television stations, but there are numerous ways for consumers to access entertainment and educational programming. There is a mind-boggling array of alternatives, most of them delivered through electronic media and on the Internet. As a result, many Canadians are relying less and less on conventional print and broadcast media for their news and entertainment.
- ***Impact on service delivery:*** Technology has had a very definite impact on the delivery of customer service. On the one hand, some argue that the introduction of such technology as automated banking machines, interactive voice-response telephone systems, and call-management software has created an impenetrable barrier between some companies and their customers. This suggests that, at a time when companies are generally interested in establishing close relationships with customers, there is a very real danger that technology will get in the way of a company being able to do so. On the other hand, this is a very good example of the "two-edged sword" nature of technology. At the same time that technology seems to be getting in the way of service delivery, there are many examples of how technology actually facilitates service delivery.
- ***Customer monitoring:*** Technology has made it possible for companies to get to know far more about their customers than has ever been the case in the past. Retail scanners and other forms of technology essentially observe the purchase patterns and behaviour of customers and maintain a running record of what has been purchased, where, and when. The result is the comprehensive databases that can be used to identify opportunities and to improve the efficiency of direct marketing programs.

Growth of customer information Marketers have the ability to pinpoint trends and individual customers as never before. Using scanner data that produces detailed purchase behaviour on a store-by-store basis, Statistics Canada data that provide demographic information down to the city block and, a variety of other sources such as warranty registration cards, contest entries, and rebate requests, firms can build detailed customer and prospective customer databases. With this information, they are able to design products and assortments tailored specifically to a customer's needs.

market fragmentation
The identification of smaller and smaller market segments with individualized communications approaches.

Knowing more about the market has led to **market fragmentation** and to niche marketing — the identification of smaller and smaller market segments This enables a marketer to tailor the marketing approach so that it appeals to very small groups of customers. As a result, we see a dramatically increased number of product varieties in many product categories, such as breakfast cereals, laundry detergents, and toothpaste. Using personally-tailored communication through the Internet and other targeted channels, marketers can now reach individual customers with personalized messages.

There was a time when a packaged-goods manufacturer could develop a quality product, advertise it nationally using the national media, stock retailers' shelves, and have a reasonable chance of success. But the situation has changed — marketers can no longer expect large numbers of consumers to compromise their needs and wants and buy standardized products. Rather, they must tailor goods and services to meet the needs of small market segments. The strategy of niche marketing significantly complicates the marketer's job. One version of a product is replaced by several. Different ads must be produced and new media must be found to reach different consumers. Retailers must choose among many product variations, not all of which can be stocked. The added variety complicates inventory management, distribution, and personal selling.

There are no indications that the trend toward niche marketing will end. In fact, with more sophisticated electronic data collection methods being developed and the diversity of the population increasing, all indications point to even greater fragmentation in the future. The reaching of smaller and smaller market segments is facilitated largely through advances in technology that make it possible to design a unique marketing program to address the needs of individual customers.

How Marketing is Responding: 7 Steps to Success

One common response to change is simply to react as it occurs. However, realizing that change is always occurring, marketers should initiate strategic proactive efforts to improve performance. Seven are described in this section.

1. Instilling a customer-centric orientation Describing the approach to marketing that we have presented in this book and implementing it in an organization are two different things. The concept — combining a customer orientation with co-ordinated marketing and organizational goals — certainly has intuitive appeal, yet many organizations seem unable to practise it consistently. What does practising a truly customer-centric orientation require?

- The marketing concept involves a philosophy of business that focuses on the customer's needs. However, when faced with the choice of putting the customer first or meeting their own needs, some companies and employees often find it difficult to give the customer priority. Instilling this orientation requires top-management commitment. Lip service is not sufficient. Employees must see management putting the customer first. As a result, leadership is essential if a customer-centric orientation is to pervade a company's operations.
- Companies must create the right culture to support a customer orientation. Everything that the company does, how it communicates with its employees and others, all must be done with the customer in mind. Those companies that have been successful in instilling a customer orientation have succeeded in gaining what they call "employee buy-in" to the notion that the customer must come first in their thinking.
- There must be a reward system within the company that encourages a customer orientation. Employees must be empowered to make decisions that recognize the importance of

customers and be publicly rewarded for those decisions. Managing the employees in a customer-centric organization will increasingly be seen as a partnership between marketing and human resources.

- Organizations must stay in close contact with the market. This means having detailed, accurate market knowledge. Consumers are becoming less and less willing to compromise to satisfy their goals and objectives. Marketers must develop more programs for smaller markets. This means conducting marketing research on a regular basis. Progressive marketing research firms have helped their clients by developing research programs to measure the quality of service being delivered and to examine the health of customer relationships.
- Consumers must be offered the best value possible. Many companies have realized that offering discounts and "specials" does little to build long-term customer loyalty and have instead turned to other ways to create value for their customers. The concept of adding value is of such importance that we will return to it later in this chapter.
- The most customer-oriented companies listen to their customers. Successful companies no longer assume that they know what their customers want. Consequently, many are doing more marketing research than they have in the past. They have also learned that they can do nothing to improve the service to customers unless they know when customers are having problems or concerns.
- All exchange partners, not just customers, must be satisfied. The exchange partners of an organization include its customers, suppliers, intermediaries, owners, regulators, and anyone else with whom it interacts. If suppliers, for example, feel their interaction with an organization is unsatisfactory, they will not do everything in their power to ensure that the needs of end-customers will be met. The same is true of employees. Essential to satisfying the final customers are strong, positive relationships among all of the parties who contribute to bringing a product or service to the customer.

2. Competing more effectively Today, most businesses (and not-for-profit organizations, as well) are facing greater and more effective competition than ever before. The array of choices available to consumers today is much greater than it has ever been. As we observed earlier, competition is coming from all sides, locally, nationally, and internationally. Such a marketing environment changes how a company must compete. It is no longer sufficient (if it ever was!) to merely put products into the marketplace and hope that customers will find them attractive. We have stressed a strategic approach to marketing in this book because it is more important today than ever before for a company to have a strategy in order to compete. This means that it must understand the marketplace, the customer, and the competition better than ever before. It also means that business has to be much more creative in how it practises marketing, so that the company will stand out from the competition and give the customer a reason to deal with it.

3. Adopting a global orientation To be successful in the future, marketers must adopt a global orientation toward customers, products, and marketing strategy. In the past, most firms could be successful by focusing on the domestic market and outperforming local rivals, but that has changed: Now firms, both large and small, are going where the markets are the most attractive.

The cliché that we live in a "small world" is a reality for marketers. Virtually instantaneous communication has greatly increased global awareness. Economic, social, and political developments on one side of the world have an impact everywhere else. On the evening television

MARKETING AT WORK 16-3: RELATIONSHIPS

Flying for Free

In 1981, when American Airlines launched its mileage-based frequent-flyer program, the mileage collection mania began. Now, 25 years later, more than 130 million people around the world collect miles from more than 130 airlines that issue them. In the beginning, these "loyalty" programs were meant to reward loyal frequent flyers. Today, however, the biggest collectors of miles are frequent buyers — those who earn miles from credit card purchases, car rentals, hotel stays and retail purchases.

The frequent flyer programs have bred a form of loyalty, as they definitely cause many customers to continue to deal with the same airline. But, as with any proposition, the marketer has to be able to deliver on the promise. With so many people collecting miles, there are growing complaints from consumers that they cannot get the flights they want or have been forced to redeem twice as many miles to get a seat. And, the success rate of getting a seat varies from one airline to another.

Is there a risk that frequent-flyer miles may become worthless? With so many airlines experiencing financial trouble in recent years, it is a possibility that even those customers who earn miles from larger airlines may be at risk of losing their miles if the company folds. Already, members of loyalty programs with smaller airlines have lost all of their miles when the airlines went bankrupt.

Has this "loyalty" program gone too far then? What began as a way to reward loyal, frequent flyers has become a mainstream points program where anyone with a credit card can earn points. Those truly loyal customers must feel the devaluation of their points when they are forced to redeem twice the points to get the seat they want. That can hardly be good for the relationship.

QUESTIONS:

1. What do points-based loyalty programs have to do with customer loyalty? What's the connection?
2. Is there a danger that some points programs may "backfire" on the airlines involved?
3. What can airlines and other owners of loyalty programs do to change their programs and to create genuine customer loyalty?

SOURCE: Adapted from "Funny Money," *The Economist*, www.economist.com, December 20, 2005.

news, we are as likely to hear about developments on the Japanese stock market as we are about activity on Bay Street.

Despite problems, the trend toward global marketing will accelerate. The lure of millions of consumers, combined with an improved understanding of the markets and marketing practices necessary to be successful, will increase the attractiveness of such opportunities. Internet technology has made every marketplace an international market. Consumers and businesses can now obtain information and place and receive orders from across the continent as easily as from across the province. Prospective customers and competitors can be anywhere in the world.

4. Understanding the concept of value and its relationship to customer needs One of the most talked-about but least-understood concepts in marketing is value. We hear a great deal in marketing circles about adding value for customers. Presumably, this involves adding something over and above what the customer would normally expect, in order to make the offering more attractive than that of a competitor. Often overlooked, however, is the fact that, in order to add value, marketers must have a very good understanding of what it is that customers value most. Few companies have invested sufficiently in research to be able to answer the question: What do customers value? The provision of children's play areas and restaurants in their stores represents one way in which IKEA adds value for its customers.

This issue of adding value is very closely related to the concept of customer needs, as discussed above and in Chapter 1. Customers value what allows them to better meet their needs. Thus, to add value for clients, marketers must be able to understand their needs.

Increasingly in companies, there is an appreciation for the fact that the customer's needs extend well beyond the product or service that the company is selling. Thus, when a homeowner goes to a paint store to buy paint or to IKEA to buy furniture, those products are not what she really "needs." The paint and the furniture are simply a means to an end. What the homeowner really needs is to make her home look beautiful, to feel good about living there, and to receive positive comments from friends who visit.

With this view of the customer, companies are in a better position to meet customer needs, by being able to provide appropriate advice and direction, to assist in selecting the right colour and fabrics, and to generally act as the customer's partner in achieving the kind of success she is looking for.

5. Emphasizing quality and customer satisfaction The emphasis on quality in products and services that is sweeping businesses today requires a rethinking of the role of marketing and even of what marketing means. In fact, there may be some justification in arguing that marketing and quality really refer to the same thing — efforts to produce satisfied customers. They both refer to intrinsic values in organizations that are customer-centric: an attitude and an orientation toward doing whatever is necessary to satisfy the customer. The job of a company's marketing program is not simply to make sales. Marketing has one objective: to create satisfied customers. It is a strategic function of the organization — or, at least it should be! Quality in many forms clearly is critical to customer satisfaction and therefore must have a high priority with management.

6. Designing environmentally sound strategies Quality applies to more than making products that work better or longer and to delivering great service. A broader issue is the general quality of life and the way we treat the environment. In the past, commitments to single-issue efforts (for example, making a product biodegradable or eliminating chlorofluorocarbons) were enough to win consumer approval. In the future, however, environmental acceptance will be based on a product's entire life cycle, from design through disposal.

Firms will be forced to move away from looking for an exploitable or promotable feature to making environmental concerns an integral part of the business model. This will require a new way of thinking about consumption. One example is to make products so that the materials, components, and packages can be used longer and reused either in part or whole, a process called reconsumption that includes:[6]

- ***Reusing:*** Packaging material is often discarded long before it is unusable. Lego, the Danish toy manufacturer, delivers its products to retailers in large, durable boxes that are returned to Lego for reuse.
- ***Refilling:*** Rather than discarding a container when it is empty, if it is properly designed, it can be refilled. More than 30 million laser-printer cartridges are used and disposed of every year. Several companies have designed their cartridges so that they can be refilled.

SKF

- ***Repairing:*** With proper maintenance, products can be used longer. Thus, rather than waiting to act until after a product fails, SKF (**www.skf.se**), a Swedish bearing manufacturer, has developed a series of preventive support services and diagnostic techniques that its customers can use to greatly lengthen the life of its bearings.
- ***Restoring:*** Some products can be returned to their original condition by replacing some parts and reconditioning others. BMW and Mercedes-Benz are now restoring damaged auto parts that in the past were simply discarded.

7. Building relationships One of the most important aspects of the current new way of looking at marketing is the emphasis that many companies now put on the development of relationships with customers. There is now widespread acceptance of the fact that it costs a company a great deal more to attract a new customer than it does to keep an existing customer happy. Therefore, we have seen a change in emphasis away from getting customers and toward keeping customers. In fact, some authors have suggested that in the future marketers must pay increasing attention to the "four Rs" of marketing: relationships, retention, referrals, and recovery.[7]

There is also growing acceptance that building a real relationship with customers involves more than getting them to come back to buy from us again. That's retention, repeat buying, a behavioural concept. Real relationships involve building an emotional connection with customers by working very hard to create positive emotions and reduce negative emotions for customers.

In this new way of thinking, marketers will stress building relationships with customers who will generate long-term profits for the company, developing strategies that will keep them satisfied over the long term, so that they will stay with the company, and creating strategies that will deal with recovering from problems and mistakes when these occur. As the following box reflects, there is a considerable difference between this new way of looking at marketing and what has been practised in the past.

One final issue that should be addressed concerns the type of relationship that a company should establish with its customers. There are some who believe that having a customer's name in a database and sending regular mailings to that customer constitutes a relationship. But a genuine relationship that will last a long time requires the company to demonstrate sincere interest in customers and in their well-being — not really different from those factors that contribute to relationships between people.[8]

Old Marketing Model	New Marketing Model
• Focus on the product.	• Focus on serving customers.
• Define the target group.	• Cultivate and nourish the relationship.
• Set brand objectives.	• Extend respect and value to customers.
• Opportunity comes from analysis.	• Opportunity comes from synergy.
• Focus on brand benefit.	• Develop and refresh relevance.
• Create strategic advertising.	• Open the doors for dialogue.
• Operate against a brand plan.	• Improvise to sustain the relationship.
• Driven by a marketing group.	• A pervasive holistic attitude.

SOURCE: Adapted from John Dalla Costa, "Towards a Model Relationship," *Marketing Magazine,* June 27, 1994, p. 12. Reprinted with permission.

The New Marketing

We are seeing a balanced, holistic form of marketing in the early years of the 21st century, one driven by massive change in the environment in which the company and its customers operate. The most progressive companies are realizing that, as the world in which they operate changes before their very eyes, they must change how they deal with and serve their customers if they are to remain relevant and successful.

There has probably been more change in the past five years in marketing than has taken place in the preceding 25 years. This change has been necessitated by some of the things that we have discussed at length in earlier chapters, principally the impact of technology, global competition, and a more knowledgeable, informed and confident customer. Consequently, the best companies have become even more customer focused, placing great emphasis not just on what we can sell them — which is a company-focused view — but on what we can do to really address their needs and on what we can help them accomplish. Truly customer-centric companies, like IKEA, The Home Depot, and Running Room, are constantly thinking about what they can make possible for their customers. It is a different view of customers; one that is far removed from the old view that customers are a target toward which we are directing a marketing offensive.

In fact, there is now a great deal of research evidence that customers are rebelling against the "hard sell," against the aggressive selling efforts of some companies. They simply don't like being *sold* things. They have confidence and want to make their own decisions. As a result, companies are realizing that they have to take a different approach. Marketing in the future will have to be a "softer" form of marketing, one that involves more pull and less push, more two-way communication and conversation and less unsolicited advertising, more individualized and personalized attention and less mass marketing.

There will be increasing emphasis in marketing on the kinds of experiences companies create for their customers. This is part of a more holistic view that extends beyond the products and services that the company sells, to what they put their customers through and what they make possible. More companies are focused today on being easy to deal with, on putting friendly, knowledgeable and helpful staff in front of customers and on making sure customers get true enjoyment from the products after they take them home. All of these relate to the kinds of experiences that companies can create and fit with the notion that a company can have great products at great prices and still create upset for customers if the experience of dealing with that company is unpleasant or frustrating.

The holistic view of marketing means that the company must have the view that they are in business to make things possible for customers, to help them succeed in doing things and to make them look and feel good in their own minds and in the eyes of others. This is a far different view than one that sees marketing as selling stuff to people. It requires a different kind of thinking and a view that extends well beyond the conventional marketing mix to include every aspect of the interaction with the customer. Every employee must understand his or her role in contributing to long-term customer satisfaction and to the building of the relationship between customers and the company or brand.

Maybe marketing really is everything, after all.

PAGE UP!

1. How should companies evaluate their performance in marketing?
2. How have advances in technology changed marketing?
3. How has marketing had to change in order to respond to its changing environment and the changing customer?

Key Terms and Concepts

consumerism 475
corporate culture 465
customer-centric 464
ethics 477
holistic view of marketing 464
market fragmentation 482
social responsibility 477

Questions and Problems

1. If customers today are really less accepting of a hard-sell approach to marketing, how then should marketers in certain industries respond and change their approach to customers?
2. Give examples of how advertising and personal selling activities might be co-ordinated in a company's marketing department.
3. How can a not-for-profit organization offer value to its many different "customers"? Select a charity or other form of not-for-profit organization in your town and identify the various customer segments it is attempting to serve or attract. Then, determine how it can create value for each of them.
4. How can a company's leadership affect customer satisfaction and retention, and the long-term success of the firm?
5. What are the social and economic justifications for "paternalistic" laws such as seat-belt regulations and warnings on cigarette packages and alcoholic beverage containers?
6. Discuss some ethical implications of the fact that many companies today are able to obtain a considerable amount of data about consumers and what they buy, and other information that some consumers may wish to keep confidential. What are reasonable boundaries on the use of such information for marketing purposes?
7. What firms can you think of that you would consider to be customer-focused or customer-centric? What, in your opinion, makes them customer-centric? How do they make their customers feel?
8. Choose two retail clothing companies that you think have opposite views of marketing. How does each practise marketing? What does marketing seem to mean in these companies? Which firm would you say does not have an holistic view of marketing? What would it need to change in order to think beyond the traditional view of marketing?
9. Think of companies that you have interacted with in recent weeks that seem to be operating a Customer Relationship Management (CRM) system. What evidence do you have that these companies have adopted CRM? What difference has it made to how they deal with you and how you feel about these companies as a result?
10. How can a company take into consideration the "four Rs of marketing" and incorporate them into their strategy for interacting with customers?

Hands-On Marketing

1. Interview a marketing executive and/or consult a corporate Web site to identify how the particular company is applying the principles of CRM as discussed in the boxed item in this chapter. Identify the various components of the company's CRM system. How successful do you believe this company's investment in CRM has been in developing solid relationships with customers? In your report, identify how you believe this company should evaluate the success of its CRM program.
2. Interview three managers in companies near your campus or home and ask them:
   a. How they define marketing in their companies and how marketing may have changed in recent years.
   b. How marketing is organized and who is responsible for it.
   c. What foreseeable developments will have the greatest impact on marketing in their firms over the next five years.
   d. How they think their industry and their company should respond to these developments.

Back to the Top

When James and Anne decided to furnish their new room they had many choices of retailers who sell furniture. They chose IKEA for a number of reasons; what do you think those reasons were? Why do customers choose one company over another? Some marketers truly understand their customers' needs and show this not only by the products and services they provide but how they provide them. What was the shopping experience available at IKEA as compared with other stores where the Fergusons could have bought their furniture? Think of the factors that cause you to choose some retailers over others, one bank over another, and one cellphone provider over another. What sets these marketers apart?

Online **Learning Centre**

Want to get better grades, tips on how to study more effectively, and up-to-date information on happenings in the world of marketing? Then, visit the Online Learning Centre for practice tests, Study Smart software, *Marketing Magazine,* and much more! **www.mcgrawhill.ca/olc/sommers**

CASE 7-1:

Multimedia

Mission Hill Family Estate Winery

Rod O'Reilly is owner of the Toyota dealership in Terrace, BC, and he was visiting Kelowna for the first time in many years. He and almost 40 other dealer principals and some of their sales managers were attending the annual marketing conference of the Toyota Dealers' Association of British Columbia, a two-day event that allowed the dealers to share ideas and to learn of the latest plans from Toyota Canada. Rod and most of the others had arrived by mid-day on Sunday in preparation for an early start to the meetings on Monday.

The kick-off event for the conference was to be a bus-tour to the Mission Hill Family Estate Winery in Kelowna (**www.missionhillwinery.com**) on Sunday evening. Rod had never been on a winery tour before and was not quiet sure what to expect. While he enjoyed a glass of wine with dinner, he certainly didn't consider himself a connoisseur.

Mission Hill

Mission Hill Family Estate is an internationally-recognized, award-winning winery located in Kelowna, BC, with a series of five vineyards producing grapes as far south as Osoyoos, near the U.S. border. Anthony von Mandl, the winery's proprietor, was a successful, Vancouver-based wine merchant in the early 1980s when he realized his dream of producing his own wines and purchased a near-bankrupt winery in the Okanagan Valley.

Products

Mission Hill Family Estate produces four tiers of wines. Its Five Vineyards wines are made from grapes produced mostly in the winery's vineyards throughout the Okanagan Valley and are generally available at retail stores and restaurants across Canada. The Reserve wines are made predominantly from estate-grown grapes and involve more elaborate winemaking techniques. They are available in slightly limited supply in Canada. The Select Lot Collection (SLC) wines are produced in very small quantities, from grapes from selected areas among the best vineyards. These wines are available in very limited fine-wine accounts and in a few fine-dining restaurants in North America and international markets. Oculus is Mission Hill Family Estate's signature wine, made in very limited quantities from selected clusters of designated blocks from the best vineyard locations. These wines represent the pinnacle of everything undertaken by Mission Hill Family Estate, from vineyard regimen to winemaking. Oculus is available in very limited fine wine and top restaurant distribution in Canada and key international markets.

The Winery Tour

Rod and the other members of the BC Toyota team were met as they got off their buses by staff dressed in black trousers and white shirts, and led through the archway that marks the entrance to the Mission Hill Family Estate winery. The impressive entrance consisted of a massive set of contemporary, curved arches held together by a single keystone that had been hand-carved from a five-tonne block of Indiana limestone and featuring images taken from the von Mandl family crest. Each was offered a glass of chilled Sauvignon Blanc, as one of the guides explained the significance of the architecture of the buildings. The group walked around the property, admiring the views over the Okanagan Valley and hearing from the guide the significance of the unique climate of the region and its excellence for growing grapes. They then toured the winery's vast climate-controlled cellars with the thousands of barrels, many of them French oak, specially crafted and selected for Mission Hill Family Estate wines.

They were then ushered into a small theatre that easily accommodated the whole group, offered chilled glasses of Pinot Grigio, welcomed by more enthusiastic staff, and shown a video narrated by Anthony von Mandl that explained the history and values of Mission Hill Family Estate, its wines, the unique climate of the region, and introduced winemaker, John Simes, who had come to Mission Hill Family Estate from New Zealand in 1992.

The big surprise for Rod, however, came at the end of the video as the lights came up and the screen disappeared into the ceiling, revealing the winery's kitchen behind. The winery chef, Michael Allemeier, and his staff were ready to explain what was being served for dinner that night, extending glasses of the winery's Reserve Chardonnay and platters of parmesan gougères and rabbit rillette.

Chef Allemeier explained where the ingredients that he would be using come from, the importance of using only the best and freshest local Okanagan produce, their commitment to crafting a menu that is exactly right to complement the Mission Hill Family Estate wines being served. Following hors d'ouvres, Chef Allemeier invited them to join him for dinner.

Dinner was served in the winery's Chagall Room, with its cathedral ceiling, and an impressive Marc Chagall tapestry dominating the back wall. Chef Allemeier came out of the kitchen to introduce each course and the wine being served with it. Dinner was truly memorable: five courses of superbly prepared and presented delicacies, each accompanied by the right glass of Mission Hill Family Estate wine.

At the end of the evening, as they made their way back to the hotel in the rented coaches, Rod and his colleagues from Toyota BC were conversing among themselves about what an impressive show Mission Hill Family Estate had put on for them. They had been particularly impressed by the tremendous attention to detail; they had thought of everything. The young staff members whom they had met demonstrated an obvious passion for Mission Hill Family Estate, understood wine and the history of winemaking in the Okanagan, and clearly enjoyed working there.

The next day, they were still talking about their "Mission Hill Family Estate Experience." During the next two days of business meetings, some wondered aloud what they could learn from Mission Hill Family Estate that they could implement in their dealerships.

Please view the corporate video that accompanies this case before proceeding with the questions.

Questions

1. What business is Mission Hill Family Estate Winery really in? Who are the target segments to which Mission Hill is directing its marketing?
2. Go to **www.missionhillwinery.com** and navigate through the Guest Experience section of the Web site.
   a. What roles do the winery tours, the catered events and culinary workshops/seminars play in the marketing strategy of Mission Hill Family Estate?
   b. Is Chef Allemeire part of the marketing team? Explain your answer.
3. How is Mission Hill Family Estate differentiating itself from other wineries in the Okanagan Valley and from other wines? Can these differentiating features be easily copied by the competition? What does Mission Hill Family Estate have to do to continue differentiating itself in the marketplace?
4. While Rod O'Reilly and the other Toyota dealers may have little control over Toyota Canada's marketing strategy, they do have control over some of the marketing activities at their own dealerships. What ideas can Rod take from his visit to Mission Hill Family Estate that he can implement at his dealership in Terrace?

CASE 7-2:

Dr. Duncan's Dilemma

Dr. Pauline Duncan is a family physician whose practice is located in Kentville, Nova Scotia. Dr. Duncan graduated from Dalhousie University's Medical School in 1987 and moved shortly thereafter to the Annapolis Valley where she and her husband, Dr. Peter Morrissey, set up a joint practice. Over almost 20 years, the practice has grown and the two physicians and their young family have come to feel very much a part of the community.

Over the past year or so, Dr. Duncan has become increasingly uneasy about what she considers to be an invasion of patient privacy. She is aware of the fact that some large drug store chains are capturing certain data on prescriptions that are written by doctors and making such data available to pharmaceutical manufacturers. She and Dr. Morrissey have both observed that the sales representatives from pharmaceutical companies who call on them in their practice seem much better informed today than they were several years ago about the kinds of illnesses they are treating and the drugs that they are prescribing.

While she understands that better-informed sales reps can do a better job of recommending the pharmaceutical products that will be most effective in treating her patients, Dr. Duncan also has a nagging doubt about the use to which patient prescription information is being put. In one way, she feels the information about the drugs she prescribes for her patients should be treated as part of the private doctor-patient relationship. On the other hand, she realizes that individual patient data is not being released to the pharmaceutical companies.

Over a late dinner last week, she and her husband discussed whether they should write a letter to the Canadian Medical Association, offering their opinion on the use of data from prescriptions by drug store chains and pharmaceutical companies.

Questions:

1. Is there something special about the relationship between doctors and their patients that makes the use of "customer" data for marketing purposes a particularly sensitive topic in this situation?

2. Why is the capturing of data in his way by drug stores any different than the data captured when customers buy products from other large retailers such as Canadian Tire or The Bay?
3. Do you think Drs. Duncan and Morrissey should write to the Canadian Medical Association? Why? What should they say?
4. Do you believe the use of information from prescriptions written by Canadian doctors should be regulated? How?

SOURCE: Adapted from in part CBC *Disclosure*, "Targeting Doctors," March 5, 2002.

CASE 7-3:

Dr. Duncan's Other Dilemma

It was Thursday afternoon and Dr. Pauline Duncan had just seen her fifteenth patient of the day. It was the third time Robert McCarthy had been to see her in the past month, complaining about a persistent stiff neck and pain radiating though his right shoulder. Robert was 28 years old and otherwise quite fit and Dr. Duncan had prescribed an anti-inflammatory to deal with Robert's discomfort. Nevertheless, his pain had persisted and Robert had been off work for the past week.

But this third visit was different. Robert had arrived for his appointment with 30 or more pages that he had printed from a number of Internet sites. As soon as he entered the examining room, he said, "Doctor, I've been on the Internet for the past few days, searching through lots of medical sites, and I've found what my problem is; just look! This doctor in England says that he has seen patients with exactly my problem and that this is what is causing it. He prescribes this drug for it. So, I want you to write me a prescription for it."

Dr. Duncan has had several similar experiences in recent months, when patients have come to her office with printouts from Internet sites, pages torn from magazines, or notes that they have made about drugs that they have seen advertised on television. Invariably, they ask her to prescribe those drugs to deal with their medical problems. Dr. Duncan is becoming increasingly frustrated because the information the patients are bringing to her is not usually accurate and often does not remotely relate to the symptoms they have. In some of the cases, the drugs they are requesting are not the right ones to treat their illnesses.

Dr. Duncan believes that she simply does not have the time in her very busy practice to read the material that these patients are bringing with them to her clinic. She also knows that she does not have time to go online herself to become aware of all of the information that is currently available on medical conditions, diagnoses and remedies. But, she also has had a few patients get angry when she refused to prescribe the drugs they wanted. A couple even threatened to go to another doctor.

Questions

1. How do you suspect Dr. Duncan feels when presented with such information by patients? How should she handle such situations? How do the patients feel when she refuses to prescribe the drugs they have suggested?
2. To what extent should Dr. Duncan's patients expect to be treated like "customers?" What does this mean in terms of how the doctor deals with them? Isn't the customer always right?
3. How should Dr. Duncan handle the competition that is posed by the information now available on the Internet? How does she prevent some of her "customers" from taking their "business" elsewhere?
4. What is the increased availability of medical information on the Internet and increased exposure of Canadian consumers to advertising for prescription drugs potentially doing to the relationship between doctors and their patients?

SOURCE: Adapted in part from CBC *Marketplace*, "Direct to Consumer Advertising," February 27, 2002.

Glossary

accessory equipment: In the business market, capital goods used in the operation of a firm. p. 191.

activities, interests, and opinions: The bases of an individual's lifestyle; these characterize how people lead their lives. p. 140.

activity indicator of buying power: A market factor that is related to income generation and expenditures; sometimes, a combined indicator of purchasing power and the number of business users. p. 169.

actual self-concept: The way you really see yourself, as distinguished from *ideal self-concept*. p. 42.

administered vertical marketing system: A distribution system in which channel control is maintained through the economic power of one firm in the channel. p. 350.

advertising: All activities involved in presenting to a group a non-personal, sponsor-identified message regarding a product or organization. p. 404.

advertising agency: An independent company rendering specialized services in advertising in particular and in marketing in general. p. 425.

advertising allowance: A payment or cash discount offered by a manufacturer to a retailer to encourage the retailer to advertise or prominently display the manufacturer's product. p. 407.

advertising campaign: The total advertising program for a product or brand that involves co-ordination, a central theme, and specific goals. p. 409.

advertising media: The communications vehicles (such as newspapers, radio, and television) that carry advertising. p. 413.

advertising recall: A measure of advertising effectiveness based on the premise that an ad can have an effect only if it is perceived and remembered. p. 423.

agent wholesaler: An independent firm that primarily engages in wholesaling and does not take title to the products being distributed, but does actively negotiate their sale or purchase on behalf of other firms. p. 340.

agribusiness: The business side of farming; usually involves large, highly mechanized farming operations. p. 163.

annual marketing plan: A written document that details the planned marketing activities for a business unit or product for a given year. p. 80.

appeal: The reason, justification, or argument presented in an advertisement to cause a message receiver to be influenced. p. 412.

attention: Getting people to notice your message. p. 412.

attitude: A learned predisposition to respond to an object or class of objects in a consistently favourable or unfavourable way. p. 42.

auction company: An agent wholesaler that provides (1) auctioneers who do the selling and (2) physical facilities for displaying the sellers' products. p. 342.

automatic vending: A form of non-store retailing in which the products are sold through a machine, with no personal contact between the buyer and seller; same as *automated merchandising*. p. 327.

awareness: Stage 1 of buying readiness: The customer gains information about the product and the brand name. p. 389.

B2B marketing: The marketing of goods and services to business and organizational users, rather than to end-consumers. p. 160.

bait pricing: Attracting consumers with a low-priced feature item and then pointing out its weaknesses in order to sell a more expensive version. p. 301.

base price: The price of one unit of the product at its point of production or resale; same as list price. p. 283.

behavioural segmentation: Market segmentation based on consumers' product-related behaviour; typically, the benefits consumers desire from a product, the rate at which they use the product, and situations where it is used. p. 142.

benchmark: The process of comparing a company with its competitors and others in related industries, or comparing the results of one time period with those of another. p. 102.

benefit segments: Segments of customers defined by the benefits they seek or experience from the purchase and use of products or services. p. 142.

Boston Consulting Group (BCG) matrix: A strategic planning model that classifies strategic business units or major products according to market shares and growth rates. p. 82.

brand: The essence of a company; more than the products and services it markets — how it is presented to customers; what the company stands for; its reputation and image; and what it means to customers. p. 244.

brand awareness: The first stage in building an association between customers and a brand; they become aware of it. p. 245.

brand characteristics: The stage of the development of a brand relationship in which customers are able to associate certain characteristics with the brand. p. 246.

brand equity: The value that customers place on a company or brand; its value in their eyes. The higher the sense of loyalty, the greater the level of brand equity. pp. 8, 247.

brand extensions: New products or services that are launched by a company under an existing brand name. p. 249.

brand label: The application of the brand name alone to a product or package. p. 261.

brand loyalty: The situation in which a customer buys a certain brand on a regular basis because of its performance and appeal. p. 247.

brand mark: The part of a brand that appears in the form of a symbol, picture, design, or distinctive colour or type of lettering. p. 245.

brand name: The part of a brand that can be vocalized: words, letters, and/or numbers. p. 245.

brand personality: The acquisition by a brand of certain characteristics normally associated with people; reflects the people who are most likely to feel comfortable with and to buy the brand. p. 246.

brand recognition: The stage in a brand's association with customers where it is recognized and many customers are familiar with it. p. 245.

brand relationship: The ultimate stage of association between customers and a brand: They have an emotional attachment to it. p. 246.

brand values: The qualities that are inherent in a brand and that govern how a company or brand conducts itself. p. 246.

branding: The process that leads to a company or product acquiring a certain meaning over time; it comes to stand for something in the minds of customers. p. 244.

breadth of product mix: The number of product lines offered for sale by a firm. p. 192.

break-even point: The level of output at which revenues equal costs, assuming a certain selling price. p. 289.

broker: An independent agent wholesaler that brings buyers and sellers together and provides market information to either party. p. 341.

bundling: The process of grouping together a number of services that are sold as a single unit. p. 260.

business analysis: The stage of new-product development in which a surviving idea is expanded into a business proposal and management identifies product features; estimates market demand, competition, and profitability; establishes a development program; and assigns responsibility for further study. p. 204.

business and organizational (B2B) market: The market consisting of business and other organizational users; involves business-to-business (B2B) interaction and relationships. p. 160.

business product: A product that is intended for purchase and use in producing other products or in rendering services in a business. p. 189.

business user: An organization that buys goods or services to resell, use in its own business, or make other products. p. 132.

business-to-business advertising: Advertisements directed to businesses rather than consumers. p. 405.

buy classes: Three typical buying situations in the business market: new-task buy, straight rebuy, and modified rebuy. p. 172.

buyers: The people in a buying centre who select the suppliers, arrange the terms of sale, and process the actual purchase orders. p. 174.

buying centre: All of the people in an organization who participate in the buying-decision process. p. 173.

buying-decision process: The six stages through which a prospective customer goes when faced with a buying problem. The stages differ for consumers and organizations. p. 30.

buying motive: The reason why a person buys a specific product. p. 172.

cash cows: Strategic business units that are characterized by high market shares and do business in mature industries (those with low growth rates). p. 83.

catalogue retailing: One form of direct marketing, in which companies mail catalogues to consumers or make them available at retail stores, and consumers make their purchases from the catalogues, often ordering online. p. 326.

category-killer store: A type of retail institution that has a narrow but very deep assortment, emphasizes low prices, and offers few-to-moderate customer services; it is designed to "destroy" all competition in a specific product category. p. 322.

Census Metropolitan Area (CMA): One of the major population centres of Canada, as defined by Statistics Canada; generally contains population centres of 100,000 or more. p. 135.

channel conflict: A situation in which one channel member perceives another channel member to be acting in a way that prevents the first member from achieving its distribution objectives. p. 356.

channel control: The ability to influence the behaviour of other channel members. p. 358.

co-branding: A branding strategy that involves two or more brands appearing on the same product. Both brands benefit because they are mutually supportive and a good "fit." p. 255.

cognitive dissonance: Anxiety created by the fact that in most purchases, the alternative selected has some negative features and the alternatives not selected have some positive features. p. 37.

commercial information environment: All marketing organizations and individuals that directly or indirectly communicate with consumers. p. 45.

commercial services: The services marketed by business or professional firms with profit-making motives, as compared with the services offered by public and not-for-profit organizations. p. 222.

commission merchant: An independent agent wholesaler, used primarily in the marketing of agricultural products, that may physically handle the seller's products in central markets and has authority regarding prices and terms of sale. p. 342.

commoditization: A situation in which consumers perceive little or no difference among the products of various companies and therefore focus on price as a differentiator. p. 291.

communication: Verbal or non-verbal transmission of information, through a medium or media, between a sender and a receiver. p. 386.

company sales branch: A sales facility that carries a stock of the product being sold. p. 353.

comparative advertising: Selective-demand advertising in which the advertiser either directly (by naming a rival brand) or indirectly (through inference) points out how the advertised brand is better. p. 406.

Competition Act: The major federal legislation in Canada that governs the marketing and advertising activities of companies and organizations operating in Canada. p. 398.

competitive bidding: The characteristic form of government procurement, in which a government agency advertises both offline and online for bids, using a format that states the specifications of the intended purchase. The agency must accept the lowest bid that meets these specifications. p. 162.

consultative salesperson: A selling job in which the person engages in the creative selling of goods and services by addressing customer needs that are often not obvious, and then offering advice and solutions to those needs. p. 437.

consumer advertising: Advertisements directed to consumers. p. 405.

consumer product: A product that is intended for purchase and use by household consumers for non-business purposes. p. 189.

consumer promotion: Sales promotion that is aimed at end consumers. p. 447.

consumerism: Initiatives by consumers to identify unfairness and inefficiency in marketing, and the efforts to remedy these injustices. p. 475.

contractual vertical market system: An arrangement in which independent firms (producers, wholesalers, and retailers) operate under a contract specifying how they will try to improve their distribution efficiency and effectiveness. pp. 312, 350.

convenience goods: A class of consumer products of which the consumer has prior knowledge and purchases with minimum time and effort. p. 189.

convenience sample: A sample that is selected in a non-random way, so that every member of the universe does not have an equal chance of being included. p. 116.

convenience store: A type of retailing institution that concentrates on convenience-oriented groceries and non-foods, has higher prices than found at most grocery stores, and offers few customer services. p. 323.

conviction: Stage 5 of buying readiness: The customer makes an actual decision or commitment to purchase. p. 390.

co-operative advertising: Advertising for which two or more firms share the cost. p. 407.

core services: Services that are the main purpose or object of a transaction — the intangible essence of the offer. p. 221.

corporate chain: An organization of two or more centrally owned and managed stores that generally handle the same lines of products. p. 315.

corporate culture: The atmosphere that prevails within a company, which contributes to employees' satisfaction and influences how they treat customers. p. 465.

corporate vertical marketing system: An arrangement under which a firm at one level of a distribution channel owns the firms at the next level or owns the entire channel. p. 349.

cost-based pricing: A company uses its costs as the basis for setting its prices and does not take the customer or market into account. p. 287.

cost per thousand (CPM): The media cost of gaining exposure to one thousand people with an ad. p. 414.

culture: A complex of symbols and artifacts created by a given society and handed down from generation to generation as determinants and regulators of human behaviour. p. 45.

cumulative quantity discount: A quantity discount based on the total volume purchased over a specified period of time. p. 296.

customer: An individual or organization involved in making purchase and consumption decisions. p. 4.

customer-centric: Focused on customers and on achieving customer satisfaction; the customer is at the centre of management thinking. p. 464.

customer expectations: What customers expect to encounter when dealing with a company or buying a product or service, based on past experience and desired outcomes. pp. 6, 236.

customer experience: The entire experience a customer has in dealing with a business or organization, including many factors that have the potential to influence whether or not the customer is satisfied, such as how the customer is treated and the setting in which the interaction takes place. p. 5.

customer-interest stage: A company realizes that satisfying its customers is critical to its success; generally involves trying to know customers better. p. 11.

customer loyalty: A state achieved when a customer not only deals regularly with a company, but also feels an emotional attachment to it and recommends it to others. p. 8.

customer relationship: A close association between a company or brand and its customers, characterized by strong feelings of loyalty, trust, and commitment; the ultimate connection, based not only on quality of products and service, but also on how the company makes its customers feel. p. 8.

customer-relationship stage: A company actively tries to cultivate long-term relationships with its customers, based not only on great products, price, and service, but also on establishing an emotional connection. p. 11.

customer retention: The behavioural connection between regular customers and a company; characterized by repeat buying behaviour, but not yet a relationship because it may be lacking an emotional component. p. 22.

customer-retention strategy: The measures that a company uses to retain current customers and have them make repeat purchases; includes getting to know customers in as much detail as possible in order to communicate effectively, and rewarding those who are loyal and continue to give the company their business. p. 333.

customer satisfaction: The degree to which a customer's experience with a product or organization meets or exceeds his or her expectations. p. 4.

customer-service advertising: Advertising that presents information about the advertiser's operations. p. 405.

customer-service representatives: Employees who represent the company to customers, usually providing advice and service over the telephone from call centres. p. 430.

customer-service stage: A company at this stage places emphasis on providing excellent service to its customers, usually through improved systems and employee-customer interaction. p. 11.

data analysis: The process of extracting relevant information from data collected through research; usually associated with the application of statistical tools. p. 117.

database: A set of related data that is organized, stored, and regularly updated in computer files. Much of the data are automatically "captured" through the ongoing monitoring of card swipes, billing data, etc. p. 99.

data mining: Method used to identify patterns and meaningful relationships in masses of data that might be unrecognizable to researchers. p. 100.

data warehouse: A collection of data from a variety of internal and external sources, compiled by a firm for use in conducting transactions. p. 100.

deciders: The people in a buying centre who make the actual buying decision regarding a product and/or supplier. p. 173.

decision maker: The individual in a household or organization who has the responsibility of deciding what to buy. p. 14.

decline stage: The fourth, and final, part of a product life cycle, during which the sales of a generic product category drop and most competitors abandon the market. p. 211.

demographic segmentation Segmentation of a company's customers based on their demographic characteristics; including most often age, gender, income level, marital status, family composition, etc. p. 135.

demography: The statistical study of human population and its distribution. p. 61.

department store: A large-scale retailing institution that has a very broad and deep product assortment, prefers not to compete on the basis of price, and offers a wide array of customer services. p. 319.

depth of product line: The assortment within a product line. p. 192.

derived demand: A situation in which the demand for one product is dependent on the demand for another product. p. 165.

differential advantage/differential competitive advantage: Any feature of an organization or brand perceived by customers to be desirable and different from that of the competition. pp. 78, 407.

differentiation: The strategy of setting a company or brand apart from its competition in the minds of its customers or prospective customers. p. 152.

direct-action advertising: Product advertising that seeks a quick response. p. 405.

direct distribution: A channel consisting only of producer and final customer, with no intermediaries providing assistance. p. 345.

direct mail: An advertising medium in which the advertiser contacts prospective customers by sending some form of advertisement through the mail. p. 326.

direct marketing: A form of non-store retailing that uses non-personal media to contact consumers who, in turn, purchase products without visiting a retail store. p. 326.

direct selling: A form of non store retailing in which personal contact between a salesperson and a consumer occurs away from a retail store. p. 324.

direct tests: Measures of the sales volume produced by an ad or an entire advertising campaign. p. 423.

discount house: A large-scale retailing institution that has a broad and shallow product assortment, emphasizes low prices, and offers relatively few customer services. p. 320.

discount retailing: A retailing approach that uses price as a major selling point by combining comparatively low prices and reduced costs of doing business. p. 320.

discretionary purchasing power: The amount of disposable income remaining after fixed expenses and essential household needs are covered. p. 138.

distribution centre: A concept in warehousing that develops under one roof an efficient, fully integrated system for the flow of products, taking orders, filling them, and delivering them to customers. p. 366.

distribution channel: The set of people and firms involved in the flow of ownership of a product as it moves from producer to ultimate consumer or business user. p. 69.

dogs: Strategic business units that are characterized by low market shares and operate in industries with low growth rates. p. 84.

door-to-door selling: A kind of direct selling with the personal contact between a salesperson and an individual prospect occurring at the prospective customer's residence or business. p. 325.

driver-salesperson: A selling job in which the job is primarily to deliver the product; selling responsibilities, if any, are secondary to seeing that orders are filled correctly and on time. p. 436.

early adopters: The second group (following innovators) to adopt something new. This group includes opinion leaders, is respected, and has much influence on its peers. p. 206.

early majority: A more deliberate group of innovation adopters that adopts just before the "average" adopter. p. 206.

eco-labelling: Seals of approval awarded by a government to encourage environmentally safe products. p. 261.

economic order quantity (EOQ): The optimal quantity for reorder when replenishing inventory stocks, as indicated by the volume at which the inventory carrying cost plus the order-processing cost are at a minimum. p. 365.

electronic data interchange (EDI): Digital transmission of orders, invoices, or other business information. p. 365.

emotional value: The value that an organization is able to create for its customers that addresses the feelings that the customer has toward the company or its brands. p. 236.

end-consumers: People who buy products for their personal, non-business use. p. 132.

environmental scanning: Gathering information regarding a company's internal and external environment, analyzing it, and forecasting the impact of the conditions and trends that the analysis suggests. p. 74.

ethics: The rules and standards of moral behaviour that are generally accepted by a society. p. 477.

evaluating sales performance: The process of determining whether sales personnel have achieved objectives; important for building customer loyalty and for compensation. p. 445.

everyday low pricing (EDLP): A pricing strategy that involves consistently low prices and few if any temporary price reductions. p. 301.

exchange: The voluntary act of providing a person or organization with something of value in order to acquire something else of value in return. p. 4.

exclusive distribution: A strategy in which a producer agrees to sell its product to only one wholesaling intermediary and/or retailer in a given market. p. 356.

expected price: The price at which customers consciously or unconsciously value a product; what they think the product is worth. p. 283.

experimental method: A method of gathering primary data in which the researcher is able to observe the results of changing one variable in a situation while holding all others constant. p. 106.

export agent: An intermediary that operates either in a manufacturer's country or in the destination country, negotiating the sale of a product in another country; may provide additional services such as arranging for international financing, shipping, and insurance on behalf of the manufacturer. p. 353.

export merchant: An intermediary operating in a manufacturer's country that buys goods and exports them. p. 353.

exporting: The activities by which a firm sells its product in another country, either directly to foreign importers or through import-export intermediaries. p. 353.

express warranty: A statement in written or spoken words regarding restitution from seller to customer if the seller's product does not perform up to reasonable expectations. p. 264.

external macro-environmental forces: Market forces that are mostly beyond the control of companies: demographics, social and cultural trends, economic conditions, competition, technological developments, and political and legal forces. p. 60.

external micro-environmental forces: Forces affecting a particular firm that can be readily influenced by the company: the sets of marketing relationships a firm has with its customers, its suppliers, and the wholesalers and retailers through which the company sells its products and services to customers. p. 60.

fabricating parts and materials: Materials that become part of other finished products, distinguished from raw materials in that they have already been processed and bought by manufacturers for assembly into their final products. Some undergo further processing and may be referred to as *fabricating materials*. p. 191.

factory outlet: A special type of off-price retail institution that is owned by a manufacturer and usually sells only that manufacturer's clearance items, regular merchandise, and perhaps even otherwise unavailable items. p. 322.

family: A group of two or more people related by blood, marriage, adoption, or common practice, living together in a household. p. 51.

family-brand strategy: A branding strategy in which a group of related products is given a single brand. p. 257.

family life cycle: The series of life stages that a family goes through, starting with young, single people and progressing through married stages with young and then older children, then ending with older married and single people. p. 138.

family packaging: A strategy of using either similar packages for all products or packages with a common and clearly noticeable feature. p. 260.

fashion: A style that is popularly accepted by groups of people over a reasonably long period of time. p. 331.

fashion-adoption process: The process by which a style becomes popular in a market; similar to diffusion of an innovation. p. 331.

flexible-price strategy: A pricing strategy under which a company sells similar quantities of merchandise to similar buyers at different prices; same as *variable-price strategy*. p. 300.

f.o.b. factory pricing: A geographic pricing strategy whereby the buyer pays all freight charges from the selling facility location to the destination. p. 299.

focus group: An approach to qualitative research that involves interviewing customers in groups of 8 to 10, usually lasting 90 minutes or more, intended to reveal deeply held views. p. 102.

forward dating: A combination of a seasonal discount and a cash discount under which a buyer places an order and receives shipment during the off-season, but does not have to pay the bill until after the season has started and some sales revenue has been generated. p. 297.

"four RS" of marketing: Guideposts for the new way of thinking in marketing: customer retention, relationships, referrals, and recovery from negative experiences. p. 22.

fragmentation: The break-up of the mass audience for television or other media into smaller audiences as the result of technological innovations, such as the proliferation of channels, channel-zapping, skip devices, use of VCRS and DVD players. p. 416.

franchising: A type of contractual marketing system that involves a continuing relationship in which a franchiser (the parent company) provides the right to use a trademark plus management assistance in opening and operating a services business in return for financial considerations from a franchisee (the owner of the individual business unit). p. 229.

freight-absorption pricing: A geographic pricing strategy whereby the seller pays for (absorbs) some of the freight charges in order to penetrate more distant markets. p. 300.

functional value: The value that a company creates for its customers that is based on the quality of its products and the efficiency of its services. p. 236.

gatekeepers: The people in a buying centre who control the flow of purchasing information within the organization and between the buying firm and potential vendors. p. 174.

geographic segmentation: The process of segmenting a market into geographic regions and developing a different marketing strategy for each region. p. 134.

"give and get": An illustration of the exchange process as both customer and company giving something and getting something in return. p. 5.

government market: The segment of the business market that includes federal, provincial, and local government units buying for government institutions such as schools, offices, hospitals, and research facilities. p. 162.

grade label: Identification of the quality (grade) of a product by means of a letter, number, or word. p. 261.

growth stage: The second part of a product life cycle, during which the sales and profits of a generic product category rise and competitors enter the market; profits start to decline near the end of this part of the cycle. p. 211.

heterogeneity (of a service): A characteristic of a service indicating that the nature and quality of the service is different each time it is delivered. p. 224.

high-involvement level: A purchase decision that involves all six stages of the buying-decision process. p. 32.

holistic view of marketing: The view that virtually everything a company does has an impact on long-term customer satisfaction and is, therefore, part of marketing. p. 464.

horizontal business market: A situation in which a given product is usable in a wide variety of industries. p. 168.

horizontal conflict: A form of channel conflict occurring between firms on the same level of distribution, between intermediaries of the same type, or between different types of intermediaries. p. 356.

horizontal co-operative advertising: Advertising that involves firms on the same level of distribution sharing the cost. p. 407.

household: A single person, a family, or any group of unrelated persons who occupy a housing unit. p. 51.

ideal self-concept: The way you want to be seen or would like to see yourself, as distinguished from *actual self-concept*. p. 42.

implied warranty: An intended but unstated assurance regarding restitution from seller to customer if the seller's product does not perform up to reasonable expectations. p. 264.

import-export agent: An agent wholesaler that arranges for distribution of goods in a foreign country. p. 342.

impulse buying: Low-involvement purchase made with little or no advance planning. p. 33.

independent retailer: A company with a single retail store that is not affiliated with any type of contractual VMS. p. 314.

indirect-action advertising: Product advertising that is intended to inform or remind consumers about a product and its benefits. p. 405.

indirect distribution: A channel consisting of producer, final customer, and at least one level of intermediary. p. 345.

indirect tests: Measures of advertising effects that use something other than sales volume. p. 423.

individual depth interview: An approach to qualitative research that involves a one-on-one interview with a customer, usually lasting 90 minutes or more, intended to explore attitudes and opinions in considerable depth. p. 102.

inelastic demand: A price-volume relationship in which a change of one unit on the price scale results in a change of less than one unit on the volume scale. p. 165.

influence: The ability to cause a change in a person's beliefs, attitudes, or intentions. p. 412.

influencers: The people in a buying centre who set the specifications and aspects of buying decisions because of their technical expertise, financial position, or political power in the organization. pp. 14, 173.

informal investigation: The stage in a marketing research study at which information is gathered from people outside the company, such as distribution channel members, competitors, advertising agencies, and customers. p. 110.

innovation-adopter categories: Five categories, based on the point in time when individuals adopt a given innovation, comprising innovators, early adopters, early majority, late majority, and laggards. p. 206.

innovator: The first member of a reference group who is most likely to adopt something new (good, service). p. 50.

innovators: The first group of people (in the innovation-adopter categories) — a venturesome group — to adopt a new product or service. p. 206.

inseparability: A characteristic of a service indicating that the service cannot be separated from the creator or seller of the service. p. 223.

inside order taker: A selling job in which the primary function of the salesperson is to take orders in person or by telephone inside a store or other type of business. p. 436.

inside selling: The kind of selling in which customers come to the salespeople; primarily face-to-face retail selling, but also includes phone-in ordering. p. 432.

installations: In the business market, long-lived, expensive, major industrial capital goods that directly affect the scale of operation of an industrial firm. p. 191.

institutional advertising: Advertising designed either to present information about the advertiser's business or to create a good impression to build goodwill toward the organization. p. 405.

intangibility: A characteristic of a service indicating that it has no physical attributes and, as a result, is impossible for customers to taste, feel, see, hear, or smell before buying. p. 223.

integrated marketing communications (IMC): A strategic business process used to plan, develop, execute, and evaluate co-ordinated communication with an organization's customers and the general public. p. 383.

intensity of distribution: The number of intermediaries used by a producer at the retailing and wholesaling levels of distribution. p. 355.

intensive distribution: A strategy in which a producer sells its product in every available outlet where a consumer might reasonably look for it. p. 355.

internal marketing: The process of directing programs to staff members with the intention of encouraging them to deliver superior service to customers and generally to adopt a customer focus in all that they do. p. 233.

internal non-marketing forces: The environment within a firm composed of working relationships between employees and departments. p. 60.

Internet research: Customer research conducted through the use of surveys administered through the Internet, either by sending questionnaires by e-mail or by having customers enter a secure Web site. p. 113.

Internet shopping: Use of the Internet to offer products for sale, providing information that can assist in sales being made elsewhere, but also offering an alternative way to purchase products. p. 327.

interview guide: The equivalent of a questionnaire used in qualitative research; a list of semi-structured questions or areas of enquiry designed to guide the depth interview or focus group. p. 115.

introduction stage: The first part of a product life cycle, during which a generic product category is launched into the market in a full-scale marketing program. p. 210.

inventory control: Involves maintaining control over the size and composition of inventories in order to fill customers' orders promptly, completely, and accurately while minimizing both the investment and fluctuations in inventories. p. 365.

inverse demand: A price-volume relationship: The higher the price, the greater the unit sales. p. 285.

just-in-time (JIT) inventory control: An inventory control system that involves buying parts and supplies in small quantities just in time for use in production and then producing in quantities just in time for sale. p. 366.

knowledge: Stage 2 of buying readiness: A customer learns about a product's features and how it can meet a need. p. 390.

label: The part of a product that carries written information about the product or the seller. p. 261.

laggards: Tradition-bound people who are the last to adopt an innovation. p. 207.

late majority: The sceptical group of innovation adopters who adopt a new idea late in the game. p. 206.

leader pricing: Involves temporarily reducing the prices of well-known items; the price cuts are made with the idea that these "specials" (leaders) will attract customers to the store. p. 294.

learning: Changes in attitudes and behaviour resulting from previous experiences. p. 40.

lifestyle: The way in which a person conducts his or her life — activities, interests, and opinions. p. 43.

lifetime value of customers: The value to a company of a customer over the lifetime of that customer's association with the firm; more than direct current purchases. p. 12.

liking: Stage 3 of buying readiness: The knowledgeable customer moves from being indifferent about the brand to having positive feelings about it. p. 390.

limited-line store: A type of retailing institution that has a narrow but deep product assortment; its customer services tend to vary from store to store. p. 321.

line extension: One form of product-mix expansion in which a company adds a similar item to an existing product line with the same brand name. p. 195.

logistics: Activities involved in the flow of products as they move physically from producer to consumer or industrial user. p. 361.

logistics management: The cost efficient organizing and managing of the flow of raw materials, in-process inventory, finished goods, and related information from point of origin to point of consumption to satisfy customer requirements. p. 361.

low-involvement level: A purchase decision in which the consumer moves directly from need recognition to purchase, skipping the stages in between. p. 32.

mail survey: Gathering data by means of a questionnaire mailed to respondents and, when completed, returned by mail. p. 113.

mall intercept: A method of gathering data by conducting personal interviews in central locations, typically regional shopping centres. p. 112.

manufacturer's agent: An independent agent wholesaler that sells part or all of a manufacturer's product mix in an assigned geographic territory. p. 340.

market: People or organizations with needs or wants to satisfy, money to spend, and the willingness to spend it. p. 14.

market fragmentation: The identification of smaller and smaller market segments with individualized communications approaches. p. 482.

market-penetration pricing: A pricing strategy in which a low initial price is set to reach the mass market immediately. p. 295.

market response system: A form of inventory control in which a purchase by a final customer activates a process to produce and deliver a replacement item to inventory. p. 366.

market segmentation: The process of dividing the total market for a product into several customer groups, each of which tends to be homogeneous. p. 127.

market share targets: When a company sets a certain share of the market as its objective when setting prices. p. 281.

market-skimming pricing: A pricing strategy in which the initial price is set high in the target market's range of expected prices. p. 294.

market tests: The stage of new-product development that involves tests with actual consumers. p. 204.

marketer: Any business or other organization that desires to create long-term satisfaction among the customer groups it serves. p. 6.

marketing: An integrated series of activities oriented toward achieving long-term customer satisfaction; involves planning, pricing, promoting, and distributing need-satisfying products and services to target markets in order to achieve success for both customers and businesses/organizations. p. 4.

marketing communications: All of the elements of an organization's marketing (usually advertising, publicity, public relations, personal sales, and sales promotion) that serve to inform existing and potential customers. p. 379.

marketing communications mix: The combination of personal selling, advertising, sales promotion, publicity, and public relations that is intended to help an organization achieve its marketing objectives. p. 389.

marketing concept: A philosophy of doing business that emphasizes a customer orientation and co-ordination of marketing activities in order to achieve customer satisfaction and the organization's performance objectives. p. 12.

marketing intermediaries: Firms that render services directly related to the purchase and/or sale of a product as it flows from producer to consumer. p. 68.

marketing mix: A combination of the elements — traditionally including product, pricing, distribution system, and promotional activities — that comprise a company's marketing program. Many marketers now consider the service and experience provided to customers to be an additional and extremely important component of the marketing mix. p. 7.

marketing research: The process of specifying, assembling, and analyzing information used to identify and define marketing opportunities and problems; generate, refine, and evaluate marketing actions; monitor marketing performance; and improve the understanding of customers and of marketing as a process. p. 95.

mark-up: The dollar amount that is added to the acquisition cost of a product to determine the selling price. p. 280.

Maslow's hierarchy of needs: A needs structure consisting of five levels and organized according to the order in which people seek need gratification. p.38.

materials handling: The subsystem of logistics management that involves selecting and operating the equipment and warehouse building used in physically handling products. p. 366.

maturity stage: The third part of a product life cycle, during which sales of a generic product category continue to increase (but at a decreasing rate), profits decline largely due to price competition, and some firms leave the market. p. 211.

merchant wholesaler: An independently owned firm that primarily engages in wholesaling and ordinarily takes title to the products being distributed; same as *wholesaler*. p. 340.

missionary salesperson: A selling job in which the salespeople are not expected to solicit orders but rather to influence decision makers by building goodwill, performing promotional activities, and providing service to customers; called a detail salesperson in pharmaceuticals marketing. p. 436.

mission statement: Indicates the boundaries of an organization's activities. p. 71.

mix extension: A way of expanding the product mix by adding a new product line to the company's current assortment. p. 196.

mode of transportation: The manner in which the movement of goods is carried out; leading modes of transportation are railroads, trucks, ships, and airplanes. p. 367.

modified rebuy: In the business market, a purchasing situation between a new-task rebuy and a straight rebuy in terms of time required, information needed, and alternatives considered. p. 173.

motive: A need sufficiently stimulated that an individual is moved to seek satisfaction. p. 38.

multiple-brand strategy: A strategy in which a firm has more than one brand of essentially the same product, aimed either at the same target market or at distinct target markets. p. 257.

multiple buying influences: A situation in which a purchasing decision is influenced by more than one person in the buyer's organization. p. 173.

multiple packaging: The placing of several units of the same product in one container or by physically wrapping them together. p. 260.

multiple-segment strategy: A strategy that involves the selection of two or more groups of potential customers as target markets. p. 145.

national brands: Brands of tangible products that are generally owned by manufacturers. p. 245.

needs and wants: The focus of a customer-oriented company who will want to satisfy these in order to achieve customer satisfaction. May be viewed as a combination of functional and emotional needs. p. 15.

new-product strategy: A plan that defines the role new products are to play in helping the company achieve its corporate and marketing goals. p. 203.

new-task buy: In the business market, a purchasing situation in which a company considers buying a given item for the first time. p. 172.

niche marketing: A strategy in which goods and services are tailored to meet the needs of small market segments. p. 151.

non-adopters: Consumers who never adopt an innovation. p. 207.

non-business market: Includes such diverse institutions as churches, colleges and universities, museums, hospitals and other health institutions, political parties, labour unions, and charitable organizations. p. 163.

non-cumulative quantity discount: A quantity discount based on the size of an individual order of products. p. 296.

non-price competition: A strategy in which a firm tries to compete based on some factor other than price; for example, promotion, product differentiation, or variety of services. p. 282.

non-store retailing: Retailing activities resulting in transactions that occur away from a retail store. p. 324.

North American Industry Classification System (NAICS): System that allows business marketers to locate codes for present customers and obtain coded lists of similar firms, and provides a rapid, low-cost approach to identifying changes in the growth of various industry sectors. p. 167.

objective: A desired outcome; same as *goal*. p. 71.

observational method: Gathering data by observing personally or using technology the actions of a person. p. 104.

odd pricing: A form of psychological pricing that consists of setting prices at odd amounts ($4.99 rather than $5.00, for example) in the belief that these seemingly low prices will result in larger sales volume. p. 301.

off-price retailing: A strategy of selling well-known brands below the manufacturer's recommended retail price. p. 321.

one-price strategy: A strategy under which a seller charges the same price to all customers of the same type who buy the same quantity of goods. p. 300.

operating supplies: The "convenience goods" of the business market: short-lived, low-priced items purchased with a minimum of time and effort. p. 191.

opinion leader: The member of a reference group who is the information source and who influences the decision-making of others in the group. p. 51.

order processing: Consists of the set of procedures for receiving, handling, and filling orders. p. 365.

outside order taker: A selling job in which salespeople primarily go to customers in the field. p. 436.

outside sales force: A group of sales reps engaged in field selling; that is, selling in person at a customer's place of business or home. p. 432.

outside selling: The kind of personal selling in which salespeople go to the customers, making contact by mail, telephone, or face to face. p. 432.

packaging: For products, the activities in product planning that involve designing and producing the container or wrapper for a product; for services, bundling and promotion activities are involved. p. 258.

party-plan selling: A type of direct selling in which a host or hostess invites some friends to a party at which a salesperson makes a sales presentation. p. 325.

patronage motives: The reasons why a consumer chooses to shop at a certain place or buy from a particular company. p. 35.

perception: Collecting and processing information from the environment in order to give meaning to the world around us. p. 39.

perishability: A characteristic of a service indicating that it disappears if not sold and cannot be placed in inventory as can tangible products. p. 225.

personal disposable income: Personal income remaining after all personal taxes are paid. p. 138.

personal interview: A face-to-face method of gathering data in a survey. p. 111.

personality: An individual's pattern of traits that influences behavioural responses. p. 41.

physical facilities: The location, design and layout of a retail store's site. p. 313.

pioneering advertising: Primary-demand advertising that is done in the introductory stage of the product life cycle. p. 406.

population: The group of particular interest to the researcher about which conclusions are to be drawn; usually a specific group or segment of customers. p. 116.

positioning: The strategy of creating an appropriate image for a company or brand in the minds of its target customers — what the brand stands for, what it means to customers. pp. 78, 146.

positioning map: A graphic representation of the relative positions that various brands or companies occupy in the minds of their target customers. Positioning maps are used based on data collected in customer surveys. p. 149.

predictive modelling: Procedures for analyzing data so as to predict, based on past purchase behaviour, the types of products and services customers may be interested in buying, so that targeted marketing programs may be developed. p. 100.

preference: Stage 4 of buying readiness: The customer distinguishes among brands and prefers yours. p. 390.

press release: News from a company sent to the media for publication. p. 453.

prestige pricing: Raising prices above competitive levels. p. 301.

pre-test (of commercials): An activity in which commercials in finished or nearly finished form are presented to panels of consumers in order to gauge their reactions. p. 424.

pre-testing (of questionnaires): The process of testing a questionnaire before it is used in a survey, to identify problems and areas of confusion. p. 115.

price: The amount of money and/or other resources needed to acquire some combination of a product and its accompanying services. p. 274.

price competition: A strategy in which a firm regularly offers prices that are as low as possible, usually accompanied by a minimum of services. p. 292.

price elasticity of demand: The responsiveness of quantity purchased to price changes. p. 285.

price lining: Involves selecting a limited number of prices at which a business will sell related products. p. 301.

price sensitivity: The extent to which a customer or a certain segment of customers will respond to price changes or is focused on price when buying. p. 277.

pricing objective: The goals that management tries to reach with its pricing structure and strategies. p. 280.

primary data: Original data gathered specifically for the project at hand. p. 111.

primary-demand advertising: Advertising designed to stimulate demand for a generic product. p. 406.

primary-product agents: Intermediaries who trade in primary products as opposed to manufactured goods. p. 342.

private labels: Brands that are owned by retailers. p. 245.

proactive selling: A situation in which the selling effort is initiated by the salesperson, who actively tries to interest the customer in buying. p. 432.

product: A product can be a physical item or a service, place, person, or idea; it has a set of tangible attributes, including packaging, colour, price, quality, and brand, plus the services and reputation of the seller. p. 188.

product-adoption process: The stages that an individual goes through in deciding whether to accept a new product or innovation. p. 205.

product diffusion: The process by which a new product or innovation is spread through a market or social system over time. p. 205.

product-focus stage: The stage at which a company is focused mainly on producing high-quality products and services. p. 10.

product-in-use situation: The stage in the interaction when the customer has bought the product or service and is using or experiencing it; evaluation of the success of the purchase takes place. p. 17.

product life cycle: The stages a product goes through from its introduction, to its growth and maturity, to its eventual decline and death (withdrawal from the market or deletion from the company's offerings). p. 209.

product line: A broad group of products intended for essentially similar uses and possessing reasonably similar physical characteristics. p. 192.

product mix: All products offered for sale by a company. p. 192.

product-mix contraction: The elimination of an entire line or simplification of the assortment within a line to weed out low-profit and unprofitable products. p. 200.

product-mix expansion: Increasing the depth within a particular product line and/or the number of lines a firm offers to consumers. p. 195.

product modification: Improvement of an established product as a less risky and more profitable alternative to developing a completely new product. p. 199.

profit maximization: The pricing objective of making as much money as possible in the short term. p. 280.

promotional allowance: A price reduction granted by the seller as payment for promotional services rendered by the buyer. p. 298.

prospecting: The stage in the personal-selling process that involves developing a list of potential customers. p. 440.

psychographics: A concept in consumer behaviour that describes consumers in terms of a combination of psychological and sociological influences. p. 38.

psychological pricing: Setting a price to have a special appeal to a particular segment of customers. p. 301.

public relations: A broad communications effort designed to build or maintain a favourable image for an organization with its various publics. p. 452.

public service advertising: Advertising designed to improve the quality of life and indicate that the advertiser is a responsible member of the community. p. 405.

publicity: Media presentations about a product or organization that are not paid for and have the credibility of editorial material. p. 452.

pull strategy: A communications program aimed primarily at end-users. p. 392.

purchase: Stage 6, the last stage of buying readiness: The customer overcomes any inhibitors that might delay or postpone purchase and buys the product. p. 390.

purchaser: The person in the household or organization who actually makes the purchase of a product or service. p. 14.

push strategy: A communications program aimed primarily at wholesalers and retailers. p. 392.

qualitative research: A form of marketing research intended to provide greater insight into customers' deeply held views, opinions, and feelings; includes focus group interviews and one-on-one depth interviews. p. 102.

quality: The characteristics of a product or service in relation to the expectations of the customer. p. 277.

quantitative research: A form of marketing research that is intended to obtain statistical information about a sample of customers or members of the public; usually relies on surveys to collect the data. p. 102.

quantity discount: A reduction of the list price when large quantities are purchased; offered to encourage buyers to purchase in large quantities. p. 296.

question marks: Strategic business units characterized by low market shares but high industry growth rates. p. 84.

questionnaire: A data-gathering form used to collect information in a personal, telephone, Internet, or mail survey. p. 115.

random sample: A sample that is selected in such a way that every unit in the defined universe has a known probability of being selected. It is usually not possible to obtain a completely random sample. As a result, most research projects will use a sample that is as representative as possible of the population of interest. p. 116.

raw materials: Business goods that have not been processed in any way and that will become part of another product. p. 191.

reactive selling: A situation in which the sales process is initiated by the customer and the salesperson simply processes the sale. p. 432.

reference group: A group of people who influence a person's attitudes, values, and behaviour. p. 49.

referral: The process of recommending a company or brand to others; positive word of mouth. p. 22.

relationship-insensitive forces: Forces that do not afford a firm a particular advantage or the opportunity to develop particularly strong bonds or connections with its customers. p. 61.

relationship pricing: Related to the concept of value pricing, in which benefits are shared with customers to ensure that they receive better value and therefore remain loyal. p. 294.

relationship segmentation: The process of segmenting a market on the basis of the types of relationships that customers want to have with a company or brand. p. 142.

relationship-sensitive forces: Forces that can be managed to varying degrees and therefore are part of a firm's marketing system. p. 67.

repositioning: The process of moving a company, store, or brand to a new position in the minds of target customers, usually by changing its image. p. 150.

research hypothesis: A tentative supposition that, if proven, would suggest a possible solution to a problem. p. 110.

research objectives: The purpose of conducting the research; questions the marketer and researcher want to have addressed and areas that they want to have explored. p. 108.

reseller market: Wholesaling and retailing intermediaries that buy products for resale to other business users or to consumers; a segment of the business market. p. 161.

response: The reaction (non-verbal, verbal, or behavioural) of an information receiver that serves as feedback to the sender of a communication. p. 387.

retail positioning: A retailer's strategies and actions designed to favourably distinguish itself from competitors in the minds (and hearts) of targeted groups of consumers. p. 330.

retail scanner: The electronic device at retail checkouts that reads the bar code on each item, thereby capturing detailed data on every transaction. p. 101.

retailer: A firm engaged primarily in retailing. p. 310.

retailing: The sale, and all activities directly related to the sale, of goods and services to end-consumers for personal, non-business use; same as *retail trade*. p. 310.

sales: The process of selling products and services to customers; usually involves sales personnel who interact with customers. p. 430.

sales engineer: A selling job that often involves technically trained individuals selling sophisticated equipment; the emphasis is on the salesperson's ability to explain the product to the prospect and perhaps to adapt it to the customer's particular needs. p. 437.

sales function: The part of a company that is responsible for sales. p. 430.

sales-orientation stage: The stage in the evolution of marketing in which the emphasis is on selling whatever the organization produces. p. 11.

sales promotion: Activities intended to stimulate short-term interest and purchasing, including contests for salespeople and consumers, trade shows, in-store displays, samples, premiums, and coupons; designed to supplement advertising and co-ordinate selling efforts. p. 447.

sample: A smaller group which is selected to be interviewed or from whom data are to be collected; chosen so as to be representative of the larger population. p. 116.

seasonal discount: A discount for placing an order during the seller's slow season. p. 297.

secondary data: Information already gathered by somebody else for some other purpose. They represent a valuable starting point to a research project to provide the marketer with top-line information about a marketing problem or opportunity. p. 108.

segments: Parts of markets or customer groups. p. 77.

selective attention: The process that limits our perceptions so that, of all of the marketing stimuli to which our senses are exposed, only those able to capture and hold our attention have the potential of being perceived. p. 40.

selective-demand advertising: Advertising intended to stimulate demand for specific brands. p. 406.

selective distortion: The process of mentally altering information that is inconsistent with one's beliefs or attitudes. p. 40.

selective distribution: A strategy in which a producer sells its product through multiple, but not all, wholesalers and/or retailers in a market where a consumer might reasonably look for it. p. 355.

selective retention: The process of retaining in memory some portion of what is perceived. p. 40.

self-concept: A person's self-image. p. 41.

selling: The communication of information to persuade a prospective customer to buy a product, service, or idea. Increasingly being seen to include the offering of advice and the creation of solutions for customers. p. 430.

selling agent: A type of independent intermediary that essentially takes the place of a manufacturer's marketing department, marketing the manufacturer's entire output, and often influencing the design and/or pricing of the products. p. 342.

service encounter: In services marketing, a customer's interaction with any service employee or with any tangible element, such as a service's physical surroundings or through technology. p. 230.

service experience: That part of a company's value proposition that addresses how the company interacts with its customers; the kind of experience the customer has during his or her encounters with the company. p. 232.

service failure: The failure of a service to meet customer expectations or standards, resulting in disappointment, frustration, or similar emotions. p. 234.

service guarantees: Guarantees that companies offer to their customers that attest to the quality of their service. p. 264.

service quality: The value that consumers perceive they are receiving from their purchase of services; generally very difficult to control and measure. p. 232.

service recovery: The process of correcting the situation when a customer is dissatisfied with service provided. A company may attempt to recover from a poor service experience by apologizing or by offering the customer a price reduction or other form of compensation. pp. 24, 234.

services: Identifiable, intangible activities that are sometimes the main object of a transaction and at other times support the sale of tangible products or other services. p. 221.

services market: The market for service activities, including all transportation carriers and public utilities; communications firms, financial, insurance, legal, and real estate firms; and organizations that produce and sell services such as rental housing, recreation and entertainment, repairs, health care, personal care, and business services. p. 162.

services value proposition: The value proposition of a services company, which must include core and support elements of the service provided to customers and the service experience delivered to customers. p. 226.

share of wallet: The share of a customer's total spending in a product or service category that is given to a particular company or brand. p. 22.

shopping centre: A planned grouping of retail stores in a multi-unit structure, with the physical structure usually owned by a single organization. p. 313.

shopping goods: A class of consumer products purchased after the buyer has spent some time and effort comparing price, quality, colour, and/or other attributes of alternative products. p. 189.

single-segment strategy: The selection of one homogeneous segment from within a total market to be the target market. p. 144.

situation analysis: The stage in strategic company planning that involves gathering and studying information that is important to the strategies and tactics of an organization. p. 74.

situational influences: Temporary forces, associated with the immediate purchase environment, which affect behaviour. p. 53.

slotting allowance: A fee that some retailers demand from manufacturers to place manufacturers' products on store shelves. p. 358.

social information environment: Family, friends, and acquaintances who directly or indirectly provide information about products. p. 45.

social responsibility: The commitment on the part of a company to improving the well-being of society. p. 477.

specialty goods: A class of consumer products with perceived unique characteristics; consumers are willing to expend special effort to buy them. p. 189.

specialty store: A type of retail institution that concentrates on a specialized product line or even part of a specialized product line. p. 321.

stabilizing prices: A pricing goal designed to achieve steady, non-volatile prices in an industry. p. 281.

stages in the product-adoption process: The six stages a prospective user goes through in deciding whether to purchase something new, including awareness, interest, evaluation, trial, adoption, and confirmation. p. 206.

stars: Strategic business units characterized by high market shares and high industry growth rates. p. 83.

statutory labelling requirements: Federal and provincial laws regulating packaging and labelling. p. 261.

stimulus-response theory: The theory that learning occurs as a person responds to some stimulus and is rewarded with need satisfaction for a correct response or penalized for an incorrect one. p. 41.

straight rebuy: In the business market, a routine purchase with minimal information needs. p. 173.

strategic business unit (SBU): A separate division for a major product or market in a multi-product or multi-business organization. p. 82.

strategic company planning: The level of planning that consists of defining the organization's mission, analyzing the situation the company is facing, setting organizational objectives, and selecting strategies to achieve the organization's objectives. p. 73.

strategic marketing planning: The level of planning that consists of conducting a situation analysis, determining marketing objectives, identifying target markets and measuring the market, deciding on positioning and differential advantage, and designing a marketing mix. p. 74.

strategy: Broad, basic plan of action by which an organization intends to achieve its objectives. p. 72.

style: A distinctive presentation or construction of any art, product, or activity. p. 331.

subculture: Groups that exhibit characteristic behaviour patterns sufficient to distinguish them from other groups within the same culture. p. 46.

supermarket: A type of retailing institution that has a moderately broad and moderately deep product assortment, spanning groceries and some non-food lines, that offers relatively few customer services and ordinarily emphasizes price in either an offensive or defensive way. p. 322.

supermarket retailing: A retailing method that features several related product lines, a high degree of self-service, largely centralized checkout, and competitive prices. p. 322.

supplementary services: Services that support or facilitate the sale of a tangible product or a core service. p. 221.

supply chain: The sequence of organizations that perform the logistics and related activities required to create and deliver a product to consumers or industrial users. p. 362.

supply chain management: The integration and organization of information and logistics activities across firms in a supply chain to create and deliver goods and services that have customer value. p. 362.

supply partnership: A partnership that occurs when a buyer and seller with mutual trust and interests adopt certain policies, procedures, and co-ordinated relationships to lower production and supply costs and increase consumer product value. p. 176.

survey: A method of gathering data by interviewing a limited number of people (a sample) in person, by telephone or mail, or over the Internet. p. 102.

SWOT assessment: Identifying and evaluating an organization's most significant **s**trengths, **w**eaknesses, **o**pportunities, and **t**hreats. p. 74.

syndicated data: Research information that is purchased from a research supplier on a shared-cost basis by a number of clients. p. 111.

tactic: An operational means by which a strategy is implemented or activated. p. 72.

target market: A group of customers (people or organizations) to whom a seller aims its marketing efforts. p. 77.

target return: A pricing goal that involves setting prices to achieve a certain percentage return on investment or on net sales. p. 280.

target segment: A group of customers (people or firms) to whom a company specifically directs its marketing efforts. p. 129.

team selling: Use of a number of sales personnel to represent a company, often calling on several people in the same account. p. 438.

telemarketing: A form of non-store retailing in which a salesperson initiates contact with a prospect and attempts to close the sale over the telephone. Usually involves outbound calls from a company to prospective customers. pp. 325, 433.

telephone survey: A method of gathering data in a survey by interviewing people over the telephone. p. 112.

television shopping: A form of direct marketing in which TV channels show consumer electronics, jewellery, and other products for sale at relatively low prices. p. 327.

test marketing: A marketing research technique in which, before committing to a major marketing effort, a firm markets its product in a limited geographic area, measures the sales, and then, from this sample, projects (a) the company's sales over a larger area and/or (b) consumer response to a strategy. p. 107.

trademark: A brand that is legally protected. p. 245.

trade promotion: Sales promotion that is directed to members of a distribution channel. p. 447.

trading down: A product-line strategy in which a company adds a lower-priced item to its line of prestige goods in order to reach a market that cannot afford the higher-priced items. p. 198.

trading up: A product-line strategy in which a company adds a higher-priced, prestige product to its line in order to increase sales of the existing lower-priced products in that line and attract a higher-income market. p. 198.

uniform delivered pricing: A geographic pricing strategy whereby the same delivered price is quoted to all buyers, regardless of their location; same as *postage-stamp pricing*. p. 299.

unsought goods: A type of consumer product that consists of new products of which the consumer is not yet aware or products that the consumer does not yet want. p. 189.

usage rate: The rate at which people use or consume a product, or participate in the use of a service. p. 142.

users: The people in a buying centre who actually use a particular product. p. 173.

value: A measure of what customers receive and what companies provide in the exchange. Should be very broadly defined. p. 6.

value chain: The relationships by which the roles of suppliers, producers, distributors, and end-users contribute to the final product. p. 175.

value for money: A customer's perception of what is received for the price paid. p. 278.

value of a customer: The categorization of customers based on their value to the firm. p. 236.

value of a product/service (to consumer): The ratio of perceived benefits of a product or service to perceived costs, including price and other incurred costs. p. 274.

value pricing: A strategy that is aimed at justifying a higher price based on offering the customer additional forms of value. p. 293.

value proposition: The sum total of what the company offers the customer, including much more than product and price. p. 19.

value strategy: An overall strategy of a company to offer value to its customers; price is part of this strategy. p. 279.

values (as distinct from *value*): The principles that individuals hold to be important and by which they lead their lives. p. 140.

vertical business market: A situation in which a given product is usable by virtually all of the firms in only one or two industries. p. 168.

vertical conflict: A form of channel conflict occurring between firms at different levels of the same channel, typically producer versus wholesaler or producer versus retailer. p. 357.

vertical co-operative advertising: Advertising for which firms at different levels of the distribution channel share the cost. p. 407.

vertical marketing system (VMS): A tightly co-ordinated distribution channel designed to achieve operating efficiencies and marketing effectiveness. p. 349.

viral marketing: The planned promotion of a product or service by a company taking advantage of the attention and credibility that often accompanies word of mouth communication. p. 23.

warehouse club: A combined retailing and wholesaling institution that has a very broad but very shallow product assortment; offers very low prices but few customer services, and is open only to members (same as *wholesale club*). p. 324.

warehousing: A broad range of logistics activities that include assembling, doing any necessary repacking, storing products, and then preparing them for reshipping. p. 366.

warranty: An assurance given to buyers that they will be compensated in case the product does not perform up to reasonable expectations. p. 264.

wholesaling: All activities directly related to the sale of goods and services to parties for resale, use in producing other goods and services, or operating an organization. p. 338.

word of mouth: The process of customers discussing companies and brands with which they have come in contact; may be either positive or negative. p. 23.

zone-delivered pricing: A geographic pricing strategy whereby the same delivered price is charged at any location within each geographic zone. p. 300.

Notes and References

Chapter 1

1. James L. Heskett, Thomas O. Jones, Gary W. Loveman, W. Earl Sasser Jr., and Leonard A. Schlesinger, "Putting the Service–Profit Chain to Work," *Harvard Business Review*, March–April 1994, pp. 164–174.
2. Kevin Cox, "The art of the toy business," *The Globe and Mail*, May 4, 2005, p. B4.
3. www.gap.com/asp/cs_returns
4. Michelle Halpern, "Sweet Whispers," *Marketing Magazine Online*, www.marketingmag.ca, January 10, 2005.

Chapter 2

1. A. H. Maslow, *Motivation and Personality* (New York: Harper & Row, 1954), pp. 80–106.
2. Keith McArthur, "Blue Jays deliver new advertising pitch," *The Globe and Mail*, April 8, 2005, p. B3.
3. World News, *Gulf Marketing Review*, January 2005, p 22.
4. Other schools of thought on learning, principally the cognitive approach and gestalt learning, are discussed in books on *consumer behaviour*. See David Louden and Albert J. Della Bitta, *Consumer Behavior*, 3rd ed. (New York: McGraw-Hill, 1988).
5. Daniel Greeno, Montrose Sommers, and Jerome Kernan, "Personality and Implicit Behaviour Patterns," *Journal of Marketing Research*, February 1973, vol. 10, pp. 63–69.
6. R. Craig Endicott, "Advertising Fact Book," *Advertising Age*, January 6, 1992, p. S-11.
7. Clyde Kluckholn, *Culture and Behaviour* (New York: Free Press, 1962), p. 26.
8. Jo Marney, "Counting Ethnic Canadians In," *Marketing Magazine*, June 4, 2001, p. 24.
9. "The Marketing Report on Multicultural Marketing," *Marketing Magazine*, September 14, 1998, pp. 15–25; Chris Daniels, "Shopping Mosaic," *Marketing Magazine Online*, www.marketingmag.ca, May 17, 2004.
10. Rebecca Harris, "Ethnic Approaches," *Marketing Magazine Online*, www.marketingmag.ca, March 14, 2005,
11. Tony Pigott and Michael Sullivan, "Including Visible Minorities," *Marketing Magazine*, June 4, 2001, p. 24.
12. Rebecca Harris, "Ethnic Approaches," *Marketing Magazine Online*, www.marketingmag.ca, March 14, 2005.
13. Madonna Harris, "Embrace and Prosper," *Marketing Magazine Online*, (http://www.marketingmag.ca/magazine/current/multicultural_report/article. January 23, 2006.
14. For statistical information regarding languages spoken in Canada, see the Statistics Canada Web site at www.statcan.ca. The information reported is based on the most recent 1996 Canadian census data.
15. For more information see, Dwight Thomas, "Culture and Consumption Behavior in English and French Canada," in Bent Stidsen, ed., *Marketing in the 70s and Beyond* (Edmonton: Marketing Division, 1975), pp. 255–261. Also, Francois Vary, "Quebec Consumer Has Unique Buying Habits," *Marketing Magazine*, March 23, 1992, p. 28; Louise Gagnon, "Eaton's Quebec Ads Target Hip Shoppers," *Marketing Magazine*, June 16, 1997, and "Price Cuts Escalate Beer Battle," *Marketing Magazine*, June 30, 1997.
16. *CIA World Fact Book:* www.cia.gov/publications/factbook, June 3, 2002.
17. Julie Look, "Understanding Tween Culture," *Marketing Magazine*, August 2, 1999, p. 16.
18. Anita Lahey, "Bauer Gets A Boost at World Cup of Hockey," *Marketing Magazine*, September 2, 1996, p. 2; Daniel Greeno, Montrose Sommers, and Jerome Kernan, "Personality and Implicit Behaviour Patterns," *Journal of Marketing Research*, February 1973, vol. 10, pp. 63–69; "McDonald's Global Campaign to Focus on Healthy Living," *Marketing Magazine Online*, www.marketingmag.ca, March 9, 2005; "Reebok signs deal with junior hockey star," *Marketing Magazine Online*, www.marketingmag.ca, March 9, 2005.
19. See Elihu Katz and Paul Lazarsfeld, *Personal Influence* (New York: Free Press, 1955), especially p. 325.
20. Sara Curtis, "Radio Show Targets Children 8 to 12," *Marketing Magazine*, October 7, 1996, p. 3; Michelle Halpern, "Cute But Scary," *Marketing Magazine Online*, www.marketingmag.ca, August 9, 2004.
21. Kathleen Martin, "Where the boys are," *Marketing Magazine Online*, www.marketingmag.ca, January 17, 2005; Paul-Mark Rendon, "Zellers adds Duff's stuff," *Marketing Magazine*, March 8, 2004; Mikala Folb, "Totally Girl," *Marketing Magazine*, January 4/11, 1999, pp. 10, 12.
22. Andrew Poon and Dawn Walton, "Tables Turning on Fast Food," *The Globe and Mail*, July 5, 1997, pp. B1, B3.

Chapter 3

1. Scott Deveau, "Gear makers rush aboard the iPod express," *The Globe and Mail*, January 19, 2006, p. B10.
2. Garth Turner, "The Turner Report: the boom and the bust," *The Online Edition of The Brooks Bulletin*, www.brooksbulletin.com/news/business.asp?itemid=48389, January 24, 2006.

3. "Population Projections," *The Daily,* December 15, 2005.
4. "Dorel aims to age gracefully — from car seats to walkers," *The Globe and Mail*, May 19, 2005, p. B7.
5. Data obtained from Statistics Canada Web site, www.statcan.ca, 2000.
6. Michelle Halpern, "Cute, But Scary," *Marketing Magazine Online*, www.marketingmag.ca, August 9, 2004.
7. Robert Thompson, "Breakfast, lunch, desert," *National Post*, April 28, 2005, p. FP8.
8. Milton Parissis and Michael Helfinger, "Ethnic Shoppers Share Certain Values," *Marketing Magazine*, January 11, 1993, p. 16.
9. Eve Lazarus, "Mrs. Fix-it," *Marketing Magazine Online*, www.marketingmag.ca, November 28, 2005.
10. http://moneycentral.msn.com/content/invest/extra/P76640.asp…, March 3, 2004.
11. Aveda Corporation Web site: http://aveda.aveda.com/about/beliefs_vision/default.asp.
12. Ontario Transportation Capital Corporation, "Ontario Transportation Minister Registers for a Highway 407 Transponder," Press Release, Canada NewsWire, May 30, 1997.
13. Stan Sutter, "Me and my iPod," *Marketing Magazine Online*, www.marketingmag.ca, January 23, 2006.
14. Peter A. Dunne and James G. Barnes, "Internal Marketing: A Relationships, Value-Creation View," in Barbara R. Lewis and Richard J. Varey, *Internal Marketing: Directions for Management* (London: Routledge, 2000).
15. "Smart Moves into Canada," *Marketing Magazine Online*, www.marketingmag.ca, October 5, 2004; "Diesel Gets Smart for Mercedes-Benz," *Marketing Magazine Online*, www.marketingmag.ca, April 30, 2004; Mercedes-Benz Canada, "Mercedes-Benz Canada reports new sales record for 2005 and best December in the company's history," Press Release, Canada NewsWire, January 4, 2006, www.newswire.ca/en/releases/archive/January2006/04/c4919.html.
16. "Coke to Launch Another Diet Drink," *Gulf Marketing News*, March 28, 2005, p. 5.

Chapter 4

1. Carolyn Abraham, "MS's Pitch-and-Swing Days are Over," *The Globe and Mail*, February 25, 2005, p. A6.
2. Natalia Williams, "Big Moves at HBC" *Strategy*, February 2005, p. 19; Patty Summerfield, "Behavioural Studies," *Strategy*, January 2005, p. 25; Lisa D'Innocenzo, "Next Wave Custom Pubs: The New Black," *Strategy*, November 2004, p. 26.
3. Rebecca Harris, "Do Focus Groups Have a Future?" *Marketing Magazine Online*, http://www.marketingmag.ca/magazine/current/market_research_rpt/article.jsp?content=20050606_68883_68883, June 6, 2005.
4. Lisa D'Innocenzo, "Focus Groups for a New Age," *Strategy,* April 2005, p. 10; Paula Baker, "Online Research – Faster, Easier…Better?" *Strategy*, February 2005, p. 25; Statistics Canada, "Internet Use in Canada," www.statcan.ca/bsolc/english/bsolc?catno=56F0003X, September 23, 2004.
5. Justin Martin, "Ignore Your Customer," *Fortune*, May 1, 1995, pp. 121–126; Astrid Van Den Broek, "Are You Sure They Want It?" *Strategy*, July 15, 2002, p. 29.
6. Colin Tener, "A Practical Approach to Internet Privacy," *Strategy*, January 29, 2001, p. D11.
7. Robert Everett-Green, "The Great Canadian Hunt for Home-Grown Movies," *The Globe and Mail*, June 13, 1996, p. A13.
8. Ivor Thompson, "Why Response Rates Matter," *Marketing Magazine*, May 27, 2002, p.18.
9. Industry Canada Web site, http://privacyforbusiness.ic.gc.ca updated December 12, 2005; Robert Gillelan, "How to Stop Worrying and Love PIPEDA," *Strategy,* February 9, 2004, p. 12.

Chapter 5

1. Natalia Williams, "The Metrics of it All," *Strategy,* April 2005, p. 35 and Patti Summerfield, "What's up with the Web?" *Strategy*, March 2005, p. 25.
2. Natalia Williams, "Brilliant! Shopping Bags," *Strategy*, February 2005, p. 6; Natalia Williams, "Who are they Wearing? Why Chanel, Dahling," *Strategy,* October 2004, p. 13.
3. Mark Maremont, "They're All Screaming for Häagen-Dazs," *Business Week*, October 14, 1991, p. 121.
4. www.statcan.ca, January 29, 2006.
5. www.statcan.ca, January 29, 2006.
6. www.statcan.ca, May 22, 2005.
7. www.heinz.com, January 26, 2006.
8. www.lululemon.com, January 29, 2006.
9. www.aritzia.com, January 29, 2006.
10. www.drmartens.com, January 29, 2006.
11. www.quiksilver.com, May 24, 2005.
12. Lisa D'Innocenzo, "Top Three Beer Ads," *Strategy*, p. 9; Dave Scholz, "The Fickle Beer Consumer," *Marketing Magazine Online*, www.marketingmag.ca, May 9, 2005.
13. Allan J. Magrath, "Niche Marketing: Finding a Safe, Warm Cave," *Sales and Marketing Management in Canada*, May 1987, p. 40; Robert E. Linneman and John L. Stanton Jr., "Mining For Niches," *Business Horizons*, May/June 1992, pp. 43–51.
14. www.gatorade.com, January 29, 2006.

Chapter 6

1. Statistics Canada, *Market Research Handbook*, catalogue 63-224 (Ottawa, 2005).
2. Statistics Canada, *Market Research Handbook*, catalogue 63-224 (Ottawa, 2004).

3. Danny Skenkman, "Are You Ready to Join the iPod Nation?" *Strategy*, February 2005, p. 32; Symbian Limited Company Web site, www.symbian.com, May 7, 2005.
4. Sang-Lin Han, David Wilson, and Shirlish P. Dant, "Buyer-Seller Relationships Today," *Industrial Marketing Management,* November 1993, pp. 331–338.
5. Background on relationship-building is described in F. Robert Dwyer, Paul H. Schurr, and Sejo Oh, "Developing Buyer-Seller Relationships," *Journal of Marketing,* April 1987, pp. 11–27. See also Patricia Doney and Joseph Cannon, "An Examination of the Nature of Trust in Buyer-Seller Relationships," *Journal of Marketing,* April 1997, pp. 31–51.
6. www.ford.media.com, January 29, 2006.
7. An interesting description of value imaging, the psychological influences on business buying behaviour, can be found in Paul Sherlock, "The Irrationality of 'Rational' Business Buying Decisions," *Marketing Management*, Spring 1992, pp. 8–15.
8. Robert D. McWilliams, Earl Naumann, and Stan Scott, "Determining Buying Center Size," *Industrial Marketing Management*, February 1992, pp. 43–49.
9. "The Battle for Online B2B," *Marketing Magazine Online*, www.marketingmag.ca, February 21, 2005.
10. Ken Yamada, "Apple to Unveil Mail Order Catalog and Sell Directly to Big Companies," *The Wall Street Journal*, September 17, 1992, p. B7.
11. For examples of benefit segmentation as used in the business market, see Mark L. Bennion Jr., "Segmentation and Positioning in a Basic Industry," *Industrial Marketing Management*, February 1987, pp. 9–18. Also, Cornelius A. de Kluyver and David B. Whitlark, "Benefit Segmentation for Industrial Products," *Industrial Marketing Management,* November 1986, pp. 273–286.
12. For an excellent discussion on industrial market segmentation, see Richard E. Plank, "A Critical Review of Industrial Market Segmentation," *Industrial Marketing Management*, May 1985, pp. 75–91. Also, detailed coverage of the topic is contained in Thomas V. Bonoma and Benson P. Shapiro, *Segmenting the Industrial Market* (Lexington, MA: Lexington Books, 1983).

Chapter 7

1. Paul Lima, "Home desktop's Swiss Army knife slices into office market," *The Globe and Mail*, April 7, 2005, p. B10.
2. Natalia Williams, "The McCain Makeover," *Strategy*, January 2005, p. 15; Rebecca Harris, "Zwak Attack," *Marketing Magazine Online*, www.marketingmag.ca, February 21, 2005.
3. Marina Strauss, "Canada Rated 6th in Quality of Its Manufactured Goods," *The Globe and Mail*, February 10, 1994, p. B6.
4. Jan Field, "Ice With Edge," *Marketing Magazine*, February 7, 2000, p. 17.
5. Natalia Williams, "I Want My TMN," *Strategy*, April 2005, p. 19.
6. Kathy Tyrer, "Selling Hockey in the Land of La La and Disney," *Marketing Magazine*, November 8, 1993, p. 5.
7. Lisa D'Innocenzo, "Virgin Appears To Crowd in Toronto," *Strategy*, March 2005, p. 6.
8. Samson Okalow, "Dove: A Clean Slate," *Strategy*, November 2004, p. 31.
9. Samson Okalow, "X Marks the Spot: Nissan's New SUV Hits the Road Driving," *Strategy*, January 2005, p. 37.
10. Glenn Collins, "The Cola War Is Expected to Heat Up," *The New York Times*, January 25, 1997, pp. 37, 39.
11. James Pollack, "Ikea Puts Focus on Office Furniture," *Marketing Magazine*, November 4, 1996, p. 4.
12. "Gap Opens New Store for Boomer Women," *Marketing Magazine Online*, www.marketingmag.ca, April 26, 2005; Susan Caminiti, "Will Old Navy Fill the Gap," *Fortune*, March 18, 1996, p. 59.
13. Natalia Williams, "Shiny Happy Marketers," *Strategy*, March 2005, p. 45.
14. Jo Marney, "Too Much of a Good Thing," *Marketing Magazine*, January 24, 1999, p. 21.
15. Samson Okalaw, "Shoppers Adds Some Karacter to Life Designs," *Strategy*, October 2004, p. 37; "Kraft Buzzing About Honey Cereal," *Marketing Magazine*, August 2, 1999, p. 1.
16. David Menzies, "The Museum of Mortal Marketing Mistakes," *Marketing Magazine*, April 23, 2001, pp. 9–11.
17. Eugene Carlson, "Some Forms of Identification Can't Be Handily Faked," *The Wall Street Journal*, September 14, 1993, p. B2.
18. Geoffrey York, "We, Robots," *The Globe and Mail* Online, www.globeandmail.com, March 31, 2005.
19. Axel Law, "B-Class F-Cell Takes Fuel Cells to a New Level, *Maclean's Online*, www.macleans.ca, March 3, 2005.
20. Andrew Stodart, "The Road More Traveled," *Marketing Magazine Online*, www.marketingmag.ca, July 19/26, 1999.
21. The benefits cited are from a study reported in Robert G. Cooper and Elko J. Kleinschmidt, "New Product Processes at Leading Industrial Firms," *Industrial Management*, May 1991, pp. 137–147. For an approach to improve the management of multiple new-product development projects, see Steven C. Wheelwright and Kim B. Clark, "Creating Project

Plans to Focus Product Development Stages," *Harvard Business Review,* March-April 1992, pp. 70–82.

22. For a report on the criteria used in making "go-no-go" decisions in the product-development process, see Ilkka A. Ronkainen, "Criteria Changes Across Product Development Stages," *Industrial Marketing Management*, August 1985, pp. 171–178.
23. "Study: Launching New Products Is Worth the Risk," *Marketing News*, January 20, 1992, p. 2.
24. For more on the first two stages, see Linda Rochford, "Generating and Screening New Product Ideas," *Industrial Marketing Management*, November 1991, pp. 287–296.
25. For the foundations of diffusion theory of innovation, see Everett M. Rogers, *Diffusion of Innovations*, 3rd ed. (New York: Free Press, 1983).
26. The Gillette Company Web site, www.gillette.com, retrieved May 9, 2005.
27. The Gillette Company Web site, www.gillette.com, retrieved January 30, 2006.
28. Kevin Coughlin, "Are CD's Days Numbered? Two New Technologies Join the Battle for the World's Ear," *St. Louis Post-Dispatch*, September 5, 1999, p. E1; Robert A. Starrett, "Burning Down the House: Home Recorders are Here," *E-Media Professional,* May 1999, p. 50.
29. Lucy Saddleton, "Anti-Aging Products Are Multiplying Like Tribbles," *Strategy*, March 11, 2002, p. 2.
30. For more on this subject, see Steven P. Schnaars, "When Entering Growth Markets, Are Pioneers Better Than Poachers?" *Business Horizons*, March-April 1986, pp. 27–36.
31. "Microsoft brainstorms every angle of Xbox 360," www.ctv.ca, January 30, 2006; Reiji Yoshida, "Sega Plays Survival Game with Dreamcast," *Japan Times Weekly, International Edition,* December 14–20, 1998, p. 13; Chris Daniels, "Xbox's Inner Workings," *Marketing Magazine*, November 19, 2001, pp. 8–9.
32. Lesley Daw, "How to Market A Milestone," *Marketing Magazine*, March 10, 1997, pp. 10–11.
33. Mikala Folb, "Playskool Beats Bacteria," *Marketing Magazine*, March 17, 1997, p. 3.
34. MSN Encarta Web site, http://encarta.msn.com, May 9, 2005.

Chapter 8

1. Leonard L. Berry and Terry Clark, "Four Ways to Make Services More Tangible," *Business*, October/December 1986, p. 53. Also see Betsy D. Gelb, "How Marketers of Intangibles Can Raise the Odds for Consumer Satisfaction," *Journal of Service Marketing*, Summer 1987, pp. 11–17.
2. Leonard A. Schlesinger and James L. Heskett, "The Service-Driven Service Company," *Harvard Business Review*, September-October 1991, pp. 71–81.
3. Natalia Williams, "Truly Interactive TV," *Strategy*, April 2005, p. 33.

Chapter 9

1. "Tim Hortons," "The First Goal Is Having Fun" and "Timbits" are registered trademarks of The TDL Marks Corporation and are used under license by The TDL Group Corp. Printed with permission of The TDL Group Corp.
2. The 1993 study of personal computers was summarized in Kyle Pope, "Computers: They're No Commodity," *The Wall Street Journal*, October 15, 1993, p. B1.
3. George Stalk Jr. "What's in a Brand? It's the Experience," *The Globe and Mail*, May 23, 1997, p. B11.
4. Marina Strauss, "Gap a tired brand in new old clothing," *The Globe and Mail*, August 16, 2002, p. B9.
5. www. gapinc.com, January 28, 2006.
6. Suzanne Hogan, "Positioning a Brand in the Marketplace," www.lippincottmercer.com, accessed January 28, 2006.
7. Elizabeth Nickson, "The American founders of Roots have been accused of branding the wilderness," *The Globe and Mail*, March 23, 2000.
8. *Marketing Magazine Online*, www.marketingmag.ca, January 20, 2006.
9. For an in-depth discussion of the value of branding, see David Arnold, *The Handbook of Brand Management* (London: Pitman Publishing, 1992).
10. Jamie Beckett, "Inventing a Product Name Is Part Science, Part Art," *The Globe and Mail*, October 27, 1992, p. B4.
11. Kim Robertson, "Strategically Desirable Brand Name Characteristics," *The Journal of Product and Brand Management*, Summer 1992, pp. 62–72.
12. Kanran Kashani, "A Future for Brands," *Financial Times, Mastering Management* (London: Pitman, 1997), pp. 171–174.
13. For a look at the success of Loblaws' private-label business and at the developer of the program, Dave Nichol, see Mark Stevenson, "Global Gourmet," *Canadian Business*, July 1993, pp. 22–23; see also Anne Kingston, *The Edible Man: Dave Nichol, President's Choice and the Making of Popular Taste* (Toronto: Macfarlane Walter & Ross, 1994).
14. *Marketing Magazine Online*, www.marketingmag.ca, November 15, 2005.
15. www.trendwatching.com, February 9, 2006.

16. Lesley Young, "Gatorade Targets Pint-Sized Jocks," *Marketing Magazine Online*, www.marketingmag.ca, August 19, 2002.
17. For information related to this Act, the government has set up the Competition Bureau, which can answer any questions. You can write to Industry Canada, 50 Victoria Street, Hull, PQ, K1A 0C9 (1-800-248-5358). Industry Canada's Web site is www.ic.gc.ca. All federal government departments can be reached through www.canada.gc.ca.
18. For further information on any federal acts or regulations, access the Government of Canada Web page at www.canada.gc.ca.
19. "Will Gross Cigarette Labels Stop Smoking," *Toronto Star*, February 8, 2000, p. C4.
20. www.apple.com, January, 21, 2006.
21. www.apple.com, January 21, 2006.
22. For a more detailed discussion of service guarantees, see Valarie A. Zeithaml and Mary Jo Bitner, *Services Marketing*, 3rd ed. (New York: McGraw-Hill Irwin, 2003) pp. 205–211.

Chapter 10

1. Sarah Smith, "Toy Versus Toy," *Marketing Magazine Online*, www.marketingmag.ca, January 17, 2000.
2. For a review of pricing strategies, see Nessim Hanna and H. Robert Dodge, *Pricing: Policies and Procedures* (London: McMillan Press, 1995).
3. Thomas L. Powers, "Break-Even Analysis with Semi-Fixed Costs," *Industrial Marketing Management*, February 1987, pp. 25–41.
4. Patti Summerfield, "Wipeout! Convenience Checkmates Conservation for Canadian Consumers," *Strategy*, March 11, 2002, p. 6.
5. Discussions on relationship pricing are included in Tony Cram, *The Power of Relationship Marketing: Keeping Customers for Life* (London: Pitman Publishing, 1994). Also Leonard L. Berry, "Relationship Marketing," in Adrian Payne, Martin Christopher, Moira Clark, and Helen Peck, *Relationship Marketing for Competitive Advantage: Winning and Keeping Customers* (Oxford: Butterworth-Heinemann, 1996), pp. 65–74.
6. Robert M. Schindler and Lori S. Warren, "Effects of Odd Pricing on Price Recall," *Journal of Business*, June 1989, pp. 165–177; Robert Blattberg and Kenneth Wisniewski, "How Retail Price Promotions Work: Empirical Results," *Marketing Working Paper No. 42* (Chicago: University of Chicago, 1987).

Chapter 11

1. Adapted from Shirley Won, "Analysts still upbeat on Canadian Tire," *The Globe and Mail*, April 11, 2005, p. B11; Shirley Won, "Canadian Tire set to launch expansion," *The Globe and Mail*, April 7, 2005, p. B3; "Canadian Tire Maps Future," *Metro*, April 7, 2005, p. 11; Lisa D' Innocenzo, "Going to the Q," *Strategy*, January 2006, p. 28.
2. Terence Belford, "Retail investors soak up mall's success," *The Globe and Mail*, April 5, 2005, p. B11.
3. *Marketing Magazine Online*, www.marketingmag.ca, January 31, 2006.
4. For an interesting insight into how a small family-owned kitchenware retailer in Calgary operates with an emphasis on personalized service, see Cathryn Motherwell, "Where the Business Is Cooking," *The Globe and Mail*, August 24, 1993, p. B28.
5. David Eggleston, "Zellers Freshens Up Gen Z," *Strategy*, May 22, 2000, p. D3; Scott Gardiner, "A Truly Awesome Database," *Marketing Magazine*, April 29, 2002, p. 12.
6. James Pollack, "Specialists Thrive on High-End Positioning," *Marketing News*, March 10, 1997, p. 3.
7. Sonja Rasula, "Beyond Clothes," *Marketing Magazine*, May 10, 1999, pp. 16–17.
8. Shawna Cohen, "One-Stop Shopping for Dinner," *Marketing Magazine*, February 1, 1999, pp. 10, 12; Jennifer Bain, "Raw Fish and Piano Bars," *The Globe and Mail*, January 29, 2000, p. R15.
9. Shawna Cohen, "One-Stop Shopping for Dinner," *Marketing Magazine*, February 1, 1999, pp. 10, 12.
10. Eve Lazarus, "Chevron Reimages Town Pantry Brand," *Marketing Magazine*, July 12, 1999, p. 2; Brian Dunn, "The King of Bread, Butts, and Beer," *Marketing Magazine*, October 25, 1999, p. 23.
11. Peter Verberg, "Party Time: Tupperware Has Been Keeping Food Fresh for Over 50 Years," *Canadian Business*, March 18 2002, p. 27.
12. Fantasia home page: www.kwic.com, August 20 2002.
13. "Challenging Times for Fundraisers," *Marketing Magazine*, April 29 2002, p. MD6.
14. Calmetta W. Coleman, "Retailers Strive for Shopping Synergy," *The Wall Street Journal*, December 20, 1999, pp. B1, B6; also "Lands' End, Bean Lead Pack," *Daily News Record*, November 3, 1999, p. 12.
15. Statistics Canada, *Vending Machine Operators*, 1997, cat. no. 63-213; Mary Gooderham, "Your Supermarket Knows Who You Are," *The Globe and Mail*, August 17, 1993, pp. A1, A4.
16. "Coke Tests Machine That Adjusts Prices," *St. Louis Post-Dispatch*, October 28, 1999.
17. Tavia Grant, "More turning to e-business transactions," *The Globe and Mail*, April 22, 2005, p. B4.
18. Howard Solomon, "Pick a Niche, Study Warns E-tailers," *eBusiness Journal*, June 2001, p. 7; Timothy Hune, "Beyond Point and Click," *National Post Business*, May 2001, pp. 50–56.
19. Howard Solomon, "Customers in the crosshairs," *eBusiness Journal*, January 2002, p. 4.

20. Chris Daniels, "Turning Browsers into Buyers," *Digital Marketing*, March 2002, pp. 7–8.
21. Cristine Lourosa-Ricardo, "Picking the product," *The Wall Street Journal*, November 22, 1999, pp. R8, R10.
22. Positioning based on price and service is discussed in George H. Lucas Jr. and Larry G. Gresham, "How to Position for Retail Success," *Business*, April-June 1988, pp. 3–13. Positioning that combines all three variables is presented in Laurence H. Wortzel, "Retailing Strategies for Today's Mature Marketplace," *The Journal of Business Strategy*, Spring 1987, pp. 45–56.

Chapter 12

1. Adapted from Dow Jones and Reuters, "Roynat Capital presents a series of business profiles celebrating the success of Canadian companies," *National Post*, April 15, 2005, p. FP 20, and the Padinox Incorporated Web site, www.paderno.com, accessed May 22, 2005.
2. An alternative approach that emphasizes market analysis is presented in Allan J. Magrath and Kenneth G. Hardy, "Six Steps to Distribution Network Design," *Business Horizons*, January-February 1991, pp. 48–52.
3. An excellent discussion of distribution channels for business goods and services is found in Michael D. Hutt and Thomas W. Speh, *Business Marketing and Management,* 4th ed. (Ft. Worth, TX: Dryden Press, 1992), pp. 359–392. For a review of emerging issues on business channels, see Al McGrath, "Managing Distribution Channels," *Business Quarterly*, Spring 1996, pp. 57–65.
4. For a discussion of this topic, see Donald H. Light, "A Guide for New Distribution Channel Strategies for Service Firms," *The Journal of Business Strategy,* Summer 1986, pp. 54–64.
5. Rowland T. Moriarty and Ursula Moran, "Managing Hybrid Marketing Systems," *Harvard Business Review*, November-December 1990, pp. 146–155.
6. For extensive discussion of this strategy, see John A. Quelch, "Why Not Exploit Dual Marketing?," *Business Horizons*, January-February 1987, pp. 52–60.
7. Ibid.
8. For more on the idea that market considerations should determine a producer's channel structure, see Louis W. Stern and Frederick D. Sturdivant, "Customer-Driven Distribution Systems," *Harvard Business Review*, July-August 1987, pp. 34–41.
9. For further discussion of the strategies that either create or offset conflict between manufacturers and retailers, see Allan J. Magrath and Kenneth G. Hardy, "Avoiding the Pitfalls in Managing Distribution Channels," *Business Horizons*, September-October 1987, pp. 29–33.
10. Allan J. Magrath, "The Hidden Clout of Middlemen," *Journal of Business Strategy*, March/April 1990, pp. 38–41.
11. Adapted from *What It's All About.* (Oakbrook, IL: Council of Logistics Management, 1993).
12. Adapted from David Sinchi-Levy, Philip Kaminsky and Edith Sinchi-Levy, *Designing and Managing the Supply Chain* (Burr Ridge, IL: McGraw-Hill/Irwin, 2000) p.5.
13. Adapted from Hau L. Lee, "The Triple-A Supply Chain," *Harvard Business Review,* October 2004, pp. 1-12.
14. "Out of the Box at UPS," *Business Week*, January 10, 2000, p. 76; and Douglas A. Blackmon, "Overnight, Everything Changed for FedEx; Can It Reinvent Itself?" *The Wall Street Journal*, November 4, 1999, pp. A1, A16.

Chapter 13

1. Adapted from "Team," Indiantelevision.com, January 16, 2006; "Disney cautious in marketing Narnia," beyondmadisonavenue.com, Nov. 2005; Merissa Marr, "Selling Narnia," *The Wall Street Journal Online*, Nov. 25, 2005.
2. "Guerrilla Tactics Get Panasonic Noticed," *Strategy*, March 27, 2000, p. BMP10.
3. "Campbell's Debuts Snacking Soup," *Marketing Magazine Online*, www.marketingmag.ca, October 25, 2000; www.Campbellkitchen.com, July 15, 2002.
4. Jo Marney, "What's in Your Face Counts," *Marketing Magazine*, September 11, 2000, p. 24.
5. "Corby's C.C.&G. Just For Guys," *Marketing Magazine*, April 1, 2002, p. 1.
6. "What's Hot: Tune In, Turn On Your Customers," *Strategy*, July 19, 1999, p. 5.
7. This is a condensed version of the definition offered by Don E. Shultz and Heidi F. Shultz, "Transitioning Marketing Communications into the Twenty-First Century," *Journal of Marketing Communications*, March 1998, pp. 9–26.
8. Ford Motor Company home page, www.ford.com, July 16, 2002.
9. This example is based on information in Bradley Johnson, "Abe Kohnstann: IBM," *Advertising Age*, June 26, 1995 and Sloane Lucas, "One on One," *Brandweek*, September 20, 1999, p. 16.
10. Adapted from Lara Mills, "Coke May Move Toward Localizing," *Marketing Magazine*, February 7, 2000, p. 3. Also, Lara Mills, "Coke Is Thinking and Acting Locally," *Marketing Magazine*, March 20, 2000, p. 3.
11. Russ Green, "Making Measuring Simple: Plan Marcomm, Evaluate Criteria," *Advertising Age's Business Marketing*, September 1999, p. 49.

12. Dan Thompson, "Bigger, Fewer, Better," *Strategy*, March 11, 2002, p. 30.
13. "Tiny Lipsticks Sent Direct," *Marketing Magazine*, October 18, 1999, p. 17.
14. Eve Lazarus, "B.C. Hydro to Slash 2002 Ad Budget," *Marketing Magazine*, December 17, 2001, p. 3.
15. "Bait and switch" advertising is prohibited by the Competition Bureau of Industry Canada. The Bureau's role is to promote and maintain fair competition so that Canadians can benefit from lower prices, product choice, and quality services. For more information or to report unfair business practices, you can contact the Competition Bureau at 1-800-348-5358 or access its Internet site at www.cb-bc.gc.ca.
16. See "Marketer's Guide to Liquor Advertising Regulations," *Marketing Magazine*, August 21/28, 1997, pp. 14–16.

Chapter 14

1. Adapted from Keith McArthur, "Olympic strategy key to branding gold," *The Globe and Mail*, February 13, 2006, p. B3; Keith McArthur, "Piggybacking on Olympic ads losing favour," *The Globe and Mail Online,* www.theglobeandmail.com, February 14, 2006; Keith McArthur, "Sponsors expand efforts to market Olympic cachet," *The Globe and Mail*, February 21, 2006, p. B7.
2. *2006, Media Digest*. Published by *Marketing Magazine* as compiled by TVB from Statistics Canada, CRTC, CNA, CCNA/Les Hebos du Québec, Magazines Canada, CARD, CAN, Tele-Direct, Canada Post, IAB, and industry estimates.
3. David Eggleston, "summedia Turns Coupon Clippers into Coupon Clickers," *Strategy*, November 8, 1999, p. D10; also, David Todd, "Savingumoney.com Builds Awareness Offline," *Strategy*, February 28, 2000, p. NP7.
4. Doug Sanders, "Advertisers Aim to Fragment TV Audience," *The Globe and Mail*, August 9, 1997, p. C3.
5. Carey Toane, "Teen Internet Use Survey Challenged," *Marketing Magazine*, June 5, 2000, p. 4; also, Bernadette Johnson, "Teen Study Raises Debate," *Strategy*, June 5, 2000, p. 3.
6. Bernadette Johnson, "Westminster Links Direct Mail Back to Internet," *Strategy*, July 19, 1999, p. D5.
7. Doug Checkeris, "Leaner, Meaner and Better?" *Marketing Magazine*, November 18, 1996, p. 11.
8. "Canadian E-tailers Lagging Behind U.S.," *Strategy*, March 13, 2000, p. 6.
9. Bernadette Johnson, "E-mail Comes into Its Own," *Strategy*, March 25, 2002, p. D8.

Chapter 15

1. Yankelovich Partners Inc., *2005 Market Receptivity Study*, www.yankelovich.com/thought/TL2005 marketreceptivitystudy.pdf. April 18, 2005.
2. Rebecca Harris, "Do-not-call legislation becomes law," *Marketing Magazine Online*, www.marketingmag.ca, November 30, 2005; Industry Canada, "Legislation to Establish National Do Not Call List Adopted by Parliament," Press Release, November 28, 2005, www.ic.gc.ca.
3. Neil Rackham and John R. DeVincentis, *Rethinking the Sales Force: redefining selling to create and capture customer value* (New York: McGraw-Hill, 1999) pp. 16-18.
4. Robert N. McMurray, "The Mystique of Super-Salesmanship," *Harvard Business Review,* March-April 1961, pp. 113–122; Derek A. Newton, *Sales Force Performance and Turnover* (Cambridge, MA: Marketing Science Institute, 1973).
5. Annette Bourdeau, "Training Day: Mike Nedec, VP of strategic marketing. Best Buy Canada," *Strategy*, November 2005, p. 16.
6. Wayne Mouland, "Coupon convenience," *Marketing Magazine Online*, www.marketingmag.ca, May 9, 2005.
7. Wayne Mouland, "How to Use Coupons to Get More Trial," *Marketing Magazine Online*, www.marketingmag.ca, November 22, 1999.
8. Chris Powell, "Click and Save," *Marketing Magazine*, July 23, 2001, p. 8.
9. *Marketing Magazine Online*, www.marketingmag.ca, April 6, 2005.
10. Lisa D'Innocenzo, "Marketers Ramp Up Activity in Canadian Skateboard Scene," *Strategy*, June 3, 2002, p. 1.
11. Lisa D'Innocenzo, "Absolut Considers TV Advertising as Competition Heats Up," *Strategy*, March 11, 2002, p. 1; Holly Wyatt, "Finding the Absolut Fit," *Strategy*, March 11, 2002, p. 32.

Chapter 16

1. Jim Stengel, "The Future of Marketing." Presentation to the AAAA Media Conference, February 12, 2004. Accessed at: www.pg.com/content/pdf/04_news/stengel_feb_12_2004.pdf.
2. James G. Barnes, *Secrets of Customer Relationship Management: It's All About How you Make Them Feel,* Chapter 8 (New York: McGraw-Hill Companies, 2001).
3. Jennifer Kirkby, "Welcome to the Blogosphere," www.insightexec.com, March 22, 2006.
4. For a very good overview of the ethical issues involved in marketing and advertising, see Jack Mahoney, "Buyer Beware: Are Marketing and Advertising Always Ethical?" *Financial Post*,

December 14/16, 1996, pp. MM10–MM12; reprinted in *Financial Times Mastering Management* (London: Pitman Publishing, 1997), pp. 375–378.

5. Yankelovich Partners Inc. *2005 Market Receptivity Study*, www.yankelovich.com/thought/TL2005marketreceptivitystudy.pdf, April 18, 2005, p. 3.
6. Sandra Vandermerwe and Michael Oliff, "Corporate Challenges for an Age of Reconsumption," *Columbia Journal of World Business*, Fall 1991, pp. 23–28.
7. James G. Barnes, "Close to the Customer: But Is It Really a Relationship," *Journal of Marketing Management*, 1994, vol. 10, pp. 561–570.
8. Daphne A. Sheaves and James G. Barnes, "The Fundamentals of Relationships," in Teresa A. Swartz, David E. Bowen, and Stephen W. Brown, eds., *Advances in Services Marketing and Management,* vol. 5 (Greenwich, CT: JAI Press, Inc., 1996); and James G. Barnes, "Closeness, Strength and Satisfaction: Examining the Nature of Relationships Between Providers of Financial Services and Their Retail Customers," *Psychology and Marketing* (Special Issue on Relationship Marketing), 1997.

Credits

Chapter 1

Page 3, Antonio Mo/Getty Images; page 14, Tom Hanson/Canadian Press; page 15, Tim Hall/Getty Images; page 17, The McGraw-Hill Companies, Inc./Andrew Resek, photographer; page 18, CP PHOTO/Jacques Boissinot; page 20, Running Room Canada, Inc.; page 23, Ryan McVay/Getty Images.

Chapter 2

Page 29, BananaStock/JupiterImages; page 36, The McGraw-Hill Companies, Inc./Christopher Kerrigan, photographer; page 46, © The McGraw-Hill Companies, Inc./Lars A. Niki, photographer; page 48, PR Newswire Lexus; page 50, CP PHOTO/Olivier Douliery/©Abaca Press (2004) All rights reserved; page 52, McGraw-Hill Companies, Inc./Gary He, photographer; page 52, © Brand X Pictures/PictureQuest; page 54, Courtesy of Earls.

Chapter 3

Page 59, Courtesy of Apple Computer Inc.; page 62, Photo taken by Mark Burnham, Burnham Photography Ltd.; page 63, Courtesy of L'Oreal; page 75, PR Newswire/Subaru of America, Inc.; page 75, © Bo Zaunders/CORBIS; page 77, Ford Motor Company of Canada, Limited and Ford Motor Company trademarks and branded product images are used with permission; page 78, © Issei Kato/Reuters/Corbis; page 83, Photograph courtesy of Sony of Canada, Ltd.

Chapter 4

Page 93, Getty Images/Mark Thornton; page 101, Courtesy of Indigo Books and Music, Inc.; page 104, *National Post*; page 110, PR Newswire NINTENDO; page 112, Photodisc Collection Getty Images.

Chapter 5

Page 125, © Alan Schein Photography/CORBIS; page 130, Courtesy of Heather Tulk; page 130, Courtesy of Alliant; page 136, BananaStock/JupiterImages; page 137, Rob Melnychuk/Getty Images; page 142, Courtesy of P&G; page 143, The McGraw-Hill Companies, Inc./Andrew Resek, photographer; page 144, lululemon athletica; page 145, © AirWair International Ltd.; page 147, Photographer: Tiffany Alonzo; page 147, Courtesy of Quiksilver; page 154, © 2006 Primus Telecommunications Canada, Inc.

Chapter 6

Page 159, © Jon Feingersh; page 161, Courtesy of Terra; page 170, Alison Derry; page 174, Courtesy of Purchasing Management Association of Canada; page 177, *Kraft* is a trademark of Kraft Foods. Reproduced with permission.

Chapter 7

Page 187, Derek Wuenschirs; page 192, Courtesy of Panasonic Canada Inc. Panasonic is the registered trademark of Matsushita Electric Industrial Co. Ltd.; page 193, © C Squared Studios/Getty Images; page 194 Associated Press AP; page 196, © Bradley Dorfman/Handout/Reuters/Corbis; page 197, Courtesy of Apple Computer Inc.; page 198, The McGraw-Hill Companies, Inc./Andrew Resek, photographer; page 199, PRNewsWire/BMW of North America, LLC; page 201, © Haruyoshi Yamaguchi/Corbis; page 215, PRNewsFoto/Microsoft Corp.

Chapter 8

Page 219, Courtesy of Aveda; page 222, courtesy of Virgin Mobile; page 224, The McGraw-Hill Companies, Inc./Lars A. Niki, photographer; page 227, Courtesy of Petcare Insturance; page 228, Courtesy of Booster Juice.

Chapter 9

Page 243, Printed with permission of The TDL Group Corp.; page 248, Courtesy of Bruce Hunter; page 248, *Kraft* is a trademark of Kraft Foods. Reproduced with permission; page 250, Reproduced with the permission of Cadbury Adams; page 250 Courtesy of Swiffer; page 251, AP; page 256, Courtesy of Loblaws; page 260, Courtesy of Campbell Soup Company; page 262, Manon Boyer, photographer. www.debbietravis.com

Chapter 10

Page 273, John A. Rizzo/Getty Images; page 278, © 2005 Rogers Communications Inc. *Rogers* and *Better Choice Bundles* are trademarks of Rogers Communications Inc. used with permission; page 283, Courtesy of L'Oreal; page 284, Courtesy of Greg Pope; page 284, Courtesy of Boston Pizza; page 286, Royalty-Free/CORBIS; page 291, PR Newswire Godiva Chocolatier.

Chapter 11

Page 309, CP/Steve White; page 317, © Alison Derry; page 321, The McGraw-Hill Companies, Inc./Lars A. Niki, photographer; page 325, Ryan McVay/Getty Images; page 328, © Barry Sweet/epa/Corbis; page 332, Photo courtesy of Mountain Equipment Co-op.

Chapter 12

Page 337, Courtesy of Paderno; page 343, Courtesy of Westin Hotels & Resorts; page 354, © 2006 Mega Brands Inc. All rights reserved; page 360, Courtesy of John Gardner; page 360, The McGraw-Hill Companies, Inc./John Flournoy, photographer; page 364, CP/Macleans/Peter Bregg.

Chapter 13

Page 377, CP; page 378, BECEL and TAKES YOUR HEALTH TO HEART are registered trade-marks owned by Unilever Canada Inc. These marks are used with permission of Unilever Canada; page 379, Courtesy of Fido; page 382, Courtesy of P&G Beauty; page 382, CP/Dimitios Papadopoulos; page 385, CP/Stuart Nimmo; page 389, Courtesy of GM; page 391, Staples Business Depot/Derek Wuenschirs photographer; page 398, CP/Jacques Boissinot.

Chapter 14

Page 403, CP Photo/Jacques Boissinot; page 405, Ad courtesy of Life Fitness; page 406, Newfoundland and Labrador Tourism; page 406, CP Photo/*Toronto Star* — Bernard Weil; page 407, Courtesy of BC Hothouse Foods, Inc.; page 409, Courtesy of Toyota; page 413, Courtesy of MADD Canada; page 419, Courtesy of Ralph van Dyck; page 419, © BananaStock/PunchStock.

Chapter 15

Page 429, Courtesy of Ray Murphy; page 431, © Rick Friedman/Corbis; page 433, © Royalty-Free/Corbis; page 439, Imagesource/PictureQuest; page 447, The McGraw-Hill Companies, Inc./Andrew Resek, photographer; page 448, PRNewswire/Gatorade; page 454, Courtesy of L'Oreal.

Chapter 16

Page 463, CP/Steve White; page 466, Courtesy of Salvation Army; page 471, Royalty-Free/Corbis; page 477, The McGraw-Hill Companies, Inc./John Flournoy, photographer; page 478, Photographer; Mits Naga; page 484, CP/Adrian Brown.

Subject Index

C

G

H

I

M

Q

T

U

V

W

Y

Z

Company and Brand Name Index

C

D

W

X

Y

Z